We're Shifting the Demand.

ECON
Are you in?

In Demand

Affordable Texts

ECON is under $60!

Concise Chapters

Concepts and key terms are presented in a concise, engaging, and efficient format.

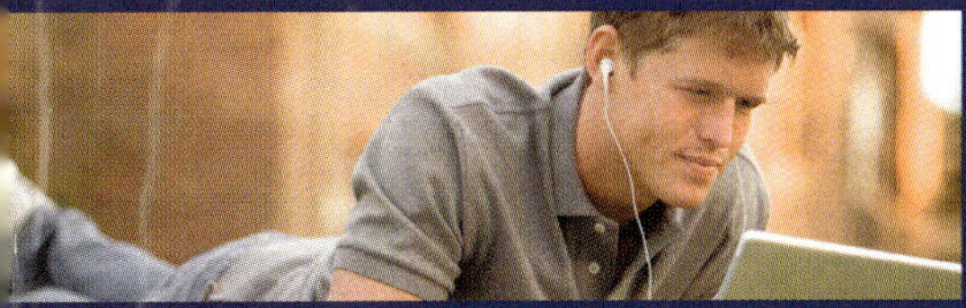

Online Study Resources

Students can practice and review with interactive online quizzing and video clips at 4ltrpress.cengage.com/econ.

Superior Instructor Resources

You'll find PowerPoint® Slides, the Instructor's Manual, News Articles, information about Aplia™, details about our Tomlinson Economics Videos, and more at 4ltrpress.cengage.com/econ.

Interactive Graphing Workshops

Students learn the basics of graphing as they manipulate graphs in this interactive online workshop.

Flash Cards and Chapter Reviews

Students can print flash cards for extra study options. Chapter Reviews help make study time more focused and efficient.

4ltrpress.cengage.com/econ

SOUTH-WESTERN
CENGAGE Learning™

ECON Micro ***2008–2009 Edition***
William A. McEachern

EVP/Publisher: Ed Moura

VP/Editorial Director: Jack W. Calhoun

VP/Director of Marketing: Bill Hendee

Editor-in-Chief: Alex von Rosenberg

Director: Neil Marquardt

Sr. Acquisitions Editor: Steve Scoble

Sr. Developmental Editor: Susanna C. Smart

Developmental Editors: Jamie Bryant and David Ferrell, B-books, Ltd.

Research Coordinator: Clara Kuhlman

Editorial Assistant: Laura Cothran

Executive Marketing Manager: Kimberly Kanakes

Sr. Marketing Manager: John Carey

Marketing Communications Manager: Sarah Greber

Production Director: Amy McGuire, B-books, Ltd.

Managing Media Editor: Pam Wallace

Media Editor: Deepak Kumar

Sr. Manufacturing Coordinator: Sandee Milewski

Production Service: B-books, Ltd.

Sr. Art Director: Michelle Kunkler

Internal Designer: Beckmeyer Design

Cover Designer: Ted Knapke/Ke Design

Cover Image: © Tetra Images/Alamy

Photography Manager: Deanna Ettinger

Photo Researcher: Charlotte Goldman

Library of Congress Control Number: 2008922017

SE Package ISBN-13: 978-0-324-58738-8
SE Package ISBN-10: 0-324-58738-4
SE Book Only ISBN-13: 978-0-324-58739-5
SE Book Only ISBN-10: 0-324-58739-2
IE Package ISBN-13: 978-0-324-58816-3
IE Package ISBN-10: 0-324-58816-X
IE Book Only ISBN-13: 978-0-324-58818-7
IE Book Only ISBN-10: 0-324-58818-6

South-Western Cengage Learning
5191 Natorp Boulevard
Mason, OH 45040
USA

Cengage Learning products are represented in Canada by Nelson Education, Ltd.

For your course and learning solutions, visit **academic.cengage.com**
Purchase any of our products at your local college store or at our preferred online store **www.ichapters.com**

Printed in the United States of America
1 2 3 4 5 6 7 11 10 09 08

MICRO
ECON

Brief Contents

CAUTION
Drinks

MICRO

ECON

Contents

PART 1 Introduction to Economics

crispy
special
SNACK WRAP
special
crispy
honey mustard
SNACK WRAP
honey mustard

Perrier
"A Whisky and Perrier — a Perfect Entente.

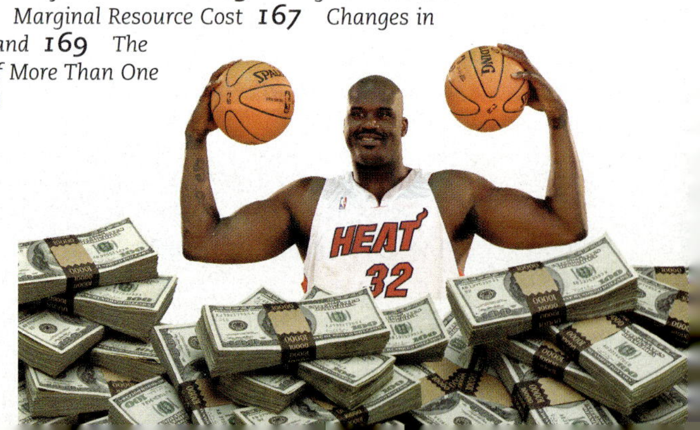
HEAT
32

PART 5 Market Failure and Public Policy

PART 6 International Microeconomics

CHAPTER

1

The Art *and* Science of Economic Analysis

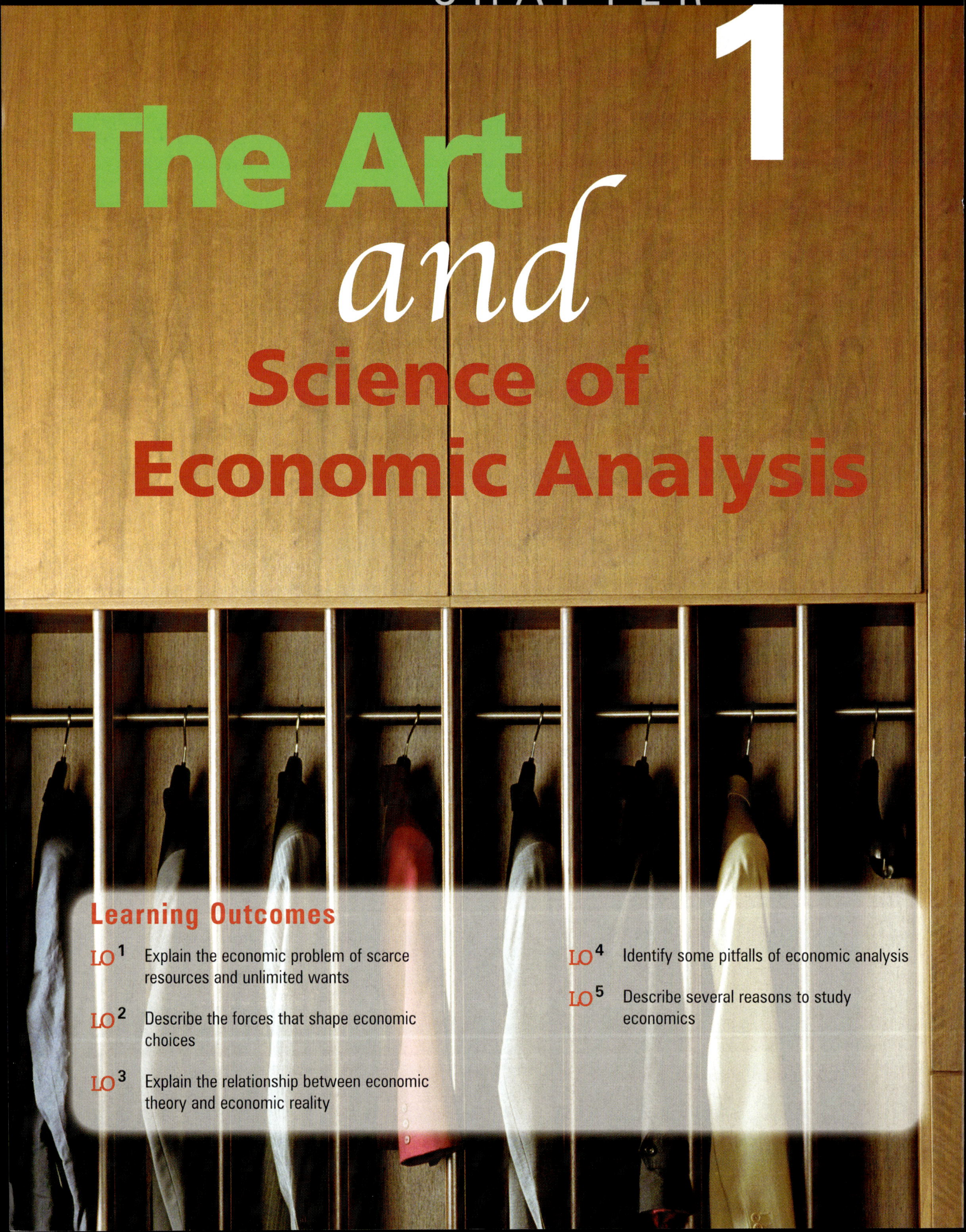

Learning Outcomes

LO 1 Explain the economic problem of scarce resources and unlimited wants

LO 2 Describe the forces that shape economic choices

LO 3 Explain the relationship between economic theory and economic reality

LO 4 Identify some pitfalls of economic analysis

LO 5 Describe several reasons to study economics

"Why is a good theory like a California Closet?"

Why are comic-strip characters like Hagar the Horrible, Hi and Lois, Cathy, Monty, and FoxTrot missing a finger on each hand? And where is Dilbert's mouth? Why does Japan have nearly ten times more vending machines per capita than does Europe? In what way are people who pound on vending machines relying on theory? Why is a good theory like a California Closet? What's the big idea with economics? Finally, how can it be said that in economics "what goes around comes around"? These and other questions are answered in this chapter, which introduces the art and science of economic analysis.

What do you think?

Lots of things work in theory but not in practice.

Strongly Disagree ... *Strongly Agree*

1 2 3 4 5 6 7

You have been reading and hearing about economic issues for years—unemployment, inflation, poverty, federal deficits, college tuition, airfares, stock prices, computer prices, gas prices. When explanations of these issues go into any depth, your eyes may glaze over and you may tune out, the same way you do when a weather forecaster tries to provide an in-depth analysis of high-pressure fronts colliding with moisture carried in from the coast.

What many people fail to realize is that economics is livelier than the dry accounts offered by the news media. Economics is about making choices, and you make economic choices every day—choices about whether to get a part-time job or focus on your studies, live in a dorm or off campus, take a course in accounting or one in history, get married or stay single, pack a lunch or grab a sandwich. You already know much more about economics than you realize. You bring to the subject a rich personal experience, an experience that will be tapped throughout the book to reinforce your understanding of the basic ideas.

Topics discussed in Chapter 1 include:

- The economic problem
- Marginal analysis
- Rational self-interest
- Scientific method
- Normative versus positive analysis
- Pitfalls of economic thinking

© STOCKBYTE/GETTY IMAGES

LO[1] The Economic Problem: Scarce Resources, Unlimited Wants

Would you like a new car, a nicer home, better meals, more free time, a more interesting social life, more spending money, more leisure, more sleep? Who wouldn't? But even if you can satisfy some of these desires, others keep popping up. *The problem is that, although your wants, or desires, are virtually unlimited, the resources available to satisfy these wants are scarce.* A resource is *scarce* when it is not freely available—that is, when its price exceeds zero. Because resources are scarce, you must choose from among your many wants, and whenever you choose, you must forgo satisfying some other wants. The problem of scarce resources but unlimited wants exists to a greater or lesser extent for each of the 6.6 billion people on earth. Everybody—cab driver, farmer, brain surgeon, dictator, shepherd, student, politician—faces the problem. For example, a cab driver uses time and other scarce resources, such as the taxi, knowledge of the city, driving skills, and gasoline, to earn income. That income, in turn, buys housing, groceries, clothing, trips to Disney World, and thousands of other goods and services that help satisfy some of the driver's unlimited wants. **Economics** examines how people use their scarce resources to satisfy their unlimited wants. Let's pick apart the definition, beginning with resources, then goods and services, and finally focus on the heart of the matter—economic choice, which arises from scarcity.

economics
the study of how people use their scarce resources to satisfy their unlimited wants

resources
the inputs, or factors of production, used to produce the goods and services that people want; resources consist of labor, capital, natural resources, and entrepreneurial ability

labor
the physical and mental effort used to produce goods and services

capital
the buildings, equipment, and human skills used to produce goods and services

natural resources
all "gifts of nature" used to produce goods and services; includes renewable and exhaustible resources

Resources

Resources are the inputs, or factors of production, used to produce the goods and services that people want. *Goods and services are scarce because resources are scarce.* Resources sort into four broad categories: labor, capital, natural resources, and entrepreneurial ability. **Labor** is human effort, both physical and mental. Labor includes the effort of the cab driver and the brain surgeon. Labor itself comes from a more fundamental resource: *time*. Without time we can accomplish nothing. We allocate our time to alternative uses: we can *sell* our time as labor, or we can *spend* our time doing other things, like sleeping, eating, studying, playing sports, going online, watching TV, or just relaxing with friends.

Capital includes all human creations used to produce goods and services. Economists often distinguish between physical capital and human capital. *Physical capital* consists of factories, tools, machines, computers, buildings, airports, highways, and other human creations used to produce goods and services. Physical capital includes the cab driver's taxi, the surgeon's scalpel, and the building where your economics class meets. *Human capital* consists of the knowledge and skill people acquire to increase their productivity, such as the cab driver's knowledge of city streets, the surgeon's knowledge of human anatomy, and your knowledge of economics.

Natural resources are all *gifts of nature,* including bodies of water, trees, oil reserves, minerals, and even animals. Natural resources can be divided into renewable resources and exhaustible resources. A *renewable resource* can be drawn on indefinitely if used conservatively. Thus, timber is a renewable resource if felled trees are replaced to provide a steady supply. The air and rivers are renewable resources if they are allowed suffient time to clean themselves of any pollutants. More generally, biological resources like fish, game, livestock, forests, rivers, groundwater, grasslands, and soil are renewable if managed properly. An *exhaustible resource*—such as oil, coal, or copper ore—does not renew itself

There's no such thing as a free napkin.

and so is available in a limited amount. Once burned, each barrel of oil or ton of coal is gone forever. The world's oil and coal deposits are exhaustible.

A special kind of human skill called **entrepreneurial ability** is the talent required to dream up a new product or find a better way to produce an existing one. This special skill comes from an entrepreneur. An **entrepreneur** is a profit-seeking decision maker who starts with an idea, then organizes an enterprise to bring that idea to life, and assumes the risk of operation. An entrepreneur pays resource owners for the opportunity to employ their resources in the firm. Every firm in the world today, such as Ford, Microsoft, Google, and Dell, began as an idea in the mind of an entrepreneur.

Resource owners are paid **wages** for their labor, **interest** for the use of their capital, and **rent** for the use of their natural resources. Entrepreneurial ability is rewarded by **profit**, which equals the *revenue* from items sold minus the *cost* of the resources employed to make those items. The word *profit* comes from the Latin *proficere,* which means "to benefit." The entrepreneur benefits from what's left over after paying other resource suppliers. Sometimes the entrepreneur suffers a loss. Resource earnings are usually based on the *time* these resources are employed. Resource payments therefore have a time dimension, as in a wage of $10 *per hour,* interest of 6 percent *per year,* rent of $600 *per month,* or profit of $10,000 *per year.*

Goods and Services

Resources are combined in a variety of ways to produce goods and services. A farmer, a tractor, 50 acres of land, seeds, and fertilizer combine to grow the good: corn. One hundred musicians, musical instruments, chairs, a conductor, a musical score, and a music hall combine to produce the service: Beethoven's Fifth Symphony. Corn is a **good** because it is something you can see, feel, and touch; it requires scarce resources to produce; and it satisfies human wants. The book you are now holding, the chair you are sitting in, the clothes you are wearing, and your next meal are all goods. The performance of the Fifth Symphony is a **service** because it is intangible, yet it uses scarce resources to satisfy human wants. Lectures, movies, concerts, phone service, broadband connections, yoga lessons, dry cleaning, and haircuts are all services.

Making choices in a world of scarcity means we must pass up some goods and services.

Because goods and services are produced using scarce resources, they are themselves scarce. *A good or service is scarce if the amount people desire exceeds the amount available at a zero price.* Because we cannot have all the goods and services we would like, we must continually choose among them. We must choose among more pleasant living quarters, better meals, nicer clothes, more reliable transportation, faster computers, and so on. Making choices in a world of **scarcity** means we must pass up some goods and services. But not everything is scarce. In fact some things we would prefer to have less of. For example, we would prefer to have less garbage, less spam email, and less pollution. Things we want none of even at a zero price are called *bads.* Think of a bad as the opposite of a good.

A few goods and services seem *free* because the amount available at a zero price exceeds the amount people want. For example, air and seawater often seem

entrepreneurial ability
managerial and organizational skills needed to start a firm, combined with the willingness to take the risk of profit or loss

entrepreneur
a profit-seeking decision maker who starts with an idea, organizes an enterprise to bring that idea to life, and assumes the risk of the operation

wages
payment to resource owners for their labor

interest
payment to resource owners for the use of their capital

rent
payment to resource owners for the use of their natural resources

profit
reward for entrepreneurial ability; sales revenue minus resource cost

good
a tangible product used to satisfy human wants

service
an activity, or intangible product, used to satisfy human wants

scarcity
occurs when the amount people desire exceeds the amount available at a zero price

free because we can breathe all the air we want and have all the seawater we can haul away. Yet, despite the old saying "The best things in life are free," most goods and services are scarce, not free, and even those that appear to be free come with strings attached. For example, *clean* air and *clean* seawater have become scarce. *Goods and services that are truly free are not the subject matter of economics. Without scarcity, there would be no economic problem and no need for prices.*

Sometimes we mistakenly think of certain goods as free because they involve no apparent cost to us. Napkins seem to be free at Starbucks. Nobody stops you from taking a fistful. Supplying napkins, however, costs the company millions each year and prices reflect that cost. Some restaurants make special efforts to keep napkin use down—such as packing them tightly into the dispenser or making you ask for them.

You may have heard the expression "There is no such thing as a free lunch." There is no free lunch because all goods and services involve a cost to someone. The lunch may seem free to us, but it draws scarce resources away from the production of other goods and services, and whoever provides a free lunch often expects something in return. A Russian proverb makes a similar point but with a bit more bite: "The only place you find free cheese is in a mousetrap." Albert Einstein once observed, "Sometimes one pays the most for things one gets for nothing."

Economic Decision Makers

There are four types of decision makers in the economy: households, firms, governments, and the rest of the world. Their interaction determines how an economy's resources are allocated. *Households* play the starring role. As consumers, households demand the goods and services produced. As resource owners, households supply labor, capital, natural resources, and entrepreneurial ability to firms, governments, and the rest of the world. *Firms, governments,* and *the rest of the world* demand the resources that households supply and then use these resources to supply the goods and services that households demand. The rest of the world includes foreign households, firms, and governments that supply resources and products to U.S. markets and demand resources and products from U.S. markets.

market
a set of arrangements by which buyers and sellers carry out exchange at mutually agreeable terms

product market
a market in which a good or service is bought and sold

resource market
a market in which a resource is bought and sold

circular-flow model
a diagram that traces the flow of resources, products, income, and revenue among economic decision makers

Markets are the means by which buyers and sellers carry out exchange. By bringing together the two sides of exchange, markets determine price and quantity. Markets are often physical places, such as supermarkets, department stores, shopping malls, or yard sales. But markets also include other mechanisms by which buyers and sellers communicate, such as classified ads, radio and television ads, telephones, bulletin boards, online sites, and face-to-face bargaining. These market mechanisms provide information about the quantity, quality, and price of products offered for sale. Goods and services are bought and sold in **product markets**. Resources are bought and sold in **resource markets**. The most important resource market is the labor, or job, market. Think about your own experience looking for a job, and you get some idea of that market.

A Simple Circular-Flow Model

Now that you have learned a bit about economic decision makers, consider how they interact. Such a picture is conveyed by the **circular-flow model**, which describes the flow of resources, products, income, and revenue among economic decision makers. The simple circular-flow model focuses on the primary interaction in a market economy—that between households and firms. Exhibit 1 shows households on the left and firms on the right; please take a look.

Exhibit 1

The Simple Circular-Flow Model for Households and Firms

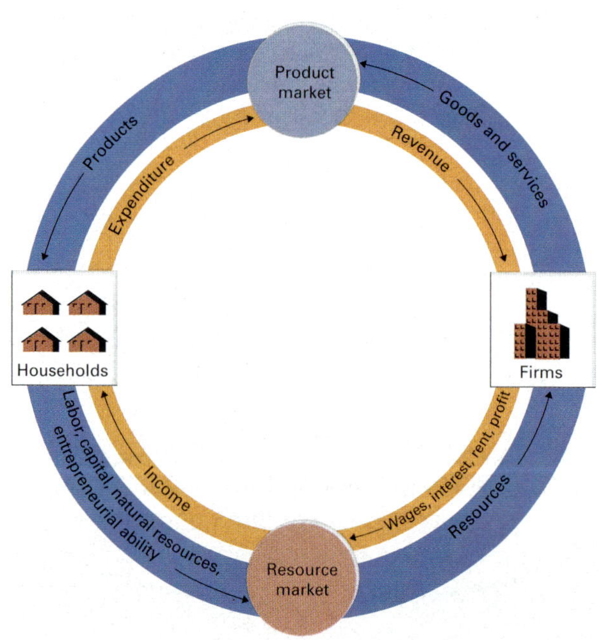

Households supply labor, capital, natural resources, and entrepreneurial ability to firms through resource markets, shown in the lower portion of the exhibit. In return, households demand goods and services from firms through product markets, shown on the upper portion of the exhibit. Viewed from the business end, firms demand labor, capital, natural resources, and entrepreneurial ability from households through resource markets, and firms supply goods and services to households through product markets.

The flows of resources and products are supported by the flows of income and expenditure—that is, by the flow of money. So let's add money. The demand and supply of resources come together in resource markets to determine what firms pay for resources. These resource prices—wages, interest, rent, and profit—flow as *income* to households. The demand and supply of products come together in product markets to determine what households pay for goods and services. These product prices of goods and services flow as *revenue* to firms. Resources and products flow in one direction—in this case, counterclockwise—and the corresponding payments flow in the other direction—clockwise. What goes around comes around. Take a little time now to trace the logic of the circular flows.

LO2 The Art of Economic Analysis

An economy results from the choices that millions of individuals make in attempting to satisfy their unlimited wants. Because these choices lie at the heart of the economic problem—coping with scarce resources but unlimited wants—they deserve a closer look. Learning about the forces that shape economic choice is the first step toward mastering the art of economic analysis.

Rational Self-Interest

A key economic assumption is that individuals, in making choices, rationally select alternatives they perceive to be in their best interests. By *rational*, economists mean simply that people try to make the best choices they can, given the available information. People may not know with certainty which alternative will turn out to be the best. They simply select the alternatives they *expect* will yield the most satisfaction and happiness. In general, rational self-interest means that individuals try to maximize the expected benefit achieved with a given cost or to minimize the expected cost of achieving a given benefit.

Rational self-interest should not be viewed as blind materialism, pure selfishness, or greed. We all know people who are tuned to radio station WIIFM (What's In It For Me?). For most of us, however, self-interest often includes the welfare of our family, our friends, and perhaps the poor of the world. Even so, our concern for others is influenced by the cost of that concern. We may readily volunteer to drive a friend to the airport on Saturday afternoon but are less likely to offer a ride if the plane leaves at 6:00 A.M. When we donate clothes to an organization such as Goodwill Industries, they are more likely to be old and worn than brand new. People tend to give more to charities when their contributions are tax deductible. TV stations are more likely to donate airtime for public-service announcements during the dead of night than during prime time (in fact, 80 percent of such announcements air between 11:00 P.M. and 7:00 A.M.[1]). In Asia some people burn money to soothe the passage of a departed loved one. But they burn fake money, not real money. The notion of self-interest does not rule out concern for others; it simply means that concern for others is influenced by the same economic forces that affect other economic choices. *The lower the personal cost of helping others, the more help we offer.*

Choice Requires Time and Information

Rational choice takes time and requires information, but time and information are scarce and therefore valuable. If you have any doubts about the time and information required to make choices, talk to someone who recently purchased a home, a car, or a personal computer. Talk to a corporate official trying to decide whether to introduce a new product, sell online, build a new factory, or buy another firm. Or think back to your own experience of choosing a college. You probably talked to friends, relatives, teachers, and guidance counselors. You likely used school catalogs, college guides, and Web sites. You may have visited some campuses to see the admissions staff and anyone else willing to talk. The decision

1. Sally Goll Beatty, "Media and Agencies Brawl Over Do-Good Advertising," *Wall Street Journal,* 29 September 1997.

rational self-interest
individuals try to maximize the expected benefit achieved with a given cost or to minimize the expected cost of achieving a given benefit

> > After armed guards escorted the shipment of *Harry Potter and the Deathly Hallows* to Amazon, the online retailer, it deposited the top-secret books in a guarded security zone. The zone had one entrance, and employees required a special badge to enter. Only longtime employees were allowed to pack the books, and counts were taken multiple times a day to ensure that no copies "went missing." The marginal cost for distributing such a hot title were certainly not insignificant.

took time and money, and it probably involved aggravation and anxiety.

Because information is costly to acquire, we are often willing to pay others to gather and digest it for us. College guidebooks, stock analysts, travel agents, real estate brokers, career counselors, restaurant critics, movie reviewers, specialized Web sites, and *Consumer Reports* magazine attest to our willingness to pay for information that improves our choices. As we'll see next, *rational decision makers continue to acquire information as long as the additional benefit expected from that information exceeds the additional cost of gathering it.*

Economic Analysis Is Marginal Analysis

Economic choice usually involves some adjustment to the existing situation, or status quo. Amazon.com must decide whether to add an additional line of products. The school superintendent must decide whether to hire another teacher. Your favorite jeans are on sale, and you must decide whether to buy another pair. You are wondering whether to carry an extra course next term. You just finished lunch and are deciding whether to have dessert.

> **marginal**
> incremental, additional, or extra; used to describe a change in an economic variable
>
> **microeconomics**
> the study of the economic behavior in particular markets, such as that for computers or unskilled labor

Economic choice is based on a comparison of the *expected marginal benefit* and the *expected marginal cost* of the action under consideration. **Marginal** means incremental, additional, or extra. Marginal refers to a change in an economic variable, a change in the status quo. *A rational decision maker changes the status quo if the expected marginal benefit from the change exceeds the expected marginal cost.* For example, Amazon.com compares the marginal benefit expected from adding a new line of products (the additional sales revenue) with the marginal cost (the additional cost of the resources required). Likewise, you compare the marginal benefit you expect from eating dessert (the additional pleasure or satisfaction) with its marginal cost (the additional money, time, and calories).

Typically, the change under consideration is small, but a marginal choice can involve a major economic adjustment, as in the decision to quit school and find a job. For a firm, a marginal choice might mean building a plant in Mexico or even filing for bankruptcy. By focusing on the effect of a marginal adjustment to the status quo, the economist is able to cut the analysis of economic choice down to a manageable size. Rather than confront a bewildering economic reality head-on, the economist begins with a marginal choice to see how this choice affects a particular market and shapes the economic system as a whole. Incidentally, to the noneconomist, *marginal* usually means relatively inferior, as in "a movie of marginal quality." Forget that meaning for this course and instead think of *marginal* as meaning incremental, additional, or extra.

Microeconomics and Macroeconomics

Although you have made thousands of economic choices, you probably seldom think about your own economic behavior. For example, why are you reading this book right now rather than doing something else? **Microeconomics** is the study of your economic behavior and the economic behavior of others who make choices about such matters as how much to study and how much to party, how much to borrow and how much to save, what to buy and what to sell. Microeconomics examines individual economic choices and how markets coordinate the choices of various decision makers. Microeconomics explains how price and quantity are determined in individual markets—the market for breakfast cereal, sports equipment, or used cars, for instance.

> "A good theory helps us understand a messy and confusing world."

You have probably given little thought to what influences your own economic choices. You have likely given even less thought to how your choices link up with those made by millions of others in the U.S. economy to determine economy-wide measures such as total production, employment, and economic growth. **Macroeconomics** studies the performance of the economy as a whole. Whereas microeconomics studies the individual pieces of the economic puzzle, as reflected in particular markets, macroeconomics puts all the pieces together to focus on the big picture.

To review: The art of economic analysis focuses on how people use their scarce resources in an attempt to satisfy their unlimited wants. Rational self-interest guides individual choice. Choice requires time and information and involves a comparison of the marginal benefit and marginal cost of alternative actions. Microeconomics looks at the individual pieces of the economic puzzle; macroeconomics fits the pieces together to shape the big picture.

LO3 The Science of Economic Analysis

Economists use scientific analysis to develop theories, or models, that help explain economic behavior. An **economic theory**, or **economic model**, is a simplification of economic reality that is *used to make predictions about the real world*. A theory, or model, such as the circular-flow model, captures the important elements of the problem under study but need not spell out every detail and interrelation. In fact, adding more details may make a theory more unwieldy and, therefore, less useful. For example, a wrist watch is a model that tells time, but a watch festooned with extra features is harder to read at a glance and is therefore less useful as a time-telling model. The world is so complex that we must simplify to make sense of things. Store mannequins simplify the human form (some even lack arms and heads). Comic strips simplify characters—leaving out fingers or a mouth, for instance. You might think of economic theory as a stripped-down, or streamlined, version of economic reality.

A good theory helps us understand a messy and confusing world. Lacking a theory of how things work, our thinking can becomes cluttered with facts, one piled on another as in a messy closet. You could think of a good theory as a closet organizer for the mind. A good theory offers a helpful guide to sorting, saving, and understanding information.

The Role of Theory

Most people don't understand the role of theory. Perhaps you have heard, "Oh, that's fine in theory, but in practice it's another matter." The implication is that the theory in question provides little aid in practical matters. People who say this fail to realize that they are merely substituting their own theory for a theory they either do not believe or do not understand. They are really saying, "I have my own theory that works better."

All of us employ theories, however poorly defined or understood. Someone who pounds on the Pepsi machine that just ate a quarter has a crude theory about how that machine works. One version of that theory might be "The quarter drops through a series of whatchamacallits, but sometimes it gets stuck. *If* I pound on the machine, *then* I can free up the quarter and send it on its way." Evidently, this theory is widespread enough that people continue to pound on machines that fail to perform (a real problem for the vending machine industry and one reason newer machines are fronted with glass). Yet, if you were to ask these mad pounders to explain their "theory" about how the machine operates, they would look at you as if you were crazy.

macroeconomics the study of the economic behavior of entire economies

economic theory (economic model) a simplification of reality used to make predictions about cause and effect in the real world

Exhibit 2

The Scientific Method: Step by Step

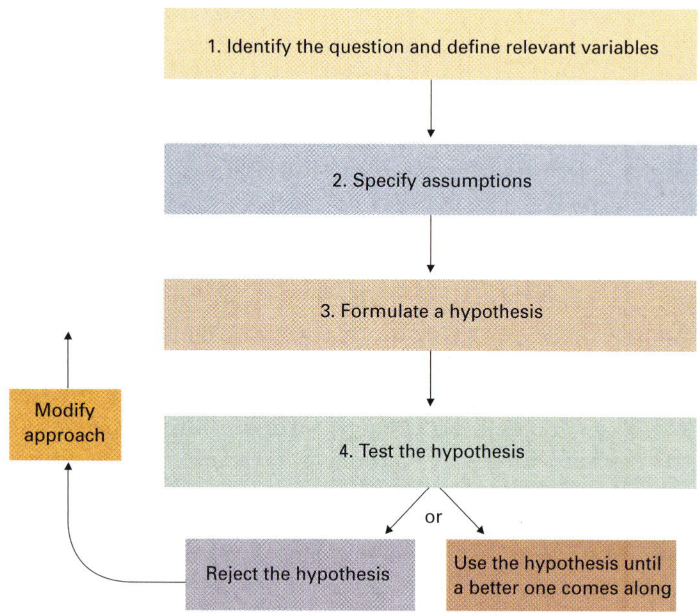

The Scientific Method

To study economic problems, economists employ a process of theoretical investigation called *the scientific method,* which consists of four steps, as outlined in Exhibit 2.

Step One: Identify the Question and Define Relevant Variables

variable
a measure, such as price or quantity, that can take on different values at different times

other-things-constant assumption
the assumption, when focusing on the relation among key economic variables, that other variables remain unchanged; in Latin, *ceteris paribus*

behavioral assumption
an assumption that describes the expected behavior of economic decision makers—what motivates them

hypothesis
a theory about how key variables relate

The scientific method begins with curiousity: Someone wants to answer a question. Thus, the first step is to identify the economic question and define the variables relevant to a solution. For example, the question might be "What is the relationship between the price of Pepsi and the quantity of Pepsi purchased?" In this case, the relevant variables are price and quantity. A **variable** is a measure that can take on different values at different times. The variables of concern become the elements of the theory, so they must be selected with care.

Step Two: Specify Assumptions

The second step is to specify the assumptions under which the theory is to apply. One major category of assumptions is the **other-things-constant assumption**—in Latin, the *ceteris paribus* assumption. The idea is to identify the variables of interest and then focus exclusively on the relationships among them, assuming that nothing else important changes—that other things remain constant. Again, suppose we are interested in how the price of Pepsi influences the amount purchased. To isolate the relation between these two variables, we assume that there are no changes in other relevant variables such as consumer income, the average temperature, or the price of Coke.

© MARTIN LEE/MEDIABLITZIMAGES (UK) LIMITED/ALAMY

We also make assumptions about how people behave; these are called **behavioral assumptions**. The primary behavioral assumption is rational self-interest. Earlier we assumed that individual decision makers pursue self-interest rationally and make choices accordingly. Rationality implies that each consumer buys the products expected to maximize his or her level of satisfaction. Rationality also implies that each firm supplies the products expected to maximize the firm's profit. These kinds of assumptions are called behavioral assumptions because they specify how we expect economic decision makers to behave—what makes them tick, so to speak.

Step Three: Formulate a Hypothesis

The third step in the scientific method is to formulate a **hypothesis**, which is a theory about how key variables relate to each other. For example, one hypothesis holds that if the price of Pepsi goes up, other things constant, then the quantity purchased declines. The hypothesis becomes a prediction of what happens to the quantity purchased if the price increases. *The purpose of this hypothesis, like that of any theory, is to help make predictions about cause and effect in the real world.*

Step Four: Test the Hypothesis

In the fourth step, by comparing its predictions with evidence, we test the validity of a hypothesis. To test a hypothesis, we must focus on the variables in question, while carefully controlling for other effects assumed not to change. The test leads us either to (1) reject the hypothesis, or theory, if it predicts worse than the best alternative theory or (2) use the hypothesis, or theory, until a better one comes along. If we reject the hypothesis, we can go back and modify our approach in light of the results. Please spend a moment now reviewing the steps of the scientific method in Exhibit 2.

Scientific Method:

1. Identify the question and define relevant variables
2. Specify assumptions
3. Formulate a hypothesis
4. Test the hypothesis

Normative Versus Positive

Economists usually try to explain how the economy works. Sometimes they concern themselves not with how the economy *does* work but how it *should* work. Compare these two statements: "The U.S. unemployment rate is 4.6 percent" and "The U.S. unemployment rate should be lower." The first, called a **positive economic statement**, is an assertion about economic reality that can be supported or rejected by reference to the facts. Positive economics, like physics or biology, attempts to understand the world around us. The second, called a **normative economic statement**, reflects an opinion. And an opinion is merely that—it cannot be shown to be true or false by reference to the facts. Positive statements concern what *is;* normative statements concern what, in someone's opinion, *should be.* Positive statements need not necessarily be true, but they must be subject to verification or refutation by reference to the facts. Theories are expressed as positive statements such as "If the price of Pepsi increases, then the quantity demanded decreases."

Most of the disagreement among economists involves normative debates—such as the appropriate role of government—rather than statements of positive analysis. To be sure, many theoretical issues remain unresolved, but economists generally agree on most fundamental theoretical principles—that is, about positive economic analysis. For example, in a survey of 464 U.S. economists, only 6.5 percent disagreed with the statement "A ceiling on rents reduces the quantity and quality of housing available." This is a positive statement because it can be shown to be consistent or inconsistent with the evidence. In contrast, there was much less agreement on normative statements such as "The distribution of income in the United States should be more equal." Half the economists surveyed "generally agreed," a quarter "generally disagreed," and a quarter "agreed with provisos."[2]

© PHOTOS.COM/JUPITERIMAGES

Normative statements, or value judgments, have a place in a policy debate such as the proper role of government, provided that statements of opinion are distinguished from statements of fact. In such policy debates, you are entitled to your own opinion, but you are not entitled to your own facts.

> "Economists explain their theories by telling stories about how they think the economy works."

Economists Tell Stories

Despite economists' reliance on the scientific method for developing and evaluating theories, economic analysis is as much art as science. Formulating a question, isolating the key variables, specifying the assumptions, proposing a theory to answer the question, and devising a way to test the predictions all involve more than simply an understanding of economics and the scientific method. Carrying out these steps requires good intuition and the imagination of a storyteller. Economists explain their theories by telling stories about how they think the economy works. To tell a compelling story, an economist relies on case studies, anecdotes, parables, the personal experience of the listener, and supporting data. Throughout this book, you'll hear stories that bring you closer to the ideas under consideration. The stories, such as the one about the Pepsi machine, breathe life into economic theory and help you personalize abstract ideas.

positive economic statement
a statement that can be proved or disproved by reference to facts

normative economic statement
a statement that reflects an opinion, which cannot be proved or disproved by reference to the facts

2. Richard M. Alston, et al., "Is There a Consensus Among Economists in the 1990s?" *American Economic Review* 82 (May 1992): pp. 203–209, Table 1.

Predicting Average Behavior

The goal of an economic theory is to predict the impact of an economic event on economic choices and, in turn, the effect of these choices on particular markets or on the economy as a whole. Does this mean that economists try to predict the behavior of particular consumers or producers? Not necessarily, because a specific individual may behave in an unpredictable way. But the unpredictable actions of numerous individuals tend to cancel one another out, so the *average behavior* of groups can be predicted more accurately. For example, if the federal government cuts personal income taxes, certain households may decide to save the entire tax cut. On average, however, household spending increases. Likewise, if Burger King cuts the price of Whoppers, the manager can better predict how much sales will increase than how a specific customer coming through the door will respond. *The random actions of individuals tend to offset one another, so the average behavior of a large group can be predicted more accurately than the behavior of a particular individual.* Consequently, economists tend to focus on the average, or typical, behavior of people in groups—for example, as average taxpayers or average Whopper consumers—rather than on the behavior of a specific individual.

LO[4] Some Pitfalls of Faulty Economic Analysis

Economic analysis, like other forms of scientific inquiry, is subject to common mistakes in reasoning that can lead to faulty conclusions. Here are three sources of confusion.

association-is-causation fallacy the incorrect idea that if two variables are associated in time, one must necessarily cause the other

fallacy of composition the incorrect belief that what is true for the individual, or part, must necessarily be true for the group, or the whole

secondary effects unintended consequences of economic actions that may develop slowly over time as people react to events

The Fallacy That Association Is Causation

In the last two decades, the number of physicians specializing in cancer treatment increased sharply. At the same time, the incidence of some cancers increased. Can we conclude that physicians cause cancer? No. To assume that event A caused event B simply because the two are associated in time is to commit the **association-is-causation fallacy**, a common error. The fact that one event precedes another or that the two events occur simultaneously does not necessarily mean that one causes the other. Remember: Association is not necessarily causation.

The Fallacy of Composition

Perhaps you have been to a rock concert where everyone stands to get a better view. At some concerts, most people even stand on their chairs. But even standing on chairs does not improve the view if others do the same. Likewise, arriving early to buy game tickets does not work if many others have the same idea. These are examples of the **fallacy of composition**, which is an erroneous belief that what is true for the individual, or the part, is also true for the group, or the whole.

The Mistake of Ignoring the Secondary Effects

In many cities, public officials have imposed rent controls on apartments. The primary effect of this policy, the effect policy makers focus on, is to keep rents from rising. Over time, however, fewer new apartments get built because renting them becomes less profitable. Moreover, existing rental units deteriorate because owners have plenty of customers anyway. Thus, the quantity and quality of housing may decline as a result of what appears to be a reasonable measure to keep rents from rising. The mistake was to ignore the **secondary effects**, or the unintended consequences, of the policy. Economic actions have secondary effects that often turn out to be more important than the primary effects. Secondary effects may develop more slowly and may not be immediately obvious, but good economic analysis tries to anticipate them and take them into account.

LO[5] Why Study Economics (Or, If Economists Are So Smart, Why Aren't They Rich?)

Why aren't economists rich? Well, some are, earning over $25,000 per appearance on the lecture circuit. Others top $2 million a year as consultants and expert witnesses.[3] Economists have been appointed to federal cabinet posts, such as Secretaries of Commerce, Defense, Labor, State, and Treasury, and to head the U.S. Federal Reserve System. Economics is the only

3. As reported by George Anders, "An Economist's Courtroom Bonanza," *Wall Street Journal*, 19 March 2007.

social science and the only business discipline for which the prestigious Nobel Prize is awarded, and pronouncements by economists are reported in the media daily. *The Economist,* a widely respected news weekly from London, has argued that economic ideas have influenced policy "to a degree that would make other social scientists drool."[4]

The economics profession thrives because its models usually do a better job of making economic sense out of a confusing world than do alternative approaches. But not all economists are wealthy, nor is personal wealth the goal of the discipline. In a similar vein, not all doctors are healthy (some even smoke), not all carpenters live in perfectly built homes, not all marriage counselors are happily married, and not all child psychologists have well-adjusted children. Still, those who study economics do reap financial rewards.

Famous Economics Majors

© AP IMAGES

Are you the next successful economics major?

A number of world leaders majored in economics, including three of the last six U.S. presidents, Philippines President Gloria Macapagal-Arroyo, who earned a Ph.D. in the subject, U.S. Supreme Court Justices Steven Breyer and Anthony Kennedy, and former Justice Sandra Day O'Connor. Other economics majors include billionaire Donald Trump, eBay President (and billionaire) Meg Whitman, Microsoft chief executive officer (and billionaire) Steve Ballmer, CNN founder (and billionaire) Ted Turner, Intel President Paul Otellini, NFL Patriot's coach Bill Belichick, Governor Arnold Schwarzenegger, high-tech guru Esther Dyson, and Scott Adams, creator of Dilbert, the mouthless wonder.

SOURCE: "The World's Billionaires," *Forbes,* 8 March 2007.

Among college graduates, all kinds of factors affect earnings, such as general ability, occupation, college attended, college major, and highest degree earned. To isolate the effects of the college major on earnings, a National Science Foundation study surveyed people in specific age groups who worked full time and had earned a bachelor's as their highest degree. Exhibit 3 shows the median earnings by major for men and women ages 35 to 44. As a point of reference, the *median* annual earnings for men was $43,199 (half earned more and half earned less). The median earnings for women was $32,155, only 74 percent that of men. Among men, the top pay was the $53,286 median earned by engineering majors; that pay was 23 percent above the median for all men surveyed. Among women, the top pay was the $49,170 median earned by economics majors; that pay was 53 percent above the median for all women surveyed.

Incidentally, men who majored in economics earned a median of $49,377, ranking them seventh among 27 majors and 14 percent above the median for all men surveyed. Thus, even though the median pay for all women was only 74 percent of the median pay for all men, women who majored in economics earned about the same as men who majored in economics. We can say that *economics majors earned more than most, and they experienced no pay difference based on gender.*

Note that among both men and women, the majors ranked toward the top of the list tend to be more quantitative and analytical. According to the study's author, "Employers may view certain majors as more difficult and may assume that graduates in these fields are more able and hard working, whereupon they offer them higher salaries."[5] The selection of a relatively more challenging major such as economics sends a favorable signal to future employers.

The study also examined the kinds of jobs different majors actually found. Those who majored in economics became mid- and top-level managers, executives, and administrators. They also worked in sales, computer fields, financial analysis, and economic analysis. Remember, the survey was limited to those whose highest degree was the baccalaureate, so it excluded the many economics majors who went on to pursue graduate studies in law, business administration, economics, public administration, journalism, and other fields.[6]

Final Word

This textbook describes how economic factors affect individual choices and how all these choices come together to shape the economic system. Economics is not the whole story, and economic

4. "The Puzzling Failure of Economics," *The Economist,* 23 August 1997, p. 11.

5. Daniel E. Hecker, "Earnings of College Graduates, 1993," *Monthly Labor Review* (December 1995): p. 15.

6. For a survey of employment opportunities, go to the U.S. Labor Department's Occupational Outlook Handbook at http://www.bls.gov/oco/.

Exhibit 3

Median Annual Earnings of 35-to-44-Year-Olds with Bachelor's as Highest Degree, by Major

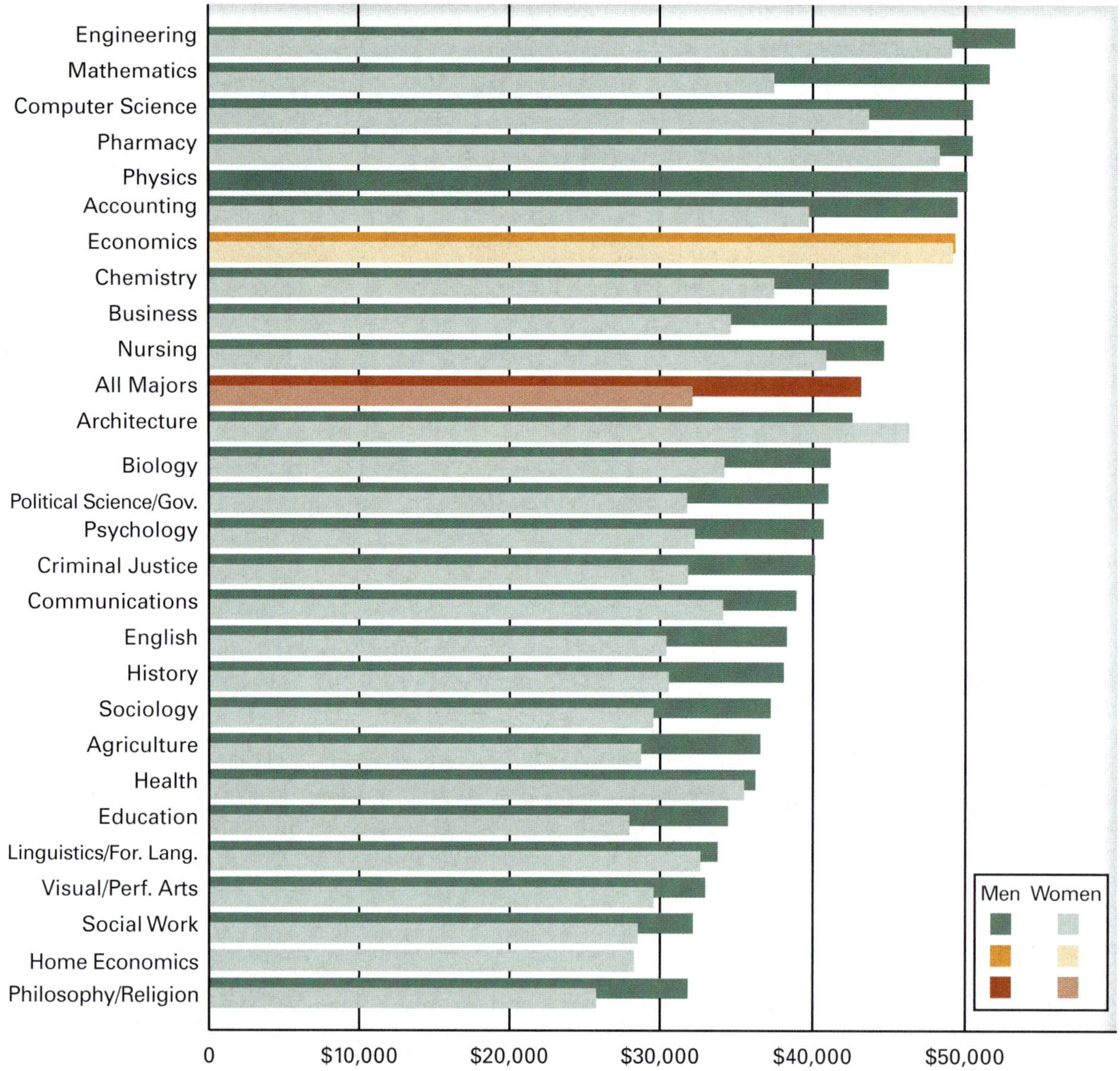

SOURCE: Earnings are for 1993 based on figures reported by Daniel Hecker in "Earnings of College Graduates, 1993." *Monthly Labor Review* (December 1995): 3–17.

factors are not always the most important. But economic considerations have important and predictable effects on individual choices, and these choices affect the way we live.

Sure, economics is a challenging discipline, but it is also an exciting and rewarding one. The good news is that you already know a lot about economics. To use this knowledge, however, you must cultivate the art and science of economic analysis. You must be able to simplify the world to formulate questions, isolate the relevant variables, and then tell a persuasive story about how these variables relate.

An economic relation can be expressed in words, represented as a table of quantities, described by a mathematical equation, or illustrated as a graph. The appendix to this chapter introduces graphs. You may find this unnecessary. If you are already familiar with relations among variables, slopes, tangents, and the like, you can probably just browse. But if you have little recent experience with graphs, you might benefit from a more careful reading with pencil and paper in hand.

The next chapter introduces key tools of economic analysis. Subsequent chapters use these tools to explore economic problems and to explain economic behavior that may otherwise seem puzzling. You must walk before you can run, however, and in the next chapter, you take your first wobbly steps.

Appendix

Understanding Graphs

Take out a pencil and a blank piece of paper. Go ahead. Put a point in the middle of the paper. This is your point of departure, called the origin. With your pencil at the origin, draw a straight line off to the right. This line is called the horizontal axis. The value of the variable x measured along the horizontal axis increases as you move to the right of the origin. Now mark off this line from 0 to 20, in increments of 5 units each. Returning to the origin, draw another line, this one straight up. This line is called the vertical axis. The value of the variable y measured along the vertical axis increases as you move upward. Mark off this line from 0 to 20, in increments of 5 units each.

Within the space framed by the two axes, you can plot possible combinations of the variables measured along each axis. Each point identifies a value measured along the horizontal, or *x*, axis *and* a value measured along the vertical, or *y*, axis. For example, place point *a* in your graph to reflect the combination where x equals 5 units and y equals 15 units. Likewise, place point *b* in your graph to reflect 10 units of x and 5 units of y. Now compare your results with points shown in Exhibit 4.

A graph is a picture showing how variables relate, and a picture can be worth a thousand words. Take a look at Exhibit 5, which shows the annual U.S. unemployment rate since 1900. The years are measured along the horizontal axis and the unemployment rate is measured as a percentage along the vertical axis. Exhibit 5 is a *time-series graph*, which shows the value of a variable, in this case the percentage of the labor force unemployed, over time. If you had to describe the information presented in Exhibit 5 in words, the explanation could take many words. The picture shows not only how one year compares to the next but also how one decade compares to another and how the rate trends over time. The sharply higher unemployment rate during the Great Depression of the 1930s is unmistakable. *Graphs convey information in a compact and efficient way.*

Exhibit 4

Basics of a Graph

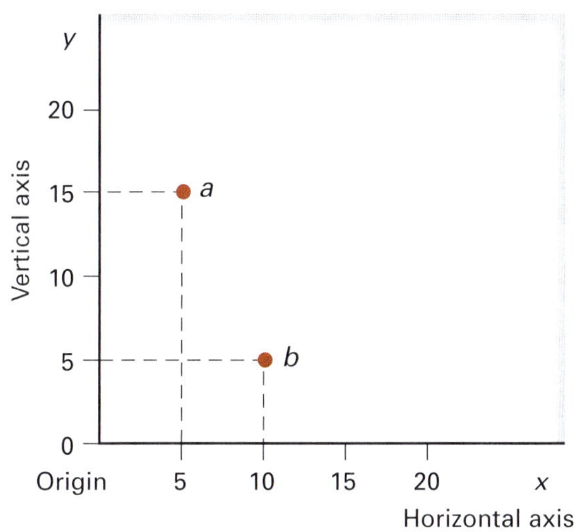

This appendix shows how graphs express a variety of possible relations among variables. Most graphs of interest in this book reflect the relationship between two economic variables, such as the unemployment rate and the year, the price of a product and the quantity demanded, or the price of production and the quantity supplied. Because we focus on just two variables at a time, we usually assume that other relevant variables remain constant.

One variable often depends on another. The time it takes you to drive home depends on your average speed. Your weight depends on how much you eat. The amount of Pepsi people buy depends on its price. A *functional relation* exists between two variables when the value of one variable *depends* on the value of another variable. The value of the dependent variable depends on the value of the independent variable. The task of the economist is to isolate economic relations and determine the direction of causality, if any. Recall that one of the pitfalls of economic thinking is the erroneous belief that association is causation. We cannot conclude that, simply because two events relate in time, one causes the other. There may be no relation between the two events.

Drawing Graphs

Let's begin with a simple relation. Suppose you are planning to drive across country and want to determine how far you will travel each day. You plan to average 50 miles per hour. Possible combinations of driving time and distance traveled per day appear in Exhibit 6. One column lists the hours driven per day, and the next column lists

origin
on a graph depicting two-dimensional space, the zero point

horizontal axis
line on a graph that begins at the origin and goes to the right and left; sometimes called the *x* axis

vertical axis
line on a graph that begins at the origin and goes up and down; sometimes called the *y* axis

graph
a picture showing how variables relate in two-dimensional space; one variable is measured along the horizontal axis and the other along the vertical axis

dependent variable
a variable whose value depends on that of the independent variable

independent variable
a variable whose value determines that of the dependent variable

Exhibit 5

U.S. Unemployment Rate Since 1900

A time-series graph depicts the behavior of some economic variable over time.

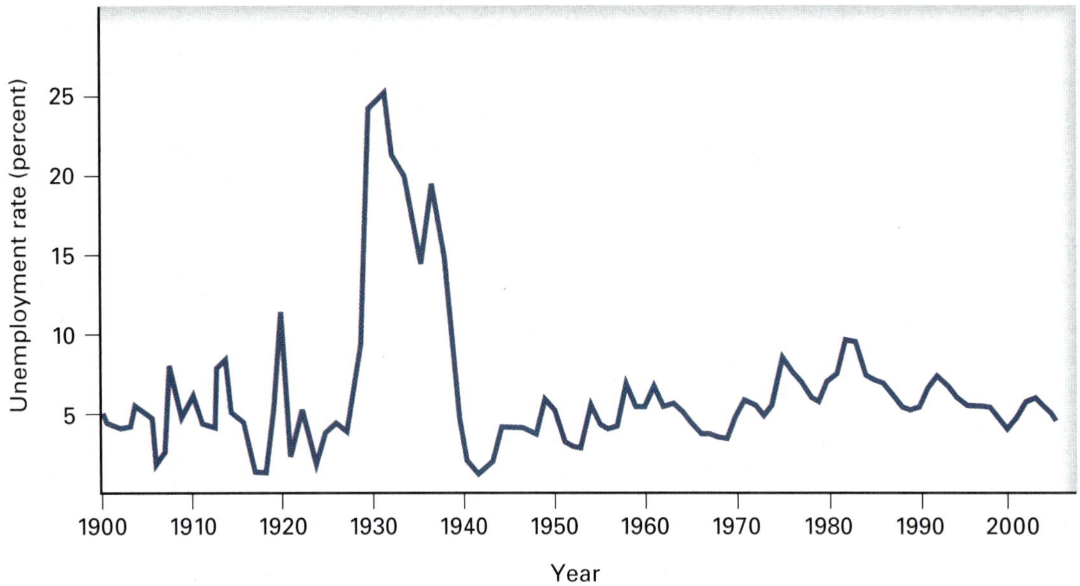

the number of miles traveled per day, assuming an average speed of 50 miles per hour. The distance traveled, the *dependent* variable, depends on the number of hours driven, the *independent* variable. Combinations of hours driven and distance traveled are shown as *a, b, c, d,* and *e*. Each combination of hours driven and distance traveled is represented by a point in Exhibit 7. For example, point *a* shows that if you drive for 1 hour, you travel 50 miles. Point *b* indicates that if you drive for 2 hours, you travel 100 miles. By connecting the points, or possible combinations, we create a line running upward and to the right. This makes sense, because the longer you drive, the farther you travel. Assumed constant along this line is your average speed of 50 miles per hour.

positive relation (direct relation) occurs when two variables increase or decrease together; the two variables move in the same direction

negative relation (inverse relation) occurs when two variables move in opposite directions; when one increases, the other decreases

slope of a line a measure of how much the vertical variable changes for a given increase in the horizontal variable; the vertical change between two points divided by the horizontal increase

Types of relations between variables include the following:

1. As one variable increases, the other increases— as in Exhibit 7; this is called a **positive**, or **direct**, **relation** between the variables.
2. As one variable increases, the other decreases; this is called a **negative**, or **inverse**, **relation**.

Exhibit 6

Schedule Relating Distance Traveled to Hours Driven

The distance traveled per day depends on the number of hours driven per day, assuming an average speed of 50 miles per hour. This table shows combinations of hours driven and distance traveled. These combinations are shown as points in Exhibit 7.

	Hours Driven per Day	Distance Traveled per Day (miles)
a	1	50
b	2	100
c	3	150
d	4	200
e	5	250

3. As one variable increases, the other remains unchanged; the two variables are said to be *independent*, or *unrelated*. One of the advantages of graphs is that they easily convey the relation between variables. We do not need to examine the particular combinations of numbers; we need only focus on the shape of the curve.

The Slopes of Straight Lines

A more precise way to describe the shape of a curve is to measure its slope. The **slope of a line** indicates how much the vertical variable changes for a given increase in the horizontal variable. Specifically, the

Exhibit 7

Graph Relating Distance Traveled to Hours Driven

Points *a* through *e* depict different combinations of hours driven per day and the corresponding distances traveled. Connecting these points graphs a line.

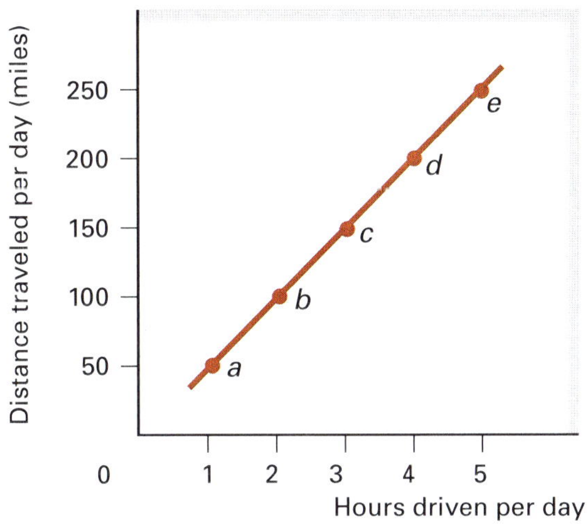

slope between any two points along any straight line is the vertical change between these two points divided by the horizontal increase, or

$$\text{Slope} = \frac{\text{Change in the vertical distance}}{\text{Increase in the horizontal distance}}$$

Each of the four panels in Exhibit 8 indicates a vertical change, given a 10-unit increase in the horizontal variable. In panel (a), the vertical distance increases by 5 units when the horizontal distance increases by 10 units. The slope of the line is therefore 5/10, or 0.5. Notice that the slope in this case is a positive number because the relation between the two variables is positive, or direct. This slope indicates that for every 1-unit increase in the horizontal variable, the vertical variable increases by 0.5 units. The slope, incidentally, does not imply causality; the increase in the horizontal variable does not necessarily *cause* the increase in the vertical variable. The slope simply measures the relation between an increase in the horizontal variable and the associated change in the vertical variable.

Exhibit 8

Alternative Slopes for Straight Lines

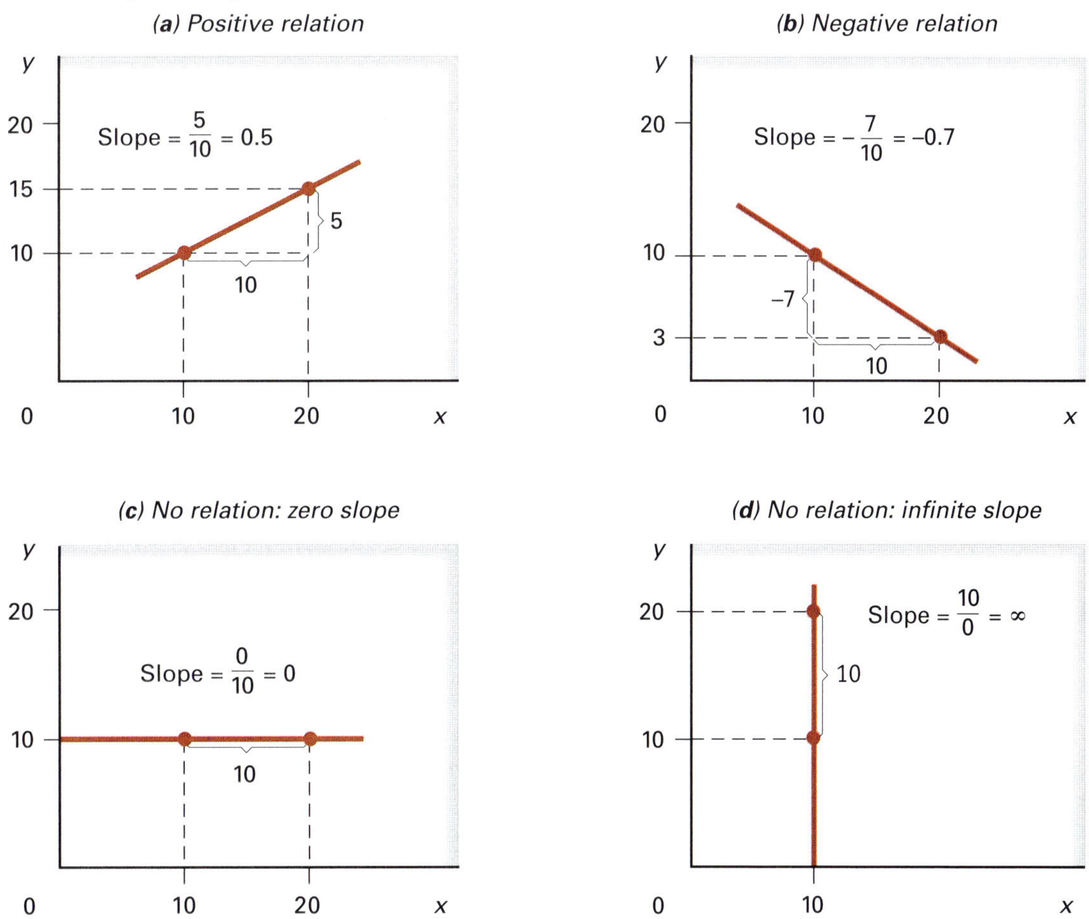

In panel (b) of Exhibit 8, the vertical distance declines by 7 units when the horizontal distance increases by 10 units, so the slope equals –7/10, or –0.7. The slope in this case is a negative number because the two variables have a negative, or inverse, relation. In panel (c), the vertical variable remains unchanged as the horizontal variable increases by 10, so the slope equals 0/10, or 0. These two variables are not related. Finally, in panel (d), the vertical variable can take on any value, although the horizontal variable remains unchanged. Again, the two variables are not related. In this case, any change in the vertical measure, for example a 10-unit change, is divided by 0, because the horizontal value does not change. Any change divided by 0 is infinitely large, so we say that the slope of a vertical line is infinite.

The Slope, Units of Measurement, and Marginal Analysis

The mathematical value of the slope depends on the units measured on the graph. For example, suppose copper tubing costs $1 a foot. Graphs depicting the relation between total cost and quantity purchased are shown in Exhibit 9. In panel (a), the total cost increases by $1 for each 1-foot increase in the amount of tubing purchased. Thus, the slope equals 1/1, or 1. If the cost per foot remains the same but units are measured not in *feet* but in *yards*, the relation between total cost and quantity purchased is as depicted in panel (b). Now total cost increases by $3 for each 1-*yard* increase in output, so the slope equals 3/1, or 3. Because different units are used to measure the copper tubing, the two panels reflect different slopes, even though the cost is $1 per foot in each panel. Keep in mind that *the slope depends in part on the units of measurement.*

Economic analysis usually involves *marginal analysis,* such as the marginal cost of one more unit of output. The slope is a convenient device for measuring marginal effects because it reflects the change in total cost, measured along the vertical axis, for each 1-unit change in output, measured along the horizontal axis. For example, in panel (a) of Exhibit 9, the marginal cost of another *foot* of copper tubing is $1, which also equals the slope of the line. In panel (b), the marginal cost of another *yard* of tubing is $3, which again is the slope of that line. Because of its applicability to marginal analysis, the slope has special relevance in economics.

The Slopes of Curved Lines

The slope of a straight line is the same everywhere along the line, but the slope of a curved line differs along the curve, as shown in Exhibit 10. To find the slope of a curved line at a particular point, draw a straight line that just touches the curve at that point but does not cut or cross the curve. Such a line is called a **tangent** to the curve at that point. The slope of the tangent gives the slope of the curve at that point. Look at line *A*, which is tangent to the curve at point *a*. As the horizontal value increases from 0 to 10, the vertical value drops along *A* from 40 to 0. Thus, the vertical change divided by the horizontal change equals –40/10, or –4, which is the slope of the curve at point *a*. This slope is negative because the vertical value decreases as the horizontal value increases. Line *B*, a line tangent to the curve at point *b*, has the slope –10/30, or –0.33. As you can see, the curve depicted in Exhibit 10 gets flatter as the horizontal variable increases, so the value of its slope approaches zero.

Other curves, of course, will reflect different slopes as well as different changes in the slope along the curve. Downward-sloping curves have negative slopes, and upward-sloping curves, positive slopes. Sometimes curves, such as those in Exhibit 11, are

tangent
a straight line that touches a curve at a point but does not cut or cross the curve; used to measure the slope of a curve at a point

Exhibit 9

Slope Depends on the Unit of Measure

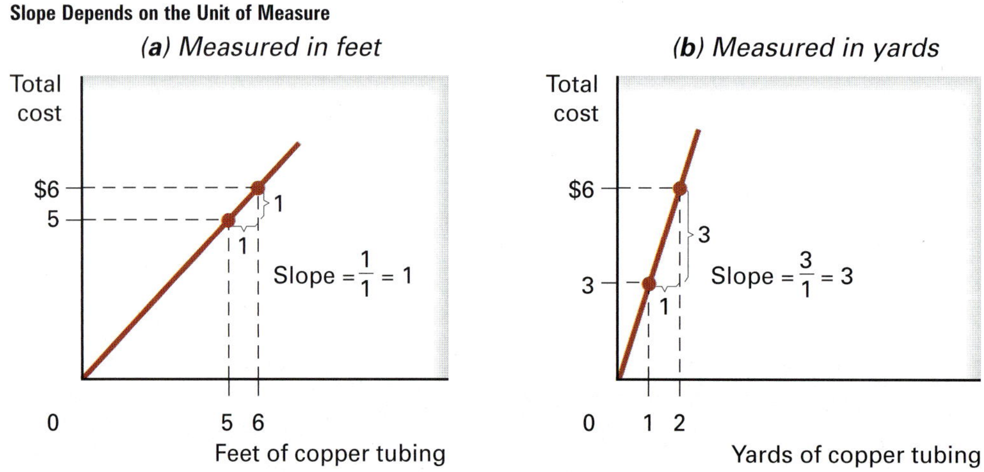

Exhibit 10

Slope at Different Points on a Curved Line

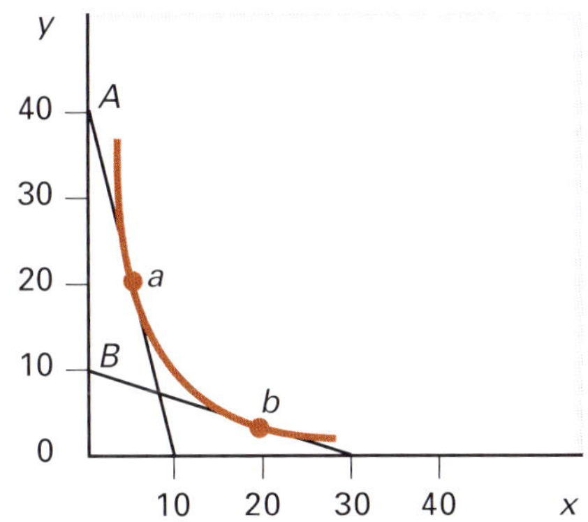

more complex, having both positive and negative ranges, depending on the horizontal value. In the hill-shaped curve, for small values of *x*, there is a positive relation between *x* and *y*, so the slope is positive. As the value of *x* increases, however, the slope declines and eventually becomes negative. We can divide the curve into two segments: (1) the segment between the origin and point *a*, where the slope is positive, and (2) the segment of the curve to the right of point *a*, where the slope is negative. The slope of the curve at point *a* is 0. The U-shaped curve in Exhibit 11 represents the opposite relation: *x* and *y* are negatively related until point *b* is reached; thereafter, they are positively related. The slope equals 0 at point *b*.

Line Shifts

Let's go back to the example of your cross-country trip, where we were trying to determine how many miles you would travel per day. Recall that we measured hours driven per day on the horizontal axis and miles traveled per day on the vertical axis, assuming an average speed of 50 miles per hour. That same relation is shown as line *T* in Exhibit 12. What happens if the average speed is 40 miles per hour? The entire relation between hours driven and distance traveled would change, as shown by the shift to the right of line *T* to *T*′. With a slower average speed, any distance traveled per day now requires more driving time. For example, 200 miles traveled requires 4 hours of driving when the average speed is 50 miles per hour (as shown by point *d* on curve *T*), but 200 miles takes 5 hours when your speed averages 40 miles per hour (as shown by point *f* on curve *T*′). Thus, *a change in the assumption about average speed changes the relationship between the two variables observed.* This changed relationship is expressed by a shift of the line that shows how the two variables relate.

That ends our once-over of graphs. Return to this appendix when you need a review.

Exhibit 11

Curves with Both Positive and Negative Slopes

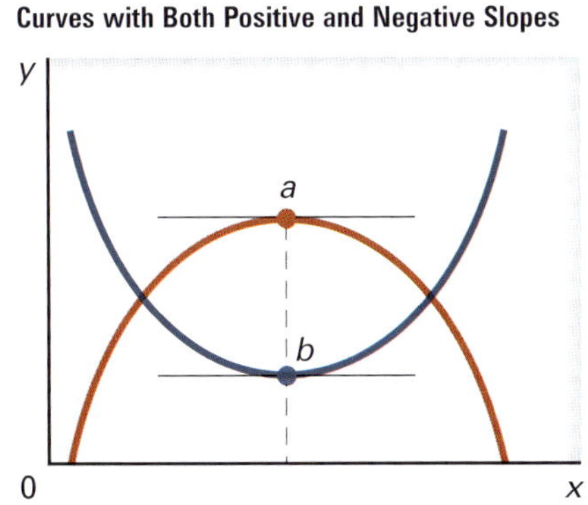

Exhibit 12

Shift of Line Relating Distance Traveled to Hours Driven

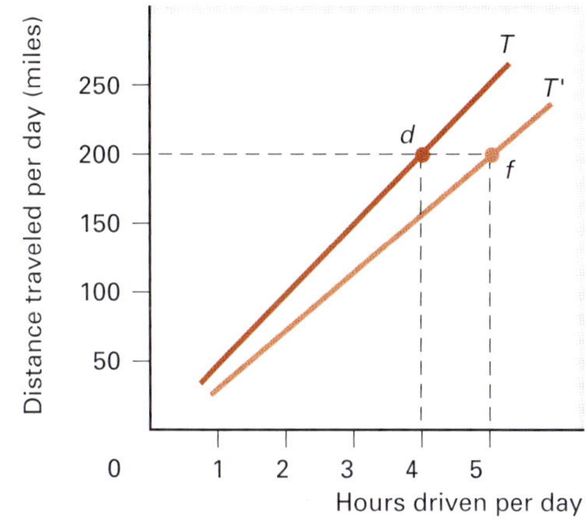

CHAPTER 2

Economic Tools and Economic Systems

Learning Outcomes

LO 1 Describe the impact of choice on opportunity

LO 2 Explain how comparative advantage, specialization, and exchange affect economic outcomes (output)

LO 3 Outline how economies function as production systems

LO 4 Describe different economic systems and the decision-making rules that define them

“Why is there no sense crying over spilt milk?”

Why are you reading this book right now rather than doing something else? What is college costing you? Why will you eventually major in one subject rather than continue to take courses in different ones? Why is fast food so fast? Why is there no sense crying over spilt milk? These and other questions are addressed in this chapter, which introduces some tools of economic analysis—some tools of the trade.

Chapter 1 introduced the idea that scarcity forces us to make choices, but the chapter said little about how to make economic choices. This chapter develops a framework for evaluating economic alternatives. First, we consider the cost involved in selecting one alternative over others. Next, we develop tools to explore the choices available to individuals and to the economy as a whole. Finally, we examine the questions that different economies must answer—questions about what goods and services to produce, how to produce them, and for whom to produce them.

What do you think?

People take better care of their personal belongings than they do of public property.

Strongly Disagree 1 2 3 4 5 6 7 *Strongly Agree*

Topics discussed in Chapter 2 include:

- Opportunity cost
- Division of labor
- Comparative advantage
- Specialization
- Production possibilities frontier
- Three economic questions
- Economic systems

LO1 Choice and Opportunity Cost

Think about a decision you just made: the decision to begin reading this chapter right now rather than use the time to study for another course, play sports, watch TV, go online, get some sleep, hang with friends, or do something else. Suppose your best alternative to reading right now is getting some sleep. The cost of reading is passing up the opportunity of sleep. Because of scarcity, whenever you make a choice, you must pass up another opportunity; you must incur an *opportunity cost*.

Opportunity Cost

What do we mean when we talk about the cost of something? Isn't it what we must give up—must forgo—to get that thing? The **opportunity cost** of the chosen item or activity is *the value of the best alternative that is forgone*. You can think of opportunity cost as the *opportunity lost*. Sometimes opportunity cost can be measured in terms of money, although, as we shall see, money is usually only part of opportunity cost.

How many times have you heard people say they did something because they "had nothing better to do"? They actually mean they had nothing else going on. Yet, according to the idea of opportunity cost, people *always* do what they do because they have nothing better to do. The choice selected seems, at the time, preferable to any other possible alternative. You are reading this chapter right now because you have nothing better to do. In fact, you are attending college for the same reason: College appears more attractive than your best alternative.

Opportunity Cost Is Subjective

Like beauty, opportunity cost is in the eye of the beholder. It is subjective. Only the individual making the choice can identify the most attractive alternative. But the chooser seldom knows the actual value of the best alternative forgone, because that alternative is "the road not taken." If you give up an evening of pizza and conversation with friends to work on a term paper, you will never know exactly what you gave up. You know only what you *expected*. Evidently, you expected the value of working on that paper to exceed the value of the best alternative. (Incidentally, focusing on the best alternative forgone makes all lesser alternatives irrelevant.)

Calculating Opportunity Cost Requires Time and Information

Economists assume that people rationally choose the most valued alternative. This does not mean you exhaustively assess the value of all possibilities. You assess alternatives as long as the expected marginal benefit of gathering more information about your options exceeds the expected marginal cost (even if you are not aware of making such conscious calculations). In other words, you do the best you can for yourself.

opportunity cost the value of the best alternative forgone when an item or activity is chosen

Because learning about alternatives is costly and time consuming, some choices are based on limited or even wrong information. Indeed, some choices may turn out badly (you went for a picnic but it rained; the movie you rented stank; your new shoes pinch; your new exercise equipment gets no exercise; the stock you bought tanked). Regret about lost opportunities is captured in the common expression "coulda, woulda, shoulda." At the time you made the choice, however, you thought you were making the best use of all your scarce resources, including the time required to gather and evaluate information about your alternatives.

Time: The Ultimate Constraint

The Sultan of Brunei is among the richest people on earth, with wealth topping $20 billion based on huge oil revenues that flow into his tiny country. He and his royal family (which has ruled for six centuries) live in a palace with 1,788 rooms, 250 toilets, and a throne room the size of a football field. The family owns hundreds of cars, including dozens of Rolls-Royces. Supported by such wealth, the Sultan would appear to have overcome the economic problem of scarcity. Though he can buy just about whatever he wants, he lacks the time to enjoy his stuff. If he pursues one activity, he cannot at the same time do something else. Each activity involves an opportunity cost. Consequently, the Sultan must choose from among the competing uses of his scarcest resource, time. Although your alternatives are less exotic, you too face time constraints, especially toward the end of the college term.

Opportunity Cost Varies with Circumstance

Opportunity cost depends on your alternatives. This is why you are more likely to study on a Tuesday night than on a Saturday night. On a Tuesday night, the opportunity cost of studying is lower because

© R. IAN LLOYD/MASTERFILE

Scarcity of Money? No. Scarcity of Time? Yes

© ANTHONY NESTE/TIME & LIFE PICTURES/GETTY IMAGES

your alternatives are less attractive than on a Saturday night, when more is happening. Suppose you go to a movie on Saturday night. Your opportunity cost is the value of your best alternative forgone, which might be attending a college game. For some of you, studying on Saturday night may be well down the list of alternatives—perhaps ahead of reorganizing your closet but behind doing your laundry.

Opportunity cost is subjective, but in some cases, money paid for goods and services is a reasonable approximation. For example, the opportunity cost of the new DVD player you bought is the value of spending that $100 on the best forgone alternative. The money measure may leave out some important elements, however, particularly the value of the time involved. For example, renting a movie costs you not just the $4 rental fee but the time and travel required to get it, watch it, and return it.

Even religious practices are subject to opportunity cost. For example, about half the U.S. populations attends religious services at least once a month. In some states, so called "blue laws" prohibit retail activity on Sunday. Many states have repealed these laws in recent years, thus raising the opportunity cost of church attendance. Researchers have found that when a state repeals its blue laws, religious attendance declines as do church donations. These results do not seem to be linked to any decline in religiousity before the repeal.[1]

Sunk Cost and Choice

Suppose you have just finished grocery shopping and are wheeling your cart toward the checkout counters. How do you decide which line to join? Easy. You pick the shortest one. Suppose that it barely moves for 10 minutes, when you notice that a cashier has opened a new line and invites you to check out. Do you switch to the open cashier, or do you think, "Since I've already spent 10 minutes in this line, I'm staying put"? The 10 minutes you waited represents a sunk cost, which is a cost that has already been incurred and cannot be recovered, regardless of what you do next. You should ignore sunk cost in making economic choices. Hence, you should switch. *Economic decision makers should consider only those costs that are affected by the choice. Sunk costs have already been incurred and are not affected by the choice, so they are irrelevant.* Likewise, you should walk out on a bad movie, even if you spent $10 to get in. Your $10 is gone, and sitting through that stinker only makes you worse off. The irrelevance of sunk costs is underscored by proverbs such as "Don't throw good money after bad," "Let bygones be bygones," "That's water over the dam," and "There's no sense crying over spilt milk." The milk has already spilled, so whatever you do now cannot change that. Or, as Tony Soprano would say, "Fuhgeddaboutit!"

You should ignore sunk cost in making economic choices.

Now that you have some idea about opportunity cost, let's see how it helps solve the economic problem.

LO2 Comparative Advantage, Specialization, and Exchange

Suppose you live in a dormitory. You and your roommate have such tight schedules that you each can spare only about an hour a week for mundane tasks like ironing shirts and typing papers (granted, in reality you may not iron shirts or type papers, but this example will help you understand some important principles). Each of you must turn in a typed three-page paper every week, and you each prefer ironed shirts when you have the time. Let's say it takes you a half hour to type a handwritten paper. Your roommate is from the hunt-and-peck school and takes about an hour. But your roommate is

sunk cost a cost that has already been incurred in the past, cannot be recovered, and thus is irrelevant for present and future economic decisions

1. See Jonathan Gruber and Daniel Hungerman, "The Church vs. the Mall: What Happens When Religion Faces Increased Secular Competition?" NBER Working Paper No. 124110 (July 2006).

a talented ironer and can iron a shirt in 5 minutes flat (or should that be, iron it flat in 5 minutes?). You take twice as long, or 10 minutes, to iron a shirt.

During the hour set aside each week for typing and ironing, typing takes priority. If you each do your own typing and ironing, you type your paper in a half hour and iron three shirts in the remaining half hour. Your roommate takes the entire hour typing the paper, leaving no time for ironing. Thus, if you each do your own tasks, the combined output is two typed papers and three ironed shirts.

The Law of Comparative Advantage

Before long, you each realize that total output would increase if you did all the typing and your roommate did all the ironing. In the hour available for these tasks, you type both papers and your roommate irons 12 shirts. As a result of specialization, total output increases by 9 shirts! You strike a deal to exchange your typing for your roommate's ironing, so you each end up with a typed paper and 6 ironed shirts. Thus, *each of you is better off as a result of specialization and exchange*. By specializing in the task that you each do better, you are using the **law of comparative advantage**, which states that the individual with the lower opportunity cost of producing a particular output should specialize in producing that output. You face a lower opportunity cost of typing than does your roommate, because in the time it takes to type a paper, you could iron 3 shirts whereas your roommate could iron 12 shirts in the time it takes your roomate to type the paper. And if you face a lower opportunity cost of typing, your roommate must face a lower opportunity cost of ironing (try working that out).

Absolute Advantage Versus Comparative Advantage

The gains from specialization and exchange so far are obvious. A more interesting case is if you are faster at both tasks. Suppose the example changes only in one respect: your roommate takes 12 minutes to iron a shirt compared with your 10 minutes. You now have an *absolute advantage* in both tasks, meaning each task takes you less time than it does your roommate. More generally, having an **absolute advantage** means making something using fewer resources than other producers require.

Does your absolute advantage in both activities mean specialization is no longer a good idea? Recall that the law of comparative advantage states that the individual with *the lower opportunity cost* of producing a particular good should specialize in that good. You still take 30 minutes to type a paper and 10 minutes to iron a shirt, so your opportunity cost of typing the paper remains at three ironed shirts. Your roommate takes an hour to type a paper and 12 minutes to iron a shirt, so your roommate could iron five shirts in the time it takes to type a paper. Your opportunity cost of typing a paper is ironing three shirts; for your roommate it's ironing five shirts. *Because your opportunity cost of typing is lower than your roommate's, you still have a comparative advantage in typing*. Consequently, your roommate must have a comparative advantage in ironing (again, try working this out to your satisfaction). Therefore, you should do all the typing and your roommate, all the ironing. Although you have an absolute advantage in both tasks, your **comparative advantage** calls for specializing in the task for which you have the lower opportunity cost—in this case, typing.

law of comparative advantage
the individual, firm, region, or country with the lowest opportunity cost of producing a particular good should specialize in that good

absolute advantage
the ability to make something using fewer resources than other producers use

comparative advantage
the ability to make something at a lower opportunity cost than other producers face

> "Does your absolute advantage in both activities mean specialization is no longer a good idea?"

If neither of you specialized, you could type one paper and iron three shirts. Your roommate could still type just the one paper. Your combined output would be two papers and three shirts. If you each specialized according to comparative advantage, in an hour you could type both papers and your roommate could iron five shirts. Thus, specialization increases total output by two ironed shirts. Even though you are better at both tasks than your roommate, you are comparatively better at typing. Put another way, your roommate, although worse at both tasks, is not quite as bad at ironing as at typing.

Don't think that this is just common sense. Common sense would lead you to do your own ironing and typing, because you are better at both. *Absolute advantage focuses on who uses the fewest resources, but comparative advantage focuses on what else those resources could produce—that is, on the opportunity cost of those resources.* Comparative advantage is the better guide to who should do what.

> "The degree of specialization is limited by the extent of the market."

The law of comparative advantage applies not only to individuals but also to firms, regions of a country, and entire nations. Individuals, firms, regions, or countries with the lowest opportunity cost of producing a particular good should specialize in producing that good. Because of such factors as climate, workforce skills, natural resources, and capital stock, certain parts of the country and certain parts of the world have a comparative advantage in producing particular goods. From Washington State apples to Florida oranges, from software in India to hardware in Taiwan—*resources are allocated most efficiently across the country and around the world when production and trade conform to the law of comparative advantage.*

Specialization and Exchange

In the previous example, you and your roommate specialized and then exchanged output. No money was involved. In other words, you engaged in **barter**, where products are traded directly for other products. Barter works best in simple economies with little specialization and few traded goods. But for economies with greater specialization, *money* facilitates exchange. Money—coins, bills, checks, and debit cards—is a *medium of exchange* because it is the one thing that everyone accepts in return for goods and services.

Because of specialization and comparative advantage, most people consume little of what they produce and produce little of what they consume. Each individual specializes, then exchanges that product for money, which in turn is exchanged for goods and services. Did you make anything you are wearing? Probably not. Think about the degree of specialization that went into your cotton shirt. A farmer in a warm climate grew the cotton and sold it to someone who spun it into thread, who sold it to someone who wove it into fabric, who sold it to someone who sewed the shirt, who sold it to a wholesaler, who sold it to a retailer, who sold it to you. Many specialists created that shirt.

Evidence of specialization is all around us. Shops at the mall specialize in products ranging from luggage to lingerie. Restaurants range from subs to sushi. Or let your fingers do the walking through the help-wanted ads or *Yellow Pages*, where you will find thousands of specializations. Without moving a muscle, you can observe the division of labor within a single industry by watching the credits roll at the end of a movie. The credits show scores of specialists—from gaffer (lighting electrician) to assistant location scout. TV is no different. A typical TV drama, such as *Grey's Anatomy*, requires hundreds of specialists.

Some specialties may seem odd. For example, professional mourners in Taiwan are sometimes hired by grieving families to scream, wail, and otherwise demonstrate the deep anguish befitting a proper funeral. The degree of specialization is perhaps most obvious online, where the pool of potential customers is so vast that individual sites become sharply focused. For example, you can find sites specializing in musical bowls, tongue studs, toe rings, brass knuckles, mouth harps, ferret toys, and cat bandannas—just to name a few of the hundreds of thousands of specialty sites. You won't find such precise specialization at the mall. Adam Smith said the degree of specialization is limited by the extent of the market. Online sellers draw on the broadest customer base in the world to find a market niche.

Division of Labor and Gains from Specialization

Picture a visit to McDonald's: "Let's see, I'll have a Big Mac, an order of fries, and a chocolate shake." Less than a minute

barter
the direct exchange of one good for another without using money

later your order is ready. It would take you much longer to make a homemade version of this meal. Why is the McDonald's meal faster, cheaper, and—for some people—tastier than one you could make yourself? Why is fast food so fast? McDonald's takes advantage of the gains resulting from the **division of labor**. Each worker, rather than preparing an entire meal, specializes in separate tasks. This division of labor allows the group to produce much more.

How is this increase in productivity possible? First, the manager can assign tasks according to *individual preferences and abilities*—that is, according to the law of comparative advantage. The worker with the toothy smile and pleasant personality can handle the customers up front; the one with the strong back but few social graces can handle the heavy lifting out back. Second, a worker who performs the same task again and again gets better at it (experience is a good teacher). The worker filling orders at the drive-through, for example, learns to deal with special problems that arise. As another example, consider the experience gained by someone screening bags at the airport. Experience helps the screener distinguish the harmful from the harmless. Third, specialization means no time is lost moving from one task to another. Finally, and perhaps most importantly, the **specialization of labor** allows for the introduction of more sophisticated production techniques—techniques that would not make sense on a smaller scale. For example, McDonald's large shake machine would be impractical in the home. *Specialized machines make workers more productive.*

To review: The specialization of labor (a) takes advantage of individual preferences and natural abilities, (b) allows workers to develop more experience at a particular task, (c) reduces the need to shift between different tasks, and (d) permits the introduction of laborsaving machinery. Specialization and the division of labor occur not only among individuals but also among firms, regions, and indeed entire countries. The cotton shirt mentioned earlier might involve growing cotton in one country, turning it into cloth in another, making the shirt in a third, and selling it in a fourth.

We should also acknowledge the downside of specialization. Doing the same thing all day can become tedious. Consider, for example, the assembly-line worker whose sole task is to tighten a particular bolt. Such a job could drive that worker bonkers or lead to repetitive motion injury. Thus, the gains from dividing production into individual tasks must be weighed against any problems caused by assigning workers to repetitive, tedious, and potentially harmful jobs. Fortunately, many routine tasks, particularly on assembly lines, can be turned over to robots.

division of labor
breaking down the production of a good into separate tasks

specialization of labor
focusing work effort on a particular product or a single task

LO3 The Economy's Production Possibilities

The focus to this point has been on how individuals choose to use their scarce resources to satisfy their unlimited wants or, more specifically, how they specialize based on comparative advantage. This emphasis on the individual has been appropriate because the economy is shaped by the choices of individual decision makers, whether they are consumers, producers, or public officials. Just as resources are scarce for the individual, they are also scarce for the economy as a whole (no fallacy of composition here). An economy has millions of different resources that can be combined in all kinds of ways to produce millions of different goods and services. This section steps back from the immense complexity of the real economy to develop another model, which explores the economy's production options.

Efficiency and the Production Possibilities Frontier

Let's develop a model to get some idea of how much an economy can produce with the resources available. What are the economy's production capabilities? Here are the model's assumptions:

1. To simplify matters, output is limited to just two broad classes of products: consumer goods and capital goods.
2. The focus is on production during a given period—in this case, a year.
3. The economy's resources are fixed in both quantity and quality during that period.
4. Society's knowledge about how these resources combine to produce output—that is, the available *technology*—does not change during the year.
5. Also assumed fixed during the period are the "rules of the game" that facilitate production and exchange. These include such things as the legal system, property rights, tax laws, patent laws, and the manners, customs, and conventions of the market.

The point of these simplifying assumptions is to freeze in time the economy's resources, technology, and rules of the game so we can focus on the economy's production options.

Given the resources, technology, and rules of the game available in the economy, the **production possibilities frontier**, or **PPF**, identifies possible combinations of the two types of goods that can be produced when all available resources are employed efficiently. *Resources are employed efficiently when there is no change that could increase the production of one good without decreasing the production of the other good.* **Efficiency** involves getting the most from available resources.

The economy's PPF for consumer goods and capital goods is shown by the curve *AF* in Exhibit 1. Point *A* identifies the amount of consumer goods produced per year if all the economy's resources are used efficiently to produce consumer goods. Point *F* identifies the amount of capital goods produced per year if all the economy's resources are used efficiently to produce capital goods. Points along the curve between *A* and *F* identify possible combinations of the two goods that can be produced when *all* the economy's resources *are used efficiently.*

Exhibit 1

The Economy's Production Possibilities Frontier

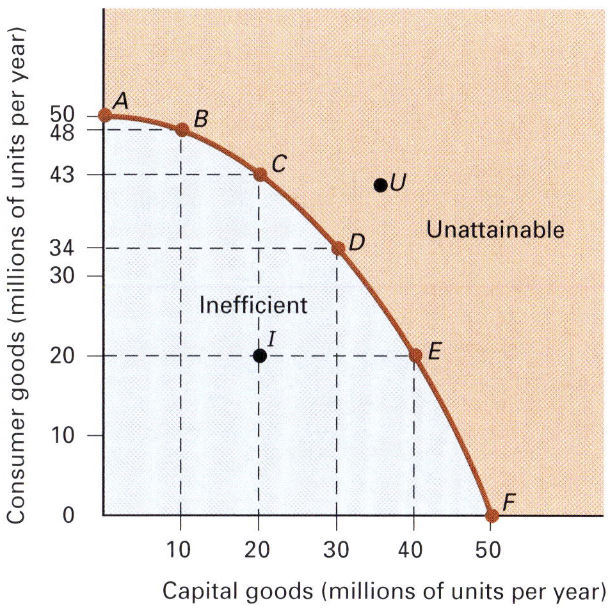

Inefficient and Unattainable Production

Points inside the PPF, such as *I* in Exhibit 1, identify combinations that do not employ resources efficiently. Note that point *C* yields more consumer goods and no fewer capital goods than *I*. And point *E* yields more capital goods and no fewer consumer goods than *I*. Indeed, any point along the PPF between *C* and *E*, such as point *D*, yields both more consumer goods and more capital goods than *I*. Hence, point *I* is *inefficient*. By using resources more efficiently, the economy can produce more of at least one good without reducing the production of the other good. Points outside the PPF, such as *U* in Exhibit 1, identify *unattainable* combinations, given the availability of resources, technology, and rules of the game. Thus, *the PPF not only shows efficient combinations of production but also serves as the boundary between inefficient combinations inside the frontier and unattainable combinations outside the frontier.*

The Shape of the Production Possibilities Frontier

Focus again on point *A* in Exhibit 1. Any movement along the PPF involves giving up some of one good to get more of the other. Movements down along the curve indicate that the opportunity cost of more capital goods is fewer consumer goods. For example, moving from point *A* to point *B* *increases* capital production from none to 10 million units but *reduces* consumer units from 50 million to 48 million. Increasing capital to 10 million units reduces consumer goods only a little. Capital production initially employs resources (such as heavy machinery used to build factories) that add few consumer units but are quite productive in making capital.

As shown by the dashed lines in Exhibit 1, each additional 10 million capital units reduces consumer units by a successively larger amount. The resources used to produce more capital were increasingly better suited to producing consumer goods. *The opportunity cost of making more capital goods inceases, because resources in the economy are not all perfectly adaptable to the production of both types of goods.* The shape of the production possibilities frontier reflects the **law of increasing opportunity cost**. If the economy uses all resources efficiently, the law of increasing opportunity cost states that each additional increment of one good requires the economy to sacrifice successively larger and larger increments of the other good.

production possibilities frontier (PPF) a curve showing alternative combinations of goods that can be produced when available resources are used efficiently; a boundary line between inefficient and unattainable combinations

efficiency the condition that exists when there is no way resources can be reallocated to increase the production of one good without decreasing the production of another; getting the most from available resources

law of increasing opportunity cost to produce more of one good, a successively larger amount of the other good must be sacrificed

The PPF derives its bowed-out shape from the law of increasing opportunity cost. For example, whereas the first 10 million units of capital have an opportunity cost of only 2 million consumer units, the final 10 million units of capital—that is, the increase from point E to point F—have an opportunity cost of 20 million consumer units. Notice that the slope of the PPF shows the opportunity cost of an increment of capital. As the economy moves down the curve, the curve becomes steeper, reflecting the higher opportunity cost of capital goods in terms of forgone consumer goods. The law of increasing opportunity cost also applies when moving from the production of capital goods to the production of consumer goods. If resources were perfectly adaptable to alternative uses, the PPF would be a straight line, reflecting a constant opportunity cost along the PPF.

Exhibit 2

Shifts of the Economy's Production Possibilities Frontier

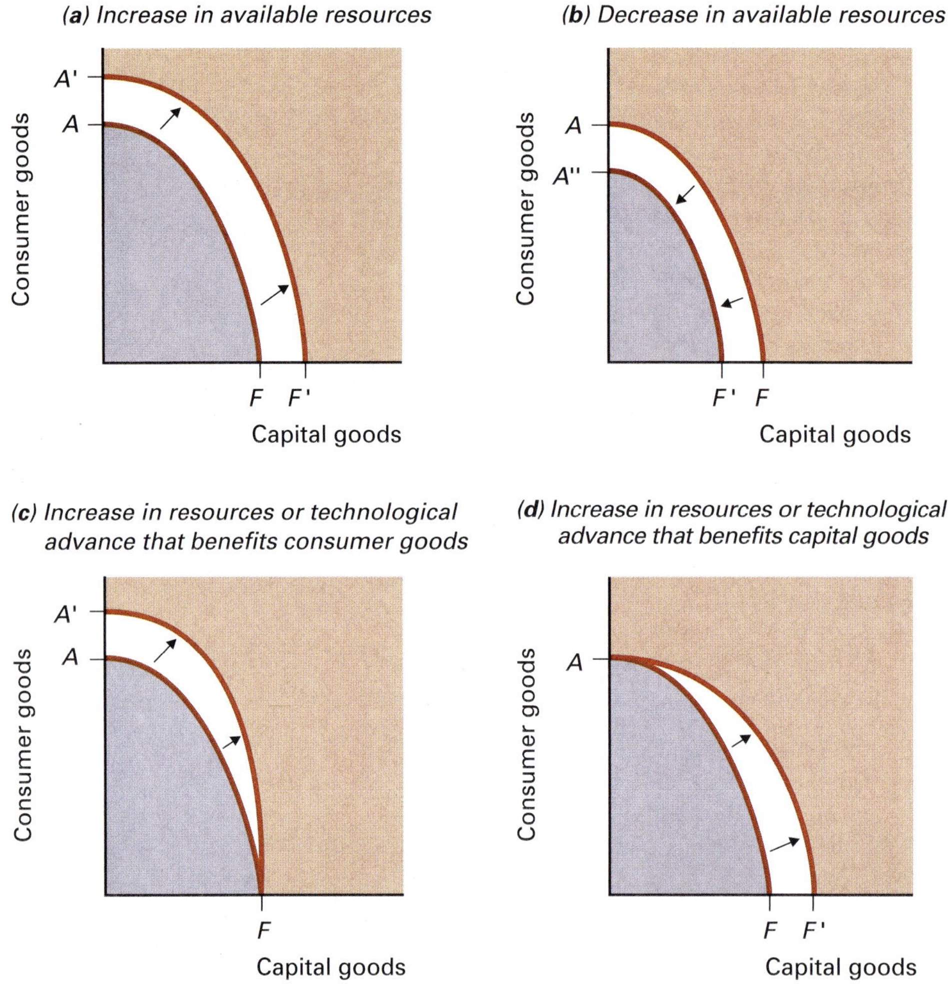

What Can Shift the Production Possibilities Frontier?

Any production possibilities frontier assumes the economy's resources and technology are fixed during the period under consideration. Over time, however, the PPF may shift if resources, technology, or the rules of the game change. Economic growth is an expansion in the economy's production possibilities as reflected by an outward shift of the PPF.

economic growth an increase in the economy's ability to produce goods and services; reflected by an outward shift of the economy's production possibilities frontier

Changes in Resource Availability

If people decide to work longer hours, the PPF shifts outward, as shown in panel (a) of Exhibit 2. An increase in the size or health of the labor force, an increase in the skills of the labor force, or an increase in the availability of other resources, such as new oil discoveries, also shifts the PPF outward. In contrast, a decrease of resources shifts the PPF inward, as depicted in panel (b). For example, in 1990 Iraq invaded Kuwait, setting oil fields ablaze and destroying much of Kuwait's physical capital. In West Africa, the encroaching sands of the Sahara destroy thousands of square miles of farmland each year. And in northwest China, a rising tide of wind-blown sand has claimed grasslands, lakes, and forests and swallowed entire villages, forcing tens of thousands of people to flee.

The new PPFs in panels (a) and (b) appear to be parallel to the original ones, indicating that the resources that changed could produce both capital goods and consumer goods. For example, an increase in electrical power can enhance the production of both, as shown in panel (a). If a resource such

Disasters cause an inward shift or retraction of the PPF.

© REUTERS/LANDOV

as farmland benefits just consumer goods, then increased availability or productivity of that resource shifts the PPF more along the consumer goods axis, as shown in panel (c). Panel (d) shows the effect of an increase in a resource such as construction equipment that is suited only to capital goods.

Increases in the Capital Stock

An economy's PPF depends in part on the stock of human and physical capital. The more capital an economy produces during one period, the more output can be produced in the next period. Thus, producing more capital goods this period (for example, more machines in the case of physical capital or more education in the case of human capital) shifts the economy's PPF outward the next period. The choice between consumer goods and capital goods is really the choice between present consumption and future production. Again, the more capital goods produced this period, the greater the economy's production possibilities next period.

Technological Change

A technological discovery that employs resources more efficiently could shift the economy's PPF outward. Some discoveries enhance the production of both consumer goods and capital goods, as shown in panel (a) of Exhibit 2. For example, the Internet has increased each firm's ability to identify available resources. A technological discovery that benefits consumer goods only, such as more disease resistant crops, is reflected by a rotation outward of the PPF along the consumer goods axis, as shown in panel (c). Note that point *F* remains unchanged because the breakthrough does not affect the production of capital goods. Panel (d) shows a technological advance in the production of capital goods, such as better software for designing heavy machinery.

Improvements in the Rules of the Game

The **rules of the game** are the formal and informal institutions that support the economy—the laws, customs, manners, conventions, and other institutional underpinnings that encourage people to pursue productive activity. A more stable political environment and more reliable property rights increase the incentive to work and to invest, and thus help the economy grow. For example, people have more incentive to work if taxes claim less of their paychecks. People have more incentive to invest if they are more confident that their investment will not be appropriated by government, stolen by thieves, destroyed by civil unrest, or blown up by terrorists. Improvements in the rules of the game shift the economy's PPF outward. On the other hand, greater instability reduces the economy's productive capacity, as reflected by in inward shift of the PPF. Rankings like the ones in Exhibit 3 illustrate how rules of the game of a particular country affect the how easy it is to conduct business there.

What We Learn from the PPF

The PPF demonstrates several ideas introduced so far. The first is *efficiency:* The PPF describes efficient combinations of outputs, given the economy's resources, technology, and rules of the game. The second idea is *scarcity:* Given the resources, technology, and rules of the game, the economy can produce only so much. The PPF slopes downward, so more of one good means less of the other good, thus demonstrating *opportunity cost.* The PPF's bowed-out shape reflects the *law of increasing opportunity cost,* which arises because some resources are not perfectly adaptable to the production of each good. And a shift outward in the PPF reflects *economic growth.*

Finally, because society must somehow select a specific combination of output—a single point—along the PPF, the PPF also underscores the need for *choice.*

rules of the game the formal and informal institutions that support the economy—the laws, customs, manners, conventions, and other institutional underpinnings that encourage people to pursue productive activity

© JONATHAN DRAKE/ BLOOMBERG NEWS/LANDOV

In 2007, *Inc.* magazine published an interactive map with information on doing business around the world. The map shows annual GDP growth; identifies places with little regulation; and provides useful factoids. Most importantly, though, the map highlights the worst countries in which to do business: Afghanistan, Burkina Faso, Chad, Congo, Djibouti, East Timor, Egypt, Eritrea, and Venezuela. Three countries were singled out as the worst of the worst, where businesspeople "must proceed very carefully": Belarus, Guinea-Bissau, and Zimbabwe. See if the map is still online at http://www.inc.com/keyword/globalmap.

SOURCE: M. Chafkin and N. Tiku, "The 21st Century Treasure Map," *Inc.,* April 2007, unpaginated pullout.

Exhibit 3

Best 10 and Worst 10 Among 175 Countries Based on Ease of Doing Business, According to the World Bank

Best 10	Worst 10
1. Singapore	166. Burundi
2. New Zealand	167. Central African Republic
3. United States	168. Sierra Leone
4. Canada	169. São Tomé and Principe
5. Hong Kong	170. Eritrea
6. United Kingdom	171. Republic of Congo
7. Denmark	172. Chad
8. Australia	173. Guinea-Bissau
9. Norway	174. East Timor
10. Ireland	175. Democratic Republic of Congo

SOURCE: *Doing Business in 2007: Comparing Business Regulations,* World Bank Publications, http://www.doingbusiness.org/

Selecting a particular combination determines not only consumer goods available this period but also the capital stock available next period. One thing the PPF does not tell us is which combination to choose. The PPF tells us only about the costs, not the benefits, of the two goods. To make a selection, we need to know about both costs *and* benefits. How society goes about choosing a particular combination depends on the nature of the economic system, as you will see next.

LO4 Economic Systems

Each point along the economy's production possibilities frontier is an efficient combination of outputs. Whether the economy produces efficiently and how the economy selects the most preferred combination depends on the decision-making rules employed. But regardless of how decisions are made, each economy must answer three fundamental questions.

© COMSTOCK IMAGES/JUPITERIMAGES

economic system the set of mechanisms and institutions that resolve the what, how, and for whom questions

Three Questions Every Economic System Must Answer

What goods and services are to be produced? How are they to be produced? And for whom are they to be produced? An **economic system** is the set of mechanisms and institutions that resolve the *what, how,* and *for whom* questions. Some criteria used to distinguish among economic systems are (1) who owns the resources, (2) what decision-making process is used to allocate resources and products, and (3) what types of incentives guide economic decision makers.

What Goods and Services Are to Be Produced?

Most of us take for granted the incredible number of choices that go into deciding what gets produced—everything from which new kitchen appliances are introduced, which roads get built, to which of the 10,000 movie scripts purchased by U.S. studios each year get to be among the 500 movies made.[2] Although different economies resolve these and millions of other questions using different decision-making rules and

2. As reported in Ian Parker, "The Real McKee," *New Yorker,* 20 October 2003.

mechanisms, all economies must somehow make such choices.

How Are Goods and Services to Be Produced?

The economic system must determine how output gets produced. Which resources should be used, and how should they be combined to produce each product? How much labor should be used and at what skill levels? What kinds of machines should be used? What new technology should be incorporated into the latest video games? Should the office complex be built in the city or closer to the interstate highway? Millions of individual decisions determine which resources are employed and how these resources are combined.

For Whom Are Goods and Services to Be Produced?

Who will actually consume the goods and services produced? The economic system must determine how to allocate the fruits of production among the population. Should everyone receive equal shares? Should the weak and the sick get more? Should those willing to wait in line get more? Should goods be allocated according to height? Weight? Religion? Age? Gender? Race? Looks? Strength? Political connections? The value of resources supplied? The question "For whom are goods and services to be produced?" is often referred to as the *distribution question*.

Although the three economic questions were discussed separately, they are closely related. The answer to one depends on the answers to the others. For example, an economy that distributes goods and services uniformly to all will, no doubt, answer the what-will-be-produced question differently than an economy that somehow allows more personal choice. As we have seen, laws about resource ownership and the role of government determine the "rules of the game"—the set of conditions that shape individual incentives and constraints. Along a spectrum ranging from the freest to the most regimented types of economic systems, *pure capitalism* would be at one end and the *pure command system* at the other.

Pure Capitalism

Under pure capitalism, the rules of the game include the private ownership of resources and the market distribution of products. Owners have *property rights* to the use of their resources and are therefore free to supply those resources to the highest bidder. Private property rights allow individuals to use resources or to charge others for their use. Any income derived from supplying labor, capital, natural resources, or entrepreneurial ability goes to the individual resources owners. Producers are free to make and sell whatever they think will be profitable. Consumers are free to buy whatever goods they can afford. All this voluntary buying and selling is coordinated by unrestricted markets, where buyers and sellers make their intentions known. Market prices guide resources to their most productive use and channel goods and services to the consumers who value them the most.

Under pure capitalism, markets answer the what, how, and for whom questions. That's why capitalism is also referred to as a *market system*. Markets transmit information about relative scarcity, provide individual incentives, and distribute income among resource suppliers. No individual or small group coordinates these activities. Rather, it is the voluntary choices of many buyers and sellers responding only to their individual incentives and constraints that direct resources and products to those who value them the most.

According to Adam Smith (1723–1790), market forces allocate resources as if by an "invisible hand"—an unseen force that harnesses the pursuit of self-interest to direct resources where they earn the greatest payoff. According to Smith, *although each individual pursues his or her self-interest, the "invisible hand" of markets promotes the general welfare*. Capitalism is sometimes called *laissez-faire;* translated from the French, this phrase means "to let do," or to let people do as they choose without government intervention. Thus, under capitalism, voluntary choices based on rational self-interest are made in unrestricted markets to answer the questions what, how, and for whom.

As we will see in later chapters, pure capitalism has its flaws. The most notable market failures are:

1. No central authority protects property rights, enforces contracts, and otherwise ensures that the rules of the game are followed.
2. People with no resources to sell could starve.
3. Some producers may try to monopolize markets by eliminating the competition.
4. The production or consumption of some goods involves side effects that can harm or benefit people not involved in the market transaction.
5. Private firms have no incentive to produce so-called *public goods,* such as national defense, because private firms cannot prevent nonpayers from enjoying the benefits of public goods.

Because of these limitations, countries have modified pure capitalism to allow some role for government.

pure capitalism
an economic system characterized by the private ownership of resources and the use of prices to coordinate economic activity in unregulated markets

private property rights
an owner's right to use, rent, or sell resources or property

Even Adam Smith believed government should play a role. The United States is among the most market-oriented economies in the world today.

Pure Command System

In a pure command system, resources are directed and production is coordinated not by market forces but by the "command," or central plan, of government. In theory at least, instead of private property, there is public, or *communal*, ownership of property. That's why central planning is sometimes called *communism*. Government planners, as representatives of all the people, answer such questions through *central plans* spelling out how much steel, how many cars, and how much housing to produce. They also decide how to produce these goods and who gets them.

pure command system
an economic system characterized by the public ownership of resources and centralized planning

mixed system
an economic system characterized by the private ownership of some resources and the public ownership of other resources; some markets are regulated by government

In theory, the pure command system incorporates individual choices into collective choices, which, in turn, are reflected in the central plans. In fact, command economies often have names that focus on collective choice, such as the People's Republic of China and the Democratic People's Republic of Korea (North Korea). In practice, the pure command system also has flaws, most notably:

1. Running an economy is so complicated that some resources are used inefficiently.
2. Because nobody in particular owns resources, each person has less incentive to employ them in their highest-valued use, so some resources are wasted.
3. Central plans may reflect more the preferences of central planners than those of society.
4. Because government is responsible for all production, the variety of products tends to be more limited than in a capitalist economy.
5. Each individual has less personal freedom in making economic choices.

Because of these limitations, countries have modified the pure command system to allow a role for markets. North Korea is perhaps the most centrally planned economy in the world today.

Mixed and Transitional Economies

No country on earth exemplifies either type of economic system in its pure form. Economic systems have grown more alike over time, with the role of government increasing in capitalist economies and the role of markets increasing in command economies. The United States represents a mixed system, with government directly accounting for about one-third of all economic activity. What's more, government regulates the private sector in a variety of ways. For example, local zoning boards determine lot sizes, home sizes, and the types of industries allowed. Federal bodies regulate workplace safety, environmental quality, competitive fairness, food and drug quality, and many other activities.

Although both ends of the spectrum have moved toward the center, capitalism has gained the most converts in recent decades. Perhaps the benefits of markets are no better illustrated than where a country, as a result of war or political upheaval, became divided by ideology into a capitalist economy and a command economy, such as with Taiwan and China or South Korea and North Korea. In each case, the economies began with similar human and physical resources, but once they went their separate ways, economic growth diverged sharply, with the capitalist economies outperforming the command economies. For example, Taiwan's production per capita in 2006 was four times that of China, and South Korea's production per capita was 12 times that of North Korea.

Consider the experience of the pilgrims in 1620 while establishing Plymouth Colony. They first tried communal ownership of the land. That turned out badly. Crops were neglected and food shortages developed. After three years of near starvation, the system was changed so that each family was assigned a private plot of land and granted the fruits of that plot. Yields increased sharply. The pilgrims learned that people take better care of what they own individually; common ownership often leads to common neglect.

Recognizing the incentive power of property rights and markets, some of the most die-hard central planners are now allowing a role for markets. For example, about one fifth of the world's population lives in China, which grows more market oriented each day, even going so far as to give private property constitutional protection on a par with state property. In a poll of Chinese citizens, 74 percent agreed that "the free enterprise system is the best system on which to base the future of the world." Among Americans polled, 71 percent agreed with that statement.[3] More than a decade ago, the former Soviet Union dissolved into 15 independent republics; most converted state-owned enterprises into private firms. From Moscow to Beijing, from Hungary to Mongolia, the transition to mixed economies now under way in former command economies will shape the world for decades to come.

Economies Based on Custom or Religion

Finally, some economic systems are molded largely by custom or religion. For example, caste systems in India and elsewhere restrict occupational choices. Charging interest is banned under Islamic law. Family relations also play significant roles in organizing and coordinating economic activity. Even in the United States, some occupations are still dominated by women, others by men, largely because of tradition. Your own pattern of consumption and choice of occupation may be influenced by some of these considerations.

Final Word

Although economies can answer the three economic questions in a variety of ways, this book focuses primarily on the mixed market system, such as exists in the United States. This type of economy blends *private choice,* guided by the price system in competitive markets, with *public choice,* guided by democracy in political markets. The study of mixed market systems grows more relevant as former command economies try to develop markets. The next chapter focuses on the economic actors in a mixed economy and explains why government gets into the act.

3. As reported in "Capitalism, Comrade," *Wall Street Journal,* 18 January 2006.

Rooms in the Royal Palace of Brunei> 1,788

Scripts bought by Hollywood studios each year> 10,000

Main questions every economic system must answer> 3

Notable limitations of pure command and pure capitalism> 5

CHAPTER 3

Economic Decision Makers

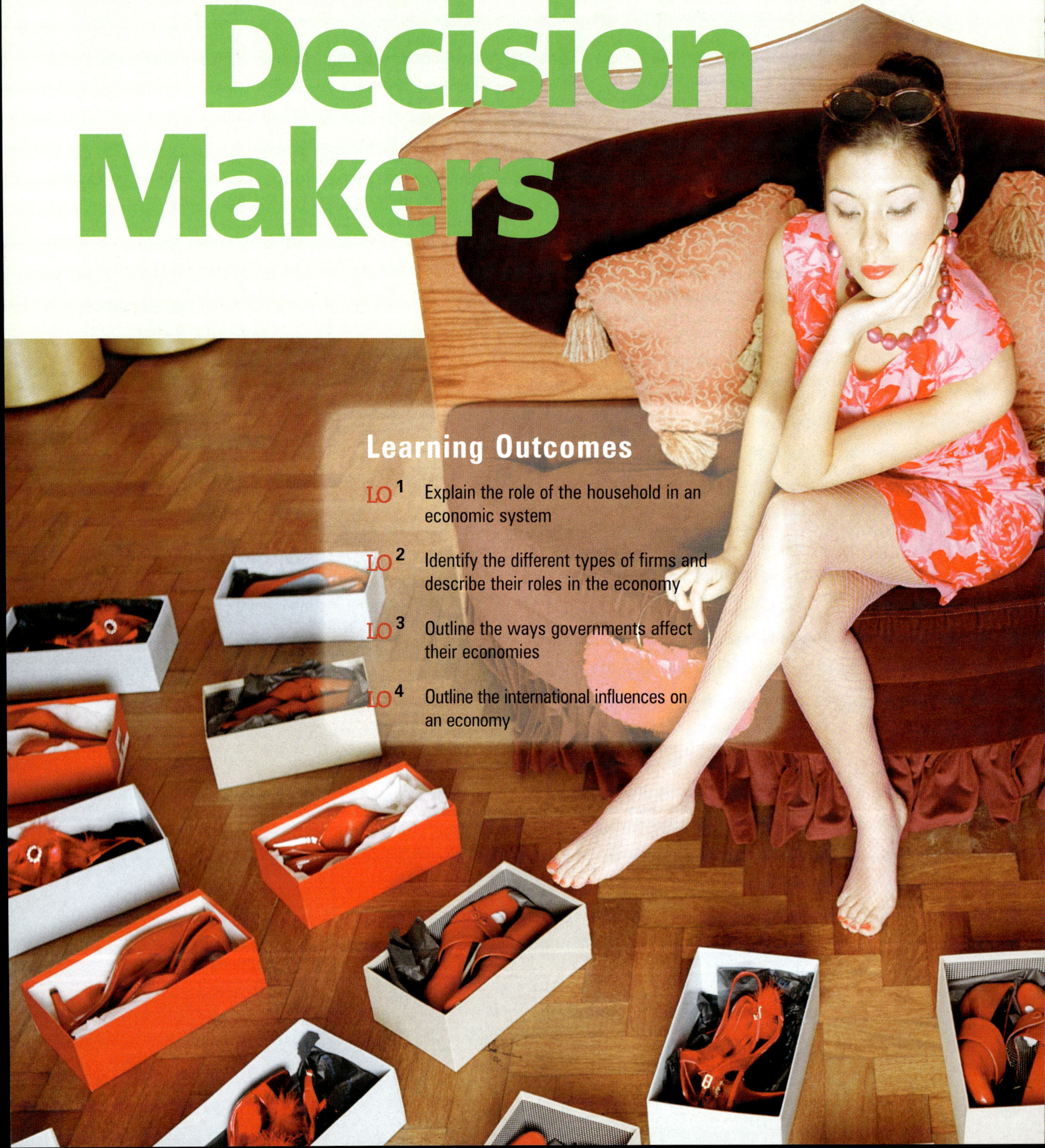

Learning Outcomes

LO 1 Explain the role of the household in an economic system

LO 2 Identify the different types of firms and describe their roles in the economy

LO 3 Outline the ways governments affect their economies

LO 4 Outline the international influences on an economy

“What happens to personal income once it comes into the household?”

If we live in the age of specialization, then why haven't specialists taken over all production? For example, why do most of us still do our own laundry and perform dozens of other tasks for ourselves? In what sense has production moved from the household to the firm and then back to the household? If the "invisible hand" of competitive markets is so efficient, why does government get into the act? Answers to these and other questions are addressed in this chapter, which discusses the four economic decision makers: households, firms, governments, and the rest of the world.

What do you think?

Governments are effective managers of national economies.

Strongly Disagree						*Strongly Agree*
1	2	3	4	5	6	7

To develop a better feel for how the economy works, you must get more acquainted with the key players. You already know more about them than you may realize. You grew up in a household. You have dealt with firms all your life, from Sony to Subway. You know much about governments, from taxes to public schools. And you have a growing awareness of the rest of the world, from online sites, to imports, to foreign travel. This chapter draws on your abundant personal experience with economic decision makers to consider their makeup and objectives.

Topics discussed in Chapter 3 include:

- Evolution of the household
- Evolution of the firm
- Types of firms
- Market failures and government remedies
- Taxing and public spending
- International trade and finance

LO1 The Household

Households play the starring role in a market economy. Their demand for goods and services determines what gets produced. And their supplies of labor, capital, natural resources, and entrepreneurial ability produce that output. As demanders of goods and services and suppliers of resources, households make all kinds of choices, such as what to buy, how much to save, where to live, and where to work. Although a household usually consists of several individuals, we will view each household as acting like a single decision maker.

The Evolution of the Household

In earlier times, when the economy was primarily agricultural, a farm household was largely self-sufficient. Each family member specialized in a specific farm task—cooking meals, making clothes, tending livestock, planting crops, and so on. These early households produced what they consumed and consumed what they produced. With the introduction of new seed varieties, better fertilizers, and laborsaving machinery, farm productivity increased sharply. Fewer farmers were needed to grow enough food to feed a nation. At the same time, the growth of urban factories increased the demand for factory labor. As a result, workers moved from farms to cities, where they became more specialized but less self-sufficient.

Households evolved in other ways. For example, in 1950, only about 15 percent of married women with young children were in the labor force. Since then, higher levels of education among women and a growing demand for their labor increased women's earnings, thus raising their opportunity cost of working in the home. This higher opportunity cost contributed to their growing labor force participation. Today 70 percent of women with children under 18 are in the labor force.

utility
the satisfaction received from consumption; sense of well-being

The rise of two-earner households has affected the family as an economic unit. Households produce less for themselves and demand more from the market. For example, child-care services and fast-food restaurants have displaced some household production (Americans consume about one-third of their calories away from home). The rise in two-earner families has reduced specialization within the household—a central feature of the farm family. Nonetheless, some production still occurs in the home, as we'll explore later.

Households Maximize Utility

There are more than 115 million U.S. households. All those who live together under one roof are considered part of the same household. What exactly do households attempt to accomplish in making decisions? Economists assume that people try to maximize their level of satisfaction, sense of well-being, happiness, and overall welfare. In short, households attempt to maximize **utility**. Households, like other economic decision makers, are viewed as rational, meaning that they try to act in their best interests and do not deliberately make themselves less happy. Utility maximization depends on each household's subjective goals, not on some objective standard. For example, some households maintain neat homes with well-groomed lawns; others pay little attention to their homes and use their lawns as junkyards.

© REGINE MAHAUX/STONE/GETTY IMAGES

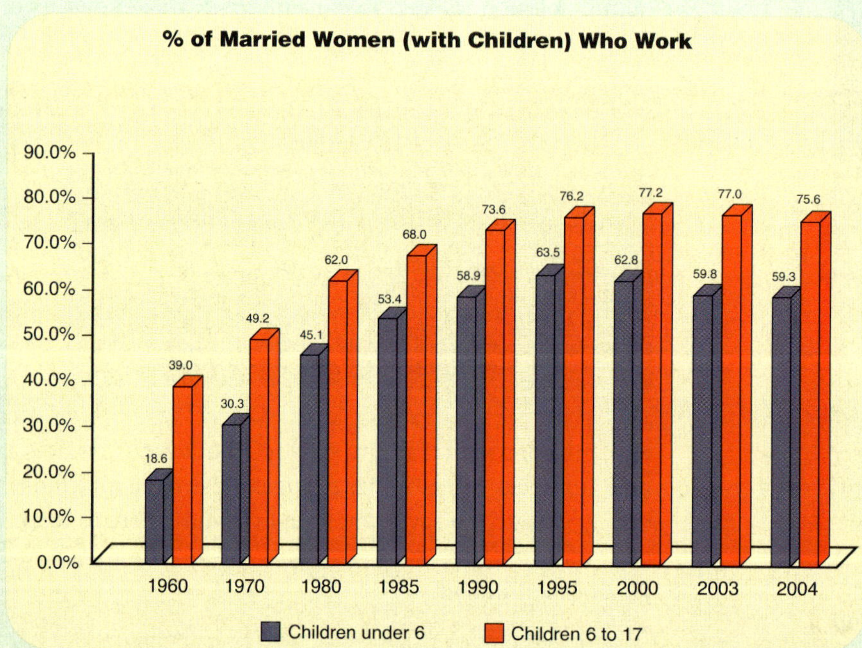

Households as Resource Suppliers

Households use their limited resources—labor, capital, natural resources, and entrepreneurial ability—in an attempt to satisfy their unlimited wants. They can use these resources to produce goods and services in their homes. For example, they can prepare meals, mow the lawn, and fix a leaky faucet. They can also sell these resources in the resource market and use the income to buy goods and services in the product market. The most valuable resource sold by most households is labor.

Panel (a) of Exhibit 1 shows the sources of personal income received by U.S. households in 2006, when personal income totaled $10.9 trillion. As you can see, 61 percent of personal income came from wages and salaries. A distant second was transfer payments (to be discussed next), at 14 percent of personal income, followed by personal interest at 9 percent, and proprietors' income also at 9 percent. *Proprietors* are people who work for themselves rather than for employers; farmers, plumbers, and doctors are often self-employed. Proprietors' income should also be considered a form of labor income. *Over two-thirds of personal income in the United States comes from labor earnings rather than from the ownership of other resources such as capital or natural resources.*

Because of a poor education, disability, discrimination, time demands of caring for small children, or bad luck, some households have few resources that are valued in the market. Society has made the political decision that individuals in such circumstances should receive short-term public assistance. Consequently, the government gives some households **transfer payments**, which are outright grants. *Cash transfers* are monetary payments, such as welfare benefits, Social Security, unemployment compensation, and disability benefits. *In-kind transfers* provide for specific goods and services, such as food stamps, health care, and housing.

Households as Demanders of Goods and Services

What happens to personal income once it comes into the household? Most goes to personal consumption, which sorts into three broad spending categories: (1) *durable goods*—that is, goods expected to last three or more years—such as an automobile or a refrigerator; (2) *nondurable goods,* such as food, clothing, and gasoline; and (3) *services,* such as haircuts, air travel, and medical care. As you can see from panel (b) of Exhibit 1, spending on durable goods in 2006 claimed 10 percent of U.S. personal income; nondurables, 25 percent; and services, 50 percent. Taxes claimed 10 percent, and all

transfer payments
cash or in-kind benefits given to individuals as outright grants from the government

Exhibit 1

Where U.S. Personal Income Comes From and Where It Goes

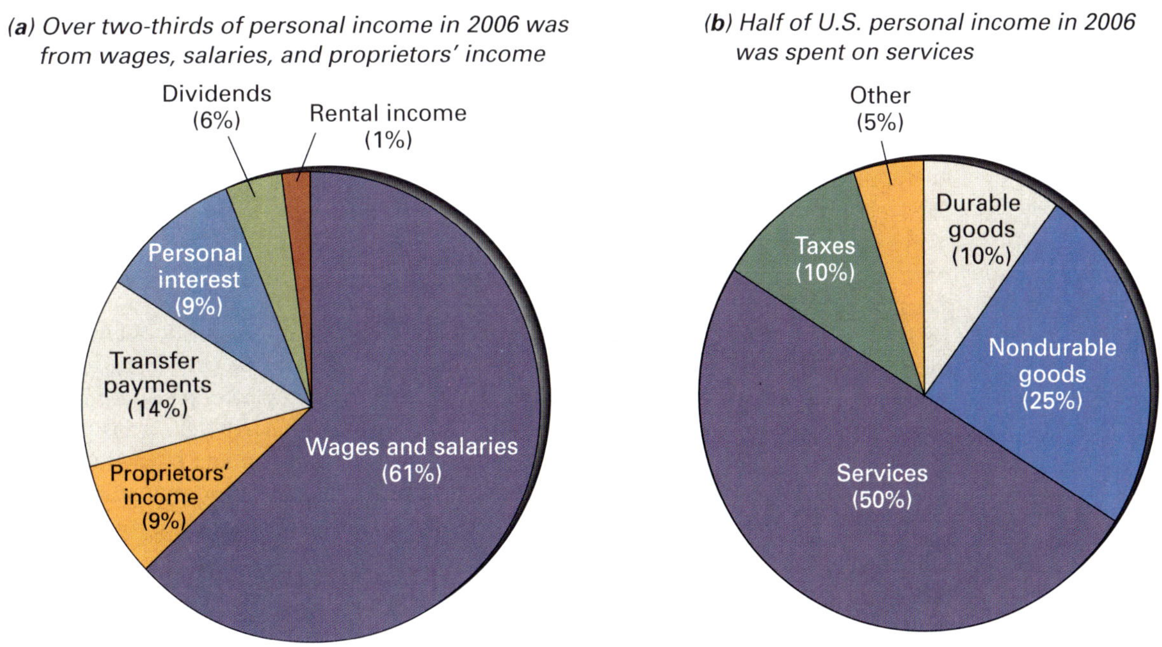

SOURCE: Based on figures from *Survey of Current Business,* Bureau of Economic Analysis, February 2007, Tables 1.5.5 and 2.1. For the latest figures, go to http://www.bea.gov/scb/index.htm.

other categories, including savings, claimed just 5 percent. So half of all personal income went for services—the fastest growing sector, because many services, such as child care, are shifting from do-it-yourself home production to market production.

LO2 The Firm

Households members once built their own homes, made their own clothes and furniture, grew their own food, and amused themselves with books, games, and hobbies. Over time, however, the efficiency arising from comparative advantage resulted in a greater specialization among resource suppliers. This section takes a look at firms, beginning with their evolution.

The Evolution of the Firm

Specialization and comparative advantage explain why households are no longer self-sufficient. But why is a firm the natural result? For example, rather than make a woolen sweater from scratch, couldn't a consumer take advantage of specialization by negotiating with someone who produced the wool, another who spun the wool into yarn, and a third who knitted the yarn into a sweater? Here's the problem with that model: If the consumer had to visit each of these specialists and strike an agreement, the resulting *transaction costs* could easily erase the gains from specialization.

© PHOTOS.COM/JUPITERIMAGES

Instead of visiting and bargaining with each specialist, the consumer can pay someone to do the bargaining—an entrepreneur, who hires all the resources necessary to make the sweater. *An entrepreneur, by contracting for many sweaters rather than just one, is able to reduce the transaction costs per sweater.*

For about two hundred years, profit-seeking entrepreneurs relied on "putting out" raw material, like wool and cotton, to rural households that turned it into finished products, like woolen goods made from yarn. The system developed in the British Isles, where workers' cottages served as tiny factories, especially during winter months, when farming chores were light (so the opportunity cost was low). This approach, which came to be known as the *cottage industry system,* still exists in some parts of the world. You might think of this system as part way between household self-sufficiency and the modern firm.

As the British economy expanded in the 18th century, entrepreneurs began organizing the stages of production under one roof. Technological developments, such as waterpower and later steam power, increased the productivity of each worker and contributed to the shift of employment from rural areas to urban factories. *Work, therefore, became organized in large, centrally powered factories that (1) promoted a more efficient division of labor, (2) allowed for the direct supervision of production, (3) reduced transportation costs, and (4) facilitated the use of machines far bigger than anything used in the home.* The development of large-scale factory production, known as the **Industrial Revolution**, began in Great Britain around 1750 and spread to the rest of Europe, North America, and Australia.

Production, then, evolved from self-sufficient rural households to the cottage industry system, where specialized production occurred in the household, to production in a firm. Today, entrepreneurs combine resources in firms such as factories, mills, offices, stores, and restaurants. **Firms** are economic units formed by profit-seeking entrepreneurs who combine labor, capital, and natural resources to produce goods and services. Just as we assume that households try to maximize utility, we assume that firms try to *maximize profit.* Profit, the entrepreneur's reward, equals sales revenue minus the cost of production.

Industrial Revolution
development of large-scale factory production that began in Great Britain around 1750 and spread to the rest of Europe, North America, and Australia

firms
economic units formed by profit-seeking entrepreneurs who employ resources to produce goods and services for sale

sole proprietorship
a firm with a single owner who has the right to all profits but who also bears unlimited liability for the firm's losses and debts

Types of Firms

There are about 30 million for-profit businesses in the United States. Two-thirds are small retail businesses, small service operations, part-time home-based businesses, and small farms. Each year more than a million new businesses start up and many fail. Firms are organized in one of three ways: as a sole proprietorship, as a partnership, or as a corporation.

Sole Proprietorships

The simplest form of business organization is the **sole proprietorship**, a single-owner firm. Examples are self-employed plumbers, farmers, and dentists.

Most sole proprietorships consist of just the self-employed proprietor—there are no hired employees. To organize a sole proprietorship, the owner simply opens for business by, for example, taking out a classified ad announcing availability for plumbing or whatever. The owner is in complete control. But he or she faces unlimited liability and could lose everything, including a home and other personal assets, to settle business debts or other claims against the business. Also, since the sole proprietor has no partners or other financial backers, raising enough money to get the business going can be a challenge. One final disadvantage is that a sole proprietorship usually goes out of business when the proprietor dies or leaves the business. Still, a sole proprietorship is the most common type of business, accounting most recently for 72 percent of all U.S. businesses. Nonetheless, because this type of firm is typically small, proprietorships generate just a tiny portion of all U.S. business sales—only 4 percent.

EACH YEAR MORE THAN A MILLION NEW BUSINESSES START UP AND MANY FAIL.

Partnerships

A more complicated form of business is the **partnership**, which involves two or more individuals who agree to combine their funds and efforts in return for a share of the profit or loss. Law, accounting, and medical partnerships typify this business form. Partners have strength in numbers and often find it easier than sole proprietors to raise enough funds to get the business going. But partners may not always agree. Also, each partner usually faces unlimited liability for any debts or claims against the partnership, so one partner could lose everything because of another's mistake. Finally, the death or departure of one partner can disrupt the firm's continuity and require a complete reorganization. The partnership is the least common form of U.S. business, making up only 10 percent of all firms and 12 percent of all business sales.

Corporations

By far the most influential form of business is the corporation. A **corporation** is a legal entity established through articles of incorporation. Shares of stock confer corporate ownership, thereby entitling stockholders to a claim on any profit. A major advantage of the corporate form is that many investors—hundreds, thousands, even millions—can pool their funds, so incorporating represents the easiest way to amass large sums to finance the business. Also, stockholder liability for any loss is limited to the value of their stock, meaning stockholders enjoy *limited liability*. A final advantage of this form of organization is that the corporation has a life apart from its owners. The corporation survives even if ownership changes hands, and it can be taxed, sued, and even charged with a crime as if it were a person.

The corporate form has some disadvantages as well. A stockholder's ability to influence corporate policy is limited to voting for a board of directors, which oversees the operation of the firm. Each share of stock usually carries with it one vote. The typical stockholder of a large corporation owns only a tiny fraction of the shares and thus has little say. Whereas the income from sole proprietorships and partnerships is taxed only once, corporate income gets whacked twice—first as corporate profits and second as stockholder income, either as corporate dividends or as realized capital gains. A *realized capital gain* is any increase in the market price of a share that occurs between the time the share is purchased and the time it is sold.

A hybrid type of corporation has evolved to take advantage of the limited liability feature of the corporate structure while reducing the impact of double taxation. The *S corporation* provides owners with limited liability, but profits are taxed only once—as income on each shareholder's personal income tax return. To qualify as an S corporation, a firm must have no more than 100 stockholders and no foreign stockholders.

Corporations make up only 18% of all U.S. businesses.

Corporations make up only 18 percent of all U.S. businesses, but because they tend to be much larger than the other two business forms, corporations account for 84 percent of all business sales. Exhibit 2 shows, by business type, the percentages of U.S. firms and the percentages of U.S. sales. *The sole proprietorship is the most important in sheer numbers, but the corporation is the most important in terms of total sales.*

Cooperatives

A **cooperative**, or "co-op" for short, is a group of people who cooperate by pooling their resources to buy and sell more efficiently than

partnership a firm with multiple owners who share the profits and bear unlimited liability for the firm's losses and debts

corporation a legal entity owned by stockholders whose liability is limited to the value of their stock ownership

cooperative an organization consisting of people who pool their resources to buy and sell more efficiently than they could individually

Exhibit 2

Number and Sales of Each Type of Firm

*(**a**) Most firms are sole proprietorships* | *(**b**) Corporations account for most sales*

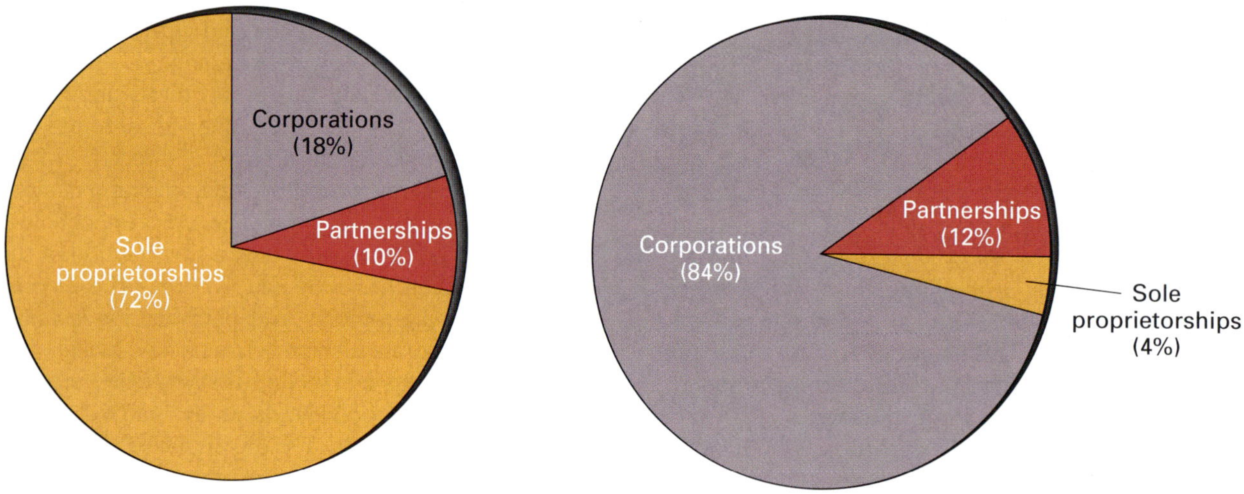

SOURCE: U.S. Census Bureau, *Statistical Abstract of the United States: 2007.* U.S. Bureau of the Census, Table No. 724 and Table No. 806. For the latest figures go to http://www.census.gov/compendia/statab/.

they could independently. Cooperatives try to minimize costs and operate with limited liability of members. The government grants most cooperatives tax-exempt status. There are two types: consumer cooperatives and producer cooperatives.

Consumer Cooperatives

A *consumer cooperative* is a retail business owned and operated by some or all of its customers in order to reduce costs. Some cooperatives require members to pay an annual fee and others require them to work a certain number of hours each year. Members sometimes pay lower prices than other customers or may share in any revenues that exceed costs. In the United States, consumer cooperatives operate credit unions, electric-power facilities, health plans, apartment buildings, and grocery stores, among other businesses. Many college bookstores are cooperatives. For example, the UConn Co-op is owned by about 30,000 students, faculty, and staff. These members receive discounts on their purchases.

Producer Cooperatives

In a *producer cooperative,* producers join forces to buy supplies and equipment and to market their output. Each producer's objective is to reduce costs and increase profits. Federal legislation allows farmers to cooperate without violating antitrust laws. Firms in other industries could not do this legally. Farmers pool their funds to purchase machinery and supplies, provide storage and processing facilities, and transport goods to market. Sunkist, for example, is a farm

>> Ocean Spray is one of the best known producer cooperatives in the United States. Through product development (think Craisins), Ocean Spray has been able to increase the price it pays its farmers 100 percent over a three year period.

© MATHIEU BELANGER/REUTERS/LANDOV

cooperative owned and operated by 6,500 citrus growers in California and Arizona.

Not-for-Profit Organizations

So far, you have learned about organizations that try to maximize profits or, in the case of cooperatives, to minimize costs. Some organizations have neither as a goal. Not-for-profit organizations engage in charitable, educational, humanitarian, cultural, professional, and other activities, often with a social purpose. Government agencies do not have profit as a goal either, but governments are not included in this definition of not-for-profit organizations.

Like businesses, not-for-profit organizations evolved to help people accomplish their goals. Examples include nonprofit hospitals, private schools and colleges, religious organizations, the Red Cross, Greenpeace, charitable foundations, soup kitchens, orchestras, museums, labor unions, and professional organizations. There are about two million not-for-profit organizations in the United States. They employ about 10 million workers, with not-for-profit hospitals being the biggest employer. But even not-for-profit organizations must somehow pay the bills. Revenues typically include some combination of voluntary contributions and service charges, such as college tuition and hospital charges. In the United States, not-for-profit organizations are usually exempt from taxes.

© COMSTOCK IMAGES/JUPITERIMAGES

> “Although you wouldn't hire someone to brush your teeth, dental work is not for amateurs.”

Why Does Household Production Still Exist?

If firms are so efficient at reducing transaction and production costs, why don't they make everything? Why do households still perform some tasks, such as cooking and cleaning? *If a household's opportunity cost of performing a task is below the market price, then the household usually performs that task.* People with a lower opportunity cost of time do more for themselves. For example, janitors are more likely to mow their lawns than are physicians. Let's look at some reasons for household production.

No Skills or Special Resources Are Required

Some activities require so few skills or special resources that householders find it cheaper to do the jobs themselves. Sweeping the kitchen floor requires only a broom and some time, so it's usually performed by household members. Sanding a wooden floor, however, involves special machinery and expertise, so this service is usually left to professionals. Similarly, although you wouldn't hire someone to brush your teeth, dental work is not for amateurs. *Households usually perform domestic chores that demand neither expertise nor special machinery.*

Household Production Avoids Taxes

Suppose you are deciding whether to pay someone $3,000 to paint your house or to do it yourself. If the income tax rate is one-third, you must earn $4,500 before taxes to have the $3,000 after taxes to pay for the job. And the painter who charges you $3,000 nets only $2,000 after paying $1,000 in taxes. Thus, you must earn $4,500 so that the painter can take

not-for-profit organizations
groups that do not pursue profit as a goal; they engage in charitable, educational, humanitarian, cultural, professional, or other activities, often with a social purpose

home $2,000. If you paint the house yourself, no taxes are involved. The tax-free nature of do-it-yourself activity favors household production over market transactions.

Household Production Reduces Transaction Costs

Getting estimates, hiring a contractor, negotiating terms, and monitoring job performance all take time and require information. Doing the job yourself reduces these transaction costs. Household production also allows for more personal control over the final product than is usually available through the market. For example, some people prefer home-cooked meals, because they can season home-cooked meals to individual tastes.

Technological Advances Increase Household Productivity

Technological breakthroughs are not confined to market production. Vacuum cleaners, washers and dryers, dishwashers, microwave ovens, and other modern appliances reduce the time and often the skill required to perform household tasks. Also, new technologies such as DVD players, HDTV, broadband downloads, and computer games enhance home entertainment. Indeed, microchip-based technologies have shifted some production from the firm back to the household.

LO3 The Government

You might think that production by households and firms could satisfy all consumer wants. Why must yet another economic decision maker get into the act? After all, governments play some role in every nation on earth.

market failure a condition that arises when the unregulated operation of markets yields socially undesirable results

monopoly a sole supplier of a product with no close substitutes

natural monopoly one firm that can supply the entire market at a lower per-unit cost than could two or more firms

The Role of Government

Sometimes the unrestrained operation of markets yields undesirable results. Too many of some goods and too few of other goods get produced. This section discusses the sources of **market failure** and how society's overall welfare may be improved through government intervention.

Establishing and Enforcing the Rules of the Game

Market efficiency depends on people like you using your resources to maximize your utility. But what if you were repeatedly robbed of your paycheck on your way home from work? Or what if, after you worked two weeks in a new job, your boss called you a sucker and said you wouldn't get paid? Why bother working? The market system would break down if you could not safeguard your private property or if you could not enforce contracts. Governments safeguard private property through police protection and enforce contracts through a judicial system. More generally, governments try to make sure that market participants abide by the rules of the game. These rules are established through government laws and regulations and also through the customs and conventions of the marketplace.

Promoting Competition

Although the "invisible hand" of competition usually promotes an efficient allocation of resources, some firms try to avoid competition through *collusion,* which is an agreement among firms to divide the market and fix the price. Or an individual firm may try to eliminate the competition by using unfair business practices. For example, to drive out local competitors, a large firm may temporarily sell at a price below cost. Government antitrust laws try to promote competition by prohibiting collusion and other anticompetitive practices.

Regulating Natural Monopolies

Competition usually keeps the product price below what it would be without competition—that is, below the price charged by a **monopoly**, a sole supplier to the market. In rare instances, however, a monopoly can produce and sell the product for less than could competing firms. For example, electricity is delivered more efficiently by a single firm that wires the community than by competing firms each stringing its own wires. When it is cheaper for one firm to serve the market than for two or more firms to do so, that one firm is called a **natural monopoly**. Since a natural monopoly faces no competition, it maximizes profit by charging a higher price than would be optimal from society's point of view. A lower price and greater output would improve social welfare. Therefore, the government usually regulates the natural monopoly, forcing it to lower its price and increase output.

Providing Public Goods

So far this book has been talking about private goods, which have two important features. First, private goods are *rival* in consumption, meaning that

> THE SUPPLIER OF A PRIVATE GOOD CAN EASILY EXCLUDE THOSE WHO FAIL TO PAY.

the amount consumed by one person is unavailable for others to consume. For example, when you and some friends share a pizza, each slice they eat is one less available for you. Second, the supplier of a private good can easily exclude those who fail to pay. Only paying customers get pizza. Thus, private goods are said to be *exclusive*. So **private goods**, such as pizza, are both rival in consumption and exclusive. In contrast, **public goods** are *nonrival* in consumption. For example, your family's benefit from a safer neighborhood does not reduce your neighbor's benefit. What's more, once produced, public goods are available to all. Suppliers cannot easily prevent consumption by those who fail to pay. For example, reducing terrorism is *nonexclusive*. It benefits all in the community, regardless of who pays for it and who doesn't. Because public goods are *nonrival* and *nonexclusive*, private firms cannot sell them profitably. The government, however, has the authority to enforce tax collections for public goods. Thus, the government provides public goods and funds them with taxes.

Dealing with Externalities

Market prices reflect the private costs and private benefits of producers and consumers. But sometimes production or consumption imposes costs or benefits on third parties—on those who are neither suppliers nor demanders in a market transaction. For example, a paper mill fouls the air breathed by nearby residents, but the price of paper fails to reflect such costs. Because these pollution costs are outside, or external to, the market, they are called *externalities*. An **externality** is a cost or a benefit that falls on a third party. A negative externality imposes an external cost, such as factory pollution or auto emissions. A positive externality confers an external benefit, such as getting a good education or driving carefully. Because market prices do not reflect externalities, governments often use taxes, subsidies, and regulations to discourage negative externalities and encourage positive externalities. For example, a polluting factory often faces taxes and regulations aimed at curbing that pollution. And because more educated people can read road signs and have options that pay better than crime, governments try to encourage education with free public schools and subsidized higher education and by keeping people in school until their 16th birthdays.

A More Equal Distribution of Income

As mentioned earlier, some people, because of poor education, mental or physical disabilities, or perhaps the need to care for small children, are unable to support themselves and their families. Because resource markets do not guarantee even a minimum level of income, transfer payments reflect society's attempt to provide a basic standard of living to all households. Most citizens agree that government should redistribute income to the poor (note the normative nature of this statement). Opinions differ about who should receive benefits, how much they should get, what form benefits should take, and how long benefits should last.

Full Employment, Price Stability, and Economic Growth

Perhaps the most important responsibility of government is fostering a healthy economy, which benefits just about everyone. The government—through its ability to tax, to spend, and to control the money supply—attempts to promote full employment, price stability, and economic growth. Pursuing these objectives by taxing and spending is called **fiscal policy**. Pursuing them by regulating the money supply is called **monetary policy**. Macroeconomics examines both policies.

Government's Structure and Objectives

The United States has a *federal system* of government, meaning that responsibilities are shared across levels of government. State governments grant some powers to local governments and surrender some powers to the national, or federal, government. As the system has evolved, the federal government has primary responsibility for national security, economic stability, and market competition. State governments fund public higher education, prisons, and—with aid from the federal government—highways and welfare. Local governments

private good
a good that is both rival in consumption and exclusive, such as pizza

public good
a good that, once produced, is available for all to consume, regardless of who pays and who doesn't; such a good is nonrival and nonexclusive, such as a safer community

externality
a cost or a benefit that affects neither the buyer or seller, but instead affects people not involved in the market transaction

fiscal policy
the use of government purchases, transfer payments, taxes, and borrowing to influence economy-wide variables such as inflation, employment, and economic growth

monetary policy
regulation of the money supply to influence economy-wide variables such as inflation, employment, and economic growth

Roles of Government

Here's a quick review of beneficial government interventions in markets:

- Establishing and enforcing the rules of the game
- Promoting competition
- Regulating natural monopolies
- Providing public goods
- Dealing with externalities
- Distributing income more equally
- Pursuing full employment, price stability, and economic growth

provide primary and secondary education with aid from the state, plus police and fire protection. Here are some distinguishing features of government.

Difficulty in Defining Government Objectives

We assume that households try to maximize utility and firms try to maximize profit, but what about governments—or, more specifically, what about government decision makers? What do they try to maximize? One problem is that our federal system consists of not one but many governments—more than 87,600 separate jurisdictions in all including 1 nation, 50 states, 3,034 counties, 35,933 cities and towns, 13,506 school districts, and 35,052 special districts. What's more, because the federal government relies on offsetting, or countervailing, powers across the executive, legislative, and judicial branches, government does not act as a single, consistent decision maker. Even within the federal executive branch, there are so many agencies and bureaus that at times they seem to work at cross-purposes. For example, at the same time as the U.S. Surgeon General required health warnings on cigarette packages, the U.S. Department of Agriculture pursued policies to benefit tobacco growers. Given this thicket of jurisdictions, branches, and bureaus, one useful theory of government behavior is that elected officials try to maximize the number of votes they will get in the next election. So let's assume that elected officials are vote maximizers. In this theory, vote maximization guides the decisions of elected officials who, in turn, oversee government employees.

There is no necessary link between the cost of a program and the benefit.

Voluntary Exchange Versus Coercion

Market exchange relies on the voluntary behavior of buyers and sellers. Don't like tofu? No problem—don't buy it. But in political markets, the situation is different. Any voting rule except unanimous consent must involve some government coercion. Public choices are enforced by the police power of the state. Those who fail to pay their taxes could go to jail, even though they may object to some programs those taxes support, such as the war in Iraq or capital punishment.

No Market Prices

Another distinguishing feature of governments is that public output is usually offered at either a zero price or at a price below the cost of providing it. If you now pay in-state tuition at a public college or university, your tuition probably covers only about half the state's cost of providing your education. Because the revenue side of the government budget is usually separate from the expenditure side, there is no necessary link between the cost of a program and the benefit. In the private sector, the expected marginal benefit is at least as great as marginal cost; otherwise, market exchange would not occur.

The Size and Growth of Government

One way to track the impact of government over time is by measuring government outlays relative to the U.S. *gross domestic product,* or *GDP,* which is the total value of all final goods and services produced in the United States. In 1929, the year the Great Depression began, all government outlays, mostly by state and local governments, totaled about 10 percent of GDP. At the time, the federal government played a minor role. In fact, during the

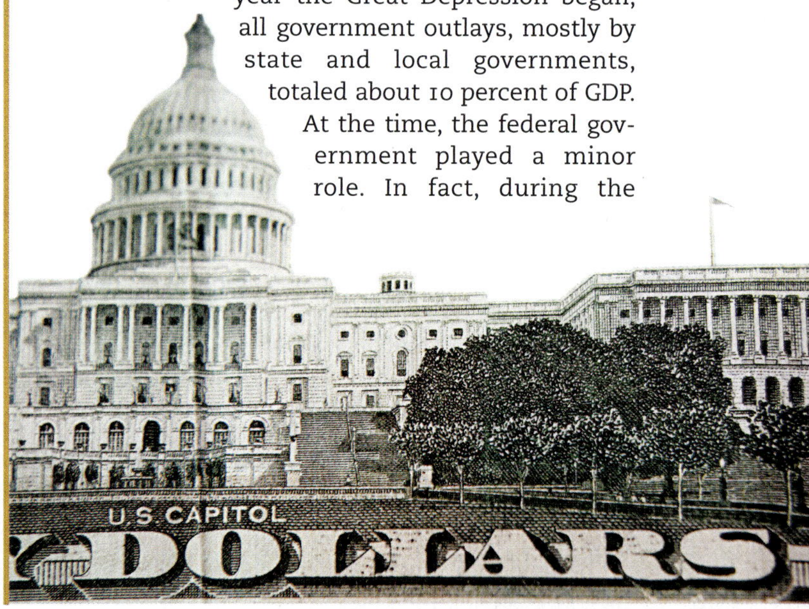

nation's first 150 years, federal outlays, except during war years, never exceeded 3 percent relative to GDP.

The Great Depression, World War II, and a change in macroeconomic thinking boosted the share of government outlays to 37 percent of GDP in 2007, with about two-thirds of that by the federal government.[1] In comparison, government outlays relative to GDP were 36 percent in Japan; 40 percent in Canada; 45 percent in the United Kingdom, Germany, and Italy; and 53 percent in France. Government outlays by the 28 largest industrial economies averaged 40 percent of GDP in 2007.[1] Thus, government outlays in the United States relative to GDP are below those of most other advanced economies.

Exhibit 3

Redistribution Has Grown and Defense Has Declined as Share of Federal Outlays Since 1960

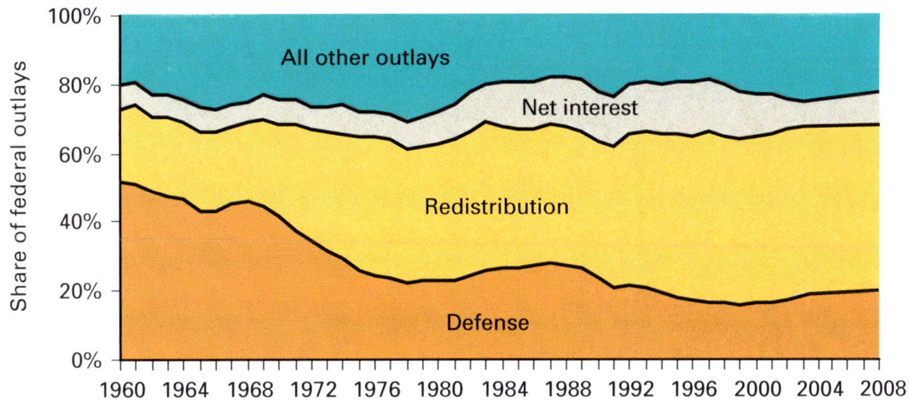

SOURCE: Computed based on figures from the *Economic Report of the President,* February 2007. Table B-80. For the latest figures, go to http://gpoaccess.gov/eop/.

Let's look briefly at the composition of federal outlays. Since 1960, defense spending has declined from over half of federal outlays to about one-fifth by 2008, as shown in Exhibit 3. Redistribution—Social Security, Medicare, and welfare programs—has been the mirror image of defense spending, jumping from only about one-fifth of federal outlays in 1960 to nearly half by 2008.

Sources of Government Revenue

Taxes provide the bulk of revenue at all levels of government. The federal government relies primarily on the individual income tax, state governments rely on income and sales taxes, and local governments rely on the property tax. Other revenue sources include user charges, such as highway tolls, and borrowing. For additional revenue, some states also monopolize certain markets, such as for lottery tickets and liquor.

Exhibit 4 focuses on the composition of federal revenue since 1960. The share made up by the individual income tax has remained relatively constant, ranging from a low of 42 percent in the mid-1960s to 47 percent in 2008. The share from payroll taxes more than doubled from 15 percent in 1960 to 35 percent in 2008. *Payroll taxes* are deducted from paychecks to support Social Security and Medicare, which funds medical care for the elderly. Corporate taxes and revenue from other sources, such as excise (sales) taxes and user charges, have declined as a share of the total since 1960.

Exhibit 4

Payroll Taxes Have Grown as a Share of Federal Revenue Since 1960

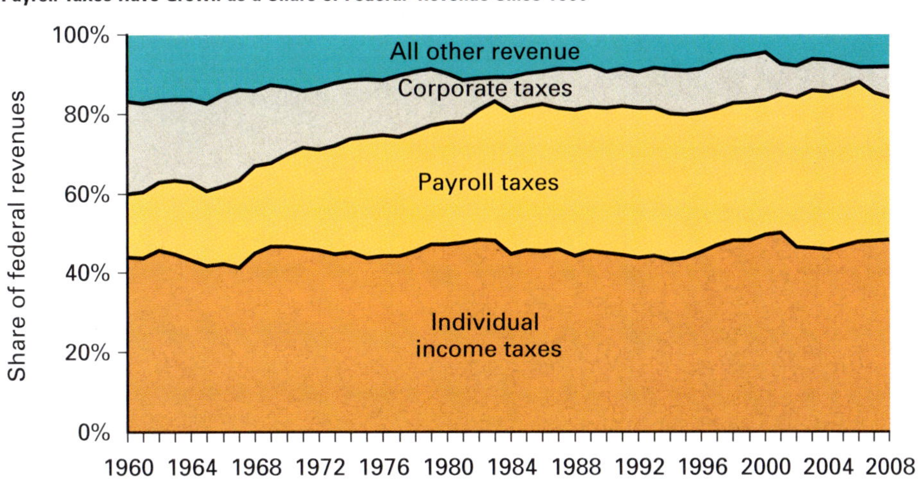

SOURCE: Computed based on figures from the *Economic Report of the President,* February 2007. Table B-80. For the latest figures, go to http://gpoaccess.gov/eop/.

Tax Principles and Tax Incidence

The structure of a tax is often justified on the basis of one of two general

1. The Organization of Economic Cooperation and Development, OECD *Economic Outlook* (May 2007): Annex Table 25.

principles. First, a tax could relate to the individual's ability to pay, so those with a greater ability pay more taxes. Income or property taxes often rely on this **ability-to-pay tax principle**. Alternatively, the **benefits-received tax principle** relates taxes to the benefits taxpayers receive from the government activity funded by the tax. For example, the tax on gasoline funds highway construction and maintenance, thereby linking tax payment to road use, since those who drive more pay more gas taxes.

Exhibit 5

Top Marginal Rate on Federal Personal Income Tax Since 1913

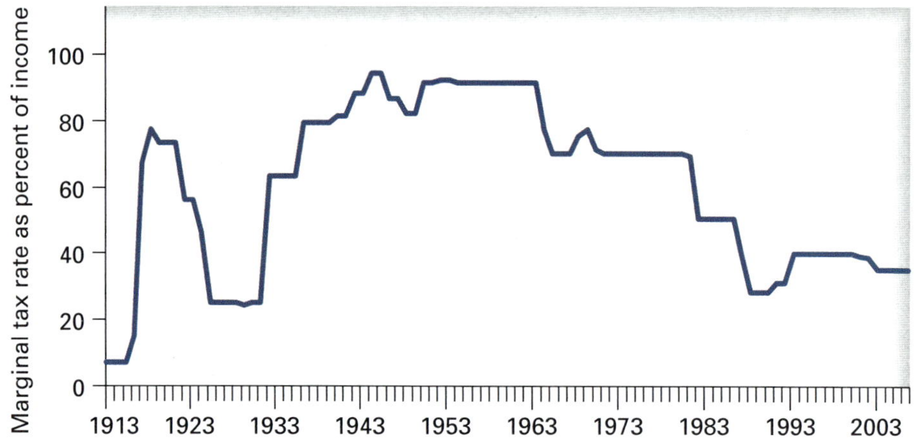

SOURCE: U.S. Internal Revenue Service. For the latest figures on the personal income tax go to http://www.irs.gov/individuals/index.html.

Tax incidence indicates who actually bears the burden of the tax. One way to evaluate tax incidence is by measuring the tax as a percentage of income. Under **proportional taxation**, taxpayers at all income levels pay the same percentage of their income in taxes. A proportional income tax is also called a flat tax, since the tax as a percentage of income remains constant, or flat, as income increases. Note that under proportional taxation, although taxes remain constant as a percentage of income, the dollar amount of taxes increases as income increases.

ability-to-pay tax principle those with a greater ability to pay, such as those earning higher incomes or those owning more property, should pay more taxes

benefits-received tax principle those who get more benefits from the government program should pay more taxes

tax incidence the distribution of tax burden among taxpayers; who ultimately pays the tax

proportional taxation the tax as a percentage of income remains constant as income increases; also called a flat tax

progressive taxation the tax as a percentage of income increases as income increases

marginal tax rate the percentage of each additional dollar of income that goes to the tax

Under **progressive taxation**, the percentage of income paid in taxes increases as income increases. The **marginal tax rate** indicates the percentage of each additional dollar of income that goes to taxes. Because high marginal rates reduce the after-tax return from working or investing, high marginal rates can reduce people's incentives to work and invest. The six marginal rates applied to the U.S. personal income tax ranged from 10 to 35 percent in 2007, down from a range of 15 to 39.6 percent in 2000.

The top marginal tax bracket each year during the history of the personal income tax is shown by Exhibit 5. Although the top marginal rate is now

{ Decoding the taxes on your pay stub }

FICA (aka Social Security) stands for Federal Insurance Contributions Act: 6.2% paid by you, 6.2% paid by your employer

FUTA (aka unemployment) stands for Federal Unemployment Tax Act: 6.2% of taxable wages, paid by your employer lower than it was during most other years, high income households still pay most of the federal income tax collected. For example, according to the U.S. Internal Revenue Service, the top 1 percent of tax filers, based on income, paid 36.9 percent of all income taxes collected in 2004. Their average tax rate was 23.5 percent. And the top 10 percent of tax filers paid 68.2 percent of all income taxes collected. Their average tax rate was 18.6 percent. In contrast, the bottom 50 percent of tax filers paid only 3.3 percent of all income taxes collected. Their tax rate averaged only 3.0 percent. Whether we look at marginal tax rates or average tax rates, the U.S. income tax is progressive. High-income filers pay the overwhelming share of income taxes.

Finally, under regressive taxation, the percentage of income paid in taxes decreases as income increases, so the marginal tax rate declines as income increases. Most U.S. payroll taxes are regressive, because they impose a flat rate up to a certain level of income, above which the marginal rate drops to zero. For example, Social Security taxes were levied on the first $97,500 of workers' pay in 2007. Half of the 12.4 percent tax is paid by employers and half by employees (the self-employed pay the entire 12.4 percent).

Taxes often do more than fund public programs. Some taxes discourage certain activity. For example, a pollution tax can help clean the air. A tax on gasoline can encourage people to work at home, carpool, or use public transportaion. Some taxes have unintended consequences. For example, in Egypt a property tax is not imposed until a building is complete. To avoid such taxes, builders never finish the job; multistory dwellings are usually missing the top floor. As another example of how taxes can distort the allocation of resources, property taxes in Amsterdam and Vietnam were originally based on the width of the building. As a result, buildings in those places are extremely narrow.

This discussion of revenue sources brings to a close, for now, our examination of the role of government in the U.S. economy. Government has a pervasive influence on the economy, and its role is discussed throughout the book.

regressive taxation the tax as a percentage of income decreases as income increases

>>In France, a house's property taxes used to be assessed on the basis of the number stories of livable space in the building. Attic space was not counted as livable space, so houses designed with Mansard roofs became increasingly popular. (More usable space, less taxes.)

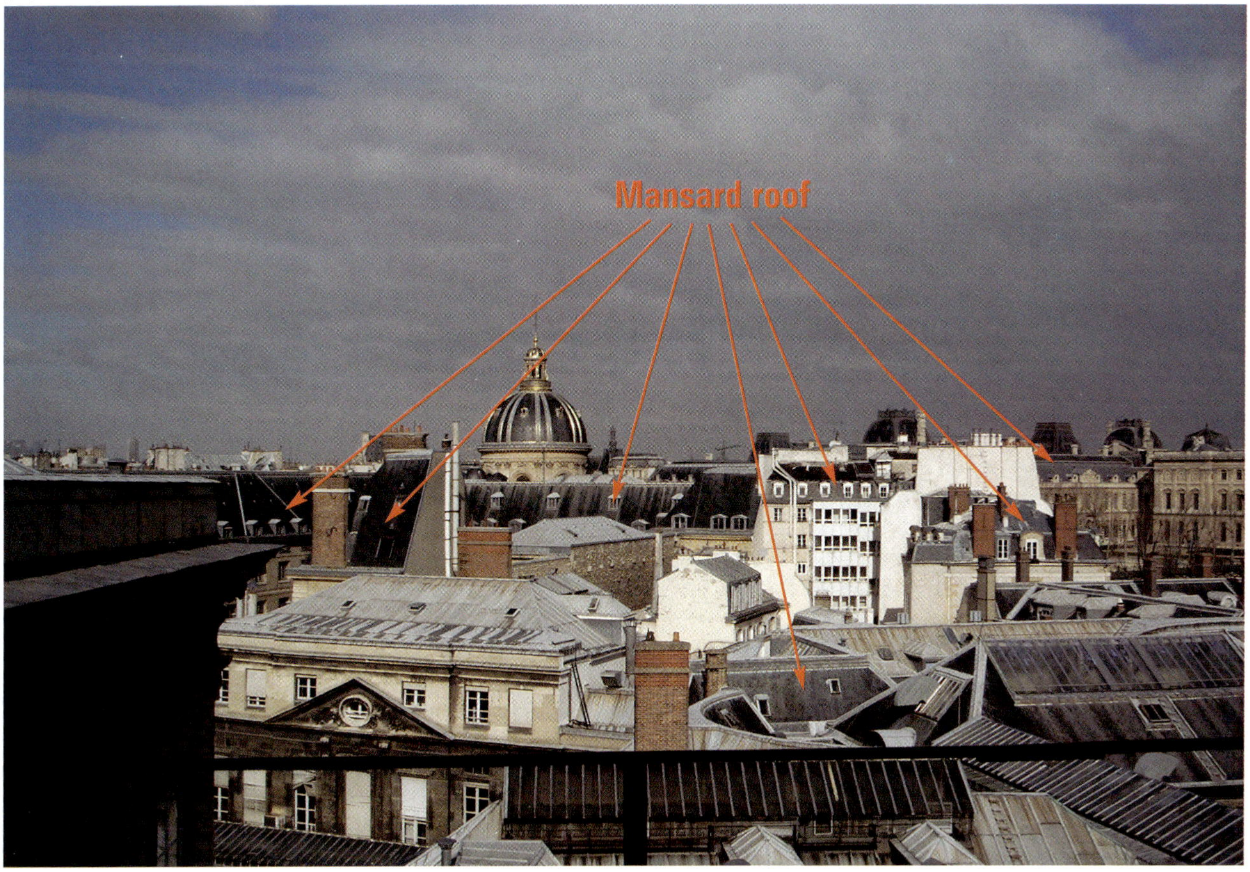

CHAPEL HOUSE PHOTOGRAPHY

LO4 The Rest of the World

So far, the focus has been on institutions within the United States—that is, on *domestic* households, firms, and governments. This focus is appropriate because our primary objective is to understand the workings of the U.S. economy, by far the largest in the world. But the rest of the world affects what U.S. households consume and what U.S. firms produce. For example, Japan and China supply us with all kinds of manufactured goods, thereby affecting U.S. prices, wages, and profits. Likewise, political events in the Persian Gulf can affect what Americans pay for oil. Foreign decision makers, therefore, influence the U.S. economy—what we produce and what we consume. The *rest of the world* consists of the households, firms, and governments in the two hundred or so sovereign nations throughout the world.

International Trade

In the previous chapter, you learned about comparative advantage and the gains from specialization. These gains explain why householders stopped doing everything for themselves and began to specialize. International trade arises for the same reasons. *International trade occurs because the opportunity cost of producing specific goods differs across countries.* Americans import raw materials like crude oil, diamonds, and coffee beans and finished goods like cameras, DVD players, and automobiles. U.S. producers export sophisticated products like computer software, aircraft, and movies, as well as agricultural products like wheat and corn.

Trade between the United States and the rest of the world has increased in recent decades. In 1970, U.S. exports of goods and services amounted to only 6 percent of the gross domestic product. That has increased to 10 percent. The top 10 destinations for U.S. exports in order of importance are Canada, Mexico, Japan, China, United Kingdom, Germany, South Korea, Netherlands, France, and Taiwan.

The **merchandise trade balance** equals the value of exported goods minus the value of imported goods. Goods in this case are distinguished from services, which show up in another trade account. For the last quarter century, the United States has imported more goods than it has exported, resulting in a merchandise trade deficit. Just as a household must pay for its spending, so too must a nation. The merchandise trade deficit must be offset by a surplus in one or more of the other *balance-of-payments* accounts. A nation's **balance of payments** is the record of all economic transactions between its residents and residents of the rest of the world.

Exchange Rates

The lack of a common currency complicates trade between countries. How many U.S. dollars buy a Porsche? An American buyer cares only about the dollar cost; the German carmaker cares only about the *euros* (€) received (the common currency of 13 European countries). To facilitate trade funded by different currencies, a market for foreign exchange has developed. **Foreign exchange** is foreign currency needed to carry out international transactions. The supply and demand for foreign exchange comes together in *foreign exchange markets* to determine the exchange rate. The *exchange rate* measures the price of one cur-

merchandise trade balance
the value during a given period of a country's exported goods minus the value of its imported goods

balance of payments
a record of all economic transactions during a given period between residents of one country and residents of the rest of the world

foreign exchange
foreign money needed to carry out international transactions

On the Porsche Web site, the base price of a 2008 Turbo Cayenne is $93,700. As the euro strengthens against the dollar, that figure only rises.

rency in terms of another. For example, the exchange rate between the euro and the dollar might indicate that one euro exchanges for $1.20. At that exchange rate, a Porsche selling for €100,000 costs $120,000. The exchange rate affects the prices of imports and exports and thus helps shape the flow of foreign trade.

Trade Restrictions

Despite clear gains from international specialization and exchange, nearly all nations restrict trade to some extent. These restrictions can take the form of (1) tariffs, which are taxes on imports; (2) quotas, which are limits on the quantity of a particular good that can be imported from a country; and (3) other trade restrictions. If specialization according to comparative advantage is so beneficial, why do most countries restrict trade? Restrictions benefit certain domestic producers that lobby their governments for these benefits. For example, U.S. growers of sugar cane have benefited from legislation restricting imports, thereby raising U.S. sugar prices. These higher prices hurt domestic consumers, but consumers are usually unaware of this harm. Trade restrictions interfere with the free flow of products across borders and tend to hurt the overall economy.

Final Word

This chapter examined the four economic decision makers: households, firms, governments, and the rest of the world. Domestic households are by far the most important, for they supply resources and demand goods and services.

If you were to stop reading right now, you would already know more economics than most people. But to understand market economies, you must learn how markets work. The next chapter introduces demand and supply.

tariff
a tax on imports

quota
a legal limit on the quantity of a particular product that can be imported

$10.9 < Trillion of personal income in the United States

72% < Of all U.S. businesses are sole proprietorships

Start of Industrial Revolution in Britain > 1750

Base price of Porsche Cayenne Turbo > $93,700

Student owners of UConn bookstore co-op> 30,000

CHAPTER

4

Demand, Supply, *and* Markets

Learning Outcomes

LO[1] Explain how the law of demand affects market activity

LO[2] Explain how the law of supply affects market activity

LO[3] Describe how the interaction between supply and demand creates markets

LO[4] Describe how markets reach equilibrium

LO[5] Explain how markets react during periods of disequilibrium

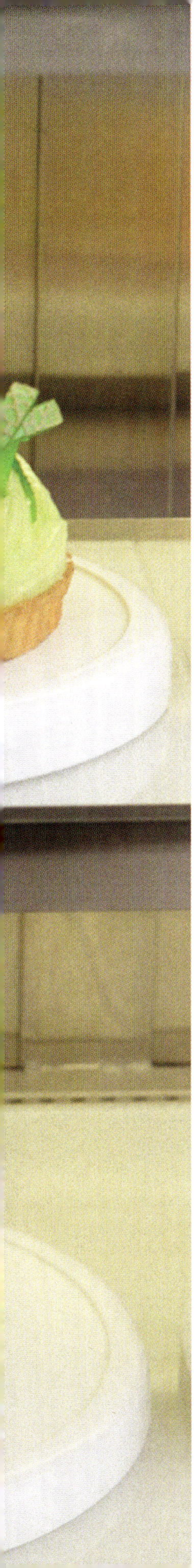

© YOKO INOUE/NONSTOCK/JUPITERIMAGES

"Why does the bakery never have enough of the cakes you want and plenty of the ones you don't?"

Why do roses cost more on Valentine's Day than during the rest of the year? Why do TV ads cost more during the Super Bowl ($2.6 million for 30 seconds in 2007) than during *Nick at Nite* reruns? Why do Miami hotels charge more in February than in August? Why do surgeons earn more than butchers? Why do basketball pros earn more than hockey pros? Why do economics majors earn more than most other majors? Answers to these and most economic questions boil down to the workings of demand and supply—the subject of this chapter.

What do you think?

Professional athletes should earn comparable salaries regardless of the sport they play.

Strongly Disagree 1 2 3 4 5 6 7 *Strongly Agree*

This chapter introduces demand and supply and shows how they interact in competitive markets. *Demand and supply are the most fundamental and the most powerful of all economic tools*—important enough to warrant a chapter. Indeed, some believe that if you program a computer to answer "demand and supply" to every economic question, you could put many economists out of work. An understanding of the two ideas will take you far in mastering the art and science of economic analysis. This chapter uses graphs, so you may need to review the Chapter 1 appendix as a refresher.

Topics discussed in Chapter 4 include:

- Demand and quantity demanded
- Movement along a demand curve
- Shift of a demand curve
- Supply and quantity supplied
- Movement along a supply curve
- Shift of a supply curve
- Markets and equilibrium
- Disequilibrium

LO1 Demand

How many six packs of Pepsi will people buy each month at a price of $3? What if the price is $2? What if it's $4? The answers reveal the relationship between the price of Pepsi and the quantity demanded. Such a relationship is called the *demand* for Pepsi. Demand indicates the quantity consumers are both *willing and able* to buy at each possible price during a given time

demand
a relation between the price of a good and the quantity that consumers are willing and able to buy per period, other things constant

period, other things constant. Because demand pertains to a specific period—a day, a week, a month—think of demand as the *amounts purchased per period* at each possible price. Also, notice the emphasis on *willing and able*. You may be *able* to buy a new Harley-Davidson XL 883 for $6,600 because you can afford one, but you may not be *willing* to buy one if motorcycles don't interest you.

The Law of Demand

In 1962, Sam Walton opened his first store in Rogers, Arkansas, with a sign that read "Wal-Mart Discount City. We sell for less." Wal-Mart now sells more than any other retailer in the world because prices are among the lowest around. As a consumer, you understand why people buy more at a lower price. Sell for less, and the world will beat a path to your door. Wal-Mart, for example, sells on average over 20,000 pairs of shoes *an hour*. This relation between the price and the quantity demanded is an economic law. The **law of demand** says that quantity demanded varies inversely with price, other things constant. Thus, the higher the price, the smaller the quantity demanded; the lower the price, the greater the quantity demanded.

law of demand
the quantity of a good that consumers are willing and able to buy per period relates inversely, or negatively, to the price, other things constant

substitution effect of a price change
when the price of a good falls, that good becomes cheaper compared to other goods so consumers tend to substitute that good for other goods

money income
the number of dollars a person receives per period, such as $400 per week

real income
income measured in terms of the goods and services it can buy; real income changes when the price changes

income effect of a price change
a fall in the price of a good increases consumers' real income, making consumers more able to purchase goods; for a normal good, the quantity demanded increases

Demand, Wants, and Needs

Consumer demand and wants are not the same. As we have seen, wants are unlimited. You may want a new Mercedes SL600 Roadster convertible, but the $132,500 price tag is likely beyond your budget (that is, the quantity you demand at that price is zero). Nor is demand the same as need. You may need a new muffler for your car, but a price of $300 is just too high for you. If, however, the price drops enough—say, to $200—then you become both willing and able to buy one.

The Substitution Effect of a Price Change

What explains the law of demand? Why, for example, is more demanded at a lower price? The explanation begins with unlimited wants confronting scarce resources. Many goods and services could satisfy particular wants. For example, you can satisfy your hunger with pizza, tacos, burgers, chicken, or hundreds of other foods. Similarly, you can satisfy your desire for warmth in the winter with warm clothing, a home-heating system, a trip to Hawaii, or in many other ways. Clearly, some alternatives have more appeal than others (a trip to Hawaii is more fun than warm clothing). In a world without scarcity, everything would be free, so you would always choose the most attractive alternative. Scarcity, however, is a reality, and the degree of scarcity of one good relative to another helps determine each good's relative price.

Notice that the definition of *demand* includes the other-things-constant assumption. Among the "other things" assumed to remain constant are the prices of other goods. For example, if the price of pizza declines while other prices remain constant, pizza becomes relatively cheaper. Consumers are more *willing* to purchase pizza when its relative price falls; they substitute pizza for other goods. This principle is called the **substitution effect of a price change**. On the other hand, an increase in the price of pizza, other things constant, increases the opportunity cost of pizza. This higher opportunity cost causes consumers to substitute other goods for the now higher-priced pizza, thus reducing their quantity of pizza demanded. Remember that *it is the change in the relative price—the price of one good relative to the prices of other goods—that causes the substitution effect*. If all prices changed by the same percentage, there would be no change in relative prices and no substitution effect.

The Income Effect of a Price Change

A fall in the price increases the quantity demanded for a second reason. Suppose you earn $30 a week from a part-time job, so $30 is your money income. **Money income** is simply the number of dollars received per period, in this case, $30 per week. Suppose you spend all that income on pizza, buying three a week at $10 each. What if the price drops to $6? At the lower price you can now afford five pizzas a week. Your money income remains at $30 per week, but the decrease in the price has increased your **real income**—that is, your income measured in terms of what it can buy. The price reduction, other things constant, increases the purchasing power of your income, thereby increasing your ability to buy pizza. The quantity of pizza you demand will likely increase because of this **income effect of a price change**. You may not increase your quantity demanded to five pizzas, but you could. If you decide to purchase four pizzas a week when the price drops to $6, you would still have $6 remaining to buy other goods. Thus, the income effect of a lower price increases your real income and thereby increases your ability to purchase all goods. Because of the income effect, consumers typically increase their quantity demanded when the price declines.

Conversely, an increase in the price of a good, other things constant, reduces real income, thereby reducing the *ability* to purchase all goods. Because of the income effect, consumers typically reduce their quantity demanded when the price increases. Again, note that money income, not real income, is assumed to remain constant along a demand curve. A change in price changes your real income, so real income varies along a demand curve. The lower the price, the greater your real income.

The Demand Schedule and Demand Curve

Demand can be expressed as a *demand schedule* or as a *demand curve*. Exhibit 1a shows a hypothetical demand schedule for pizza. In describing demand, we must specify the units measured and the period considered. In our example, the unit is a 12-inch regular pizza and the period is a week. The schedule lists possible prices, along with the quantity demanded at each price. At a price of $15, for example, consumers demand 8 million pizzas per week. As you can see, the lower the price, other things constant, the greater the quantity demanded. Consumers substitute pizza for other foods. And as the price falls, real income increases, causing consumers to increase the quantity of pizza they demand. If the price drops as low as $3, consumers demand 32 million per week.

Exhibit 1a

The Demand Schedule for Pizza

	Price per Pizza	Quantity Demanded per Week (millions)
a	$15	8
b	12	14
c	9	20
d	6	26
e	3	32

© THINKSTOCK IMAGES/JUPITERIMAGES

The demand schedule in Exhibit 1a appears as a demand curve in Exhibit 1b, with price measured on the vertical axis and the quantity demanded per week on the horizontal axis. Each price-quantity combination listed in the demand schedule in Exhibit 1a becomes a point in Exhibit 1b. Point *a*, for example, indicates that if the price is $15, consumers demand 8 million pizzas per week. These points connect to form the demand curve for pizza, labeled *D*. (By the way, some demand curves are straight lines, some are curved lines, and some are even jagged lines, but all are called demand *curves*.)

Exhibit 1b

The Demand Curve for Pizza

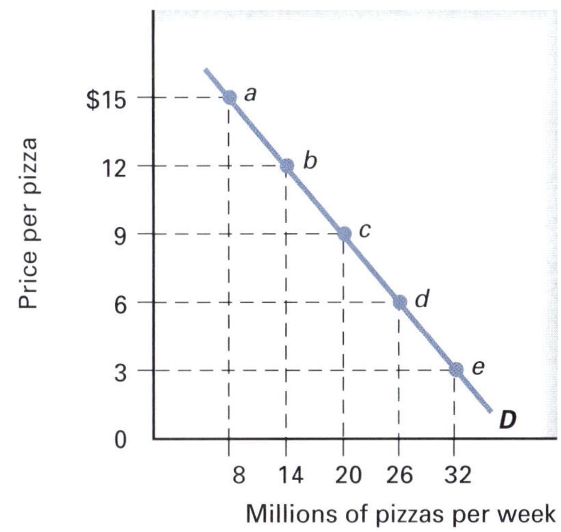

A demand curve slopes downward, reflecting the *law of demand*: Price and quantity demanded are inversely related, other things constant. Besides money income, also assumed constant along the demand curve are the prices of other goods. Thus, along the demand curve for pizza, the price of pizza changes *relative to the prices of other goods*. The demand curve shows the effect of a change in the *relative price* of pizza—that is, relative to other prices, which do not change.

Take care to distinguish between *demand* and *quantity demanded*. The *demand* for pizza is not a specific amount, but rather the *entire relationship* between price and quantity demanded—represented by the demand schedule or the demand curve. An individual point on the demand

demand curve a curve showing the relation between the price of a good and the quantity consumers are willing and able to buy per period, other things constant curve indicates the quantity demanded at a particular price. For example, at a price of $12, the quantity demanded is 14 million pizzas per week. If the price drops from $12 to, say, $9, this is shown in Exhibit 1b by *a movement along the demand curve*—in this case from point *b* to point *c*. Any movement along a demand curve reflects a *change in quantity demanded,* not a change in demand.

The law of demand applies to the millions of products sold in grocery stores, department stores, clothing stores, shoe stores, drugstores, music stores, bookstores, hardware stores, travel agencies, and restaurants, as well as through mail-order catalogs, the *Yellow Pages,* classified ads, online sites, stock markets, real estate markets, job markets, flea markets, and all other markets. The law of demand applies even to choices that seem more personal than economic, such as whether or not to own a pet. For example, after New York City passed an anti-dog-litter law, law-abiding owners had to follow their dogs around the city with scoopers, plastic bags—whatever would do the job. Because the law raised the personal cost of owning a dog, the quantity of dogs demanded decreased. Some owners simply abandoned their dogs, raising the number of strays in the city. The number of dogs left at animal shelters doubled. The law of demand predicts this inverse relation between cost, or price, and quantity demanded.

© RADIUS IMAGES/JUPITERIMAGES

It is useful to distinguish between individual demand, which is the demand of an individual consumer, and market demand, which is the sum of the individual demands of all consumers in the market. In most markets, there are many consumers, sometimes millions. Unless otherwise noted, when we talk about demand, we are referring to market demand, as shown in Exhibit 1.

quantity demanded
the amount of a good consumers are willing and able to buy per period at a particular price, as reflected by a point on a demand curve

individual demand
a relation between the price of a good and the quantity purchased by an individual consumer per period, other things constant

market demand
the relation between the price of a good and the quantity purchased by all consumers in the market during a given period, other things constant; sum of the individual demands in the market

Shifts of the Demand Curve

A demand curve isolates the relation between the price of a good and quantity demanded when other factors that could affect demand remain unchanged. What are those other factors, and how do changes in them affect demand? Variables that can affect market demand are (1) the money income of consumers, (2) prices of other goods, (3) consumer expectations, (4) the number or composition of consumers in the market, and (5) consumer tastes. How do changes in each affect demand?

Changes in Consumer Income

Exhibit 2 shows the market demand curve *D* for pizza. This demand curve assumes a given level of money income. Suppose consumer income increases. Some consumers will then be willing and able to buy more pizza at each price, so market demand increases. The demand curve shifts to the right from *D* to *D*′. For example, at a price of $12, the amount of pizza demanded increases from 14 million to 20 million per week, as indicated by the movement from point *b* on demand curve *D* to point *f* on demand curve *D*′. In short, *an increase in demand—that is, a rightward shift of the demand curve—means that consumers are willing and able to buy more pizza at each price.*

Goods are classified into two broad categories, depending on how demand responds to changes in

Exhibit 2

An Increase in the Market Demand for Pizza

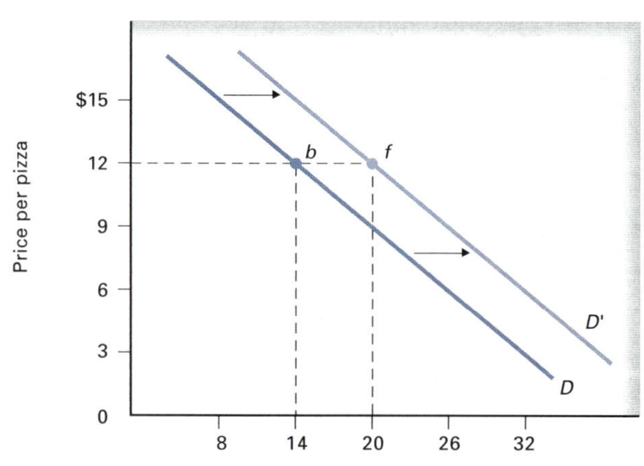

money income. The demand for a normal good increases as money income increases. Because pizza is a normal good, its demand curve shifts rightward when money income increases. Most goods are normal. In contrast, demand for an inferior good actually decreases as money income increases, so the demand curve shifts leftward. Examples of inferior goods include bologna sandwiches, used furniture, and used clothing. As money income increases, consumers tend to switch from these inferior goods to normal goods (such as roast beef sandwiches, new furniture, and new clothing).

Changes in the Prices of Other Goods

Again, the prices of other goods are assumed to remain constant along a given demand curve. Now let's bring these other prices into play. Consumers have various ways of trying to satisfy any particular want. Consumers choose among substitutes based on relative prices. For example, pizza and tacos are substitutes, though not perfect ones. An increase in the price of tacos, other things constant, reduces the quantity of tacos demanded along a given taco demand curve. An increase in the price of tacos also increases the demand for pizza, shifting the demand curve for pizza to the right. Two goods are considered substitutes if an increase in the price of one shifts the demand for the other rightward and, conversely, if a decrease in the price of one shifts demand for the other leftward.

Goods used in combination are called *complements*. Examples include Coke and pizza, milk and cookies, computer software and hardware, and airline tickets and rental cars. Two goods are considered complements if an increase in the price of one decreases the demand for the other, shifting that demand curve leftward. For example, an increase in the price of pizza shifts the demand curve for Coke leftward. But most pairs of goods selected at random are *unrelated*—for example, pizza and housing, or milk and gasoline. Still, an increase in the price of an unrelated good reduces the consumer's real income and can reduce the demand for pizza and other goods. For example, a sharp increase in housing prices reduces the amount of income people have to spend on other goods, such as pizza.

Changes in Consumer Expectations

Another factor assumed constant along a given demand curve is consumer expectations about factors that influence demand, such as incomes or prices. A change in consumers' *income expectations* can shift the demand curve. For example, a consumer who learns about a pay raise might increase demand well before the raise takes effect. A college senior who lands that first real job may buy a new car even before graduation. Likewise, a change in consumers' *price expectations* can shift the demand curve. For example, if you expect the price of pizza to jump next week, you may buy an extra one today for the freezer, shifting this week's demand for pizza rightward. Or if consumers come to believe that home prices will climb next month, some will increase their demand for housing now, shifting this month's demand for housing rightward. On the other hand, if housing prices are expected to fall next month, some consumers will postpone purchases, thereby shifting this month's housing demand leftward.

Changes in the Number or Composition of Consumers

As mentioned earlier, the market demand curve is the sum of the individual demand curves of all consumers in the market. If the number of consumers changes, the demand curve will shift. For example, if the population grows, the demand curve for pizza will shift rightward. Even if total population remains unchanged, demand could shift with a change in the composition of the population. For example, a bulge in the teenage population could shift pizza demand rightward. A baby boom would shift rightward the demand for car seats and baby food. A growing Latino population would affect the demand for Latino foods.

Changes in Consumer Tastes

Do you like anchovies on your pizza? How about sauerkraut on your hot

normal good
a good, such as new clothes, for which demand increases, or shifts rightward, as consumer income rises

inferior good
a good, such as used clothes, for which demand decreases, or shifts leftward, as consumer income rises

substitutes
goods, such as Coke and Pepsi, that relate in such a way that an increase in the price of one shifts the demand for the other rightward

complements
goods, such as milk and cookies, that relate in such a way that an increase in the price of one shifts the demand for the other leftward

dogs? Are you into tattoos and body piercings? Is music to your ears more likely to be rock, country, hip-hop, reggae, R&B, jazz, funk, Latin, gospel, new age, or classical? Choices in food, body art, music, clothing, books, movies, TV—indeed, all consumer choices—are influenced by consumer tastes. Tastes are nothing more than your likes and dislikes as a consumer. What determines tastes? Your desires for food when hungry and drink when thirsty are largely biological. So too is your desire for comfort, rest, shelter, friendship, love, status, personal safety, and a pleasant environment. Your family background affects some of your tastes—your taste in food, for example, has been shaped by years of home cooking. Other influences include the surrounding culture, peer pressure, and religious convictions. So economists can say a little about the origin of tastes, but they claim no special expertise in understanding how tastes develop and change over time. Economists recognize, however, that tastes have an important impact on demand. For example, although pizza is popular, some people just don't like it, and those who are lactose intolerant can't stomach the cheese topping. Thus, most people like pizza but some don't.

tastes consumer preferences; likes and dislikes in consumption; assumed to remain constant along a given demand curve

movement along a demand curve change in quantity demanded resulting from a change in the price of the good, other things constant

shift of a demand curve movement of a demand curve right or left resulting from a change in one of the determinants of demand other than the price of the good

supply a relation between the price of a good and the quantity that producers are willing and able to sell per period, other things constant

law of supply the amount of a good that producers are willing and able to sell per period is usually directly related to its price, other things constant

supply curve a curve showing the relation between the price of a good and the quantity producers are willing and able to sell per period other things constant

In our analysis of consumer demand, *we will assume that tastes are given and are relatively stable.* Tastes are assumed to remain constant along a given demand curve. A change in the tastes for a particular good would shift that good's demand curve. For example, a discovery that the tomato sauce and cheese combination on pizza promotes overall health could change consumer tastes, shifting the demand curve for pizza to the right. But because a change in tastes is so difficult to isolate from other economic changes, we should be reluctant to attribute a shift of the demand curve to a change in tastes. We try to rule out other possible reasons for a shift of the demand curve before accepting a change in tastes as the explanation.

That wraps up our look at changes in demand. Before we turn to supply, you should remember the distinction between a movement along a given demand curve and a shift of a demand curve. A change in *price,* other things constant, causes a *movement along a demand curve,* changing the quantity demanded. A change in one of the determinants of demand other than price causes a *shift of a demand curve,* changing demand.

LO2 Supply

Just as demand is a relation between price and quantity demanded, supply is a relation between price and quantity supplied. Supply indicates how much producers are *willing* and *able* to offer for sale per period at each possible price, other things constant. The law of supply states that the quantity supplied is usually directly related to its price, other things constant. Thus, the lower the price, the smaller the quantity supplied; the higher the price, the greater the quantity supplied.

The Supply Schedule and Supply Curve

Exhibit 3 presents the market *supply schedule* and market supply curve S for pizza. Both show the quantities supplied per week at various possible prices by the thousands of pizza makers in the economy. As you can see, price and quantity supplied are directly, or positively, related. Producers offer more at a higher price than at a lower price, so the supply curve slopes upward.

© THINKSTOCK IMAGES/JUPITERIMAGES

There are two reasons why producers offer more for sale when the price rises. First, as the price increases, other things constant, a producer becomes more *willing* to supply the good. Prices act as signals to existing and potential suppliers about the rewards for producing various goods. A higher pizza price attracts resources from lower-valued uses. *A higher price makes producers more willing to increase quantity supplied.*

Higher prices also increase the producer's *ability* to supply the good. The law of increasing opportunity

Exhibit 3

The Supply Schedule and Supply Curve for Pizza

(a) Supply schedule

Price per Pizza	Quantity Supplied per Week (millions)
$15	28
12	24
9	20
6	16
3	12

(b) Supply curve

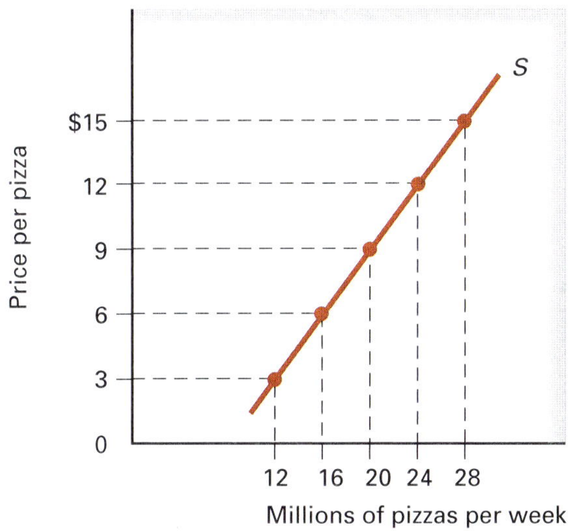

cost, as noted in Chapter 2, states that the opportunity cost of producing more of a particular good rises as output increases—that is, the *marginal cost* of production increases as output increases. Because producers face a higher marginal cost for additional output, they need to get a higher price for that output to be *able* to increase the quantity supplied. *A higher price makes producers more able to increase quantity supplied.* As a case in point, a higher price for gasoline increases oil companies' ability to extract oil from tar sands, to drill deeper, and to explore in less accessible areas, such as the remote jungles of the Amazon, the stormy waters of the North Sea, and the frozen tundra above the Arctic Circle. For example, at a market price of $20 per barrel, extracting oil from tar sands is unprofitable, but at price of $25 per barrel, producers are able to supply millions of barrels per month from tar sands.

Thus, a higher price makes producers more *willing* and more *able* to increase quantity supplied. Producers

© DAVID MCLAIN/AURORA/GETTY IMAGES

<<Supply of crude oil is not the only supply affecting the final price at the pump. A low supply of refineries (refining capacity) also has a hand in higher gas prices.

are more *willing* because production becomes more profitable than other uses of the resources involved. Producers are more *able* because they can afford to cover the higher marginal cost that typically results from increasing output.

As with demand, we distinguish between *supply* and **quantity supplied**. *Supply* is the entire relationship between prices and quantities supplied, as reflected by the supply schedule or supply curve. *Quantity supplied* refers to a particular amount offered for sale at a particular price, as reflected by a point on a given supply curve. We also distinguish between **individual supply**, the supply of an individual producer, and **market supply**, the sum of individual supplies of all producers in the market. Unless otherwise noted, the term *supply* refers to market supply.

Shifts of the Supply Curve

The supply curve isolates the relation between the price of a good and the quantity supplied, other things constant. Assumed constant along a supply curve are the determinants of supply other than the price of the good, including (1) the state of technology, (2) the prices of relevant resources, (3) the prices of alternative goods, (4) producer expectations, and (5) the number of producers

quantity supplied the amount offered for sale per period at a particular price, as reflected by a point on a given supply curve

individual supply the relation between the price of a good and the quantity an individual producer is willing and able to sell per period, other things constant

market supply the relation between the price of a good and the quantity all producers are willing and able to sell per period, other things constant in the market. Let's see how a change in each affects the supply curve.

Changes in Technology

Recall from Chapter 2 that the state of technology represents the economy's knowledge about how to combine resources efficiently. Along a given supply curve, technology is assumed to remain unchanged. If a better technology is discovered, production costs will fall, so suppliers will be more willing and able to supply the good at each price. Consequently, supply will increase, as reflected by a rightward shift of the supply curve. For example, suppose a new high-tech oven that costs the same as existing ovens bakes pizza in half the time. Such a breakthrough would shift the market supply curve rightward, as from S to S′ in Exhibit 4, where more is supplied at each possible price. For example, at a price of $12, the amount supplied increases from 24 million to 28 million pizzas, as shown in Exhibit 4 by the movement from point *g* to point *h*. In short, *an increase in supply—that is, a rightward shift of the supply curve—means that producers are willing and able to sell more pizza at each price.*

Exhibit 4

An Increase in the Supply of Pizza

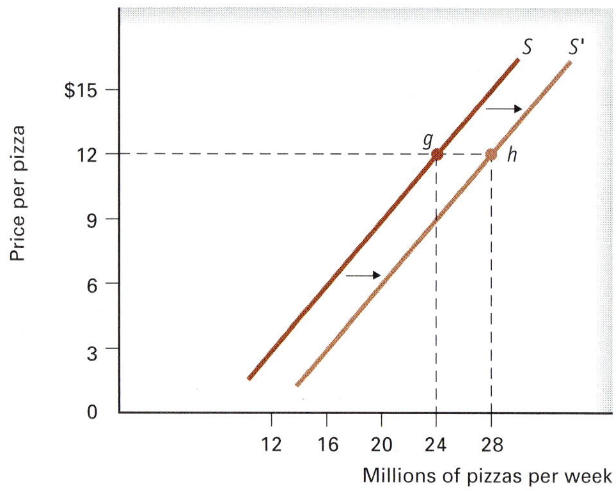

Changes in the Prices of Relevant Resources

Relevant resources are those employed in the production of the good in question. For example, suppose the price of mozzarella cheese falls. This price decrease reduces the cost of making pizza, so producers are more willing and better able to supply it. The supply curve for pizza shifts rightward, as shown in Exhibit 4. On the other hand, an increase in the price of a relevant resource reduces supply, meaning a shift of the supply curve leftward. For example, a higher price of mozzarella increases the cost of making pizza. Higher production costs decrease supply, as reflected by a leftward shift of the supply curve.

relevant resources resources used to produce the good in question

alternative goods other goods that use some or all of the same resources as the good in question

Changes in the Prices of Alternative Goods

Nearly all resources have alternative uses. The labor, building, machinery, ingredients, and knowledge needed to run a pizza business could produce other baked goods. **Alternative goods** are those that use some of the same resources employed to produce the good under consideration. For example, a decrease in the price of Italian bread reduces the opportunity cost of making pizza. As a result, some bread makers become pizza makers so the supply of pizza increases, shifting the supply curve of pizza rightward as in Exhibit 3. On the other hand, if the price of an alternative good, such as Italian bread, increases, supplying pizza becomes relatively less attractive compared to supplying Italian bread. As resources shift from pizza to bread, the supply of pizza decreases, or shifts to the left.

Changes in Producer Expectations

Changes in producer expectations can shift the supply curve. For example, a pizza maker expecting higher pizza prices in the future may expand his or her pizzeria now, thereby shifting the supply of pizza rightward. When a good can be easily stored (crude oil, for example, can be left in the ground), expecting higher prices in the future might prompt some producers to *reduce* their current supply while awaiting the higher price. Thus, an expectation of higher prices in the future could either increase or decrease current supply, depending on the good. More generally, any change affecting future profitability, such as a change in business taxes, could shift the supply curve now.

Changes in the Number of Producers

Because market supply sums the amounts supplied at each price by all producers, market supply depends on the number of producers in the market. If that number increases, supply will increase, shifting supply to the right. If the number of producers decreases, supply will decrease, shifting supply to the left. As an example of increased supply, the number of gourmet coffee bars in the United States has more than quadrupled since 1990 (think Starbucks), shifting the supply curve of gourmet coffee to the right.

Finally, note again the distinction between a movement along a supply curve and a shift of a supply curve. A change in *price,* other things constant, causes *a movement along a supply curve,* changing the quantity supplied. A change in one of the determinants of supply other than price causes a *shift of a supply curve,* changing supply.

You are now ready to bring demand and supply together.

LO3 Demand and Supply Create a Market

Demanders and suppliers have different views of price. Demanders pay the price and suppliers receive it. Thus, a higher price is bad news for consumers but good news for producers. As the price rises, consumers reduce their quantity demanded along the demand curve and producers increase their quantity supplied along the supply curve. How is this conflict between producers and consumers resolved?

Markets

A market sorts out differences between demanders and suppliers. A *market,* as you know from Chapter 1, includes all the arrangements used to buy and sell a particular good or service. Markets reduce transaction costs—the costs of time and information required for exchange. For example, suppose you are looking for a summer job. One approach might be to go from employer to employer looking for openings. But this could have you running around for days or weeks. A more efficient strategy would be to pick up a copy of the local newspaper or go online and look for openings. Classified ads and Web sites, which are elements of the job market, reduce the transaction costs of bringing workers and employers together.

The coordination that occurs through markets takes place not because of some central plan but because of Adam Smith's "invisible hand." For example, the auto dealers in your community tend to locate together, usually on the outskirts of town, where land is cheaper. The dealers congregate not because they all took an economics course or because they like one another's company but because together they become a more attractive destination for car buyers. A dealer who makes the

movement along a supply curve
change in quantity supplied resulting from a change in the price of the good, other things constant

shift of a supply curve
movement of a supply curve left or right resulting from a change in one of the determinants of supply other than the price of the good

transaction costs
the costs of time and information required to carry out market exchange

© JOHN FOXX/STOCKBYTE/GETTY

mistake of locating away from the others misses out on a lot of business. Similarly, stores locate together so that more shoppers will be drawn by the call of the mall. From Orlando theme parks to Broadway theaters to Las Vegas casinos, suppliers congregate to attract demanders. Some groupings can be quite specialized. For example, shops selling dress mannequins cluster along Austin Road in Hong Kong. And diamond merchants congregate within a few city blocks in New York City.

Market Equilibrium

To see how a market works, let's bring together market demand and supply. Exhibit 5 shows the market for pizza, using schedules in panel (a) and curves in panel (b). Suppose the price initially is $12. At that price, producers supply 24 million pizzas per week, but consumers demand only 14 million, resulting in an *excess quantity supplied,* or a **surplus**, of 10 million pizzas per week. Suppliers don't like getting stuck with unsold pizzas. Their desire to eliminate the surplus puts downward pressure on the price, as shown by the arrow pointing down in the graph. As the price falls, producers reduce their quantity supplied and consumers increase their quantity demanded. The price continues to fall as long as quantity supplied exceeds quantity demanded.

surplus
at a given price, the amount by which quantity supplied exceeds quantity demanded; a surplus usually forces the price down

shortage
at a given price, the amount by which quantity demanded exceeds quantity supplied; a shortage usually forces the price up

Alternatively, suppose the price initially is $6. You can see from Exhibit 5 that at that price, consumers demand 26 million pizzas but producers supply only 16 million, resulting in an *excess quantity demanded,* or a **shortage**, of 10 million pizzas per week. Producers quickly notice that they have sold out and those customers still demanding pizzas are grumbling. Profit-maximizing producers and frustrated consumers create market pressure for a higher price, as shown by the arrow pointing up in the graph. As the price rises, producers increase their quantity supplied and consumers reduce their quantity demanded. The price continues to rise as long as quantity demanded exceeds quantity supplied.

Thus, *a surplus creates downward pressure on the price, and a shortage creates upward pressure.* As long as quantity demanded differs from quantity supplied, this difference forces a price change. Note that a shortage or a surplus depends on the price. There is no such thing as a general shortage or a general surplus, only a shortage or a surplus at a particular price.

Exhibit 5

Equilibrium in the Pizza Market

(a) Market schedules

	Millions of Pizzas per Week			
Price per Pizza	Quantity Demanded	Quantity Supplied	Surplus or Shortage	Effect on Price
$15	8	28	Surplus of 20	Falls
12	14	24	Surplus of 10	Falls
9	20	20	Equilibrium	Remains the same
6	26	16	Shortage of 10	Rises
3	32	12	Shortage of 20	Rises

(b) Market curves

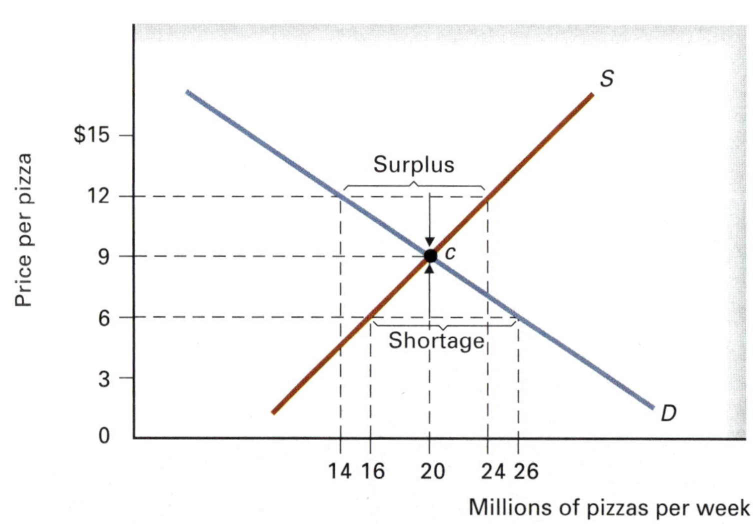

A market reaches equilibrium when the quantity demanded equals quantity supplied. In equilibrium, the independent plans of both buyers and sellers exactly match, so market forces exert no pressure for change. In Exhibit 5, the demand and supply curves intersect at the *equilibrium point*, identified as point *c*. The *equilibrium price* is \$9 per pizza, and the *equilibrium quantity* is 20 million per week. At that price and quantity, the market *clears*. Because there is no shortage or surplus, there is no pressure for the price to change. The demand and supply curves form an "x" at the intersection. The equilibrium point is found where "x" marks the spot.

A market finds equilibrium through the independent actions of thousands, or even millions, of buyers and sellers. In one sense, the market is personal because each consumer and each producer makes a personal decision about how much to buy or sell at a given price. In another sense, the market is impersonal because it requires no conscious communication or coordination among consumers or producers. The price does all the talking. *Impersonal market forces synchronize the personal and independent decisions of many individual buyers and sellers to achieve equilibrium price and quantity.*

The market is impersonal because it requires no conscious communication or coordination among consumers or producers.

LO4 Changes in Equilibrium Price and Quantity

Equilibrium occurs when the intentions of demanders and suppliers exactly match. Once a market reaches equilibrium, that price and quantity prevail until something happens to demand or supply. A change in any determinant of demand or supply usually changes equilibrium price and quantity in a predictable way, as you'll see.

Shifts of the Demand Curve

© THINKSTOCK IMAGES/JUPITERIMAGES

In Exhibit 6, demand curve D and supply curve S intersect at point *c* to yield the initial equilibrium price of \$9 and the initial equilibrium quantity of 20 million 12-inch regular pizzas per week. Now suppose that one of the

Exhibit 6

Effects of an Increase in Demand

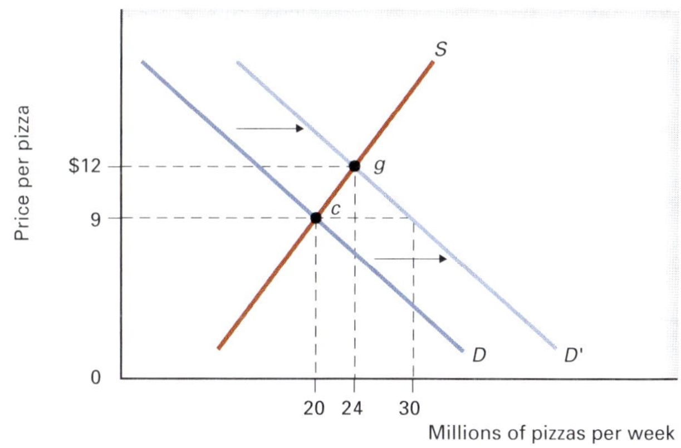

determinants of demand changes in a way that increases demand, shifting the demand curve to the right from *D* to *D*′. Any of the following could shift the demand for pizza rightward: (1) an increase in the money income of consumers (because pizza is a normal good); (2) an increase in the price of a substitute, such as tacos, or a decrease in the price of a complement, such as Coke; (3) a change in consumer expectations that causes people to demand more pizzas now; (4) a growth in the number of pizza consumers; or (5) a change in consumer tastes—based, for example, on a discovery that the tomato sauce on pizza has antioxidant properties that improve overall health.

After the demand curve shifts rightward to *D*′ in Exhibit 6, the amount demanded at the initial price of \$9 is 30 million pizzas, which exceeds the amount supplied of 20 million by 10 million pizzas. This shortage puts upward pressure on the price. As the price increases, the quantity demanded decreases along the new demand curve *D*′, and the quantity supplied increases along the existing supply curve S until the two quantities are equal once again at equilibrium point *g*. The new equilibrium price is \$12, and the new equilibrium quantity is 24 million pizzas per week. Thus, given an upward-sloping supply curve, an increase in demand increases both equilibrium price and quantity. A decrease in demand would lower both equilibrium price and quantity. These results can be

equilibrium the condition that exists in a market when the plans of buyers match those of sellers, so quantity demanded equals quantity supplied and the market clears summarized as follows: *Given an upward-sloping supply curve, a rightward shift of the demand curve increases both equilibrium price and quantity and a leftward shift decreases both equilibrium price and quantity.*

Shifts of the Supply Curve

Let's consider shifts of the supply curve. In Exhibit 7, as before, we begin with demand curve *D* and supply curve *S* intersecting at point *c* to yield an equilibrium price of $9 and an equilibrium quantity of 20 million pizzas per week. Suppose one of the determinants of supply changes, increasing supply from *S* to *S*′. Changes that could shift the supply curve rightward include (1) a technological breakthrough in pizza ovens; (2) a reduction in the price of a relevant resource, such as mozzarella cheese; (3) a decline in the price of an alternative good, such as Italian bread; (4) a change in expectations that encourages pizza makers to expand production now; or (5) an increase in the number of pizzerias.

After the supply curve shifts rightward in Exhibit 7, the amount supplied at the initial price of $9 increases from 20 million to 30 million, so producers now supply 10 million more pizzas than consumers demand. This surplus forces the price down. As the price falls, the quantity supplied declines along the new supply curve but the quantity demanded increases along the existing demand curve until a new equilibrium point *d* is established. The new equilibrium price is $6, and the new equilibrium quantity is 26 million pizzas per week. In short, an increase in supply reduces the price and increases the quantity. On the other hand, a decrease in supply increases the price but decreases the quantity. Thus, *given a downward-sloping demand curve, a rightward shift of the supply curve decreases price but increases quantity, and a leftward shift increases price but decreases quantity.*

Exhibit 7

Effects of an Increase in Supply

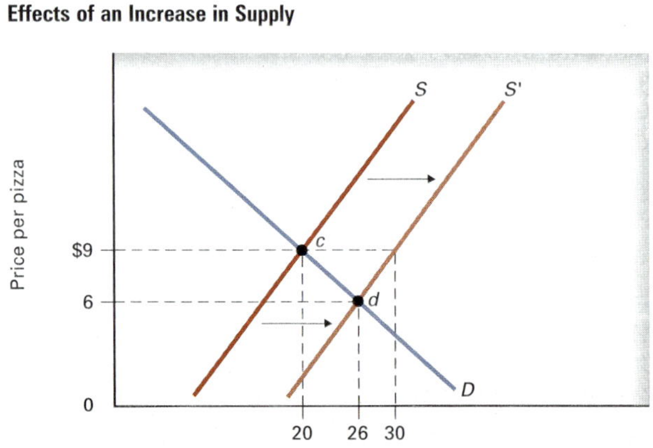

Simultaneous Shifts of Demand and Supply Curves

© THINKSTOCK IMAGES/JUPITERIMAGES

As long as only one curve shifts, we can say for sure how equilibrium price and quantity will change. If both curves shift, however, the outcome is less obvious. For example, suppose both demand and supply increase, or shift rightward, as in Exhibit 8. Note that in panel (a), demand shifts more than supply, and in panel (b), supply shifts more than demand. In both panels, equilibrium quantity increases. The change in equilibrium price, however, depends on which curve shifts more. If demand shifts more, as in panel (a), equilibrium price increases. For example, between 1995 and

Exhibit 8

Indeterminate Effect of an Increase in Both Demand and Supply

(a) Shift of demand dominates

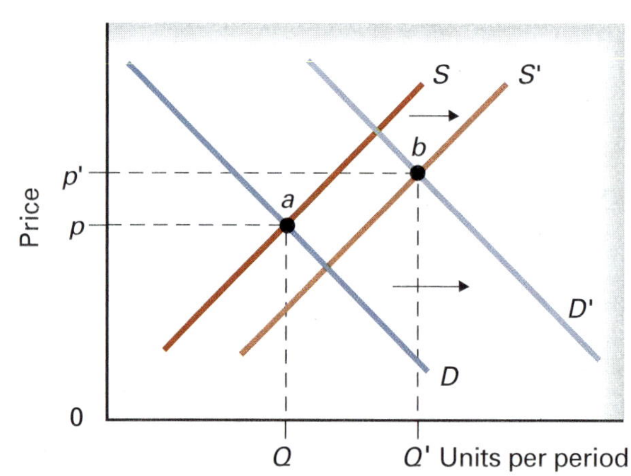

(b) Shift of supply dominates

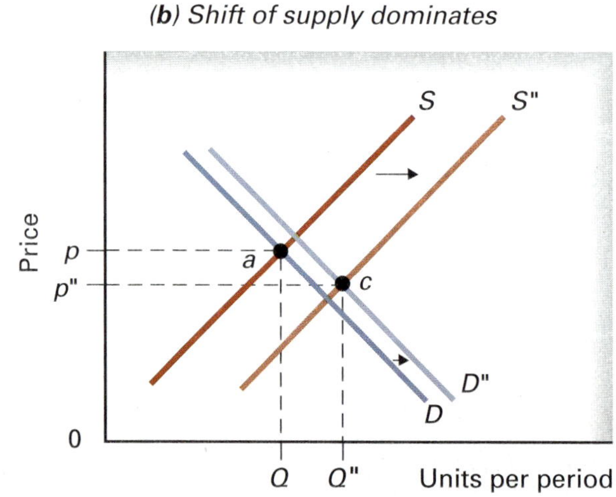

Average annual pay $4.9 million.

2005, the demand for housing increased more than the supply, so both price and quantity increased. But if supply shifts more, as in panel (b), equilibrium price decreases. For example, in the last decade, the supply of personal computers has increased more than the demand, so price has decreased and quantity increased.

Conversely, if both demand and supply decrease, or shift leftward, equilibrium quantity decreases. But, again, we cannot say what will happen to equilibrium price unless we examine relative shifts. (You can use Exhibit 8 to consider decreases in demand and supply by viewing D' and S' as the initial curves.) If demand shifts more, the price will fall. If supply shifts more, the price will rise.

If demand and supply shift in opposite directions, we can say what will happen to equilibrium price. Equilibrium price will increase if demand increases and supply decreases. Equilibrium price will decrease if demand decreases and supply increases. Without reference to particular shifts, however, we cannot say what will happen to equilibrium quantity.

These results are no doubt confusing, but Exhibit 9 summarizes the four possible combinations of changes. Using Exhibit 9 as a reference, please take the time right now to work through some changes in demand and supply to develop a feel for the results.

Exhibit 9

Effects of Shifts of Both Demand and Supply

Change in supply	Change in demand: Demand increases	Change in demand: Demand decreases
Supply increases	Equilibrium price change is indeterminate. Equilibrium quantity increases.	Equilibrium price falls. Equilibrium quantity change is indeterminate.
Supply decreases	Equilibrium price rises. Equilibrium quantity change is indeterminate.	Equilibrium price change is indeterminate. Equilibrium quantity decreases.

The Market for Professional Basketball

Take a look at Exhibit 10 depicting the market for NBA players, with demand and supply in 1980 as D_{1980} and S_{1980}. The intersection of these two curves generated an average pay in 1980 of $170,000, or $0.17 million, for the 300 or so players in the league. Since

Exhibit 10

NBA Pay Leaps

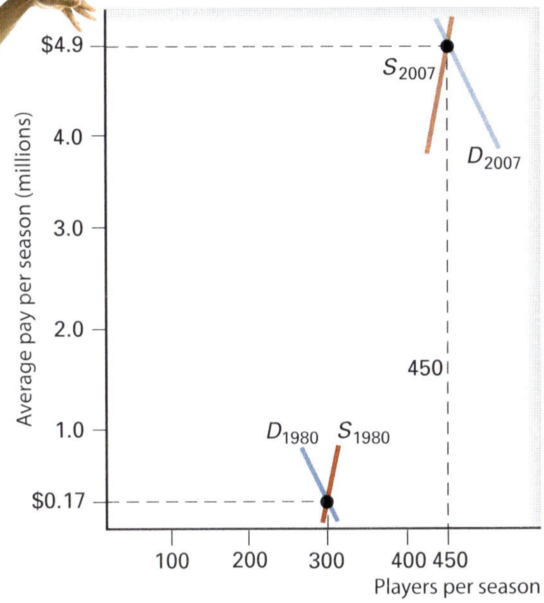

1980, the talent pool expanded somewhat, shifting the supply curve a bit rightward from S_{1980} to S_{2007} (almost by definition, the supply of the top few hundred players in the world is limited). But demand exploded from D_{1980} to D_{2007}. With supply relatively fixed, the greater demand boosted average pay for NBA players to $4.9 million by 2007 for the 450 or so players in the league. Such pay attracts younger and younger players. NBA players are now the highest-paid team athletes in the world—earning 60 percent more than pro baseball's average and at least double that for pro football and pro hockey.

But rare talent alone does not command high pay. Top rodeo riders, top bowlers, and top women basketball players also possess rare talent, but the demand for their talent is not sufficient to support pay anywhere near NBA levels. Some sports aren't even popular enough to support professional leagues (for example, the U.S. women's pro soccer league folded).

LO5 Disequilibrium

A surplus exerts downward pressure on the price, and a shortage exerts upward pressure. Markets, however, don't always reach equilibrium quickly. During the time required to adjust, the market is said to be in disequilibrium. **Disequilibrium** is usually temporary as the market gropes for equilibrium. But

disequilibrium the condition that exists in a market when the plans of buyers do not match those of sellers; a temporary mismatch between quantity supplied and quantity demanded as the market seeks equilibrium

Rare talent alone doesn't command high pay. Only the 300 or so top riders can earn a living. Only the top 50 or so make more than $100,000.

sometimes, often as a result of government intervention, disequilibrium can last a while, perhaps decades, as we will see next.

Price Floors

price floor
a minimum legal price below which a product cannot be sold; to have an impact, a price floor must be set above the equilibrium price

price ceiling
a maximum legal price above which a product cannot be sold; to have an impact, a price ceiling must be set below the equilibrium price

Sometimes public officials set prices above their equilibrium levels. For example, the federal government regulates some agriculture prices in an attempt to ensure farmers a higher and more stable income than they would otherwise earn. To achieve higher prices, the federal government sets a price floor, or a *minimum* selling price that is above the equilibrium price. Exhibit 11a shows the effect of a $2.50 per gallon price floor for milk. At that price, farmers supply 24 million gallons per week, but consumers demand only 14 million gallons, yielding a surplus of 10 million gallons. This surplus milk will pile up on store shelves, eventually souring. To take it off the market, the government usually agrees to buy the surplus milk. The federal government, in fact, spends billions buying and storing surplus agricultural products. Note, to have an impact, a price floor must be set above the equilibrium price. A price floor set at or below below the equilibrium price would be nonbinding (how come?). Price floors distort markets and reduce economic welfare.

Price Ceilings

Sometimes public officials try to keep a price below the equilibrium level by setting a price ceiling, or a *maximum* selling price. Concern about the rising cost of rental housing in some cities has prompted city officials to impose rent ceilings. Exhibit 11b depicts the demand and supply of rental housing. The vertical axis shows monthly rent, and the horizontal axis shows the quantity of rental units. The equilibrium, or market-clearing, rent is $1,000 per month, and the equilibrium quantity is 50,000 housing units. Suppose city officials set a maximum rent of $600 per month.

Exhibit 11a

Price Floors for Milk

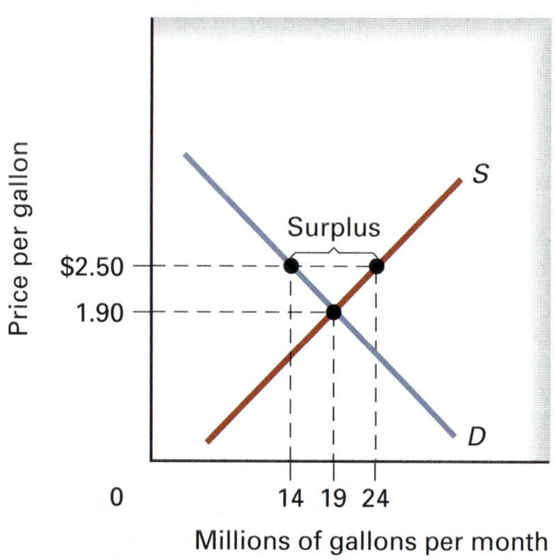

Exhibit 11b

Price Ceilings for Rent

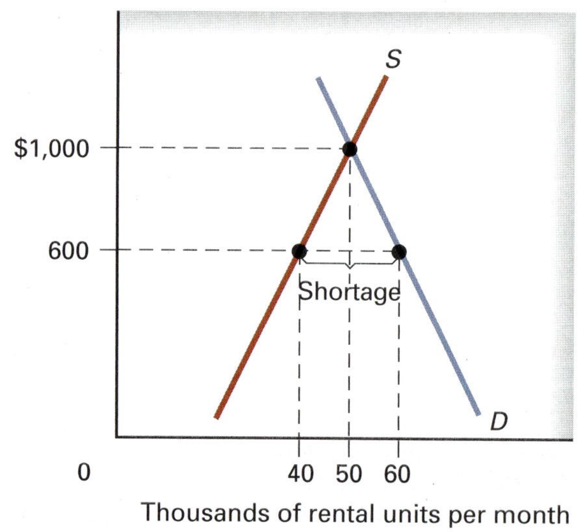

At that ceiling price, 60,000 rental units are demanded, but only 40,000 supplied, resulting in a housing shortage of 20,000 units. Because of the price ceiling, the rental price no longer rations housing to those who value it the most. Other devices emerge to ration housing, such as long waiting lists, personal connections, and the willingness to make under-the-table payments, such as "key fees," "finder's fees," high security deposits, and the like. To have an impact, a price ceiling must be set below the equilibrium price. A price ceiling set at or above the equilibrium level would be nonbinding. Price floors and ceilings distort markets and reduce economic welfare.

Government intervention is not the only source of market disequilibrium. Sometimes, when new products are introduced or when demand suddenly changes, it takes a while to reach equilibrium. For example, popular toys, best-selling books, and chart-busting CDs sometimes sell out. On the other hand, some new products attract few customers and pile up unsold on store shelves, awaiting a "clearance sale."

Final Word

Demand and supply are the building blocks of a market economy. Although a market usually involves the interaction of many buyers and sellers, few markets are consciously designed. Just as the law of gravity works whether or not we understand Newton's principles, market forces operate whether or not participants understand demand and supply. These forces arise naturally, much the way car dealers cluster on the outskirts of town to attract more customers.

Markets have their critics. Some observers may be troubled, for example, that an NBA star like Kevin Garnett earns a salary that could pay for 500 new schoolteachers, or that corporate executives, such as the head of Lehman Brothers, a financial firm, earn enough to pay for 1,000 new schoolteachers, or that U.S. consumers spend over $40 billion on their pets. On your next trip to the supermarket, notice how much shelf space goes to pet products—often an entire aisle. PetSmart, a chain store, sells over 12,000 pet items. Veterinarians offer cancer treatment, cataract removal, root canals, even acupuncture. Kidney dialysis for a pet can cost over $75,000 per year.

In a market economy, consumers are kings and queens. Consumer sovereignty rules, deciding what gets produced. Those who don't like the market outcome usually look to government for a solution through price ceilings and price floors, regulations, income redistribution, and public finance more generally.

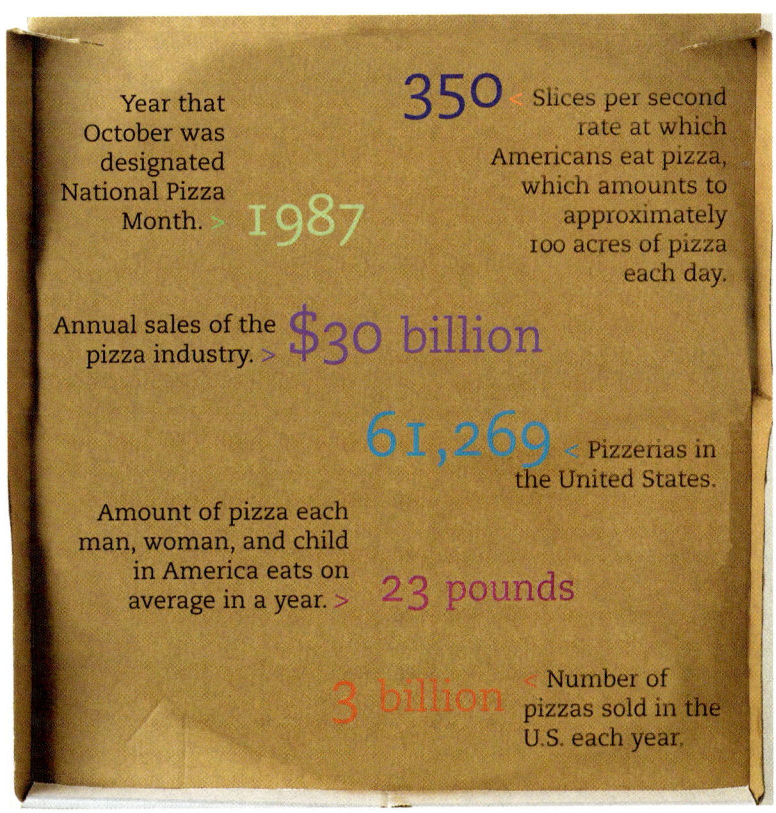

SOURCES: *Pizza Today* magazine; National Association of Pizza Operators; www.francopizza.com/trivia; American Business Lists, Omaha, NE; Packaged Facts, New York.

CHAPTER 5

Elasticity of Demand *and* Supply

Learning Outcomes

LO 1 Define and graph the price elasticity of demand

LO 2 Identify the determinants of the price elasticity of demand

LO 3 Define and graph the price elasticity of supply

LO 4 Describe other measures of elasticity

© MICHAEL OCHS ARCHIVES/GETTY IMAGES

“What does the supply curve look like for Cadillacs once owned by Elvis Presley?”

What does the demand curve look like when price is no object? What does the supply curve look like for Cadillacs once owned by Elvis Presley? Why do higher cigarette taxes cut smoking by teenagers more than by other age groups? Why are consumers more sensitive to the price of Post Raisin Bran than to the price of cereal more generally? Why does a good harvest often spell trouble for farmers? Answers to these and other questions are explored in this chapter, which takes a closer look at demand and supply.

What do you think?

If I were rich, I wouldn't shop at consignment stores.

Strongly Disagree					Strongly Agree	
1	2	3	4	5	6	7

As you learned in Chapter 1, macroeconomics concentrates on aggregate markets—on the big picture. But the big picture is a mosaic pieced together from individual decisions made by households, firms, governments, and the rest of the world. To understand how a market economy works, you must take a closer look at these individual decisions, especially at the role of prices. In a market economy, prices tell producers and consumers about the relative scarcity of products and resources.

A downward-sloping demand curve and an upward-sloping supply curve combine to form a powerful analytical tool. But to use this tool wisely, you need to learn more about demand and supply curves. The more you know, the better you can predict the effects of a change in the price on quantity. Decision makers are willing to pay dearly for such knowledge. For example, Taco Bell would like to know what happens to sales if taco prices change. Governments would like to know how a hike in cigarette taxes affects teenage smoking. Colleges would like to know how tuition increases affect enrollments. And subway officials would like to know how fare changes affect ridership. To answer such questions, you must learn how responsive consumers and producers are to price changes. This chapter introduces the idea of *elasticity*, a measure of *responsiveness*.

Topics discussed in Chapter 5 include:

- Price elasticity of demand
- Determinants of price elasticity
- Price elasticity and total revenue
- Price elasticity of supply
- Income elasticity of demand
- Cross-price elasticity of demand

LO1 Price Elasticity of Demand

Just before Thanksgiving 2006, Delta Airlines cut fares for some seats on more than 10,000 domestic flights. Was that a good idea? A firm's success or failure often depends on how much it knows about the demand for its product. For Delta's total revenue to increase, the gain in tickets sold would have to more than make up for the decline in ticket prices. Likewise, the operators of Taco Bell would like to know what happens to sales if the price drops from, say, \$1.10 to \$0.90 per taco. The law of demand tells us that a lower price increases quantity demanded, but by how much? How sensitive is quantity demanded to a change in price? After all, if quantity demanded increases enough, a price cut could be a profitable move for Taco Bell.

price elasticity of demand measures how responsive quantity demanded is to a price change; the percentage change in quantity demanded divided by the percentage change in price

price elasticity formula percentage change in quantity demanded divided by the percentage change in price; the average quantity and the average price are used as bases for computing percentage changes in quantity and in price

Calculating Price Elasticity of Demand

Let's get more specific about how sensitive changes in quantity demanded are to changes in price. Take a look at the demand curve in Exhibit 1. At the initial price of \$1.10 per taco, consumers demand 95,000 per day. If the price drops to \$0.90, quantity demanded increases to 105,000. Is such a response a little or a lot? The *price elasticity of demand* measures, in a standardized way, how responsive consumers are to a change in price. *Elasticity* is another word for *responsiveness*. In simplest terms, the **price elasticity of demand** measures the percentage change in quantity demanded divided by the percentage change in price, or:

> "*Elasticity* is another word for *responsiveness.*"

$$\text{Price elasticity of demand} = \frac{\text{Percentage change in quantity demanded}}{\text{Percentage change in price}}$$

So what's the price elasticity of demand when the price of tacos falls from \$1.10 to \$0.90—that is, what's the price elasticity of demand between points *a* and *b* in Exhibit 1? For price elasticity to be a clear and reliable measure, we should get the same result between points *a* and *b* as we get between points *b* and *a*. To ensure that consistency, we must take the average of the initial price and the new price and use that as the base for computing the percentage change in price. For example, in Exhibit 1, the base used to calculate the percentage change in price is the average of \$1.10 and \$0.90, which is \$1.00. The percentage change in price is therefore the change in price, –\$0.20, divided by \$1.00, which works out to be –20 percent.

The same holds for changes in quantity demanded. In Exhibit 1, the base used for computing the percentage change in quantity demanded is the average of 95,000 and 105,000, which is 100,000. So the percentage increase in quantity demanded is the change in quantity demanded, 10,000, divided by 100,000, which works out to be 10 percent. So the resulting price elasticity of demand between points *a* and *b* (and between points *b* and *a*) is the percentage increase in quantity demanded, 10 percent, divided by the percentage decrease in price, –20 percent, which is –0.5 (=10%/–20%).

Let's generalize the **price elasticity formula**. If the price changes from p to p', other things constant, the quantity demanded changes from q to q'. The change in price can be represented as Δp and the change in quan-

Exhibit 1

Demand Curve for Tacos

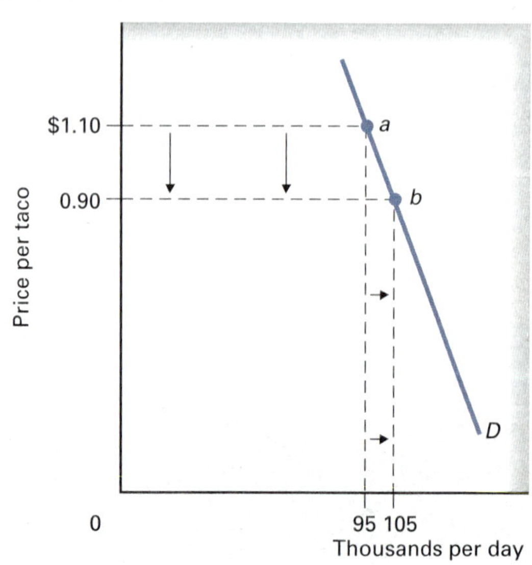

tity as Δq. The formula for calculating the price elasticity of demand E_D between the two points is the percentage change in quantity demanded divided by the percentage change in price, or:

$$E_D = \frac{\Delta q}{(q + q')/2} \div \frac{\Delta p}{(p + p')/2}$$

Again, because the average quantity and average price are used as the bases for computing percentage change, the same elasticity results whether going from the higher price to the lower price or the other way around.

Elasticity expresses a relationship between two amounts: the percentage change in quantity demanded and the percentage change in price. Because the focus is on the *percentage change,* we don't need to be concerned with how output or price is measured. For example, suppose the good in question is apples. It makes no difference in the elasticity formula whether we measure apples in pounds, bushels, or even tons. All that matters is the percentage change in quantity demanded. Nor does it matter whether we measure price in U.S. dollars, Mexican pesos, Zambian kwacha, or Vietnamese dong. All that matters is the percentage change in price.

$$E_D = \frac{\Delta q}{(q + q')/2} \div \frac{\Delta p}{(p + p')/2}$$

Finally, the law of demand states that price and quantity demanded are inversely related, so the change in price and the change in quantity demanded move in opposite directions. In the elasticity formula, the numerator and the denominator have opposite signs, leaving the price elasticity of demand with a negative sign. Because constantly referring to elasticity as a negative number gets old fast, from here on we treat the price elasticity of demand as an absolute value, or as a positive number. For example, the absolute value of the elasticity measured in Exhibit 1 is 0.5. Still, from time to time, you will be reminded that we are discussing absolute values.

Categories of Price Elasticity of Demand

As you'll see, the price elasticity of demand usually varies along a demand curve. Ranges of elasticity can be divided into three categories, depending on how responsive quantity demanded is to a change in price. If the percentage change in quantity demanded is smaller than the percentage change in price, the resulting elasticity has an absolute value between 0 and 1.0. That portion of the demand curve is said to be **inelastic**, meaning that quantity demanded is relatively *unresponsive* to a change in price. For example, the elasticity derived in Exhibit 1 between points *a* and *b* was 0.5, so that portion of the demand curve is inelastic. If the percentage change in quantity demanded just equals the percentage change in price, the resulting elasticity has an absolute value of 1.0, and that portion of a demand curve is **unit-elastic**. Finally, if the percentage change in quantity demanded exceeds the percentage change in price, the resulting elasticity has an absolute value exceeding 1.0, and that portion of a demand curve is said to be **elastic**.

In summary, *the price elasticity of demand is inelastic if its absolute value is between 0 and 1.0, unit elastic if equal to 1.0, and elastic if greater than 1.0.*

Elasticity and Total Revenue

Knowledge of price elasticity of demand is especially valuable to producers, because it indicates the effect of a price change on total revenue. **Total revenue** (*TR*) is the price (*p*) multiplied by the quantity demanded (*q*) at that price, or $TR = p \times q$. What happens to total revenue when price decreases? Well, according to the law of demand, a lower price increases quantity demanded, which tends to increase total revenue. But, a lower price means producers get less for each

$$TR = p \times q$$

inelastic demand
a change in price has relatively little effect on quantity demanded; the percentage change in quantity demanded is less than the percentage change in price; the resulting price elasticity has an absolute value less than 1.0

unit-elastic demand
the percentage change in quantity demanded equals the percentage change in price; the resulting price elasticity has an absolute value of 1.0

elastic demand
a change in price has a relatively large effect on quantity demanded; the percentage change in quantity demanded exceeds the percentage change in price; the resulting price elasticity has an absolute value exceeding 1.0

total revenue
price multiplied by the quantity demanded at that price

unit sold, which tends to decrease total revenue. The overall impact of a lower price on total revenue therefore depends on the net result of these opposite effects. *If the positive effect of a greater quantity demanded more than offsets the negative effect of a lower price, then total revenue rises.* More specifically, if demand is *elastic*, the percentage increase in quantity demanded exceeds the percentage decrease in price, so total revenue increases. If demand is *unit elastic*, the percentage increase in quantity demanded just equals the percentage decrease in price, so total revenue remains unchanged. Finally, if demand is *inelastic*, the percentage increase in quantity demanded is more than offset by the percentage decrease in price, so total revenue decreases.

Exhibit 2

Demand, Price Elasticity, and Total Revenue

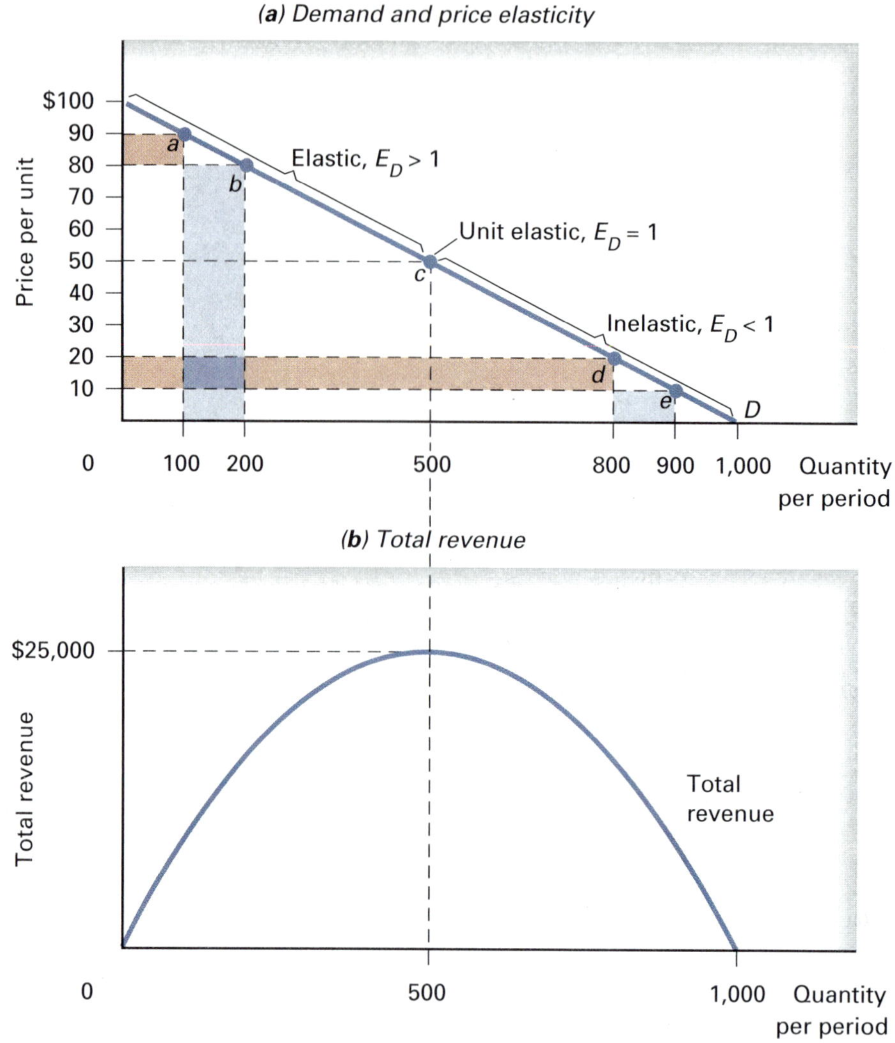

Price Elasticity and the Linear Demand Curve

A look at elasticity along a particular type of demand curve, the linear demand curve, ties together the ideas discussed so far. A **linear demand curve** is simply a straight-line demand curve, as in panel (a) of Exhibit 2. Panel (b) shows the total revenue generated by each price-quantity combination along the demand curve in panel (a). Recall that total revenue equals price times quantity. Please take a moment to see how the demand curve and total revenue curve relate.

Because the demand curve is linear, its slope is constant, so a given decrease in price always causes the same unit increase in quantity demanded. For example, along the demand curve in Exhibit 2, a $10 drop in price always increases quantity demanded by 100 units. But the price elasticity of demand is larger on the higher-price end of the demand curve than on the lower-price end. Here's why. Consider a movement from point *a* to point *b* on the upper end of the demand curve in Exhibit 2. The $10 price drop is a percentage change of 10/85, or 12 percent. The 100-unit increase in quantity demanded is a percentage change of 100/150, or 67 percent. Therefore, the price elasticity of demand between points *a* and *b* is 67%/12%, which equals 5.6. Between points *d* and *e* on the lower end, however, the $10 price decrease is a percentage change of 10/15, or 67 percent, and the 100-unit quantity increase is a percentage change of 100/850, or only 12 percent. The price elasticity of demand is 12%/67%, or 0.2. In other words, *if the demand curve is linear, consumers are more responsive to a given price change when the initial price is high than when it's low.*

linear demand curve
a straight-line demand curve; such a demand curve has a constant slope but usually has a varying price elasticity

Demand becomes less elastic as we move down the curve. At a point halfway down the linear demand curve in Exhibit 2, the elasticity is 1.0. *This halfway point divides a linear demand curve into an elastic upper half and an inelastic lower half.* You can observe a clear relationship between the elasticity of demand in panel (a) and total revenue in panel (b). Notice that where demand is elastic, a decrease in price increases total revenue because the gain in revenue from selling more units (represented by the large blue rectangle) exceeds the loss in revenue from selling all units at the lower price (the small pink rectangle). But where demand is inelastic, a price decrease reduces total revenue because the gain in revenue from selling more units (the small blue rectangle) is less than the loss in revenue from selling all units at the lower price (the large pink rectangle). And where demand is unit elastic, the gain and loss of revenue exactly cancel each other out, so total revenue at that point remains constant (thus, total revenue peaks in the lower panel).

THE SLOPE OF A DEMAND CURVE IS NOT THE SAME AS THE PRICE ELASTICITY OF DEMAND.

To review, total revenue increases as the price declines until the midpoint of the linear demand curve is reached, where total revenue peaks. In Exhibit 2, total revenue peaks at $25,000 where quantity demanded equals 500 units. To the right of the midpoint of the demand curve, total revenue declines as the price falls. More generally, regardless of whether demand is straight or curved, there is a consistent relationship between the price elasticity of demand and total revenue: A *price decline increases total revenue if demand is elastic, has no effect on total revenue if demand is unit elastic, and decreases total revenue if demand is inelastic.* Finally, note that a downward-sloping linear demand curve has a constant slope but a varying elasticity, so *the slope of a demand curve is not the same as the price elasticity of demand.*

Constant-Elasticity Demand Curves

Again, price elasticity measures the responsiveness of consumers to a change in price. The shape of the demand curve for a firm's product is key in the pricing and output decision. This responsiveness varies along a linear demand curve unless the demand curve is horizontal or vertical, as in panels (a) and (b) of Exhibit 3. These two demand curves, along with the special demand curve in panel (c), are all called *constant-elasticity demand curves* because the elasticity does not change along the curves.

Perfectly Elastic Demand Curve

The horizontal demand curve in panel (a) indicates that consumers demand all that is offered for sale at the given price *p* (the quantity actually demanded depends on the amount supplied at that price). If the price rises above *p*, however, quantity demanded drops to zero. This is a **perfectly elastic demand curve**, and its elasticity value is infinity, a number too large to be defined. You may think this an odd sort of demand curve: Consumers, as a result of a small increase in price, go from demanding as much as is supplied to demanding none of the good. Consumers are so sensitive to price changes that they tolerate no price increase. As you will see in a later chapter, this behavior reflects the demand for the output of any individual producer when many producers supply identical products at the market price of *p*.

Exhibit 3a

Constant-Elasticity Demand Curves: Perfectly Elastic

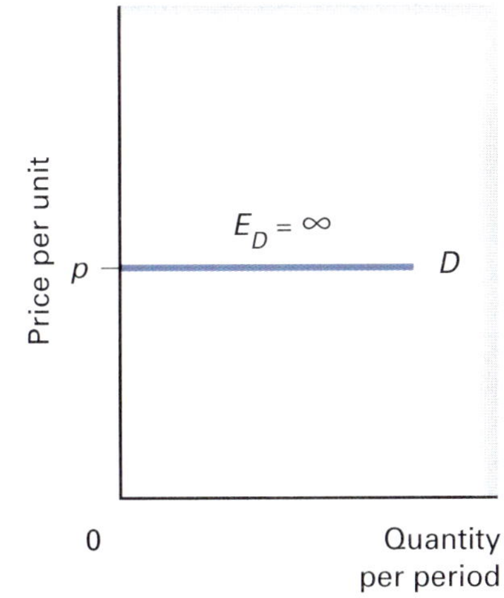

Perfectly Inelastic Demand Curve

Along the vertical demand curve in panel (b) of Exhibit 3, quantity demanded does not vary when the price changes. This demand curve expresses consumer sentiment when "price is no object." For example, if you are extremely rich and need insulin to survive, price would be no object. No matter how high the price, you would continue to demand whatever it takes. And if the price of insulin should drop, you would not increase your quantity demanded. Because the percentage change in quantity

perfectly elastic demand curve
a horizontal line reflecting a situation in which any price increase would reduce quantity demanded to zero; the elasticity has an absolute value of infinity

demanded is zero for any given percentage change in price, the numerical value of the price elasticity is zero. A vertical demand curve is called a **perfectly inelastic demand curve**.

Exhibit 3b

Constant-Elasticity Demand Curves: Perfectly Inelastic

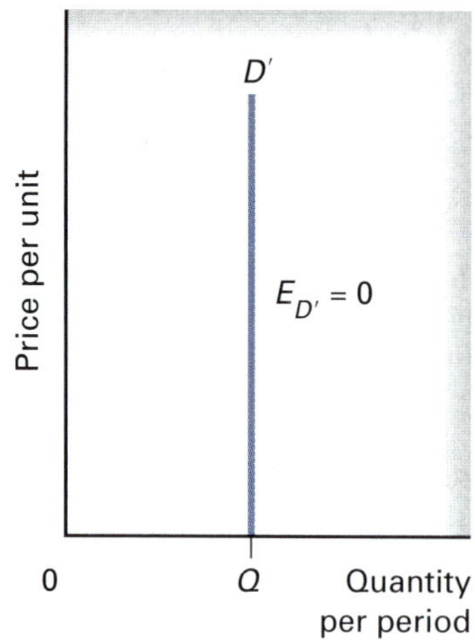

© PICTURE POST/HULTON ARCHIVE/GETTY IMAGES

My kingdom for a horse

Another example of perfectly inelastic demand comes from Shakespeare's play *Richard III*. After his horse is slain in battle, the king, at the mercy of the enemy, cries out, "A horse! A horse! My kingdom for a horse!" The king is willing to pay a high price indeed—his kingdom—for a horse. On a less lofty level, Ben Franklin expressed a similar sentiment when he observed, "Necessity never made a good bargain."

Unit-Elastic Demand Curve

Panel (c) in Exhibit 3 presents a demand curve that is unit elastic everywhere. Along a **unit-elastic demand curve**, any percentage change in price causes an exact opposite percentage change in quantity demanded. Because changes in price and in quantity demanded are offsetting, total revenue remains constant for every price-quantity combination along the curve. For example, when the price falls from \$10 to \$6, the quantity demanded increases from 60 to 100 units. The price drops by \$4/\$8, or 50 percent, and the quantity increases by 40/80, or 50 percent. The pink shaded rectangle shows the loss in total revenue from cutting the price; the blue shaded rectangle shows the gain in total revenue from selling more at the lower price. Because the demand curve is unit elastic, the revenue gained from selling more just offsets the revenue lost from lowering the price, so total revenue remains unchanged at \$600.

perfectly inelastic demand curve a vertical line reflecting a situation in which any price change has no effect on the quantity demanded; the elasticity value is zero

unit-elastic demand curve everywhere along the demand curve, the percentage change in price causes an equal but offsetting percentage change in quantity demanded, so total revenue remains the same; the elasticity has an absolute value of 1.0

constant-elasticity demand curve the type of demand that exists when price elasticity is the same everywhere along the curve; the elasticity value is constant

Each demand curve in Exhibit 3 is called a **constant-elasticity demand curve** because the elasticity is the same all along the curve. In contrast, the downward-sloping linear demand curve examined earlier had a different elasticity value at each point along the curve. Exhibit 4 lists the absolute values for the five categories of price elasticity we have discussed, summarizing the effects of a 10 percent price increase on quantity demanded and on total revenue. Give this exhibit some thought now, and see if you can draw a demand curve for each category of elasticity.

Exhibit 3c

Constant-Elasticity Demand Curves: Unit Elastic

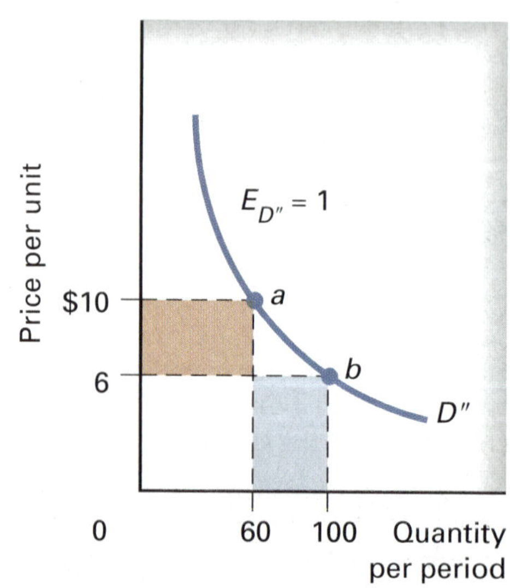

Exhibit 4

Summary of Price Elasticity of Demand

Effects of a 10 Percent Increase in Price

Absolute Value of Price Elasticity	Type of Demand	What Happens to Quantity Demanded	What Happens to Total Revenue
$E_D = 0$	Perfectly inelastic	No change	Increases by 10 percent
$0 < E_D < 1$	Inelastic	Drops by less than 10 percent	Increases by less than 10 percent
$E_D = 1$	Unit elastic	Drops by 10 percent	No change
$1 < E_D < \infty$	Elastic	Drops by more than 10 percent	Decreases
$E_D = \infty$	Perfectly elastic	Drops to 0	Drops to 0

LO2 Determinants of the Price Elasticity of Demand

So far we have explored the technical properties of demand elasticity and discussed why price elasticity varies along a downward-sloping demand curve. But we have yet to consider why price elasticities of demand are different for different goods. Several factors influence the price elasticity of demand for a good.

Availability of Substitutes

As we saw in Chapter 4, your particular wants can be satisfied in a variety of ways. A rise in the price of pizza makes other food relatively cheaper. If close substitutes are available, an increase in the price of pizza prompts some consumers to buy substitutes. But if nothing else satisfies like pizza, the quantity of pizza demanded does not decline as much. *The greater the availability of substitutes and the more similar these substitutes are to the good in question, the greater that good's price elasticity of demand.*

© JUSTIN SULLIVAN/GETTY IMAGES

The number and similarity of substitutes depend on how the good is defined. *The more narrow the definition, the more substitutes and, thus, the more elastic the demand.* For example, the demand for Post Raisin Bran is more elastic than the demand for raisin bran more generally because there are more substitutes for Post Raisin Bran, including Kellogg's Raisin Bran and Total Raisin Bran, than for raisin bran more generally. The demand for raisin bran, however, is more elastic than the demand for breakfast cereal more generally because the consumer has many substitutes for raisin bran, such as cereals made from corn, rice, wheat, or oats, and processed with or without honey, nuts, fruit, or chocolate. To give you some idea of the range of elasticities, the price elasticity of demand for Post Raisin Bran has been estimated to be -2.5 versus -0.9 for all breakfast cereal.[1]

Certain goods—some prescription drugs, for instance—have no close substitutes. The demand for such goods tends to be less elastic than for goods with close substitutes, such as Bayer aspirin. Much advertising is aimed at establishing in the consumer's mind the uniqueness of a particular product—an effort to convince consumers "to accept no substitutes." Why might a firm want to make the demand for its product less elastic?

As an example of the impact of substitutes on price elasticity, consider the timing of commercial breaks during network TV movies. When the movie begins, viewers have several substitutes available, including other shows and perhaps movies on other networks. To keep viewers from switching channels, the first movie segment is longer than usual, perhaps 20 or 25 minutes before a commercial break. But once viewers get interested in the movie, shows on other channels are no longer good substitutes, so broadcasters inject commercials sooner with less fear of losing viewers. Toward the end of the movie, networks insert commercials with even greater frequency, confident that viewers will hang on to see how things turn out.

Share of the Consumer's Budget Spent on the Good

Recall that a higher price reduces quantity demanded in part because a higher price reduces the real spending power of consumer income. Because spending on some goods claims a large share of the consumer's budget, a change in the price of such a good has a substantial impact on the consumer's *ability* to buy it. An increase in the price of housing, for example, reduces consumers' ability to buy housing. The income effect of a higher price reduces the quantity demanded. In contrast, the income effect of an increase in the price

1. See Jerry A. Hausman, "The Price Elasticity of Demand for Breakfast Cereal," in *The Economics of New Goods,* T. F. Bresnahan and J.J. Gordon, eds. (University of Chicago Press, 1997).

of, say, paper towels is trivial because paper towels represent such a tiny share of any budget. *The more important the item is as a share of the consumer's budget, other things constant, the greater is the income effect of a change in price, so the more price elastic is the demand for the item.* Hence, the quantity of housing demanded is more responsive to a given percentage change in price than is the quantity of paper towels demanded.

Length of Adjustment Period

Consumers can substitute lower-priced goods for higher-priced goods, but finding substitutes usually takes time. Suppose your college announces a sharp increase in room and board fees, effective next term. Some students will move off campus before the next term begins; others may wait until the next academic year. Over time, the college may get fewer applicants and more incoming students will choose off-campus housing. The longer the adjustment period, the greater the consumers' ability to substitute away from relatively higher-priced products toward lower-priced substitutes. Thus, *the longer the period of adjustment, the more responsive the change in quantity demanded is to a given change in price.* Here's another example: Between 1973 and 1974, OPEC (Organization of Petroleum Exporting Countries) raised gasoline prices 45 percent, but the quantity demanded initially decreased only 8 percent. As more time passed, however, people bought smaller cars and made greater use of public transportation. They also bought more energy-efficient appliances and added more insulation to their homes. Thus, the percentage change in quantity demanded was greater the longer consumers adjusted to the price hike.

Exhibit 5 shows how demand becomes more elastic over time. Given an initial price of $1.00 at point *e*, let D_w be the demand curve one week after a price change; D_m, one month after; and D_y, one year after. Suppose the price increases to $1.25. The more time consumers have to respond to the price increase, the greater the reduction in quantity demanded. The demand curve D_w shows that one week after the price increase, the quantity demanded has not declined much—in this case, from 100 to 95 per day. The demand curve D_m indicates a reduction to 75 per day after one month, and demand curve D_y shows a reduction to 50 per day after one year. Notice that among these demand curves and over the range starting from point *e*, the flatter the demand curve, the more price elastic the demand. Here, elasticity seems linked to the slope because we begin from a common point—the price-quantity combination at point *e*.

Exhibit 5

Demand Becomes More Elastic over Time

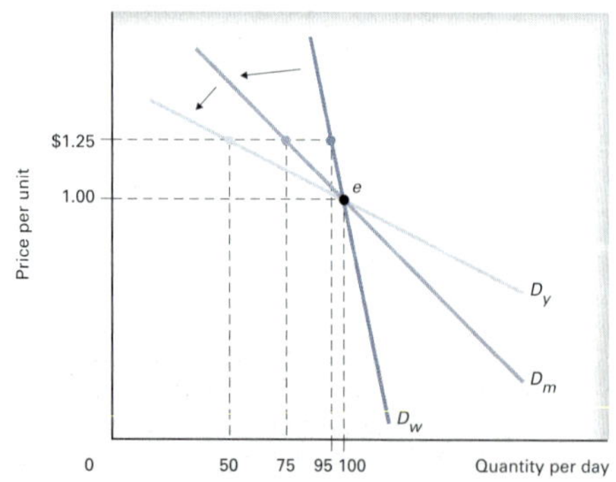

Elasticity Estimates

Let's look at some estimates of the price elasticity of demand for particular goods and services. Remember, finding alternatives when the price increases takes time. Thus, when estimating price elasticity, economists often distinguish between a period during which consumers have little time to adjust—let's call it the *short run*—and a period during which consumers can more fully adjust to a price change—let's call it the *long run*. Exhibit 6 provides some short-run and long-run price elasticity estimates for selected products.

Exhibit 6

Selected Price Elasticities of Demand (absolute values)

Product	Short Run	Long Run
Cigarettes (among adults)	—	0.4
Electricity (residential)	0.1	1.9
Air travel	0.1	2.4
Medical care and hospitalization	0.3	0.9
Gasoline	0.4	1.5
Milk	0.4	—
Fish (cod)	0.5	—
Wine	0.7	1.2
Movies	0.9	3.7
Natural gas (residential)	1.4	2.1
Automobiles	1.9	2.2
Chevrolets	—	4.0

SOURCES: F. Chaloupka, "Rational Addictive Behavior and Cigarette Smoking," *Journal of Political Economy* (August 1991); Hsaing-tai Cheng and Oral Capps, Jr., "Demand for Fish," *American Journal of Agricultural Economics* (August 1998); J. Johnson et al., "Short-Run and Long-Run Elasticities for Canadian Consumption of Alcoholic Beverages," *Review of Economics and Statistics* (February 1992); Douglas Young et al., "Alcohol Consumption, Measurement Error, and Beverage Prices," *Journal of Studies on Alcohol* (March 2003); J. Griffin, *Energy Conservation in the OECD, 1980–2000* (Cambridge, Mass.: Balinger, 1979); H. Houthakker and L. Taylor, *Consumer Demand in the United States: Analysis and Projections,* 2nd ed. (Cambridge, Mass.: Harvard University Press, 1970); and G. Lakshmanan and W. Anderson, "Residential Energy Demand in the United States," *Regional Science and Urban Economics* 10 (August 1980).

Smoke Out

There are no close substitutes for cigarettes, even in the long run, so the demand for cigarettes among adults is price inelastic. For teens, however, demand for cigarettes is more price elastic. Why are teenagers more sensitive to price changes than adults?

1. Because teen income is relatively low, the share spent on cigarettes usually exceeds the share spent by adult smokers.
2. Peer pressure shapes a young person's decision to smoke more than an adult's decision to continue smoking (if anything, adults face negative peer pressure for smoking). Thus, the effect of a higher price gets magnified among young smokers because that higher price also reduces smoking by peers. With fewer peers smoking, teens face less pressure to smoke, and so on.
3. Young people not yet addicted to nicotine are more sensitive to price increases than are adult smokers, who are more likely to be already hooked. Increasing taxes on cigarettes, then, can have a significant impact on teen smoking. A large tax increase on cigarettes in Canada cut youth smoking by two-thirds.

SOURCES: John Tauras, "An Empirical Analysis of Adult Cigerette Demand," *Eastern Economic Journal* 31(3) (Summer 2005): pp. 361–375; Phillip Cook and Rebecca Hutchinson, "Smoke Signals: Adolescent Smoking and School Continuation," *NBER Working Paper 12462,* (August 2006); and Hana Ross and Frank Chaloupka, "The Effects of Public Policies and Prices on Youth Smoking," *Southern Economic Journal* (April 2004).

The price elasticity of demand is greater in the long run because consumers have more time to adjust. For example, if the price of electricity rose today, consumers in the short run might cut back a bit in their use of electrical appliances, and those in homes with electric heat might lower the thermostat in winter. Over time, however, consumers would switch to more energy-efficient appliances, insulate their homes better, and perhaps switch from electric heat. So the demand for electricity is more elastic in the long run than in the short run, as shown in Exhibit 6. In fact, in every instance where estimates for both the short run and the long run are listed, demand is more elastic in the long run than the short run. Notice also that the demand for Chevrolets is more elastic than the demand for automobiles more generally. Chevrolets have many more substitutes than do automobiles in general.

LO3 Price Elasticity of Supply

Prices signal both sides of the market about the relative scarcity of products. Higher prices discourage consumption but encourage production. Lower prices encourage consumption but discourage production. The price elasticity of demand measures how responsive consumers are to a price change. Likewise, the price elasticity of supply measures how responsive producers are to a price change. Supply elasticity is calculated in the same way as demand elasticity. In simplest terms, the price elasticity of supply equals the percentage change in quantity supplied divided by the percentage change in price. Because a higher price usually increases quantity supplied, the percentage change in price and the percentage change in quantity supplied move in the same direction, so the price elasticity of supply is usually a positive number.

Exhibit 7 depicts a typical upward-sloping supply curve. As you can see, if the price increases from p to p', the quantity supplied increases from q to q'. Price and quantity supplied move in the same direction. Let's look at the elasticity formula for the supply curve. The price elasticity of supply is:

price elasticity of supply a measure of the responsiveness of quantity supplied to a price change; the percentage change in quantity supplied divided by the percentage change in price

$$E_S = \frac{\Delta q}{(q + q')/2} \div \frac{\Delta p}{(p + p')/2}$$

Exhibit 7

Price Elasticity of Supply

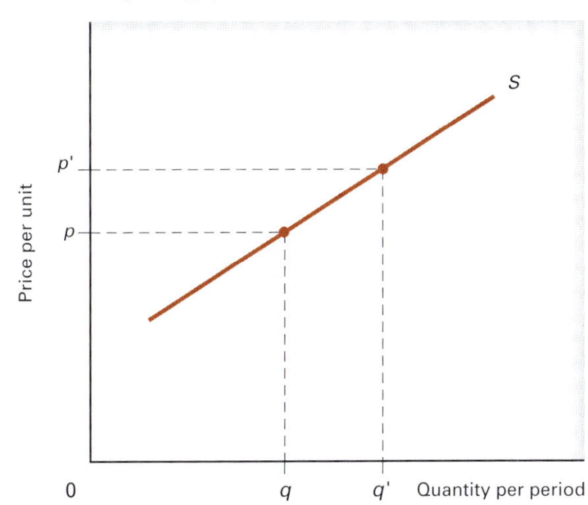

$$E_S = \frac{\Delta q}{(q + q')/2} \div \frac{\Delta p}{(p + p')/2}$$

where Δq is the change in quantity supplied and Δp is the change in price. This is the same formula used to compute the price elasticity of demand except that q here is quantity supplied, not quantity demanded. The terminology for supply elasticity is the same as for demand elasticity: If supply elasticity is less than 1.0, supply is inelastic; if it equals 1.0, supply is unit elastic; and if it exceeds 1.0, supply is elastic.

Constant-Elasticity Supply Curves

inelastic supply a change in price has relatively little effect on quantity supplied; the percentage change in quantity supplied is less than the percentage change in price; the price elasticity of supply has a value less than 1.0

unit-elastic supply the percentage change in quantity supplied equals the percentage change in price; the price elasticity of supply equals 1.0

elastic supply a change in price has a relatively large effect on quantity supplied; the percentage change in quantity supplied exceeds the percentage change in price; the price elasticity of supply exceeds 1.0

perfectly elastic supply curve a horizontal line reflecting a situation in which any price decrease drops the quantity supplied to zero; the elasticity value is infinity

perfectly inelastic supply curve a vertical line reflecting a situation in which a price change has no effect on the quantity supplied; the elasticity value is zero

Again, price elasticity of supply measures the responsiveness of producers to a change in price. This responsiveness varies along a linear supply curve unless the curve is horizontal or vertical, as in panels (a) and (b) of Exhibit 8, or passes through the origin, as in panel (c). These three supply curves are called *constant-elasticity supply curves* because the elasticity does not change along the curves.

Perfectly Elastic Supply Curve

At one extreme is the horizontal supply curve, such as supply curve S in panel (a) of Exhibit 8. In this case, producers supply none of the good at a price below p but supply any amount at price p (the quantity actually supplied at price p depends on the amount demanded at that price). Because a tiny increase from a price just below p to a price of p results in an unlimited quantity supplied, this is called a perfectly elastic supply curve, which has a numerical value of infinity. As individual consumers, we typically face perfectly elastic supply curves. When we go to the supermarket, we usually can buy as much as we want at the prevailing price but none at a lower price. Obviously all consumers together could not buy an unlimited amount at the prevailing price (recall the fallacy of composition from Chapter 1).

Exhibit 8a

Constant-Elasticity Supply Curves: Perfectly Elastic

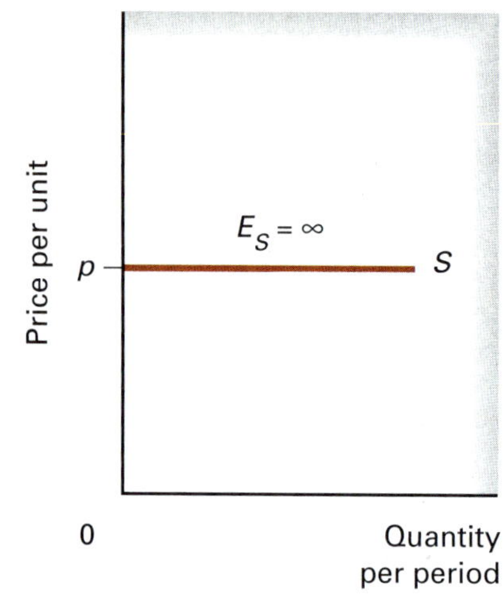

Perfectly Inelastic Supply Curve

The least responsive relationship is where there is no change in the quantity supplied regardless of the price, as shown by the vertical supply curve S′ in panel (b) of Exhibit 8. Because the percentage change in quantity supplied is zero, regardless of the change in price, the price elasticity of supply is zero. This is a perfectly inelastic supply curve. Any good in fixed supply, such as Picasso paintings, 1995 Dom Perignon champagne, or Cadillacs once owned by Elvis Presley, has a perfectly inelastic supply curve.

Exhibit 8b

Constant-Elasticity Supply Curves: Perfectly Inelastic

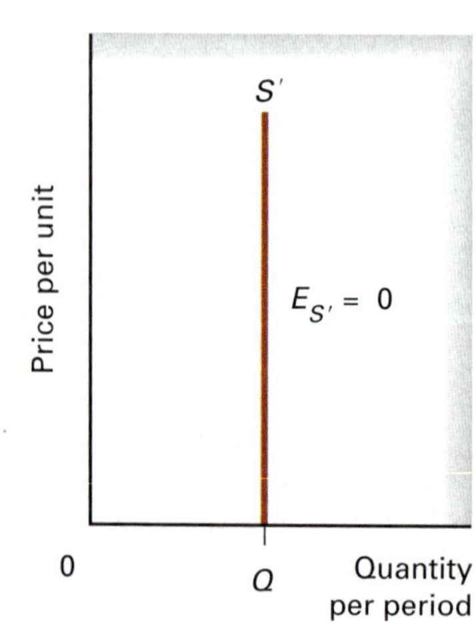

Unit-Elastic Supply Curve

Any supply curve that is a straight line from the origin—such as S″ in panel (c) of Exhibit 8—is a **unit-elastic supply curve**. This means a percentage change in price always generates an identical percentage change in quantity supplied. For example, along S″ a doubling of the price results in a doubling of the quantity supplied. Note that unit elasticity is based not on the slope of the line but on the fact that the linear supply curve is a ray from the origin.

Exhibit 8c

Constant-Elasticity Supply Curves: Unit Elastic

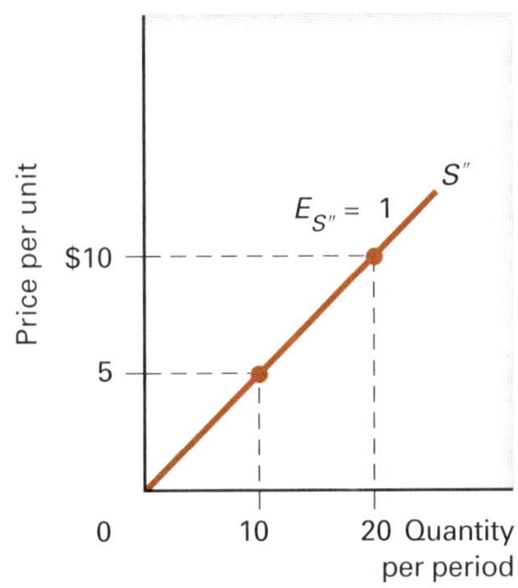

Determinants of Supply Elasticity

The elasticity of supply indicates how responsive producers are to a change in price. Their response depends on how easy it is to alter quantity supplied when the price changes. If the cost of supplying additional units rises sharply as output expands, then a higher price causes little increase in quantity supplied, so supply tends to be inelastic. But if the marginal cost rises slowly as output expands, the lure of a higher price prompts a large increase in quantity supplied. In this case, supply is more elastic.

One determinant of supply elasticity is the length of the adjustment period under consideration. Just as demand becomes more elastic over time as consumers adjust to price changes, supply also becomes more elastic over time as producers adjust to price changes. The longer the adjustment period under consideration, the more able producers are to adapt to a price change. Exhibit 9 presents different supply curves for each of three periods. S_w is the supply curve when the period of adjustment is a week. As you can see, a higher price generates little response in quantity supplied because firms have little time to adjust. This supply curve is inelastic between $1.00 to $1.25.

S_m is the supply curve when the adjustment period under consideration is a month. Firms have more time to vary output. Thus, supply is more elastic when the adjustment period is a month than

Exhibit 9

Supply Becomes More Elastic over Time

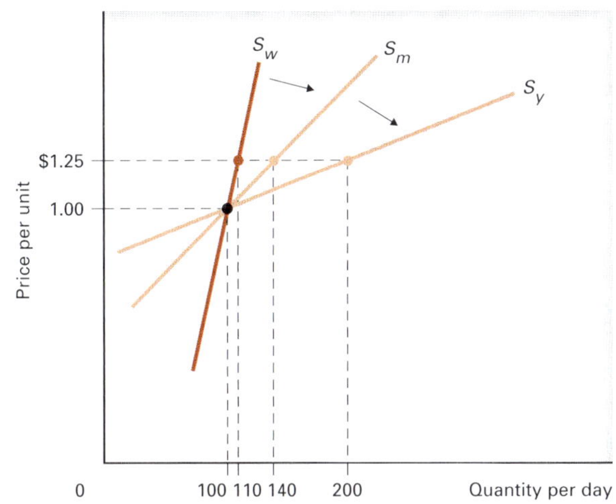

when it's a week. Supply is yet more elastic when the adjustment period is a year, as is shown by S_y. As the adjustment period lengthens, the supply response increases. For example, if the price of oil increases, oil producers in the short run can try to pump more from existing wells, but in the long run, a higher price stimulates more exploration. Research confirms the positive link between the price elasticity of supply and the length of the adjustment period. *The elasticity of supply is typically greater the longer the period of adjustment.*

The ability to increase quantity supplied in response to a higher price differs across industries. For example, oil was

unit-elastic supply curve
a percentage change in price causes an identical percentage change in quantity supplied; depicted by a supply curve that is a straight line from the origin; the elasticity value equals 1.0

© BURKE/TRIOLO PRODUCTIONS/BOTANICA/JUPITERIMAGES

>> Demand for used goods actually declines as income increases. But this does not consider the entertainment aspects of shopping garage and yard sales, the largest of which stretches 450 miles through 5 states down US 127 for 4 days in August each year. What do you think the income elasticity of used goods is when shopping for them is for entertainment rather than necessity?

discovered on Alaska's north slope in 1967; but oil did not begin to flow south until a decade later. More generally, the response time is slower for suppliers of oil, electricity, and timber (where expansion may take years, if not decades) than for suppliers of window-washing service, lawn maintenance, and hot-dog vending (where expansion may take only days).

LO4 Other Elasticity Measures

Price elasticities of demand and supply are frequently used in economic analysis, but two other elasticity measures also provide valuable information.

Income Elasticity of Demand

What happens to the demand for new cars, fresh vegetables, or computer software if consumer income increases by, say, 10 percent? The answer is of great interest to producers because it helps them predict the effect of changing consumer income on quantity sold and on total revenue. The **income elasticity of demand** measures how responsive demand is to a change in consumer income. Specifically, *the income elasticity of demand measures the percentage change in demand divided by the percentage change in income that caused it.*

As noted in Chapter 4, the demand for some products, such as used furniture and used clothing, actually declines, or shifts leftward, as income increases. Thus, the income elasticity of demand for such goods is negative. Goods with income elasticities less than zero are called *inferior goods*. But the demand for most goods increases, or shifts rightward, as income increases. These are called *normal goods* and have income elasticities greater than zero.

income elasticity of demand
the percentage change in demand divided by the percentage change in consumer income; the value is positive for normal goods and negative for inferior goods

Let's take a closer look at normal goods. Suppose demand increases as income increases but by a smaller percentage than income increases. In such cases, the income elasticity is greater than 0 but less than 1. For example, people buy more food as their incomes rise, but the percentage increase in demand is less than the percentage increase in income. Normal goods with income elasticities less than 1 are called *income inelastic*. *Necessities* such as food, housing, and clothing often have income elasticities less than 1. Goods with income elasticity greater than 1 are called *income elastic*. *Luxuries* such as high-end cars, vintage wines, and meals at upscale restaurants have income elasticities greater than 1. By the way, the terms *inferior goods, necessities,* and *luxuries* are not value judgment about the merits of particular goods; these terms are simply convenient ways of classifying economic behavior.

Exhibit 10 presents income elasticity estimates for some goods and services. The figures indicate, for example, that as income increases, consumers spend proportionately more on wine, restaurant meals, and owner-occupied housing. Spending on food and rental housing also increases as income increases, but less than proportionately. Spending on beer declines with rising income. So as income rises, the demand for restaurant meals increases more in percentage terms than does the demand for food, and the demand for owner-occupied housing increases more in percentage terms than does the demand for rental housing. The demand for wine increases sharply, while the demand for beer declines. Flour also has negative income elasticity. According to these estimates, beer and flour are inferior goods.

Exhibit 10

Selected Income Elasticities of Demand

Product	Income Elasticity	Product	Income Elasticity
Wine	5.03	Physicians' services	0.75
Private education	2.46	Coca-Cola	0.68
Automobiles	2.45	Beef	0.62
Owner-occupied housing	1.49	Food	0.51
Furniture	1.48	Coffee	0.51
Dental service	1.42	Cigarettes	0.50
Restaurant meals	1.40	Gasoline and oil	0.48
Spirits ("hard" liquor)	1.21	Rental housing	0.43
Shoes	1.10	Pork	0.18
Chicken	1.06	Beer	–0.09
Clothing	0.92	Flour	–0.36

SOURCES: Ivan Bloor, "Food for Thought," *Economic Review* (September 1999); F. Gasmi et al., "Econometric Analysis of Collusive Behavior in a Soft-Drink Market," *Journal of Economics and Management Strategy* (Summer 1992); X. M. Gao et al., "A Microeconomic Model Analysis of U.S. Consumer Demand for Alcoholic Beverages," *Applied Economics* (January 1995); H. Houthakker and L. Taylor, *Consumer Demand in the United States: Analyses and Projections*, 2nd ed. (Cambridge, Mass.: Harvard University Press, 1970); C. Huang et al., "The Demand for Coffee in the United States, 1963–77," *Quarterly Review of Economics and Business* (Summer 1980); and G. Brester and M. Wohlgenant, "Estimating Interrelated Demands for Meats Using New Measures for Ground and Table Cut Beef," *American Journal of Agricultural Economics* (November 1991).

Cross-Price Elasticity of Demand

A firm that produces an entire line of products has a special interest in how a change in the price of one item affects the demand for another. For example, the Coca-Cola Company needs to know how changing the price of Lemon Coke affects sales of Classic Coke. The company also needs to know the relationship between the price of Coke and the demand for Pepsi and vice versa. The responsiveness of the demand for one good to changes in the price of another good is called the **cross-price elasticity of demand**. This is defined as the percentage change in the demand of one good divided by the percentage change in the price of another good. Its numerical value can be positive, negative, or zero, depending on whether the two goods in question are substitutes, complements, or unrelated, respectively.

Substitutes

If an increase in the price of one good leads to an increase in the demand for another good, their cross-price elasticity is positive and the two goods are *substitutes*. For example, an increase in the price of Coke, other things constant, shifts the demand for Pepsi rightward, so the two are substitutes. The cross-price elasticity between Coke and Pepsi has been estimated at about 0.7, indicating that a 10 percent increase in the price of one increases the demand for the other by 7 percent.[2]

Complements

If an increase in the price of one good leads to a decrease in the demand for another, their cross-price elasticity is negative and the goods are *complements*. For example, an increase in the price of gasoline, other things constant, shifts the demand for tires leftward because people drive less and replace their tires less frequently. Gasoline and tires have a negative cross-price elasticity and are complements.

In summary: *The cross-price elasticity of demand is positive for substitutes and negative for complements*. Most pairs of goods selected at random are unrelated, so their cross-price elasticity is zero.

Final Word

Because this chapter has been more quantitative than earlier ones, the mechanics may have overshadowed the intuitive appeal and neat simplicity of elasticity. *Elasticity measures the willingness and ability of buyers and sellers to alter their behavior in response to changes in their economic circumstances*. Firms try to estimate the price elasticity of demand for their products. Governments also have an ongoing interest in various elasticities. For example, state governments want to know the effect of an increase in the sales tax on total tax receipts, and local governments want to know how an increase in income affects the demand for real estate and thus the revenue generated by a property tax. International groups are interested in elasticities; for example, OPEC is concerned about the price elasticity of demand for oil—in the short run and in the long run. Because a corporation often produces an entire line of products, it also has a special interest in certain cross-price elasticities. Some corporate economists estimate elasticities for a living. The appendix to this chapter shows how price elasticities of demand and supply shed light on who ultimately pays a tax.

2. F. Gasmi, J. Laffont, and Q. Vuong, "Econometric Analysis of Collusive Behavior in a Soft-Drink Market," *Journal of Economics and Management Strategy* (Summer 1992).

cross-price elasticity of demand
the percentage change in the demand of one good divided by the percentage change in the price of another good; it's negative for substitutes, positive for complements, and zero for unrelated goods

Why Good Harvests . . . Spell Trouble for Farmers

© ANDY SACKS/STONE/GETTY IMAGES

Many of the forces that determine farm production are beyond a farmer's control. Temperature, rainfall, pests, and other natural forces affect crop size and quality. For example, favorable weather boosted crop production 16 percent in one recent year. Such increases create special problems for farmers because the demand for most farm crops, such as milk, eggs, corn, potatoes, oats, sugar, and beef, is price inelastic.

Demand for food is *income* inelastic, and it also tends to be *price* inelastic. As household incomes grow over time, spending on food may increase because consumers substitute prepared foods and restaurant meals for home cooking. But this switch has little effect on the total demand for farm products. (This modest increase in demand from *D* to *D′* is reflected in Exhibit 11.)

Because of technological improvements in production, however, the supply of farm products has increased sharply. Developments such as more sophisticated machines, better fertilizer, and healthier seeds have increased farm output per hour of labor 11-fold since 1950. Exhibit 11 shows a big increase in the supply of grain from *S* to *S′*. Because the supply increase exceeds the demand increase, the price declines. And because the demand for grain is price inelastic, the percentage drop in price exceeds the percentage increase in output. The combined effect in our example is lower total revenue.

SOURCES: Bruce L. Gardner, "Changing Economic Perspective on the Farm Problem," *Journal of Economic Literature* 30 (March 1992): 62–105; and *Economic Report of the President*, February 2007, Tables B-99 at http://www.gpoaccess.gov/eop/. For current economic research at the U.S. Department of Agriculture, go to http://www.ers.usda.gov/.

Exhibit 11

The Effect of Increases in Demand and Supply on Farm Revenue

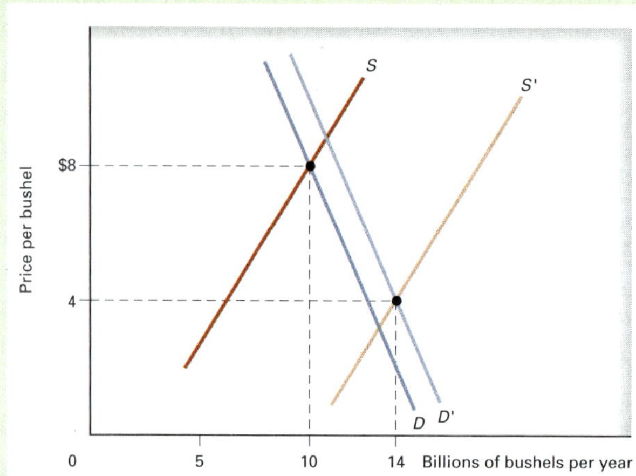

---

450 miles < Length of World's Longest Yard Sale

-0.9 < Price elasticity of breakfast cereal

Year oil was discovered on Alaska's north slope > **1967**

Price elasticity of Post Raisin Bran > **-2.5**

Reduction in youth smoking after large tax increase on cigarettes > **67%**

CHAPTER 6

Consumer Choice *and* Demand

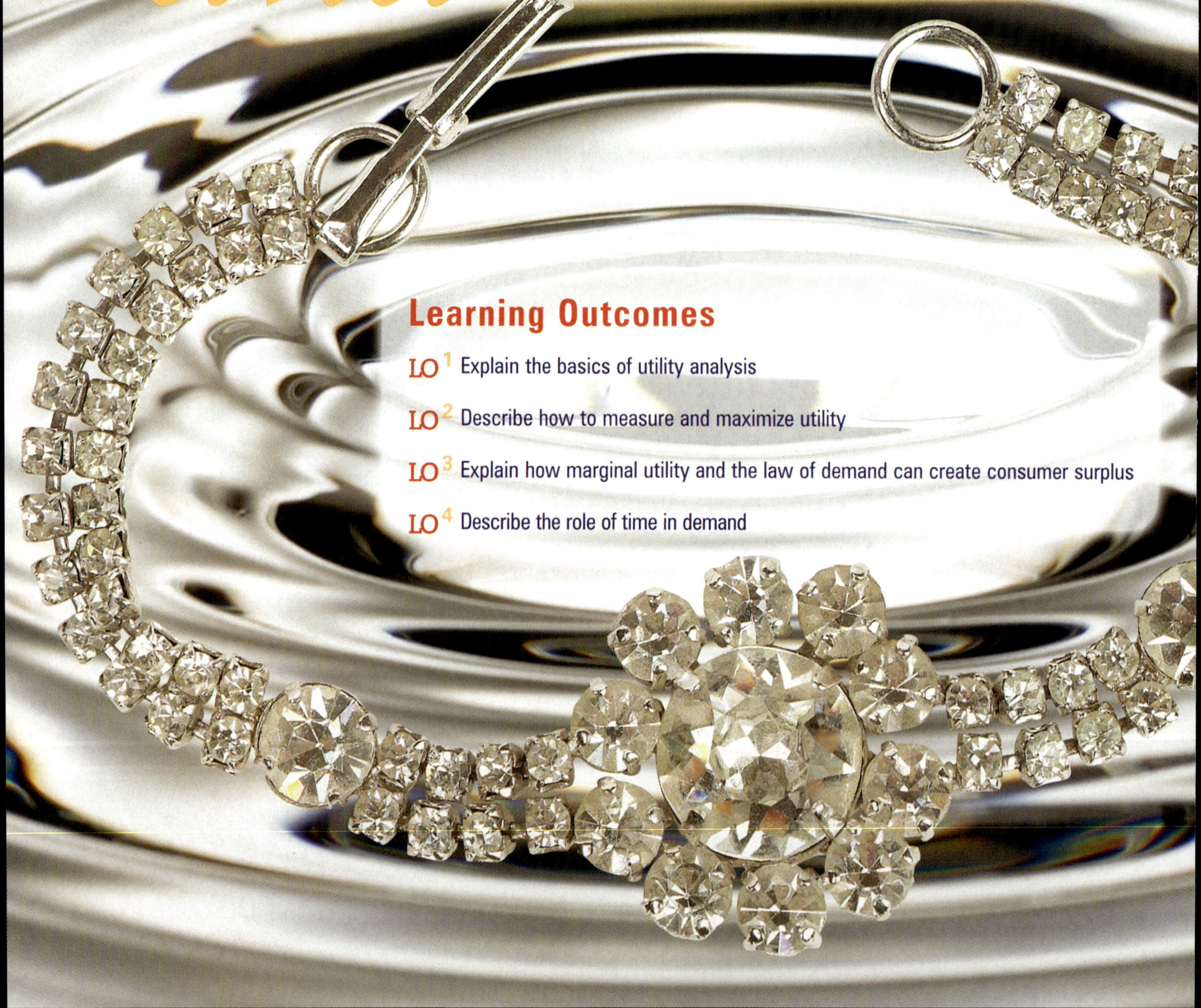

Learning Outcomes

- LO 1 Explain the basics of utility analysis
- LO 2 Describe how to measure and maximize utility
- LO 3 Explain how marginal utility and the law of demand can create consumer surplus
- LO 4 Describe the role of time in demand

“Why is water cheaper than diamonds even though water is essential to life and diamonds are simply bling?”

Why are newspapers sold in vending machines that allow you to take more than one? How much do you eat when you can eat all you want? Why don’t restaurants allow doggie bags with their all-you-can-eat specials? What are cures for cabin fever and for spring fever? Why is water cheaper than diamonds even though water is essential to life and diamonds are simply bling? To answer these and other questions, we take a closer look at consumer demand, a key building block in economics.

What do you think?

I'm willing to pay a premium for goods and services that save me time.

Strongly Disagree — *Strongly Agree*

1 2 3 4 5 6 7

You have already learned two reasons why demand curves slope downward. The first is the *substitution effect* of a price change. When the price of a good falls, consumers substitute that now-cheaper good for other goods. The second is the *income effect* of a price change. When the price of a good falls, real incomes increase, boosting consumers’ ability to buy more.

Demand is so important that it needs more attention. This chapter develops the law of demand based on the utility, or satisfaction, of consumption. As usual, the assumption is that you and other consumers try to maximize utility, or satisfaction. The point of this chapter is not to teach you how to maximize utility—that comes naturally. But learning the theory behind your behavior will help you understand the implications of that behavior, making predictions more accurate.

Topics discussed in Chapter 6 include:

- Total and marginal utility
- Law of diminishing marginal utility
- Measuring utility
- Time price of goods
- Utility-maximizing condition
- Consumer surplus
- Role of time in demand

LO[1] Utility Analysis

Suppose you and a friend are dining out. After dinner, your friend asks how you liked your meal. You wouldn’t say, “I liked mine twice as much as you liked yours.” Nor would you say, “It deserves a rating of 86 on the Consumer Satisfaction Index.”

The utility, or satisfaction, you derive from that meal cannot be compared with another person's experience, nor can your utility be measured based on some uniform standard. But you might say something such as, "I liked it better than my last meal here" or "I liked it better than campus food." More generally, you can say whether one of your experiences is more satisfying than another. Even if you say nothing about your likes and dislikes, we can draw conclusions about your preferences by observing your behavior. For example, we can conclude that you prefer apples to oranges if, when the two are priced the same, you buy apples every time.

> "Different people may have different tastes, but an individual's tastes are not constantly in flux."

Tastes and Preferences

As introduced in Chapter 3, *utility* is the sense of pleasure, or satisfaction, that comes from consumption. Utility is subjective. The utility you derive from a particular good, service, or activity depends on your *tastes and preferences*—your likes and dislikes in consumption. Some things are extremely appealing to you and others are not. You may not understand, for example, why someone would pay good money for sharks' fin soup, calves' brains, polka music, or martial arts movies. Why are most baby carriages sold in the United States navy blue, whereas they are yellow in Italy and chartreuse in Germany? And why do Australians favor chicken-flavored potato chips and chicken-flavored salt?

total utility the total satisfaction you derive from consumption; this could refer to either your total utility of consuming a particular good or your total utility from all consumption

marginal utility the change in your total utility from a one-unit change in your consumption of a good

law of diminishing marginal utility the more of a good a person consumes per period, the smaller the increase in total utility from consuming one more unit, other things constant

As noted in Chapter 4, your desires for food and drink are largely biological, as is your desire for comfort, rest, shelter, friendship, love, status, personal safety, and a pleasant environment. Your family background shapes some of your tastes, such as food preferences. Other influences include your surrounding culture, peer pressure, and religious convictions. So economists can say something about the origin of tastes, but they claim no special expertise. *Economists assume simply that tastes are given and are relatively stable—that is, different people may have different tastes, but an individual's tastes are not constantly in flux.* To be sure, tastes for some products do change over time. Here are three examples: (1) over the last two decades, hiking boots and work boots replaced running shoes as everyday footwear among many college students, (2) Americans began consuming leaner cuts of beef after a report linked the fat in red meat to a greater risk of cancer, and (3) because of the decline in the popularity of baseball cards, the number of shops that sell and trade these cards fell from about 10,000 in the early 1990s to only about 1,600 in 2007.

Although some tastes do change over time, economists believe they are stable enough to allow us to examine relationships such as that between price and quantity demanded. If tastes were not relatively stable, then we could not reasonably make the other-things-constant assumption required for demand analysis. We could not even draw a demand curve.

The Law of Diminishing Marginal Utility

Suppose it's a hot summer day and you are extremely thirsty after jogging four miles. You pour yourself an 8-ounce glass of ice water. That first glass is wonderful, and it puts a serious dent in your thirst. The next glass is not quite as wonderful, but it is still pretty good. The third one is just fair; and the fourth glass you barely finish.

What can we say about the *utility*, or satisfaction, you get from water. Let's first distinguish between *total utility* and *marginal utility*. **Total utility** is the total satisfaction you derive from consumption. In this example, total utility is the total satisfaction you get from four glasses of water. **Marginal utility** is the change in total utility resulting from a one-unit change in consumption. For example, the marginal utility of a third glass of water is the change in total utility resulting from that third glass.

Your experience with water reflects an economic law—the **law of diminishing marginal utility**. This law states that the more of a good you consume per period, other things constant, the smaller the increase in your total utility from additional consumption—that is, the smaller the marginal utility of each additional unit consumed. The marginal utility you derive from each additional glass of water declines as you drink more. You enjoy the first glass a lot, but each additional glass provides less and less marginal utility. If forced to drink a fifth glass, you

wouldn't enjoy it; your marginal utility would be negative—you would experience *disutility.*

Diminishing marginal utility is a feature of all consumption. A second foot-long sub sandwich at one meal, for most people, would provide little or no marginal utility. You might still enjoy a second movie on Friday night, but a third would probably be too much to take. In fact, almost anything repeated enough could become torture, such as being forced to watch the same movie or listen to the same song over and over and over. Yes, variety is the spice of life.

A long cold winter spent cooped up inside can cause "cabin fever." Each additional cold day brings more disutility. But the fever breaks with the arrival of the first warm day of spring, which is something wonderful. That first warm, glorious day causes such delirious joy that this jump in marginal utility has its own fevered name—"spring fever." Spring fever is eventually "cured" by many warm days like the first. By the time August rolls around, you attach much less marginal utility to yet another warm day.

For some goods, the drop in marginal utility with additional consumption is greater. A second copy of the same daily newspaper would likely provide you no marginal utility (in fact, the design of newspaper vending machines relies on the fact that people will take no more than one).[1] Likewise, a second viewing of the same movie at one sitting usually yields no additional utility. More generally, expressions such as "Been there, done that" and "Same old, same old" convey the idea that, for many activities, things start to get old after the first time. Restaurants depend on the law of diminishing marginal utility when they hold all-you-can-eat specials—and no doggie bags allowed, because the deal is all you can eat now, not now and the next few days.

LO2 Measuring Utility

So far, the description of utility has used such words as *wonderful, good,* and *fair.* The analysis can't be pushed very far with such subjective language. To predict consumer behavior, we need to develop a consistent way of viewing utility.

Units of Utility

Let's go back to the water example. Although there really is no objective way of measuring utility, if pressed, you could be more specific about how much you enjoyed each glass of water. For example, you might say the second glass was half as good as the first, the third was half as good as the second, the fourth was half as good as the third, and you passed up a fifth glass because you expected no positive utility. To get a handle on this, let's assign arbitrary numbers to the utility you get from water, so the pattern of numbers reflects your expressed level of satisfaction. Let's say the first glass provides you with 40 units of utility, the second glass with 20, the third with 10, and the fourth with 5. A fifth glass, if you were forced to drink it, would yield negative utility, or disutility—in this case, say, −2 units. *Developing numerical values for utility allows us to be more specific about the utility from consumption.* If it would help, you could think of these units more playfully as thrills, kicks, or jollies—as in, getting your kicks from consumption.

Each person has a uniquely subjective utility scale.

By attaching a numerical measure to utility, we can compare the total utility a particular consumer gets from different goods as well as the marginal utility that consumer gets from additional consumption. Thus, we can employ units of utility to evaluate a consumer's preferences. Note, however, that we cannot compare utility levels across consumers. *Each person has a uniquely subjective utility scale.*

The first column of Exhibit 1 lists possible quantities of water you might consume after running four miles on a hot day. The second column presents the total utility derived from that consumption, and the third column shows the marginal utility of each additional glass of water. Recall that marginal utility is the change in total utility from an additional unit of the good. You can see from the second column that total

1. This example appears in Marshall Jevons, *The Fatal Equilibrium* (Cambridge, Mass.: MIT Press, 1985).

Exhibit 1

Utility Derived from Drinking Water After Jogging Four Miles

Amount Consumed (8-ounce glasses)	Total Utility	Marginal Utility
0	0	—
1	40	40
2	60	20
3	70	10
4	75	5
5	73	−2

utility increases with each of the first four glasses but by smaller and smaller amounts. The third column shows that the first glass of water yields 40 units of utility, the second glass yields an additional 20 units, and so on. Marginal utility declines after the first glass of water, becoming negative with the fifth glass. *At any level of consumption, marginal utilities sum to total utility.* Total utility is graphed in panel (a) of Exhibit 2. Again, because of diminishing marginal utility, each additional glass of water adds less to total utility, so

Exhibit 2

Total Utility and Marginal Utility You Derive from Drinking Water after Jogging Four Miles

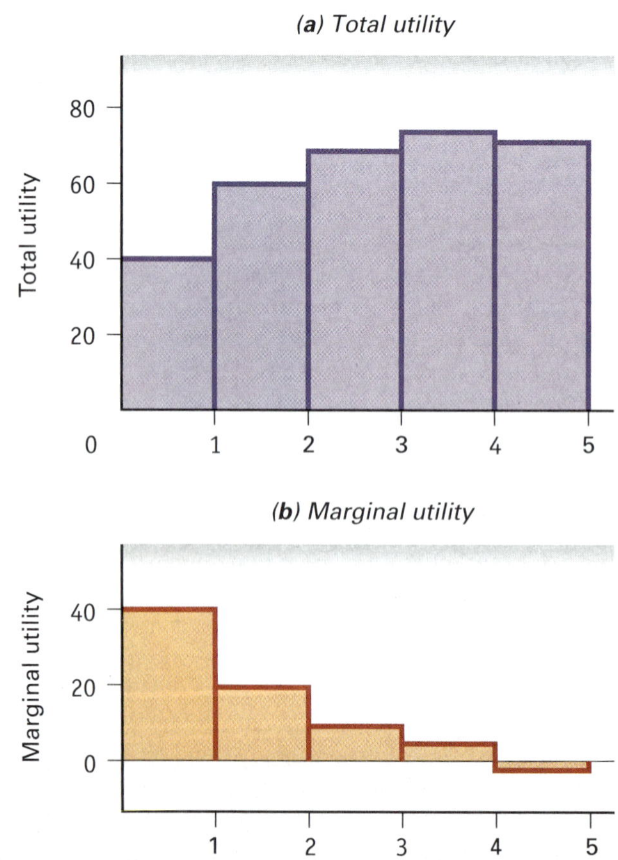

total utility increases for the first four glasses but at a decreasing rate. Panel (b) shows the law of diminishing marginal utility.

Utility Maximization in a World Without Scarcity

Economists assume that your purpose for drinking water, as with all consumption, is to *maximize your total utility.* So how much water do you consume? If the price of water is zero, you drink water as long as doing so increases total utility. Each of the first four glasses of water adds to your total utility. *If a good is free, you increase consumption as long as marginal utility is positive.* Let's broaden the analysis to a world of only two goods—pizza and video rentals. We continue to translate the satisfaction you receive from consumption into units of utility. Based on your tastes and preferences, suppose your total utility and marginal utility from consumption are as presented in Exhibit 3. The first four columns apply to pizza and the second four to video rentals. Please take a little time right now with each column.

Notice from columns (3) and (7) that each good shows diminishing marginal utility. Given this set of preferences, how much of each good would you consume per week? At a zero price, you would increase consumption as long as marginal utility is positive. Thus, you would consume at least the first six pizzas and first six videos because the sixth unit of each good yields marginal utility. Did you ever go to a party where the food and drinks were free to you? How much did you eat and drink? You ate and drank until you didn't want any more—that is, until the marginal utility of each additional bite and each additional sip fell to zero. Your consumption was determined not by prices or your income but simply by your tastes.

Utility Maximization in a World of Scarcity

Alas, goods are usually scarce, not free. Suppose the price of a pizza is $8, the rental price of a video is $4, and your part-time job pays $40 per week after taxes. Your utility is still based on your tastes, but you now buy goods with your limited income. How do you allocate your income between the two goods to maximize utility? To get the ball rolling, suppose you start off spending your entire budget of $40 on pizza, purchasing five pizzas a week, which yields a total of 142 units of utility. You quickly realize that if you buy one less pizza, you free up enough in your budget to rent two movies. Would total utility increase? Sure. You give up 12 units of utility, the marginal utility of the fifth pizza, to get 68 units of utility from the first two videos. Total utility zooms from 142 to 198. Then you notice that if you reduce purchases to three pizzas, you give up 18 units of utility from the fourth pizza but gain a total of 32 units of utility from the third and fourth videos. This is another utility-increasing move.

Further reductions in pizza, however, would reduce your total utility because you would give up 24 units of utility from the third pizza but gain only 14 units from the fifth and sixth videos. Thus, you quickly find that the utility-maximizing combination is three pizzas and four videos per week, for a total utility of 212. This means spending $24 on pizza and $16 on videos. *You are in equilibrium when consuming this combination because any affordable change would reduce your utility.*

Exhibit 3

Total and Marginal Utilities from Pizza and Videos

Pizza				Video Rentals			
(1) Consumed per Week	(2) Total Utility	(3) Marginal Utility	(4) Marginal Utility per Dollar if p = $8	(5) Viewed per Week	(6) Total Utility	(7) Marginal Utility	(8) Marginal Utility per Dollar if p = $4
0	0	—	—	0	0	—	—
1	56	56	7	1	40	40	10
2	88	32	4	2	68	28	7
3	**112**	**24**	**3**	3	88	20	5
4	130	18	2¼	**4**	**100**	**12**	**3**
5	142	12	1½	5	108	8	2
6	150	8	1	6	114	6	1½

© LAWRENCE MANNING/CORBIS

Utility-Maximizing Conditions

Once a consumer is in equilibrium, there is no way to increase utility by reallocating the budget. Any change in consumption decreases utility. But, wait, there's more: *In equilibrium, the last dollar spent on each good yields the same marginal utility.* Let's see how this works. Column (4) shows the marginal utility of pizza divided by its price of \$8. Column (8) shows the marginal utility of videos divided by its price of \$4. The equilibrium combination of three pizzas and four videos exhausts the \$40 budget and adds 3 units of utility for the last dollar spent on each good. **Consumer equilibrium** is achieved when the budget is exhausted and the last dollar spent on each good yields the same marginal utility. In equilibrium, pizza's marginal utility divided by its price equals video's marginal utility divided by its price. In short, the consumer gets the same bang from the last buck spent on each good. This equality can be expressed as:

$$\frac{MU_P}{p_p} = \frac{MU_V}{p_v}$$

where MU_P is the marginal utility of pizza, p_p is the price of pizza, MU_V is the marginal utility of videos, and p_v is the rental price. The consumer reallocates spending until the last dollar spent on each product yields the same marginal utility. Although this example considers only two goods, the logic of utility maximization applies to any number of goods.

In equilibrium, higher-priced goods must yield more marginal utility than lower-priced goods—enough additional utility to compensate for their higher price. Because a pizza costs twice as much as a video rental, the marginal utility of the final pizza purchased must, in equilibrium, be twice that of the final video rented. Indeed, the marginal utility of the third pizza, 24, is twice that of the fourth video, 12. Economists do not claim that you consciously equate the ratios of marginal utility to price, but they do claim that you act as if you had made such calculations. *Thus, you decide how much of each good to purchase by considering your tastes, market prices, and your income. Consumers maximize utility by equalizing the marginal utility from the last dollar spent on each good.*

$$\frac{MU_P}{p_p} = \frac{MU_V}{p_v}$$

consumer equilibrium
the condition in which an individual consumer's budget is spent and the last dollar spent on each good yields the same marginal utility; therefore, utility is maximized

Water for Diamonds

Q: Diamonds are bling—certainly not a necessity of life in any sense. Water is essential to life and has hundreds of valuable uses. For the price of a one-carat diamond, you could buy enough water to last a lifetime. So why are diamonds expensive and water cheap? How can something as useful as water cost so much less than something of such limited use as diamonds? The *diamonds-water paradox* discussed by Adam Smith in 1776 holds the answer.

:A Because water is essential to life, the total utility derived from water greatly exceeds the total utility derived from diamonds. Yet the market value of a good is based not on its total utility but its marginal utility. Because water is so abundant in nature, we consume it to the point where the marginal utility of the last gallon purchased is relatively low. Because diamonds are relatively scarce compared to water, the marginal utility of the last diamond purchased is relatively high. Thus, water is cheap and diamonds expensive. As Ben Franklin said, "We will only know the worth of water when the well is dry."

LO3 Marginal Utility and the Law of Demand

How does utility analysis relate to your demand for pizza? The discussion so far yields a single point on your demand curve for pizza: At a price of \$8, you demand three pizzas per week. This is based on income of \$40 per week, a price of \$4 per video, and your tastes reflected by the utility tables in Exhibit 3. Knowing that three pizzas are demanded when the price is \$8 offers no clue about the shape of your demand curve for pizza. To generate another point, let's see what

Exhibit 4

Total and Marginal Utilities from Pizza and Videos After the Price of Pizza Decreases from $8 to $6

Pizza				Video Rentals			
(1) Consumed per Week	(2) Total Utility	(3) Marginal Utility	(4) Marginal Utility per Dollar if p = $6	(5) Viewed per Week	(6) Total Utility	(7) Marginal Utility	(8) Marginal Utility per Dollar if p = $4
0	0	—	—	0	0	—	—
1	56	56	9⅓	1	40	40	10
2	88	32	5⅓	2	68	28	7
3	112	24	4	3	88	20	5
4	**130**	**18**	**3**	**4**	**100**	**12**	**3**
5	142	12	2	5	108	8	2
6	150	8	1⅓	6	114	6	1½

happens to quantity demanded if the price of pizza changes, while keeping other things constant (such as tastes, income, and the price of video rentals). Suppose the price of a pizza drops from $8 to $6.

Exhibit 4 is the same as Exhibit 3, except the price per pizza is $6. Your original choice was three pizzas and four video rentals. At that combination and with the price of pizza now $6, the marginal utility per dollar spent on the third pizza is 4, while the marginal utility per dollar spent on the fourth video remains at 3. The marginal utilities of the last dollar spent on each good are no longer equal. What's more, the original combination of three pizzas and four videos now leaves $6 unspent. So you could still buy your original combination but have $6 left to spend (this, incidentally, shows the income effect of the lower price). You can increase utility by adjusting your consumption. Take a moment now to see if you can figure out what the new equilibrium should be.

In light of your utility schedules in Exhibit 4, you would increase your consumption to four pizzas per week. This strategy exhausts your budget and equates the marginal utilities of the last dollar expended on each good. Your video rentals remain the same. The marginal utility of the fourth pizza, 18, divided by the price of $6 yields 3 units of utility per dollar of expenditure, the same as you get from the fourth video. You are in equilibrium once again. Total utility increases by the 18 units you derive from the fourth pizza. Thus, you are clearly better off as a result of the price decrease.

We now have a second point on your demand curve for pizza—if the price of pizza is $6, you demand four pizzas. The two points are presented as *a* and *b* in Exhibit 5. We could continue to change the price of pizza and thereby generate additional points on the demand curve, but you can get some idea of the demand curve's downward slope from these two points. The shape of the demand curve for pizza

Exhibit 5

Demand for Pizza Generated from Marginal Utility

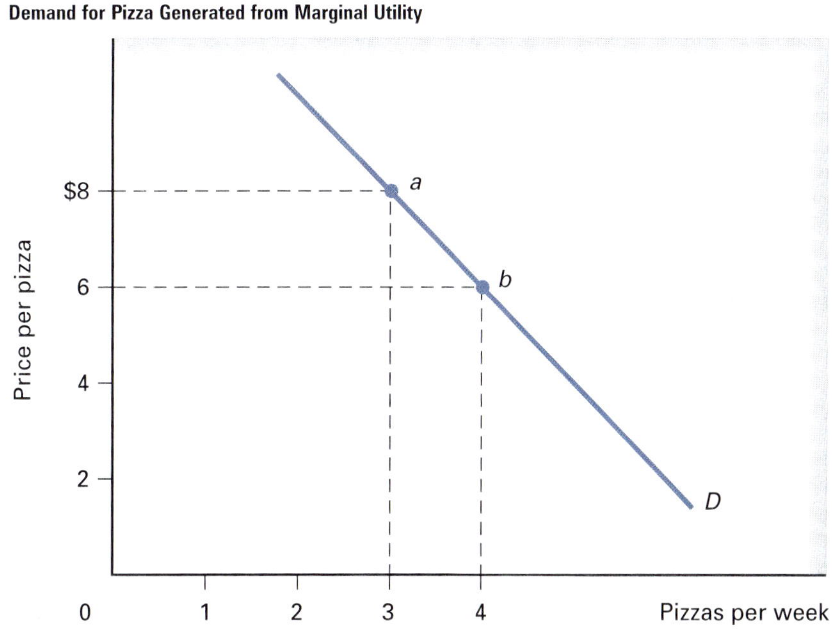

matches our expectations based on the law of demand: Price and quantity demanded are inversely related. (Try estimating your price elasticity of demand between points *a* and *b*. Hint: What does your total spending on pizza tell you?)

We have gone to some lengths to see how you (or any consumer) maximize utility. Given prices and your income, your tastes and preferences naturally guide you to the best bundle. You are not even conscious of your behavior. The urge to maximize utility is like the force of gravity—both work whether or not you understand them. Even animal behavior seems consistent with the law of demand. Wolves, for example, exhibit no territorial concerns when game is plentiful. But when game becomes scarce, wolves carefully mark their territory and defend it against intruders. Thus, wolves appear to value game more when it is scarce.

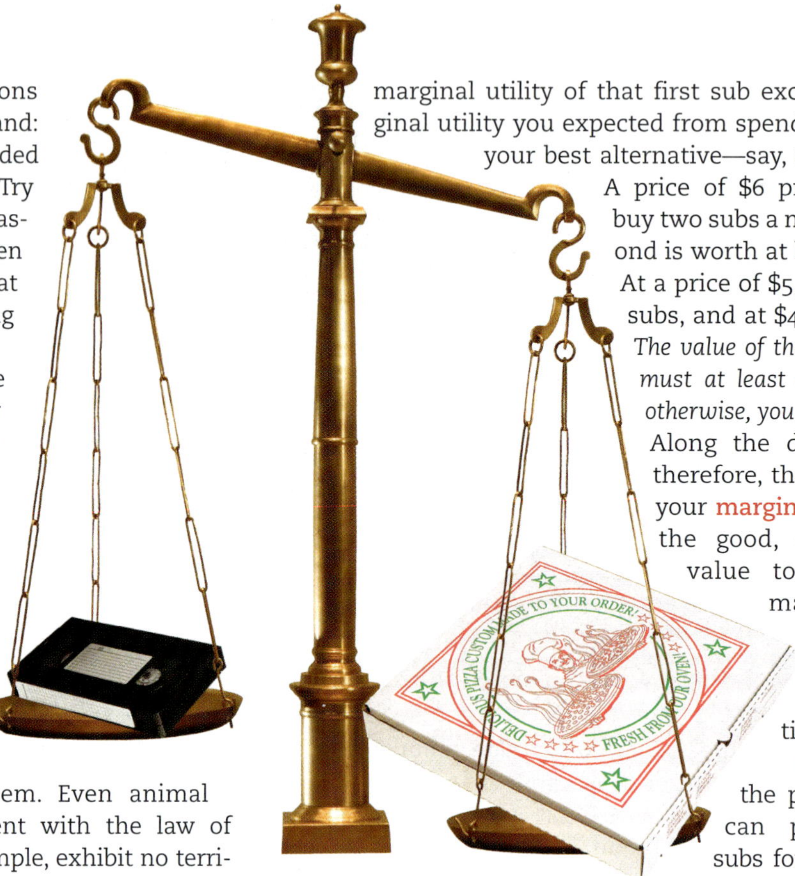

Now that you have some idea of utility, let's consider an application of utility analysis.

Consumer Surplus

In our earlier example, total utility increased when the price of pizza fell from $8 to $6. In this section, we take a closer look at how consumers benefit from a lower price. Suppose your demand for foot-long sub sandwiches is as shown in Exhibit 6. Recall that in constructing an individual's demand curve, we hold tastes, income, and the prices of related goods constant. Only the price varies. At a price of $8 or above, you find that the marginal utility of other goods that you could buy for $8 is higher than the marginal utility of a sub sandwich. Consequently, you buy no subs. At a price of $7, you are willing and able to buy one per month, so the marginal utility of that first sub exceeds the marginal utility you expected from spending that $7 on your best alternative—say, a movie ticket. A price of $6 prompts you to buy two subs a month. The second is worth at least $6 to you. At a price of $5, you buy three subs, and at $4, you buy four. *The value of the sub purchased must at least equal the price; otherwise, you wouldn't buy it.* Along the demand curve, therefore, the price reflects your **marginal valuation** of the good, or the dollar value to you of the marginal utility derived from consuming each additional unit.

Notice that if the price is $4, you can purchase four subs for $4 each, even though you would have been willing to pay more for each of the first three subs. The first sandwich provides marginal utility that you valued at $7; the second you valued at $6; and the third you valued at $5. In fact, if you had to, rather than go without subs, you would have been willing to pay $7 for the first, $6 for the second, and $5 for the third. The dollar value of the total utility of the first four sandwiches is $7 + $6 + $5 + $4 = $22 per month. But when the price is $4, you get four for a total of $16. Thus, a price of $4 confers a **consumer surplus**, or a consumer bonus, equal to the difference between the maximum amount you would have been willing to pay

marginal valuation the dollar value of the marginal utility derived from consuming each additional unit of a good

consumer surplus the difference between the most a consumer would pay for a given quantity of a good and what the consumer actually pays

Exhibit 6

Consumer Surplus from Sub Sandwiches

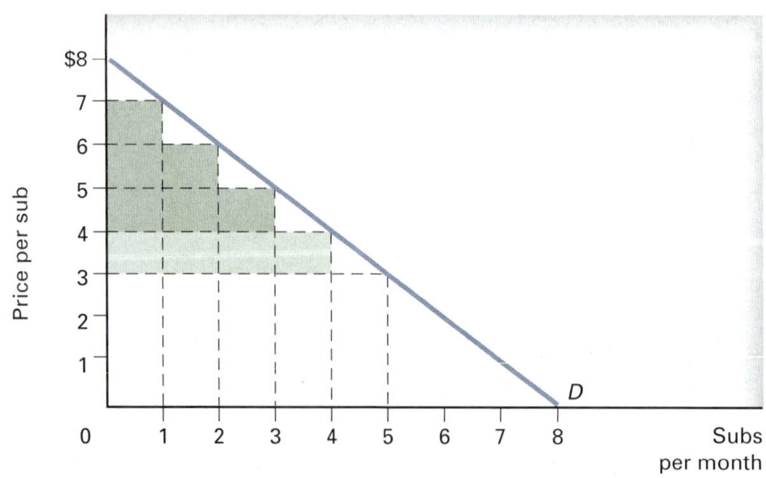

($22) rather than go without subs altogether and what you actually pay ($16). When the price is $4, your consumer surplus is $22 − $16 = $6, as approximated by the six darker shaded blocks in Exhibit 6. Consumer surplus equals the value of the total utility you receive from consuming the sandwiches minus your total spending on them. Consumer surplus is reflected by the area under the demand curve but above the price.

If the price falls to $3, you buy five subs a month. Apparently, you feel that the marginal utility from the fifth one is worth at least $3. The lower price means that you get all five for $3 each, even though each except the fifth one is worth more to you than $3. Your consumer surplus when the price is $3 is the value of the total utility from the first five, which is $7 + $6 + $5 + $4 + $3 = $25, minus your cost, which is $3 × 5 = $15. Thus, your consumer surplus is $25 − $15 = $10, as indicated by both the dark and the light shaded blocks in Exhibit 6. So if the price declines to $3, your consumer surplus increases by $4, as reflected by the four lighter-shaded blocks in Exhibit 6. You can see how consumers benefit from lower prices.

Incidentally, in some cases your consumer surplus is huge, such as from a bottle of water if you are dying of thirst, a winter coat if you are at risk of freezing, or a pair of glasses if you can't see without them.

Market Demand and Consumer Surplus

Let's talk now about the market demand for a good, assuming the market consists of you and two other consumers. *The market demand curve is simply the horizontal sum of the individual demand curves for all consumers in the market.* Exhibit 7 shows how the demand curves for three consumers in the market for sub sandwiches sum horizontally to yield the market demand. At a price of $4, for example, you demand four subs per month, Brittany demands two, and Chris demands none. The market demand at a price of $4 is therefore six sandwiches. At a price of $2, you demand six per month, Brittany four, and Chris two, for a market demand of 12. *The market demand curve shows the total quantity demanded per period by all consumers at various prices.* Consumer surplus can be used to examine market demand as well as individual demand. *At a given price, consumer surplus for the market is the difference between the most consumers would pay for that quantity and the amount they do pay.*

Instead of just three consumers in the market, suppose there are many. Exhibit 8 presents market demand for a good with millions of consumers. If the price is $2 per unit, each person adjusts his or her quantity demanded until the marginal valuation of the final unit purchased equals $2. But each consumer gets to buy all other units for $2 each as well. In Exhibit 8, the dark shading, bounded above by the demand curve and below by the price line at $2, depicts the consumer surplus. The light shading shows the gain in consumer surplus if the price drops to $1. Notice that if this good were given away, the consumer surplus would not be that much greater than when the price is $1.

Consumer surplus is the net benefit consumers get from market exchange. It can be used to measure economic welfare and to compare the effects of different market structures, different tax structures, and different public programs.

Exhibit 7

Summing Individual Demand Curves to Derive the Market Demand for Sub Sandwiches

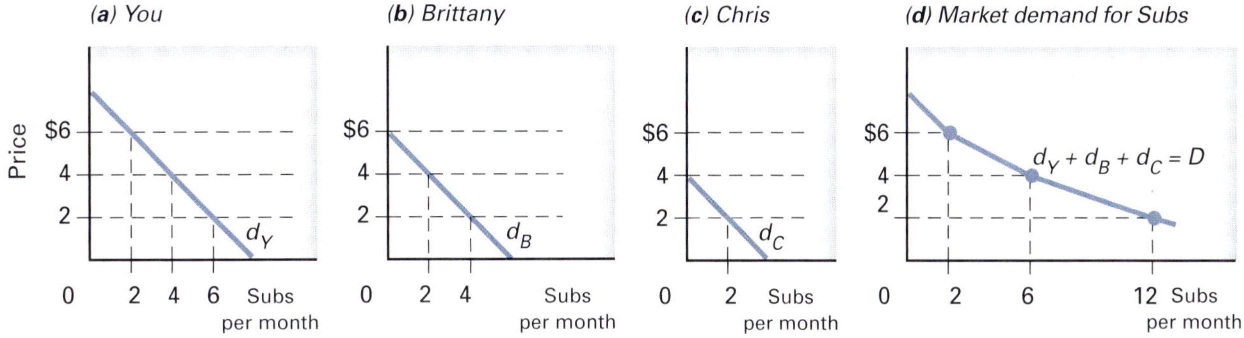

Exhibit 8

Market Demand and Consumer Surplus

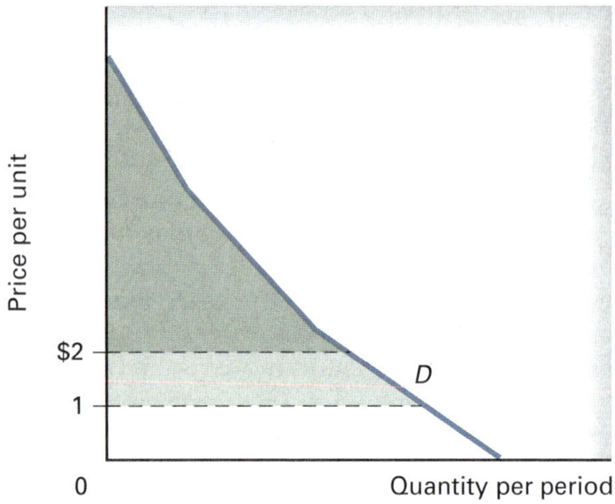

LO[4] The Role of Time in Demand

Because consumption does not occur instantly, time plays a role in demand analysis. Consumption takes time and, as Ben Franklin said, time is money—time has a positive value for most people. Consequently, consumption has a *money price* and a *time price*. Goods are demanded because of the benefits they offer. It is not the microwave oven, personal computer, airline trip, or headache medicine that you value but the services they provide. Other things constant, you would gladly pay more to get the same benefit in less time, as with faster ovens, computers, airline trips, and headache relief. Likewise, you are willing to pay more for seedless grapes, seedless oranges, and seedless watermelon.

Your willingness to pay a premium for time-saving goods and services depends on the opportunity cost of your time. Differences in the value of time among consumers help explain differences in the consumption patterns observed in the economy. For example, a retired couple has more leisure time than a working couple and may clip discount coupons and search the newspapers for bargains, sometimes even going from store to store for particular grocery items on sale that week. The working couple tends to ignore the coupons and sales, eats out more often, and shops more at convenience stores, where they pay more for the "convenience." The retired couple is more inclined to drive to a vacation destination, whereas the working couple flies.

Just inside the gates at Disneyland, Disney World, and Universal Studios are boards listing the waiting times of each attraction and ride. At that point, the dollar cost of admission has already been paid, so the marginal dollar cost of each ride and attraction is zero. The waiting times offer a menu of the mar-

ginal *time costs* of each ride or attraction. Incidentally, people who were willing to pay up to $55 an hour at Disney World and $60 an hour at Disneyland (plus the price of admission), until recently, could take VIP tours that bypass the lines.[2] How much would you pay to avoid the lines?

Differences in the opportunity cost of time among consumers shape consumption patterns and add another dimension to our analysis of demand.

Final Word

This chapter has analyzed consumer choice by focusing on utility, or satisfaction. We assumed that utility could be measured in some systematic way for a particular consumer, even though utility measures could not be compared across consumers. The goal has been to explore utility maximization and predict how consumers react to a change in price. We judge a theory not by the realism of its assumptions but by the accuracy of its predictions. Based on this criterion, the theory of consumer choice presented in this chapter has proven to be quite useful.

Again, to maximize utility, you or any other consumer do not need to understand the material presented in this chapter. Economists assume that the urge to maximize utility is natural and instinctive. In this chapter, we simply tried to analyze that process.

2. For example, see Nancy Keates, "Tourists Learn How to Mouse around Disney's Long Lines," *Wall Street Journal,* 27 March 1998.

Tough Crowd

In recent years the retail movie rental industry, characterized by the brick-and-mortar stores operated by industry leaders such as Blockbuster and Movie Gallery, has come under a lot of pressure from alternative sources for movie rentals. Here are some figures on the kind of competition these companies are facing:

Online Movie Rental

- In 2006 the online movie rental industry counted 8.8 million subscribers and $1.2 billion in revenue.
- Netflix offers a selection of about 90,000 different titles.
- Blockbuster's Total Access program offers 75,000 titles along with in-store DVD exchange.
- DVD Avenue offers 25,000 titles along with over 600 video game titles.

Kiosk Rentals

- DVD rental kiosks, such as those operated by Redbox and The New Release in locations like grocery stores and McDonald's, each carry roughly 500 DVDs and 150 different titles at $1 per night.
- Redbox operates nearly 5,000 rental kiosks in 46 states.
- The New Release operates 1,900 rental kiosks in 26 states.

Paid Video Downloads

- In 2006 paid video downloads, such as those offered by Apple's iTunes store and Amazon's Unbox, were estimated at $98 million. For 2007 they were projected at $279 million (May 2007).
- Netflix online viewing service currently offers over 5,000 titles.

SOURCES: Stephen Williams, "Which Online Movie Rental Company Is Right for You?" *Newsday* (Melville, NY), 7 November 2007; http://ir.netflix.com/; Catherine Holahan, "Netflix May Have a New Direction; The Online DVD Rental Store's Shares Saw Some Action This Week on Speculation of a Sale to Amazon, a Move that Could Amp Its Subscriber Base," *Business Week Online,* 11 June 2007; Michael Levensohn, "DVD Renters Seeing Redbox," *Times Herald-Record,* 20 November 2007; http://www.thenewrelease.com/newspress061207.htm.

CHAPTER 7

Production *and* Cost in the Firm

Learning Outcomes

LO 1. Explain the relationship between cost and profit

LO 2 Identify the elements that affect production in the short term

LO 3 Explain how the costs of production vary with output in the short run

LO 4 Describe how firms use the long-run average cost curve to make choices about production

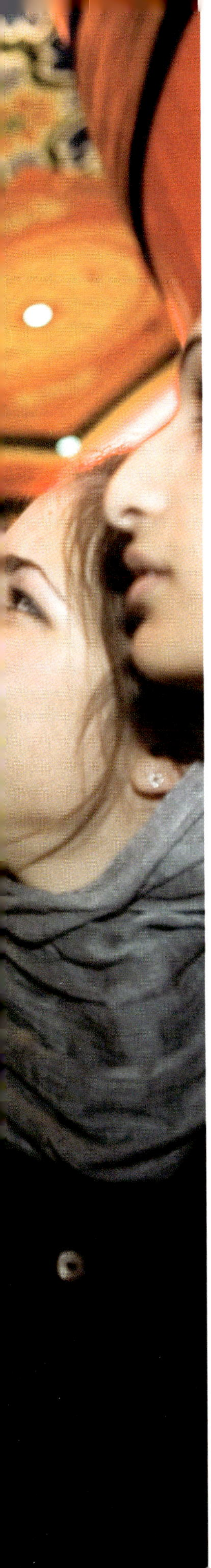

“Why do movie theaters have so many screens? Why don’t they add even more?”

Why do too many cooks spoil the broth? Why do movie theaters have so many screens? Why don’t they add even more? If you go into business for yourself, how much must you earn just to break even? Why might your grade point average fall even though you improved from the previous term? Answers to these and other questions are discovered in this chapter, which introduces production and cost in the firm.

The previous chapter explored the consumer behavior shaping the demand curve. You were asked to think like a consumer, or demander. This chapter examines the producer behavior shaping the supply curve. You must now think like a producer, or supplier. You may feel more natural as a consumer (after all, you *are* one), but you already know a lot more about producers than you may realize. You have been around them all your life—Wal-Mart, Blockbuster, Starbucks, Google, Exxon, Amazon.com, Home Depot, McDonald’s, MySpace, Facebook, Pizza Hut, FedEx Kinko’s, Ford, Gap, and hundreds more. So you already have some idea how businesses operate. They all have the same goal—they try to maximize profit, which is revenue minus cost. This chapter introduces the cost side of the profit equation.

What do you think?

I’d rather go to a movie theater with lots of screens than to a one-screen movie house.

Strongly Disagree						Strongly Agree
1	2	3	4	5	6	7

Topics discussed in Chapter 7 include:

- Explicit and implicit costs
- Economic and normal profit
- Increasing and diminishing returns
- Short-run costs
- Long-run costs
- Economies and diseconomies of scale

LO[1] Cost and Profit

With demand, we assume that consumers try to maximize utility, a goal that motivates their behavior. With supply, we assume that producers try to maximize *profit,* and this goal motivates their behavior. *Firms try to earn a profit by transforming resources into salable products.* Over time, firms that survive and grow are those that are more profitable. Unprofitable firms eventually fail. Each year, millions of new firms enter the marketplace and many leave. The firm's decision makers must choose what goods and services to produce and what resources to employ. They must make plans while confronting uncertainty about consumer demand, resource availability, and the intentions of other firms in the market. *The lure of profit is so strong, however, that eager entrepreneurs are always ready to pursue their dreams.*

Explicit and Implicit Costs

To hire a resource, a firm must pay at least the resource's *opportunity cost*—that is, at least what the resource could earn in its best alternative use. For most resources, a cash payment approximates the opportunity cost. For example, the $3 per pound that Domino's Pizza pays for cheese must at least equal the cheese producer's opportunity cost of supplying it. Firms do not make direct cash payments for resources they own. For example, a firm pays no rent to operate in a company-owned building. Similarly, small-business owners usually don't pay themselves an hourly wage. Yet these resources are not free. *Whether hired in resource markets or owned by the firm, all resources have an opportunity cost.* Company-owned buildings can be rented or sold; small-business owners can find other work.

A firm's **explicit costs** are its actual cash payments for resources: wages, rent, interest, insurance, taxes, and the like. In addition to these direct cash outlays, or explicit costs, the firm also incurs **implicit costs**, which are the opportunity costs of using resources owned by the firm or provided by the firm's owners. Examples include the use of a company-owned building, use of company funds, or the time of the firm's owners. Like explicit costs, implicit costs are opportunity costs. But unlike explicit costs, implicit costs require no cash payment and no entry in the firm's *accounting statement*, which records its revenues, explicit costs, and accounting profit.

explicit cost
opportunity cost of resources employed by a firm that takes the form of cash payments

implicit cost
a firm's opportunity cost of using its own resources or those provided by its owners without a corresponding cash payment

accounting profit
a firm's total revenue minus its explicit costs

economic profit
a firm's total revenue minus its explicit and implicit costs

Alternative Measures of Profit

An example may help clarify the distinction between explicit and implicit costs. Wanda Wheeler earns $50,000 a year as an aeronautical engineer with the Skyhigh Aircraft Corporation. On her way home from work one day, she gets an idea for a rounder, more friction-resistant airplane wheel. She decides to quit her job and start a business, which she calls Wheeler Dealer. To buy the necessary machines and equipment, she withdraws $20,000 from a savings account earning interest of $1,000 a year. She hires an assistant and starts producing the wheel using the spare bay in her condominium's parking garage, which she had been renting to a neighbor for $100 a month.

Sales are slow at first—people keep telling her she is just trying to reinvent the wheel—but her wheel eventually gets rolling. When Wanda reviews the firm's performance after the first year, she is pleased. As you can see in the top portion of Exhibit 1, company revenue in 2007 totaled $105,000. After paying her assistant and for materials and equipment, the firm shows an accounting profit of $64,000. **Accounting profit** equals total revenue minus explicit costs. Accountants use this profit to determine a firm's taxable income.

Exhibit 1

Wheeler Dealer Accounts, 2007

Total revenue		$105,000
Less explicit costs:		
Assistant's salary	−$21,000	
Material and equipment	−$20,000	
Equals accounting profit		$64,000
Less implicit costs:		
Wanda's forgone salary	−$50,000	
Forgone interest on savings	−$1,000	
Forgone garage rental	−$1,200	
Equals economic profit		$11,800

But accounting profit ignores the opportunity cost of Wanda's own resources used in the firm. First is the opportunity cost of her time. Remember, she quit a $50,000-a-year job to work full time on her business, thereby forgoing that salary. Second is the $1,000 in annual interest she passes up by funding the operation with her own savings. And third, by using the spare bay in the garage for the business, she forgoes $1,200 per year in rental income. The forgone salary, interest, and rental income are implicit costs because she no longer earns income from the best alternative uses of these resources.

Economic profit equals total revenue minus all costs, both implicit and explicit; *economic profit takes into account the opportunity cost of all resources used in* *production*. In Exhibit 1, accounting profit of $64,000 less implicit costs of $52,200 yields an economic profit of $11,800. What would happen to the accounting statement if Wanda decided to pay herself a salary of $50,000 per year? Explicit costs would increase by $50,000, and implicit costs would decrease by $50,000. Thus, accounting profit would decrease by $50,000, but economic profit would not change because it already reflects both implicit and explicit costs.

© MINT PHOTOGRAPHY/ALAMY

There is one other profit measure to consider. The accounting profit just sufficient to ensure that *all* resources used by the firm earn their opportunity cost is called a **normal profit**. Wheeler Dealer earns a normal profit when accounting profit equals implicit costs—the sum of the salary Wanda gave up at her regular job ($50,000), the interest she gave up by using her own savings ($1,000), and the rent she gave up on her garage ($1,200). Thus, if the accounting profit is $52,200 per year—the opportunity cost of resources Wanda supplies to the firm—the company earns a normal profit. *Any accounting profit in excess of a normal profit is economic profit*. If accounting profit is large enough, it can be divided into normal profit and economic profit. The $64,000 in accounting profit earned by Wanda's firm consists of (1) a normal profit of $52,200, which covers her implicit costs—the opportunity cost of resources she supplies the firm, and (2) an economic profit of $11,800, which is over and above what these resources, including Wanda's time, could earn in their best alternative use.

As long as economic profit is positive, Wanda is better off running her own firm than working for Skyhigh Aircraft. If total revenue had been only $50,000, an accounting profit of only $9,000 would cover less than one-fifth of her salary, to say nothing of her forgone rent and interest. Because Wanda would not have covered her implicit costs, she would not be earning even a normal profit and would be better off back in her old job.

To understand profit maximization, you must develop a feel for both revenue and cost. In this chapter, you begin learning about the cost of production, starting with the relationship between inputs and outputs.

LO2 Production in the Short Run

We shift now from a discussion of profit, which is why firms exist, to a discussion of how firms operate. Suppose a new McDonald's just opened in your neighborhood and business is booming far beyond expectations. The manager responds to the unexpected demand by quickly hiring more workers. But cars are still backed up into the street waiting for a parking space. The solution is to add a drive-through window, but such an expansion takes time. What to do?

Fixed and Variable Resources

Some resources, such as labor, are called **variable resources** because they can be varied quickly to change the output rate. But adjustments in other resources take more time. Resources that cannot be altered easily—the size of the building, for example—are called **fixed resources**. When considering the time required to change the quantity of resources employed, economists distinguish between the short run and the long run. In the **short run**, at least one resource is fixed. In the **long run**, no resource is fixed.

Output can be changed in the short run by adjusting variable resources, but the size, or *scale*, of the firm is fixed in the short run. In the long run, all resources can be varied. The length of the long run differs from industry to industry because the nature of production differs. For example, the size of a McDonald's outlet can be increased more quickly than can the size of an auto plant. Thus, the long run for that McDonald's is shorter than the long run for an automaker.

normal profit the accounting profit earned when all resources earn their opportunity cost

variable resource any resource that can be varied in the short run to increase or decrease production

fixed resource any resource that cannot be varied in the short run

short run a period during which at least one of a firm's resources is fixed

long run a period during which all resources under the firm's control are variable

The Law of Diminishing Marginal Returns

Let's focus on the short-run link between resource use and the rate of output by considering a hypothetical moving company called Smoother Mover. Suppose the company's fixed resources, such as a warehouse, are already in place and that labor is the only variable resource. Exhibit 2 relates the amount of labor employed to the amount of output produced. Labor is measured in worker-days, which is one worker for one day, and output is measured in tons of furniture moved per day. The first column shows the amount of labor employed, which ranges from 0 to 8 worker-days. The second column shows the tons of furniture moved per day, or the **total product**, at each level of employment. The relationship between the amount of resources employed and total product is called the firm's **production function**. The third column shows the **marginal product** of each worker—that is, the the change in total product resulting from an additional unit of labor, assuming other resources remain unchanged. Spend a little time now getting acquainted with the three columns.

total product a firm's total output

production function the relationship between the amount of resources employed and a firm's total product

marginal product the change in total product that occurs when the use of a particular resource increases by one unit, all other resources constant

increasing marginal returns the marginal product of a variable resource increases as each additional unit of that resource is employed

law of diminishing marginal returns as more of a variable resource is added to a given amount of a fixed resource, marginal product eventually declines and could become negative

Exhibit 2

The Short-Run Relationship Between Units of Labor and Tons of Furniture Moved

Units of the Variable Resource (worker-days)	Total Product (tons moved per day)	Marginal Product (tons moved per day)
0	0	—
1	2	2
2	5	3
3	9	4
4	12	3
5	14	2
6	15	1
7	15	0
8	14	−1

Increasing Marginal Returns

Without labor, nothing gets moved, so total product is 0. If one worker is hired, that worker must do all the driving, packing, crating, and moving. Some of the larger items, such as couches and major appliances, cannot easily be moved by a single worker. Still, in our example one worker moves 2 tons of furniture per day. When a second worker is hired, some division of labor occurs, and two together can move the big stuff more easily, so production more than doubles to 5 tons per day. The marginal product of the second worker is 3 tons per day. Adding a third worker allows for a finer division of labor. For example, one worker can pack fragile items while the other two do the heavy lifting. Total product is 9 tons per day, 4 tons more than with two workers. Because the marginal product increases, the firm experiences **increasing marginal returns** from labor as each of the first three workers is hired.

Diminishing Marginal Returns

A fourth worker's marginal product is less than that of a third worker. Hiring still more workers increases total product by successively smaller amounts, so the marginal product declines after three workers. With that fourth worker, the **law of diminishing marginal returns** takes hold. This law states that as more of a variable resource is combined with a given amount of another resource, marginal product eventually declines. *The law of diminishing marginal returns is the most important feature of production in the short run.* As more labor is hired, marginal product could turn negative, so total product would decline. For example, when Smoother Mover hires an eighth worker, workers start getting in each other's way, and workers take up valuable space in the moving van. As a result, an eighth worker actually subtracts from total output, yielding a negative marginal product. Likewise, a McDonald's outlet can hire only so many workers before congestion and confusion in the work area cut total product ("too many cooks spoil the broth").

Exhibit 3

The Total and Marginal Product of Labor

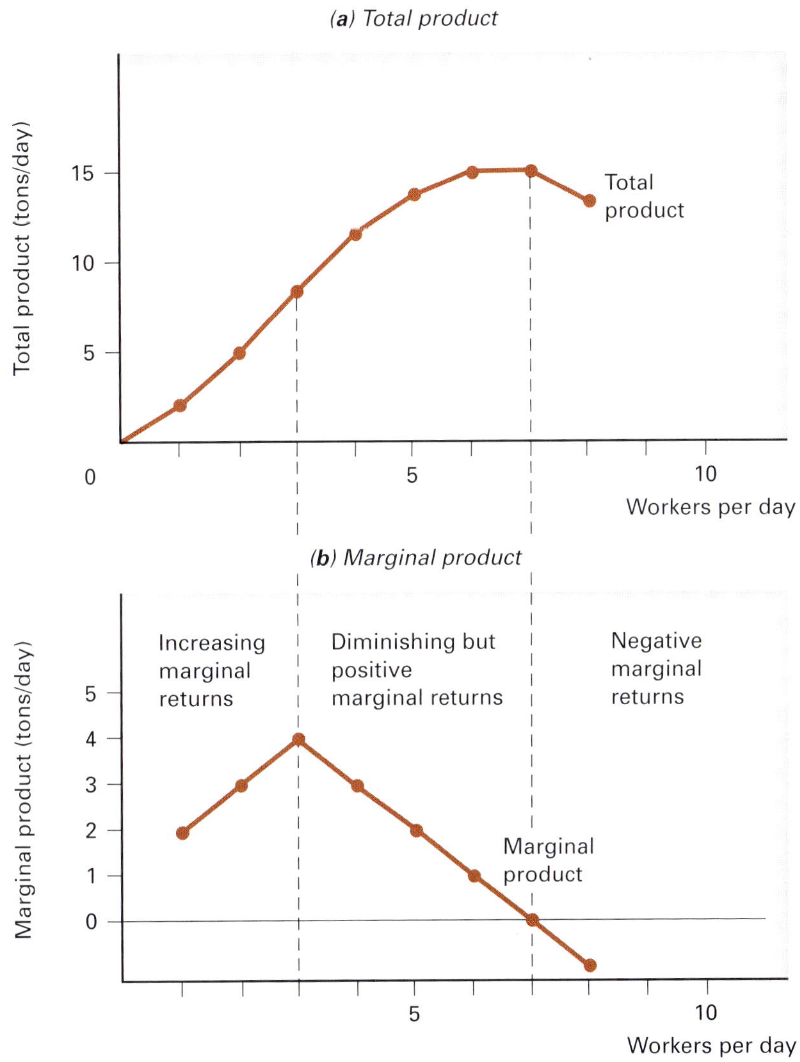

The Total and Marginal Product Curves

Exhibit 3 illustrates the relationship between total product and marginal product, using data from Exhibit 2. Note that because of increasing marginal returns, marginal product in panel (b) increases with each of the first three workers. With marginal product increasing, total product in panel (a) increases at an increasing rate (although this is hard to see in Exhibit 3). But once decreasing marginal returns set in, which begins with the fourth worker, marginal product declines. Total product continues to increase but at a decreasing rate. As long as marginal product is positive, total product increases. Where marginal product turns negative, total product starts to fall. Exhibit 3 summarizes all this by sorting production into three ranges: increasing marginal returns, diminishing but positive marginal returns, and negative marginal returns. These ranges for marginal product correspond with total product that increases at an increasing rate, increases at a decreasing rate, and declines.

LO3 Costs in the Short Run

Now that we have examined the relationship between the amount of resources used and the rate of output, let's consider how the cost of production varies as output varies. There are two kinds of costs in the short run: fixed and variable. Fixed cost pays for fixed resources and variable cost pays for variable resources. A firm must pay a **fixed cost** even if no output is produced. Even if Smoother Mover hires no labor and moves no furniture, it incurs property taxes, insurance, vehicle registration, plus any opportunity cost for warehouse and equipment. By definition, fixed cost is just that: fixed—it does not vary with output in the short run. Suppose the firm's *fixed cost* is $200 per day.

Variable cost, as the name implies, is the cost of variable resources—in this

fixed cost
any production cost that is independent of the firm's rate of output

variable cost
any production cost that changes as the rate of output changes

case, labor. When no labor is employed, output is zero, as is variable cost. As workers are hired, output increases, as does variable cost. Variable cost depends on the amount of labor employed and on the wage. If the wage is $100 per day, *variable cost* equals the number of workers hired times $100.

> "Total cost includes a normal profit but not an economic profit."

Total Cost and Marginal Cost in the Short Run

Exhibit 4 offers cost data for Smoother Mover. The table lists the cost of production associated with alternative rates of output. Column (1) shows possible rates of output in the short run, measured in tons of furniture moved per day.

Total Cost

Column (2) shows the fixed cost (FC) at each rate of output. Note that fixed cost, by definition, remains constant at $200 per day regardless of output. Column (3) shows the labor needed to produce each rate of output based on the productivity figures reported in the previous two exhibits. For example, moving 2 tons a day requires one worker, 5 tons requires two workers, and so on. Only the first six workers are listed because additional workers would add nothing to output and would not be hired. Column (4) lists variable cost (VC) per day, which equals $100 times the number of workers employed. For example, the variable cost of moving 9 tons of furniture per day is $300 because this output rate requires three workers. Column (5) lists the **total cost** (TC), the sum of fixed cost and variable cost: $TC = FC + VC$. As you can see, when output is zero, variable cost is zero, so total cost consists entirely of the fixed cost of $200. Incidentally, because total cost is the opportunity cost of all resources used by the firm, total cost includes a normal profit but not an economic profit. Think about that.

$$TC = FC + VC$$
$$MC = \Delta TC/\Delta q$$

total cost the sum of fixed cost and variable cost, or $TC = FC + VC$

marginal cost the change in total cost resulting from a one-unit change in output; the change in total cost divided by the change in output, or $MC = \Delta TC/\Delta q$

Marginal Cost

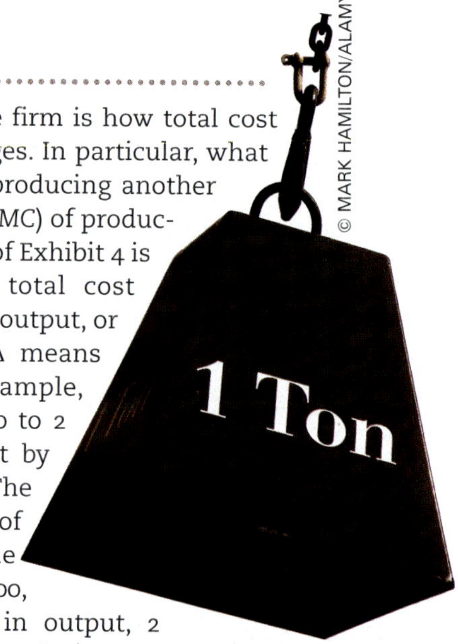

© MARK HAMILTON/ALAMY

Of special interest to the firm is how total cost changes as output changes. In particular, what is the marginal cost of producing another unit? The **marginal cost** (MC) of production listed in column (6) of Exhibit 4 is simply the change in total cost divided by the change in output, or $MC = \Delta TC/\Delta q$, where Δ means "change in." For example, increasing output from 0 to 2 tons increases total cost by $100 (= $300 − $200). The marginal cost of each of the first 2 tons is the change in total cost, $100, divided by the change in output, 2 tons, or $100/2, which equals $50. The marginal cost of each of the next 3 tons is $100/3, or $33.33.

Notice in column (6) that marginal cost first decreases, then increases. *Changes in marginal cost reflect changes in the marginal productivity of the variable resource.* Because of increasing marginal returns, each of the first three workers produces more than the previous one. This greater productivity

Exhibit 4

Short-Run Total and Marginal Cost Data for Smoother Mover

(1) Tons Moved per day (q)	(2) Fixed Cost (FC)	(3) Workers per day	(4) Variable Cost (VC)	(5) Total Cost ($TC = FC + VC$)	(6) Marginal Cost ($MC = \Delta TC/\Delta q$)
0	$200	0	$ 0	$200	—
2	200	1	100	300	$ 50.00
5	200	2	200	400	33.33
9	200	3	300	500	25.00
12	200	4	400	600	33.33
14	200	5	500	700	50.00
15	200	6	600	800	100.00

results in a falling marginal cost for the first 9 tons moved. Beginning with the fourth worker, the firm experiences diminishing marginal returns from labor, so the marginal cost of output increases. *When the firm experiences increasing marginal returns, the marginal cost of output falls; when the firm experiences diminishing marginal returns, the marginal cost of output increases.* Thus, marginal cost in Exhibit 4 first falls and then rises, because marginal returns from labor first increase and then diminish.

Total and Marginal Cost Curves

Exhibits 5a and 5b show cost curves for the data in Exhibit 4. Because fixed cost does not vary with output, the fixed cost curve is a horizontal line at the $200 level in panel (a). Variable cost is zero when

Exhibit 5a

Total and Marginal Cost Curves for Smoother Mover

(a) Total cost curve

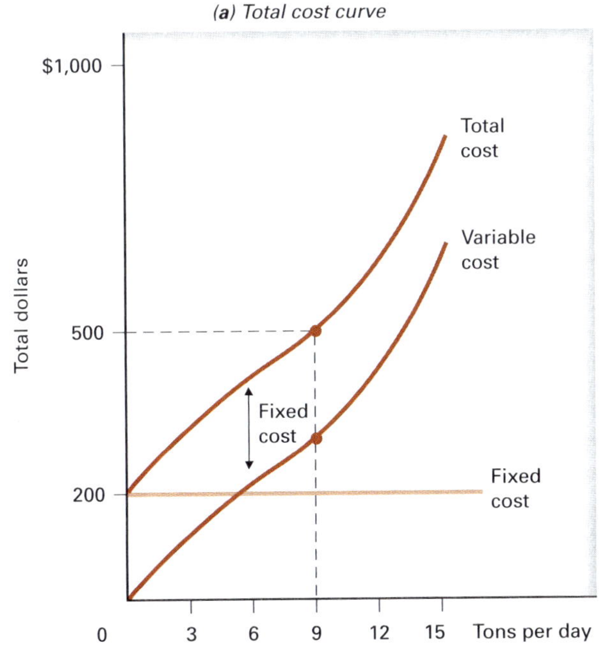

output is zero, so the *variable cost curve* starts from the origin. The *total cost curve* sums the fixed cost curve and the variable cost curve. Because a constant fixed cost is added to variable cost, the total cost curve is simply the variable cost curve shifted vertically by the fixed cost.

In panel (b) of Exhibit 5, marginal cost declines until the ninth unit of output and then increases, reflecting labor's increasing and then diminishing marginal returns. There is a relationship between the two panels because the change in total cost resulting from a one-unit change in production equals the marginal cost. With each successive unit of output, total cost increases by the marginal cost of that unit. Thus, *the slope of the total cost curve at each rate of output equals the marginal cost at that rate of output.* The total cost curve can be divided into two sections, based on what happens to marginal cost:

Exhibit 5b

Total and Marginal Cost Curves for Smoother Mover

(b) Marginal cost curve

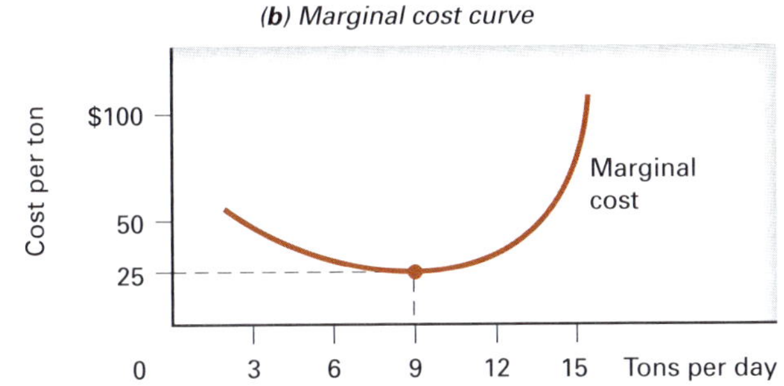

1. Because of increasing marginal returns from labor, marginal cost at first declines, so total cost initially increases by successively smaller amounts and the total cost curve becomes less steep.
2. Because of diminishing marginal returns from labor, marginal cost starts increasing after the ninth unit of output, so total cost increases by successively larger amounts and the total cost curve becomes steeper.

Keep in mind that economic analysis is marginal analysis. Marginal cost is the key to economic decisions. *Marginal cost indicates how much total cost increases if one more unit is produced or how much total cost drops if production declines by one unit.*

Average Cost in the Short Run

Although marginal cost is of most interest, the average cost per unit of output is also useful. We can distinguish between average variable cost and average total cost. These measures appear in columns (5) and (6) of Exhibit 6. Column (5) lists average variable cost, or AVC, which equals variable cost divided by output, or $AVC = VC/q$. The final column lists average total cost, or ATC, which equals total cost divided by output, or $ATC = TC/q$. Each measure of average cost first declines as output expands and then increases.

average variable cost variable cost divided by output, or $AVC = VC/q$

average total cost total cost divided by output, or $ATC = TC/q$; the sum of average fixed cost and average variable cost, or $ATC = AFC + AVC$

Exhibit 6

Short-Run Total, Marginal, and Average Cost Data for Smoother Mover

Marginal cost first falls then increases because of increasing then diminishing marginal returns from labor. As long a marginal cost is below average cost, average cost declines. Once marginal cost exceeds average cost, average cost increases. Columns (4), (5), and (6) show the relation between marginal and average costs.

(1) Tons Moved per day (q)	(2) Variable Cost (VC)	(3) Total Cost ($TC = FC + VC$)	(4) Marginal Cost ($MC = \Delta TC/\Delta q$)	(5) Average Variable Cost ($AVC = VC/q$)	(6) Average Total Cost ($ATC = TC/q$)
0	\$ 0	\$200	\$ 0	\$ —	∞
2	100	300	50.00	50.00	\$ 150.00
5	200	400	33.33	40.00	80.00
9	300	500	25.00	33.33	55.55
12	400	600	33.33	33.33	50.00
14	500	700	50.00	35.71	50.00
15	600	800	100.00	40.00	53.33

$AVC = VC/q$
$ATC = AFC + ATC$
(which means $ATC = TC/q$)

The Relationship Between Marginal Cost and Average Cost

To understand the relationship between marginal cost and average cost, let's begin with an example of college grades. Think about how your grades each term affect your grade point average (GPA). Suppose you do well your first term, starting your college career with a 3.4 (out of 4.0). Your grades for the second term drop to 2.8, reducing your GPA to 3.1. You slip again in the third term to a 2.2, lowering your GPA to 2.8. Your fourth-term grades improve a bit to 2.4, but your GPA continues to slide to 2.7. In the fifth term, your grades improve to 2.7, leaving your GPA unchanged at 2.7. And in the sixth term, you get 3.3, pulling your GPA up to 2.8. Notice that when your term grades are below your GPA, your GPA falls. Even when your term performance improves, your GPA does not improve until your term grades exceed your GPA. Your term grades first pull down your GPA and then eventually pull it up.

Let's now take a look at the relationship between marginal cost and average cost. In Exhibit 6, marginal cost has the same relationship to average cost as your term grades have to your GPA. You can observe this marginal-average relationship in columns (4) and (5). Because of increasing marginal returns from the first three workers, the marginal cost falls for the first 9 tons of furniture moved. Because marginal cost is below average cost, marginal cost pulls down average cost. Marginal cost and average cost are equal when output equals 12 tons, and marginal cost exceeds average cost when output exceeds 12 tons, so marginal cost pulls up average cost.

Exhibit 7 shows the same marginal cost curve first presented in Exhibit 5, along with average cost curves based on data in Exhibit 6. At low rates of output, marginal cost declines as output expands because of increasing marginal returns from labor. As long as marginal cost is below average cost, marginal cost pulls down average cost as output expands. At higher rates of output, marginal cost increases because of diminishing marginal returns from labor. Once marginal cost exceeds average cost, marginal cost pulls up average cost. The fact that marginal cost first pulls average cost down and then pulls it up explains why the average cost curves have a U shape. The shapes of the average variable cost curve and the

Exhibit 7

Average and Marginal Cost Curves for Smoother Mover

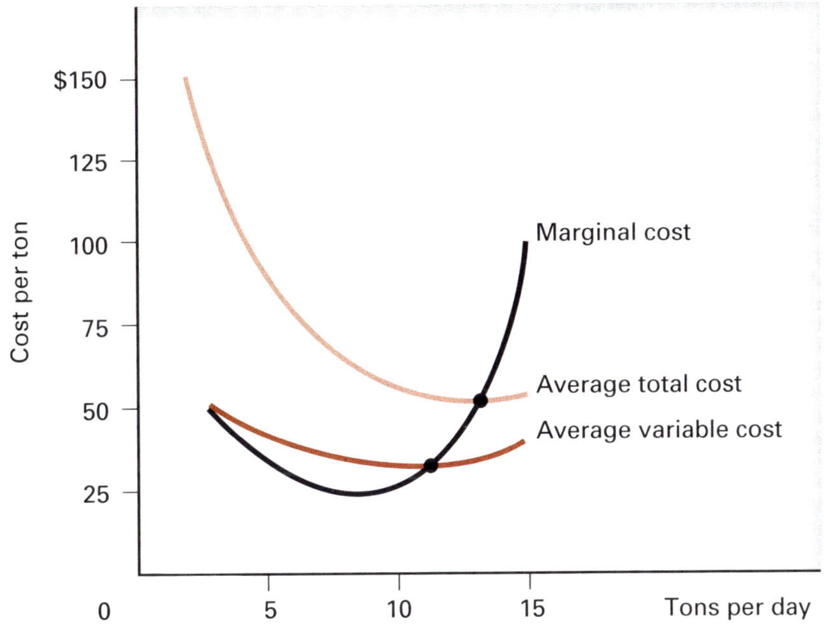

average total cost curve are determined by the shape of the marginal cost curve, so each is shaped by increasing then diminishing marginal returns.

Notice also that the rising marginal cost curve intersects both the average variable cost curve and the average total cost curve where these average curves reach their minimum. This occurs because the marginal pulls down the average where the marginal is below the average and pulls up the average where the marginal is above the average. One more thing: The distance between the average variable cost curve and the average total cost curve is *average fixed cost*, which gets smaller as the rate of output increases. (Why does average fixed cost get smaller?)

The law of diminishing marginal returns determines the shapes of short-run cost curves. When the marginal product of labor increases, the marginal cost of output falls. Once diminishing marginal returns take hold, the marginal cost of output rises. Thus, marginal cost first falls and then rises. And the marginal cost curve dictates the shapes of the average cost curves. When marginal cost is less than average cost, average cost declines. When marginal cost is above average cost, average cost increases. Got it? If not, please reread this paragraph.

> "The long run is not just a succession of short runs. The long run is best thought of as a planning horizon."

LO4 Costs in the Long Run

So far, the analysis has focused on how costs vary as the rate of output expands in the short run for a firm of a given size. In the long run, all inputs that are under the firm's control can be varied, so there is no fixed cost. The long run is not just a succession of short runs. The long run is best thought of as a *planning horizon*. In the long run, the choice of input combinations is flexible. But once the size of the plant has been selected and the concrete has been poured, the firm has fixed costs and is operating in the short run. Firms plan for the long run, but they produce in the short run. We turn now to long-run costs.

Economies of Scale

Like short-run average cost curves, the firm's long-run average cost curve is U-shaped. Recall that the shape of the short-run average total cost curve is determined primarily by increasing and diminishing marginal returns of the variable resource. A different principle shapes the long-run cost curve. If a firm experiences economies of scale, long-run average cost falls as output expands. Consider some sources of economies of scale. *A larger size often allows for larger, more specialized machines and greater specialization of labor.* For example, compare the household-size kitchen of a small restaurant with the kitchen at a McDonald's. At low rates of output, the smaller kitchen produces meals at a lower average cost than does McDonald's. But if production in the smaller kitchen increases beyond, say, 100 meals per day, a kitchen on the scale of McDonald's would make meals at a lower average cost. Thus, because of economies of scale, the long-run average cost for a restaurant may fall as size increases. As an example, the idea for McDonald's snack wrap started when a

economies of scale forces that reduce a firm's average cost as the scale of operation increases in the long run

© DANIEL BARRY/BLOOMBERG NEWS/LANDOV

franchisee suggested that the company find more uses for the strips of chicken served with dipping sauce. Selling more chicken allowed each restaurant to cook new batches more frequently, which meant customers got a fresher product.[1]

A larger scale of operation allows a firm to use larger, more efficient machines and to assign workers to more specialized tasks. Production techniques such as the assembly line can be introduced only if the rate of output is suffiently large. Typically, as the scale of firm increases, capital substitutes for labor and complex machines substitute for simpler machines.

Diseconomies of Scale

Often another force, called diseconomies of scale, may eventually take over as a firm expands its plant size, increasing long-run average cost as output expands. As the amount and variety of resources employed increase, so does the *task of coordinating all these inputs*. As the workforce grows, additional layers of management are needed to monitor production. In the thicket of bureaucracy that develops, communications may get mangled. Top executives have more difficulty keeping in touch with the factory floor because information is distorted as it moves up and down the chain of command. Indeed, in large organizations, rumors may become a primary source of information, reducing efficiency and increasing average cost. Note that *diseconomies of scale result from a larger firm size, whereas diminishing marginal returns result from using more variable resources in a firm of a given size.*

1. As reported by Janet Adamy, "For McDonald's It's a Wrap," *Wall Street Journal*, 30 January 2007.

diseconomies of scale
forces that may eventually increase a firm's average cost as the scale of operation increases in the long run

The Long-Run Average Cost Curve

Because of the special nature of technology in the industry, suppose a firm must choose from among three possible plant sizes: small, medium, and large. Exhibit 8 presents this simple case. The average cost curves for the three sizes are *SS'*, *MM'*, and *LL'*. Which size should the firm build to minimize average cost? The appropriate size, or scale, for the firm depends on how much output the firm wants to produce. For example, if q is the desired output, average cost is lowest with a small plant size. If the desired output is q', the medium plant size offers the lowest average cost. With the medium plant, the firm experiences economies of scale. With the large plant, the firm experiences diseconomies of scale.

More generally in Exhibit 8, for output less than q_a, average cost is lowest when the plant is small. For output between q_a and q_b, average cost is lowest for the

Exhibit 8

Short-Run Average Total Cost Curves Form the Long-Run Average Cost Curve, or Planning Curve

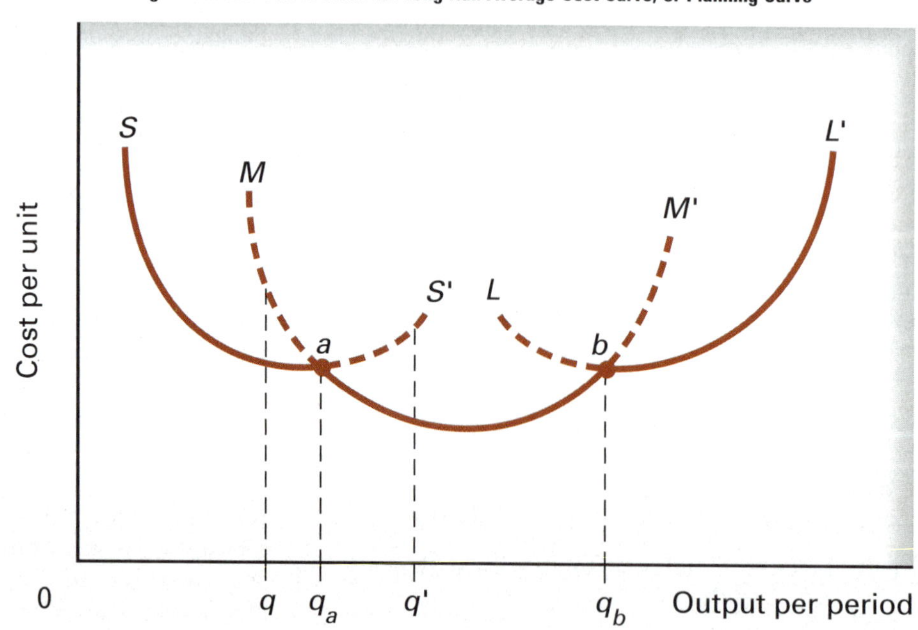

medium plant. And for output that exceeds q_b, average cost is lowest when the plant is large. The long-run average cost curve, or *LRAC* curve, sometimes called the firm's *planning curve*, connects portions of the three short-run average cost curves that are lowest for each output rate. In Exhibit 8, that curve consists of the line segments connecting *S*, *a*, *b*, and *L'*. So even though the firm experiences diseconomies of scale with the largest plant size, the large firm is the one to build if the firm needs to produce more than q_b.

Now suppose there are many possible plant sizes. Exhibit 9 presents a sample of short-run cost curves shown in pink. The long-run average cost curve, shown in red, is formed by connecting the points on the various short-run average cost curves that represent the lowest per-unit cost for each rate of output. Each of the short-run average cost curves is tangent to the long-run average cost curve, or *planning curve*. If we could display enough short-run cost curves, we would have a different plant size for each rate of output. *These points of tangency represent the least-cost way of producing each particular rate of output, given resource prices and the technology.* For example, the short-run average total cost curve ATC_I is tangent to the long-run average cost curve at point a, where $11 is the lowest average cost of producing output *q*. Note, however, that other output rates along ATC_I have a lower average cost. For example, the average cost of producing *q'* is only $10, as identified at point *b*. Point *b* depicts the lowest average cost along ATC_I. So, while the point of tangency reflects the least-cost way of producing a particular rate of output, that tangency point does not reflect the minimum average cost for this particular plant size.

If the firm decides to produce *q'*, which size plant should it choose to minimize the average cost of production? Output rate *q'* could be produced at point *b*, which represents the minimum average cost along ATC_I. But average cost is lower with a larger plant. With the plant size associated with ATC_2, the average cost of producing *q'* would be minimized at $9 per unit at point *c*. *Each point of tangency between a short-run average cost curve and the long-run average cost curve represents the least-cost way of producing that particular rate of output.*

In the long run, a firm can vary the inputs under its control. Some resources, however, are not under the firm's control, and the inability to vary them may contribute to diseconomies of scale.

It is possible for average cost to neither increase nor decrease with changes in firm size. If neither economies of scale nor diseconomies of scale are apparent over some range of output, a firm experiences constant long-run average cost. Perhaps economies and diseconomies of scale exist simultaneously in the firm but have offsetting effects. Exhibit 10 presents a firm's long-run average cost curve, or *LRAC* curve, which is divided into output segments reflecting economies of scale, constant long-run average costs, and diseconomies of scale. Output must reach quantity A for the firm to achieve the minimum efficient scale, which is the lowest rate of output at which long-run average cost is at a minimum.

Exhibit 9

Many Short-Run Average Total Cost Curves Form a Firm's Long-Run Average Cost Curve, or Planning Curve

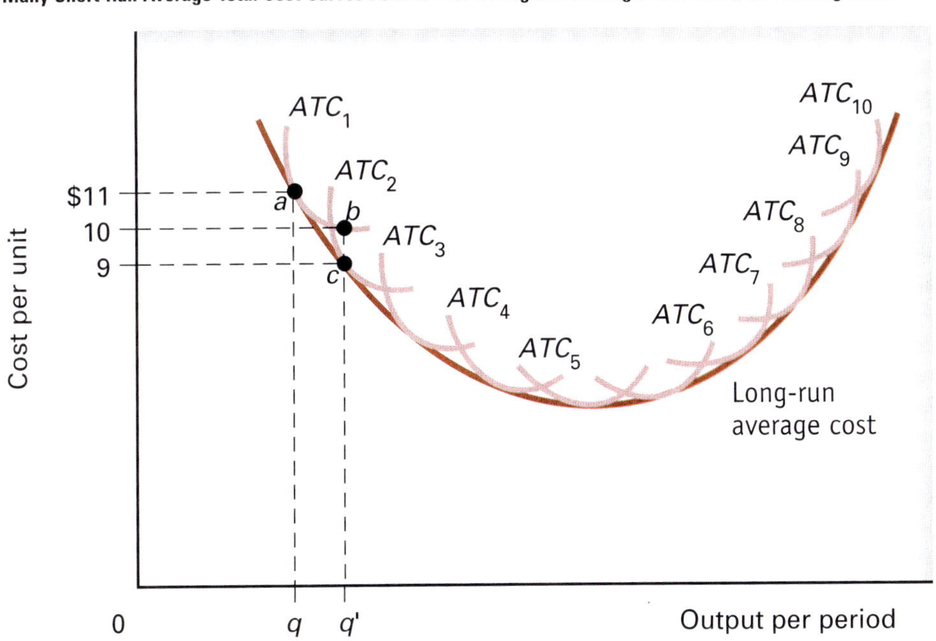

long-run average cost curve a curve that indicates the lowest average cost of production at each rate of output when the size, or scale, of the firm varies; also called the *planning curve*

constant long-run average cost a cost that occurs when, over some range of output, long-run average cost neither increases nor decreases with changes in firm size

minimum efficient scale the lowest rate of output at which a firm takes full advantage of economies of scale

{Economics at the Movies}

Movie theaters add screens to achieve economies of scale. Consider this: A theater with one screen needs three people to run it: one person to sell tickets, one to sell popcorn (concession stand sales account for well over half the profit at most theaters), and one to operate the movie projector. But if a second screen is added, the same staff of three can perform these tasks for both screens (an increase in productivity). Other factors that further increase **economies of scale**:

- construction costs per screen are reduced because only one lobby and one set of rest rooms are required;
- the theater may get a better deal from movie distributors;
- the theater can run bigger, more noticeable newspaper ads;
- and the theater can spread the cost over more films.

If adding more screens is good, then adding many more screens is better, right? But why stop at, say, 10 or even 20 screens per theater? Why not 30 screens, particularly in thickly populated areas with sufficient demand? The answer is simple: **diseconomies of scale**.

- Traffic congestion around the theater grows with the number of screens at that location. Public roads are a resource the theater cannot control.
- The supply of popular films may not be large enough to fill so many screens.
- Time itself is a resource that the firm cannot easily control. Only certain hours are popular with moviegoers. Scheduling becomes more difficult because the manager must space out starting and ending times to avoid the crush that occurs when too many customers come and go at the same time. No more "prime time" can be created. (To spread out the customers, theaters offer discounts for morning or early afternoon showings.)

Thus, theater owners lack control over such inputs as the public roads, the supply of films, and the amount of "prime time" in the day. These factors contribute to diseconomies of scale.

SOURCES: Shirley Won, "Cineplex Sees Past the Big Picture," *Globe and Mail,* 8 February 2007; Scott Bowles, "ShoWest: Movie Theaters Look to Keep the Streak Alive," *USA Today,* 12 March 2007; Sandy Cohen, "Movie Fans Prefer the Theater Experience," *Forbes,* 7 March 2007; and *Statistical Abstract of the United States: 2007,* U.S. Census Bureau, http://www.census.gov/compendia/statab/.

Economies and Diseconomies of Scale at the Firm Level

Our discussion so far has referred to a particular plant—a movie theater or a restaurant, for example. But a firm could also be a collection of plants, such as the hundreds of movie theaters in a chain or the thousands of McDonald's restaurants. More generally, we can distinguish between economies and diseconomies of scale at the *plant level*—that is, at a particular location—and at the *firm level,* where the firm is a collection of plants.

McDonald's experiences economies of scale at the plant, or restaurant, level because of its specialization of labor and machines, but it also benefits from economies of scale at the firm level. Experience gained from decades of selling hamburgers can be shared with new managers through centralized training programs. Costly research and efficient production techniques can also be shared across thousands of locations. For example, McDonald's took three years to decide on the exact temperature of the holding cabinets for its hamburger patties. What's more, the cost of advertising and promoting McDonald's through sponsorship of world events such as the Olympics can be spread across 30,000 restaurants in more than 100 countries.

Some diseconomies may also arise in such large-scale operations. The fact that the menu must be reasonably uniform across thousands of locations means that if customers in some parts of the country or the world do not like a product, it may not get on the menu, even though it might be popular elsewhere. Another problem with a uniform menu is that the ingredients must be available around the world and cannot be subject to droughts or sharp swings in price. For example, McDonald's considered adding a shrimp salad to the menu but decided not to when

Exhibit 10

A Firm's Long-Run Average Cost Curve

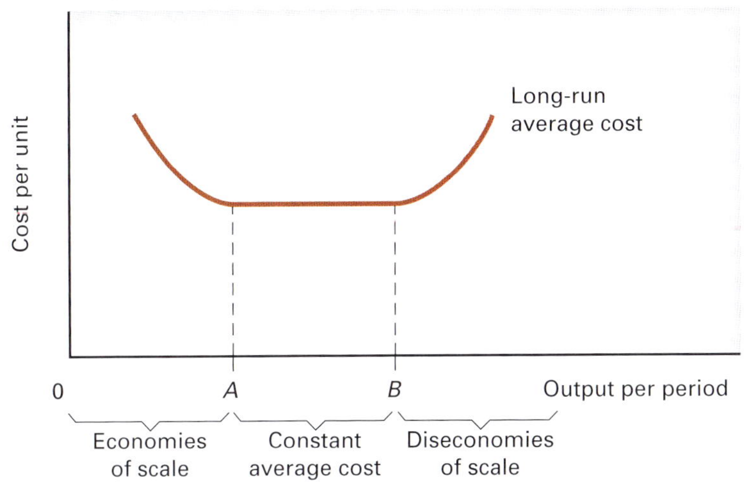

advised the move could deplete the nation's shrimp supply.[2]

Other large firms do what they can to reduce diseconomies of scale at the firm level. For example, IBM undertook a massive restructuring program to decentralize into six smaller decision-making groups. Some big corporations have even spun off parts of their operation to form new corporations. For example, Hewlett-Packard split off Agilent Technologies, AT&T created Lucent Technologies, and DaimlerChrysler, the international auto maker sold its Chrysler side of the business to a private equity group.

Final Word

By considering the relationship between production and cost, we have developed the foundation for a theory of firm behavior. Despite what may appear to be a tangle of short-run and long-run cost curves, *only two relationships between resources and output underlie all the curves. In the short run, it's increasing and diminishing returns from the variable resource. In the long run, it's economies and diseconomies of scale.* If you understand the sources of these two phenomena, you grasp the central ideas of the chapter. Our examination of production and cost in the short run and long run lays the groundwork for a firm's supply curve, to be covered in the next chapter.

Fast Facts

How many movie screens are there in the U.S.? The industry average is 6.2 screens per location, but some U.S. companies boast more than twice that.

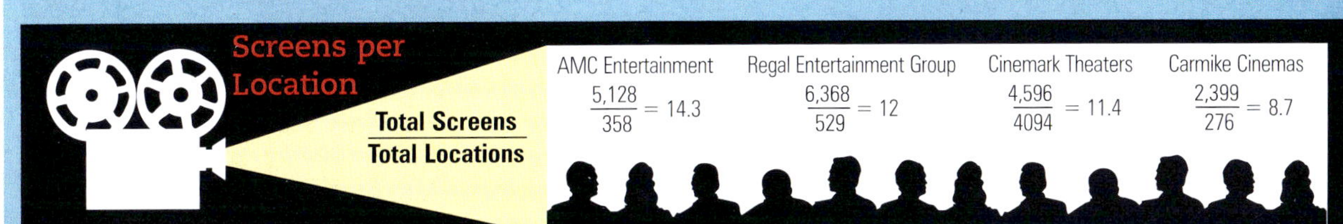

Other quick stats:

4.8 admissions per capita per year (so, on average, Americans go to the movies about 5 times a year)

1.45 billion tickets sold annually

$9.49 billion in annual box office sales

http://phx.corporate-ir.net/phoenix.zhtml?c=192773&p=irol-irhome
http://investor.regalcinemas.com/ReleaseDetail.cfm?ReleaseID=256638
http://www.carmike.com/secfilings/CARMIKE_CINEMAS_REPORTS_SECOND_QUARTER_2007_RESULTS.pdf
http://www.investor.amctheatres.com/downloads/AMCfactsheetOct07.pdf

2. Janet Adamy, "For McDonald's It's a Wrap," *Wall Street Journal,* 30 January 2007; Andrew Martin, "McDonald's Says Latest Results Are Strongest in 30 Years," *New York Times,* 25 January 2007; James L. Watson, ed., *Golden Arches East: McDonald's in East Asia* (Palo Alto, Calif.: Stanford University Press, 1998); and McDonald's Web site at http://www.mcdonalds.com/.

CHAPTER 8

Perfect Competition

Learning Outcomes

LO 1 Define a perfectly competitive market and explain its effect on demand LO 2 Explain how firms maximize profit in the short run LO 3 Identify ways firms minimize short-run losses LO 4 Explain how firms manage short-run supply LO 5 Describe how taking the long-run view affects economic factors
LO 6 Describe how different cost structures influence an industry's long-run supply curve
LO 7 Identify how concepts of efficiency are used to judge market performance

"What's so perfect about perfect competition?"

What do wheat and Google stock have in common? Why might a firm continue to operate even though it's losing money? Why do many firms fail to earn an economic profit? How can it be said that the more competitive the industry, the less individual firms compete with each other? What's the difference between making stuff right and making the right stuff? And what's so perfect about perfect competition? To answer these and other questions, we examine our first market structure—perfect competition.

What do you think?

The increasing demand for alternative fuel will create perfect competition among farmers.

Strongly Disagree *Strongly Agree*

1 2 3 4 5 6 7

The previous chapter developed cost curves for an individual firm in the short run and in the long run. In light of these costs, how much should a firm produce and what price should it charge? To discover the firm's profit-maximizing output and price, we revisit an old friend—demand. Demand and supply, together, guide the firm to maximum economic profit. In the next few chapters, we examine how firms respond to their economic environments in deciding what to supply, in what quantities, and at what price. We continue to assume that firms try to maximize profit.

LO1 An Introduction to Perfect Competition

Market structure describes the important features of a market, such as the number of suppliers (are there many or few?), the product's degree of uniformity (do firms in the market supply identical products, or are there differences across firms?), the ease of entry into the market (can new firms enter easily or is entry blocked?), and the forms of competition among firms (do firms compete based only on price, or do they also compete through advertising and product differences?). Incidentally, the word *compete* derives from Latin words *con*, which means "with," and *petere*, which means "to strive." A firm that competes strives with other firms to earn a profit by satisfying consumer wants. The various features will become clearer as we examine each market structure in the next few chapters. *A firm's decisions about how much to produce or what price to charge depend on the structure of the market.*

Topics discussed in Chapter 8 include:

- Market structure
- Price takers
- Marginal revenue
- Golden rule of profit maximization
- Loss minimization
- Short-run supply curve
- Long-run supply curve
- Competition and efficiency
- Producer surplus
- Gains from exchange

Before we get started, a few words about terminology. An *industry* consists of all firms that supply output to a particular *market*, such as the auto market, the shoe market, or the wheat market. The terms *industry* and *market* are used interchangeably throughout this chapter.

market structure important features of a market, such as the number of firms, product uniformity across firms, firm's ease of entry and exit, and forms of competition

Perfectly Competitive Market Structure

We begin with perfect competition, in some ways the most basic of market structures. A *perfectly competitive* market is characterized by (1) many buyers and sellers—so many that each buys or sells only a tiny fraction of the total amount in the market; (2) firms sell a commodity, which is a standardized product, such as a bushel of wheat, an ounce of gold, or a share of Google stock; such a product does not differ across suppliers; (3) buyers and sellers are fully informed about the price and availability of all resources and products; and (4) firms and resources are freely mobile—that is, over time they can easily enter or leave the industry without facing obstacles like patents, licenses, and high capital costs.

If these conditions exist in a market, an individual buyer or seller has no control over the price. Price is determined by market demand and supply. Once the market establishes the price, any individual firm is free to supply whatever quantity maximizes profit. *A perfectly competitive firm is so small relative to the market that the firm's supply decision does not affect the market price.* Examples of perfectly competitive markets include those for most agricultural products, such as wheat, corn, and livestock; markets for basic commodities, such as gold, silver, and copper; markets for widely traded stock, such as Google, Citibank, and General Electric; and markets for foreign exchange, such as yen, euros, and pesos. Again, there are so many buyers and sellers that the actions of any one cannot influence the market price. For example, about 150,000 farmers in the United States raise hogs, and tens of millions of U.S. households buy pork products. The model of perfect competition allows us to make a number of predictions that hold up pretty well when compared to the real world. Perfect competition is also an important benchmark for evaluating the efficiency of other types of markets. Let's look at demand under perfect competition.

Demand Under Perfect Competition

Suppose the market in question is the world market for wheat and the firm in question is a wheat farm. In the world market for wheat, there are hundreds of thousands of farms, so any one supplies only a tiny fraction of market output. For example, the thousands of wheat farmers in Kansas together produce less than 3 percent of the world's supply of wheat. In Exhibit 1, the market price of wheat of $5 per bushel is determined in panel (a) by the intersection of the market demand curve *D* and the market supply curve S. Once the market determines the price, any farmer can sell all he or she wants to at that market price.

Each farm is so small relative to the market that each has no impact on the market price. Because all

Exhibit 1

Market Equilibrium and a Firm's Demand Curve in Perfect Competition

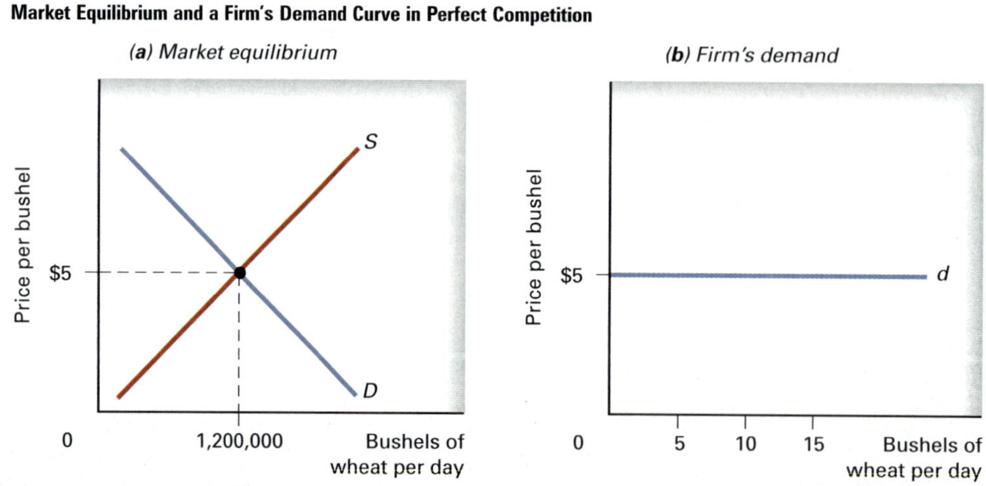

perfect competition
a market structure with many fully informed buyers and sellers of a standardized product and no obstacles to entry or exit of firms in the long run

commodity
a standardized product, a product that does not differ across producers, such as bushels of wheat or an ounce of gold

farmers produce an identical product—bushels of wheat, in this case—anyone who charges more than the market price sells no wheat. For example, a farmer charging $5.05 per bushel would find no buyers. Of course, any farmer is free to charge less than the market price, but why do that when all wheat can be sold at the market price? Farmers aren't stupid (if they are, they don't last long). *The demand curve facing an individual farmer is, therefore, a horizontal line drawn at the market price.* In our example, the demand curve facing an individual farmer, identified as *d* in panel (b), is drawn at the market price of $5 per bushel. Thus, each farmer faces a horizontal, or a *perfectly elastic,* demand curve for wheat. A perfectly competitive firm is called a price taker because that firm must "take," or accept, the market price—as in "take it or leave it."

It has been said, "In perfect competition there is no competition." Ironically, two neighboring wheat farmers in perfect competition are not really rivals. They both can sell all they want at the market price. The amount one sells has no effect on the market price or amount the other can sell.

Exhibit 2

Short-Run Cost and Revenue for a Perfectly Competitive Firm

(1) Bushels of Wheat per day (q)	(2) Marginal Revenue (Price) (p)	(3) Total Revenue ($TR = q \times p$)	(4) Total Cost (TC)	(5) Marginal Cost ($MC = \Delta TC/\Delta q$)	(6) Average Total Cost ($ATC = TC/q$)	(7) Economic Profit or Loss = $TR - TC$
0	—	$ 0	$15.00	—	—	−$15.00
1	$5	5	19.75	$4.75	$19.75	−14.75
2	5	10	23.50	3.75	11.75	−13.50
3	5	15	26.50	3.00	8.83	−11.50
4	5	20	29.00	2.50	7.25	−9.00
5	5	25	31.00	2.00	6.20	−6.00
6	5	30	32.50	1.50	5.42	−2.50
7	5	35	33.75	1.25	4.82	1.25
8	5	40	35.25	1.50	4.41	4.75
9	5	45	37.25	2.00	4.14	7.75
10	5	50	40.00	2.75	4.00	10.00
11	5	55	43.25	3.25	3.93	11.75
12	**5**	**60**	**48.00**	**4.75**	**4.00**	**12.00**
13	5	65	54.50	6.50	4.19	10.50
14	5	70	64.00	9.50	4.57	6.00
15	5	75	77.50	13.50	5.17	−2.50
16	5	80	96.00	18.50	6.00	−16.00

LO[2] Short-Run Profit Maximization

Each firm tries to maximize economic profit. Firms that ignore this strategy don't survive for long. Economic profit equals total revenue minus total cost, including both explicit and implicit costs. Implicit cost, remember, is the opportunity cost of resources owned by the firm and includes a normal profit. Economic profit is any profit above normal profit. How do firms maximize profit? You have already learned that the perfectly competitive firm has no control over price. What the firm does control is its rate of output—the quantity. The question each wheat farmer asks is this: *How much should I produce to earn the most profit?*

Total Revenue Minus Total Cost

The firm maximizes economic profit by finding the quantity at which total revenue exceeds total cost by the greatest amount. The firm's total revenue is simply its output times the price. Column (1) in Exhibit 2 shows the farmer's output possibilities measured in bushels of wheat per day. Column (2) shows the market price of $5 per bushel, a price that does not vary with the the farmer's output. Column (3) shows the farmer's total revenue, which is output times price, or column (1) times column (2). And column (4) shows the farmer's total cost of supplying each quantity shown. Total cost already includes a normal profit, so total cost includes all opportunity costs. Although the table does not distinguish between fixed and variable costs, fixed cost must equal $15 per day, because total cost is $15 when output is zero. The presence of fixed cost tells us that at least one resource is fixed, so the farm must be operating in the short run.

At each output rate, total revenue in column (3) minus total cost in column (4) yields the farmer's economic profit or economic loss in column (7). As you can see, total revenue exceeds total

price taker
a firm that faces a given market price and whose quantity supplied has no effect on that price; a perfectly competitive firm that decides to produce must accept, or "take," the market price

cost at rates of output between 7 and 14 bushels, so the farm earns an *economic profit* at those output rates. Economic profit is maximized at $12 per day when the farm produces 12 bushels of wheat per day (the $12 and 12 bushels combination here is just a coincidence).

These results are graphed in Exhibit 3a, which shows the total revenue and total cost curves. As output increases by 1 bushel, total revenue increases by $5, so the farm's total revenue curve is a straight line emanating from the origin, with a slope of 5. The short-run total cost curve has the backward S shape introduced in the previous chapter, showing increasing and then diminishing marginal returns from the variable resource. Total cost always increases as more output is produced.

Subtracting total cost from total revenue is one way to find the profit-maximizing output. For output less than 7 bushels and greater than 14 bushels, total cost exceeds total revenue. The economic loss is measured by the vertical distance between the two curves. Between 7 and 14 bushels per day, total revenue exceeds total cost. The economic profit, again, is measured by the distance between the two curves. *Profit is maximized at the rate of output where total revenue exceeds total cost by the greatest amount.* Profit is greatest when 12 bushels are produced per day.

Exhibit 3a

Short-Run Profit Maximization: Total Revenue Minus Total Cost

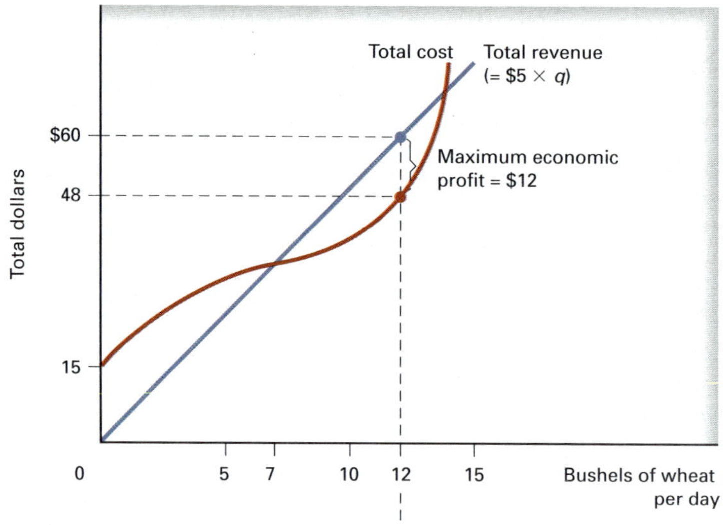

Marginal Revenue Equals Marginal Cost

Another way to find the profit-maximizing rate of output is to focus on marginal revenue and marginal cost. **Marginal revenue**, or ***MR***, is the change in total revenue from selling another unit of output. In perfect competition, each firm is a price taker, so selling one more unit increases total revenue by the market price. Thus, *in perfect competition, marginal revenue is the market price*—in this example, $5. Column (2) of Exhibit 2 presents the farm's marginal revenue for each bushel of wheat.

marginal revenue (*MR*)
the firm's change in total revenue from selling an additional unit; a perfectly competitive firm's marginal revenue is also the market price

golden rule of profit maximization
to maximize profit or minimize loss, a firm should produce the quantity at which marginal revenue equals marginal cost; this rule holds for all market structures

In the previous chapter, you learned that *marginal cost* is the change in total cost from producing another unit of output. Column (5) of Exhibit 2 shows the farm's marginal cost for each bushel of wheat. Marginal cost first declines, reflecting increasing marginal returns in the short run as more of the variable resource is employed. Marginal cost then increases, reflecting diminishing marginal returns from the variable resource.

The firm increases production as long as each additional unit adds more to total revenue than to total cost—that is, as long as marginal revenue exceeds marginal cost. Comparing columns (2) and (5) in Exhibit 2, we see that marginal revenue exceeds marginal cost for each of the first 12 bushels of wheat. The marginal cost of bushel 13, however, is $6.50, compared with its marginal revenue of $5. Therefore, producing bushel 13 would reduce economic profit by $1.50. The farmer, as a profit maximizer, limits output to 12 bushels per day. More generally, a firm expands output as long as marginal revenue exceeds marginal cost and stops expanding before marginal cost exceeds marginal revenue. A shorthand expression for this approach is the **golden rule of profit maximization**, which says that a profit-maximizing firm produces where *marginal revenue equals marginal cost.*

Economic Profit in the Short Run

Per-unit revenue and cost data from Exhibit 2 are graphed in Exhibit 3b. Because marginal revenue in perfect competition equals the market price, the marginal revenue curve is a horizontal line at the

market price of $5, which is also the perfectly competitive firm's demand curve. At any quantity measured along the demand curve, marginal revenue is the price. Because the perfectly competitive firm can sell any amount for the same price per unit, marginal revenue is also average revenue, or *AR*. Average revenue equals total revenue divided by quantity, or $AR = TR/q$. Regardless of the output rate, therefore, the following equality holds along a perfectly competitive firm's demand curve:

Market price = Marginal revenue = Average revenue

The marginal cost curve intersects the marginal revenue curve at point *e*, where output is about 12 bushels per day. At lower rates of output, marginal revenue exceeds marginal cost, so the farm could increase profit by expanding output. At higher rates of output, marginal cost exceeds marginal revenue, so the farm could increase profit by reducing output. Profit itself appears as the shaded rectangle. The height of that rectangle, *ae*, equals the price (or average revenue) of $5 minus the average total cost of $4. Price minus average total cost yields an average profit of $1 per bushel. Profit per day, $12, equals the average profit per bushel, $1 (denoted by *ae*), times the 12 bushels produced.

Note that with the total cost and total revenue curves, we measure economic profit by the vertical *distance* between the two curves, as shown in Exhibit 3a. But with the per-unit curves of Exhibit 3b, we measure economic profit by an *area*—that is, by multiplying the average profit of $1 per bushel times the 12 bushels sold.

Exhibit 3b

Short-Run Profit Maximization: Marginal Cost Equals Marginal Revenue

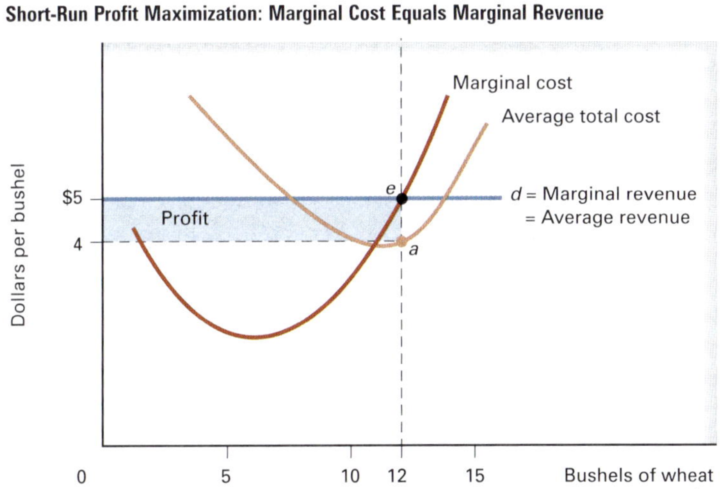

LO3 Minimizing Short-Run Losses

A firm in perfect competition has no control over the market price. Sometimes that price may be so low that a firm loses money no matter how much it produces. Such a firm can either continue to produce at a loss or temporarily shut down. But even if the firm shuts down, it cannot, *in the short run,* go out of business or produce something else. The short run is by definition a period too short to allow existing firms to leave the industry. In a sense, firms are stuck in their industry in the short run.

Fixed Cost and Minimizing Losses

When facing a loss, should a firm temporarily shut down? Intuition suggests the firm should. But keep in mind that the firm faces two types of cost in the short run: fixed cost, such as property taxes and fire insurance, which must be paid even if the firm produces nothing, and variable cost, such as labor, which depends on the amount produced. A firm that shuts down in the short run must still pay fixed cost. But, by producing, a firm's revenue may cover variable

average revenue total revenue divided by quantity, or $AR = TR/q$; in all market structures, average revenue equals the market price

Exhibit 4

Minimizing Short-Run Losses

(1) Bushels of Wheat per day (q)	(2) Marginal Revenue (Price) (p)	(3) Total Revenue ($TR = q \times p$)	(4) Total Cost (TC)	(5) Marginal Cost ($MC = \Delta TC/\Delta q$)	(6) Average Total Cost ($ATC = TC/q$)	(7) Average Variable Cost ($AVC = VC/q$)	(8) Economic Profit or Loss = $TR - TC$
0	—	$ 0	$15.00	—	—	—	−$15.00
1	$3	3	19.75	$4.75	$19.75	$4.75	−16.75
2	3	6	23.50	3.75	11.75	4.25	−17.50
3	3	9	26.50	3.00	8.83	3.83	−17.50
4	3	12	29.00	2.50	7.25	3.50	−17.00
5	3	15	31.00	2.00	6.20	3.20	−16.00
6	3	18	32.50	1.50	5.42	2.92	−14.50
7	3	21	33.75	1.25	4.82	2.68	−12.75
8	3	24	35.25	1.50	4.41	2.53	−11.25
9	3	27	37.25	2.00	4.14	2.47	−10.25
10	3	30	40.00	2.75	4.00	2.50	−10.00
11	3	33	43.25	3.25	3.93	2.57	−10.25
12	3	36	48.00	4.75	4.00	2.75	−12.00
13	3	39	54.50	6.50	4.19	3.04	−15.50
14	3	42	64.00	9.50	4.57	3.50	−22.00
15	3	45	77.50	13.50	5.17	4.17	−32.50
16	3	48	96.00	18.50	6.00	5.06	−48.00

cost and a portion of fixed cost. *A firm produces rather than shuts down if total revenue exceeds the variable cost of production.* After all, if total revenue exceeds variable cost, that excess covers at least a portion of fixed cost.

Let's look at the same cost data presented in Exhibit 2, but now suppose the market price of wheat is $3 a bushel, not $5. This new situation is presented in Exhibit 4. Because of the lower price, total cost in column (3) exceeds total revenue in column (4) at all output rates. Each quantity thus yields a loss, as indicated by column (8). If the firm produces nothing, it loses the fixed cost of $15 per day. But, by producing anywhere from 6 and 12 bushels, the firm can cut that loss. From column (8), you can see that the loss is minimized at $10 per day where 10 bushels are produced. Compared to shutting down, producing 10 bushels adds $5 more to total revenue than to total cost. That $5 pays some of the firm's fixed cost.

Panel (a) of Exhibit 5 presents the firm's total cost and total revenue curves for data in Exhibit 4. The total cost curve remains as in Exhibit 3. Because the price is $3, the total revenue curve now has a slope of 3, so it's flatter than at a price of $5. The total revenue curve now lies below the total cost curve for all output rates. The vertical distance between the two curves measures the loss at each output rate. If the farmer produces nothing, the loss is the fixed cost of $15 per day. The vertical distance between the two curves is minimized at 10 bushels, where the loss is $10 per day.

Marginal Revenue Equals Marginal Cost

We get the same result using marginal analysis. The per-unit data from Exhibit 4 are graphed in panel (b) of Exhibit 5. First we find the rate of output where marginal revenue equals marginal cost. Marginal revenue equals marginal cost at an output of 10 bushels per day. At that output, the market price of $3 exceeds the average variable cost of $2.50. Because price exceeds average variable cost, total revenue covers variable cost plus a portion of fixed cost. Specifically, $2.50 of the price pays the average variable cost, and the remaining $0.50 helps pay some of average fixed cost (average fixed cost equals average total cost of $4.00 minus average variable cost of $2.50). This still leaves a loss of $1 per bushel, which when multiplied by 10 bushels yields an economic loss of $10 per day, identified in panel (b) by the pink-shaded rectangle. *The bottom line is that the firm produces rather than shuts down if there is some rate of output where the price at least covers average variable cost.* (Why is the farmer in the short run better off operating at a loss rather than shutting down?)

Exhibit 5

Short-Run Loss Minimization

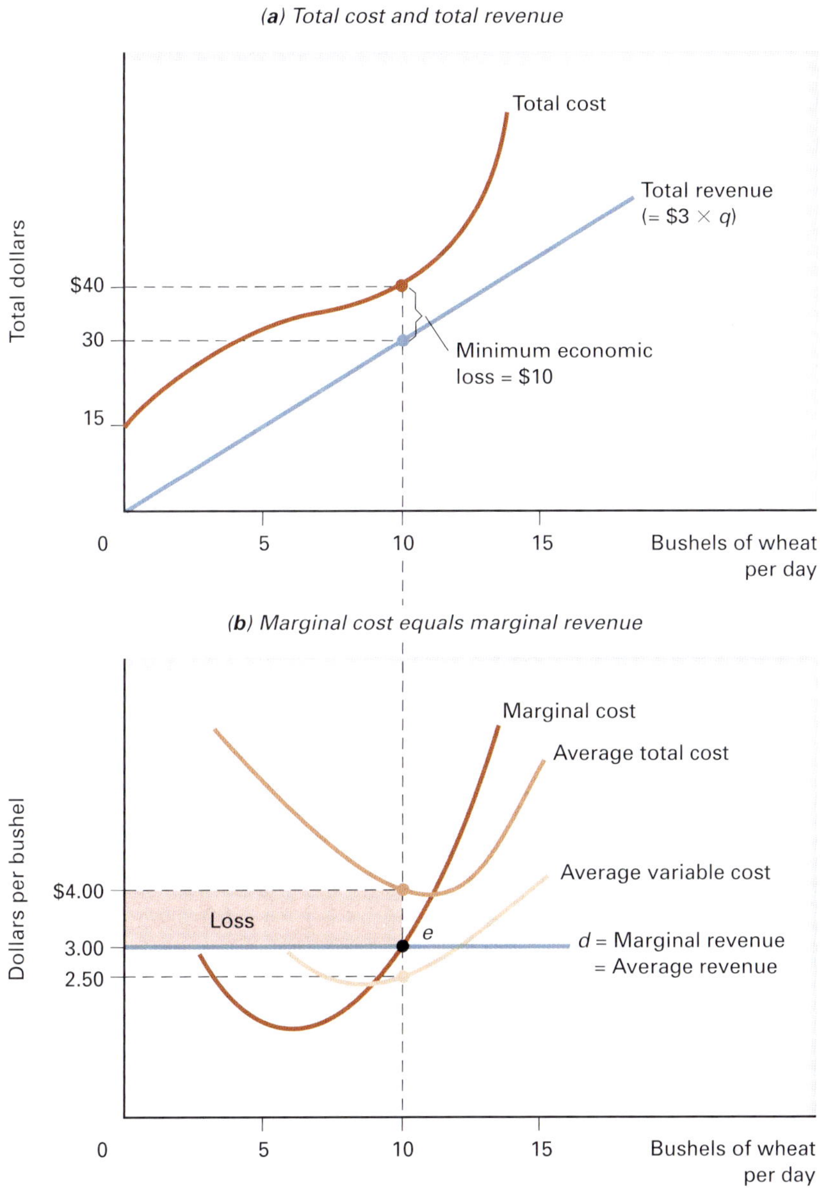

Shutting Down in the Short Run

If total revenue exceeds variable costs, the farmer produces in the short run. You may have read or heard of firms reporting a loss; most continue to operate. In fact, many new firms lose money during the first few years of operations. Still, they hang on because they hope to be profitable eventually (for example, the TV network UPN lost more than $1 billion during its first 11 years before merging with the WB network in 2006 to form the CW network). But *if the average variable cost exceeds the price at all rates of output, the firm shuts down*. After all, why produce if doing so only increases the loss? For example, a wheat price of $2 would fall below the average variable cost at all rates of output. Faced with such a low price, a farmer would shut down and lose just fixed cost, rather than produce and lose both fixed cost plus some variable cost.

From column (7) of Exhibit 4, you can also see that the lowest price at which the farmer would just cover average variable cost is $2.47 per bushel, when output is 9 bushels per day. At this price, the farmer is indifferent between producing and shutting down, because either way the loss is the $15 per day in fixed cost. Any price above $2.47 allows the farmer, by producing, to also cover some fixed cost.

Shutting down is not the same as going out of business. In the short run, even a firm that shuts down keeps productive capacity intact—paying rent, insurance, and property taxes, keeping water pipes from freezing in the winter, and so on. For example, Dairy Queen shuts down for the winter in cooler climates, a business serving a college community may close during term breaks, and an auto plant responds to slack sales by temporarily halting production. These firms do not escape fixed cost by shutting down. When demand picks up again, production resumes. If the market outlook remains grim, the firm may decide to leave the market, but that's a long-run decision. The short run is defined as a period during which some costs are fixed, so a firm cannot escape those costs in the short run, no matter what it does. *Fixed cost is sunk cost in the short run, whether the firm produces or shuts down.*

Likewise, a concert promoter may cancel an event because of poor ticket sales even though the hall has been rented. And a movie producer may pull the plug on a nearly completed film that looks like a turkey to avoid sinking millions more on advertising.

>>Dairy bar closing in winter = shutting down in the short run.

Concert promoters and movie producers want to cut their losses. They don't want to throw more good money after bad.

LO4 The Firm and Industry Short-Run Supply Curves

If average variable cost exceeds price at all output rates, the firm shuts down in the short run. But if price exceeds average variable cost, the firm produces the quantity at which marginal revenue equals marginal cost. As we'll see, a firm changes the rate of output if the market price changes.

The Short-Run Firm Supply Curve

The relationship between price and quantity is summarized in Exhibit 6. Points 1, 2, 3, 4, and 5 identify where the marginal cost curve intersects alternative marginal revenue, or demand, curves. At a price as low as p_1, the firm shuts down rather than produce at point 1 because that price is below average variable cost. So the loss-minimizing output rate at price p_1 is zero, as identified by q_1. At price p_2, the price just equals average variable cost, so the firm is indifferent between producing q_2 and shutting down; either way the firm loses fixed cost. Point 2 is called the *shutdown point*. If the price is p_3, the firm produces q_3 to minimize its loss (see if you can identify that loss in the diagram). At p_4, the firm produces q_4 to earn a normal profit, because price equals average total cost. Point 4 is called the *break-even point*. If the price rises to p_5, the firm earns short-run economic profit by producing q_5 (see if you can identify that economic profit in the diagram).

At prices below p_2, the firm shuts down in the short run. The quantity supplied when the price is p_2 or higher is determined by the intersection of the firm's marginal cost curve and its demand, or marginal revenue, curve. As long as the price covers average variable cost, the firm supplies the quantity at which the upward-sloping marginal cost curve intersects the marginal revenue, or demand, curve. Thus, that portion of the firm's marginal cost curve that intersects and rises above the lowest point on its average variable cost curve becomes the **short-run firm supply curve**. In Exhibit 6, the short-run supply curve is the upward-sloping portion of the marginal cost curve, beginning at point 2, the shutdown point. The

short-run firm supply curve
a curve that shows how much a firm supplies at each price in the short run; in perfect competition, that portion of a firm's marginal cost curve that intersects and rises above the low point on its average variable cost curve

Exhibit 6

Summary of Short-Run Output Decisions

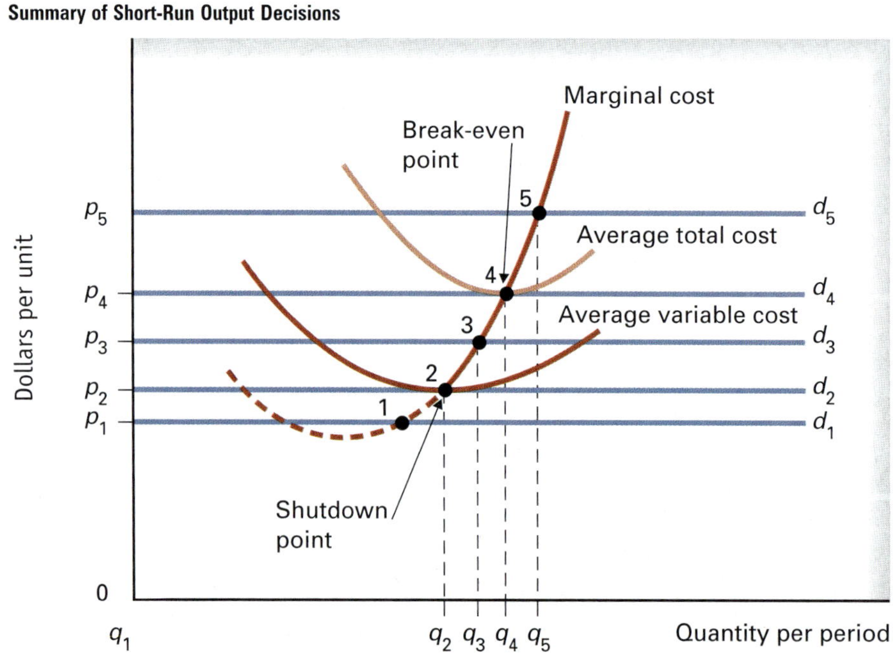

solid portion of the short-run supply curve indicates the quantity the firm offers for sale at each price.

The Short-Run Industry Supply Curve

Exhibit 7 presents examples of how supply curves for three firms with identical marginal cost curves can be summed *horizontally* to form the short-run industry supply curve (in perfect competition, there are many more firms). The **short-run industry supply curve** is the horizontal sum of all firms' short-run supply curves. At a price below *p*, no output is supplied. At price *p*, each of the three firms supplies 10 units, so the market supplies 30 units. At *p*′, which is above *p*, each firm supplies 20 units, so the market supplies 60 units.

Firm Supply and Market Equilibrium

Exhibit 8 shows the relationship between the short-run profit-maximizing output of the individual firm and market equilibrium price and quantity. Suppose there are 100,000 identical wheat farmers in this industry. Their individual supply curves (represented by the portions of the marginal cost curve at or rising above the average variable cost) are summed horizontally to yield the market, or industry, supply curve. The market supply curve appears in panel (b), where it intersects the market demand curve to determine the market price of $5 per bushel. At that price, each farmer supplies 12 bushels per day, as shown in panel (a), which sums to 1,200,000 bushels for the market, as shown in panel (b). Each farmer in the short run earns an economic profit of $12 per day, represented by the shaded rectangle in panel (a).

In summary: *A perfectly competitive firm supplies the short-run quantity that maximizes profit or minimizes loss. When confronting a loss, a firm either produces an output that minimizes that loss or shuts down temporarily.* Given the conditions for perfect competition, the market converges toward the equilibrium price and quantity.

But how is that equilibrium actually reached? In the real world, markets operate based on customs and conventions, which vary across markets. For example, the rules acceptable on the New York Stock Exchange are not the same as those followed in the market for fresh fish.

One mechanism for reaching equilibrium is an auction. In a *Dutch auction*, prices start high and work down. Dutch auctions are more common when selling multiple lots of similar, though not identical, items, such as flowers in Amsterdam, tobacco in Canada, and fish in seaports around the world. Because there is some difference among the products for sale in a given market—for example, some flower lots are in better condition than others—this is not quite perfect competition because perfectly competitive markets sell identical products.

More common than the Dutch auction is the *English open outcry auction*, where bidding starts at a low price and moves up until only one buyer remains. Products sold this way include stocks, bonds, wine, art (think

short-run industry supply curve
a curve that indicates the quantity supplied by the industry at each price in the short run; in perfect competition, the horizontal sum of each firm's short-run supply curve

Exhibit 7

Aggregating Individual Supply to Form Market Supply

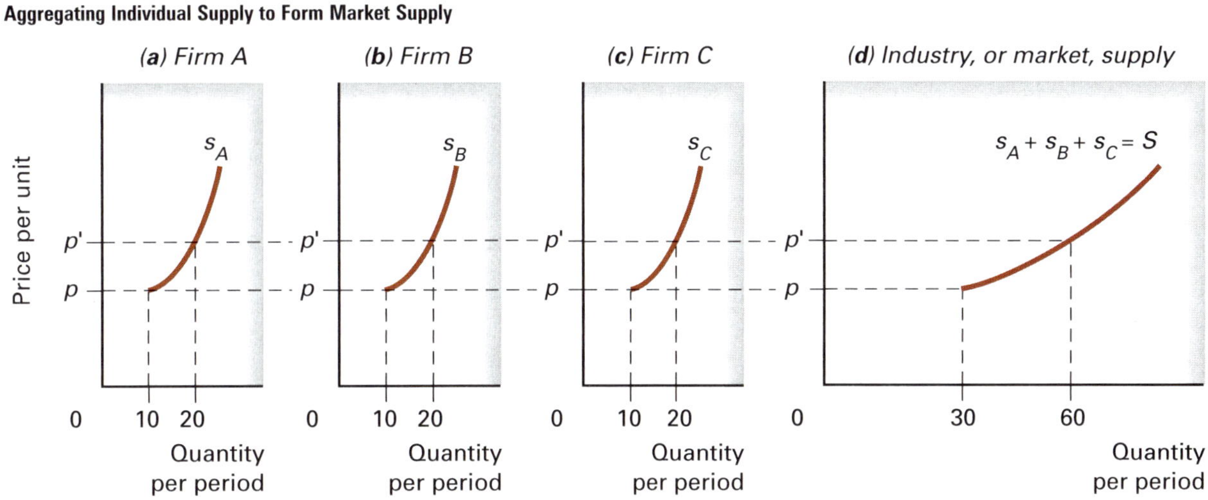

Exhibit 8

Short-Run Profit Maximization and Market Equilibrium

The firm's demand curve also equals its marginal revenue curve.

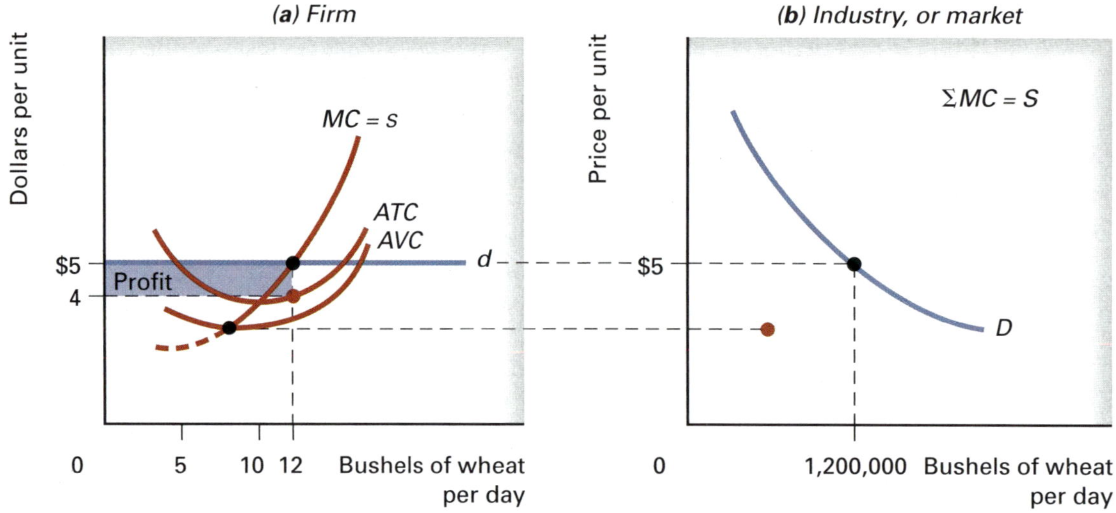

Sotheby's and Christie's), antiques, and livestock. On markets, such as the Chicago Board of Trade, prices for commodities such as wheat, gold, and coffee beans are continuously determined in the trading pits using variations of an open outcry auction.

The birth of the Internet has breathed new life into auctions. Web sites such as eBay, uBid, Yahoo!, and hundreds more hold online auctions for old maps, used computers, wine, airline tickets, antiques, military memorabilia, comic books, paperweights—you name it. As you can probably guess, eBay is the largest online auction and offers over 2,000 categories in a forum that mimics a live auction. Internet auctions allow specialized sellers to reach a world of customers. A listing on eBay, for example, could reach millions of people in more than 100 countries.

LO5 Perfect Competition in the Long Run

In the short run, the quantity of variable resources can change, but other resources, which mostly determine firm size, are fixed. In the long run, however, a firm has time to enter and leave and to adjust its size—that is, to adjust its *scale* of operations. In the long run, there is no distinction between fixed and variable cost because all resources under the firm's control are variable.

Short-run economic profit, in the long run, encourages new firms to enter the market and may prompt existing firms to get bigger. Economic profit attracts resources from industries where firms are losing money or earning only a normal profit. This expansion in the number and size of firms shifts the industry supply curve rightward in the long run, driving down the price. New firms continue to enter a profitable industry

{ Going, Going, Sold! }

Five days a week, in a huge building 10 miles outside Amsterdam, some 2,500 buyers gather to participate in Flower Auction Aalsmeer, the largest auction of its kind in the world. Over 20 million flowers and 2 million potted plants from 8,000 growers around the globe are auctioned off each day in the world's largest roofed building, spread across the equivalent of 100 football fields. Flowers are grouped and auctioned off by type—long-stemmed roses, tulips, and so on. Hundreds of buyers sit in theater settings with their fingers on buttons. Once the flowers are presented, a clock-like instrument starts ticking off descending prices until a buyer pushes a button. The winning bidder gets to choose how many and which items to take. The clock starts again until another buyer stops it, and so on, until all flowers are sold. Buyers can also bid online from remote locations. Auctions occur rapidly—on average a transaction takes place every 4 seconds.

SOURCES: Constance Cacey, "Petal Pushers," *New York Times,* 25 February 2007; Keith Bradsher, "Bouquet of Flowers May Have Note: 'Made In China,'" *New York Times,* 25 September 2007; and Lynette Evans, "Following the Flowers," *San Francisco Chronicle,* 3 March 2007.

and existing firms continue to expand as long as economic profit is greater than zero. Entry and expansion stop only when the resulting increase in supply drives down the price enough to erase economic profit. In the case of wheat farming, economic profit attracts new wheat farmers and may encourage existing wheat farmers to expand. *Short-run economic profit attracts new entrants in the long run and may cause existing firms to expand. Market supply thereby increases, driving down the market price until economic profit disappears.*

On the other hand, a short-run loss, in the long run, forces some firms to leave the industry or to reduce their scale of operation. In the long run, departures and reductions in scale shift the market supply curve to the left, thereby increasing the market price until remaining firms just break even—that is, earn a normal profit.

Zero Economic Profit in the Long Run

In the long run, firms in perfect competition earn just a normal profit, which means zero economic profit. Exhibit 9 shows a firm and the market in long-run equilibrium. Market supply adjusts as firms enter or leave or change their size. *This long-run adjustment continues until the market supply curve intersects the market demand curve at a price that corresponds to the lowest point on each firm's long-run average cost curve, or LRAC curve.* Because the long run is a period during which all resources under a firm's control are variable, a *firm in the long run is forced by competition to adjust its scale until average cost is minimized.* A firm that fails to minimize average cost will not survive in the long run. At point *e* in panel (a) of Exhibit 9, the firm is in equilibrium, producing *q* units per period and earning just a normal profit. At point *e*, price, marginal cost, short-run average total cost, and long-run average cost are all equal. No firm in the market has any reason to change its output, and no outside firm has any incentive to enter this industry, because firms in this market are earning normal, but not economic, profit. In other words, resources employed in this industry earn their opportunity costs.

The Long-Run Adjustment to a Change in Demand

To explore the long-run adjustment process, let's consider how a firm and an industry respond to an increase in market demand. Suppose that the costs facing each firm do not depend on the number of firms in the industry (an assumption explained soon).

Effects of an Increase in Demand

Exhibit 10 shows a perfectly competitive firm and industry in long-run equilibrium, with the market supply curve intersecting the market demand curve at point *a* in panel (b). The market-clearing price is *p*, and the market quantity is Q_a. The firm, shown in panel (a), supplies *q* units at that market price, earning a normal profit. This representative firm produces where price, or marginal revenue, equals marginal cost, short-run average total cost, and long-run average cost. (Remember, a normal profit is included in the firm's average cost curves.)

Exhibit 9

Long-Run Equilibrium for a Firm and the Industry

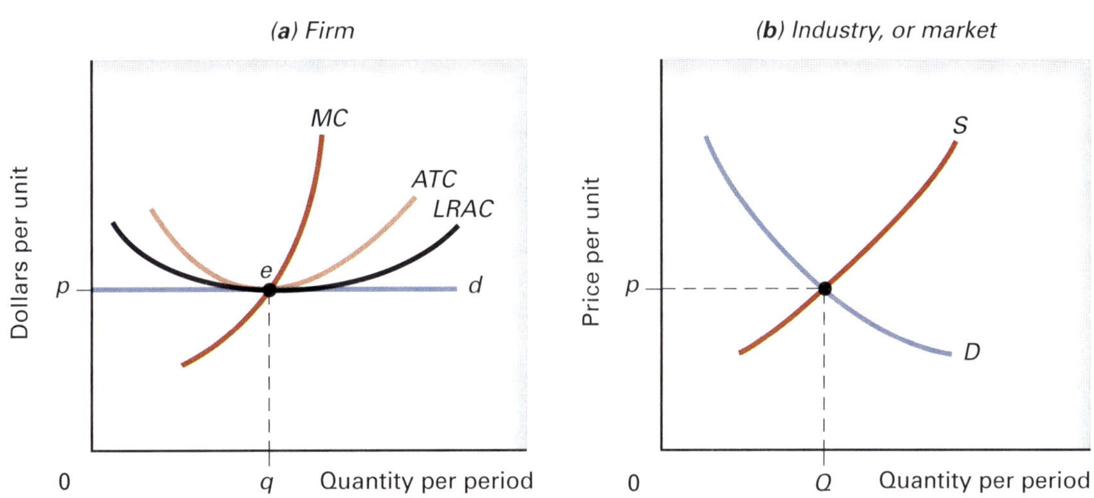

Exhibit 10

Long-Run Adjustment to an Increase in Demand

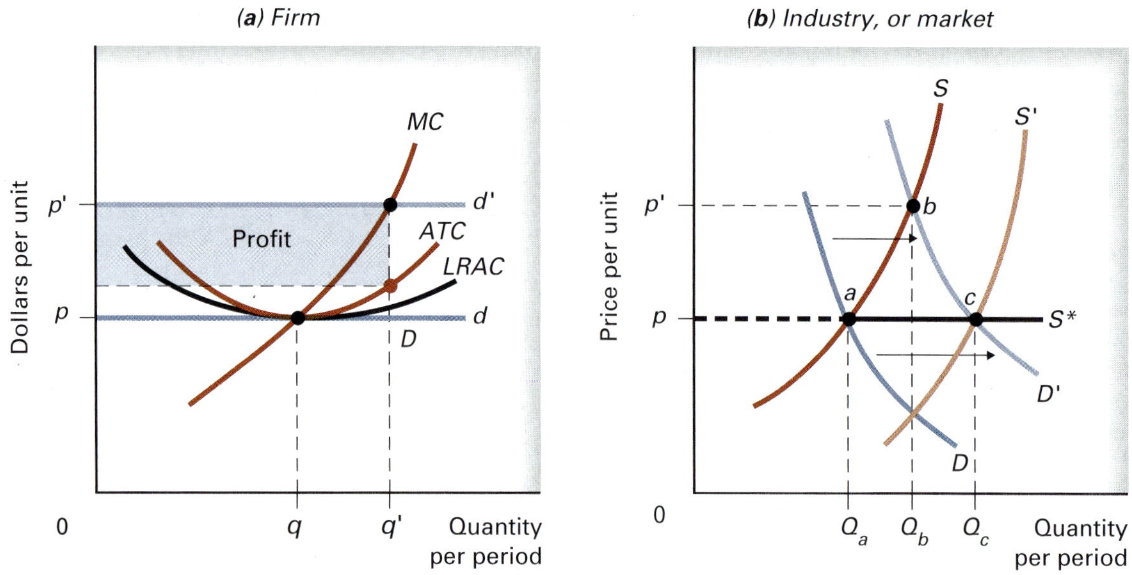

Now suppose market demand increases, as reflected by a rightward shift of the market demand curve, from *D* to *D*′ in panel (b), causing the market price to increase in the short run to *p*′. Each firm responds to the higher price by expanding output along its short-run supply, or marginal cost, curve until its quantity supplied increases to *q*′, shown in panel (a) of Exhibit 10. At that output, the firm's marginal cost curve intersects the new marginal revenue curve, which is also the firm's new demand curve, *d*′. Note that in the short run, each firm now earns an economic profit, shown by the shaded rectangle. Because all firms increase their quantity supplied, industry quantity supplied increases to Q_b in panel (b).

Economic profit attracts new firms in the long run. Their entry shifts the market supply curve to the right, which forces the price down. Firms continue to enter as long as they can earn economic profit. The market supply curve eventually shifts out to *S*′, where it intersects *D*′ at point *c*, returning the price to its initial equilibrium level, *p*. The firm's demand curve drops from *d*′ back down to d. As a result, each firm reduces output from *q*′ back to *q*, and once again, each earns just a normal profit. Notice that although industry output increases from Q_a to Q_c, each firm's output returns to *q*. In this example, the additional output comes entirely from new firms drawn to the industry rather than from more output by existing firms (existing firms don't expand in this example because an increase in scale would increase average cost).

New firms are attracted to the industry by short-run economic profits resulting from the increase in demand. But this new entry shifts out market supply, forcing the market price down until economic profit disappears. In panel (b) of Exhibit 10, the short-run adjustment to increased demand is from point *a* to point *b*; the long-run adjustment moves to point c.

Effects of a Decrease in Demand

Next, let's trace the effects of a decrease of demand on the long-run market adjustment process. The initial long-run equilibrium in Exhibit 11 is the same as in Exhibit 10. Market demand and supply curves intersect at point a in panel (b), yielding an equilibrium price *p* and an equilibrium quantity Q_a. As shown in panel (a), each firm earns a normal profit in the long run by producing output rate *q*, where price, or marginal revenue, equals marginal cost, short-run average total cost, and long-run average cost.

Now suppose that market demand declines, as reflected in panel (b) by a leftward shift of the market demand curve, from *D* back to *D*″. In the short run, this forces the market price down to *p*″. With the market price lower, the demand curve facing each individual firm drops from *d* to *d*″. Each firm responds in the short run by reducing quantity supplied to *q*″ where the firm's marginal cost equals its now-lower marginal revenue, or price. Market output falls to Q_f. Because the lower market price is below average total cost, each firm operates at a loss. This loss is shown by the shaded rectangle in Exhibit 11. Note, the price must still be above the average variable cost, because the firm's short-run supply curve,

Exhibit 11

Long-Run Adjustment to a Decrease in Demand

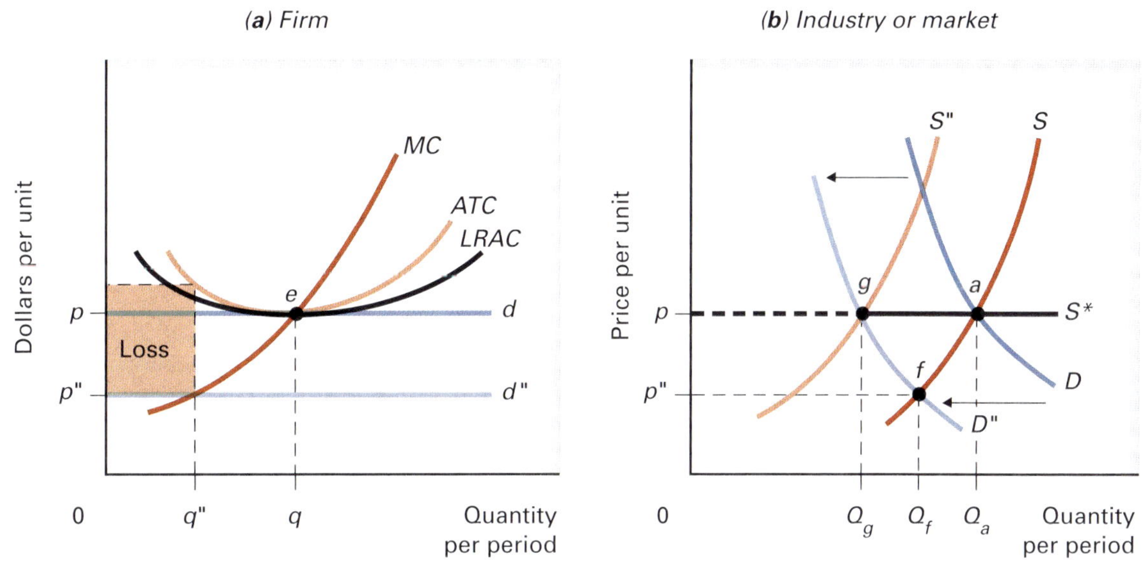

MC, is defined as that portion of the firm's marginal cost curve at or above its average variable cost curve.

A short-run loss forces some firms out of business in the long run. As firms exit, market supply decreases, or shifts leftward, so the price increases along market demand curve *D″*. Firms continue to leave until the market supply curve decreases to *S″*, where it intersects *D″* at point *g*. Market output has fallen to Q_g, and price has returned to *p*. With the price back up to *p*, remaining firms once again earn a normal profit. When the dust settles, each remaining firm produces *q*, the initial equilibrium quantity. But, because some firms have left the industry, market output has fallen from Q_a to Q_g. Again, note that the adjustment involves the departure of firms from the industry rather than a reduction in the scale of firms, as a reduction in scale would increase each firm's long-run average cost.

LO6 The Long-Run Industry Supply Curve

Thus far, we have looked at a perfectly competitive firm's and industry's response to changes in demand, distinguishing between a short-run adjustment and a long-run adjustment. In the short run, a firm alters quantity supplied by moving up or down its marginal cost curves (that portion at or above average variable cost) until marginal cost equals marginal revenue, or price. If the price is too low to cover minimum average variable cost, a firm shuts down in the short run. An economic profit (or loss), in the long run, prompts some firms to enter (or leave) the industry or to adjust firm size until remaining firms earn a normal profit.

In Exhibits 10 and 11, we began with an initial long-run equilibrium point; then, in response to a shift of the demand curve, we found a new long-run equilibrium point. In each case, the price changed in the short run but not in the long run. Market output increased in Exhibit 10 and decreased in Exhibit 11. Connecting these long-run equilibrium points yields the *long-run industry supply curve,* labeled S^* in Exhibits 10 and 11. The long-run industry supply curve shows the relationship between price and quantity supplied once firms fully adjust to any short-term economic profit or loss resulting from a change in demand.

Constant-Cost Industries

The industry we have examined thus far is called constant-cost industry because each firm's long-run average cost curve does not shift up or down as industry output changes. In a constant-cost industry, each firm's per-unit costs are independent of the number of firms in the industry. The *long-run supply curve for a constant-cost industry is horizontal,* as is depicted by S^* in Exhibits 10 and 11. A constant-cost industry uses such a small portion of the resources available that increasing industry output does not bid up resource prices. For example, output in the pencil industry can expand without bidding up the prices of wood, graphite, and rubber, because the pencil industry uses such a tiny share of the market supply of these resources.

Increasing-Cost Industries

The firms in some industries encounter higher average costs as industry output expands in the long run. Firms in these increasing-cost industries find that expanding output bids up the prices of some resources or otherwise increases per-unit production costs, and these higher costs shift up each firm's cost curves. For example, a market expansion of oil production could bid up the prices of drilling rigs and the wages of petroleum engineers and geologists, raising per-unit production costs for each oil producer. Likewise, more housing construction could bid up what developers must pay for land, carpenters, lumber, and other building materials.

long-run industry supply curve
a curve that shows the relationship between price and quantity supplied by the industry once firms adjust in the long run to any change in market demand

constant-cost industry
an industry in which each firm's long-run average cost curve does not shift up or down as industry output changes

increasing-cost industries
industries in which firms encounter higher average costs as industry output expands in the long run

To illustrate the equilibrium adjustment process for an increasing-cost industry, we begin again in long-run equilibrium in Exhibit 12, with the firm shown in panel (a) and the industry in panel (b). Market demand curve D in panel (b) intersects short-run market supply curve S at equilibrium point a to yield market price p_a and market quantity Q_a. When the price is p_a, the demand (and marginal revenue) curve facing each firm is d_a as shown in panel (a). The firm supplies quantity q, where the price, or marginal revenue, equals marginal cost. At that output, average total cost equals the price, so the firm earns no economic profit in this long-run equilibrium.

Suppose an increase in the demand for this product shifts the market demand curve in panel (b) to the right from D to D'. The new demand curve intersects the short-run market supply curve S at point b, yielding the market price p_b and market quantity Q_b. With this price increase, each firm's demand curve shifts from d_a up to d_b. The firm's new short-run equilibrium occurs at point b in panel (a), where the marginal cost curve intersects the new demand curve, which is also the marginal revenue curve. Each firm produces output q_b. In the short run, each firm earns an economic profit equal to q_b times the difference between price p_b and the average total cost at that rate of output. So far, the sequence of events is the same as for a constant-cost industry.

Economic profit attracts new firms. Because this is an increasing-cost industry, new entrants drive up the cost of production, raising each firm's marginal and average cost curves. In panel (a) of Exhibit 12, *MC* and *ATC* shift up to *MC′* and *ATC′*. (We assume for simplicity that new average cost curves are vertical shifts of the initial ones, so the minimum efficient plant size remains the same.)

The entry of new firms also shifts the short-run industry supply curve to the right in panel (b), thus reducing the market price along D'. *New firms enter the industry until the combination of a higher production cost and a lower price squeezes economic profit to zero.* This long-run equilibrium occurs when the entry of new firms has shifted the short-run industry supply curve out to S', which lowers the price until it equals the minimum on each firm's new average total cost curve. The market price does not fall back to the initial equilibrium level because each firm's average total cost curve has increased, or shifted up, with the expansion of industry output. The intersection of the new short-run market supply curve, S', and the new market demand curve, D', determines the new long-run market equilibrium point, c. Points a and c in panel (b) are on the *upward-sloping* long-run supply curve S^* for this increasing-cost industry.

In constant-cost industries, each firm's costs depend simply on the scale of its plant and its rate of output. For increasing-cost industries, each firm's costs depend also on the number of firms in the market. By bidding up the price of resources, long-run expansion in an increasing-cost industry increases each firm's marginal and aver-

Exhibit 12

An Increasing-Cost Industry

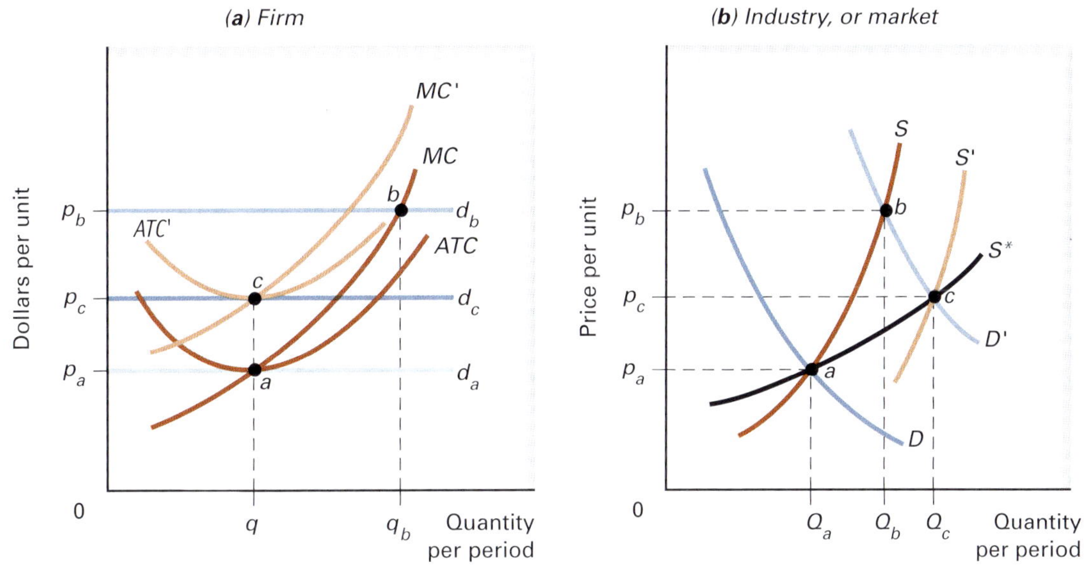

age costs. The long-run supply curve slopes upward, like S* in Exhibit 12.

To review: Firms in perfect competition can earn an economic profit, a normal profit, or an economic loss in the short run. But in the long run, the entry or exit of firms and adjustments in each firm's size force economic profit to zero. Competitive firms earn only a normal profit in the long run. This is true whether the industry in question experiences constant costs or increasing costs in the long run. Notice that, regardless of the nature of costs in the industry, the market supply curve is more elastic in the long run than in the short run. In the long run, firms can adjust all their resources, so they are better able to respond to changes in price. One final point: Firms in an industry could theoretically experience a lower average cost as output expands in the long run, resulting in a downward-sloping long-run industry supply curve. But such an outcome is considered so rare that we do not examine it.

As mentioned at the outset, perfect competition provides a useful benchmark for evaluating the efficiency of markets. Let's examine the qualities of perfect competition that make it so useful.

LO7 Perfect Competition and Efficiency

How does perfect competition stack up as an efficient user of resources? Two concepts of efficiency are used to judge market performance. The first, called *productive efficiency,* refers to producing output at the least possible cost. The second, called *allocative efficiency,* refers to producing the output that consumers value the most. *Perfect competition guarantees both productive efficiency and allocative efficiency in the long run.*

Productive Efficiency: Making Stuff Right

Productive efficiency occurs when the firm produces at the minimum point on its long-run average cost curve, so the market price equals the minimum average cost. The entry and exit of firms and any adjustment in the scale of each firm ensure that each firm produces at the minimum of its long-run average cost curve. Firms that do not reach minimum long-run average cost must, to avoid continued losses, either adjust their scale or leave the industry. Thus, *perfect competition produces output at minimum average cost in the long run.*

Allocative Efficiency: Making the Right Stuff

Just because *production* occurs at the least possible cost does not mean that the *allocation* of resources is the most efficient one possible.

productive efficiency the condition that exists when production uses the least-cost combination of inputs; minimum average cost in the long run

<< The Egokast belt buckle is a 3.5″ LCD screen that displays videos you make and load into the buckle. Retailing for $289, the Egokast boasts a crystal clear picture (i.e., it's made right). If the unique buckle becomes popular, then marketers will have launched a successful new product (i.e., it's the right stuff).

COURTESY OF SHAW KAAKE, EGOKAST

The products may not be the ones consumers want. This situation is akin to that of the airline pilot who informs passengers that there's good news and bad news: "The good news is that we're making record time. The bad news is that we're lost!" Likewise, firms may be producing goods efficiently but producing the wrong goods—that is, making stuff right but making the wrong stuff.

Allocative efficiency occurs when firms produce the output that consumers value most. How do we know that perfect competition guarantees allocative efficiency? The answer lies with the market demand and supply curves. Recall that the demand curve reflects the marginal value that consumers attach to each unit of the good, so the market price is the amount people are willing and able to pay for the final unit they consume. We also know that, in both the short run and the long run, the equilibrium price in perfect competition equals the marginal cost of supplying the last unit sold. Marginal cost measures the opportunity cost of resources employed to produce that last unit sold. Thus, the demand and supply curves intersect at the combination of price and quantity at which *the marginal value, or the marginal benefit, that consumers attach to the final unit purchased, just equals the opportunity cost of the resources employed to produce that unit.*

allocative efficiency
the condition that exists when firms produce the output most preferred by consumers; marginal benefit equals marginal cost

As long as marginal benefit equals marginal cost, the last unit produced is valued by consumers as much as, or more than, any other good those resources could have produced. There is no way to reallocate resources to increase the total value of all output in the economy. Thus, there is no way to reallocate resources to increase the total utility or total benefit consumers reap from production. *When the marginal benefit that consumers derive from a good equals the marginal cost of producing that good, that market is said to be allocatively efficient.*

Marginal benefit = Marginal cost

Firms not only are making stuff right, they are making the right stuff.

What's So Perfect About Perfect Competition?

If the marginal cost of supplying a good just equals the marginal benefit to consumers, does this mean that market exchange confers no net benefits to participants? No. Market exchange usually benefits both consumers and producers. Recall that consumers enjoy a surplus from market exchange because the most they would be willing and able to pay for each unit of the good exceeds what they actually do pay. Exhibit 13 depicts a market in short-run equilibrium. The *consumer surplus* in this exhibit is represented by blue shading, which is the area below the demand curve but above the market-clearing price of $10.

Producers in the short run also usually derive a net benefit, or a surplus, from market exchange, because what they receive for their output exceeds the least they would accept to supply that quantity in the short run. Recall that the short-run market supply curve is the sum of each firm's marginal cost curve at or above its minimum average variable cost. Point *m* in Exhibit 13 is the minimum point on the market supply curve; it indicates that at a price of $5, quantity supplied is 100,000 units. At prices below $5, quantity supplied would be zero because firms could not cover average variable cost. A price of $5 just covers average variable cost.

If the market price rises to $6, quantity supplied increases until marginal cost equals $6. Market output increases from 100,000 to 120,000 units. Total rev-

Exhibit 13

Consumer Surplus and Producer Surplus for a Competitive Market

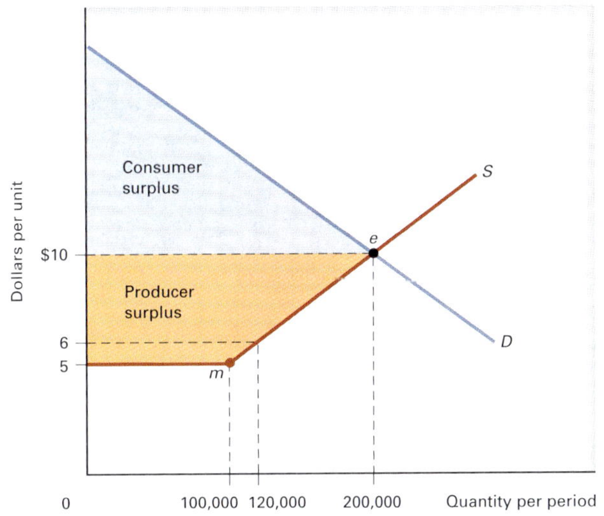

enue in this market increases from $500,000 to $720,000. Part of the higher revenue covers the higher marginal cost of production. But the rest provides a bonus to producers. After all, suppliers would have offered the first 100,000 units for only $5 each. If the price is $6, firms get to supply these 100,000 units for $6 each. Producer surplus at a price of $6 is the gold-shaded area between the prices of $5 and $6.

In the short run, producer surplus equals the total revenue producers are paid minus their variable cost of production. In Exhibit 13, the market-clearing price is $10 per unit, and producer surplus is depicted by the gold-shaded area between a price of $5 and the market price of $10. The most the firm can lose in the short run is to shut down. Any price that exceeds average variable cost, which is $5 in this example, reduces that short-run loss, and generates a producer surplus. A high enough price could yield economic profit.

The combination of consumer surplus and producer surplus shows the gains from voluntary exchange. Productive and allocative efficiency in the short run occurs at equilibrium point *e*, which also is the combination of price and quantity that maximizes the sum of consumer surplus and producer surplus, thus maximizing social welfare. Social welfare is the overall well-being of people in the economy. Even though marginal cost equals marginal benefit for the final unit produced and consumed, both producers and consumers usually derive a surplus, or a bonus, from market exchange.

Final Word

Let's review the assumptions of a perfectly competitive market and see how each relates to ideas developed in this chapter. *First,* there are many buyers and many sellers. This assumption ensures that no individual buyer or seller can influence the price (although recent experiments show that competition occurs even with few buyers and sellers). *Second,* firms produce a commodity, or a uniform product. If consumers could distinguish between the products of different suppliers, they might prefer one firm's product even at a higher price, so different producers could sell at different prices. In that case, not every firm would be a price taker—that is, each firm's demand curve would no longer be horizontal. *Third,* market participants have full information about all prices and all production processes. Otherwise, some producers could charge more than the market price, and some uninformed consumers would pay that higher price. Also, through ignorance, some firms might select outdated technology or fail to recognize opportunities for short-run economic profits. *Fourth,* all resources are mobile in the long run, with nothing preventing firms in the long run from entering profitable markets or leaving losing markets. If firms couldn't enter profitable markets, then some firms already in that market could earn economic profit in the long run.

Perfect competition is not the most common market structure observed in the real world. The markets for agricultural products, commodities such as gold and silver, widely traded stocks, and foreign exchange come close to being perfect. But even if not a single such industry could be found, the model would still be useful for analyzing market behavior. As you will see in the next two chapters, perfect competition provides a valuable benchmark for evaluating the efficiency of other market structures.

producer surplus
a bonus for producers in the short run; the amount by which total revenue from production exceeds variable cost

social welfare
the overall well-being of people in the economy; maximized when the marginal cost of production equals the marginal benefit to consumers

CHAPTER

Monopoly 9

Learning Outcomes

LO 1 List and describe barriers to market entry

LO 2 Explain sources of revenue for the monopolist

LO 3 Describe a firm's costs and its opportunities for profit maximization

LO 4 Explain monopoly and the allocation of resources

LO 5 Describe the problems that interfere with estimating the deadweight loss of a monopoly

LO 6 Describe conditions that create price discrimination

"Why aren't most markets monopolized? And why don't monopolies charge the highest possible price?"

How can a firm monopolize a market? Why aren't most markets monopolized? Why don't most monopolies last? Why don't monopolies charge the highest possible price? How has China monopolized the world market for pandas? Why is the head of Starbucks worried about his coffee becoming a commodity? Do student and senior discounts come from corporate generosity? Why are there so many air fares for the same flight? These and other questions are answered in this chapter, which looks at our second market structure—monopoly.

What do you think?

Monopolies can benefit society and business.

Strongly Disagree					Strongly Agree	
1	2	3	4	5	6	7

Monopoly is from the Greek, meaning "one seller." In some parts of the United States, monopolists sell electricity, cable TV service, and local phone service. Monopolists also sell postage stamps, hot dogs at sports arenas, some patented products, some prescription drugs, and other goods and services with no close substitutes. You have probably heard about the evils of monopoly. You may have even played the board game *Monopoly* on a rainy day. Now we sort out fact from fiction.

Like perfect competition, pure monopoly is not as common as other market structures. But by understanding monopoly, you grow more familiar with market structures that lie between the extremes of perfect competition and pure monopoly. This chapter examines the sources of monopoly power, how a monopolist maximizes profit, differences between monopoly and perfect competition, and why a monopolist sometimes charges different prices for the same product.

Topics discussed in Chapter 9 include:

- Barriers to entry
- Price elasticity and marginal revenue
- Profit maximization and loss minimization
- Monopoly and resource allocation
- Welfare cost of monopoly
- Price discrimination
- The monopolist's dream

LO[1] Barriers to Entry

As noted in Chapter 3, a *monopoly* is the sole supplier of a product with no close substitutes. Why do some markets come to be dominated by a single supplier? A monopolized market is characterized by **barriers to entry**, which are restrictions on the entry of new firms into an industry. Because of barriers,

barrier to entry any impediment that prevents new firms from entering an industry and competing on an equal basis with existing firms new firms cannot profitably enter that market. Let's examine three types of entry barriers: legal restrictions, economies of scale, and control of an essential resource.

Governments commonly grant

Legal Restrictions

One way to prevent new firms from entering a market is to make entry illegal. Patents, licenses, and other legal restrictions imposed by the government provide some producers with legal protection against competition.

Patents and Invention Incentives

In the United States, a **patent** awards an inventor the exclusive right to produce a good or service for 20 years from the date the patent is filed with the patent office. Originally enacted in 1790, patent laws encourage inventors to invest the time and money required to discover and develop new products and processes. If others could simply copy successful products, inventors would be less interested in incurring the up-front costs of invention. Abraham Lincoln said that "the patent system added the fuel of interest to the fire of genius." Patents also provide the stimulus to turn inventions into marketable products, a process called **innovation**.

Licenses and Other Entry Restrictions

Governments often confer monopoly status by awarding an individual firm the exclusive right to supply a particular good or service. Federal licenses give certain firms the right to broadcast radio and TV signals. State licenses authorize suppliers of medical care, haircuts, and legal advice. A license may not grant a monopoly, but it does block entry and often gives firms the power to charge prices above the competitive level. Thus, a license can serve as an effective barrier against new competitors. Governments also grant monopoly rights to sell hot dogs at civic auditoriums, collect garbage, provide bus and taxi service, and supply other services ranging from electricity to cable TV. Sometimes the government itself may claim that right by outlawing competitors. For example, many state governments sell liquor and lottery tickets, and the U.S. Postal Service has the exclusive right to deliver first-class mail to your mailbox.

patent
a legal barrier to entry that grants the holder the exclusive right to sell a product for 20 years from the date the patent application is filed

innovation
the process of turning an invention into a marketable product

Economies of Scale

A monopoly sometimes occurs naturally when a firm experiences *economies of scale*, as reflected by the downward-sloping, long-run average cost curve shown in Exhibit 1. In such instances, a single firm can supply market demand at a lower average cost per unit than could two or more firms, each producing less. Put another way, market demand is not great enough to allow more than one firm to achieve sufficient economies of scale. Thus, a single firm emerges from the competitive process as the only supplier in the market. For example, even though electricity *production* has become more competitive, electricity *transmission* still exhibits economies of scale. Once wires are strung through-

Exhibit 1

Economies of Scale as a Barrier to Entry

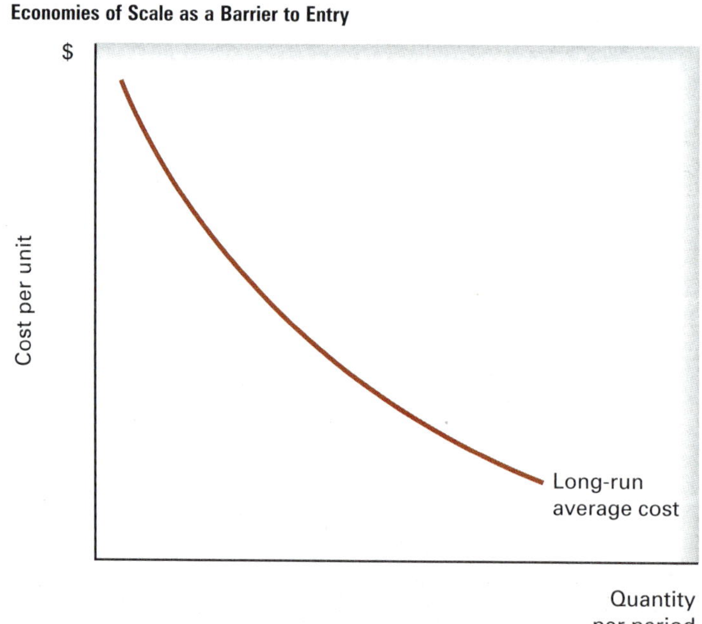

monopoly status to utility companies.

out a community, the cost of linking an additional household to the power grid is relatively small. Consequently, the average cost of delivering electricity declines as more and more households are wired into an existing system.

A monopoly that emerges from the nature of costs is called a *natural monopoly*, to distinguish it from the artificial monopolies created by government patents, licenses, and other legal barriers to entry. A new entrant cannot sell enough to experience the economies of scale achieved by an established natural monopolist. Therefore, market entry is naturally blocked. A later chapter gets into the regulation of natural monopolies.

Control of Essential Resources

Sometimes the source of monopoly power is a firm's control over some resource critical to production. Here are some examples: Alcoa was the sole U.S. maker of aluminum from the late 19th century until World War II. Its monopoly power initially stemmed from production patents that expired in 1909, but for the next three decades, it controlled the supply of bauxite, the key raw material. Professional sports leagues try to block the formation of competing leagues by signing the best athletes to long-term contracts and by seeking the exclusive use of sports stadiums and arenas. China is a monopoly supplier of pandas to the world's zoos. The National Zoo in Washington, D.C., for example, rents its pair of pandas from China for $1 million a year. Other cities have similar arrangements. To control the supply, China stipulates that any offspring becomes China's property.[1] Finally, for decades, the world's diamond trade was controlled primarily by De Beers Consolidated Mines, which mined diamonds and also bought most of the world's supply of rough diamonds.

Local monopolies are more common than national or international monopolies. In rural areas, monopolies may include the only grocery store, movie theater, restaurant, or gas station for miles around. These are natural monopolies for products sold in local markets. But long-lasting monopolies are rare because economic profit attracts competitors. Also, over time, technological change tends to break down barriers to entry. For example, the development of wireless transmission of long-distance calls created competitors to AT&T. Wireless transmission is erasing the monopoly held by local cable TV providers and even local phone service. Likewise, fax machines, e-mail, the Internet, and firms such as FedEx and UPS now compete with the U.S. Postal Service's monopoly.

1. D'Vera Cohn, "Zoos Find Pandas Don't Make the Cash to Cover the Keep," *Washington Post*, 7 August 2005.

LO2 Revenue for the Monopolist

Because a monopoly, by definition, supplies the entire market, the demand a monopolist outputs is also the market demand. The demand curve therefore slopes

© KEREN SU/SONE/GETTY IMAGES

Just Another Cup of Coffee?

Monopoly profits often arise from offering something that other producers can't match. For example, Starbucks over the years has built up a unique "experience" for the customer, including baristas who know customer orders by heart and a comfortable atmosphere that encourages patrons to relax and linger. That uniqueness has given Starbucks the market power to grow and to charge a premium price that has rocketed the company's stock price more than fortyfold since 1992. But the company chairman has warned that pressure to grow could "commoditize" Starbucks, making it more vulnerable to competition from other coffee shops and even from fast-food chains. Once a product loses its uniqueness—in this case, just another cup of coffee—the supplier loses market power and profitability.

SOURCE: Janet Adamy, "Starbucks Chairman Says Trouble May Be Brewing," *Wall Street Journal*, 24 February 2007.

downward, reflecting the law of demand—price and quantity demanded are inversely related. Let's look at demand, average revenue, and marginal revenue.

Demand, Average Revenue, and Marginal Revenue

Suppose De Beers controls the diamond market. Exhibit 2 shows the demand curve for 1-carat diamonds. De Beers, for example, can sell three diamonds a day at $7,000 each. That price-quantity combination yields total revenue of $21,000 (=$7,000 × 3). Total revenue divided by quantity is the *average revenue per diamond,* which also is $7,000. Thus, the monopolist's price equals the average revenue per unit. To sell a fourth diamond, De Beers must lower the price to $6,750. Total revenue from selling four diamonds is $27,000 (=$6,750 × 4) and average revenue is $6,750. All along the demand curve, price equals average revenue. Therefore, *the demand curve is also the monopolist's average revenue curve,* just as the perfectly competitive firm's demand curve is that firm's average revenue curve.

What's the marginal revenue from selling a fourth diamond? When De Beers drops the price from $7,000 to $6,750, total revenue increases from $21,000 to $27,000. Thus, *marginal revenue*—the change in total revenue from selling one more diamond—is $6,000, which is less than the price, or average revenue, of $6,750. *For a monopolist, marginal revenue is less than the price, or average revenue.* Recall that for a perfectly competitive firm, marginal revenue equals the price, or average revenue, because that firm can sell all it supplies at the market price.

The Gains and Loss from Selling One More Unit

A closer look at Exhibit 2 reveals why a monopolist's marginal revenue is less than the price. By selling another diamond, De Beers gains the revenue from that sale. For example, De Beers gets $6,750 from the fourth diamond, as shown by the blue-shaded vertical rectangle marked "Gain." But to sell that fourth unit, De Beers must sell all four diamonds for $6,750 each. Thus, to sell a fourth diamond, De Beers must sacrifice $250 on each of the first three diamonds, which could have been sold for $7,000 each. This loss in revenue from the first three units totals $750 (=$250 × 3) and is identified in Exhibit 2 by the pink-shaded horizontal rectangle marked "Loss." The net change in total revenue from selling the fourth diamond—that is, the marginal revenue from the fourth diamond—equals the *gain* minus the *loss,* which equals $6,750 minus $750, or $6,000. So mar-

Exhibit 2

A Monopolist's Gain and Loss in Total Revenue from Selling One More Unit

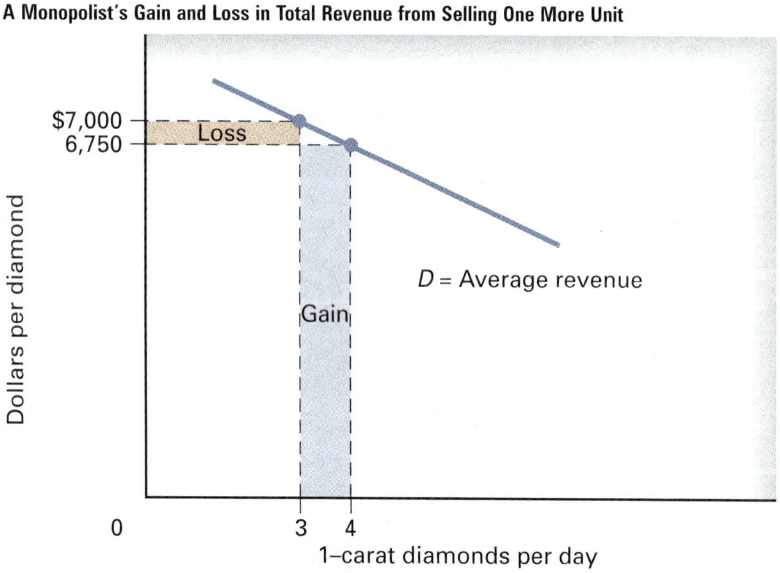

ginal revenue equals the gain minus the loss, or the price minus the revenue forgone by selling all units for a lower price. Because a monopolist's marginal revenue equals the price minus the loss, you can see why the marginal revenue is less than the price.

Incidentally, this analysis assumes that all units are sold at the market price; for example, the four diamonds are sold for $6,750 each. Although this is usually true, later in the chapter you learn how some monopolists try to increase profit by charging different customers different prices.

$TR = p \times Q$

Revenue Schedules

Let's flesh out more fully the revenue schedules behind the demand curve of Exhibit 2. Column (1) of Exhibit 3 lists the quantity of diamonds demanded per day, and column (2) lists the corresponding price, or average revenue. Together, the two columns are the demand schedule for 1-carat diamonds. The price in column (2) times the quantity in column (1) yields the monopolist's *total revenue* schedule in column (3). So $TR = p \times Q$. As De Beers sells more, total revenue increases until quantity reaches 15 diamonds.

Marginal revenue, the change in total revenue from selling one more diamond, appears in column (4). In shorthand, $MR = \Delta TR/\Delta Q$, or the change in total revenue divided by the change in quantity. Note in Exhibit 3 that after the first unit, marginal revenue is less than price. As the price declines, the gap between price and marginal revenue widens. As the price declines, the *loss* from selling all diamonds for less increases (because quantity increases) and the *gain* from selling another diamond decreases (because the price falls).

$MR = \Delta TR/\Delta Q$

Revenue Curves

The schedules in Exhibit 3 are graphed in Exhibit 4, which shows the demand and marginal revenue curves in panel (a) and the total revenue curve in panel (b). Recall that total revenue equals price times quantity. Note that *the marginal revenue curve is below the demand curve and that total revenue reaches a maximum where marginal revenue is zero.* Please take a minute now to study these relationships—they are important.

Again, along the demand curve price equals average revenue, so the demand curve is also the monopolist's average revenue curve. In Chapter 5 you learned that the price elasticity for a straight-line demand curve declines as you move down the curve. When demand is elastic—that is, when the percentage increase in quantity demanded more than offsets the percentage decrease in price—a decrease in price increases total revenue. Therefore, *where demand is elastic, marginal revenue is positive, and total revenue increases as the price falls.* On the other hand, where demand is

Exhibit 3

Revenue for De Beers, a Monopolist

To sell more, the monopolist must lower the price on all units sold. Because the revenue lost from selling all units at a lower price must be subtracted from the revenue gained from selling another unit, marginal revenue is less than the price. At some point, marginal revenue turns negative, as shown here when the price is reduced to $3,500.

(1) 1-Carat Diamonds per day (Q)	(2) Price (average revenue) (p)	(3) Total Revenue ($TR = p \times Q$)	(4) Marginal Revenue ($MR = \Delta TR/\Delta Q$)
0	$7,750	0	—
1	7,500	$ 7,500	$7,500
2	7,250	14,500	7,000
3	7,000	21,000	6,500
4	6,750	27,000	6,000
5	6,500	32,500	5,500
6	6,250	37,500	5,000
7	6,000	42,000	4,500
8	5,750	46,000	4,000
9	5,500	49,500	3,500
10	5,250	52,500	3,000
11	5,000	55,000	2,500
12	4,750	57,000	2,000
13	4,500	58,500	1,500
14	4,250	59,500	1,000
15	4,000	60,000	500
16	3,750	60,000	0
17	3,500	59,500	–500

Exhibit 4

Monopoly Demand and Marginal Total Revenue

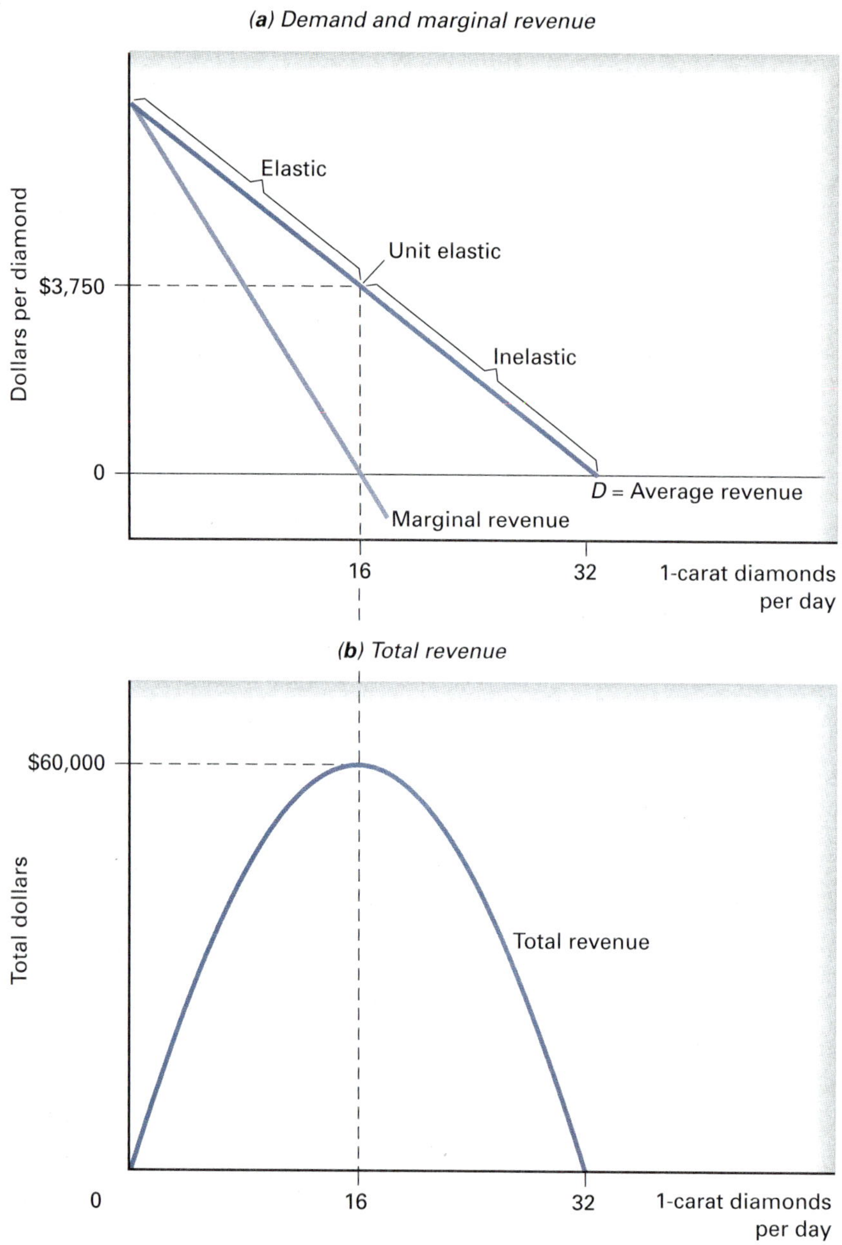

inelastic—that is, where the percentage increase in quantity demanded is less than the percentage decrease in price—a decrease in price reduces total revenue. In other words, the loss in revenue from selling all diamonds for the lower price overwhelms the gain in revenue from selling more diamonds. Therefore, *where demand is inelastic, marginal revenue is negative, and total revenue decreases as the price falls.*

price maker
a firm with some power to set the price because the demand curve for its output slopes downward; a firm with market power

From Exhibit 4, you can see that marginal revenue turns negative if the price drops below $3,750, indicating inelastic demand below that price. *A profit-maximizing monopolist would never expand output to the inelastic range of demand because doing so would reduce total revenue.* It would make no sense to sell more if total revenue drops in the process. Also note that demand is unit elastic at the price of $3,750. At that price, marginal revenue is zero and total revenue reaches a maximum.

LO3 The Firm's Costs and Profit Maximization

In perfect competition, each firm's choice is confined to *quantity* because the market has already determined the price. The perfect competitor is a *price taker. The monopolist, however, can choose either the price or the quantity, but choosing one determines the other—they come in pairs.* For example, if De Beers decides to sell 10 diamonds a day, consumers would demand that many only at a price of $5,250 per diamond. Alternatively, if De Beers decides to sell diamonds for $6,000 each, consumers would demand 7 a day. Because the monopolist can choose any price-quantity combination on the demand curve , we say the monopolist is a **price maker**. More generally, any firm that has some control over what price to charge is a price maker.

Profit Maximization

Exhibit 5 repeats revenue schedules from Exhibits 3 and 4 and also includes a short-run cost schedule similar to those already introduced in the two previous chapters. Please take a little time now to become familiar with this table. Then ask yourself this question: which price-quantity combination should De Beers select to maximize profit? As was the case

> "The monopolist, however, can choose either the price or the quantity, but choosing one determines the other—they come in pairs."

© COMSTOCK IMAGES/JUPITERIMAGES

with perfect competition, the monopolist can approach profit maximization in two ways—the total approach and the marginal approach.

Total Revenue Minus Total Cost

The profit-maximizing monopolist employs the same decision rule as the competitive firm. *The monopolist supplies the quantity at which total revenue exceeds total cost by the greatest amount.* Economic profit appears in column (8) of Exhibit 5. As you can see, maximum profit is $12,500 per day, which occurs at 10 diamonds per day. At that quantity, total revenue is $52,500 and total cost is $40,000.

Marginal Revenue Equals Marginal Cost

De Beers, as a profit-maximizing monopolist, increases output if it adds more to total revenue than to total cost. So De Beers expands output as long as marginal revenue, shown in column (4) of Exhibit 5, exceeds marginal cost, shown in column (6). But De Beers stops short of producing where marginal cost exceeds marginal revenue. Again,

Exhibit 5

Short-Run Costs and Revenue for a Monopolist

(1) Diamonds per day (*Q*)	(2) Price (*p*)	(3) Total Revenue ($TR = p \times Q$)	(4) Marginal Revenue ($MR = \Delta TR/\Delta Q$)	(5) Total Cost (*TC*)	(6) Marginal Cost ($MC = \Delta TC/\Delta Q$)	(7) Average Total Cost ($ATC = TC/Q$)	(8) Total Profit or Loss ($= TR - TC$)
0	$7,750	0	—	$15,000	—	—	−$15,000
1	7,500	$7,500	$7,500	19,750	$4,750	$19,750	−12,250
2	7,250	14,500	7,000	23,500	3,750	11,750	−9,000
3	7,000	21,000	6,500	26,500	3,000	8,833	−5,500
4	6,750	27,000	6,000	29,000	2,500	7,750	−2,000
5	6,500	32,500	5,500	31,000	2,000	6,200	1,500
6	6,250	37,500	5,000	32,500	1,500	5,420	5,000
7	6,000	42,000	4,500	33,750	1,250	4,820	8,250
8	5,750	46,000	4,000	35,250	1,500	4,410	10,750
9	5,500	49,500	3,500	37,250	2,000	4,140	12,250
10	**5,250**	**52,500**	**3,000**	**40,000**	**2,750**	**4,000**	**12,500**
11	5,000	55,000	2,500	43,250	3,250	3,930	11,750
12	4,750	57,000	2,000	48,000	4,750	4,000	9,000
13	4,500	58,500	1,500	54,500	6,500	4,190	4,000
14	4,250	59,500	1,000	64,000	9,500	4,570	−4,500
15	4,000	60,000	500	77,500	13,500	5,170	−17,500
16	3,750	60,000	0	96,000	18,500	6,000	−36,000
17	3,500	59,500	−500	121,000	25,000	7,120	−61,500

profit is maximized at $12,500 when output is 10 diamonds per day. For the tenth diamond, marginal revenue is $3,000 and marginal cost is $2,750. As you can see, if output exceeds 10 diamonds per day, marginal cost exceeds marginal revenue. An eleventh diamond's marginal cost of $3,250 exceeds its marginal revenue of $2,500. For simplicity, we say that *the profit-maximizing output occurs where marginal revenue equals marginal cost,* which, you will recall, is the golden rule of profit maximization.

Graphical Solution

The revenue and cost schedules in Exhibit 5 are graphed in Exhibit 6, with per-unit cost and revenue curves in panel (a) and total cost and revenue curves in panel (b). The intersection of the two marginal curves at point *e* in panel (a) indicates that profit is maximized when 10 diamonds are sold. At that quantity, we move up to the demand curve to find the profit-maximizing price of $5,250. Average total cost of $4,000 is identified by point *b*. The average profit per diamond equals the price of $5,250 minus the average total cost of $4,000. Economic profit is the average profit per unit of $1,250 multiplied by the 10 diamonds sold, for a total profit of $12,500 per day, as identified by the blue-shaded rectangle. So *the profit-maximizing rate of output is found where the marginal cost curve intersects the marginal revenue curve.*

In panel (b), the firm's profit or loss is measured by the vertical distance between the total revenue and total cost curves. De Beers expands output if the increase in total revenue from selling another diamond exceeds the increase in total cost. *The profit-maximizing firm produces where total revenue exceeds total cost by the greatest amount.* Again, profit is maximized where De Beers sells 10 diamonds per day. Total profit in panel (b) is measured by the *vertical distance* between the two total curves; in panel (a), total profit is measure by the shaded *area* formed by multiplying average profit per unit by the number of units sold.

One common myth about monopolies is that they charge the highest price possible. But the monopolist is interested in maximizing profit, not price. What the monopolist can charge is limited by consumer demand. De Beers, for example, could charge $7,500, but selling only one diamond would result in a big loss. Indeed, De Beers could charge $7,750 or more but would sell no diamonds. So charging the highest possible price is not consistent with maximizing profit. A monopolist may be able to set the price, but the quantity demanded at that price is determined by consumers. *Even the most powerful monopolist is subject to the law of demand.*

Exhibit 6

Monopoly Costs and Revenue

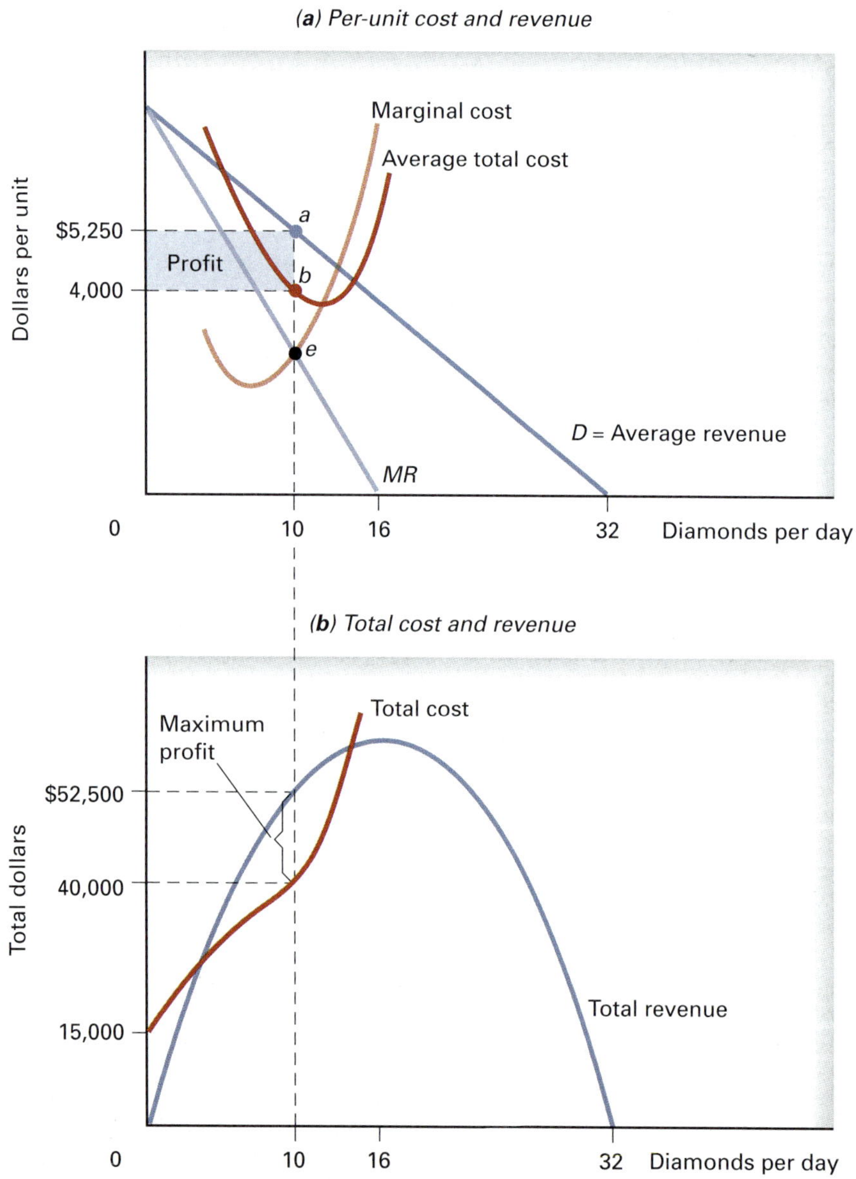

Short-Run Losses and the Shutdown Decision

A monopolist is not assured an economic profit. Although a monopolist is the sole supplier of a good with no close substitutes, the demand for that good may not generate economic profit in either the short run or the long run. After all, many new products are protected from direct competition by patents, yet most patents never turn into a profitable product. And even a monopolist that is initially profitable may eventually suffer losses because of rising costs, falling demand, or market entry of similar products. For example, Coleco, the original mass producer of Cabbage Patch dolls, went bankrupt after that craze died down. And Cuisinart, the company that introduced the food processor, soon faced many imitators and filed for bankruptcy (though its name lives on).

In the short run, the loss-minimizing monopolist, like the loss-minimizing perfect competitor, must decide whether to produce or to shut down. *If the price covers average variable cost, the monopolist produces, at least in the short run. If not, the monopolist shuts down, at least in the short run.*

Exhibit 7 brings average variable cost back into the picture. Recall from Chapter 7 that average variable cost and average fixed cost sum to average total cost. Loss minimization occurs in Exhibit 7 at point *e*, where the marginal revenue curve intersects the marginal cost curve. At the equilibrium rate of output, Q, price *p* is found on the demand curve at point *b*. That price exceeds average variable cost, at point *c*, but is below average total cost, at point *a*. Because price covers average variable cost and a portion of average fixed cost, this monopolist loses less by producing Q than by shutting down. The loss, identified by the shaded rectangle, is the average loss per unit, *ab*, times the quantity sold, Q. The firm would shut down in the short run if the average variable cost curve is above the demand curve, or average revenue curve, at all output rates.

© MICKEY PFLEGER/TIME LIFE PICTURES/GETTY IMAGES

Recall that a perfectly competitive firm's supply curve is that portion of the marginal cost curve at or above the average variable cost curve. The intersection of a monopolist's marginal revenue and marginal cost curves identifies the profit-maximizing (or loss-minimizing) quantity, but the price is found up on the demand curve. Because the equilibrium quantity can be found along a monopolist's marginal cost curve but the equilibrium price appears on the demand curve, no single curve traces points showing unique combinations of both the price and quantity supplied. Because no curve reflects combinations of price and quantity supplied, *there is no monopolist supply curve*.

Exhibit 7

The Monopolist Minimizes Losses in the Short Run

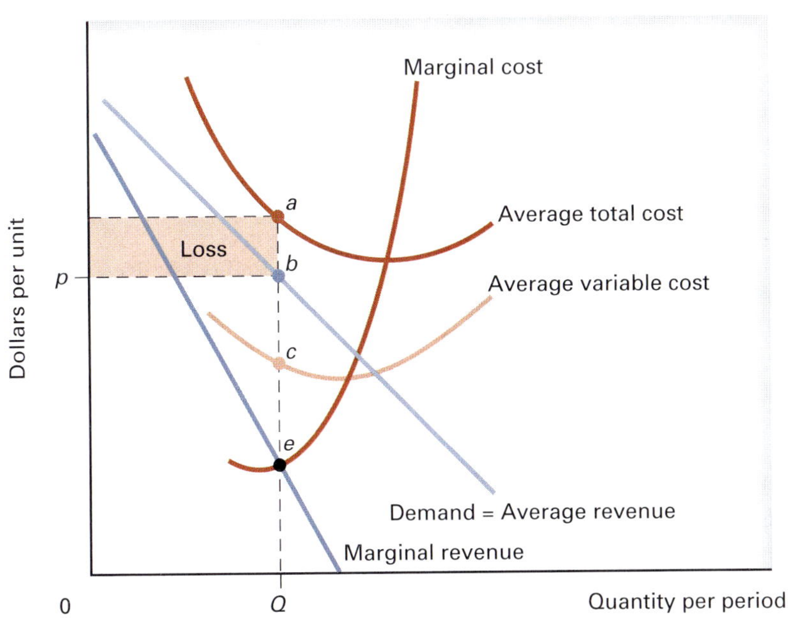

Long-Run Profit Maximization

For perfectly competitive firms, the distinction between the short run and the long run is important because entry and exit of firms can occur in the long run, erasing any economic profit or loss. For the monopolist, the distinction between the short run and long run is less relevant. *If a monopoly is insulated from competition by high barriers that block new entry, economic profit can persist into the long run.* Yet short-run profit is no guarantee of long-run profit. For example, suppose the monopoly relies on a patent. Patents last only so long and even while a product is under patent, the monopolist often must defend it in court (patent litigation increased more than 50 percent in the last decade). On the other hand, a monopolist may be able to erase a loss (most start-up firms lose money initially) or increase profit in the long run by adjusting the scale of the firm or by advertising to increase demand. A monopolist unable to erase a loss will, in the long run, leave the market.

LO4 Monopoly and the Allocation of Resources

If monopolists are no greedier than perfect competitors (because both maximize profit), if monopolists do not charge the highest possible price (because the highest price would reduce quantity demanded to zero), and if monopolists are not guaranteed a profit (because demand for the product may be weak), then what's the problem with monopoly? To get a handle on the problem, let's compare monopoly with the benchmark established in the previous chapter—perfect competition.

> THE MONOPOLIST RESTRICTS QUANTITY BELOW WHAT WOULD MAXIMIZE SOCIAL WELFARE.

Price and Output Under Perfect Competition

Let's begin with the long-run equilibrium price and output in a perfectly competitive market. Suppose the long-run market supply curve in perfect competition is horizontal, as shown by S_c in Exhibit 8. Because this is a constant-cost industry, the horizontal long-run supply curve also shows marginal cost and average total cost at each quantity. Equilibrium in perfect competition occurs at point c, where the market demand and market supply curves intersect to yield price p_c and quantity Q_c. Remember, the demand curve reflects the marginal benefit of each unit purchased. In competitive equilibrium, the marginal benefit of the final unit sold equals the marginal cost to society of producing that final unit. As noted in the previous chapter, when the marginal benefit that consumers derive from a good equals the marginal cost of producing that good, that market is said to be allocatively efficient and to maximize social welfare. There is no way of reallocating resources to increase the total value of output or to increase social welfare. Because consumers are able to purchase Q_c units at price p_c, they enjoy a net benefit from consumption, or a consumer surplus, measured by the entire shaded triangle, acp_c.

Price and Output Under Monopoly

With only one firm in the industry, the industry demand curve D in Exhibit 8 becomes the monopolist's demand curve, so the price the monopolist charges determines the market quantity. Because the monopolist's demand curve slopes downward, the marginal revenue curve also slopes downward and is beneath the demand curve, as is indicated by MR_m in Exhibit 8. Suppose the monopolist can produce at the same constant cost in the long run as can firms in the competitive industry. The monopolist maximizes profit by equating marginal revenue with marginal cost, which occurs at point b, yielding equilibrium price p_m and output Q_m. Again, the price shows the consumers' marginal benefit for unit Q_m. This marginal benefit, identified at point m, exceeds the monopolist's marginal cost, identified at point b. Because marginal benefit exceeds marginal cost, society would be better off if output expanded beyond Q_m. *The monopolist restricts quantity below what would maximize social welfare.* Even though the monopolist restricts output, consumers still derive some benefit, just not as much as with perfect competition. Consumer surplus is shown by the smaller triangle, amp_m.

Allocative and Distributive Effects

Consider the allocative and distributive effects of monopoly versus perfect competition. In Exhibit 8, consumer surplus under perfect competition is the large triangle, acp_c. Under monopoly, consumer surplus shrinks to the smaller triangle amp_m, which in this example is only one-fourth as large. The monopolist earns economic profit equal to the shaded rectangle. By comparing the situation under perfect competition with that under monopoly , you can see that the monopolist's economic profit comes entirely from what was consumer surplus under perfect competition. Because the profit rectangle reflects a transfer from consumer surplus to monopoly profit, this amount is not lost to society and so is not considered a welfare loss.

Notice, however, that consumer surplus has been reduced by more than the profit rectangle. Consumers also lose the triangle *mcb*, which is part of the consumer surplus with perfect competition. The *mcb* triangle is called the **deadweight loss of monopoly** because it is a loss to consumers but a gain to nobody. This loss results from the *allocative inefficiency arising from the higher price and reduced output of monopoly*. Again, society would be better off if output exceeded the monopolist's profit-maximizing quantity, because the marginal benefit of more output exceeds its marginal cost. Under monopoly, the price, or marginal benefit, always exceeds marginal cost. Empirical estimates of the annual deadweight loss of monopoly in the United States have ranged from about 1 percent to about 5 percent of national income. Applied to national income data for 2007, these estimates imply a deadweight loss of monopoly ranging from about $450 to $2,250 per capita—not a trivial amount.

Exhibit 8

Perfect Competition and Monopoly

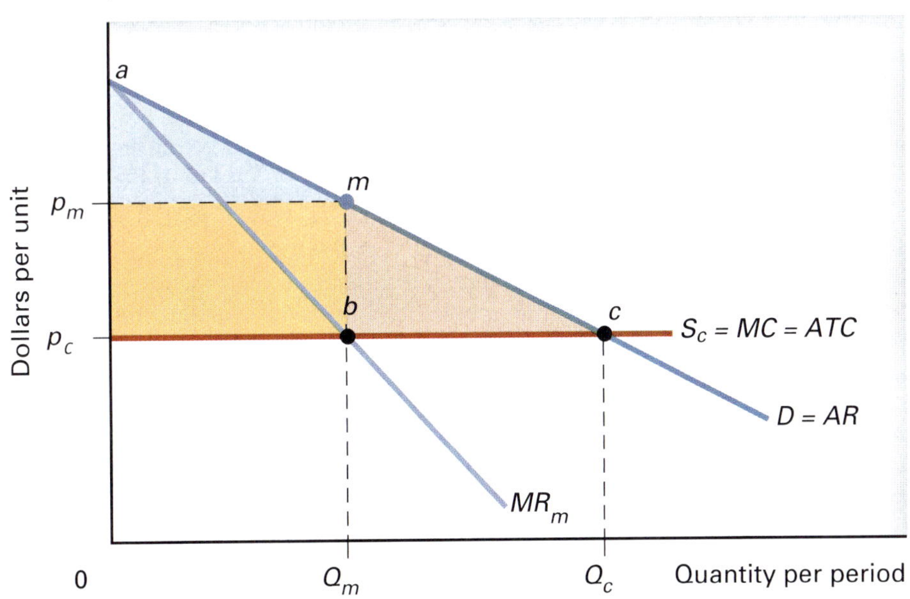

LO5 Problems Estimating the Deadweight Loss of Monopoly

The actual cost of monopoly could differ from the deadweight loss described so far. These costs could be lower or higher. Here's the reasoning.

Why the Deadweight Loss of Monopoly Might Be Lower

If economies of scale are substantial enough, a monopolist might be able to produce output at a lower cost per unit than could competitive firms. Therefore, the price, or at least the cost of production, could be lower under monopoly than under competition. The deadweight loss shown in Exhibit 8 may also overstate the true cost of monopoly because monopolists might, in response to public scrutiny and political pressure, keep prices below the profit maximizing level. Although monopolists would like to earn as much profit as possible, they realize that if the public outcry over high prices and high profit grows loud enough, some sort of government intervention could reduce or even erase that profit. For example, the prices and profit of drug companies, which individually are monopoly suppliers of patented medicines, come under scrutiny from time to time by elected officials who propose regulating drug prices or taxing "windfall profits." Drug firms might try to avoid such treatment by keeping prices below the level that would maximize profit. Finally, a monopolist might keep the price below the profit-maximizing level to avoid attracting competitors to the market. For example, some observers claim that Alcoa, when it was the only U.S. producer of aluminum, kept prices low enough to discourage new entry.

deadweight loss of monopoly
net loss to society when a firm with market power restricts output and increases the price

Why the Deadweight Loss Might Be Higher

Another line of reasoning suggests that the deadweight loss of monopoly might, in fact, be greater than shown in our simple diagram. *If resources must be devoted to securing and maintaining a monopoly position, monopolies may impose a greater welfare loss than simple models suggest.* For example, radio and TV broadcasting rights confer on the recipient the use a particular band of the scarce broadcast spectrum. In the past, these rights have been given away by government agencies to the applicants deemed most deserving. Because these rights are so valuable, numerous applicants have spent millions on lawyers' fees, lobbying expenses, and other costs associated with making themselves appear the most deserving. The efforts devoted to securing and maintaining a monopoly position are largely a social waste because they use up scarce resources but add not one unit to output. Activities undertaken by individuals or firms to influence public policy to directly or indirectly redistributes income to themselves are referred to as **rent seeking**.

© JUSTIN SULLIVAN/GETTY IMAGES

The Mail Monopoly

The U.S. Postal Service (USPS) was granted a monopoly in 1775 and has operated under federal protection ever since. USPS pays no taxes and is exempt from local zoning laws. It has a legal monopoly in delivering regular, first-class letters and has the exclusive right to use the space inside your mailbox. Other delivery services such as FedEx or UPS cannot use mail boxes or post office boxes.

Still, USPS has suffered in recent years because of rising costs and growing competition from new technologies. The price of a first-class stamp climbed from 6 cents in 1970 to 41 cents by 2007—a growth rate double that of inflation. New technologies such as email, ecards, online bill-payment, text messaging, and fax machines also displace USPS delivery services (email messages now greatly outnumber first-class letters). Because its monopoly applies only to regular first-class mail, USPS has lost chunks of other business to private firms offering lower rates and better service. The United Parcel Service (UPS), for example, is more mechanized and more containerized than the USPS and thus has lower costs and less breakage.

SOURCES: "Going Postal," *Wall Street Journal,* 13 April 2006; Katie Hafner, "Postal Service Finds a Friend in the Internet," *New York Times,* 2 August 2006; John McKinnon and Rick Brooks, "Mail Rates to Be Harnessed as Part of Postal-Overhaul Bill," *Wall Street Journal,* 11 December 2006; and the USPS home page at http://www.usps.com.

The monopolist, insulated from the rigors of competition in the marketplace, might also grow fat and lazy—and become inefficient. Because some monopolies could still earn an economic profit even if the firm is inefficient, corporate executives might waste resources by creating a more comfortable life for themselves. Long lunches, afternoon golf, plush offices, corporate jets, and excessive employee benefits might make company life more pleasant, but they increase production costs and raise prices.

Monopolists have also been criticized for being slow to adopt the latest production techniques, being reluctant to develop new products, and generally lacking innovation. Because monopolists are largely insulated from the rigors of competition, they might take it easy. It's been said "The best of all monopoly profits is a quiet life."

rent seeking activities undertaken by individuals or firms to influence public policy in a way that increases their incomes

price discrimination increasing profit by charging different groups of consumers different prices for the same product

Not all economists believe that monopolies manage their resources with any less vigilance than perfect competitors do. Some argue that because monopolists are protected from rivals, they are in a good position to capture the fruits of any innovation and therefore are more innovative than competitive firms are. Others believe that if a monopolist strays from the path of profit maximization, its share price will drop enough to attract someone who will buy a controlling interest and shape up the company. This market for corporate control is said to keep monopolists on their toes.

LO6 Price Discrimination

In the model developed so far, to sell more output a monopolist must lower the price. In reality, a monopolist can sometimes increase profit by charging higher prices to those who value the product more. This practice of charging different prices to different groups of consumers is called **price discrimination**. For example, children, students, and senior citizens often pay lower admission prices to ball games, movies, amusement parks, and other events. You may believe firms do this out of some sense of fairness to certain groups, but the primary goal is to boosts profits. Let's see how and why.

> A monopolist can sometimes increase profit by charging higher prices to those who value the product more.

Conditions for Price Discrimination

To practice price discrimination, a firm's product must meet certain conditions. First, the demand curve for the firm's product must slope downward, indicating that the firm is a price maker—the producer has some market power, some ability to set the price. Second, there must be at least two groups of consumers for the product, each with a different price elasticity of demand. Third, the firm must be able, at little cost, to charge each group a different price for essentially the same product. Finally, the firm must be able to prevent those who pay the lower price from reselling the product to those who pay the higher price.

A Model of Price Discrimination

Exhibit 9 shows the effects of price discrimination. Consumers are sorted into two groups with different demand elasticities. For simplicity, let's assume that the firm produces at a constant long-run average and marginal cost of $1.00. *At a given price,* the price elasticity of demand in panel (b) is greater than that in panel (a). Think of panel (b) as reflecting the demand of college students, senior citizens, or some other group more sensitive to the price. *This firm maximizes profit by finding the price in each market that equates marginal revenue with marginal cost.* For example, consumers with a lower price elasticity pay $3.00, and those with a higher price elasticity pay $1.50. Profit maximization means charging a lower price to the group with the more elastic demand. Despite the price difference, the firm gets the same marginal revenue of $1.00 from the last unit sold to each group. Note that charging both groups $3.00 would erase any profit from that right-hand group of consumers, who would be priced out of the market. Charging both groups $1.50 would lead to negative marginal revenue from the left-hand group, which would reduce profit. No single price could generate the profit achieved through price discrimination.

Examples of Price Discrimination

Let's look at some examples of price discrimination. Because businesspeople face unpredictable yet urgent demands for travel and because their employers pay such expenses, businesspeople tend to be less sensitive to price than are householders. In other words, businesspeople have a less elastic demand for travel than do householders, so airlines try to maximize profits by charging businesses more than households. Business-class tickets cost much more than

Exhibit 9

Price Discrimination with Two Groups of Consumers

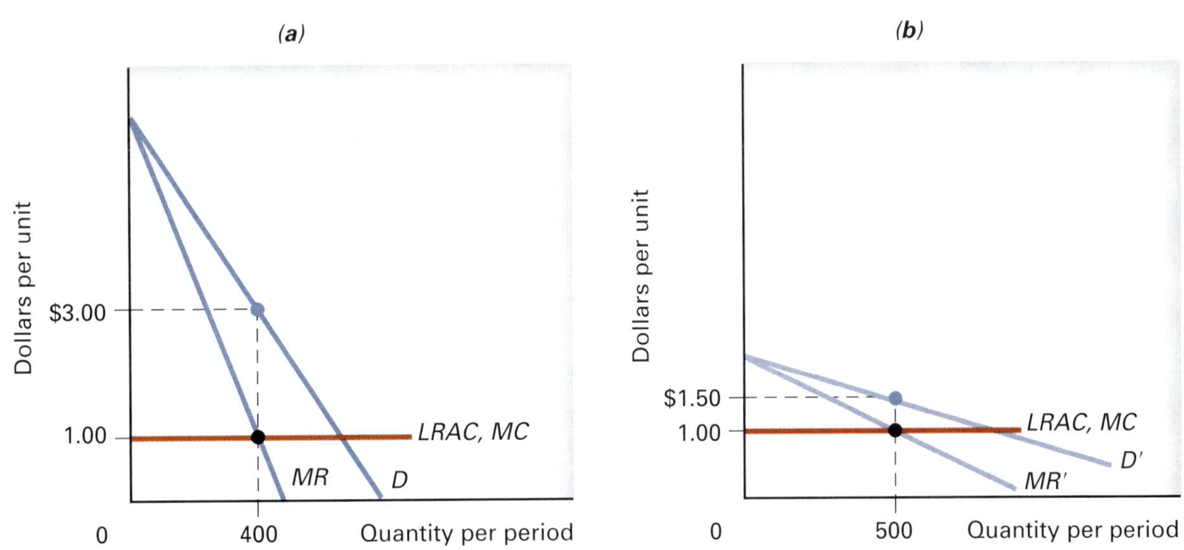

coach-class tickets. Business seats offer more room than coach seats, and the food is a little better, but the difference is ticket prices far exceeds differences in the airline's cost of providing each service. Even within a class of tickets, airlines charge different rates based on how far in advance tickets are purchased. Householders usually plan their trips well in advance and often spend the weekend. But business travel is more unpredictable, more urgent, and seldom involves a weekend stay. The airlines sort out the two groups by limiting discount fares to travelers who buy tickets well in advance. More generally, airlines use computer models to price discriminate depending on the circumstances. Still, an airline's ability to charge a higher price for a particular seat is limited by competition from other airlines.

Here are other examples of price discrimination: IBM wanted to charge business users of its laser printer more than home users. To distinguish between the two groups, IBM decided to slow down the home printer to 5 pages a minute (versus 10 for the business model). To do this, they added an extra chip that inserted pauses between pages.[2] Thus, IBM could sell the home model for less than the business model without cutting into sales of its business model. Intel offered two versions of the same computer chip; the cheaper version was the expensive version with some extra work done to reduce its speed. And Adobe stripped some features from its Photoshop CD to offer a cheaper version, Photoshop Elements. Major amusement parks, such as Disney World and Universal Studios, distinguish between local residents and out-of-towners when it comes to the price of admission. Out-of-towners typically spend substantial amounts on airlines and lodging just to be there, so they are less sensitive to the admission price than are local residents. The problem is how to charge a lower price to locals. The parks do this by making discount coupons available at local businesses, such as dry cleaners, which vacationers are less likely to visit. The Las Vegas monorail sorts out the locals from the visitors by charging $1 for those presenting a Nevada driver's license and $5 for those without one.

perfectly discriminating monopolist
a monopolist who charges a different price for each unit sold; also called the monopolist's dream

Perfect Price Discrimination: The Monopolist's Dream

The demand curve shows the marginal value of each unit consumed, which is also the maximum amount consumers would pay for each unit. If the monopolist could charge a different price for each unit sold—a price reflected by the height of the demand curve—the firm's marginal revenue from selling one more unit would equal the price of that unit. Thus, the demand curve would become the firm's marginal revenue curve. A **perfectly discriminating monopolist** would charge a different price for each unit sold.

In Exhibit 10, again for simplicity, the monopolist is assumed to produce at a constant average and marginal cost in the long run. A perfectly discriminating monopolist, like any pro-

2. Carl Shapiro and Hal Varian, *Information Rules: A Strategic Guide to the Network Economy* (Harvard Business School Press, 1999), p. 59.

ducer, would maximize profit by producing the quantity at which marginal revenue equals marginal cost. Because the demand curve is now the marginal revenue curve, the profit-maximizing quantity occurs where the demand, or marginal revenue, curve intersects the marginal cost curve, identified at point *e* in Exhibit 10. Price discrimination is a way of increasing profit. The area of the shaded triangle *aec* shows the perfectly discriminating monopolist's economic profit.

Exhibit 10

Perfect Price Discrimination

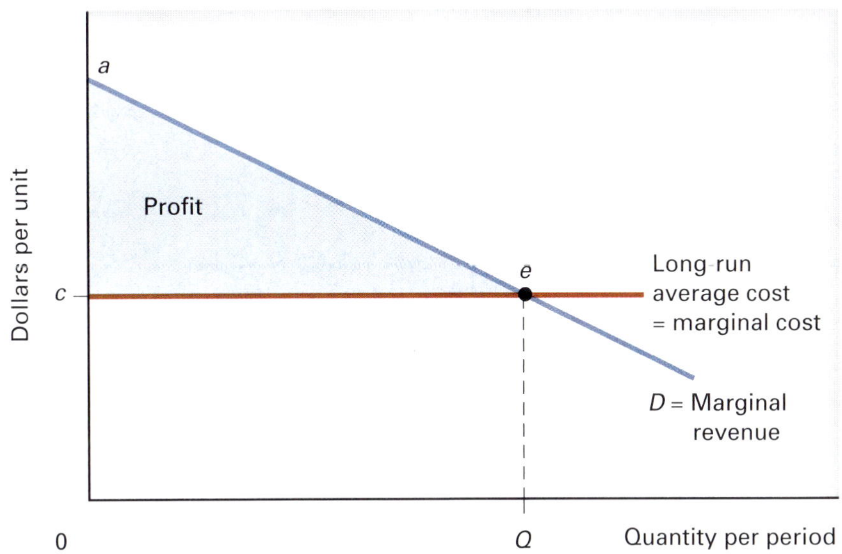

By charging a different price for each unit sold, the perfectly discriminating monopolist is able to convert every dollar of consumer surplus into economic profit. Although this practice may seem unfair to consumers, perfect price discrimination gets high marks based on allocative efficiency. Because such a monopolist does not have to lower the price to all customers to sell more, there is no reason to restrict output. In fact, because this is a constant-cost industry, Q is the same quantity produced in perfect competition (though in perfect competition, the triangle *aec* would be consumer surplus, not economic profit). As in the perfectly competitive outcome, the marginal benefit of the final unit produced and consumed just equals its marginal cost. And although perfect price discrimination yields no consumer surplus, the total benefit consumers derive from consuming this good just equals their total cost. Note also that because the monopolist does not restrict output, *there is no deadweight loss.* Thus, perfect price discrimination enhances social welfare when compared with monopoly output in the absence of price discrimination. But the monopolist reaps all net gains from production, while consumers just break even on the deal because their total benefit equals their total cost.

The pricing of cell phone service reflects a firm's effort to capture more consumer surplus as profit. Pricing alternatives include (1) a per-minute price with no basic fee, (2) a flat rate for the month plus a price per minute, and (3) a flat rate for unlimited calls. These alternatives allow the company to charge those who use fewer minutes more per minute than those who call more. Such suppliers are trying to convert some consumer surplus into profit.

Final Word

Pure monopoly, like perfect competition, is not that common. Perhaps the best examples are firms producing patented items that provide unique benefits, such as certain prescription drugs. Some firms may enjoy monopoly power in the short run, but the lure of economic profit encourages rivals to hurdle seemingly high entry barriers in the long run. Changing technology also works against monopoly in the long run. For example, the railroad monopoly was erased by the interstate highway system. AT&T's monopoly on long-distance phone service crumbled as wireless technology replaced copper wire. The U.S. Postal Service's monopoly on first-class mail is being eroded by fax machines, e-mail, e-payments, and private firms offering overnight delivery. De Beers has lost its grip on the diamond market. And cable TV is losing its local monopoly to technological breakthroughs in fiber-optics technology, wireless broadband, and the Internet.

Although perfect competition and pure monopoly are rare, our examination of them yields a framework to help understand market structures that lie between the two extremes. Many firms have some degree of monopoly power—that is, they face downward-sloping demand curves. The next chapter discusses the two market structures that lie in the gray region between perfect competition and monopoly.

CHAPTER 10

Monopolistic Competition *and* Oligopoly

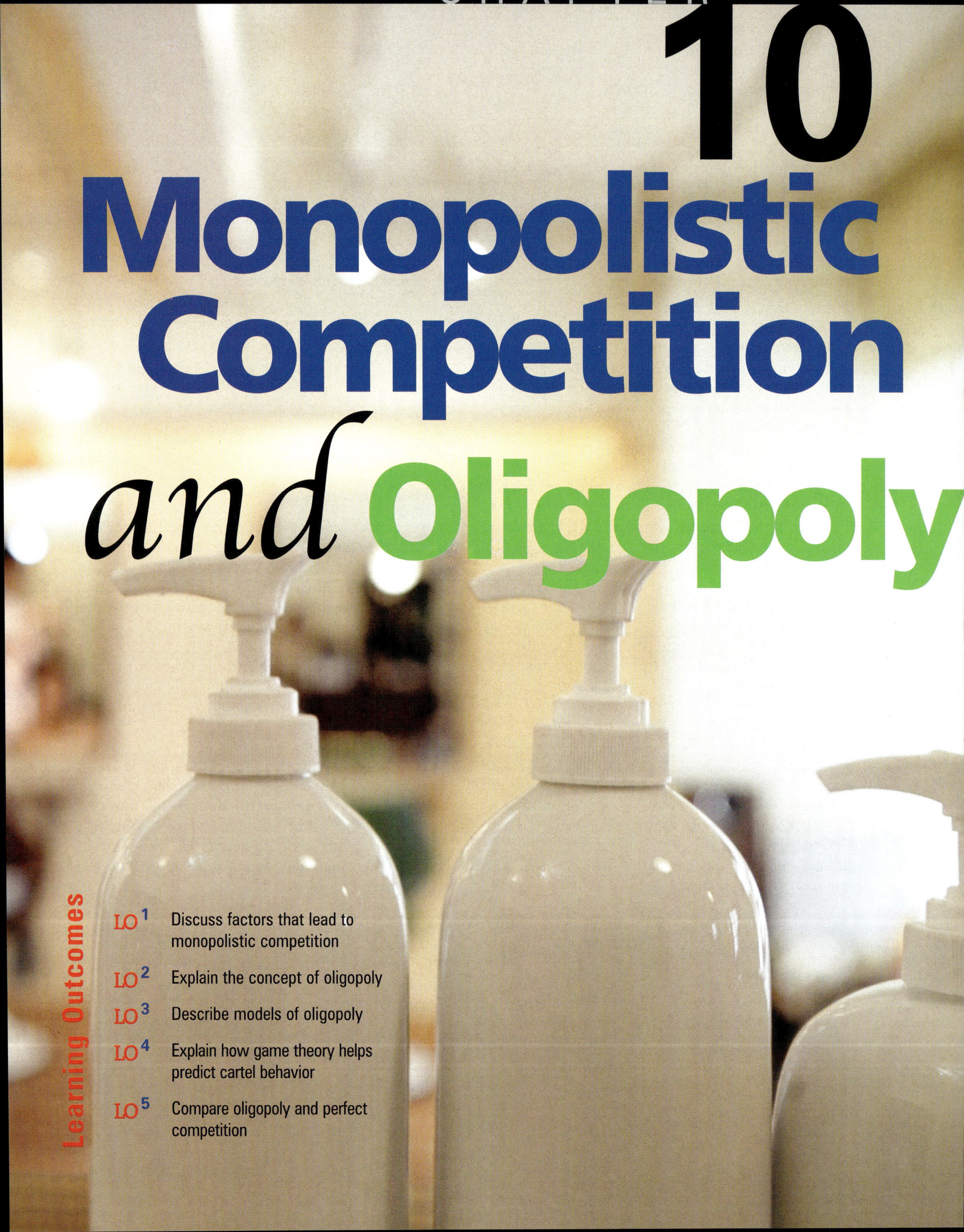

Learning Outcomes

LO 1 Discuss factors that lead to monopolistic competition

LO 2 Explain the concept of oligopoly

LO 3 Describe models of oligopoly

LO 4 Explain how game theory helps predict cartel behavior

LO 5 Compare oligopoly and perfect competition

© BLOOMIMAGE/GETTY IMAGES

“Why are some shampoos sold only in hair salons?”

Why is Perrier water sold in green, tear-shaped bottles? Why are some shampoos sold only in salons? Why do some pizza makers deliver? Which market structure is like a golf tournament and which is like a tennis match? Why do airlines engage in airfare warfare? Why was the oil cartel, OPEC, created, and why has it met with spotty success? Why is there a witness protection program? To answer these and other questions, we turn in this chapter to the vast gray area that lies between perfect competition and monopoly.

What do you think?

Perfect competition is better for consumers than monopoly.

Strongly Disagree						*Strongly Agree*
1	2	3	4	5	6	7

Perfect competition and monopoly are extreme market structures. Under perfect competition, many suppliers offer an identical product and, in the long run, entry and exit erases economic profit. A monopolist supplies a product with no close substitutes in a market where natural and artificial barriers keep out would-be competitors, so a monopolist can earn economic profit in the long run. These polar market structures are logically appealing and offer a useful description of some industries observed in the economy.

But most firms fit into neither market structure. Some markets have many sellers producing goods that vary slightly, such as the many convenience stores that abound. Other markets consist of just a few sellers that in some industries produce essentially identical products, or commodities (such as oil), and in other industries produce differentiated goods (such as automobiles). This chapter examines the two remaining market structures that together include most firms in the economy.

Topics discussed in Chapter 10 include:

- Monopolistic competition
- Product differentiation
- Excess capacity
- Oligopoly
- Collusion
- Prisoner's dilemma

LO1 Monopolistic Competition

During the 1920s and 1930s, economists began formulating models that fit between perfect competition and monopoly. Two models of *monopolistic competition* were developed independently. In 1933 Edward Chamberlin of Harvard University published *The Theory of Monopolistic Competition*. Across the Atlantic that same year, Joan Robinson of Cambridge University published *The Economics of Imperfect Competition*. Although the theories differed, their underlying principles were similar. We discuss Chamberlin's approach.

Characteristics of Monopolistic Competition

As the expression monopolistic competition suggests, this market structure contains elements of both monopoly and competition. Chamberlin used the term to describe a market in which many producers offer products that are substitutes but are not viewed as identical by consumers. Because the products of different suppliers differ slightly—for example, some convenience stores are closer to you than others—the demand curve for each is not horizontal but slopes downward. Each supplier has some power over the price it can charge. Thus, the firms that populate this market are not *price takers,* as they would be under perfect competition, but are *price makers*.

Because barriers to entry are low, firms in monopolistic competition can, in the long run, enter or leave the market with ease. Consequently, there are enough sellers that they behave competitively. There are also enough sellers that each tends to get lost in the crowd. For example, in a large metropolitan area, an individual restaurant, gas station, drugstore, video store, dry cleaner, or convenience store tends to act *independently*. In other market structures, there may be only two or three sellers in each market, so they keep an eye on one another; they act *interdependently*. You will see the relevance of this distinction later in the chapter.

Product Differentiation

In perfect competition, the product is a commodity, meaning it's identical across producers, such as a bushel of wheat. In monopolistic competition, the product differs somewhat among sellers, as with the difference between one rock radio station and another, or one convenience store and another. Sellers differentiate their products in four basic ways.

Physical Differences

The most obvious way products differ is in their physical appearance and their qualities. Packaging is also designed to make a product stand out in a crowded field, such as a distinctive bottle of water (Perrier) and instant soup in a cup (Cup O' Soup). Physical differences are seemingly endless: size, weight, color, taste, texture, and so on. Shampoos, for example, differ in color, scent, thickness, lathering ability, and bottle design. Particular brands aim at consumers with dandruff and those with normal, dry, or oily hair.

monopolistic competition
a market structure with many firms selling products that are substitutes but different enough that each firm's demand curve slopes downward; firm entry is relatively easy

>> Perrier's distinctive packaging helps it stand out in the crowded field of bottled water.

© MARY EVANS PICTURE LIBRARY/ALAMY

Location

The number and variety of locations where a product is available are other ways of differentiation—*spatial differentiation*. Some products seem to be available everywhere, including online; finding other products requires some search and travel. If you live in a metropolitan area, you are no doubt accustomed to the many convenience stores that populate the region. Each wants to be closest to you when you need milk, bread, or nachos—thus, the proliferation of stores. As the name says, these mini grocery stores are selling *convenience*. Their prices are higher and selections more limited than at regular grocery stores, but they are usually closer to customers, don't have long lines, and some are open 24/7.

Services

Products also differ in terms of their accompanying services. For example, some products are delivered to your door, such as Domino's pizza and Amazon.com books; others are cash and carry. Some products are demonstrated by a well-trained sales staff; others are mostly self-service. Some products include online support and toll-free help lines; others come with no help at all. Some sellers provide money-back guarantees; others say "no refunds." The quality and range of accompanying services often differentiate otherwise close substitutes.

Product Image

A final way products differ is in the image the producer tries to foster in the buyer's mind. Producers try to create and maintain brand loyalty through product promotion and advertising. For example, suppliers of sportswear, clothing, watches, and cosmetics often pay for endorsements from athletes, fashion models, and other celebrities. Some producers emphazise the care and attention to detail in each item. For example, Hastens, a small, family-owned Swedish bedding company, underscores the months of labor required to craft each bed by hand—as a way to justify the $65,000 price tag. Some producers try to demonstrate high quality based on where products are sold, such as shampoo sold only in salons. Some products tout their all-natural ingredients, such as Ben & Jerry's ice cream, Tom's of Maine toothpaste, and Nantucket Nectars, or appeal to environmental concerns by focusing on recycled packaging, such as the Starbucks coffee cup insulating sleeve "made from 60% post-consumer recycled fiber."

© AP IMAGES

Short-Run Profit Maximization or Loss Minimization

Because each monopolistic competitor offers a product that differs somewhat from what others supply, each has some control over the price charged. This *market power* means that each firm's demand curve slopes downward. Because many firms offer close but not identical products, any firm that raises its price can expect to lose some customers to rivals. By way of comparison, a price hike would cost a monopolist fewer customers but would cost a perfect competitor *all* customers. Therefore, a monopolistic competitor faces a demand curve that tends to be more elastic than a monopolist's but less elastic than a perfect competitor's.

Recall that the availability of substitutes for a given product affects its price elasticity of demand. The price elasticity of the monopolistic competitor's demand depends on (1) the number of rival firms that produce similar products and (2) the firm's ability to differentiate its product from those of its rivals. *A firm's demand curve is more elastic the more substitutes there are and the less differentiated its product is.*

Marginal Revenue Equals Marginal Cost

From our study of monopoly, we know that a downward-sloping demand curve means the marginal revenue curve also slopes downward and lies beneath the demand curve. Exhibit 1 depicts demand and marginal revenue curves for a monopolistic competitor. The exhibit also presents average and marginal cost curves. Remember that the forces that determine the cost of production are largely independent of the forces that shape demand, so there is nothing special about a monopolistic competitor's cost curves. In the short run, a firm that can at least cover its variable cost increases output as long as marginal revenue exceeds marginal cost. A monopolistic competitor maximizes profit just as a monopolist does: the profit-maximizing quantity occurs where marginal revenue equals marginal cost; *the profit-maximizing price for that quantity is found up on the demand curve.* Exhibit 1 shows the price and quantity combinations that maximize short-run profit in panel (a), and minimize short-run loss in panel (b). In each panel, the marginal cost and marginal revenue curves intersect at point *e*, yielding equilibrium output *q*, equilibrium price *p*, and average total cost *c*.

Maximizing Profit or Minimizing Loss in the Short Run

Recall that the short run is a period too brief to allow firms to enter or leave the market. The demand and cost conditions shown in panel (a) of Exhibit 1 indicate that this firm earns economic profit in the short run. At the firm's profit-maximizing quantity, average total cost, *c*, is below the price, *p*. Price minus average total cost is the firm's profit per unit, which, when multiplied by the quantity, yields economic profit, shown by the pink rectangle. Again, the profit-maximizing quantity is found where marginal revenue equals marginal cost; price is found up on the

Exhibit 1

Monopolistic Competitor in the Short Run

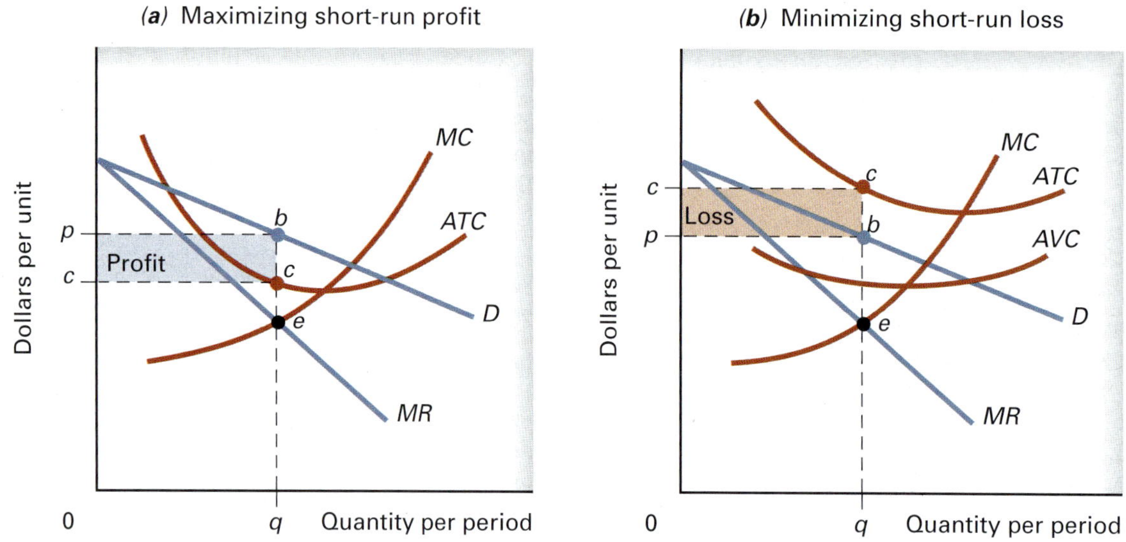

demand curve at that quantity. Thus, a monopolistic competitor, like a monopolist, has no supply curve—that is, *there is no curve that uniquely relates prices and corresponding quantities supplied.*

The monopolistic competitor, like monopolists and perfect competitors, is not guaranteed an economic profit. The firm's demand and cost curves could be as shown in panel (b), where the average total cost curve lies entirely above the demand curve, so no quantity allows the firm to escape a loss. In such a situation, the firm must decide whether to produce at a loss or to shut down in the short run. The rule here is the same as with perfect competition and monopoly: as long as price exceeds average variable cost, the firm in the short run loses less by producing than by shutting down. If no price covers average variable cost, the firm shuts down. Recall that the halt in production may be only temporary; shutting down is not the same as going out of business. Firms that expect economic losses to persist may, in the long run, leave the industry.

Short-run profit maximization in monopolistic competition is quite similar to that under monopoly. But the stories differ in the long run, as we'll see next.

Zero Economic Profit in the Long Run

Low barriers to entry in monopolistic competition mean that short-run economic profit attracts new entrants in the long run. Because new entrants offer similar products, they draw customers away from other firms in the market, thereby reducing the demand facing other firms. Entry continues in the long run until economic profit disappears. *Because market entry is easy, monopolistically competitive firms earn zero economic profit in the long run.*

On the other side of the ledger, economic losses drive some firms out of business in the long run. As firms leave the industry, their customers switch to the remaining firms, increasing the demand for those products. Firms continue to leave in the long run until the remaining firms have enough customers to earn normal profit, but not economic profit.

Exhibit 2 shows long-run equilibrium for a typical monopolistic competitor. In the long run, entry and exit shifts each firm's demand curve until economic profit disappears—that is, until price equals average total cost. In Exhibit 2, the marginal revenue curve intersects the marginal cost curve at point *a*. At the equilibrium quantity, *q*, the average total cost curve is tangent to the demand

Exhibit 2

Long-Run Equilibrium in Monopolistic Competition

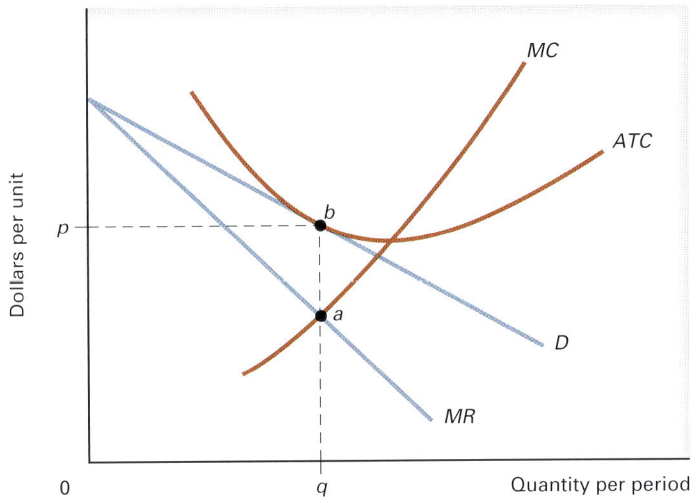

cost equals the price, the firm earns no economic profit but does earn a normal profit (how do we know this?). At all other quantities, the firm's average total cost curve lies above the demand curve, so the firm would lose money by reducing or expanding production.

Thus, because entry is easy in monopolistic competition, short-run economic profit attracts new entrants in the long run. The demand curve facing each monopolistic competitor shifts left until economic profit disappears. A short-run economic loss prompts some firms to leave the industry in the long run until remaining firms earn just a normal profit. In summary: Monopolistic competition is like monopoly in the sense that firms in each industry face demand curves that slope downward. *Monopolistic competition is like perfect competition in the sense that easy entry and exit eliminate economic profit or economic loss in the long run.*

Monopolistic Competition and Perfect Competition Compared

How does monopolistic competition compare with perfect competition in terms of efficiency? In the long run, neither earns economic profit, so what's the difference? The difference traces to the demand curves facing individual firms in each of the two market structures. Exhibit 3 presents the long-run equilibrium price and quantity for a typical firm in each market structure, assuming each firm has identical cost curves. In each case, the marginal cost curve intersects the marginal revenue curve at the quantity where the average total cost curve is tangent to the firm's demand curve.

A perfect competitor's demand curve is a horizontal line drawn at the market price, as shown in panel (a). This demand curve is tangent to the lowest point of the firm's long-run average total cost curve. Thus, a perfect competitor in the long run produces at the lowest possible average cost. In panel (b), a monopolistic competitor faces a downward-sloping demand curve because its product differs somewhat

Exhibit 3

Perfect Competition Versus Monopolistic Competition in Long-Run Equilibrium

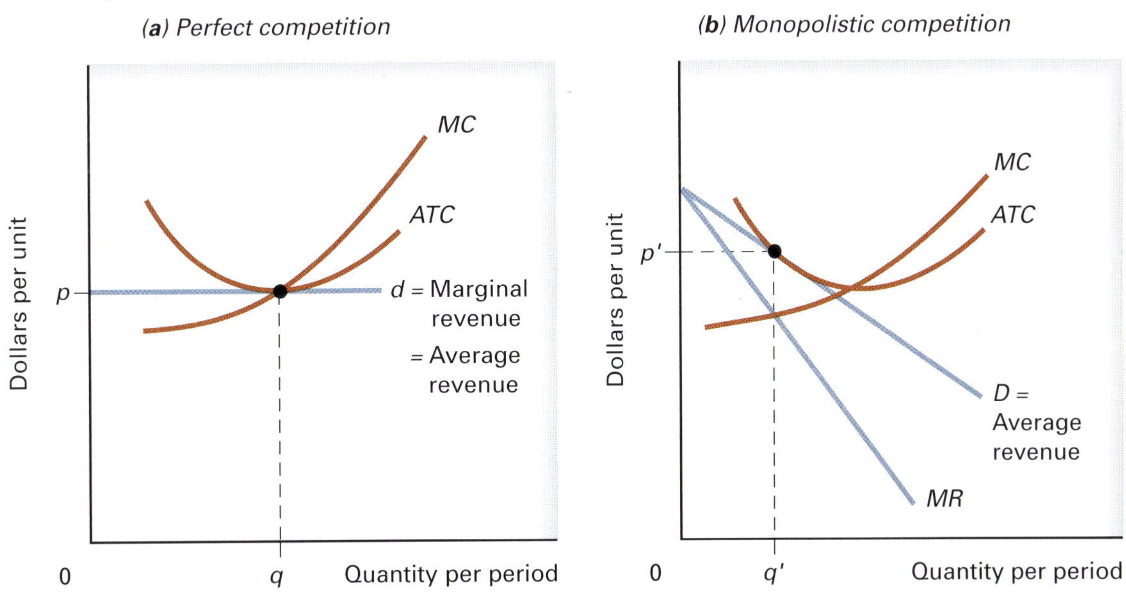

from those of other suppliers. In the long run, the monopolistic competitor produces less than required to achieve the lowest possible average cost. Thus, the price and average cost in monopolistic competition, identified as p' in panel (b), exceed the price and average cost in perfect competition, identified as p in panel (a). *If firms have the same cost curves, the monopolistic competitor produces less and charges more than the perfect competitor does in the long run, though neither earns economic profit.*

Firms in monopolistic competition are not producing at minimum average cost. They are said to have excess capacity, because production falls short of the quantity that would achieve the lowest average cost. Excess capacity means that each producer could easily serve more customers and, in the process, lower average cost. *The marginal value of increased output would exceed its marginal cost, so greater output would increase social welfare.* Such excess capacity exists with gas stations, drugstores, convenience stores, restaurants, motels, bookstores, flower shops, and firms in other monopolistic competitive industries. A specific example is the funeral business. Industry analysts argue that the nation's 22,000 funeral directors could efficiently handle 4 million funerals a year, but only about 2.4 million people die. So the industry operates at only 60 percent of capacity, resulting in a higher average cost per funeral because valuable resources remain idle much of the time.

excess capacity the difference between a firm's profit-maximizing quantity and the quantity that minimizes average cost; firms with excess capacity could reduce average cost by increasing quantity

oligopoly a market structure characterized by so few firms that each behaves interdependently

undifferentiated oligopoly an oligopoly that sells a commodity, or a product that does not differ across suppliers, such as an ingot of steel or a barrel of oil

differentiated oligopoly an oligopoly that sells products that differ across suppliers, such as automobiles or breakfast cereal

One other difference between perfect competition and monopolistic competition does not show up in Exhibit 3. Although the cost curves drawn in each panel of the exhibit are identical, firms in monopolistic competition spend more to differentiate their products than do firms in perfect competition, where products are identical. This higher cost of product differentiation shift up the average cost curve.

Some economists have argued that monopolistic competition results in too many suppliers and in artificial product differentiation. The counterargument is that consumers are willing to pay a higher price for a wider selection. According to this latter view, consumers benefit from more choice among gas stations, restaurants, convenience stores, clothing stores, video stores, drugstores, textbooks, hiking boots, and many other goods and services. For example, what if half of the restaurants in your area were to close just so the remaining ones could reduce their excess capacity? Some consumers, including you, might be disappointed if a favorite closed.

Perfect competitors and monopolistic competitors are so numerous in their respective markets that an action by any one of them has little or no effect on the behavior of others in the market. Another important market structure on the continuum between perfect competition and monopoly has just a few firms. We explore this market structure in the balance of the chapter.

LO2 An Introduction to Oligopoly

The final market structure we examine is *oligopoly,* a Greek word meaning "few sellers." When you think of "big business," you are thinking of oligopoly, an industry dominated by just a few firms. Perhaps three or four account for more than half the industry supply. Many industries, including steel, automobiles, oil, breakfast cereals, cigarettes, personal computers, and operating systems software, are oligopolistic. Because an oligopoly has only a few firms, each one must consider the effect of its own actions on competitors' behavior. Oligopolists are therefore said to be interdependent.

Varieties of Oligopoly

In some oligopolies, such as steel or oil, the product is identical, or undifferentiated, across producers. Thus, an undifferentiated oligopoly sells a commodity, such as an ingot of steel or a barrel of oil. But in other oligopolies, such as automobiles or breakfast cereals, the product is differentiated across producers. A differentiated oligopoly sells products that differ across producers, such as a Toyota Camry versus a Honda Accord.

The more similar the products, the greater the interdependence among firms in the industry. For example, because steel ingots are essentially identical, steel producers are quite sensitive to each other's pricing. A small rise in one producer's price sends customers to rivals. But with differentiated oligopoly, such as the auto industry, producers are not quite as sensitive about each other's prices. As with monopolistic competitors, oligopolists differentiate their products through (1) physical qualities, (2) sales locations, (3) services offered with the product, and (4) the image of the product established in the consumer's mind.

The more similar the products, the greater the interdependence among firms in the industry.

Because of interdependence, the behavior of any particular firm is difficult to predict. *Each firm knows that any changes in its product's quality, price, output, or advertising policy may prompt a reaction from its rivals. And each firm may react if another firm alters any of these features.* Monopolistic competition is like a professional golf tournament, where each player strives for a personal best. Oligopoly is more like a tennis match, where each player's actions depend on how and where the opponent hits the ball. Here's another analogy to help you understand the effects of interdependence: Did you ever find yourself in an awkward effort to get around someone coming toward you on a sidewalk? You each end up turning this way and that in a brief, clumsy encounter. You each are trying to figure out which way the other will turn. But since neither can read the other's mind, neither can work out the problem independently. The solution is for one of you to put your head down and just walk. The other then easily adjusts.

Why have some industries evolved into oligopolies, dominated by only a few firms? Although the reasons are not always clear, *an oligopoly can often be traced to some form of barrier to entry, such as economies of scale, legal restrictions, brand names built up by years of advertising, or control over an essential resource.* In the previous chapter, we examined barriers to entry as they applied to monopoly. Those same principles apply to oligopoly.

Economies of Scale

Perhaps the most important barrier to entry is economies of scale. Recall that the minimum efficient scale is the lowest output at which the firm takes full advantage of economies of scale. If a firm's minimum efficient scale is relatively large compared to industry output, then only a few firms are needed to satisfy industry demand. For example, an automobile plant of minimum efficient scale could make enough cars to supply nearly 10 percent of the U.S. market. If there were 100 auto plants, each would supply such a tiny portion of the market that the average cost per car would be higher than if only 10 plants manufacture autos. In the automobile industry, economies of scale create a barrier to entry. To compete with existing producers, a new entrant must sell enough automobiles to reach a competitive scale of operation.

Exhibit 4 presents the long-run average cost curve for a typical firm in the industry. If a new entrant sells only S cars, the average cost per unit, c_a, far exceeds the average cost, c_b, of a manufacturer that sells enough cars to reach the minimum efficient size, M. If autos sell for less than c_a, a potential entrant can expect to lose money, and this prospect discourages entry. For example, John Delorean tried to break into the auto industry in the early 1980s with a modern design featured in the *Back to the Future* movies. But his company managed to build and sell only 8,583 Deloreans before going bankrupt.

Exhibit 4

Economies of Scale as a Barrier to Entry

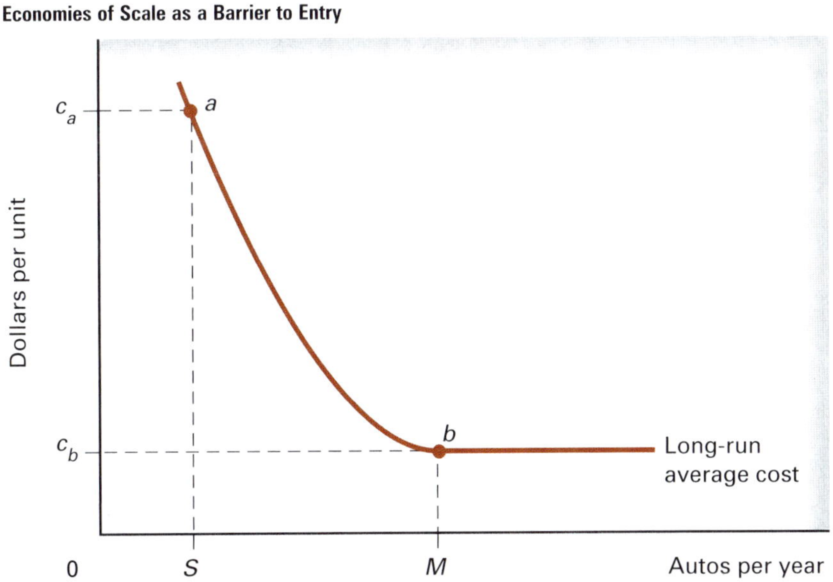

The High Cost of Entry

Potential entrants into oligopolistic industries could face another problem. The total investment needed to reach the minimum efficient size is often gigantic. A new auto plant or new semiconductor plant can cost over $3 billion. The average cost of developing and testing a new drug exceeds $800 million (only 1 in 25 drug candidates identified by the industry ever makes it to market).[1] Advertising a new product enough to compete with established brands may also require enormous outlays.

High start-up costs and established brand names create huge barriers to entry, especially because the market for new products is so uncertain (four out of five new consumer products don't survive). An unsuccessful product could cripple an upstart firm. The prospect of such a loss discourages many potential entrants. That's why most new products come from established firms. For example, Colgate-Palmolive spent $100 million introducing Total toothpaste, as did McDonald's in its failed attempt to sell the Arch Deluxe. Unilever lost $160 million when its new detergent, Power, washed out.

Firms often spend millions and sometimes billions trying to differentiate their products. Some of these outlays offer consumers useful information and wider choice. But some spending seems to offer neither. For example, Pepsi and Coke spend billions on messages such "It's the Cola" or "Life is Good." *Regardless, product differentiation expenditures create a barrier to entry.*

"Multiple products from the same brand dominate shelf space and attempt to crowd out new entrants."

Crowding Out the Competition

Oligopolies compete with existing rivals and try to block new entry by offering a variety of products. Entrenched producers may flood the market with new products in part to crowd out other new entries. For example, a few cereal makers offer more than a dozen products each. Many of these variations offer little that is new. One study of 25,500 new products introduced during one year found only 7 percent offered new or added benefits.[2] *Multiple products from the same brand dominate shelf space and attempt to crowd out new entrants.*

1. As reported in "Little Big Pharma," *Wall Steet Journal,* 6 December 2006.
2. The study was carried out by Market Intelligence Service and was reported in "Market Makers," *The Economist,* 14 March 1998.

LO3 Models of Oligopoly

Because oligopolists are interdependent, analyzing their behavior is complicated. No single model or single approach explains oligopoly behavior completely. At one extreme, oligopolists may try to coordinate their behavior so they act collectively as a single monopolist, forming a cartel, such as OPEC. At the other extreme, oligopolists may compete so fiercely that price wars erupt, such as those that break out among airlines, tobacco companies, computer chip makers, and wireless service providers.

Several theories have been developed to explain oligopoly behavior. We will study three of the better-known approaches: collusion, price leadership, and game theory. As you will see, each has some relevance in explaining observed behavior, although none is entirely satisfactory as a general theory of oligopoly. Thus, *there is no general theory of oligopoly but rather a set of theories, each based on the diversity of observed behavior in an interdependent market.*

>> **Potential entrants to oligopolistic industries face significant barriers to entry.**

© JOE CORNISH/STONE/GETTY IMAGES

Collusion and Cartels

In an oligopolistic market, there are just a few firms so, to decrease competition and increase profits, these firms may try to *collude*, or conspire to rig the market. **Collusion** is an agreement among firms in the industry to divide the market and fix the price. A **cartel** is a group of firms that agree to collude so they can act as a monopoly to increase economic profit. Cartels are more likely among sellers of a commodity, like oil or steel. *Colluding firms, compared with competing firms, usually produce less, charge more, block new firms, and earn more profit. Consumers pay higher prices, and potential entrants are denied the opportunity to compete.*

Collusion and cartels are illegal in the United States. Still, monopoly profit can be so tempting that some U.S. firms break the law. For example, top executives at Archer Daniels Midland were convicted of conspiring with four Asian competitors to rig the $650 million world market for lysine, an amino acid used in animal feed. Some other countries are more tolerant of cartels and a few even promote cartels, as with the 13 member-nations of OPEC. If OPEC ever met in the United States, its representatives could be arrested for price fixing. Cartels can operate worldwide because there are no international laws against them.

Suppose all firms in an industry formed a cartel. The market demand curve, *D*, appears in Exhibit 5. What price maximizes the cartel's profit, and how is output allocated among participating firms? The first task of the cartel is to determine its marginal cost of production. Because a cartel acts like a monopoly that runs many plants, the marginal cost curve for the cartel in Exhibit 5 is the horizontal sum of each firm's marginal cost curve. The cartel's marginal cost curve intersects the market's marginal revenue curve to determine output that maximizes the cartel's profit. This intersection yields quantity Q. The cartel's price, *p*, is read off the demand curve at that quantity.

So far, so good. To maximize cartel profit, output Q must be allocated among cartel members so that each member's marginal cost equals c. Any other allocation would lower cartel profit. Thus, *for cartel profit to be maximized, output must be allocated so that the marginal cost for the final unit produced by each firm is identical.* Let's look at why this is easier said than done.

Differences in Average Cost

If all firms have identical average cost curves, output and profit would be easily allocated across firms (each firm would produce the same amount), but if costs differ, as they usually do, problems arise. The greater the difference in average costs across firms,

Exhibit 5

Cartel as a Monopolist

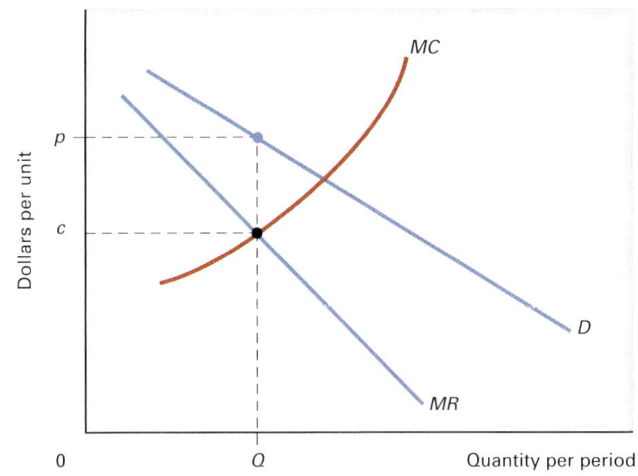

the greater the differences in economic profits among them. If cartel members try to equalize each firm's total profit, a high-cost firm would need to sell more than would a low-cost firm. But this allocation scheme would violate the cartel's profit-maximizing condition. Thus, *if average costs differ across firms, the output allocation that maximizes cartel profit yields unequal profit across cartel members.* Firms earning less profit could drop out of the cartel, thereby undermining it. Usually, the allocation of output is the result of haggling among cartel members. Firms that are more influential or more adept at bargaining get a larger share of output and profit. Allocation schemes are sometimes based on geography or on the historical division of output among firms. OPEC, for example, allocates output in proportion to each member country's share of estimated oil reserves. Cartel members of Norway's cement market base output on each firms share of industry capacity.[3]

Number of Firms in the Cartel

The more firms in an industry, the more difficult it is to negotiate an acceptable allocation of output among them. *Consensus becomes harder to achieve as the number of firms grows.* And the more firms in the industry, the more likely that some will become dissatisfied and bolt from the cartel.

3. Lars-Hendrik Roller and Frode Steen, "On the Workings of a Cartel: Evidence from the Norwegian Cement Industry," *American Economic Review* 96 (March 2006), p. 322.

collusion
an agreement among firms to increase economic profit by dividing the market and fixing the price

cartel
a group of firms that agree to coordinate their production and pricing decisions to earn monopoly profit

New Entry into the Industry

If a cartel can't prevent new entry into the market, new firms will eventually force prices down, squeeze economic profit, and disrupt the cartel. The profit of the cartel attracts entry, entry increases market supply, and increased supply forces the price down. A cartel's success therefore depends on barriers that block the entry of new firms.

Cheating

Perhaps the biggest problem in keeping the cartel together is the powerful temptation to cheat on the agreement. Because oligopolists usually operate with excess capacity, some cheat on the price. By offering a price slightly below the fixed price, any cartel member can usually increase sales and profit. Even if cartel members keep an eagle eye on each firm's price, one firm can increase sales by offering extra services, secret rebates, or other concessions. Cartels collapse once cheating *becomes widespread*.

OPEC's Spotty History

The problems of establishing and maintaining a cartel are reflected in the spotty history of OPEC. Many members are poor countries that rely on oil as their major source of revenue, so they argue over the price and their market share. OPEC members also cheat on the cartel. In 1980, the price of oil exceeded $80 a barrel. During the 1990s, the price averaged $32 a barrel and dipped as low as $10 a barrel. Oil prices hit what was a record high of $100 a barrel in early 2008, but then fell back to around $90 a barrel. Like other cartels, OPEC has difficulty with new entrants. The high prices resulting from OPEC's early success attracted new oil supplies from non-OPEC members operating in the North Sea, Mexico, and Siberia. The high price also made extraction from Canadian oil sands economical. As a result of new exploration and other oil sources, about 60 percent of the world's oil now comes from non-OPEC sources.

In summary: Establishing and maintaining an effective cartel is more difficult if (1) the product is differentiated among firms, (2) average costs differ among firms, (3) there are many firms in the industry, (4) entry barriers are low, or (5) cheating on the cartel agreement becomes widespread. Efforts to cartelize the world supply of a number of products, including bauxite, copper, tin, and coffee, have failed so far. Russia is trying to form a natural gas cartel with other gas exporters, but obstacles abound.

Price Leadership

An informal, or *tacit*, form of collusion occurs if there is a **price leader** who sets the price for the rest of the industry. Typically, a dominant firm sets the market price, and other firms follow that lead, thereby avoiding price competition. The price leader also initiates any price changes, and, again, others follow. The steel industry was an example of the price-leadership form of oligopoly. Typically, U.S. Steel, the largest firm in the industry, would set the price for various products. Public pressure on U.S. Steel not to raise prices eventually shifted the price-leadership role onto less prominent producers, resulting in a rotation of leadership among firms. Although the rotating price leadership reduced price conformity, price leadership kept prices high.

Like other forms of collusion, price leadership faces obstacles. Most importantly, the practice violates U.S. antitrust laws. Second, the greater the product differentiation among sellers, the less effective price leadership is as a means of collusion. Third, there is no guarantee that other firms will follow the leader. Firms that fail to follow a price increase take business away from firms that do. Fourth, unless there are barriers to entry, a profitable price attracts new entrants, which could destabilize the price-leadership agreement. And finally, as with formal cartels, some firms are tempted to cheat on the agreement to boost sales and profits.

price leader
a firm whose price is matched by other firms in the market as a form of tacit collusion

Cartels collapse once cheating becomes widespread.

LO4 Game Theory

How do firms act when they recognize their interdependence but either cannot or do not collude? Because oligopoly involves interdependence among a few firms, we can think of interacting firms as players in a game. **Game theory** examines oligopolistic behavior as a series of strategic moves and countermoves among rival firms. This approach analyzes the behavior of decision makers, or players, whose choices affect one another. Game theory is not really a separate model of oligopoly but a general approach, an approach that focuses on each player's incentives to cooperate—say, through cartels or price leaders—or to compete, in ways to be discussed now.

To get some feel for game theory, let's work through the **prisoner's dilemma**, the most widely examined game. The game originally considered a situation in which two thieves, let's call them Ben and Jerry, are caught near the crime scene and brought to police headquarters, where they are interrogated in separate rooms. The police know the two guys did it but can't prove it, so they need a confession. Each thief faces a choice of confessing, thereby "squealing" on the other, or "clamming up," thereby denying any knowledge of the crime. If one confesses, turning state's evidence, he is granted immunity from prosecution and goes free, while the other guy is put away for 10 years. If both clam up, each gets only a 1-year sentence on a technicality. If both confess, each gets 5 years.

What will Ben and Jerry do? The answer depends on the assumptions about their behavior—that is, what *strategy* each pursues. A **strategy** reflects a player's game plan. In this game, suppose each player tries to save his own skin—each tries to minimize his time in jail, regardless of what happens to the other (after all, there is no honor among thieves). Exhibit 6 shows the *payoff matrix* for the prisoner's dilemma. A **payoff matrix** is a table listing the rewards (or, in this case, the penalties) that Ben and Jerry can expect based on the strategy each pursues.

Exhibit 6

The Prisoner's Dilemma Payoff Matrix (years in jail)

Ben \ Jerry	Confess	Clam up
Confess	Ben: 5, Jerry: 5	Ben: 0, Jerry: 10
Clam up	Ben: 10, Jerry: 0	Ben: 1, Jerry: 1

Ben's choices are shown down the left margin and Jerry's across the top. Each prisoner can either confess or clam up. The numbers in the matrix indicate the prison time in years each can expect based on the corresponding strategies. Ben's numbers are in red and Jerry's in blue. Take a moment now to see how the matrix works. Notice that the sentence each player receives depends on the strategy he chooses and on the strategy the other player chooses.

What strategies are rational assuming that each player tries to minimize jail time? For example, put yourself in Ben's shoes. You know that Jerry, who is being questioned in another room, will either confess or clam up. If Jerry confesses, the left column of Exhibit 6 shows the penalties. If you confess too, you both get 5 years in jail, but if you clam up, you get 10 years and Jerry "walks." So, if you think Jerry will confess, you should too.

What if you believe Jerry will clam up? The right-hand column shows the two possible outcomes. If you confess, you do no time, but if you clam up too, you each get 1 year in jail. Thus, if you think Jerry will clam up, you're better off confessing. In short, whatever Jerry does, Ben is better

game theory an approach that analyzes oligopolistic behavior as a series of strategic moves and countermoves by rival firms

prisoner's dilemma a game that shows why players have difficulty cooperating even though they would benefit from cooperation

strategy in game theory, the operational plan pursued by a player

payoff matrix in game theory, a table listing the payoffs that each player can expect from each move based on the actions of the other player off confessing. The same holds for Jerry. He's better off confessing, regardless of what Ben does. So each has an incentive to confess and each gets 5 years in jail. This is called the **dominant-strategy equilibrium** of the game because each player's action does not depend on what he thinks the other player will do.

But notice that if each crook could just hang tough and clam up, both would be better off. After all, if both confess, each gets 5 years, but if both clam up, the police can't prove otherwise, so each gets only 1 year in jail. If each could trust the other to clam up, they both would be better off. But there is no way for the two to communicate or to coordinate their actions. That's why police investigators keep suspects apart, that's why organized crime threatens "squealers" with death, and that's why the witness protection program tries to shield "squealers."

Price-Setting Game

The prisoner's dilemma applies to a broad range of economic phenomena including pricing policy and advertising strategy. For example, consider the market for gasoline in a rural community with only two gas stations, Texaco and Exxon. Here the oligopoly consists of two sellers, or a **duopoly**. Suppose customers are indifferent between the brands and focus only on the price. Each station posts its daily price early in the morning before learning about the other station's price. To keep things simple, suppose only two prices are possible—a low price or a high price. If both charge the low price, they split the market and each earns a profit of $500 per day. If both charge the high price, they also split the market, but profit jumps to $700 each. If one charges the high price but the other the low one, the low-price station gets most of the business, earning a profit of $1,000, leaving the high-price station with only $200.

Exhibit 7 shows the payoff matrix, with Texaco's strategy down the left margin and Exxon's across the top. Texaco's profit appears in red, and Exxon's in blue. Suppose you are running the Texaco station and are trying to decide what to charge. If Exxon charges the low price, you earn $500 charging the low price but only $200 charging the high price. So you earn more charging the low price. If, instead, Exxon charges the high price, you earn $1,000 charging the low price and $700 charging the high price. Again, you earn more charging the low price. Exxon faces the same incentives. Thus, each charges the low price, regardless of what the other does.

dominant-strategy equilibrium
in game theory, the outcome achieved when each player's choice does not depend on what the other player does

duopoly
a market with only two producers; a special type of oligopoly market structure

Nash equilibrium
a situation in which a firm, or a player in game theory, chooses the best strategy given the strategies chosen by others; no participant can improve his or her outcome by changing strategies even after learning of the strategies selected by other participants

Exhibit 7

Price-Setting Payoff Matrix (profit per day)

Texaco \ Exxon	Low price	High price
Low price	$500 (Texaco) / $500 (Exxon)	$1,000 (Texaco) / $200 (Exxon)
High price	$200 (Texaco) / $1,000 (Exxon)	$700 (Texaco) / $700 (Exxon)

The prisoner's dilemma outcome is an equilibrium because each player maximizes profit, given the price chosen by the other. Neither gas station can increase profit by changing its price, given the price chosen by the other firm. A situation in which a player chooses its best strategy given the strategies chosen by other firms is called a **Nash equilibrium**, named after Nobel Prize winner and former Princeton professor John Nash. He inspired the award-winning movie *A Beautiful Mind* starring Russell Crowe as Nash.

In this prisoner's dilemma, each charges the low price, earning $500 a day, although each would earn $700 charging the high price. Think of yourself as a member of the oil cartel discussed earlier, where the cartel determines the price and sets production quotas for each member. If you think other firms in the cartel will stick with their quotas, you can increase your profit by cutting your price and thereby increasing quantity sold. If you think the other firms will cheat on the cartel by cutting the price, then you should too—otherwise, you will get your clock cleaned by those cheaters. Either way, your incentive as a cartel member is to cheat on the quota. All members have an incentive to cheat, although all would earn more by sticking with the agreement that maximizes joint profit. Cheating is a Nash equilibrium, unless the cartel has real teeth to keep members in line—that is, unless cartel members have the strategy imposed on them.

This incentive to cut prices suggests why price wars sometimes break out among oligopolists. Even in industries with just two or three firms, competition often locks these rivals in a steel-cage death match for survival. For example, in recent years automakers have aggressively matched and exceeded one another's price cuts and rebate programs, cutting auto prices sharply. For example, the Cadillac DeVille had a sticker price of $48,000 but sold for less than $35,000. General Motors eked out just $15 in profit on each car and truck sold; Ford lost money on each vehicle.[4] A bitter price war with Dell cut Hewlett-Packard's earnings on each $500 personal computer sold to a razor-thin $1.75.[5] Early profits in the animated movie business attracted entry, which over time cut profit and led to some bankruptcies. And just before a recent Thanksgiving weekend, a price war erupted in airfares. American Airlines first announced holiday discounts. Delta responded with cuts of up to 50 percent. Within hours, American, United, and other major carriers said they would match Delta's reductions. All these airlines were losing money at the time. So go the price wars.

> EVEN IN INDUSTRIES WITH JUST TWO OR THREE FIRMS, COMPETITION OFTEN LOCKS THESE RIVALS IN A STEEL-CAGE DEATH MATCH FOR SURVIVAL.

Cola War Game

As a final example of a prisoner's dilemma, consider the marketing strategies of Coke and Pepsi. Suppose each is putting together a promotional budget for the coming year, not knowing the other's plans. The choice boils down to adopting either a moderate budget or a big budget—one that involves multiple Super Bowl ads, showy in-store displays, and other marketing efforts aimed mostly at attracting customers from each other. If each adopts a big budget, their costly efforts will, for the most part, cancel each other out and limit each company's profit to $2 billion a year. If each adopts a moderate promotional budget, the money saved boosts profit for each to $3 billion a year. And if one adopts a big budget but the other does not, the heavy promoter captures a bigger market share and earns $4 billion, while the other loses market share and earns only $1 billion. What to do, what to do?

Exhibit 8 shows the payoff matrix for the two strategies, with Pepsi's choices listed down the left margin and Coke's across the top. In each cell of the matrix, Pepsi's profit appears in blue, and Coke's in red. Let's look at Pepsi's decision. If Coke adopts a big promotional budget, Pepsi earns $2 billion by doing the same but only $1 billion by adopting a moderate budget. Thus, if Coke adopts a big budget, so should Pepsi. If Coke adopts a moderate budget, Pepsi earns $4 billion with a big budget and $3 billion with a moderate one. Again, Pepsi earns more with a big budget. Coke faces the same incentives, so both adopt big budgets, earning $2 billion each in profit, even though each would have earned $3 billion with a moderate budget.

Exhibit 8

Cola War Payoff Matrix (annual profit in billions)

Pepsi \ Coke	Big budget	Moderate budget
Big budget	$2 (Pepsi) / $2 (Coke)	$4 (Pepsi) / $1 (Coke)
Moderate budget	$1 (Pepsi) / $4 (Coke)	$3 (Pepsi) / $3 (Coke)

One-Shot Versus Repeated Games

The outcome of a game often depends on whether it is a *one-shot game* or a *repeated game*. The classic prisoner's dilemma is a one-shot game. If the game is to be played just once, the strategy of confessing makes you better off regardless of what the other player does. Your choice won't influence the other player's behavior. But if the same players repeat the prisoner's dilemma, as would likely occur with the price-setting game, the cola war game, and the OPEC cartel, other possibilities unfold. In a repeated-game setting, each player has a chance to establish a reputation for cooperation and thereby may be able to encourage other players to do the same. After all, the

4. Micheline Maynard, "Car Sticker Prices Mask Some Big Bargains," *New York Times,* 29 October 2003.
5. David Bank, "H-P Posts 10% Increase in Revenue," *Wall Street Journal,* 20 November 2003.

cooperative solution—whether that involves clamming up, maintaining a high price, or adopting a moderate marketing budget—makes both players better off than if both fail to cooperate.

Experiments have shown that the strategy with the highest payoff in repeated games turns out to be the simplest—tit-for-tat. You begin by cooperating in the first round. On every round thereafter, you cooperate if the other player cooperated in the previous round, and you cheat if your opponent cheated in the previous round. In short, in any given round, you do whatever your opponent did in the previous round. The tit-for-tat strategy offers the other player immediate rewards for cooperation and immediate punishment for cheating. Some cartels seem to employ tit-for-tat strategies.

Coordination Game

In the coordination game, a Nash equilibrium occurs when each player chooses the same strategy. For example, you are driving on a country road and have to decide whether to drive on the right or the left side. Suppose you decide to drive on your left. If the driver coming from the opposite direction drives on his or her left, you pass each other without incident, so the cost to each of you is zero. But if the other player drives on the right-hand side, the probability of a crash increases. If, instead, you choose to drive on the right-hand side, you encounter no problems if the oncoming driver does the same, but face a greater likelihood of crashing if the other driver chooses the left-hand side. In this game, cost is mimimized when both players choose to drive either on the left or on the right. And each strategy is a Nash equilibrium because no player can improve on that outcome, given the other player's choice. So if you choose the left-hand side and the other player chooses his or her left-hand side, then you can do no better and would do worse choosing the right-hand side.

tit-for-tat
in game theory, a strategy in repeated games when a player in one round of the game mimics the other player's behavior in the previous round; an optimal strategy for getting the other player to cooperate

coordination game
a type of game in which a Nash equilibrium occurs when each player chooses the same strategy; neither player can do better than matching the other player's strategy

Our discussion has given you some idea of game theory by focusing mostly on the prisoner's dilemma. Other games can be more complicated and involve more strategic interaction. Because firms are interdependent, oligopoly gives rise to all kinds of behavior and many approaches. Each approach helps explain certain behavior observed in oligopolistic markets. The *cartel,* or *collusion,* model shows why oligopolists might want to cooperate in fixing the market price; but that model also explains why a cartel is hard to establish and maintain. The *price-leadership* model explains why and how firms may charge the same price without explicitly establishing a formal cartel. Finally, *game theory,* expressed here mostly by the prisoner's dilemma, shows how difficult a cooperative solution might be even though cooperation benefits both sides. Game theory is more of an approach to oligopoly rather than a distinct model.

LO5 Comparison of Oligopoly and Perfect Competition

As we have seen, each approach explains a piece of the oligopoly puzzle. But each has limitations, and none provides a complete picture of oligopoly behavior. Because there is no typical, or representative, model of oligopoly, "the" oligopoly model cannot be compared with the competitive model. We might, however, imagine an experiment in which we took the many firms that populate a competitive industry and, through a series of giant mergers, combined them to form, say, four firms. We would thereby transform the industry from perfect competition to oligopoly. How would firms in this industry behave before and after the massive merger?

Price Is Usually Higher Under Oligopoly

With fewer competitors after the merger, remaining firms would become more interdependent. Oligopoly models presented in this chapter suggest why firms may try to coordinate their pricing policies. *If oligopolists engaged in some sort of implicit or explicit collusion, industry output would be smaller and the price would be higher than under perfect competition.* Even if oligopolists did not collude but simply operated with excess capacity, the price would be higher and the quantity lower with oligopoly than with perfect competition. The price could become lower under oligopoly compared with perfect competition if a price war broke out among oligopolists. Two rivals, Intel and Advanced Micro Devices (AMD), together account for the entire market for a specific type of computer chip, yet these two are always at each other's throat, thereby keeping prices and profits down. Behavior also depends on whether there are barriers to entry. The lower the barriers to entry into the oligopoly, the more oligopolists act like perfect competitors.

© MIGUEL VIDAL/REUTERS/LANDOV

Firms boost market power (and profits) by offering a differentiated product. Zara, Europe's largest fashion retailer, launches about 10,000 new designs a year, which it makes at its network of 14 Spanish factories like this one.

Higher Profits Under Oligopoly

In the long run, easy entry prevents perfect competitors from earning more than a normal profit. With oligopoly, however, there may be barriers to entry, such as economies of scale or a way to differentiate a product such as with brand names, which allow firms in the industry to earn long-run economic profit. *With barriers to entry, we should expect profit in the long run to be higher under oligopoly than under perfect competition.* Profit rates do in fact appear to be higher in industries where a few firms account for a high proportion of industry sales. Some economists view these higher profit rates as troubling evidence of market power. But not all economists share this view. Some note that the largest firms in oligopolistic industries tend to earn the highest rate of profit. Thus, the higher profit rates observed in oligopolistic industries do not necessarily stem from market power per se. Rather, these higher profit rates stem from the greater efficiency arising from economies of scale in these large firms. An individual firm can also achieve greater market power and higher profit by differentiating its product.

Final Word

Firms in monopolistic competition and in oligopoly face a downward-sloping demand curve for their products. With monopolistic competition, there are so many firms in the market that each tends to get lost in the crowd. Each behaves independently. But with oligopoly, there are so few firms in the market that each must consider the impact its pricing, output, and marketing decisions will have on other firms. Each oligopolist behaves interdependently, and this makes oligopoly difficult to analyze. As a result, there are different models and approaches to oligopoly, three of which were discussed in this chapter.

The analytical results derived in this chapter are not as clear-cut as for the polar cases of perfect competition and monopoly. Still, we can draw some general conclusions using perfect competition as a guide. In the long run, perfect competitors operate at minimum average cost, while other types of firms usually operate with excess capacity. Therefore, given identical cost curves, monopolists, monopolistic competitors, and oligopolists tend to charge higher prices than perfect competitors do, especially in the long run. In the long run, monopolistic competitors, like perfect competitors, earn only a normal profit because entry barriers are low. Monopolists and oligopolists can earn economic profit in the long run if new entry is restricted. In a later chapter, we examine government policies aimed at increasing competition. *Regardless of the market structure, however, profit maximization prompts firms to produce where marginal revenue equals marginal cost.*

This chapter has moved us from the extremes of perfect competition and monopoly to the gray area inhabited by most firms. Exhibit 9 compares features and examples of the four market structures. Please take a moment now to review these key distinctions. Some of these issues are revisited later when we explore the government's role in promoting market competition.

Exhibit 9

Comparison of Market Structures

	Perfect Competition	Monopoly	Monopolistic Competition	Oligopoly
Number of firms	Most	One	Many	Few
Control over price	None	Complete	Limited	Some
Product differences	None	None	Some	None or some
Barriers to entry	None	Insurmountable	Low	Substantial
Examples	Wheat	Local electricity	Convenience stores	Automobiles

CHAPTER 11

Resource Markets

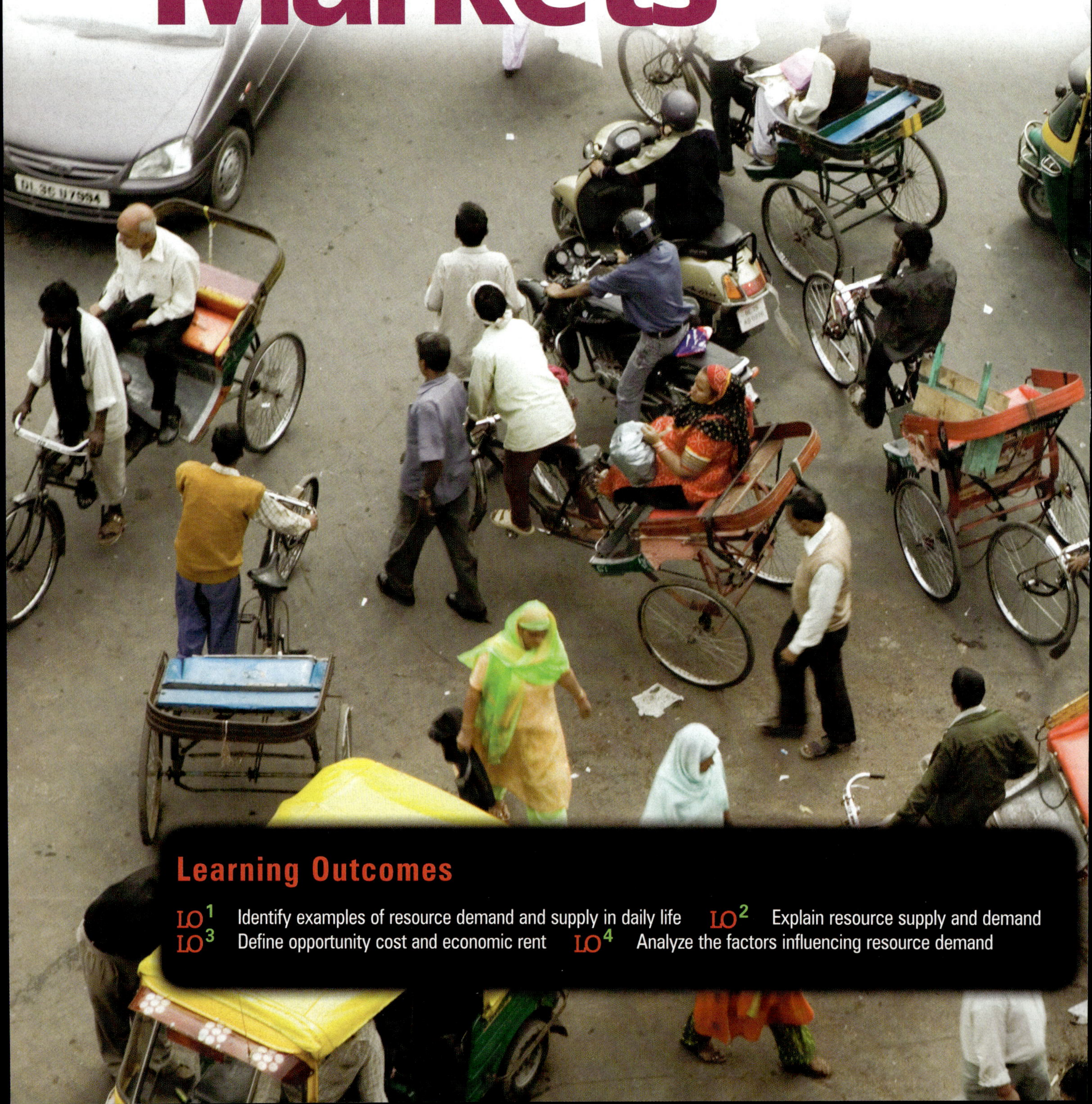

Learning Outcomes

LO 1 Identify examples of resource demand and supply in daily life

LO 2 Explain resource supply and demand

LO 3 Define opportunity cost and economic rent

LO 4 Analyze the factors influencing resource demand

“Why do truck drivers in the United States earn at least 20 times more than bicycle-rickshaw drivers in India?”

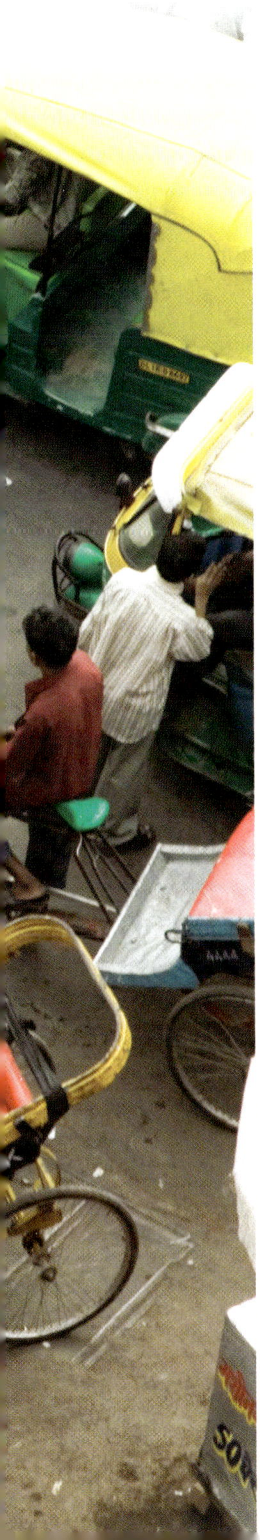

Why do surgeons earn twice as much as general practitioners? Why do truck drivers in the United States earn at least 20 times more than bicycle-rickshaw drivers in India? Why does prime Iowa corn acreage cost more than scrubland in the high plains of Montana? Why are buildings taller in downtown Chicago than those in the city's suburbs? To answer these and other questions, we turn to the demand and supply of resources.

You say you've been through this demand-and-supply drill already? True. But the earlier focus was on the product market—that is, on the market for final goods and services. Goods and services are produced by resources—labor, capital, natural resources, and entrepreneurial ability. Demand and supply in resource markets determine the price and quantity of resources. And the ownership of resources determines the distribution of earnings throughout the economy.

Because your earnings depend on the market value of your resources, you should find a study of resource markets particularly relevant to your future. Certainly one consideration in your career choice is the expected earnings associated with alternative careers. The next three chapters examine how demand and supply interact to establish market prices for various resources.

What do you think?

I'd be willing to work more hours for an increased hourly wage.

Strongly Disagree 1 2 3 4 5 6 7 *Strongly Agree*

LO[1] The Once-Over

Just to prove you already know more about resource markets than you may think, try answering the questions that arise in the following examples of resource demand and supply.

Topics discussed in Chapter 11 include:

- Demand and supply of resources
- Opportunity cost and economic rent
- Marginal revenue product
- Marginal resource cost
- Changes in resource demand

Resource Demand

Let's begin with the demand for labor. The manager of Wal-Mart estimates that hiring another sales clerk would increase total revenue by $500 per week but increase total cost by $400 per week. Should Wal-Mart hire another sales clerk? Sure, because profit would increase by $100 per week. *As long as the additional revenue from employing another worker exceeds the additional cost, the firm should hire that worker.*

© WINDSOR & WIEHAHN/STONE/GETTY IMAGES

What about capital? Suppose that you run a lawn service during the summer, getting an average of $50 per lawn. You have all the business you can handle. You mow about 15 lawns a week, for total revenue of $750 a week. You are thinking of upgrading to a larger, faster mower called the Lawn Monster, but it would cost you an extra $500 per week. The bigger mower would cut your time per lawn in half, enabling you to mow 30 lawns per week, so your total revenue would double to $1,500. Should you make the switch? Because the additional revenue of $750 exceeds the additional cost of $500, you should move up to the Monster.

What about natural resources? A neighbor offers Farmer Jones the chance to lease 100 acres of farmland. Jones figures that farming the extra land would cost $70 per acre but would yield $60 per acre in additional revenue. Should Jones lease the extra land? What do you think? Because the additional cost of farming that land would exceed the additional revenue, the answer is no.

These examples show that a *producer demands another unit of a resource as long as its marginal revenue exceeds its marginal cost.*

Resource Supply

You likely also understand the logic behind resource supply. Suppose you are trying to decide between two jobs that are identical except that one pays more than the other. Is there any question which one you'll take? If the working conditions are equally attractive, you would choose the higher-paying job. Now let's say your choice is between two jobs that pay the same. One has normal 9-to-5 hours, but the other starts at 5 A.M., an hour when your body tends to reject conscious activity. Which would you choose? You would pick the one that suits your tastes.

People supply their resources to the highest-paying alternative, other things constant. Because other things are not always constant, people must be paid more for jobs less suited to their tastes. Your utility depends on both monetary and nonmonetary aspects of the job. Generally, people must be paid more for jobs that are dirty, dangerous, dull, exhausting, illegal, low status, have no future, have no benefits, and involve inconvenient hours than for jobs that are clean, safe, interesting, energizing, legal, high status, have bright prospects, have good benefits, and involve convenient hours.

PEOPLE SUPPLY THEIR RESOURCES TO THE HIGHEST-PAYING ALTERNATIVE, OTHER THINGS CONSTANT.

LO2 The Demand and Supply of Resources

In the market for goods and services—that is, in the product market—households are the demanders and firms are suppliers. Households demand the goods and services that maximize utility, and firms supply the goods and services that maximize profit. In the resource market, roles are reversed: Firms are demanders and households are suppliers. Firms demand resources to maximize profit, and households supply resources to maximize utility. *Any differences between the profit-maximizing goals of firms and the utility-maximizing goals of households are sorted out through voluntary exchange in markets.*

Exhibit 1 presents the market for a particular resource—in this case, carpenters. As you can see, the demand curve slopes downward and the supply curve slopes upward. *Like the demand and supply for final goods and services, the demand and supply for resources depend on the willingness and ability of buyers and sellers to engage in market exchange.* This market converges to the equilibrium wage, or the market price, for this type of labor.

Exhibit 1

Resource Market for Carpenters

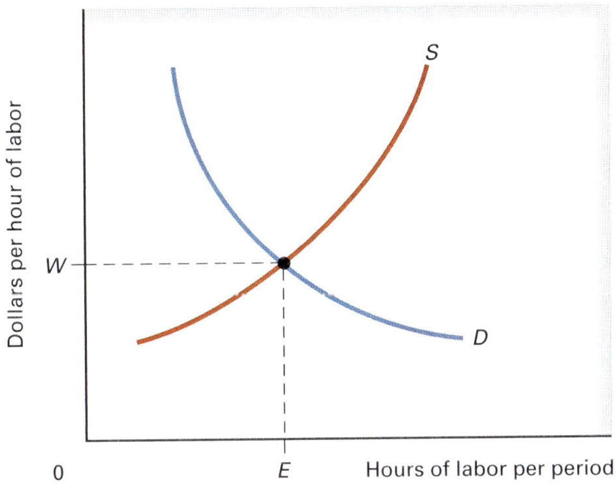

The Market Demand for Resources

Why do firms employ resources? Resources produce goods and services, which firms try to sell for a profit. A firm values not the resource itself but the resource's ability to produce goods and services. Because the value of any resource depends on what it produces, the demand for a resource is said to be a **derived demand**—arising from the demand for the final product. For example, a carpenter's pay derives from the demand for the carpenter's output, such as a cabinet or a new deck. A professional baseball player's pay derives from the demand for ballgames. A truck driver's pay derives from the demand for transporting goods. The derived nature of resource demand helps explain why professional baseball players usually earn more than professional hockey players, why brain surgeons earn more than tree surgeons, and why drivers of big rigs earn more than drivers of delivery vans. Derived demand also explains why, in the face of an industry-wide slump in box office sales, Hollywood stars like Tom Cruise, Brad Pitt, and Cameron Diaz accepted pay cuts.[1]

The market demand for a particular resource is the sum of demands for that resource in all its different uses. For example, the market demand for carpenters adds together the demands for carpenters in residential and commercial construction, remodeling, cabinetmaking, and so on. Similarly, the market demand for timber sums the demand for this resource as lumber, railway ties, furniture, pencils, toothpicks, paper products, firewood, and so on. The demand curve for a resource, like the demand for the goods produced by that resource, slopes downward, as depicted in Exhibit 1.

As the price of a resource falls, producers are more willing and able to employ that resource. Consider first the producer's greater *willingness* to hire resources as the resource price falls. In developing the demand curve for a particular resource, we assume the prices of other resources remain constant. So if the price of a particular resource falls, it becomes cheaper compared with other resources that could produce the same output. Firms therefore are more willing to hire this resource rather than hire other, now relatively more costly, resources. Thus, we observe *substitution in production*—carpenters for masons, coal for oil, security alarms for security guards, and backhoes for grave diggers, as the relative prices of carpenters, coal, security alarms, and backhoes fall.

A lower price for a resource also increases a producer's *ability* to hire that resource. For example, if the wage of carpenters falls, home builders can hire more carpenters for the same total cost. The lower resource price means the firm is *more able* to employ the resource.

The Market Supply of Resources

The market supply curve for a resource sums all the individual supply curves for that resource. Resource suppliers are more *willing* and more *able* to increase quantity supplied as the resource price increases, so the market supply curve slopes upward, as in Exhibit 1. Resource suppliers are more *willing* because a higher resource price, other things constant, means more goods and services can be purchased with the earnings from each unit of the resource supplied. Resource prices are signals about the rewards for supplying resources. A high resource price tells the resource owner, "The market will reward you more for what you supply." Higher prices draw resources from lower-valued uses, including leisure. For example, as the wage for carpenters increases, the quantity of labor supplied increases. Some carpenters give up leisure to work more.

The second reason a resource supply curve slopes upward is that resource owners are more *able* to increase the quantity supplied as the resource price increases. For example, a higher carpenter's wage means more apprentices can undergo the extensive

derived demand demand that arises from the demand for the product the resource produces

1. John Hiscock, "Hollywood Stars Meet the Real World," *The Independent*, 16 July 2006.

training to become carpenters. A higher wage *enables* resource suppliers to increase their quantity supplied. Similarly, a higher timber price enables loggers to harvest trees in less accessible forests, a higher gold price enables miners to extract the metal from lower grade ore, and a higher oil price enables producers to drill deeper and explore more remote parts of the world.

Temporary and Permanent Resource Price Differences

People have a strong interest in selling their resources where they are valued the most. *Resources tend to flow to their highest-valued use.* If, for example, carpenters can earn more building homes than making furniture, they shift into home building until wages in the two uses are equal. Because resource owners seek the highest pay, *other things constant,* earnings should tend toward equality across the different uses. For example, suppose carpenters who build homes earn $25 per hour, which is $5 more than carpenters who make furniture. This difference is shown in Exhibit 2 by an initial wage of $25 per hour in panel (a) and an initial wage of $20 per hour in panel (b). This gap encourages some carpenters to move from furniture making into home building, pulling up the wage in furniture making and driving down the wage in home building. Carpenters migrate into home building until wages equalize. In Exhibit 2, labor supply shifts leftward for furniture making and rightward for home building until the wage reaches $24 in both markets. Note that 2,000 hours of labor per day shift from furniture making to home building. *As long as the nonmonetary benefits of supplying resources to alternative uses are identical and as long as resources are freely mobile, resources adjust across uses until they earn the same in different uses.*

Sometimes earnings appear to differ between seemingly similar resources. For example, corporate economists on average earn more than academic economists, and land in the city goes for more than land in the country. As you will now see, these differences also reflect the workings of demand and supply.

Temporary Differences in Resource Prices

Resource prices might differ temporarily across markets because adjustment takes time. For example, sometimes wage differences occur among workers who appear equally qualified. As you have seen, however, a difference between the prices of similar resources prompts resource owners and firms to make adjustments that drive resource prices toward equality, as with the carpenters in Exhibit 2. The process may take years, but when resource markets are free to adjust, price differences trigger the reallocation of resources, which equalizes earnings for similar resources.

Exhibit 2

Market for Carpenter in Alternative Uses

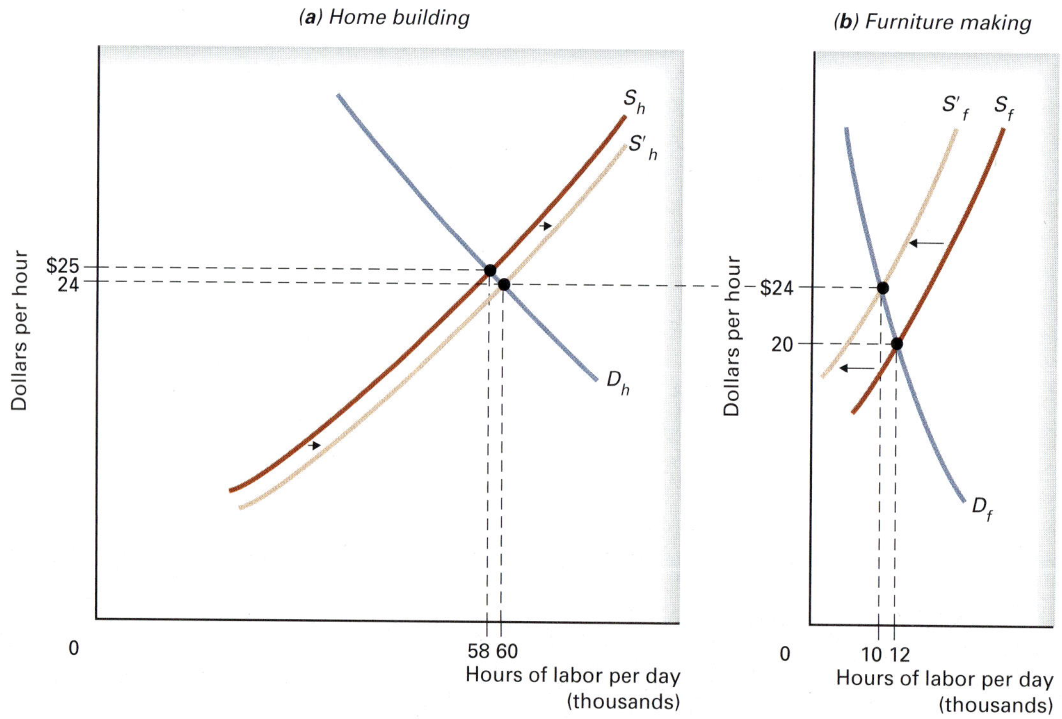

Permanent Differences in Resource Prices

Not all resource price differences cause reallocation. For example, land along New York's Fifth Avenue sells for as much as $36,000 a *square yard!* For that amount, you could buy several acres in Upstate New York. Yet such a difference does not prompt upstaters to supply their land to New York City—obviously that's impossible. Likewise, the price of farmland itself varies widely, reflecting differences in the land's fertility and location. Such differences do not trigger shifts of resource supply. Similarly, certain wage differentials stem in part from the different costs of acquiring the education and training needed to perform particular tasks. This difference explains why brain surgeons earn more than tree surgeons, why ophthalmologists earn more than optometrists, and why airline pilots earn more than truck drivers.

Differences in the nonmonetary aspects of similar jobs also lead to pay differences. For example, other things constant, most people would require higher pay to work in a grimy factory than in a pleasant office. Similarly, academic economists earn less than corporate economists, in part because academic economists typically have more freedom in their daily schedules, their attire, their choices of research topics, and even in their public statements.

Some price differences are temporary because they spark shifts of resource supply away from lower-paid uses and toward higher-paid uses. Other price differences cause no such shifts and are permanent. Permanent price differences are explained by *a lack of resource mobility* (urban land versus rural land), *differences in the inherent quality of the resource* (fertile land versus scrubland), *differences in the time and money involved in developing the necessary skills* (certified public accountant versus file clerk), or *differences in nonmonetary aspects of the job* (lifeguard at Malibu Beach versus prison guard at San Quentin).

LO3 Opportunity Cost and Economic Rent

Shaquille O'Neal earned about $20 million in 2007 playing basketball plus at least $10 million more from product endorsements, including his Nike sneakers. But he would probably have been willing

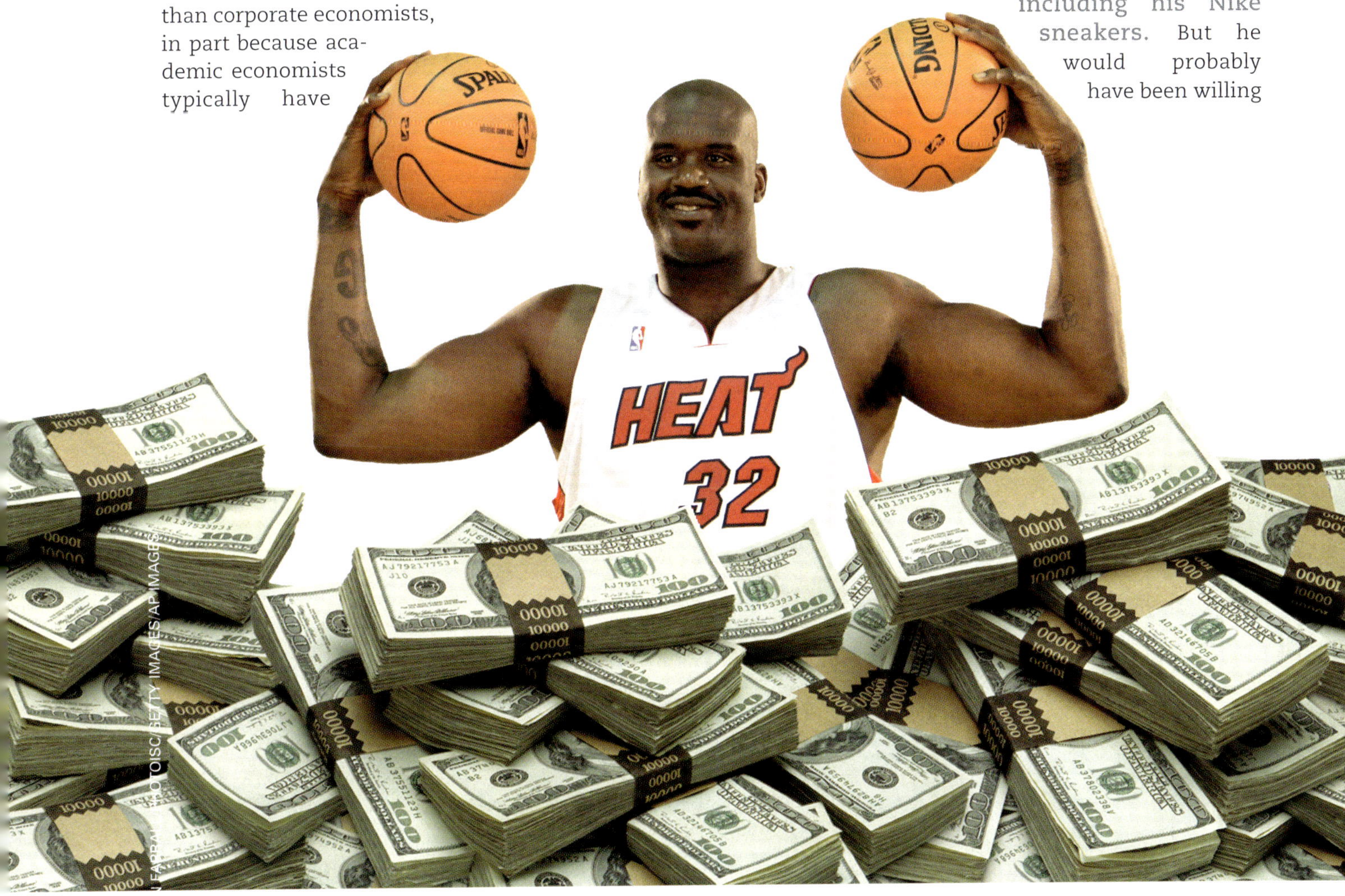

to play basketball and endorse products for less. The question is, how much less? What is his best alternative? Suppose his best alternative is to become a full-time rap artist, something he now does in his spare time (as of 2007, he had released six rap albums). Suppose, as a full-time rapper, he could earn $1 million a year, including endorsements. And suppose, aside from the pay gap, he's indifferent between basketball and rap, so the nonmonetary aspects of the two jobs even out. Thus, he must be paid at least $1 million to remain in basketball, and this represents his opportunity cost. *Opportunity cost is what that resource could earn in its best alternative use.*

> Opportunity cost is what the resource could earn in its best alternative use.

The amount O'Neal earns in excess of his opportunity cost is called *economic rent*. **Economic rent** is that portion of a resource's earnings that exceeds the amount necessary to keep the resource in its present use. Economic rent is, as the saying goes, "pure gravy." In O'Neal's case, economic rent is $29 million. Economic rent is producer surplus earned by resource suppliers. The *division of earnings between opportunity cost and economic rent depends on the resource owner's elasticity of supply. In general, the less elastic the resource supply, the greater the economic rent as a proportion of total earnings.* To develop a feel for the difference between opportunity cost and economic rent, let's consider three resource markets.

economic rent
portion of a resource's total earnings that exceeds its opportunity cost; earnings greater than the amount required to keep the resource in its present use

Resource Market A:

All Earnings Are Economic Rent

If the supply of a resource to a particular market is perfectly inelastic, that resource has no alternative use. Thus, there is no opportunity cost, and all earnings are economic rent. For example, scrubland in the high plains of Montana has no use other than for grazing cattle. The supply of this land is depicted by the red vertical line in panel (a) of Exhibit 3, which indicates that the 10 million acres have no alternative use. Because supply is fixed, the rent paid to graze cattle on this land has no effect on the quantity of land supplied. *The land's opportunity cost is zero, so all earnings are economic rent, shown by the blue-shaded area.* Here, fixed supply determines the equilibrium quantity of the resource, but demand determines the equilibrium price.

Resource Market B:

All Earnings Are Opportunity Costs

At the other extreme is the market in which a resource can earn as much in its best alternative use as in its present use. This situation is illustrated by the perfectly elastic supply curve in panel (b) of Exhibit 3, which shows the market for janitors in the local school

Exhibit 3

Opportunity Cost and Economic Rent

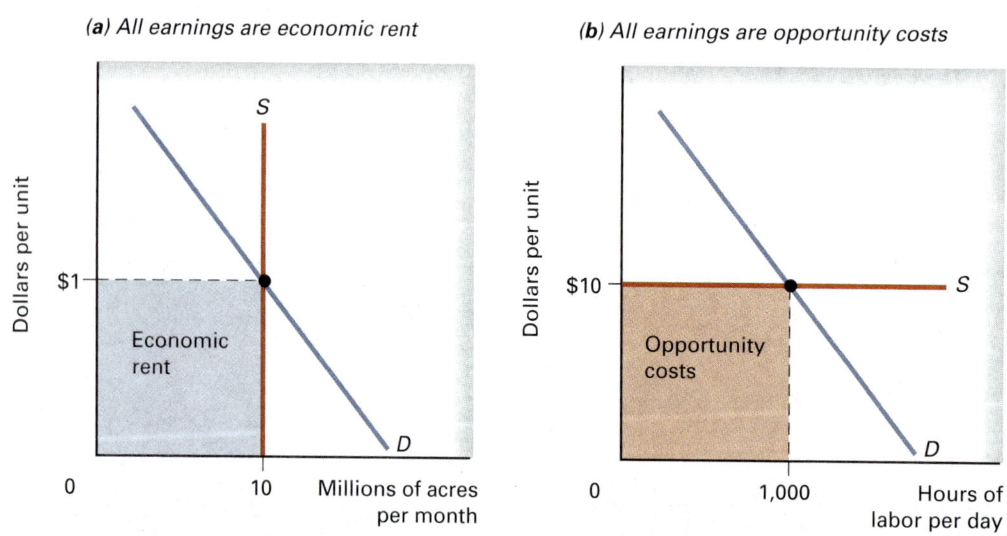

system. Here, janitors earn $10 an hour and supply 1,000 hours of labor per day. If the school system paid less than $10 per hour, janitors could find jobs elsewhere, perhaps in nearby factories, where the wage is $10 per hour. *All earnings reflect opportunity cost.* There is no economic rent. In this resource market, the horizontal supply curve determines the equilibrium wage, but demand determines the equilibrium quantity.

Resource Market C:

Earnings Include Both Economic Rent and Opportunity Costs

If the supply curve slopes upward, most resource suppliers earn economic rent in addition to their opportunity cost. For example, if the market wage for unskilled work in your college community increases from $7 to $14 per hour, the quantity of labor supplied would increase, as would the economic rent earned by these workers. This market occurs in panel (c) of Exhibit 3, where the pink shading identifies opportunity costs and the blue shading, economic rent. If the wage increases from $7 to $14 per hour, the quantity supplied increases by 5,000 hours. For those who were willing to work for $7 per hour, the difference between $7 and $14 is economic rent. *When resource supply slopes upward, as it usually does, earnings consist of both opportunity cost and economic rent.* In the case of an upward-sloping supply curve and a downward-sloping demand curve, both demand and supply determine equilibrium price and quantity.

Note that specialized resources tend to earn a higher proportion of economic rent than do resources with alternative uses. Thus, Shaquille O'Neal earns a greater *proportion* of his income as economic rent than does the janitor who cleans the Miami Heat's locker room. O'Neal would take a huge pay cut if he didn't play professional basketball, but the Heat's janitor could probably find another semi-skilled job that would pay nearly as much.

Exhibit 3, cont.

Opportunity Cost and Economic Rent

(c) Earnings divide between economic rent and opportunity cost

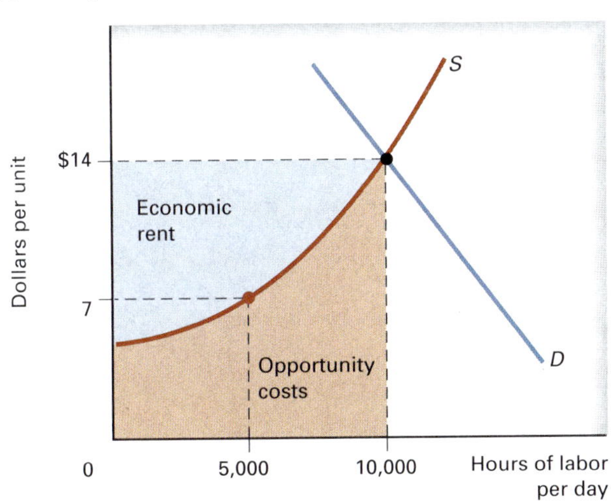

To review: Given a resource demand curve that slopes downward, when the resource supply curve is vertical (perfectly inelastic), all earnings are economic rent; when that supply curve is horizontal (perfectly elastic), all earnings are opportunity cost; and when that supply curve slopes upward (an elasticity greater than zero but less than infinity), earnings divide between economic rent and opportunity cost. Remember, *the opportunity cost of a resource is what that resource could earn in its best alternative use. Economic rent is earnings in excess of opportunity cost.* Economic rent to a resource holder is like economic profit to the firm.

> "Economic rent is earnings in excess of opportunity cost."

This completes our introduction to resource demand and supply. In the balance of this chapter, we take a closer look at resource demand. The determinants of resource demand are largely the same whether we are talking about labor, capital, or natural resources. The supply of different resources, however, has certain peculiarities depending on the resource, so the supply of resources is taken up in the next chapter.

LO4 A Closer Look at Resource Demand

Although production usually involves many resources, we cut the analysis down to size by focusing on a single resource, assuming that employment of other resources remains constant. As usual, we assume that firms try to maximize profit and households try to maximize utility.

The Firm's Demand for a Resource

You may recall that when production costs were first introduced, we considered a moving company, where labor was the only variable resource in the

© SIMON POTTER/IMAGE SOURCE

short run. We examined the relationship between the quantity of labor employed and the amount of furniture moved per day. The same approach is used in Exhibit 4, where only one resource varies. Column (1) lists possible employment levels of the variable resource, here measured as workers per day. Column (2) lists the amount produced, or total product, and column (3) lists the marginal product. The *marginal product* of labor is the change in total product from employing one more unit of labor.

With only one worker, total product is 10 units as is the marginal product. The marginal product of a second worker is 9 units. Notice in this example that diminishing marginal returns set in immediately—that is, right after the first worker.

Although labor is the variable resource here, we could examine the marginal product of any resource. For example, we could consider the number of lawns cut per week by varying the quantity of capital. We might start off with very little capital—imagine cutting grass with scissors—and then move up to a push mower, a power mower, and the Lawn Monster. By holding labor constant and varying the quantity of capital employed, we could compute the marginal product of capital. Likewise, we could compute the marginal product of natural resources by examining crop production for varying amounts of farmland, holding other inputs constant.

marginal revenue product the change in total revenue when an additional unit of a resource is hired, other things constant

Marginal Revenue Product

The important question is: what happens to the firm's *revenue* when additional workers are hired? The first three columns of Exhibit 4 show how output changes with more workers. The *marginal revenue product* of labor indicates how much total revenue changes as more labor is employed, other things constant. The **marginal revenue product** of any resource is the change in the firm's total revenue resulting from employing an additional unit of the resource, other things constant. You could think of the marginal revenue product as the firm's "marginal benefit" from hiring one more unit of the resource. *Marginal revenue product depends on how much additional output the resource produces and at what price that output is sold.*

Selling Output in Competitive Markets

The calculation of marginal revenue product is simplest when the firm sells in a perfectly competitive market, which is the assumption underlying Exhibit 4. An individual firm in perfect competition can sell as much as it wants at the market price. The marginal revenue product, listed in column (6) of Exhibit 4, is the change in total revenue that results from hiring an additional unit of the resource. For the perfectly

Exhibit 4

Marginal Revenue Product When Firm Sells in a Competitive Market

(1) Workers per day	(2) Total Product	(3) Marginal Product	(4) Product Price	(5) Total Revenue (5) = (2) × (4)	(6) Marginal Revenue Product (6) = (3) × (4)
0	0	—	$20	$ 0	—
1	10	10	20	200	$200
2	19	9	20	380	180
3	27	8	20	540	160
4	34	7	20	680	140
5	40	6	20	800	120
6	45	5	20	900	100
7	49	4	20	980	80
8	52	3	20	1040	60

competitive firm, the marginal revenue product is simply the marginal product of the resource multiplied by the product price of $20. Notice that because of diminishing returns, the marginal revenue product falls steadily as the firm employs more of the resource.

Selling Output with Some Market Power

If the firm has some market power in the product market—that is, some ability to set the price—the demand curve for that firm's output slopes downward. To sell more, the firm must lower its price. Exhibit 5 reproduces the first two columns of Exhibit 4. But column (3) now shows the price at which that output can be sold. Total output multiplied by the price yields the firm's total revenue, which appears in column (4).

The marginal revenue product of labor, which is the change in total revenue from adding another worker, appears in column (5). For example, the first worker produced 10 units per day, which sell for $40 each, yielding total revenue and marginal revenue of $400. Hiring the second worker adds 9 more units to total product, but to sell 9 more units, the firm must lower the price from $40 to $35.20. Total revenue increases to $668.80, which means the marginal revenue product from hiring a second worker is $268.80. For firms selling with some market power, the marginal revenue product curve slopes downward both because of diminishing marginal returns and because additional output can be sold only if the price falls.

Again, *marginal revenue product is the additional revenue from hiring another worker.* A profit-maximizing firm is willing and able to pay as much as the marginal revenue product for an additional unit of the resource. Thus, *the marginal revenue product curve can be thought of as the firm's demand curve for that resource.* You could think of the marginal revenue product curve as the marginal benefit to the firm of hiring each additional unit of the resource.

To review: Whether a firm sells its product in a competitive market or sells with some market power, the marginal revenue product of a resource is the change in total revenue resulting from a 1-unit change in that resource, other things constant. The marginal revenue product curve of a resource is also the demand curve for that resource—it shows the most a firm would be willing and able to pay for each additional unit of the resource. For firms selling in competitive markets, the marginal revenue product curve slopes downward only because of diminishing marginal returns to the resource. For firms selling with some market power, the marginal revenue product curve slopes downward both because of diminishing marginal returns and because additional output can be sold only if the price falls. *For all types of firms, the marginal revenue product is the change in total revenue resulting from hiring an additional unit of the resource.*

Exhibit 5

The Marginal Revenue Product When a Firm Sells with Market Power

(1) Workers per day	(2) Total Product	(3) Product Price	(4) Total Revenue (4) = (2) × (3)	(5) Marginal Revenue Product
0	0	—	—	—
1	10	$40.00	$ 400.00	$400.00
2	19	35.20	668.80	268.80
3	27	31.40	847.80	179.00
4	34	27.80	945.20	97.40
5	40	25.00	1000.00	54.80
6	45	22.50	1012.50	12.50
7	49	20.50	1004.50	−8.00
8	52	19.00	988.00	−16.50

Marginal Resource Cost

If we know a firm's marginal revenue product, can we determine how much labor that firm should employ to maximize profit? Not yet, because we also need to know how much labor costs the firm. Specifically, what is the **marginal resource cost**—what does another unit of labor cost the firm? The typical firm hires such a tiny fraction of the available resource that its hiring decision has no effect on the market price of the resource. Thus, each firm usually faces a given market price for the resource and decides only on how much to hire at that price.

For example, panel (a) of Exhibit 6 shows the market for factory workers, measured as workers per day. The intersection of market demand and market supply determines the market wage of $100 dollars per day. Panel (b) shows the situation for the firm. The market wage becomes the firm's marginal resource cost of labor. The *marginal resource cost* curve is the horizontal line drawn at the $100 level in panel (b); this is the labor supply curve to the firm. Panel (b) also shows the marginal revenue product curve, or resource demand curve, based on the schedule presented in Exhibit 4. The marginal revenue product curve indicates the

marginal resource cost
the change in total cost when an additional unit of a resource is hired, other things constant

additional revenue the firm gets from adding another worker.

Given a marginal resource cost of $100 per worker per day, how much labor should the firm employ to maximize profit? *The firm hires more labor as long as doing so adds more to revenue than to cost—that is, as long as the marginal revenue product exceeds the marginal resource cost.* The firm stops hiring more labor once the two are equal. If marginal resource cost is a constant $100 per worker, the firm hires six workers per day because the marginal revenue product from hiring a sixth worker equals $100. Thus, the firm hires additional resources until

Marginal revenue product = Marginal resource cost

This equality holds for all resources employed, whether the firm sells in competitive markets or sells with some market power. Profit maximization occurs where labor's marginal revenue product equals the market wage. Based on data presented so far, we can't yet determine the firm's actual profit because we don't yet know about the firm's other costs. We do know, however, that in Exhibit 6, a seventh worker would add $100 to cost but would add less than that to revenue, so hiring a seventh worker would reduce the firm's profit (or increase its loss).

Exhibit 6

Market Equilibrium for a Resource and the Firm's Employment Decision

(a) Market

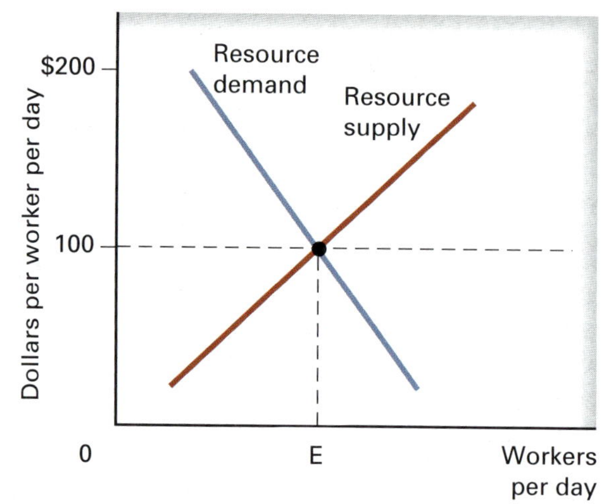

Whether a firm sells in competitive markets or with some market power, the profit-maximizing level of employment occurs where the marginal revenue product of labor equals its marginal resource cost. Similarly, profit-maximizing employment of other resources, such as natural resources and capital, occurs where their respective marginal revenue products equal their marginal resource costs. Each unit of a resource must "pull its own weight"—that is, each unit must bring in additional revenue that at least equals the additional cost.

> "Maximum profit (or minimum loss) occurs where the marginal revenue from an *input* equals its marginal resource cost."

In earlier chapters, you learned how to find the profit-maximizing level of output. Maximum profit (or minimum loss) occurs where the marginal revenue from *output* equals its marginal cost. Likewise, maximum profit (or minimum loss) occurs where the marginal revenue from an *input* equals its marginal resource cost. Although the first rule focuses on output and the second on input, the two are equivalent ways of deriving the same principle of profit maximization. For example, in Exhibit 6, the firm maximizes profit by hiring six workers when the market wage

Exhibit 6, cont.

Market Equilibrium for a Resource and the Firm's Employment Decision

(b) Firm

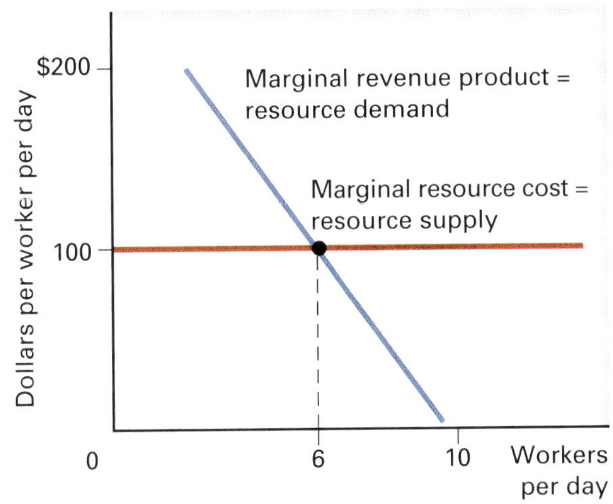

is $100 per day. Exhibit 4 indicates that a sixth worker adds five units to output, which sell for $20 each, yielding labor's marginal revenue product of $100. The *marginal revenue* of that output is the change in total revenue from selling another unit of output, which is $20. The *marginal cost* of that output is the change in total cost, $100, divided by the change in output, 5 units; so the marginal cost of output is $100/5, or $20. Thus, *in equilibrium, the marginal revenue of output equals its marginal cost.* Now that you have some idea of how to derive the demand for a resource, let's discuss what could shift the resource demand curve.

Changes in Resource Demand

As we have seen, a resource's marginal revenue product depends on the resource's marginal product and the price at which that product is sold. Two things can change a resource's marginal product: (1) a change in the amount of other resources employed and (2) a change in technology. Only one thing can change the price of the product: a change in demand for the product. Let's consider first changes that could affect marginal product, then changes that could affect demand for the product.

Change in Other Resources Employed

Although our focus so far has been on a single input, in reality the marginal product of any resource depends on the quantity and quality of other resources used in production. Sometimes resources are *substitutes*. For example, coal substitutes for oil in generating electricity. And ATMs substitute for tellers in handling bank transactions. If two resources are **substitutes**, an increase in the price of one increases the demand for the other. An increase in the price of oil increases the demand for coal, and an increase in the market wage of tellers increases the demand for ATMs.

Sometimes resources are *complements*—trucks and truck drivers, for example. If two resources are **complements**, a decrease in the price of one leads to an increase in the demand for the other. If the price of tractor-trailers decreases, the quantity demanded increases, which increases the demand for truck drivers. More generally, any increase in the quantity and quality of a complementary resource, such as trucks, raises the marginal productivity of the resource in question, such as truck drivers, and so increases the demand for that resource. A bigger and better truck makes the driver more productive. One big reason a truck driver in the United States earns much more than a bicycle-rickshaw driver in India is the truck.

resource substitutes resources that substitute in production; an increase in the price of one resource increases the demand for the other

resource complements resources that enhance one another's productivity; an increase in the price of one resource decreases the demand for the other

The McMinimum Wage

In May 2007, Congress and the president passed a law increasing the minimum hourly wage from $5.15 to $7.25 in three steps of 70 cents over two years. At the time, only about 4 percent of workers earned less than $7.25. That group included mostly young workers, the majority working part time, primarily in service and sales occupations. When 2007 the law was passed, 30 states and the District of Columbia had a minimum wage exceeding $5.15, with Washington State the highest at $7.93. In addition, dozens of municipalities across the nation have introduced so-called *living-wage laws* that set federal minimums and state minimums. One researcher found that restaurants responded to a higher minimum wage by reducing vacation time and night-shift premiums.

SOURCES: Jesse Holland, "Minimum-Wage Boost to Become Reality with Iraq Funding Bill," *Arizona Republic,* 25 May 2007: Robert Whaples, "Is There Consensus Among American Labor Economists?" *Journal of Labor Research* 27 (Fall 1996): 725–734; William Alpert, *The Minimum Wage in the Restaurant Industry* (New York: Praeger, 1986); and "A Deal on the Minimum Wage," *New York Times,* 24 April 2007.

Changes in Technology

Technological improvements can boost the productivity of some resources but make other resources obsolete. The introduction of computer-controlled machines increased the demand for computer-trained machinists but reduced the demand for machinists without computer skills. The development of synthetic fibers, such as rayon and Orlon, increased the demand for acrylics and polyesters but reduced the demand for natural fibers, such as cotton and wool. Breakthroughs in fiber-optic and satellite telecommunication increased the demand for fiberglass and satellites and reduced the demand for copper wire.

Computer programs are changing job prospects in fields such as law, medicine, accounting, and architecture. For example, Quicken's WillMaker software has written more wills than any lawyer alive. In medicine, software such as Skyscape's 5-Minute Clinical Consult helps doctors diagnose more than a thousand medical and surgical conditions. In accounting, software such as TurboTax completes tax forms with ease. And in architecture, three-dimensional modeling programs such as 3D Home Architect help configure all aspects of a structure. As software and hardware get cheaper, better, and easier to use, the demand for some professional services declines.

Increased demand for synthetic fibers reduced demand for natural fibers.

© PHOTOLINK/PHOTODISC/GETTY IMAGES

Changes in the Demand for the Final Product

Because the demand for a resource is *derived* from the demand for the final output, any change in the demand for output affects resource demand. For example, an increase in the demand for automobiles increases their market price and thereby increases the marginal revenue product of autoworkers.

In summary: The demand for a resource depends on its marginal revenue product, which is the change in total revenue resulting from employing one more unit of the resource. Any change that increases a resource's marginal revenue product increases resource demand.

The Optimal Use of More Than One Resource

As long as marginal revenue product exceeds marginal resource cost, a firm can increase profit or reduce a loss by employing more of that resource. Again, the firm hires more of a resource until the marginal revenue product just equals the marginal resource cost. This principle holds for each resource employed. The opening paragraph asked why buildings in downtown Chicago are taller than those in the suburbs. Land and capital, to a large extent, substitute in the production of building space. Because land is more expensive downtown than in the suburbs, builders downtown substitute capital for land, building up instead of out. Hence, buildings are taller closer to the center of the city and are tallest in cities where land is most expensive. Buildings in Chicago and New York City are taller than those in Salt Lake City and Tucson, for example.

The high price of land in metropolitan areas has other implications for the efficient employment of resources. For example, in New York City, as in many large cities, food vending carts seem to be on every corner. New York City has more than 3,000 of them. Why are these carts so popular? Consider the resources used to supply sidewalk food: land, labor, capital, entrepreneurial ability, plus food. Which of these do you suppose is most expensive in New York City? Retail space along Madison Avenue's Golden Mile can rent for an average $800 a year per square foot. Because operating a vending cart requires about 6 square yards (or 54 square feet), renting that space could cost as much as $43,000 a year. Aside from the necessary public permits, however, space on the public sidewalk is free to vendors. Profit-maximizing street vendors substitute public sidewalks for costly commercial space. (Incidentally, does free public space mean sidewalk vendors earn long-run economic profit?)

Final Word

A firm hires each resource until the marginal revenue product of that resource equals its marginal cost. The objective of profit maximization ensures that to produce any given level of output, firms employ the least-cost combination of resources and thereby use the economy's resources most efficiently. Although our focus has been on the marginal productivity of each resource, we should keep in mind that an orchestra of resources combine to produce output, so the marginal productivity of a particular resource depends in part on the amount and quality of other resources employed.

© DAMIR FRKOVIC/MASTERFILE

CHAPTER 12

Labor Markets *and* Labor Unions

Learning Outcomes

- LO 1 Discuss issues affecting labor supply and utility maximization
- LO 2 Explain the market supply factors that lead to differing wages
- LO 3 List types of unions and describe their collective bargaining strategies
- LO 4 Describe the relationship between union wages and employment

"How do you divide your time between work and leisure?"

How do you divide your time between work and leisure? Why do many people work *less* if the wage increases enough? For example, why do unknown rock bands play hours for peanuts, while famous bands play much less for much more? Why are butchers more likely than surgeons to mow their own lawns? What determines the wage structure in the economy? What else besides the wage affects your labor supply? In what sense have labor unions become the victims of their own success? This chapter digs deeper into labor markets and wage determination.

What do you think?

Time is money.

Strongly Disagree					Strongly Agree	
1	2	3	4	5	6	7

You can be sure of one thing: demand and supply play a central role in all this. You have already considered the demand for resources. Demand depends on a resource's marginal revenue product. The first half of this chapter focuses on the supply of labor, then brings demand and supply together to arrive at the market wage. The second half considers the role of labor unions. We examine the economic impact of unions and review recent trends in union membership.

LO1 Labor Supply

As a resource supplier, you have a labor supply curve for each of the many possible uses of your labor. To some markets, your quantity supplied is zero over the realistic range of wages. The qualifier "over the realistic range" is added because, for a high enough wage (say, $1 million per hour), you might supply labor to just about *any* activity. In most labor markets, your quantity supplied may be zero either because you are *willing* but *unable* to perform the job (professional golfer, airline pilot, novelist) or because you are *able* but *unwilling* to do so (soldier of fortune, prison guard, P.E. instructor). You have as many individual supply curves as there are labor markets, just as you have as many individual demand curves as there are markets for goods and services. Your labor supply to each market depends, among other things, on your abilities, your taste for the job,

Topics discussed in Chapter 12 include:

- Theory of time allocation
- Backward-bending labor supply curve
- Nonwage factors in labor supply
- Why wages differ
- Unions and collective bargaining
- Union wages and employment
- Trends in union membership

and the opportunity cost of your time. Your supply to a particular labor market assumes that wages in other markets are constant, just as your demand for a particular product assumes that other prices are constant.

Labor Supply and Utility Maximization

Recall the definition of economics: *the study of how people use their scarce resources in an attempt to satisfy their unlimited wants*—that is, how people use their scarce resources to maximize their utility. Two sources of utility are of special interest in this chapter: the consumption of goods and services and the enjoyment of leisure. The utility derived from consumption serves as the foundation of demand. Another valuable source of utility is leisure—time spent relaxing with friends, sleeping, eating, watching TV, and in other recreation. Leisure is a normal good that, like other goods, is subject to the law of diminishing marginal utility. Thus, the more leisure time you have, the less you value an additional hour of it. Sometimes you may have so much leisure that you "have time on your hands" and are "just killing time." As that sage of the comic page Garfield the cat once lamented, "Spare time would be more fun if I had less to spare." Or as Shakespeare wrote, "If all the year were playing holidays, to sport would be as tedious as to work." Leisure's diminishing marginal utility explains why some of the "idle rich" may grow bored in their idleness.

© RYAN McVAY/PHOTODISC/GETTY IMAGES

Three Uses of Time

Some of you are at a point in your careers when you have few resources other than your time. Time is the raw material of life. You can use your time in three ways. First, you can undertake **market work**—selling your time in the labor market. In return for a wage, you surrender control of your time to the employer. Second, you can undertake **nonmarket work**—using time to produce your own goods and services. Nonmarket work includes the time you spend doing your laundry, making a sandwich, or cleaning up after yourself. Nonmarket work also includes the time spent acquiring skills and education that enhance your productivity. Although studying and attending class may provide little immediate payoff, you expect that the knowledge and perspective so gained will enrich your future. Third, you can spend time in **leisure**—using your time in nonwork pursuits.

market work
time sold as labor

nonmarket work
time spent getting an education or on do-it-yourself production for personal consumption

leisure
time spent on nonwork activities

Work and Utility

Unless you are among the fortunate few, work is not a pure source of utility, as it often generates some boredom, discomfort, and aggravation. In short, time spent working can be "a real pain," a source of *disutility*—the opposite of utility. And work is subject to *increasing marginal disutility*—the more you work, the greater the marginal disutility of working another hour. In the extreme, you could feel burned out from overwork. You may work nonetheless, because your earnings buy goods and services. You expect the utility from these products to more than offset the disutility of work. Thus, the *net utility of work*—the utility of the consumption made possible through earnings minus the disutility of the work itself—usually makes some amount of work an attractive use of your time. In the case of market work, your income buys goods and services. In the case of nonmarket work, either you produce goods and services directly, as in making yourself a sandwich, or you invest your time in education with an expectation of higher future earnings and higher future consumption. The additional utility you expect from the sandwich and better future consumption possibilities resulting from education are the marginal benefits of nonmarket work.

Utility Maximization

Within the limits of a 24-hour day, seven days a week, you balance your time among market work, nonmarket work, and leisure to maximize utility. As a rational consumer, *you attempt to maximize utility by allocating your time so that the expected marginal utility of the last unit of time spent in each activity is identical.* Thus, in the course of a week or a month, the expected marginal utility of the last hour of leisure equals the expected net marginal utility of the last hour of market work, which equals the expected net marginal utility of the last hour of nonmarket work. In the case of time devoted to acquiring more human capital, you must consider the marginal utility expected from the future increase in earnings that result from your enhanced productivity.

Maybe at this point you are saying, "Wait a minute. I don't know what you're talking about. I don't allocate my time like that. I just sort of bump along, doing what feels good." Economists do not claim that you are even aware of making these marginal calculations. But as a rational decision maker, you allocate your scarce time trying to satisfy your unlimited wants, or trying to maximize utility. And utility maximization, or "doing what feels good," implies that you act *as if* you allocated your time to derive the same expected net marginal utility from the last unit of time spent in each alternative use.

You probably have settled into a rough plan for meals, work, entertainment, study, sleep, and so on—a plan that fits your immediate objectives. This plan is probably in constant flux as you make expected and unexpected adjustments in your use of time. For example, last weekend you may have failed to crack a book, despite good intentions. This morning you may have overslept because you were up late. Over a week, a month, or a year, however, your use of time is roughly in line with an allocation that maximizes utility as you perceive it at the time. Put another way, if you could alter your use of time to increase your utility, you would do so. Nobody's stopping you! You may emphasize immediate gratification over long-term goals, but, hey, that's your choice and you bear the consequences. *This time-allocation process ensures that at the margin, the expected net utilities from the last unit of time spent in each activity are equal.*

Because information is costly and because the future is uncertain, you sometimes make mistakes. You don't always get what you expect. Some mistakes are minor, such as going to a movie that turns out to be a waste of time. But other mistakes can be costly. For example, some people are now studying for a field that will grow crowded by the time they graduate, or some people may be acquiring skills that new technology will soon make obsolete.

Implications

The theory of time allocation described thus far has several implications for individual choice. First, consider the choices of market work, nonmarket work, and leisure. The higher your market wage, other things constant, the higher your opportunity cost of leisure and nonmarket work. For example, those who earn a high wage spend less time in nonmarket work, other things constant. Surgeons are less likely to mow their lawns than are butchers. And among those earning the same wage, those more productive in nonmarket work—handy around the house, good cooks—do more for themselves. Conversely, those who are all thumbs around the house and have trouble boiling water hire more household services and eat out more frequently.

By the same logic, the higher the expected earnings right out of high school, other things constant, the higher the opportunity cost of attending college. Most young, successful movie stars do not go to college, and many even drop out of high school, as noted earlier. Promising athletes often turn professional right after high school or before completing college. But the vast majority of people, including female basketball stars, do not face such a high opportunity cost of higher education. As one poor soul lamented, "Since my wife left me, my kids joined a cult, my job is history, and my dog died, I think now might be a good time to go back for an MBA."

Wages and Individual Labor Supply

To breathe life into the time-allocation problem, consider your choices for the summer. If you can afford to, you can take the summer off, spending it entirely on leisure, perhaps as a fitting reward for a rough academic year. Or you can supply your time to market work. Or you can undertake nonmarket work, such as cleaning the garage, painting the house, or attending summer school. As a rational decision maker, you select the combination of leisure, market work, and nonmarket work that you expect will maximize your utility. And the optimal combination is likely to involve allocating time to each activity. For example, even if you work, you might still take one or two summer courses.

Suppose the only summer job available is some form of unskilled labor, such as working in a fast-food restaurant or for the municipal parks department. For simplicity, let's assume that you view all such jobs as equally attractive (or unattractive) in terms of their nonmonetary aspects, such as working conditions, working hours, and so on. (These nonmonetary aspects are discussed in the next section.) If there is no difference among these unskilled jobs, the most important question for you in deciding how much market labor to supply is: What's the market wage?

Suppose the wage is \$6 per hour. Rather than working at a wage that low, you might decide to work

© INMAGINE/INSPIRESTOCK/JUPITERIMAGES

substitution effect of a wage increase a higher wage encourages more work because other activities now have a higher opportunity cost

income effect of a wage increase a higher wage raises a worker's income, increasing the demand for all normal goods, including leisure, so the quantity of labor supplied to market work decreases

backward-bending supply curve of labor as the wage rises, the quantity of labor supplied may eventually decline; the income effect of a higher wage increases the demand for leisure, which reduces the quantity of labor supplied enough to more than offset the substitution effect of a higher wage

around the house, attend summer school, take a really long nap, travel across the country to find yourself, or perhaps pursue some combination of these. In any case, you supply no market labor at such a low wage. The market wage must rise to $7 before you supply any market labor. Suppose at a wage of $7, you supply 20 hours per week, perhaps taking fewer summer courses and shorter naps.

As the wage increases, the opportunity cost of time spent in other activities rises, so you substitute market work for other uses of your time. You decide to work 30 hours per week at a wage of $8 per hour, 40 hours at $9, 48 hours at $10, and 55 hours at $11. At a wage of $12 you go to 60 hours per week; you are starting to earn serious money—$720 a week. If the wage hits $13 per hour, you decide to cut back to 58 hours per week. Despite the cutback, your pay rises to $754, which is more than when the wage was $12. Finally, if the wage hits $14, you cut back to 55 per week, earning $770. To explain why you may eventually reduce the quantity of labor supplied, let's consider the impact of wage increases on your time allocation.

Substitution and Income Effects

An increase in the wage has two effects on your use of time. First, because each hour of work now buys more goods and services, a higher wage increases the opportunity cost of leisure and nonmarket work. Thus, as the wage increases, you substitute market work for other activities. This is the **substitution effect of a wage increase**. Second, a higher wage means a higher income for a given number of hours. This higher income increases your demand for all normal goods. Because leisure is a normal good, a higher income increases your demand for leisure, thereby reducing your allocation of time to market work. The **income effect of a wage increase** tends to reduce the quantity of labor supplied to market work.

As the wage increases, the substitution effect causes you to work more, but the income effect causes you to work less and demand more leisure. In our example, the substitution effect exceeds the income effect for wages up to $12 per hour, resulting in more labor supplied as the wage increases. When the wage reaches $13, however, the income effect exceeds the substitution effect, causing you to reduce the quantity of labor supplied.

Backward-Bending Labor Supply Curve

The labor supply curve just described appears in Exhibit 1. As you can see, this slopes upward until a wage of $12 per hour is reached; then it bends backward. The **backward-bending supply curve** gets its shape because the income effect of a higher wage eventually dominates the substitution effect, reducing the quantity of labor supplied as the wage increases. We see evidence of a backward-bending

Exhibit 1

Individual Labor Supply Curve for Unskilled Work

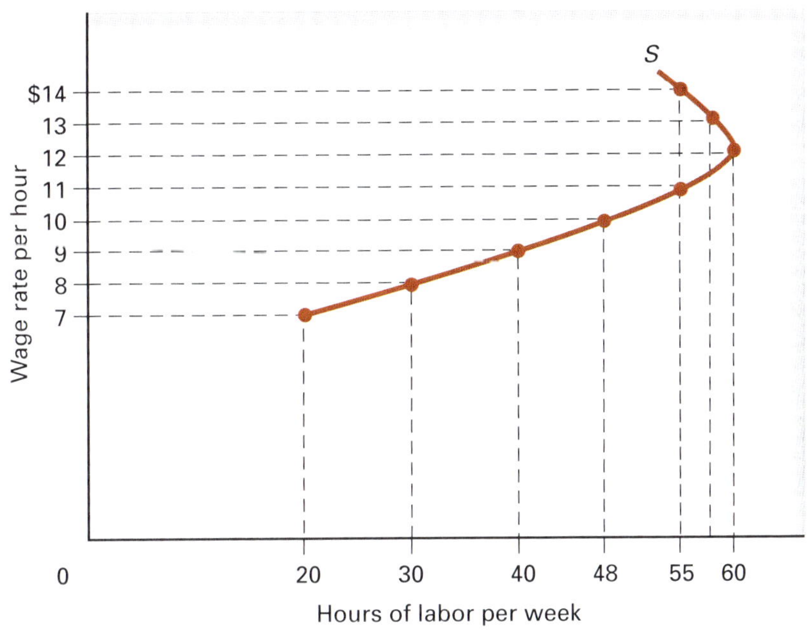

supply curve particularly among high-wage individuals, who reduce their work and consume more leisure as their wage increases. For example, entertainers typically perform less as they become more successful. Unknown musicians play for hours for hardly any money; famous musicians play much less for much more. The income effect of rising real wages helps explain the decline in the U.S. workweek from an average of 60 hours in 1900 to less than 40 hours today.

Flexibility of Hours Worked

The model we have been discussing assumes that workers have some control over the number of hours they work. Opportunities for part-time work and overtime allow workers to put together their preferred quantity of hours. Workers also have some control over the timing and length of their vacations. More generally, individuals can control how long to stay in school, when to enter or leave the workforce, and when to retire. Thus, they actually have more control over the number of hours worked than you might think if you focused simply on the benchmark of, say, a 40-hour work week.

Nonwage Determinants of Labor Supply

The supply of labor to a particular market depends on a variety of factors other than the wage, just as the demand for a particular good depends on factors other than the price. As we have already seen, the supply of labor to a particular market depends on wages in other labor markets. What nonwage factors shape a college student's labor supply for the summer?

Other Sources of Income

Although some jobs are rewarding in a variety of nonmonetary ways, the main reason people work is to earn money. Thus, the willingness to supply labor depends on income from other sources, including from family, savings, student loans, and scholarships. A student who receives a generous scholarship, for example, faces less pressure to work in the summer or during the college term. More generally, wealthy people have less incentive to work. For example, multimillion-dollar lottery winners often quit their jobs. And those who inherit a large sum are more likely to retire early.[1]

Nonmonetary Factors

Labor is a special kind of resource. Unlike capital or natural resources, which can be supplied regardless of the whereabouts of the resource owner, the supplier of labor must be where the work is performed. Because individuals must usually be physically present to supply labor, such *nonmonetary factors* as the difficulty of the job, the quality of the work environment, and the status of the position become important to labor suppliers. For example, deckhands on crab boats in the icy waters off Alaska can earn over $10,000 for five days of work, but the job is dangerous, winter temperature seldom exceeds zero, and daily shifts allow only three hours of sleep.

1. As found in research by Jeffrey Brown, Courtney Coile, and Scott Weisbenner, "The Effect of Inheritance Receipt on Retirement," *NBER Working Paper 12386*, July 2006.

© CHRISTOPHER PILLITZ/REPORTAGE/GETTY IMAGES

Consider the different working conditions you might encounter. A campus job that lets you study on the job is more attractive than one allowing no study time. Some jobs offer flexible hours; others have rigid schedules. Is the workplace air-conditioned, or do you have to sweat it out? The more attractive the working conditions, the more labor you supply to that market, other things constant. Finally, some jobs convey more status than others. For example, the president of the United States earns less than one-tenth that of corporate heads, but there is no shortage of applicants for the job. Similarly, U.S. Supreme Court justices typically take a huge pay cut to accept the job.

The Value of Job Experience

All else equal, you are more inclined to take a position that provides valuable job experience. Serving as the assistant treasurer for a local business during the summer provides better job experience and looks better on a résumé than serving mystery meat at the college cafeteria. Some people are willing to accept relatively low wages now for the promise of higher wages in the future. For example, new lawyers are eager to fill clerkships for judges, though the pay is low and the hours long, because these positions offer experience and contacts future employers value. Likewise, athletes who play in the minor leagues for little pay believe that experience will help them get to the major leagues. Thus, *the more a job enhances future earning possibilities, the greater the supply of labor, other things constant.* Consequently, the pay is usually lower than for jobs that impart less valuable experience. Sometimes the pay is zero, as with some internships.

Taste for Work

Just as the taste for goods and services differs among consumers, the taste for work also differs among labor suppliers. Some people prefer physical labor and hate office work. Some become surgeons; others can't stand the sight of blood. Some become airline pilots; others are afraid to fly. Teenagers prefer jobs at Starbucks and Gap to those at McDonald's and Burger King.[2] Many struggling writers, artists, actors, and dancers could earn more elsewhere, but prefer the creative process and the chance, albeit slim, of becoming rich and famous in the arts (for example, the 100,000 members of the Screen Actors Guild earn less than $10,000 a year on average for their professional work). Some people have such strong preferences for certain jobs that they work for free, such as auxiliary police officers or volunteer firefighters. Likewise, most computer hackers earn nothing beyond the twisted satisfaction they get from spreading viruses and causing digital mayhem.

As with the taste for goods and services, economists do not try to explain how work preferences develop. They simply argue that your preferences are relatively stable and you supply more labor to jobs you like. Based on taste, workers seek jobs in a way that tends to minimize the disutility of work. This is not to say that everyone ends up in his or her most preferred position. The transaction costs of job information and of changing jobs may prevent some matchups that might otherwise seem desirable. But in the long run, people tend to find jobs that suit them. We are not likely to find tour guides who hate to travel, zookeepers who are allergic to animals, or garage mechanics who hate getting their hands dirty.

LO2 Market Supply of Labor

In the previous section, we considered those factors, both monetary and nonmonetary, that influence individual labor supply. *The supply of labor to a particular market is the horizontal sum of all the individual supply curves.* The horizontal sum at each

2. Dirk Johnson, "For Teenagers, Fast Food Is a Snack, Not a Job," *New York Times,* 8 January 2001.

Exhibit 2

Deriving the Market Labor Supply Curve from Individual Labor Supply Curves

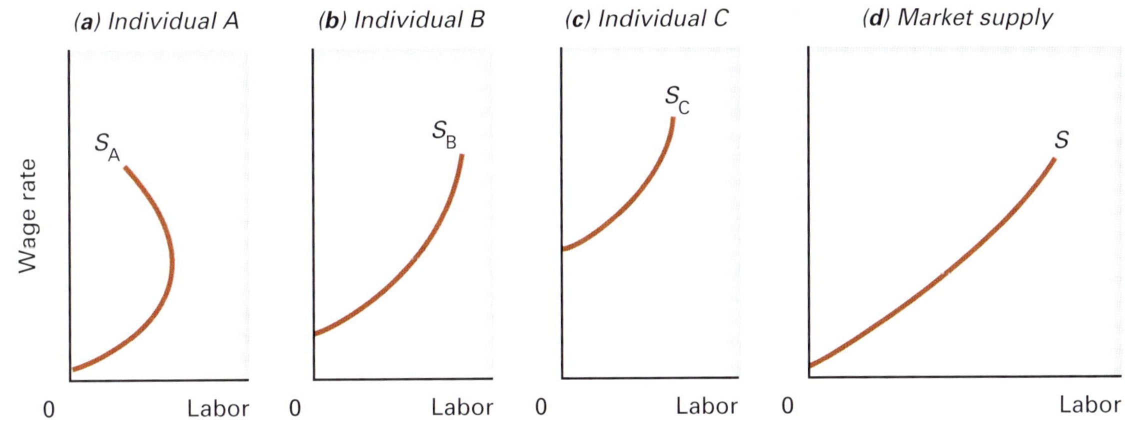

particular wage is found by adding the quantities supplied by each worker. If an individual supply curve of labor bends backward, does this mean that the market supply curve for labor also bends backward? Not necessarily. Because different individuals have different opportunity costs and different tastes for work, the bend in the supply curve occurs at different wages for different individuals. And, for some individuals, the labor supply curve may not bend backward over the realistic range of wages. Exhibit 2 shows how just three individual labor supply curves sum to yield a market supply curve that slopes upward.

Why Wages Differ

Just as both blades of scissors contribute equally to cutting paper, both labor demand and labor supply determine the market wage. Exhibit 3 shows average hourly wages for more than 130 million U.S. workers. Workers are sorted into 22 occupations from the highest to the lowest wage as of May 2006. Management earns the highest wage, at $44.20 an hour. The lowest is the $8.86 an hour averaged by workers preparing and serving food. Wage differences across labor markets trace to differences in labor demand and in labor supply, as you will see. The previous chapter discussed the elements that influence the demand for resources and examined labor in particular. In brief, *a profit-maximizing firm hires labor up to the point where labor's marginal revenue product equals its marginal resource cost*—that is, where the last unit employed increases total revenue enough to cover the added cost. Because we have already discussed what affects the demand for labor—namely, labor's marginal revenue product—let's focus more on labor supply.

Differences in Training, Education, Age, and Experience

Some jobs pay more because they require a long and expensive training period, which reduces market supply because few are willing to incur the time and expense required. But such training increases labor productivity, thereby increasing demand for the skills. Reduced supply and increased demand both raise the market wage. For example, certified public accountants (CPAs) earn more than file clerks because the extensive training of CPAs limits the supply to this field and because this training increases the productivity of CPAs compared to file clerks.

Exhibit 4 shows how education and experience affect earnings. Age groups are indicated on the horizontal axis and average annual earnings on the vertical axis. To standardize things, pay is for the highest level of education achieved. The relationship between income and education is clear. At every age, those with more education earn more. For example, among those ages 45 to 54, workers with professional degrees earned more than twice those with bachelor's degrees and nearly *six times* those without high school diplomas.

Age itself also has an important effect on income. Earnings tend to increase as workers acquire job experience and get promoted. Among educated workers, experience pays more. For example, among those with professional degrees, workers in the 45–54 age group earned on average 75 percent more than those in the 25–34 age group. But among those without high school diplomas, workers in the 45–54 age group earned on average only 17 percent more than those in the 25–34 age group. Differences in earnings reflect the normal workings of resource

Exhibit 3

Average Hourly Wage by Occupation in the United States as of May 2006

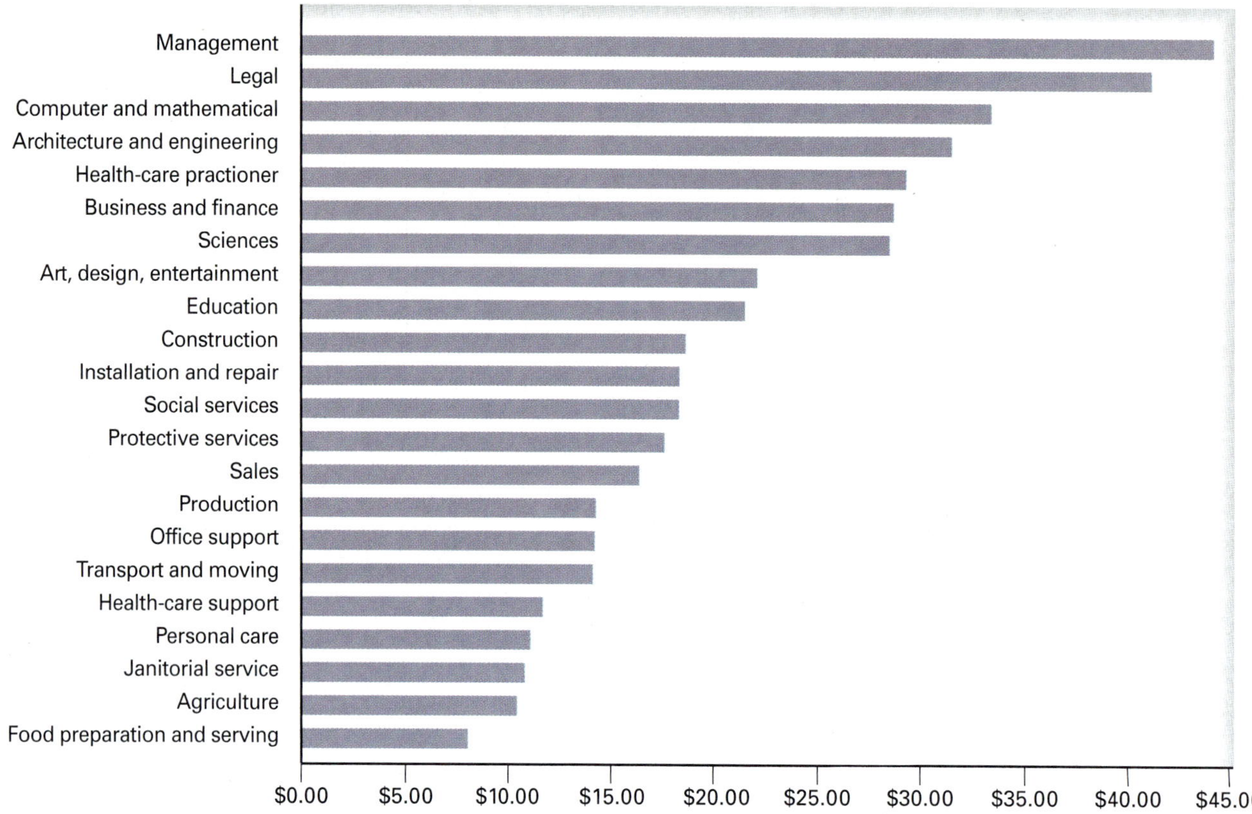

SOURCE: Developed from "Occupational Employment and Wages, May 2006," *U.S. Department of Labor News,* Chart 1, 17 May 2007, also available at http://www.bls.gov/news.release/pdf/ocwage.pdf.

markets, whereby workers are rewarded according to their marginal productivity.

Differences in Ability

Because they are more able and talented, some earn more than others with the same training and education. For example, two lawyers may have identical educations, but earnings differ because of differences in underlying ability. Most executives have extensive training and business experience, but only a few get to run large corporations. In professional sports such as basketball and baseball, some players earn up to 50 times more than others. From lawyers to executives to professional athletes, pay differences reflect differing abilities and different marginal productivities.

winner-take-all labor markets
markets in which a few key employees critical to the overall success of an enterprise are richly rewarded

Each year *Forbes* magazine lists the multimillion-dollar earnings of top entertainers and professional athletes. Entertainment and pro sports have come to be called **winner-take-all labor markets** because a few key individuals critical to the overall success of an enterprise are richly rewarded. In professional golf tournaments, attendance and TV ratings are significantly higher with Tiger Woods in the mix. Top performers generate a high marginal revenue product.[3]

The "star" treatment now extends to such fields as management, law, banking, finance, even academia. Consider, for example, corporate pay. In 1980, the chief executive officers (CEOs) of the 200 largest U.S. corporations earned about about 42 times more than the average production worker. Now, this multiple tops 400. Comparable multiples are much lower in Germany and Japan. Why the big U.S. jump?

3. Bill Livingston, "LeBron," *Cleveland Plain Dealer,* 6 May 2007; Russell Adams, "The Real Most Valuable Players," *Wall Street Journal,* 14 April 2007; Economic Report of the President, February 2007, at http://www.gpoaccess.gov/eop/.

Exhibit 4

Age, Education, and Pay

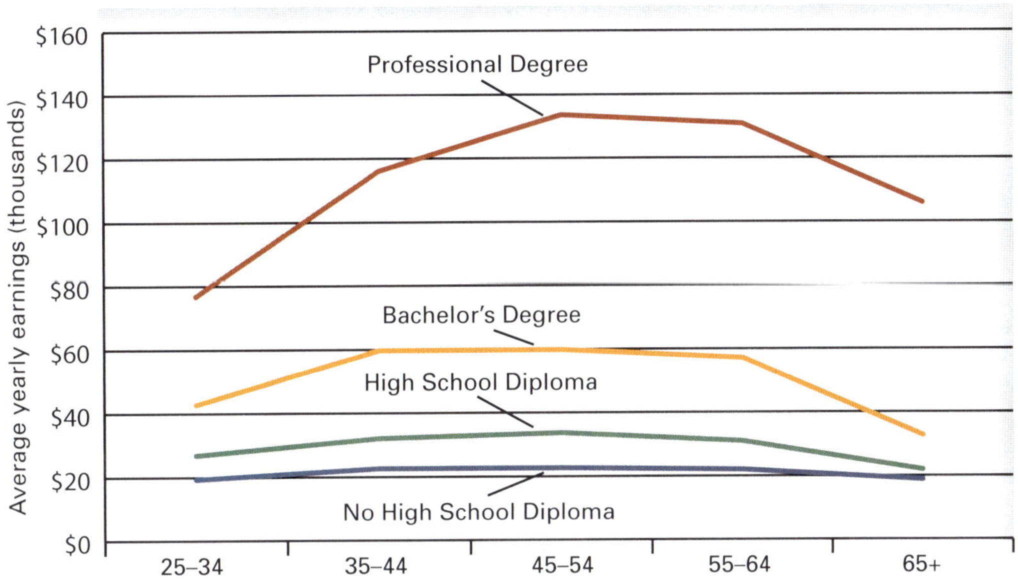

Differences in Risk

Research indicates that jobs with a higher probability of injury or death, such as coal mining, usually pay more, other things constant. Russians working at the partially disabled nuclear power plant, Chernobyl, earned 10 times the national average, but workers face continued health risk from radiation exposure. Sex workers in Mexico earn 23 percent more for unprotected sex.[4] Truck drivers for American contractors in Iraq earn over $100,000 a year, but the job is dangerous. Workers also earn more, other things constant, in seasonal jobs such as construction, where the risk of unemployment is greater.

4. See Paul Gertler, et al., "Risky Business: The Market for Unprotected Commercial Sex," *Journal of Political Economy*, vol. 113, no. 3, 2005: pp. 518–550.

Geographic Differences

People have a strong incentive to sell their resources in the market where they earn the most. For example, the National Basketball Association attracts talent from around the world. About 20 percent come from abroad. Likewise, thousands of foreign-trained physicians migrate to the United States each year for the high pay. The flow of labor is not all one way. Some Americans seek their fortune abroad, with American basketball players going to Europe and baseball players to Japan. Workers often face migration hurdles. Any reduction in these hurdles would reduce wage differentials across countries.

Discrimination

Sometimes wage differences stem from racial or gender discrimination in the job market. Although such discrimination is illegal, history shows that certain groups—including African Americans, Hispanics, and women—have systematically earned less than others of equal ability.

Union Membership

Other things equal, members of organized labor earn more than nonmembers. The balance of this chapter discusses the effects of unions on the market for labor.

LO[3] Unions and Collective Bargaining

Few aspects of labor markets make news more than labor unions. Labor negotiations, strikes, picket lines, confrontations between workers and employers—all fit TV's "action news" format. Despite media attention, only about one in eight U.S. workers is a union member and nearly all union agreements are reached without a strike. But labor unions are more important than their current membership indicates Let's examine the tools that unions use to seek higher pay and better benefits for their members.

Types of Unions

A **labor union** is a group of workers who join together to improve their terms of employment. Labor unions in the United States date back to the early days of national independence, when workers in various crafts—such as carpenters, shoemakers, and printers—formed local groups to seek higher wages and shorter work hours. A **craft union** was confined to people with a particular skill, or craft. Craft unions formed their own national organization in 1886, the *American Federation of Labor (AFL)*. The Clayton Act of 1914 exempted labor unions from antitrust laws, meaning that *unions at competing companies could legally join forces.* Unions were also tax exempt. Membership jumped during World War I but fell by half between 1920 and 1933, as the government retreated from its support of union efforts.

The *Congress of Industrial Organizations (CIO)* was formed in 1935 to serve as a national organization of unions in mass-production industries, such as autos and steel. Whereas the AFL organized workers in particular crafts, such as plumbers and carpenters, the CIO consisted of unions whose membership embraced all workers in a particular industry. These **industrial unions** included unskilled, semiskilled, and skilled workers in an industry, such as all autoworkers or all steelworkers.

labor union
a group of workers who organize to improve their terms of employment

craft union
a union whose members have a particular skill or work at a particular craft, such as plumbers or carpenters

industrial union
a union of both skilled and unskilled workers from a particular industry, such as all autoworkers or all steelworkers

collective bargaining
the process by which union and management negotiate a labor agreement

mediator
an impartial observer who helps resolve differences between union and management

binding arbitration
negotiation in which union and management must accept an impartial observer's resolution of a dispute

strike
a union's attempt to withhold labor from a firm to halt production

Collective Bargaining, Mediation, and Arbitration

Collective bargaining is the process by which representatives of union and management negotiate a mutually agreeable contract specifying wages, employee benefits, and working conditions. A tentative agreement, once reached, goes before the membership for a vote. If the agreement is rejected, the union can strike or can continue negotiations.

If negotiations reach an impasse and the public interest is involved, government officials may ask an independent mediator to step in. A **mediator** is an impartial observer who listens to each side separately and then suggests a resolution. If each side still remains open to a settlement, the mediator brings them together to work out a contract, but the mediator has no power to impose a settlement. In certain critical sectors, such as police and fire protection, where a strike could harm the public interest, differences are sometimes settled through **binding arbitration**. A neutral third party evaluates each position and issues a ruling that both sides must accept. Some disputes skip the mediation and arbitration steps and go directly from impasse to strike.

The Strike

A major source of union power is a **strike**, which is a union's attempt to withhold labor to stop production, thereby hoping to force the firm into accepting the union's position. But strikes are also risky for workers, who earn no pay or benefits during the strike and could lose their jobs. Union funds and, in some states, unemployment benefits, may aid strikers some, but incomes still fall substantially. *Although neither party usually wants a strike, both sides, rather than concede on key points, usually act as if they could endure one.* Unions usually picket to prevent or discourage so-called strikebreakers, or "scabs," from crossing the picket lines to work. But the targeted firm, by hiring temporary workers and nonstriking union workers, can sometimes continue production.

LO⁴ Union Wages and Employment

Samuel Gompers, the AFL's founder and long-time head, was once asked what unions want. "More!" he roared. Union members, like everyone else, have unlimited wants. But because resources are scarce, choices must be made. A menu of union desires includes higher wages, more benefits, greater job security, better working conditions, and so on. To keep the analysis manageable, let's focus on a single objective, higher wages, and consider three ways unions might increase wages: (1) by forming an inclusive, or industrial, union; (2) by forming an exclusive, or craft, union; and (3) by increasing the demand for union labor.

> ALTHOUGH NEITHER PARTY USUALLY WANTS A STRIKE, BOTH SIDES, RATHER THAN CONCEDE ON KEY POINTS, USUALLY ACT AS IF THEY COULD ENDURE ONE.

Inclusive, or Industrial, Unions: Negotiating a Higher Industry Wage

The market demand and supply curves for a particular type of labor are labeled *D* and *S* in panel (a) of Exhibit 5 on the next page. In the absence of a union, the market wage is *W* and industry employment is *E*. At the market wage, each firm faces a horizontal, or perfectly elastic, supply of labor, as depicted by *s* in panel (b) of Exhibit 5. Thus, each firm can hire as much labor as it wants at the market wage of *W*. The firm hires workers up to the point where labor's marginal revenue product equals its marginal resource cost, resulting in *e* units of labor in panel (b). As we saw earlier, in equilibrium, labor is paid a wage just equal to its marginal revenue product.

With the *inclusive, or industrial,* approach, the union tries to negotiate industry-wide wages for each class of labor. Suppose the union negotiates a wage above the market-clearing level. Specifically, suppose the negotiated wage is *W′* in panel (a), meaning that no labor is supplied at a lower wage. In effect, the market supply of labor is perfectly elastic at the union wage out to point *a*. To the right of point *a*, however, the wage floor no longer applies; *aS* becomes the relevant portion of the labor supply curve. For an industry facing a wage floor of *W′*, the entire labor supply curve becomes *W′aS*, which has a kink where the wage floor joins the upward-sloping portion of the original labor supply curve.

Once this wage floor is established, each firm faces a horizontal supply curve of labor at the collectively bargained wage, *W′*. Because the union wage is higher than the market-clearing wage, each firm hires less labor. Consequently, the higher wage leads to a reduction in employment; the quantity of labor demanded by the industry drops from *E* to *E′* in panel (a). At wage *W* workers in the industry would like to

Exhibit 5

Effects of Labor Union's Wage Floor

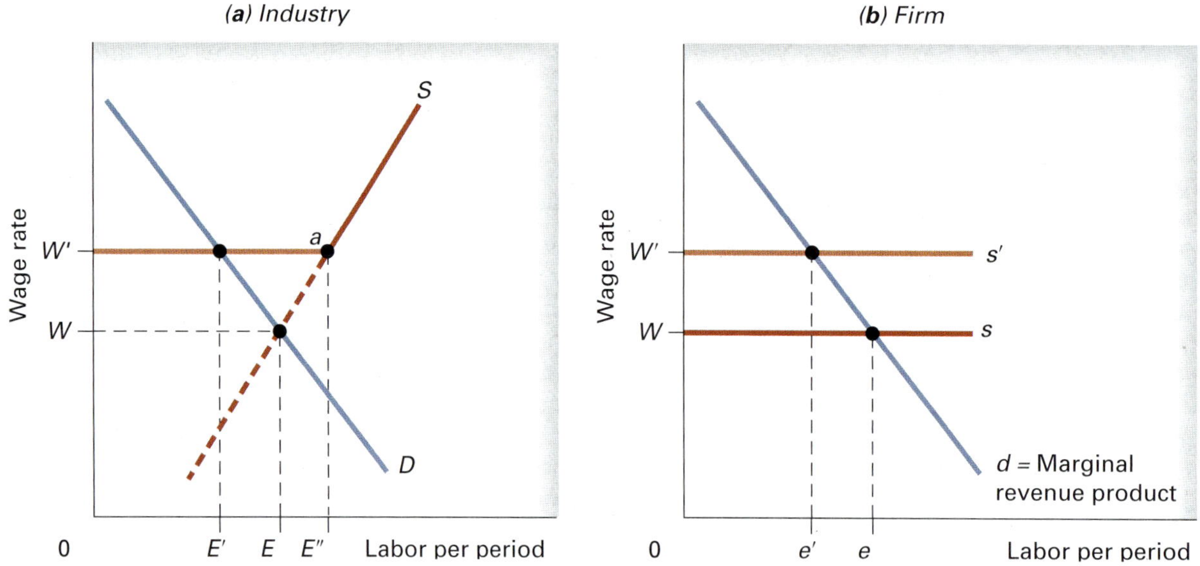

supply, E″, which exceeds the labor demanded, E′. Ordinarily this excess quantity supplied would force the wage down. But because union members agree *collectively* to the union wage, individual workers can't work for less, nor can employers hire them for less. *With the inclusive, or industrial, union, which negotiates with the entire industry, the wage is higher and employment lower than they would be in the absence of a union.*

The union must somehow ration the limited jobs available, such as by awarding them based on worker seniority, personal connections within the union, or lottery. Those who can't find union jobs must turn to the nonunion sector. *This increases the supply of labor in the nonunion sector, which drives down the nonunion wage.* So wages are relatively higher in the union sector first, because unions bargain for a wage that exceeds the market-clearing wage, and second, because those unable to find union jobs crowd into the nonunion sector. Studies show that union wages average about 15 percent above the wages of similarly qualified nonunion workers. Exhibit 6 compares median weekly earnings of union and nonunion workers. Note that unions are less successful at raising wages in more competitive sectors. For example, unions have less impact on manufacturing and service industries, where product markets tend to be competitive. Unions have greater success in government, transportation, and construction—sectors that tend to be less competitive. When there is more competition in the product market, employers cannot easily pass along higher union wages as higher product prices. New, nonunion, firms can enter the industry, pay market wages, and sell the product for less.

Exclusive, or Craft, Unions: Reducing Labor Supply

One way to increase wages while avoiding an excess quantity of labor supplied is to somehow reduce the supply of labor, shown in Exhibit 7 as a leftward shift of the labor supply curve in panel (a). This supply reduction increases the wage and reduces employment. Successful supply restrictions of this type require that the union first limit its membership and second force all employers in the industry to hire only union members. The union can restrict membership with higher initiation fees, longer apprenticeship periods, tougher qualification exams, more restrictive licensing requirements, and so on. But even if unions restrict membership, they still have difficulty unionizing all firms in the industry.

Whereas wage setting is more typical of industrial unions, restricting supply is more typical of craft unions, such as unions of carpenters, plumbers, or bricklayers. Professional groups—doctors, lawyers, and accountants, for instance—also impose entry restrictions through education, examination, and licensing requirements. These restrictions, usually defended as protecting the public, are often little more than self-serving attempts to increase wages by restricting labor supply.

Exhibit 6

Median Weekly Earnings Are Higher for Union Than Nonunion Workers

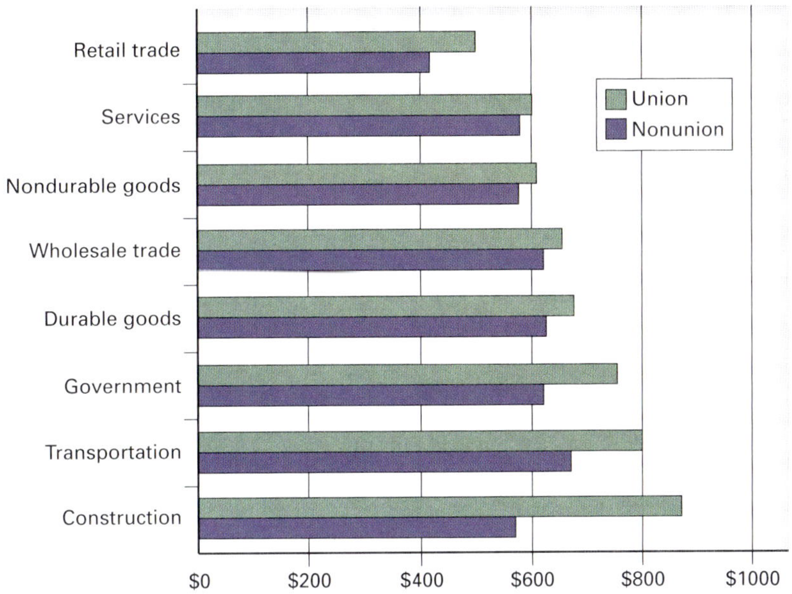

Source: U.S. Bureau of Labor Statistics, "Union Member Summary," 25 January 2007, Table 4, at http://www.bls.gov/news.release/ union2.t04.htm. Figures are for full-time workers in 2006.

Unions are less successful at raising wages in more competitive sectors.

Increasing Demand for Union Labor

A third way to increase wages is to increase the demand for union labor by somehow shifting the labor demand curve outward as from D to D″ in panel (b) of Exhibit 7. This is an attractive alternative *because it increases both the wage and employment,* so there is no need to restrict labor supply or to ration jobs among union members. Here are some ways unions try to increase the demand for union labor.

Increase Demand for Union-Made Goods

The demand for union labor may be increased through a direct appeal to consumers to buy only union-made products. Because the demand for labor is a derived demand, increasing the demand for union-made products increases the demand for union labor.

Restrict Supply of Nonunion-Made Goods

Another way to increase the demand for union labor is to restrict the supply of products that compete with union-made products. This approach relies on the derived nature of labor demand. The United Auto Workers, for example, has supported restrictions on

Exhibit 7

Effect of Reducing Labor Supply or Increasing Labor Demand

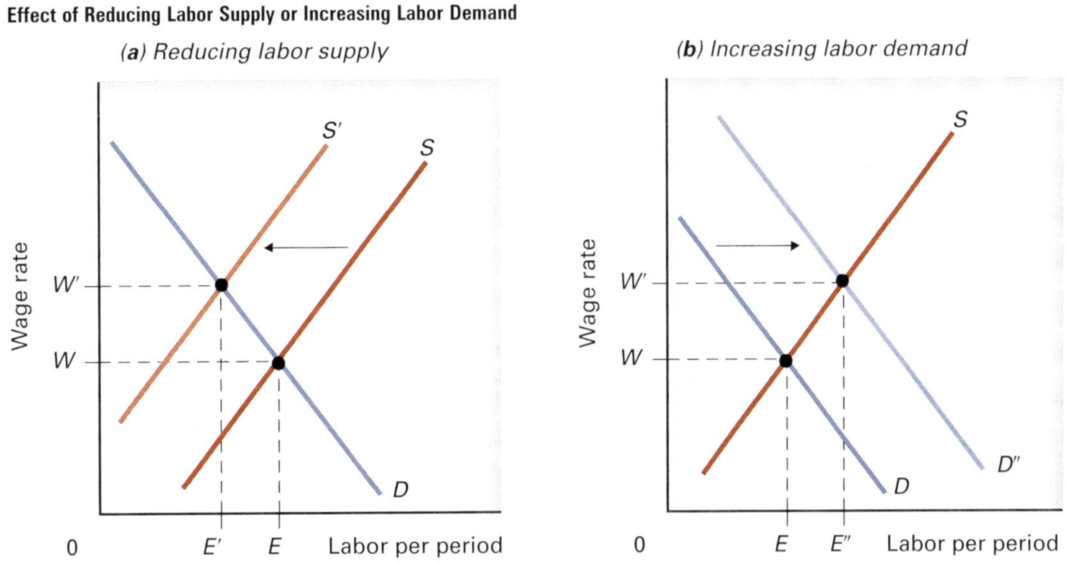

imported cars. Fewer imported cars means greater demand for cars produced by U.S. workers, who are mostly union members. This strategy has become less effective as foreign automakers, such as Toyota, establish nonunion plants in the United States.

Increase Productivity of Union Labor

Some observers claim union representation improves labor-management relations. According to this theory, unions increase worker productivity by minimizing conflicts, resolving differences, and at times even straightening out workers who goof off. In the absence of a union, a dissatisfied worker may simply quit, increasing job turnover. Turnover is costly to the firm because the departing worker leaves with company-specific, on-the-job training that increases worker productivity. With a union, however, workers can resolve matters through union channels. Quit rates are in fact significantly lower among union workers (although this could also be due to the higher pay). If unions increase the productivity of workers, the demand for union labor increases.

Featherbedding

Yet another way unions try to increase union employment is by featherbedding, which makes employers hire more labor than they demand. For example, union rules require that each Broadway theater have a permanent "house" carpenter, electrician, and property manager. Once the play opens, these workers show up only on payday. The union may require that the box office be staffed by three people.

Featherbedding does not create an increase in demand, in the sense of shifting the demand curve to the right. Instead, it forces an employer to a point to the right of its labor demand curve. The union tries to limit a firm to an all-or-none choice: Either hire so many workers for the job, or we'll strike. Thus, with featherbedding, *the union attempts to dictate not only the wage but also the quantity that must be hired at that wage, thereby moving employers to the right of their labor demand curve.*

featherbedding union efforts to force employers to hire more workers than demanded at a particular wage

right-to-work states states where workers in unionized companies do not have to join the union or pay union dues

To review: We have examined three ways that unions try to raise members' wages: (1) by negotiating a wage floor above the equilibrium wage for the industry then somehow rationing the limited jobs among union members, (2) by restricting the supply of labor, and (3) by increasing the demand for union labor. Unions try to increase the demand for union labor in four ways: (1) through a direct public appeal to buy only union-made products, (2) by restricting the supply of products made by nonunion labor, (3) by reducing labor turnover and thereby increasing labor's marginal productivity, and (4) through featherbedding, which forces employers to hire more union workers than they want or need.

Recent Trends in Union Membership

In 1955, about 35 percent of U.S. workers belonged to unions. Since then, union membership as a fraction of the workforce has declined steadily. By 2006, only 12 percent of U.S. workers belonged to unions, about the same rate as in 1900. Government workers are much more unionized than other workers—36 percent of government workers are unionized versus just 7 percent of other workers. A typical union member is a schoolteacher. Compared with other industrialized countries, the United States ranks relatively low in the extent of unionization, though rates abroad have been declining as well.

The bar graph in Exhibit 8 indicates U.S. union membership rates by age and gender in 2006. The rates for men, shown by the green bars, are higher than the rates for women, in part because women work more in the service sector, where union membership is lower. The highest membership rates are for middle-aged males. Although the exhibit does not show it, black workers have a higher union membership rate than white workers (15 percent versus 12 percent), in part because African Americans are employed more by government and by heavy industries such as autos and steel, where union representation is higher. Union membership is below average among Asians and those of Hispanic origin (10 percent each). Union membership rates also vary across states. Hawaii had the highest unionization rate at 25 percent and the Carolinas, the lowest at 3 percent each. Unionization rates in right-to-work states average only half the rates in other states. In right-to-work states, workers in unionized companies do not have to join the union or pay union dues. Over the years, the number of right-to-work states has increased and this has hurt the union movement.

The decline in union membership rates is also due to structural changes in the U.S. economy. Unions have long been more important in the industrial sector than in the service sector. But employ-

Exhibit 8

Unionization Rates by Age and Gender

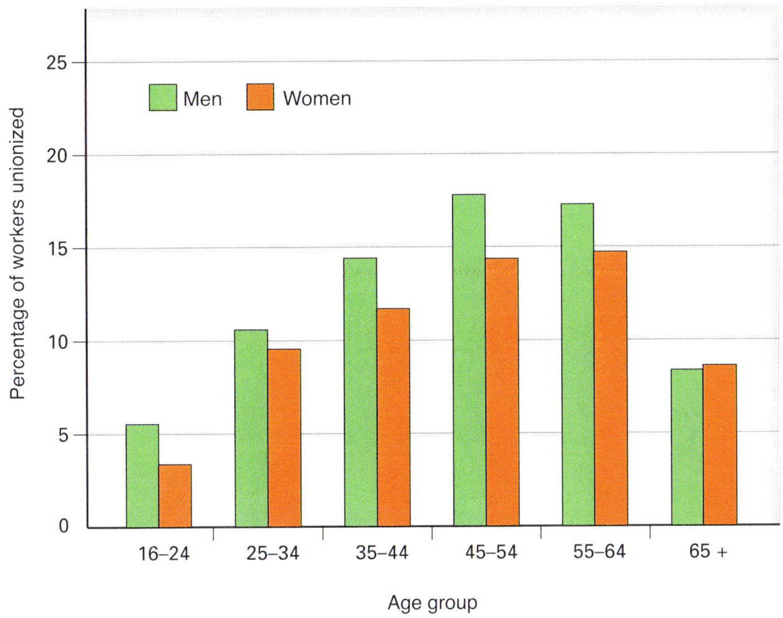

SOURCE: U.S. Bureau of Labor Statistics, "Union Members Summary," Table 1, at http://www.bls.gov/news.release/union2.t01.htm. Figures show union membership in 2006 as a percentage of all U.S. wage and salary workers.

ment in the industrial sector, which includes manufacturing, mining, and construction, has declined in recent decades as a share of all jobs. Another factor in the decline of the union movement is a growth in market competition, particularly from imports. Increased competition from nonunion employers, both foreign and domestic, has reduced the ability of unionized firms to pass on higher labor costs as higher prices. And fewer union members mean fewer voters who belong to unions, so unions have lost political clout.

Finally, the near disappearance of the strike has cut union power. During the 1970s, an average of about 300 strikes a year in the United States involved 1,000 or more workers. Since 2000, there were only about 20 such strikes a year on average. Worse still for organized labor, many recent strikes ended badly for union workers; companies such as Caterpillar, Continental Airlines, Hormel Foods, International Paper, and Phelps Dodge Copper hired replacement workers. Union members are now less inclined to strike because of the increased willingness of employers to hire strikebreakers and the increased willingness of workers—both union and nonunion—to work during a strike. Strikes also cut company profits, which hurts workers whose pay is tied to profits, thus dampening the incentive to strike. For example, a strike against General Motors cut each worker's average profit share to just $200 from more than $6,000 the year before. Because the strike and the threat of a strike have become less important, the power of unions has diminished.

Final Word

The first half of this chapter focused on labor supply and explained why wages differ across occupations and among individuals within an occupation. The interaction of labor demand and supply determines wages and employment. The second half of the chapter explored the effect of unions on the labor market. At one time unions dominated some key industries. But as global competition intensifies, employers have a harder time passing higher union labor costs along to consumers. Both in the United States and in other industrial economies, union members represent a dwindling segment of the labor force.

---

20 < Strikes per year with over 1,000 workers

15% < Union membership rate among African American workers

Average hourly wage for managers > $44.20

Yearly wage for a truck driver in Iraq > $100,000

1886 < Year AFL was founded

Workers with professional degrees can make up to 6 times more than those without a high school diploma

---

CHAPTER 13

Capital, Interest, *and* Corporate Finance

Learning Outcomes

LO[1] Discuss the role of time in production and consumption

LO[2] Describe the factors that determine optimal investment

LO[3] Explain present value and discounting

LO[4] Analyze different corporate finance strategies

© PULSE PRODUCTIONS/SUPERSTOCK/JUPITERIMAGES

"Why is a movie rental only half the price of a movie ticket?"

Why is a movie rental only half the price of a movie ticket? Why do you burn your mouth eating pizza? What's seed money and why can't Farmer Jones grow a thing without it? What's the harm in pirated software, music, and DVDs? Why are state lottery jackpots worth much less than the advertised millions? These and other questions are answered in this chapter, which examines capital and investment.

So far, our discussion of resources has focused primarily on labor markets. This emphasis is appropriate because labor generates most income—more than two-thirds of the total. The rewards to labor, however, depend in part on the amount and quality of the other resources employed, particularly capital. A farmer plowing a field with a tractor is more productive than one scraping the soil with a stick. This chapter looks at the role of capital in production—its cost and its expected return. You will learn about the optimal use of capital and how firms finance their investments.

What do you think?

I would rather receive $10 today than $100 in ten years.

Strongly Disagree						Strongly Agree
1	2	3	4	5	6	7

LO[1] The Role of Time in Production and Consumption

Topics discussed in Chapter 13 include:

- Production, saving, and time
- Consumption, saving, and time
- Optimal investment
- Corporate finance
- Loanable funds market
- Stocks, bonds, and retained earnings
- Present value and discounting

Time is important in both production and consumption. In this section, we first consider the role of time on the production decision, then show why firms borrow household savings. Next, we consider the role of time in the consumption decision and show why households are rewarded for saving, or deferring present consumption. By bringing together borrowers and savers, we find the market interest rate.

Production, Saving, and Time

Suppose Jones is a primitive farmer in a simple economy. Isolated from any neighbors or markets, he literally scratches out a living on a plot of land, using only some crude sticks. While his crop is growing, none of it is available for current consumption. Because production takes time, to survive, Jones must rely on food saved from prior

harvests. The longer the growing season, the more Jones must save. Thus, even in this simple example, it is clear that *production cannot occur without prior saving.*

With his current resources, consisting of land, labor, seed corn, fertilizer, and some crude sticks, Jones grows about 200 bushels of corn a year. He soon realizes that if he had a plow—a type of investment good, or capital—his productivity would increase. Making a plow in such a primitive setting, however, is time consuming and would keep him away from his fields for a year. Thus, the plow has an opportunity cost of 200 bushels of corn. He could not survive this drop in production without enough saved from previous harvests.

The question is: Should he invest his time in the plow? The answer depends on the cost and benefit of the plow. We already know that the plow's opportunity cost is 200 bushels—the forgone output. The benefit depends on how much the plow increases crop production and how long it lasts. Jones figures that the plow would boost annual yield by 100 bushels and would last his lifetime. In making the investment decision, he compares the current cost to the future benefit. Suppose he decides that adding 100 bushels a year outweighs the one-time cost of 200 bushels to make the plow.

In making the plow, Jones engages in *roundabout production*. Rather than working the soil with his crude sticks, he produces capital to increase his productivity. More roundabout production in an economy means more capital, so more goods can be produced in the future. Advanced industrial economies are characterized by much roundabout production and thus abundant capital accumulation.

positive rate of time preference
consumers value present consumption more than future consumption

You can see why production cannot occur without prior saving. *Production requires saving because both direct and roundabout production take time—time during which goods and services are not available from current production.* Now let's modernize the example by introducing the ability to borrow. Many farmers visit the bank each spring to borrow enough "seed money" to get by until the harvest. Likewise, other businesses often borrow at least a portion of the start-up funds needed to get going. Thus, in a modern economy, producers need not rely just on their own prior saving. Banks and other financial institutions serve as *intermediaries* between savers and borrowers. Financial markets for stocks and bonds also help channel savings to producers.

Let's take a look at the incentive to save.

Consumption, Saving, and Time

Did you ever burn the roof of your mouth eating a slice of pizza? Have you done this more than once? Why do you persist in such self-mutilation? You persist because that bite of pizza is worth more to you now than the same bite a minute from now. In fact, you are willing to risk burning your mouth rather than wait until the pizza has lost its destructive properties. In a small way, this phenomenon reflects the fact that you and other consumers value *present* consumption more than *future* consumption. You and other consumers are said to have a **positive rate of time preference**.

Because you value present consumption more than future consumption, you are willing to pay more to consume now rather than wait. And prices often reflect this greater willingness to pay. Consider the movies. You pay about twice as much for a movie ticket than to rent the DVD four months later. The same is true

> Because people value present consumption more than future consumption, they must be rewarded to postpone consumption.

for books. By waiting for the paperback, you can save more than half the hardback price. Photo developers, dry cleaners, fast-food restaurants, convenience stores, cable news networks, and other suppliers tout the speed of their services, knowing that consumers prefer earlier availability. Thus, *impatience* is one explanation for a positive rate of time preference. Another is *uncertainty*. If you wait, something might prevent you from consuming the good. A T-shirt slogan captures this point best: "Life is uncertain. Eat dessert first."

Because people value present consumption more than future consumption, they must be rewarded to postpone consumption. By saving a portion of their incomes in financial institutions such as banks, people forgo present consumption for a greater ability to consume in the future. Interest is the reward for postponing consumption. The **interest rate** is the annual reward for saving as a percentage of the amount saved. For example, if the interest rate is 5 percent, the reward, or interest, is $5 per year for each $100 saved. The higher the interest rate, other things constant, the more consumers are rewarded for saving, so the more they save. You will learn more about this later in the chapter.

LO2 Optimal Investment

In a market economy characterized by specialization and exchange, Farmer Jones no longer needs to produce his own capital, nor need he rely on his own saving. He can purchase capital with borrowed funds. Suppose he wants to buy some farm equipment. He estimates how each piece of equipment would affect his productivity. Column (1) in Exhibit 1a identifies six pieces of farm machinery that Jones has ranked from most to least productive. The total product of the equipment is listed in column (2), and the marginal product of each piece is listed in column (3). Note that other resources are assumed to remain constant.

With just his crude sticks, Jones can grow 200 bushels of corn per year. He figures that a tractor-tiller would boost the harvest to 1,200 bushels. Thus, the tractor-tiller would yield a marginal product of 1,000 bushels per year. Adding a combine would increase total output to 2,000 bushels, yielding a marginal product of 800 bushels. Note that in this example, diminishing marginal returns from capital set in with the combine. Marginal product continues to decrease as more capital is added, dropping to zero for a post-hole digger, which Jones has no use for.

Suppose Jones sells corn in a perfectly competitive market, so he can sell all he wants at the market price of $4 a bushel. The marginal product from column (3) multiplied by $4 yields capital's *marginal revenue product* listed in column (4). The marginal revenue product of machinery is its marginal product times the price of corn, or the change in total revenue resulting from adding another piece of farm equipment.

Exhibit 1a

Marginal Rate of Return per Year on Investment in Farm Equipment

(1) Farm Equipment	(2) Total Product (bushels)	(3) Marginal Product (bushels)	(4) Marginal revenue Product (4) = (3) × $4	(5) Marginal Resource Cost	(6) Marginal Rate of Return (6) = (4) / (5)
No equipment	200	—	—	—	—
Tractor-tiller	1,200	1,000	$4,000	$10,000	40%
Combine	2,000	800	3,200	10,000	32
Irrigator	2,600	600	2,400	10,000	24
Harrow	3,000	400	1,600	10,000	16
Crop sprayer	3,200	200	800	10,000	8
Post-hole digger	3,200	0	0	10,000	0

For simplicity, suppose farm equipment costs $10,000 each. Thus, the marginal resource cost is $10,000, as listed in column (5). Suppose also that the equipment is so durable that it is expected to last indefinitely, that operating expenses are negligible, and that the price of corn is expected to remain at $4 per bushel in the future. Farm equipment increases revenue not only in the first

interest rate interest per year as a percentage of the amount saved or borrowed year but every year into the future. *The optimal investment decision requires Jones to take time into account.* He can't simply equate marginal resource cost with marginal revenue product, because the marginal cost is a one-time outlay this year, whereas the marginal product is an annual amount this year and each year in the future. As we will see, markets bridge time with the interest rate.

Jones must decide how much to invest in farm equipment. His first task is to compute the *marginal rate of return* he expects to earn each year by investing in farm machinery. The **marginal rate of return on investment** is capital's marginal revenue product as a percentage of its marginal resource cost. For example, the tractor-tiller yields a marginal revenue product of $4,000 per year and has a one-time marginal resource cost of $10,000. The marginal rate of return Jones could earn on this investment is $4,000/$10,000, or 40 percent per year. Therefore, the tractor-tiller yields a *marginal rate of return* of 40 percent per year, as shown in column (6). The combine yields a marginal revenue product of $3,200 per year and has a marginal cost of $10,000, so its marginal rate of return equals $3,200/$10,000, or 32 percent per year. Dividing the marginal revenue product of capital in column (4) by the marginal resource cost of that capital in column (5) yields the marginal rate of return in column (6) for each piece of equipment.

Given the marginal rate of return, how much should Jones invest to maximize profit? Suppose he borrows the money, paying the *market interest rate*. Jones buys more capital as long as its marginal rate of return exceeds the market interest rate. He stops before capital's marginal rate of return falls below the market interest rate. For example, if the market interest rate is 20 percent, Jones invests $30,000 in three pieces of equipment. The marginal rate of return on the third item purchased, an irrigator, is 24 percent. Investing another $10,000 to buy a harrow would yield a marginal return of only 16 percent, a rate below his cost of borrowing. At a market interest rate of 10 percent, Jones would invest in the harrow as well. An interest rate of 6 percent would lead Jones to also invest in the crop sprayer.

Farmer Jones should increase his investment as long as the marginal rate of return on that investment exceeds the market interest rate. The marginal rate of return is the marginal benefit of the investment, and the market interest rate is the marginal cost, so Jones is simply maximizing profit (or minimizing loss) by investing until marginal benefit equals the marginal cost. The data in column (6) are depicted in Exhibit 1b as a step-like graph, where the solid lines reflect the amount Jones invests at each interest rate. For example, if the market interest rate is between 32 percent and 40 percent, Jones should invest in the tractor-tiller. Because the marginal rate of return shows how much should be invested at each interest rate, this step-like graph represents the farmer's demand for investment. This is a derived demand, based on the marginal productivity of each piece of equipment. *The demand curve steps down to reflect the diminishing marginal productivity of capital.*

Would the example change if Jones saved enough to buy the equipment? Not as long as he can earn the market interest rate on his savings. For example, suppose Jones saved $50,000, which is earning an interest rate of 10 percent per year. In that case, Jones should invest $40,000 in capital, with the last piece purchased, the harrow, earning a marginal return of 16 percent. The 10 percent interest Jones earns on his remaining savings of $10,000 exceeds the 8 percent he could earn by investing that amount in the crop sprayer. Thus, as long as he can borrow and save at the same interest rate, Jones ends up investing in the same equipment whether

marginal rate of return on investment
the marginal revenue product of capital expressed as a percentage of its marginal cost

Exhibit 1b

Marginal Rate of Return per Year on Investment in Farm Equipment

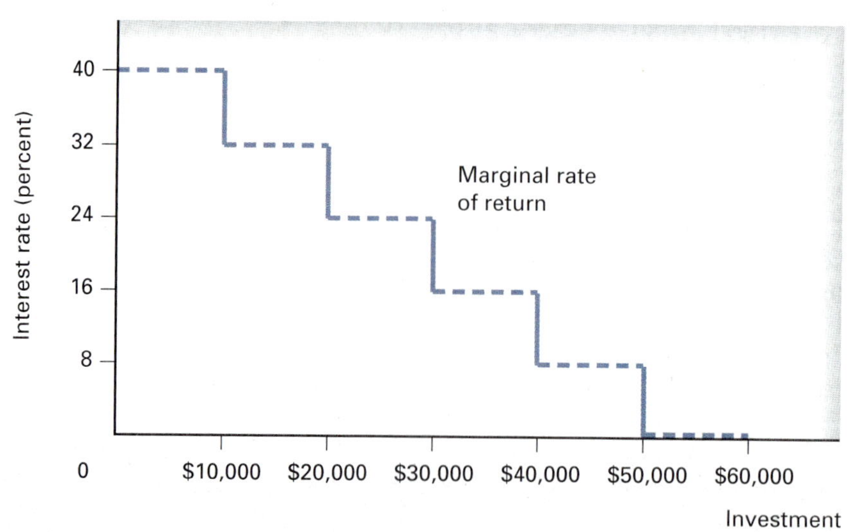

© IMAGE SOURCE/JUPITERIMAGES

he borrows funds or draws down his own savings. *Whether Jones borrows the money or draws on his savings, the market interest rate represents his opportunity cost of investing.*

Let's review the steps to determine the optimal amount of investment. First, compute the marginal revenue product of capital. Next, divide the marginal revenue product by the marginal resource cost to get the marginal rate of return. The marginal rate of return curve becomes a firm's demand curve for investment—that is, it shows the amount a firm is willing and able to invest at each interest rate. The market interest rate is the opportunity cost of investing either borrowed funds or savings, and can be thought of as the supply of investment funds to the firm. A firm should invest more as long as the marginal rate of return on capital exceeds the market rate of interest.

The Market for Loanable Funds

You learned earlier why producers are willing to pay interest to borrow money: *Money provides a command over resources, making both direct production and roundabout production possible.* The simple principles developed for Farmer Jones can be generalized to other producers. The major demanders of loans are entrepreneurs who borrow to start firms and to invest in physical capital, such as machines, trucks, and buildings, and in intellectual capital, such as patents, copyrights, and trademarks. At any time, a firm has a variety of investment opportunities. The firm ranks these opportunities from highest to lowest, based on the expected marginal rates of return. The firm increases its investment until the expected marginal rate of return just equals the market interest rate. With other inputs held constant, as they were on the farm, the demand curve for investment slopes downward.

MONEY PROVIDES A COMMAND OVER RESOURCES, MAKING BOTH DIRECT PRODUCTION AND ROUNDABOUT PRODUCTION POSSIBLE.

But entrepreneurs are not the only demanders of loans. As we have seen, households value present consumption more than future consumption; they are willing to pay extra to consume now rather than later. One way to ensure that goods and services are available now is to borrow for present consumption, as reflected by home mortgages, car loans, and credit card purchases. Some people also borrow to invest in their human capital, as reflected by college loans. The household's demand curve for loans, like the firm's demand for loans, slopes downward, indicating that consumers are more willing and able to borrow at lower interest rates, other things constant. The government sector and the rest of the world are also demanders of loans.

Demand for Loanable Funds

The **demand for loanable funds** curve shows the negative relationship between the market interest rate and the quantity of loans demanded, other things constant. This curve is based on the expected marginal rate of return these borrowed funds yield when invested in capital. Each firm has a downward-sloping demand curve for loanable funds, reflecting a declining marginal rate of return on investment. With some qualifications, the demand for loanable funds of each firm can be summed horizontally to yield the market demand for loanable funds, shown as *D* in Exhibit 2. Factors assumed constant along this demand curve include the prices of other resources, the level of technology, and the tax laws.

Supply of Loanable Funds

Banks are willing to pay interest on savings because they can, in turn, lend these savings to those who need credit, such as farmers, home buyers, college students, and entrepreneurs looking to start a new business or buy new capital. Banks play the role of *financial intermediaries* in what is known as the market for loanable funds. The higher the interest rate, other things constant, the greater the reward for saving. As people save more, the quantity of loanable funds increases. The **supply of loanable funds** curve shows the positive relationship

demand for loanable funds the negative relationship between the market interest rate and the quantity of loanable funds demanded, other things constant

supply of loanable funds the positive relationship between the market interest rate and the quantity of loanable funds supplied, other things constant

Exhibit 2

Market for Loanable Funds

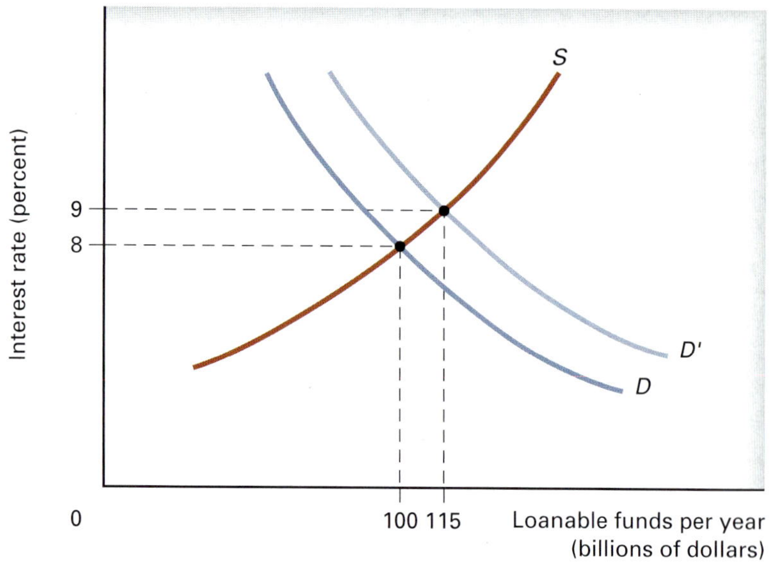

between the market interest rate and the quantity of savings supplied, other things constant, as reflected by the usual upward-sloping supply curve shown as S in Exhibit 2.

Market Interest Rate

The **loanable funds market** brings together borrowers, or demanders of loanable funds, and savers, or suppliers of loanable funds, to determine the market interest rate. The demand and supply of loanable funds come together, as in Exhibit 2, to determine the market interest rate. In this case, the equilibrium interest rate of 8 percent is the only one that exactly matches the wishes of borrowers and savers. The equilibrium quantity of loanable funds is $100 billion per year. Any change in the demand or supply of loanable funds changes the market interest rate. For example, a major technological breakthrough that increases the productivity of capital increases its marginal rate of return, shifting the demand curve for loanable funds rightward, as shown in the movement from *D* to *D'*. Such an increase in the demand for loanable funds would raise the equilibrium interest rate to 9 percent and increase the market quantity of loanable funds to $115 billion per year.

loanable funds market
the market in which savers (suppliers of loanable funds) and borrowers (demanders of loanable funds) come together to determine the market interest rate and the quantity of loanable funds exchanged

prime rate
the interest rate lenders charge their most trustworthy business borrowers

collateral
an asset pledged by the borrower that can be sold to pay off the loan in the event the borrower defaults

Why Interest Rates Differ

So far, we have been talking about *the* market interest rate, implying that only one rate prevails in the loanable funds market. At any particular time, however, a range of interest rates coexist in the economy. Exhibit 3 shows interest rates for loans in various markets. The interest rate for home mortgages is relatively low because this loan is backed up by the home itself. The so-called **prime rate** is the interest rate lenders charge their most trustworthy business borrowers. The highest is the rate charged on credit card balances, which is more than double the rate on mortgages. Let's see why interest rates differ.

Risk

Some borrowers are more likely than others to *default* on their loans—that is, not to pay them back. Before a bank lends money, it usually requires a borrower to put up **collateral**, which is an asset pledged by the borrower that can be sold to pay off the loan in the event of a default. With business loans, any valuable asset—land, buildings, machinery—the firm owns can serve as collateral. With a home mortgage, the home itself becomes collateral. And with a car loan, the car becomes collateral. The more valuable the collateral backing up the loan, other things constant, the lower the interest rate changed on that loan. For example, the interest rate charged on car loans is usually higher than on home loans. A car loses its value more quickly than a home does, and a car can be driven away by a defaulting borrower, whereas a home usually increases in value and stays put. So a car offers worse collateral than a home—hence, the interest charged on a car loan is higher. Interest rates are higher still for personal loans and credit cards, because such borrowers usually offer no collateral.

Duration of the Loan

The future is uncertain, and the further into the future a loan is to be repaid, the more uncertain that repayment becomes. Thus, as the duration of a loan

Exhibit 3

Interest Rates Charged for Different Types of Loans

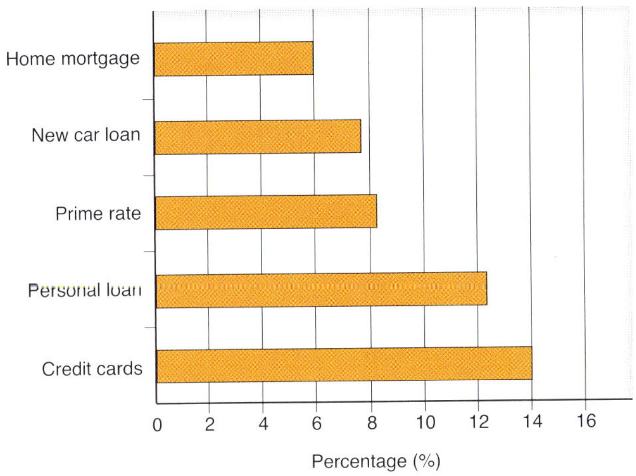

SOURCE: Federal Reserve Board. Interest rates are as of March 2007.

increases, lenders require a higher interest rate to compensate for the greater risk. The term structure of interest rates is the relationship between the duration of a loan and the interest rate charged. *The interest rate usually increases with the duration of the loan, other things constant.*

Administration Costs

The costs of executing the loan agreement, monitoring the loan, and collecting payments are called the *administration costs* of the loan. These costs, as a proportion of the loan, decrease as the size of the loan increases. For example, the cost of administering a $100,000 loan is less than 10 times the cost of administering a $10,000 loan. Consequently, that portion of the interest charge reflecting administration costs becomes smaller as the size of the loan increases, other things constant, thus reducing the interest rate for larger loans.

Tax Treatment

Differences in the tax treatment of different types of loans also affects the interest rate charged. For example, the interest earned on loans to state and local governments is not subject to federal income taxes. Because lenders focus on their after-tax rate of interest, state and local governments pay a lower interest rate than other borrowers pay.

To review: the demand and supply of loanable funds determine the market interest rate. At any given time, interest rates may differ because of differences in risk, maturity, administrative costs, and tax treatment. Now we move on to consider the value of some future benefit.

LO3 Present Value and Discounting

Because you value present consumption more than future consumption, present and future consumption cannot be compared directly. Someone who "eats like there's no tomorrow" apparently values present consumption much more than consumption tomorrow. A way of standardizing the discussion is to measure all consumption in terms of its present value. Present value is the current value of a payment or payments to be received in the future. For example, how much would you pay now to receive $100 one year from now? Put another way, what is the *present value* to you of receiving $100 one year from now?

Present Value of Payment One Year Hence

Suppose the market interest rate is 10 percent and you can either lend or borrow at that rate. One way to determine how much you would pay for the opportunity to receive $100 one year from now is to ask how much you would have to save now, at the market interest rate, to end up with $100 one year from now. Here's the problem we are trying to solve: What amount of money, if saved at an interest rate of, say, 10 percent, would accumulate to $100 one year from now? We can calculate the answer with a simple formula:

$$\text{Present value} \times 1.10 = \$100$$

or:

$$\text{Present value} = \frac{\$100}{1.10} = \$90.91$$

Thus, if the interest rate is 10 percent, $90.91 is the present value of receiving $100 one year from now; it is the most you would pay today to receive $100 one year from now. Rather than pay more than $90.91, you could simply deposit your $90.91 at the market interest rate of 10 percent and end up with $100 a year from now (ignoring taxes). Dividing the future payment by 1 plus the prevailing interest rate to express it in today's dollars is called discounting.

term structure of interest rates the relationship between the duration of a loan and the interest rate charged; typically interest rates increase with the duration of the loan, because longer loans are considered more risky

present value the value today of income to be received in the future

discounting converting future dollar amounts into present value

The present value of \$100 to be received one year from now depends on the interest rate. The more that present consumption is preferred to future consumption, the higher the interest rate that must be offered savers to defer consumption. *The higher the interest rate, the more any future payment is discounted and the lower its present value.* Put another way, the higher the interest rate, the less you need to save now to yield a given amount in the future. For example, if the interest rate is 15 percent, the present value of receiving \$100 one year from now is \$100/1.15, which equals \$86.96.

On the other hand, the less present consumption is preferred to future consumption, the less savers need to be paid to defer consumption so the lower the interest rate. The lower the interest rate, the less the future income is discounted and the greater its present value. A lower interest rate means that you must save more now to yield a given amount in the future. As a general rule, the present value of receiving an amount one year from now is:

$$\text{Present value} = \frac{\text{Amount received one year from now}}{1 + \text{interest rate}}$$

For example, when the interest rate is 5 percent, the present value of receiving \$100 one year from now is:

$$\text{Present value} = \frac{\$100}{1 + 0.05} = \frac{\$100}{1.05} = \$95.24$$

Present Value for Payments in Later Years

Now consider the present value of receiving \$100 two years from now. What amount of money, if deposited at the market interest rate of 5 percent, would yield \$100 after two years? After one year, the value would be the present value times 1.05, which would then earn the market interest rate during the second year. After two years, the deposit would have accumulated to the present value times 1.05 times 1.05. Thus, we have the equation:

$$\text{Present value} \times 1.05 \times 1.05 = \text{Present value} \times (1.05)^2 = \$100$$

Solving for the present value yields:

$$\text{Present value} = \frac{\$100}{(1.05)^2} = \frac{\$100}{1.1025} = \$90.70$$

If the \$100 were to be received three years from now, we would discount the payment over three years:

$$\text{Present value} = \frac{\$100}{(1.05)^3} = \$86.38$$

If the interest rate is i, the present value of M dollars received t years from now is:

$$\text{Present value} = \frac{M}{(1 + i)^t}$$

Because $(1 + i)$ is greater than 1, the more times it is multiplied by itself (as determined by t), the larger the denominator and the smaller the present value. Thus, *the present value of a given payment is smaller the further into the future that payment is to be received.*

Present Value of an Income Stream

So far, we have figured out the present value of a single sum to be received in the future. Most investments, however, yield a stream of income over time. In cases where the income is received for a period of years, the present value of each receipt can be computed individually and the results summed to yield the present

© RON CHAPPLE/THINKSTOCK IMAGES/JUPITERIMAGES

value of the entire income stream. For example, the present value of receiving $100 next year and $150 the year after is simply the present value of the first year's receipt plus the present value of the second year's receipt. If the interest rate is 5 percent:

$$\text{Present value} = \frac{\$100}{1.05} + \frac{\$150}{(1.05)^2} = \$231.29$$

$$\textit{Present value} = \frac{M}{(1+i)^t}$$

$$\textit{Present value of receiving M dollars each year forever} = \frac{M}{i}$$

Present Value of an Annuity

A given sum of money received each year for a specified number of years is called an **annuity**. Such an income stream is called a *perpetuity* if it continues indefinitely, as it would with indestructible farm machinery. The present value of receiving a certain amount forever seems like it should be a very large sum indeed. But because future income is valued less the more distant into the future it is to be received, the present value of receiving a particular amount forever is not much more than that of receiving it for, say, 20 years.

To determine the present value of receiving $100 a year forever, we need only ask how much money must be deposited in a savings account to yield $100 in interest each year. If the interest rate is 10 percent, a deposit of $1,000 will earn $100 per year. Thus, the present value of receiving $100 a year indefinitely when the interest rate is 10 percent is $1,000. More generally, the present value of receiving a sum each year forever equals the amount received each year divided by the interest rate.

$$\text{Present value of receiving M dollars each year forever} = \frac{M}{i}$$

The concept of present value is useful for investment decisions. Farmer Jones, by investing $10,000 in the crop sprayer, expects to earn $800 more per year. So his marginal rate of return on that investment is 8 percent. At a market interest rate of 8 percent, the present value of a cash flow of $800 per year discounted at that rate would be $800/0.08, which equals $10,000. Thus, *Jones is willing to invest capital until, at the margin, his investment yields a cash stream with a present value just equal to the marginal cost of the investment.* Jones invests until marginal benefit equals marginal cost.

What about your decision to invest in human capital—to go to college? A chart in the previous chapter showed that those with at least a college degree earned nearly twice as much as those with just a high school diploma. We could compute the present value of an education by discounting earnings based on that level of education, then summing total earnings over your working life. Even without doing the calculations, we can say with reasonable certainty that the present value of at least a college education will be nearly twice that of just a high school education.

This discussion of present value and discounting concludes our treatment of capital and interest. We now have some tools to consider how firms, especially corporations, are financed.

LO4 Corporate Finance

During the Industrial Revolution, labor-saving machinery made large-scale production more profitable, but building huge factories filled with heavy machinery required substantial investments. The corporate structure became the easiest way to finance such outlays, and by 1920, corporations accounted for most employment and output in the U.S. economy. Back in Chapter 3, you learned about the pros and cons of the corporate form of business. Thus far, however, little has been said about corporate finance. As noted in Chapter 3, a corporation is a legal entity, distinct from its shareholders. The corporation may own property, earn a profit, sue or be sued, incur debt, even be found guilty of a crime. Stockholders, the owners of the corporation, are liable only to the extent of their investment in the firm. Use of the abbreviations Inc. or Corp. in the company name serves as a warning to potential creditors that stockholders will not accept personal liability for debts of the company.

Corporate Stock and Retained Earnings

Corporations fund investment in three ways: by issuing stock, by retaining some of their profits, and by borrowing. Corporations issue and sell stock to raise money for operations and for new plants and equipment. Suppose you have developed a recipe for a hot, spicy chili that your friends have convinced you will be a best-seller. You start a company called Six-Alarm Chili. As the founder, you

annuity
a given sum of money received each year for a specified number of years

are that firm's entrepreneur. Recall that an entrepreneur is a profit-seeking decision maker who organizes an enterprise and assumes the risk of operation. An entrepreneur pays others for the opportunity to use their resources in the firm. The entrepreneur need not actually manage the firm's resources as long as he or she has the power to hire and fire the manager—that is, as long as the entrepreneur controls the manager.

Your company meets with early success, but you find that to remain competitive, you need to achieve economies of scale, which means the firm must grow fast. To fund that growth, you decide to incorporate. The newly incorporated company issues 1,000,000 shares of stock. You take 100,000 shares yourself as your *owner's equity* in the corporation. The rest are sold to the public for $10 per share, which raises $9 million for the company. You, in effect, pay for your shares with the "sweat equity" required to found the company and get it rolling. The initial sale of stock to the public is called an **initial public offering**, or **IPO**. A *share* of **corporate stock** is a claim on the net income and assets of a corporation, as well as the right to vote on corporate directors and on other important matters. A person who buys 1 percent of the 1,000,000 shares issued thereby owns 1 percent of the corporation, is entitled to 1 percent of any profit, and gets to cast 1 percent of the votes on important corporate decisions.

Corporations must pay corporate income taxes on any profit. After-tax profit is either paid as **dividends** to shareholders or reinvested in the corporation. Reinvested profit, or **retained earnings**, helps the firm fund expansion. Stockholders usually expect dividends, but the corporation is not required to pay dividends. Once shares are issued, their price tends to fluctuate directly with the firm's profit prospects. People buy stock because of the dividends and because they hope the share price will appreciate, or increase.

initial public offering (IPO)
the initial sale of corporate stock to the public

corporate stock
certificate reflecting part ownership of a corporation

dividends
after-tax corporate profit paid to stockholders rather than retained by the firm and reinvested

retained earnings
after-tax corporate profit reinvested in the firm rather than paid to stockholders as dividends

bond
certificate reflecting a firm's promise to pay the lender periodic interest and to repay the borrowed sum of money on the designated maturity date

Corporate Bonds

Again, your corporation can acquire funds by issuing stock, by retaining earnings, or by borrowing. To borrow money, the corporation can go to a bank for a loan or it can issue and sell bonds. A **bond** is the corporation's promise to pay back the holder a fixed sum of money on the designated *maturity date* plus make interest payments until that date. For example, a corporation might sell for $1,000 a bond that promises to make an annual interest payment of, say, $100 for 20 years and to repay the $1,000 at the end of 20 years.

The payment stream for bonds is more predictable than that for stocks. Unless this corporation goes bankrupt, it must pay bondholders as promised. In contrast, stockholders are last in line when resource suppliers get paid, so bondholders get paid before stockholders. Investors usually consider bonds less risky than stocks, although bonds involve risks as well. Risks include corporate bankruptcy and higher market interest rates. For example, suppose you buy a bond that pay 6 percent interest. Soon after that purchase, the market interest rate increases, so newly issued bonds pay 8 percent interest. Your 6 percent bond is less attractive than the new bonds, so the market value of your bond declines. The value of your bond declines until bond buyers are indifferent between buying your 6 percent bond and buying an 8 percent bond.

Securities Exchanges

Once stocks and bonds have been issued and sold, owners of these securities are free to resell them on *securities exchanges*. In the United States, the *Securities and Exchange Commission (SEC)* is the federal body that regulates securities markets. The largest securities market is the New York Stock Exchange, which trades the securities of about 2,800 major corporations, including about 500 non-U.S. companies. Altogether about 10,000 corporations trade on various U.S. exchanges. These are called publicly traded companies, to be distinguished from privately owned companies. Although privately owned companies, such as sole proprietors and partnerships, make up the overwhelming share of U.S. businesses in terms of numbers, corporations account for the overwhelming share of employment and sales.

Nearly all the securities traded each business day are *secondhand securities* in the sense that they have already been issued by the corporation. So the bulk of daily transactions do not finance firms in need of investment funds. Most money from daily trading goes from a securities buyer to a securities seller. *Institutional investors,* such as banks, insurance companies, and mutual funds, account for over half the trading volume on major exchanges. By providing a *secondary market* for securities, exchanges enhance the *liquidity* of securities—that is, the exchanges make the securities more readily sold for cash and thus more attractive to own. Of growing importance in securities exchanges are *hedge funds,* which often follow complex strategies to invest for institutions and wealthy clients.

The secondary markets for stocks also determine the current market value of the corporation. The market value of a firm at any given time can be found by multiplying the share price by the number of shares issued. Because the share price fluctuates throughout the trading day, so does the value of the corporation. In theory, the share price reflects the present value of the discounted stream of expected profit. Just to give you some idea, Exxon Mobil, the top-valued U.S. corporation, had a market value of $470 billion at the close of the trading day on May 25, 2007. The 2,300 U.S. corporations traded on the New York Stock Exchange had a combined market value of about $15 trillion.

Securities prices give corporate management some indication of the wisdom of raising investment funds through retained earnings, new stock issues, or new bond issues. The greater a corporation's expected profit, other things constant, the higher the value of shares on the stock market and the lower the interest rate that would have to be paid on new bond issues. Securities markets usually promote the survival of the fittest by allocating investment funds to those firms able to make the most profitable use of them. *Thus, securities markets allocate funds more readily to successful firms than to firms in financial difficulty.* Some firms may be in such poor shape that they can't issue new securities.

One final point: When economists talk about investing, they have in mind purchases of new capital, such as new machines and new buildings. When the media talk about investing, they usually mean buying stocks and bonds. To an economist, Farmer Jones is investing only when he buys new farm machinery, not when he buys stocks. As noted already, the overwhelming share of stock transactions are in secondary markets, so the money goes from buyers to sellers, and does not go toward new capital purchases.

Final Word

This chapter introduced you to capital, interest, and corporate finance. Capital is a more complicated resource than this chapter has conveyed. For example, the demand curve for investment is a moving target, not the stable relationship drawn in Exhibit 1b. An accurate depiction of the investment demand curve calls for knowledge of the marginal product of capital and the price of output in the future. But capital's marginal productivity changes with breakthroughs in technology and with changes in the employment of other resources. The future price of the product can also vary widely. Consider, for example, the dilemma of a firm contemplating an investment in oil-drilling rigs in recent years, when the price of crude oil fluctuated between $10 and $78 per barrel, as it has in the last decade.

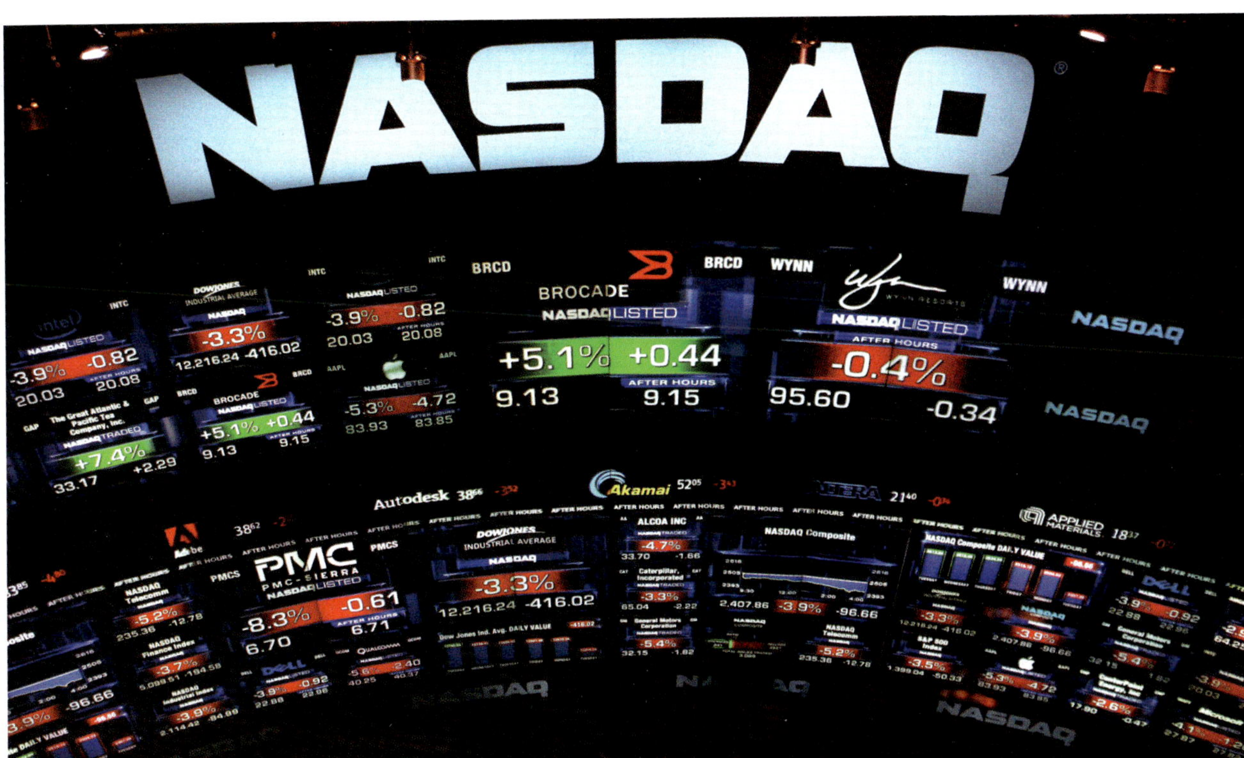

© STEPHEN HILGER/BLOOMBERG NEWS/LANDOV

CHAPTER 14

Transaction Costs, Imperfect Information, *and* Market Behavior

Learning Outcomes

LO[1] Explain the rationale for the firm and describe its scope of operation

LO[2] Discuss the ways in which imperfect information influences market behavior

LO[3] Explain how asymmetric information affects product markets

LO[4] Describe the way asymmetric information influences labor markets

“Why is buying a used car such a gamble?”

Why do some firms, such as Domino’s Pizza, specialize in a single product, while other firms, such as General Electric, make hundreds of different products? Why stop at hundreds? Why not thousands? In fact, why doesn’t a giant firm make everything? Why is proper spelling important on your résumé? Why is buying a used car such a gamble? Why do some winners of online auctions end up losers? Answers to these and other seemingly unrelated questions are addressed in this chapter, which digs deeper into assumptions about firms and the information required for competitive markets.

What do you think?

What you pay for a product depends on how much you know about it.

Strongly Disagree 1 2 3 4 5 6 7 *Strongly Agree*

In the first half of this chapter, we step inside the firm to reconsider some simplifying assumptions about how firms work. We ask: Why do firms exist? How do they decide what to make themselves and what to buy from other firms? These steps toward realism move us beyond the simple depiction of the firm employed to this point. In the second half of this chapter, we challenge some simplifying assumptions about the information available to market participants. We ask: How does the lack of certain information affect behavior and shape market outcomes? Overall, this chapter should help you develop a more realistic view of how firms and markets work.

Topics discussed in Chapter 14 include:

- Transaction costs
- Vertical integration
- Economies of scope
- Optimal search
- Winner’s curse
- Asymmetric information
- Adverse selection
- Principal-agent problem
- Moral hazard
- Signaling and screening

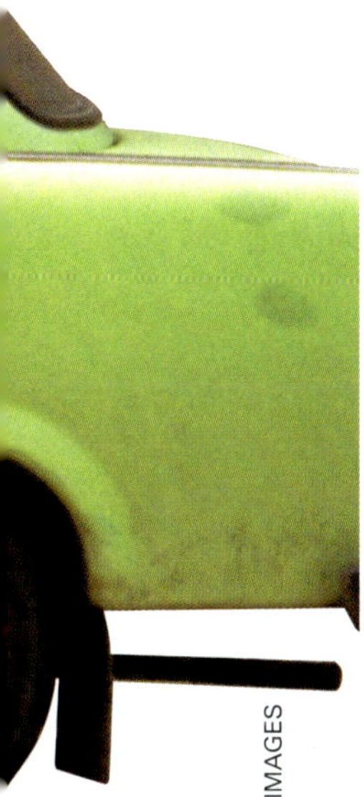

LO[1] Rationale for the Firm and Its Scope of Operation

The competitive model assumes that all participants in the market know everything they need to about the price and availability of all inputs, outputs, and production processes. The firm is assumed to be headed by a brilliant decision maker with a computer-like ability to calculate all the relevant marginal products. This individual knows everything necessary to solve complex production and pricing problems. The irony is that if the marginal products of all inputs could be measured easily and if prices for all inputs could be easily determined, there would be little reason for production to take place in firms. In a world characterized by perfect competition, perfect information, constant returns to scale, and costless exchange, the consumer could bypass the firm to deal directly with resource suppliers, purchasing inputs in the appropriate amounts. Someone who wanted a table could buy timber, have it milled, contract with a carpenter, contract with a painter, and end up with a finished product. The consumer could carry out transactions directly with each resource supplier.

The Firm Reduces Transaction Costs

So why is production carried out within firms? About 70 years ago, in a classic article entitled "The Nature of the Firm," Nobel Prize winner Ronald Coase asked the question, "Why do firms exist?"[1] Why do people organize in the hierarchical structure of the firm and coordinate their decisions through a manager rather than simply rely on market exchange? His answer would not surprise today's students of economics: *Organizing activities through the hierarchy of the firm is usually more efficient than market exchange because production requires the coordination of many transactions among many resource suppliers.* In short, firms are superior to markets when production is complicated.

Consider again the example of purchasing a table by contracting directly with all the different resource suppliers—from the logger to the painter who applied the finishing varnish. Using resource markets directly involves (1) the cost of determining what inputs are needed and how they should be combined and (2) the cost of reaching an agreement with each resource supplier *over and above* the direct costs of the timber, nails, machinery, paint, and labor required to make the table. Where inputs are easily identified, measured, priced, and hired, production can be carried out through a price-guided "do-it-yourself" approach using the market. For example, getting your house painted is a relatively simple task: You can buy the paint and brushes and hire painters by the hour. You become your own painting contractor, hiring inputs in the market and combining them to do the job.

Where the costs of identifying the appropriate inputs and negotiating for each specific contribution are high, the consumer minimizes transaction costs by purchasing the finished product from a firm. For example, although some people serve as their own contractor when painting a house, fewer do so when building a house; most buy a home already built or hire a building contractor. *The more complicated the task, the greater the ability to economize on transaction costs through specialization and centralized control.* For example, attempting to buy a car by contracting with the thousands of suppliers required to assemble one would be time consuming, costly, and impossible for most anyone. What type of skilled labor should be hired and at what wages? How much steel, aluminum, plastic, glass, paint, and other materials should be purchased? How should resources be combined and in what proportions? Anyone without a detailed knowledge of auto production couldn't do it. (General Motors and Ford, for example, each deal with some 30,000 suppliers.) That's why consumers buy assembled cars rather than contract separately with each resource supplier.

At the margin, some activities could go either way, with some consumers using firms and some hiring resources directly in markets. The choice depends on each consumer's skill and opportunity cost of time. For example, some people may not want to be troubled with hiring all the inputs to get their house painted. Instead, they simply hire a firm for an agreed-on price—they hire a painting contractor. As you will see later in the chapter, however, hiring a contractor may give rise to other problems of quality control.

The Boundaries of the Firm

So far, the chapter has explained why firms exist: *Firms minimize the transaction costs and the production costs of economic activity.* The next question is: What are

1. *Economica* 4 (November 1937): 386–405.

Three Ways to Go

One way most people take the "do-it-yourself" approach is booking travel. But there are still multiple approaches:

Traveler 1

Plans every aspect of a trip—booking flights, reserving hotel rooms, planning excursions, transportations, meals, etc.

Traveler 2

Buys a packaged tour that includes everything.

Traveler 3

Buys a land package covering hotels and excursions, but books all the flights.

What would you do?

the efficient boundaries of the firm? The theory of the firm described in earlier chapters is largely silent on the boundaries of the firm—that is, on the appropriate degree of vertical integration. **Vertical integration** is the expansion of a firm into stages of production earlier or later than those in which it specializes. For example, a steel company may decide (1) to integrate backward to mine iron ore or even mine the coal used to smelt iron ore or (2) to integrate forward to fashion raw steel into various components. A large manufacturer employs an amazing variety of production processes, but on average about half of the cost of production goes to purchase inputs from other firms. For example, General Motors and Ford each spend over $80 billion a year on parts, materials, and services. The total exceeds the annual output of most economies of the world.

How does the firm determine which activities to undertake and which to purchase from other firms? Should Dell manufacture its own computer chips or buy them from another firm? The answer depends on the benefits and costs of internal production versus market purchases. The point bears repeating: *Internal production and market purchases are alternative ways of organizing transactions.* The choice depends on which is a more efficient way of carrying out the transaction in question. Keep in mind that market prices coordinate transactions *between* firms, whereas managers coordinate activities *within* firms. The market coordinates resources by meshing the independent plans of separate decision makers, but a firm coordinates resources through the conscious direction of the manager.

> "Internal production and market purchases are alternative ways of organizing transactions."

The usual assumption is that transactions are organized by market exchange unless markets pose problems. Market exchange allows each firm to benefit from specialization and comparative advantage. For example, Dell can specialize in making computers and buy chips from Intel, a specialist. Computer chips are a standard product, but sometimes the input is not standardized or the exact performance requirements are hard to specify. For example, suppose one firm wants to hire another firm to supply research and development services. The uncertainty involved in such a nonspecific service makes it difficult to write, execute, and enforce a purchase agreement covering all possible contingencies that could arise. What if the R&D supplier, in the course of fulfilling the agreement, makes a valuable discovery for a different application? Who would have the right to that discovery—the firm that paid for the R&D service or the firm that came up with it? And who would determine if the application is different? Because incomplete contracts create potentially troublesome situations, conducting research and development *within the firm* usually involves a lower transaction cost than purchasing it in the market. At this point, it might be useful to discuss specific criteria firms consider when deciding whether to purchase a particular input from the market.

Bounded Rationality of the Manager

To direct and coordinate activity in a conscious way in the firm, a manager must understand how all the pieces of the puzzle fit together. As the firm takes on more and more activities, however, the manager may start losing track of details, so the quality of managerial decisions suffers. The more tasks the firm takes on, the longer the lines of communication between the manager and the production workers who must implement the decision. One constraint on vertical integration is the manager's **bounded rationality**, which limits the amount of information a manager can comprehend about the firm's operation. As the firm takes on more and more functions, coordination and communication become more difficult. The firm can experience diseconomies similar to those it experiences when it expands

vertical integration the expansion of a firm into stages of production earlier or later than those in which it specializes, such as a steel maker that also mines iron ore

bounded rationality the notion that there is a limit to the information that a firm's manager can comprehend and act on output beyond the efficient scale of production. The solution is for the firm to reduce its functions to those it does best. Such cutbacks occurred when automakers increased the proportion of parts they purchased from other firms.

Minimum Efficient Scale

As noted when firm costs were introduced, the *minimum efficient scale* is the minimum rate of output at which economies of scale are fully exploited. For example, suppose that minimum efficient scale in the production of personal computers is 1 million per year, as shown by the firm's long-run average cost curve in panel (a) of Exhibit 1. Suppose this also turns out to be the amount that maximizes profit. Because the computer chip is an important component in a personal computer, should the PC maker integrate backward into chip production? What if the minimum efficient scale in chip production is 5 million per year? As you can see in panel (b) of Exhibit 1, the average cost of producing 1 million chips is much higher than the average cost at the minimum efficient scale of chip production. The PC manufacturer therefore minimizes costs by buying chips from a chip maker of optimal size. More generally, *other things constant, a firm should buy an input if the market price is below what it would cost the firm to make.*

Easily Observable Quality

If an input is well defined and its quality is easily determined at the time of purchase, that input is more likely to be purchased in the market than produced internally, other things constant. For example, a flour mill typically buys wheat in the market rather than grow its own, as the quality of the wheat can be easily assessed upon inspection. In contrast, the quality of certain inputs can be determined only during production. Firms whose reputations depend on the operation of a key component are likely to produce the component, especially if the quality varies widely across producers over time and can't be easily observed by inspection. For example, suppose that the manufacturer of a sensitive measuring instrument requires a crucial gauge, the quality of which can be observed only as the gauge is assembled. If the firm produces the gauge itself, it can closely monitor quality.

Producers sometimes integrate backward so they can offer consumers a guarantee about the quality of the components or ingredients in a product. For example, some chicken suppliers such as Tyson and Purdue can advertise the upbringing of their chickens because they raise their own. KFC, however, omits this family background because the company makes no claim about raising them, focusing instead on how well it cooks the chicken.

Exhibit 1

Minimum Efficient Scale and Vertical Integration

(a) Computer manufacturer

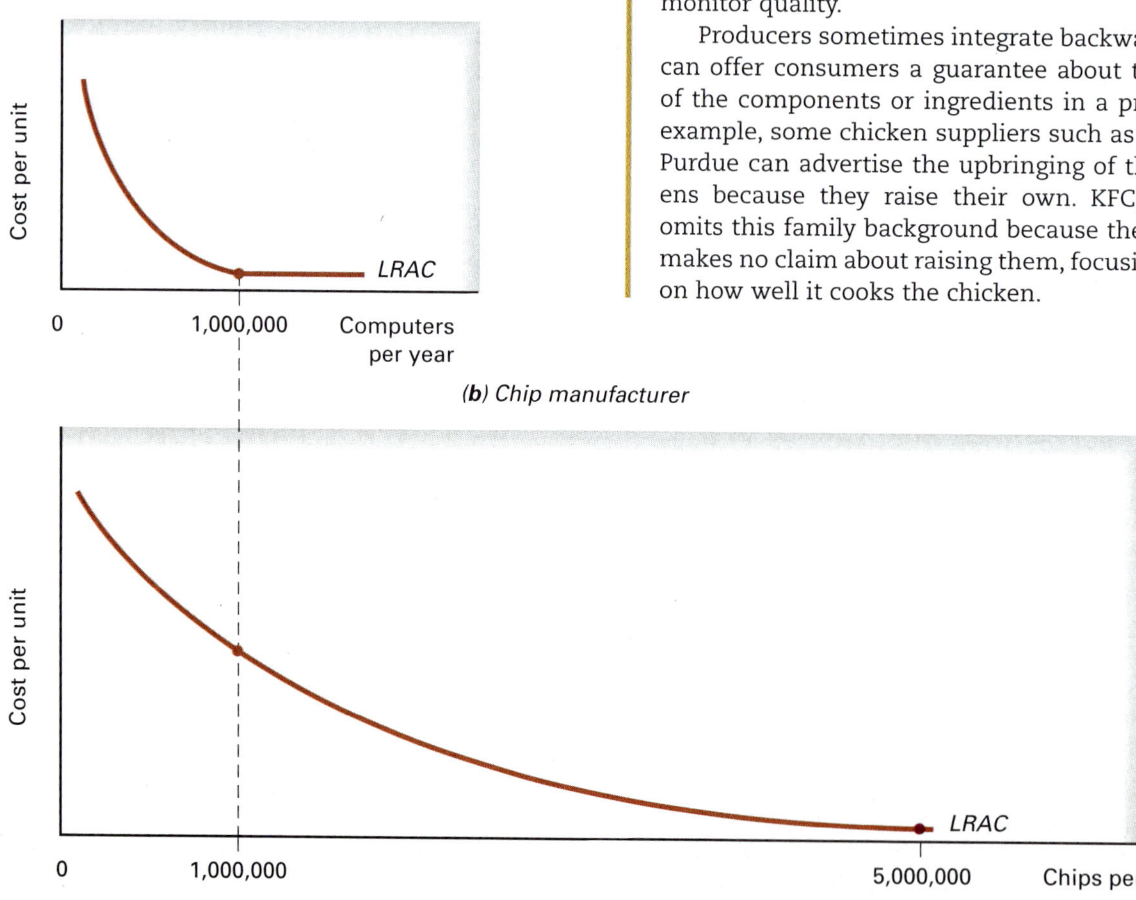

Many Suppliers

A firm wants an uninterrupted source of components. If there are many suppliers of that component, a firm is more likely to buy it than make it, other things constant. Not only do abundant suppliers ensure a dependable source of components, competition among these suppliers keeps the price down. But a firm that cannot rely on a consistent supply of components may make its own components to ensure a reliable supply.

The Trend Toward Outsourcing

Outsourcing occurs when a firm buys products, such as auto parts, or services, such as data processing, from outside suppliers. A firm relies on the division of labor and the law of comparative advantage to focus on what it does best, what it considers its **core competency**. Firms, particularly manufacturing firms, have long purchased some components from other firms, but the outsourcing movement extends this practice to a broader range of products and activities that typically were produced internally. Japanese firms pioneered outsourcing to reduce production costs and enhance quality. In the United States, outsourcing blossomed in manufacturing during the 1980s then spread to virtually every industry.

To review: If a firm relies on market purchases of inputs rather than on vertical integration, it can benefit from the specialization and comparative advantage of individual suppliers. Other things constant, the firm is more likely to buy a component rather than produce it if (1) buying the component is cheaper than making it, (2) the component is well defined and its quality easily observable, and (3) there are many suppliers of the component.

Economies of Scope

So far we have considered issues affecting the optimal degree of vertical integration in producing a particular product. Even with outsourcing, the focus is on how best to produce a particular product, such as an automobile or a computer. But some firms branch into product lines that do not have a vertical relationship. **Economies of scope** exist when it's cheaper to produce two or more different items in one firm than to produce them in separate firms. For example, General Electric produces hundreds of different products ranging from light bulbs to jet engines to NBC Universal. By spreading outlays for research and development and marketing (the company's motto is "Imagination at work") over different products, GE can reduce those costs per unit. Or consider economies of scope on the farm. A farm family often grows a variety of crops and raises different farm animals—animals that recycle damaged crops and food scraps into useful fertilizer. With economies of *scale*, the average cost per unit of output falls as the *scale* of the firm increases; *with economies of scope, average costs per unit fall as the firm supplies more types of products—that is, as the scope of the firm increases.* The cost of some fixed resources, such as specialized knowledge, can be spread across product lines.

Our focus has been on why firms exist, why they often integrate vertically, why they outsource, and why they sometimes produce a range of products. These steps toward realism move us beyond the simple picture of the firm created earlier. The rest of the chapter challenges some simplifying assumptions about the amount of information available to market participants.

LO2 Market Behavior with Imperfect Information

For the most part, our analysis of market behavior has assumed that market participants have full information about products and resources. For consumers, full information involves knowledge about a product's price, quality, and availability. For firms, full information includes knowledge about the marginal productivity of various resources, about the appropriate technology for combining them, and about the demand for the firm's product. In reality, *reliable information is often costly for both consumers and producers.* This section examines the impact of less-than-perfect information on market behavior.

Optimal Search with Imperfect Information

Suppose you want to buy a new computer. You need information about the quality and features of each model and the prices at various retail outlets and online sites. To learn more about your choices, you may talk with friends and experts, read promotional brochures and computer publications, and visit online sites. Once you narrow your choice to one or two models, you may visit the mall, or let your fingers do the walking through the *Yellow Pages*, computer

outsourcing
a firm buys inputs from outside suppliers

core competency
area of specialty; the product or phase of production a firm supplies with greatest efficiency

economies of scope
average costs decline as a firm makes a range of different products rather than specializes in just one product

catalogs, online search engines, newspaper ads, and the like. Searching for the lowest price for a particular model involves a cost, primarily the opportunity cost of your time. This cost obviously varies from individual to individual and from item to item. Some people actually enjoy shopping, but this "shop 'til you drop" attitude does not necessarily carry over to all purchases. *For most of us, the process of gathering consumer information can be considered nonmarket work.*

Marginal Cost of Search

In your quest for product information, you gather the easy and obvious information first. You may check on the price and availability at the few computer stores at the mall. But as your search widens, the *marginal cost* of information increases, both because you may have to travel greater distances to check prices and services and because the opportunity cost of your time increases as you spend more time acquiring information. Consequently, the marginal cost curve for information slopes upward, as is shown in Exhibit 2. Note that a certain amount of information, I_f, is common knowledge and is freely available, so its marginal cost is zero.

Exhibit 2

Optimal Search with Imperfect Information

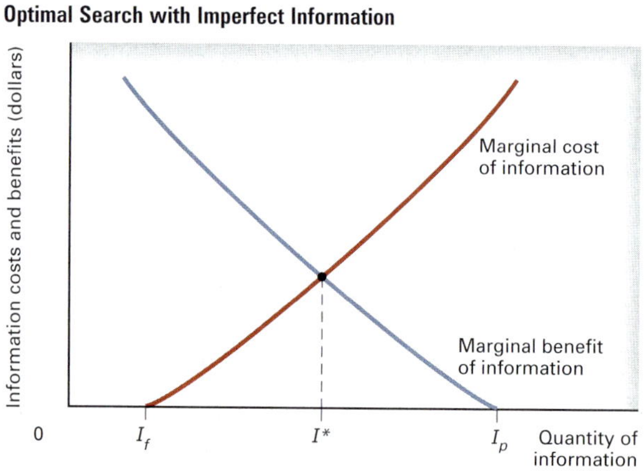

Marginal Benefit of Search

The *marginal benefit* from acquiring additional information is a better quality for a given price or a lower price for a given quality. The marginal benefit is relatively large at first, but as you gather more information and grow more acquainted with the market, additional information yields less and less marginal benefit. For example, the likelihood of uncovering valuable information, such as an added feature or a lower price, at the second store or Web site visited is greater than the likelihood of finding this information at the twentieth store or Web site visited. Thus, the marginal benefit curve for additional information slopes downward, as is shown in Exhibit 2.

Optimal Search

Market participants continue to gather information as long as the marginal benefit of additional information exceeds its marginal cost. *Optimal search occurs where the marginal benefit just equals the marginal cost,* which in Exhibit 2 is where the two marginal curves intersect. Notice that at search levels exceeding the equilibrium amount, the marginal benefit of additional information is still positive but below marginal cost. Notice also that at some point the value of additional information reaches zero, as identified by I_p on the horizontal axis. This level of information could be identified as *full information*. The high marginal cost of acquiring I_p, however, makes it impractical to become fully informed. Thus, firms and consumers, by gathering the optimal amount of information, I^*, have less-than-perfect information about the price, availability, and quality of products and resources.

Implications

This search model was developed by Nobel laureate George Stigler, who showed that the price of a product can differ among sellers because some consumers are unaware of lower prices offered by some sellers.[2] Thus, *search costs result in price dispersion, or different prices for the same product.* Some sellers call attention to price dispersions by claiming to have the lowest prices around and by promising to match any competitor's price. *Search costs also lead to quality differences across sellers, even for identically priced products, because consumers find the expected marginal cost of finding a higher quality product outweighs the expected marginal benefit.*

There are other implications of Stigler's search model. The more expensive the item, the greater the price dispersion in dollar terms, so the greater the expected marginal benefit from shopping around. You are more likely to shop around for a new car than for a new toothbrush. Also, as earnings increase, so does the opportunity cost of time, resulting in less searching and more price dispersion. On the other hand, any technological change that reduces the marginal cost of information lowers the marginal cost curve in Exhibit 2, increasing the optimal amount of information and reducing price dispersion. For example, some online sites, like mySimon.com, identify the lowest prices for books, airfares, automobiles, computers, and dozens of

2. George Stigler, "The Economics of Information," *Journal of Political Economy* (June 1961): 213–225.

other products. And some online sellers, like Buy.com, maintain the lowest prices on the Web as a way of attracting customers who undertake such searches. Thus, by reducing search costs, the Internet reduces price dispersion.

The Winner's Curse

In 1996, the federal government auctioned off leases to valuable space on the scarce radio spectrum. The space was to be used for cell phones, wireless networks, and portable fax machines. The bidding was carried out in the face of much uncertainty about what were then new markets. Bidders had little experience with the potential value of such leases. At the time, 89 companies made winning bids for 493 licenses totaling $10.2 billion. But by 1998, it became clear that many of the winning bidders couldn't pay, and many went bankrupt.[3] The auction eventually collected only half the amount of the winning bids. In auctions for products of uncertain value, such as wireless communications licenses, why do so many "winners" end up losers?

When bids were submitted, the true value of space on the radio spectrum could only be estimated. Suppose the average bid for a license was $10 million, with some higher and others lower. Suppose also that the winning bid was $20 million. The winning bid was not the average bid, which may have been the most reliable estimate of the true value, but the highest bid, which was the most optimistic estimate. Winners of such bids are said to experience the **winner's curse** because they often lose money after winning the bid, paying the price of being overly optimistic.

The winner's curse applies to all cases of bidding in which the true value is unknown at the outset. For example, movie companies often bid up the price of screenplays to what some argue are unrealistic levels (only about 5 percent of screenplays studios purchase ever become movies). Likewise, publishers get into bidding wars over book manuscripts and even book proposals that are little more than titles. Team owners bid and often overpay for athletes who become free agents. CBS lost money on the 1998 Winter Olympics. And NBC may have overbid by offering $2.3 billion for the rights to broadcast the Olympics in 2002, 2006, and 2008; at the time of the bid, Olympic cities had not even been selected. Online auctions, like eBay, often sell items of unknown value.

3. Scott Ritter, "FCC Says Several Bidders to Return Wireless Licenses," *Wall Street Journal,* 18 June 1998.

With perfect information about market value, potential buyers would never bid more than that market value. But *when competitive bidding is coupled with imperfect information, the winning bidder often ends up an overly optimistic loser.*

LO3 Asymmetric Information in Product Markets

We have considered the effects of costly information and limited information on market behavior. But the issue becomes more complicated when one side of the market knows more than the other side does, a problem of **asymmetric information**. There are two types of information that a market participant may want but lack: information about a product's *characteristics* and information about *actions* taken by the other party to the transaction. This section examines several examples of asymmetric information in the product market and the effects on market efficiency.

Hidden Characteristics: Adverse Selection

When one side of the market knows more than the other side about important product characteristics, the asymmetric information problem involves **hidden characteristics**. For example, the seller of a used car normally has abundant personal experience with important *characteristics* of that car, such as accidents, breakdowns, gas mileage, maintenance record, performance in bad weather, and so on. A prospective buyer can only guess at these characteristics based on the car's appearance and perhaps a test drive. The buyer cannot really know how well the car performs without driving it under varying traffic and weather conditions.

To simplify the problem, suppose there are only two types of used cars for sale: good ones and bad ones, or "lemons." A buyer who is certain about a car's type would be willing to pay $10,000 for a good used car but only $4,000 for a lemon. Again, only the seller knows which type is

winner's curse
the plight of the winning bidder who overestimates an asset's true value

asymmetric information
one side of the market has better information about the product than does the other side

hidden characteristics
one side of the market knows more than the other side about product characteristics that are important to the other side

for sale. Prospective buyers believe that half the used cars on the market are good ones and half are lemons and are willing to pay, say, $7,000 for a car of unknown quality (the average expected value of cars on the market). Would $7,000 become the market price of used cars?

So far, the analysis has ignored the actions of potential sellers, who know which type of car they have. Because sellers of good cars can get only $7,000 for cars they know to be worth $10,000 on average, many will keep their cars or will sell them only to friends or relatives. But sellers of lemons will find $7,000 an attractive price for a car they know to be worth only $4,000. As a result, the proportion of good cars on the market will fall and the proportion of lemons will rise, reducing the average value of used cars on the market. As buyers come to realize that the mix has shifted toward lemons, they will reduce what they are willing to pay for cars of unknown quality. As the market price of used cars falls, potential sellers of good cars become even more reluctant to sell at such a low price, so the proportion of lemons increases, leading to still lower prices. The process could continue until few good cars are for sale on the open market. More generally, *when sellers have better information about a product's quality than buyers do, lower-quality products dominate the market.*

When those on the informed side of the market self-select in a way that harms the uninformed side of the market, the problem is one of **adverse selection**. In our example, car sellers, the informed side, self-select—that is, they decide whether or not to offer their cars for sale—in a way that increases the proportion of lemons for sale. Because of adverse selection, those still willing to buy on the open market often get stuck with lemons.

adverse selection
those on the informed side of the market self-select in a way that harms those on the uninformed side of the market

hidden actions
one side of an economic relationship can do something that the other side cannot observe

principal-agent problem
the agent's objectives differ from those of the principal's, and one side can pursue hidden actions

principal
a person or firm who hires an agent to act on behalf of that person or firm

agent
a person or firm who is supposed to act on behalf of the principal

<< How do you know if the used car you're buying is a "lemon" or a "cherry"?

© STOCKBYTE/GETTY IMAGES/© MAXIMILLIAN STOCK LTD./FOODPIX/JUPITERIMAGES

Hidden Actions: The Principal-Agent Problem

A second type of problem occurs when one side of a transaction can pursue an unobservable action that affects the other side. Whenever one side of an economic relationship can take a relevant action that the other side cannot observe, the situation is described as one of **hidden actions**. In this age of specialization, there are many tasks we do not perform for ourselves because others do them better and because others have a lower opportunity cost of time. Suppose your car isn't working and you have no clue how to fix it. The mechanic you hire may have other objectives, such as maximizing on-the-job leisure or maximizing the garage's profit. But the mechanic's actions are hidden from you. Although your car's problem may be only a loose electrical wire, the mechanic could inflate the bill by charging you for work not needed or not performed. This asymmetric information problem occurs because one side of a transaction can pursue *hidden actions* that affect the other side. When buyers have difficulty monitoring and evaluating the quality of goods or services purchased, some suppliers may substitute poor-quality resources or exercise less diligence in providing the service.

The problem that arises from hidden actions is called the **principal-agent problem**, which describes a relationship in which one party, known as the **principal**, contracts with another party, known as the **agent**, in the expectation that the agent will act on behalf of the principal. *The problem arises when the goals of the agent are incompatible with those of the principal and when the agent can pursue hidden actions.* For example, you are the principal and the garage mechanic is your agent. You could also confront a principal-agent problem when you deal with a doctor, lawyer, stockbroker, plumber, or building contractor, to name a few. Any employer-employee relationship could become a principal-agent problem, with the employer as the principal and the employee as the agent. Again, the problem arises because the agent's objectives are not the same as the principal's and because the agent's actions are hidden. Not all principal-agent relationships pose a problem. For example, when you hire someone to cut your hair or your lawn, there are no hidden actions, so you can judge the results for yourself.

Asymmetric Information in Insurance Markets

Asymmetric information also creates problems in insurance markets. For example, from an insurer's point of view, the ideal candidate for health insurance is someone who leads a long, healthy life, then dies peacefully while sleeping. But many people are poor risks for health insurers because of hidden characteristics (bad genes) or hidden actions (smoking and drinking excessively, getting exercise only on trips to the refrigerator, and thinking that a balanced meal consists of beef jerky and a six-pack of beer). In the insurance market, it is the buyers, not the sellers, who have more information about the characteristics and actions that predict their likely need for insurance in the future.

If the insurance company has no way of distinguishing among applicants, it must charge those who are good health risks the same price as those who are poor ones. This price is attractive to poor risks but not to good ones, some of whom will not buy insurance. The insured group becomes less healthy on average, so rates must rise, making insurance even less attractive to healthy people. *Because of adverse selection, insurance buyers tend to be less healthy than the population as a whole.* Adverse selection has been used as an argument for national health insurance.

The insurance problem is compounded by the fact that once people buy insurance, their behavior may change in a way that increases the probability that a claim will be made. For example, those with health insurance may take less care of their health, and those with theft insurance may take less care of their valuables. This incentive problem is referred to as *moral hazard*. **Moral hazard** occurs when an individual's behavior changes in a way that increases the likelihood of an unfavorable outcome. More generally, *moral hazard is a principal-agent problem because it occurs when those on one side of a transaction have an incentive to shirk their responsibilities because the other side is unable to observe them.* The responsibility could be to repair a car, maintain one's health, or safeguard one's valuables. Both the mechanic and the insurance buyer may take advantage of the ignorant party. In the car-repair example, the mechanic is the agent; in the insurance example, the policy buyer is the principal. Thus, moral hazard arises when someone—either the agent or the principal, depending on the situation—can undertake hidden action.

Coping with Asymmetric Information

There are ways of reducing the consequences of asymmetric information. An incentive structure or an information-revealing system can be developed to reduce the problems associated with the lopsided availability of information. For example, all states now have "lemon laws" that offer compensation to buyers of new or used cars that turn out to be lemons. Used-car dealers may also offer warranties to reduce the buyer's risk of getting stuck with a lemon. Most garages provide written estimates before a job is done, and some return the defective parts to the customer as evidence that the repair was necessary and was carried out. People often get multiple estimates for major repairs.

Insurance companies deal with adverse selection and moral hazard in a variety of ways. Most require

© DARRYL LENIUK/RISER/GETTY IMAGES

>>Good Time Or Moral Hazard?

moral hazard
a situation in which one party, as a result of a contract, has an incentive to alter their behavior in a way that harms the other party to the contract

applicants to undergo a physical exam and to answer questions about their medical history and lifestyle (false information can block benefits). Preexisting medical conditions are not usually covered. To avoid adverse selection, an insurer often covers all those in a group, such as all company employees, not just those who would otherwise self-select. Insurers reduce moral hazard by making the policyholder pay, say, the first $250 of a claim as a "deductible" and by requiring the policyholder to co-pay a percentage of a claim. Also, as more claims are filed, insurance premiums go up and the policy could be canceled. Property insurers reduce premiums for those who install security systems, smoke alarms, sprinkler systems, and who take other safety precautions.

LO4 Asymmetric Information in Labor Markets

Our market analysis for particular kinds of labor typically assumes that workers are more or less interchangeable. In equilibrium, each worker in a particular labor market is assumed to be paid the same wage, a wage equal to the marginal revenue product of the last unit of labor hired. But what if ability differs across workers? Differences in ability present no particular problem as long as these differences can be readily observed by the employer. If the productivity of each worker is easily quantified through measures such as crates of oranges picked, quantity of garments sewn, or number of cars sold, these can and do serve as the basis for pay. And such incentives seem to affect output. For example, when the British National Health Service changed the pay basis of dentists from "contact hours" with patients to the number of cavities filled, dentists found more cavities and filled them in only a third of the time they took under the contact-hour pay scheme.[4]

Because production often requires a team effort, the employer may not be able to attribute specific outputs to particular workers. When information about each worker's marginal productivity is hard to come by, employers usually pay workers by the hour. Sometimes the pay combines an hourly rate and incentive pay linked to a measure of productivity. For example, a sales representative typically receives a base salary plus a commission tied to sales. At times, the task of evaluating performance is left to the consumer. Workers who provide personal services, such as waiters, barbers, beauticians, pizza deliverers, and bellhops, rely partly or mostly on tips. These services are "personal" and visible, so customers are usually in the best position to judge the quality and timeliness of service and to tip accordingly.

efficiency wage theory
the idea that offering high wages attracts a more talented labor pool and encourages those hired to perform well so as to keep their jobs

4. John Pencavel, "Piecework and On-the-Job Screening," *Working Paper,* Stanford University, June 1975.

Adverse Selection in Labor Markets

Suppose an employer wants to hire a program coordinator for a new project. The job requires imagination, organizational skills, and the ability to work independently. The employer would like to attract the most qualified person available, but the qualities demanded are not directly observable. The employer offers the going wage for such a position. Individual workers are able to evaluate this market wage in light of their own abilities and opportunities. Talented people find the wage too low and are less inclined to apply for the job. Less-talented people, however, find this wage attractive and are more inclined to seek the position. Because of this adverse selection, the employer ends up with a pool of applicants of below-average ability.

A job applicant's true abilities—motivation, work habits, skills, ability to get along with others, and the like—are, to a large extent, *hidden characteristics*. In a labor market with hidden characteristics, employers might be better off offering a higher wage. The higher the wage, the more attractive the job is to more-qualified workers. Paying a higher wage also encourages those who are hired not to goof off or otherwise jeopardize an attractive job. Paying above-market wages to attract and retain more productive workers is called paying **efficiency wages**, something that Henry Ford did.

Signaling and Screening

The person on the side of the market with hidden characteristics and hidden actions has an incentive to say the right thing. For example, a job applicant might say, "Hire me because I am hardworking, reliable, prompt, highly motivated, and just an all-around great employee." Or a manufacturer might say, "At Ford, quality is job one." But such claims appear self-serving and thus are not necessarily believable. To cut through this fog, both sides of the market try to develop credible ways of communicating reliable information about qualifications.

Signaling is the attempt by the informed side of the market to communicate information that the other side would find valuable. Consider signaling in the job market. Because some jobs require abilities that are unobservable on a résumé or in an interview, job applicants offer proxy measures, such as years of education, college grades, and letters of recommendation. A proxy measure is called a *signal*, which is an observable indicator of some hidden characteristic. A signal is sent by the informed side of the market to the uninformed side and is useful because less-qualified applicants have trouble sending the same signal.

To identify the best workers, employers try to *screen* applicants. **Screening** is the attempt by the uninformed side of the market to uncover the relevant but hidden characteristics of the informed party. An initial screen might check each résumé for spelling and typographical errors. Although not important in themselves, such errors suggest a lack of attention to detail—which could reduce labor productivity. The uninformed party must identify signals that less-productive individuals have more difficulty sending. A signal that can be sent with equal ease by all workers, regardless of their productivity, does not provide a useful way of screening applicants. But if, for example, more productive workers find it easier to graduate from college than do less-productive workers, a college degree is a measure worth using to screen workers. In this case, education may be valuable, not so much because of its direct effect on a worker's productivity, but simply because it enables employers to distinguish between types of workers. In fact, the actual pay increase resulting from a fourth year of college that results in graduation is several times the pay increase from just a third year of college. This finding is consistent with the screening theory of education.

To summarize: Because the potential productivity of job applicants cannot be measured directly, an employer must rely on proxy measures to screen applicants. The most valuable proxy is a signal that can be sent more easily by more productive workers and also is a good predictor of future productivity.

Final Word

The firm has evolved through a natural selection process as the form of organization that minimizes both transaction and production costs. The economic system selects for efficient production organizations. Attributes that yield an economic profit will thrive, and those that do not will fall away. The form of organization selected might not be optimal in the sense that it cannot be improved, but it is the most efficient of those that have been tried. If there is a way to organize production that is more efficient, some entrepreneur will stumble on it eventually, earning greater profit. The improvement may not always be the result of conscious design. Once a more efficient way of organizing production is uncovered, others will imitate it.

In conventional demand-and-supply analysis, trades occur in impersonal markets, and the buyer has no special concern about who is on the sell side. But with asymmetric information, the mix and characteristics of the other side of the market become important. When the problem of adverse selection is severe enough, some markets may cease to function. Market participants try to overcome the limitations of asymmetric information by signaling, screening, and trying to be explicit and transparent about the terms of the transaction.

signaling using a proxy measure to communicate information about unobservable characteristics the signal is more effective if more productive workers find it easier to send than do less-productive workers

screening the process used by employers to select the most qualified workers based on observable characteristics such as a job applicant's level of education and course grades

CHAPTER 15

Economic Regulation *and* Antitrust Policy

Learning Outcomes

LO 1 Describe the different types of government regulation

LO 2 Explain how natural monopolies are regulated

LO 3 Explain why producers are interested in economic regulation

LO 4 Discuss antitrust laws and their enforcement

LO 5 Describe the relationship between public policy and merger activity

LO 6 List competitive trends in the U.S. economy

"*Who benefits most when government regulates monopoly?*"

If the "invisible hand" of competition yields such desirable results for the economy, why does the government need to regulate business? Is monopoly ever better than competition? Who benefits most when government regulates monopoly? Why did the U.S. government haul Microsoft into court? Is the U.S. economy becoming more competitive or less competitive? Answers to these and other questions are addressed in this chapter, which discusses government regulation of business.

What do you think?

Government regulation provides essential protection for consumers.

Strongly Disagree 1 2 3 4 5 6 7 *Strongly Agree*

Businesspeople praise competition but they love monopoly. They praise competition because it harnesses the diverse and often conflicting objectives of various market participants and channels them into the efficient production of goods and services. Competition does this as if by "an invisible hand." Businesspeople love monopoly because it provides the surest path to economic profit in the long run—and, after all, profit is the name of the game for any business. The fruits of monopoly are so tempting that a firm might try to eliminate competitors or conspire with them to raise prices. As Adam Smith remarked more than two centuries ago, "People of the same trade seldom meet together, even for merriment or diversion, but the conversation ends in a conspiracy against the public, or in some contrivance to raise prices."

The tendency of firms to seek monopolistic advantage is understandable, but monopoly usually harms consumers and other producers. Public policy can play a role by promoting competition in those markets where competition seems desirable and by reducing the harmful effects of monopoly in those markets where the output can be most efficiently supplied by one or a few firms.

Topics discussed in Chapter 15 include:

- Regulating natural monopolies
- Theories of economic regulation
- Deregulation
- Antitrust policy
- Per se illegality
- Rule of reason
- Merger waves
- Competitive trends

LO[1] Types of Government Regulation

You'll recall that a monopolist supplies a product with no close substitutes, so a monopolist can charge a higher price than would prevail with competition. When only a few firms serve a market, those firms are sometimes able to coordinate their actions, either explicitly or implicitly, to act like a monopolist. The ability of a firm to raise the price without losing all its sales to rivals is called **market power**. Any firm facing a downward-sloping demand curve has some control over the price and thus some market power. The presumption is that a monopoly, or a group of firms acting as a monopoly, restricts output to charge a higher price than competing firms would charge. With output restricted, the marginal benefit of the final unit sold exceeds its marginal cost, so expanding output would increase social welfare. By failing to expand output to the point where marginal benefit equals marginal cost, firms with market power produce less of the good than would be socially optimal.

Other distortions have also been associated with monopolies. For example, some critics argue that because a monopoly is insulated from competition, it is not as innovative as aggressive competitors would be. Worse still, because of their size and economic importance, monopolies may influence public choices to protect and enhance their monopoly power.

Three kinds of government policies are designed to alter or control firm behavior: social regulation, economic regulation, and antitrust policy. **Social regulation** tries to improve health and safety; for example, by controling unsafe working conditions and dangerous products. Social regulation has economic consequences, but we will not discuss social regulation in this chapter. **Economic regulation** aims to control the price, output, the entry of new firms, and the quality of service *in industries in which monopoly appears inevitable or even desirable*. Government controls over *natural monopolies*, such as local electricity transmission, local phone service, and a subway system, are examples of economic regulation. Several other industries, such as land and air transportation, have also been regulated in the past. Federal, state, and local governments carry out economic regulation. **Antitrust policy** outlaws attempts to monopolize, or cartelize, markets in which competition is desirable. Antitrust policy is pursued in the courts by government attorneys and by individual firms that charge other firms with violating antitrust laws. Economic regulation and antitrust policy are examined in this chapter. Let's turn first to economic regulation—specifically, the regulation of natural monopolies.

market power the ability of a firm to raise its price without losing all its customers to rival firms

social regulation government regulations aimed at improving health and safety

economic regulation government regulation of natural monopoly, where, because of economies of scale, average production cost is lowest when a single firm supplies the market

antitrust policy government regulation aimed at preventing monopoly and fostering competition in markets where competition is desirable

LO2 Regulating a Natural Monopoly

Because of economies of scale, a natural monopoly has a long-run average cost curve that slopes downward over the range of market demand. This means that the lowest average cost is achieved when one firm serves the entire market. For example, a subway system is a natural monopoly. If two competing systems tunnel parallel routes throughout a city, the average cost per trip would be higher than if a single system provided this service.

Unregulated Profit Maximization

Exhibit 1 shows the demand and cost conditions for a natural monopoly, in this case a metropolitan subway system. A natural monopoly usually faces huge initial capital costs, such as those associated with digging a subway system, building a natural gas pipeline, launching a communcations satellite, or wiring a city for electricity or for cable TV. Once capital is in place, average cost falls as output increases, so the average cost curve slopes downward over a broad range of output. In this situation, average cost is lowest when a single firm supplies the market.

An unregulated monopolist, like any other firm, chooses the price-quantity combination that maxi-

Exhibit 1

Regulating a Natural Monopoly

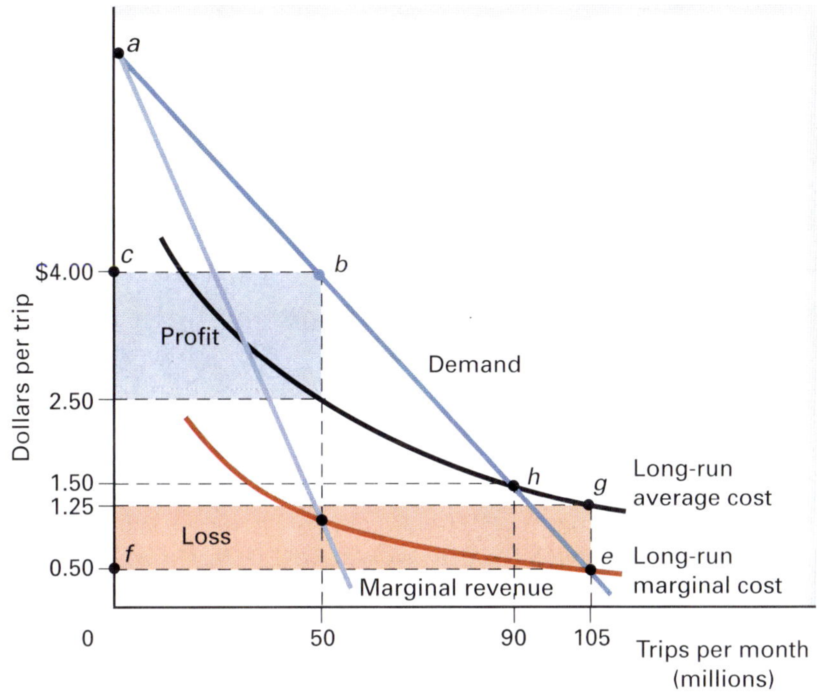

mizes profit. In Exhibit 1, the monopolist—in this case, the operator of a subway system—maximizes profit by producing where marginal revenue equals marginal cost—that is, where 50 million riders per month pay \$4 per trip. The monopolist reaps the profit identified by the blue-shaded rectangle. The *abc* triangle, which is the area below the demand curve and above the \$4 price, measures the consumer surplus—consumers' net gain from riding the subway. The problem with letting the monopolist maximize profit is that the resulting price-output combination is inefficient in terms of social welfare. Consumers pay a price that far exceeds the marginal cost of providing the service. *The marginal value of additional output exceeds its marginal cost, so social welfare would increase if output expanded.*

One option for government is to allow the monopolist to maximize profit. But government can increase social welfare by forcing the monopolist to lower the price and expand output. To accomplish this, government can either operate the monopoly itself, as it does with most urban transit systems, or government can *regulate* a privately owned monopoly, as it does with some urban transit systems, local phone services, cable TV service, and electricity transmission. Government-owned or government-regulated monopolies are called **public utilities**. Here we focus on government regulation, though the issues discussed are similar if the government chose to own and operate the monopoly.

Setting Price Equal to Marginal Cost

Many facets of a natural monopoly have been regulated, but the price-output combination gets the most attention. Suppose government regulators require the monopolist to produce the level of output that is efficient—that is, where the price, which also measures the marginal benefit to consumers, equals the marginal cost of the good. This price-output combination is depicted in Exhibit 1 as point *e*, where the demand curve, or the marginal benefit curve, intersects the marginal cost curve, yielding a price of \$0.50 per trip and quantity of 105 million trips per month. Consumers clearly prefer this price to the \$4 charged by the unregulated monopolist. The consumer surplus from riding the subway jumps from triangle *abc* without regulation to triangle *aef* with regulation.

Notice, however, that the monopolist now has a problem. The average cost of supplying each of the 105 million trips per month is \$1.25, identified by point *g* on the average cost curve. This is more than double the regulated price of \$0.50. Rather than earning a profit, the monopolist suffers a loss—in this case, \$0.75 per trip, for a total loss of \$79 million a month, identified by the pink-shaded rectangle. *Forcing a natural monopolist to produce where price, or marginal benefit, equals marginal cost results in an economic loss to the monopolist.* In the long run, the monopolist would go out of business rather than endure such a loss.

Subsidizing the Natural Monopolist

How can regulators encourage the monopolist to stay in business yet still produce where price equals marginal cost? The government can cover the loss—*subsidize* the firm so it earns a normal profit. Bus and subway fares

public utilities
government-owned or government-regulated monopolies

are typically set below the average cost of providing the service, with the difference made up by a government subsidy. For example, government susidies pay more than 40 percent of the Washington, D.C., Metro subway system. Amtrak requires a federal subsidy covering about a third of its operating budget, totalling more than $30 billion over the last three decades. One drawback with the subsidy solution is that, to provide the subsidy, the government must raise taxes or forgo public spending in some other area. Thus, the subsidy has an opportunity cost and could easily result in inefficiencies elsewhere in the economy.

Setting Price Equal to Average Cost

Although some public utilities are subsidized, most are not. Instead, regulators try to establish a price that provides the monopolist with a "fair return." Recall that the average cost curve includes a normal profit. Thus, *setting price equal to average cost* provides a normal, or "fair," profit for the monopolist. In Exhibit 1, the demand curve intersects the average cost curve at point *h*, yielding a price of $1.50 per trip and a quantity of 90 million trips a month. This price-output combination allows the monopolist to stay in business without a subsidy.

Setting price equal to average total cost enhances social welfare compared to the unregulated situation. The monopolist would prefer an economic profit but will accept a normal profit to stay in business. After all, a normal profit is the most this firm could expect if resources were redirected to their best alternative uses. But note that the marginal benefit of the 90 millionth trip exceeds its marginal cost. Therefore, expanding output beyond 90 million trips per month would increase social welfare.

The Regulatory Dilemma

Setting price equal to marginal cost yields the *socially optimal* allocation of resources because *the consumers' marginal benefit from the last unit sold equals the marginal cost of producing that last unit.* In our example, setting the price at $0.50 equates marginal benefit and marginal cost, but the monopolist faces losses unless government provides a subsidy. These losses disappear if price equals average cost, which in our example is $1.50. The higher price ensures a normal profit, but output falls 15 million trips short of the socially optimal level.

Thus, the dilemma facing the regulator is whether to set price equal to marginal cost, which is socially optimal but requires a government subsidy, or to set a break-even price even though output falls short of the socially optimal level. There is no right answer. Compared with the unregulated profit-maximizing price of $4, both reduce the price, increase output, erase economic profit, increase consumer surplus, and increase social welfare. Although Exhibit 1 lays out the options neatly, regulators usually face a cloudier picture. Demand and cost curves can only be estimated, and the regulated firm may withhold or distort information. For example, a utility may overstate costs so it can charge more.

LO3 Alternative Theories of Economic Regulation

Why do governments regulate certain industries? Why not let market forces allocate resources? There are two views of government regulation. The first has been implicit in the discussion so far—namely, economic regulation is in the *public interest.* Economic regulation promotes social welfare by keeping prices down when one or just a few firms serve a market. A second, darker, view is that economic regulation is not in the public interest but is in the *special interest* of producers. According to this view, *well-organized producer groups expect to profit from economic regulation and persuade public officials to impose restrictions that existing producers find attractive, such as limiting entry into the industry or preventing competition among existing firms.* Individual producers have more to gain or to lose from regulation than do individual consumers. Producers typically are also better organized and more focused than consumers and are therefore better able to bring about regulations that favor producers.

Producers' Special Interest in Economic Regulation

To understand how and why producer interests could influence public regulation, think back to the last time you had your hair cut. Most states regulate the training and licensing of barbers and beauticians. If any new regulation affecting the profession is proposed, who do you suppose has more interest in that legislation, you or those who cut hair for a living? *Producers have an intense interest in matters that affect their livelihood, so they try to shape such legislation.* Those who cut hair for a living often try to restrict entry by requiring thousands of hours of instruction. At any public hearings on haircut regulations, industry officials provide self-serving testimony, while consumers largely ignore the whole thing.

>> Railroads helped companies achieve economies of scale—and become monolithic.

© AP IMAGES

Regulation may be introduced under the guise of quality control, such as keeping "quacks" out of certain professions. But entry restrictions usually reduce competition and increase prices. The special-interest theory may be valid even when the initial intent of the legislation was in the consumer interest. Over time, the regulatory machinery may shift toward the special interests of producers, who, in effect, "capture" the regulating agency. This **capture theory of regulation** was discussed by George Stigler, the Nobel laureate mentioned in the previous chapter. He argued that "as a general rule, regulation is acquired by the industry and is designed and operated for its benefit."[1]

The course of regulation and deregulation raises questions about the true objectives of regulation. Recall the alternative views of regulation: one holds that regulation is in the public, or consumer, interest; the other holds that regulation is in the special, or producer, interest. In the airline industry, regulation appeared more in accord with producer interests, and producer groups fought deregulation, which benefited consumers.

As a consumer, you do not specialize in getting haircuts. You purchase haircuts, cold cuts, hardware, software, underwear, and thousands of other goods and services. You have no *special interest* in haircuts. Some economists argue that because consumers ignore such matters, business regulations often favor producer interests. Well-organized producer groups, as squeaky wheels in the legislative machinery, get the most grease in the form of favorable regulations. Such regulations are usually introduced under the guise of advancing consumer interests or protecting the public. Producer groups may argue that unbridled competition in their industry would hurt consumers. For example, the alleged problem of "cutthroat" competition among taxi drivers led to regulations that eliminated price competition and restricted the number of taxis in most large metropolitan areas. New York City has 10,000 fewer taxis now than it did 70 years ago. As a result, taxis are harder to find and fares are higher. To operate a cab in New York City, someone must purchase a "medallion." The purchase price reflects the market value to taxi owners of regulations that restrict entry and set fares above the competitive level. The average price of a taxi medallion increased from $27,000 in 1968 to more than $300,000 in 2007. Regulation gives medallion owners an abiding interest in blocking entry. If market entry and taxi fares were deregulated, cabs would become more plentiful, fares would fall to competitive levels, and medallions would become worthless.

This concludes the discussion of economic regulation, which tries to reduce the harmful consequences of monopolistic behavior in those markets where the output can be most efficiently supplied by one or a few firms. We now turn to antitrust policy, which tries to promote competition in those markets where competition seems desirable.

LO4 Antitrust Law and Enforcement

Although competition typically ensures the most efficient use of the nation's resources, an individual competitor would rather be a monopolist. If left alone, a firm might try to create a monopoly by driving competitors out of business, by merging with competitors, or by colluding with competitors. *Antitrust policy* is the government's attempt

capture theory of regulation
producers' political power and strong stake in the regulatory outcome lead them, in effect, to "capture" the regulating agency and prevail on it to serve producer interests

1. George Stigler, "The Theory of Economic Regulation," *Bell Journal of Economics and Management Science* (Spring 1971): 3.

to reduce anticompetitive behavior and promote a market structure that leads to greater competition. *Antitrust policy attempts to promote socially desirable market performance.*

Origins of Antitrust Policy

Economic developments in the last half of the nineteenth century created bigger firms serving wider markets. Perhaps the two most important developments were (1) technological breakthroughs that led to a larger optimal plant size in manufacturing and (2) the rise of the railroad from 9,000 miles of track in 1850 to 167,000 miles by 1890, which reduced transport costs. *Economies of scale and cheaper transport costs extended the geographical size of markets,* so firms grew larger to serve this bigger market.

Sharp declines in the national economy in 1873 and in 1883, however, panicked large manufacturers. Because their heavy fixed costs required large-scale production, they cut prices in an attempt to stimulate sales. Price wars erupted, creating economic turmoil. Firms desperately sought ways to stabilize their markets. One solution was for competing firms to form a *trust* by transferring their voting stock to a single board of trustees, which would vote in the interest of the industry. Early trusts were formed in the sugar, tobacco, and oil industries. Although the impact of these early trusts is still debated today, they allegedly pursued anticompetitive practices to develop and maintain a monopoly advantage. Gradually the word **trust** came to mean any firm or group of firms that tried to monopolize a market.

Trusts provoked widespread criticism and their creators were dubbed "robber barons." Farmers, especially, were hurt by these early trusts, for while farm prices were pushed down by technological change in agriculture, the prices farmers paid for supplies were often higher because of trusts. Farmers accounted for 40 percent of the U.S. workforce at the time and thus had political clout. Some states, primarily agricultural, enacted *antitrust* measures in the 1880s, outlawing trusts. But these were largely ineffective because a trust could simply move to a state without such restrictions.

trust
any firm or group of firms that tries to monopolize a market

Sherman Antitrust Act of 1890
first national legislation in the world against monopoly; prohibited trusts, restraint of trade, and monopolization, but the law was vague and, by itself, ineffective

Clayton Act of 1914
beefed up the Sherman Act; outlawed certain anticompetitive practices not prohibited by the Sherman Act, including price discrimination, tying contracts, exclusive dealing, interlocking directorates, and buying the corporate stock of a competitor

tying contract
a seller of one good requires a buyer to purchase other goods as part of the deal

exclusive dealing
a supplier prohibits its customers from buying from other suppliers of the product

interlocking directorates
a person serves on the boards of directors of two or more competing firms

Federal Trade Commission (FTC) Act of 1914
Established a federal body to help enforce antitrust laws; run by commissioners assisted by economists and lawyers

Sherman Antitrust Act of 1890

In the presidential election of 1888, the major political parties put antitrust planks in their platforms. This consensus culminated in the **Sherman Antitrust Act of 1890**, the first national legislation in the world against monopoly. The law prohibited trusts, restraint of trade, and monopolization, but the law's vague language allowed room for much anticompetitive activity.

Clayton Act of 1914

The **Clayton Act of 1914** was passed to outlaw certain practices not prohibited by the Sherman Act and to help government stop a monopoly before it develops. For example, the Clayton Act outlaws price discrimination when this practice creates a monopoly. You'll recall that *price discrimination* charges different customers different prices for the same good. The act also prohibits *tying contracts* and *exclusive dealing* if they substantially lessen competition. **Tying contracts** require the buyer of one good to purchase another good as part of the deal. For example, a seller of a patented machine might require customers to buy other supplies. **Exclusive dealing** means a customer must agree not to buy any of the product from other suppliers. For example, a manufacturer might sell computer chips to a computer maker only if the computer maker agrees not to buy chips from other manufacturers. Another prohibition of the act is **interlocking directorates**, whereby the same individual serves on the boards of directors of competing firms. Finally, the acquisition of a competing firm's corporate stock is outlawed if this would substantially lessen competition.

Federal Trade Commission Act of 1914

The **Federal Trade Commission (FTC) Act of 1914** established a federal body to help enforce antitrust laws. The president appoints the five commissioners, who are assisted by a staff of economists and lawyers. The Sherman, Clayton, and FTC acts provide the framework for U.S. antitrust laws. Subsequent amendments and court decisions have clarified and embellished these laws. A loophole in the Clayton Act was closed in 1950 with the passage of the *Celler-Kefauver Anti-Merger Act,* which prevents one firm from buying the *physical assets* of another firm if the effect is to reduce competition. This law can block both **horizontal mergers**, or the merging of firms that produce the same product, such as Coke and Pepsi, and **vertical mergers**, or the merging of firms where one supplies inputs to the other or demands output from the other, such as Microsoft software going into Dell hardware.

Key Antitrust Legislation:

- 1890 Sherman Antitrust Act
- 1914 Clayton Act
- 1914 FTC Act
- 1950 Celler-Kefauver Anti-Merger Act

Antitrust Enforcement

Any law's effectiveness depends on the vigor and vigilance of enforcement. The pattern of antitrust enforcement goes something like this. Either the Antitrust Division of the U.S. Justice Department or the FTC charges a firm or group of firms with breaking the law. Federal agencies are often acting on a complaint by a customer or a competitor. At that point, those charged with the wrongdoing may be able, without admitting guilt, to sign a **consent decree**, whereby they agree not to do whatever they had been charged with. If the accused contests the charges, evidence from both sides is presented in a court trial, and a judge decides. Some decisions may be appealed all the way to the Supreme Court, and in such cases the courts may render new interpretations of existing laws.

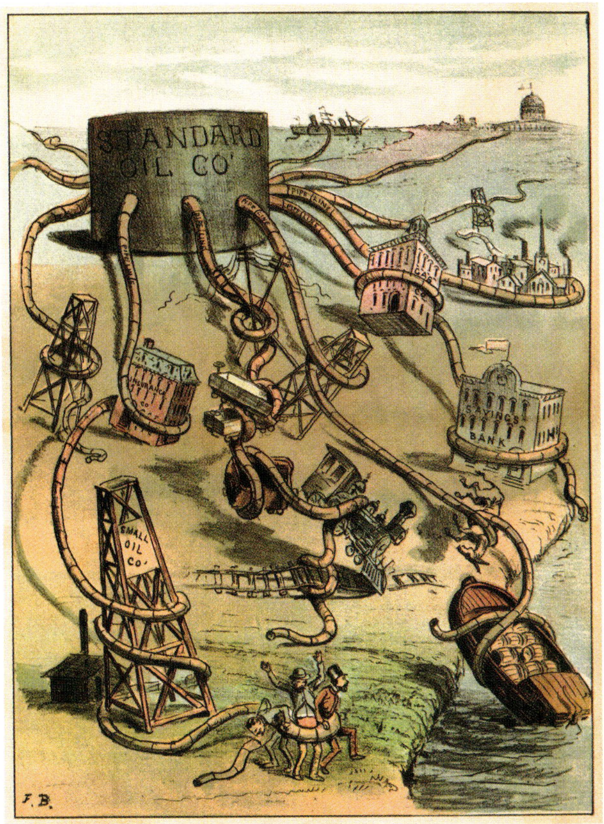

Per Se Illegality and the Rule of Reason

The courts have interpreted antitrust laws in essentially two different ways. One set of practices has been declared **per se illegal**—that is, illegal regardless of the economic rationale or consequences. For example, under the Sherman Act, all agreements among competing firms to fix prices, restrict output, or otherwise restrain competition are viewed as per se illegal. To prove guilt under a per se rule, the government need only show that the offending practice took place. Thus, the government need only examine the firm's *behavior.*

Another set of practices falls under the **rule of reason**. Here the courts take into account the facts surrounding the particular offense—namely, the reasons why the offending practice was adopted and its effect on competition. The rule of reason was first set forth in 1911, when the Supreme Court held that Standard Oil had illegally monopolized the petroleum refining industry. Standard Oil allegedly had come to dominate 90 percent of the market by acquiring more than 120 former rivals and by practicing **predatory pricing** to drive remaining rivals out of business—for example, by temporarily selling below marginal cost or dropping the price only in

horizontal merger
a merger in which one firm combines with another that produces the same type of product

vertical merger
a merger in which one firm combines with another from which it had purchased inputs or to which it had sold output

consent decree
the accused party, without admitting guilt, agrees not to do whatever it was charged with if the government drops the charges

per se illegal
in antitrust law, business practices deemed illegal regardless of their economic rationale or their consequences

rule of reason
before ruling on the legality of certain business practices, a court examines why they were undertaken and what effect they have on competition

predatory pricing
pricing tactics employed by a dominant firm to drive competitors out of business, such as temporarily selling below marginal cost or dropping the price only in certain markets

certain markets. In finding Standard Oil guilty, the Court focused on both the company's *behavior* and the *market structure* that resulted from that behavior. Based on this approach, the Court found that the company had behaved *unreasonably* and ruled that the monopoly should be broken up.

But in 1920, the rule of reason led the Supreme Court to find U.S. Steel not guilty of monopolization. In that case, the Court ruled that not every contract or combination in restraint of trade is illegal—only those that "unreasonably" restrained trade violated antitrust laws. The Court said that *mere size is not an offense.* Although U.S. Steel clearly possessed market power, the company, in the Court's view, had not violated antitrust laws because it had not unreasonably used that power. The Court switched positions in 1945, ruling that although Alcoa's conduct might be reasonable and legal, its mere possession of market power—Alcoa controlled 90 percent of the aluminum ingot market—violated antitrust laws. Here the Court was using *market structure* rather than firm *behavior* as the test of legality.

LO5 Mergers and Public Policy

Some firms have pursued rapid growth by merging with other firms or by acquiring other firms. Much of what the Antitrust Division in the U.S. Justice Department and the FTC's Bureau of Competition do is approve or deny proposed mergers and acquisitions. In determining possible harmful effects that a merger might have on competition, one important consideration is its impact on the share of sales accounted for by the largest firms in the industry. If a few firms account for a relatively large share of sales, the industry is said to be *concentrated.* As a measure of sales concentration, the Justice Department uses the **Herfindahl-Hirschman Index**, or **HHI**, which is found by squaring the percentage of market share of each firm in the market and then summing those squares. For example, if the industry consists of 100 firms of equal size, the HHI is 100 [= 100 × $(1)^2$]. If the industry is a pure monopoly, its index is 10,000 [= $(100)^2$], the largest possible value. The more firms in the industry and the more equal their size, the smaller the HHI. This index gives greater weight to firms with larger market shares, as can be seen for the three examples presented in Exhibit 2. Each industry has 44 firms, but, for ease of exposition, only the market share of the top 4 firms differs across industries. Note that the index for Industry III is nearly triple that for each of the two other industries. Please take a minute now to work through the logic of the exhibit.

Herfindahl-Hirschman Index (HHI)
a measure of market concentration that squares each firm's percentage share of the market then sums these squares

The Justice Department's guidelines sort all mergers into one of two categories: *horizontal mergers,* which involve firms in the same market, and *nonhorizontal mergers,* which include all other types of mergers. Of greatest interest for antitrust purposes are horizontal mergers, such as a merger between competing oil companies like Exxon and Mobil. The Justice Department generally challenges any merger in an industry that meets two conditions: (1) the post-merger HHI exceeds 1,800 and (2) the merger increases the index by more than 100 points. Mergers in an industry that would have a post-merger index of less than 1,000 are seldom challenged.[2] Other factors, such as the ease of entry into the market and gains in efficiency, are considered for indexes between 1,000 and 1,800.

2. Merger guidelines are laid out by the U.S. Department of Justice at http://www.usdoj.gov/atr/public/guidelines/horiz_book/hmg1.html.

Exhibit 2

Herfindahl-Hirschman Index (HHI) Based on Market Share in Three Industries

	Industry I		Industry II		Industry III	
Firm	Market Share (percent)	Market Share Squared	Market Share (percent)	Market Share Squared	Market Share (percent)	Market Share Squared
A	23	529	15	225	57	3,249
B	18	324	15	225	1	1
C	13	169	15	225	1	1
D	6	36	15	225	1	1
Remaining 40 firms	1 each	40	1 each	40	1 each	40
HHI		1,098		940		3,292

Merger Waves

There have been four merger waves in this country over the last century, as outlined in Exhibit 3. Between 1887 and 1904 some of today's largest firms, including U.S. Steel and Standard Oil, were formed. Mergers during this first wave tended to be horizontal. For example, the firm that is today the United States Steel Corporation was created in 1901 through a billion-dollar merger that involved dozens of individual steel producers and two-thirds of the industry's production capacity. This merger wave was a reaction to technological progress in transportation, communication, and manufacturing. Simply put, it became easier and cheaper to run a corporation that stretched across the nation, so firms merged to reach national markets. During this first wave, similar merger waves occurred in Canada, Great Britain, and elsewhere, creating dominant firms, some of which still exist. The U.S. merger wave cooled with the severe national recession of 1904 when antitrust laws began to have real bite.

Because antitrust laws began to restrain *horizontal* mergers, *vertical* mergers became more common during the second merger wave, between 1916 and 1929. A vertical merger is one between a firm that either supplies the other firm inputs or demands the other firm's outputs—the merger of firms at different stages of the production process. For example, a copper refiner merges with a copper fabricator. The stock market boom of the 1920s fueled this second wave, and the stock market crash stopped it cold in 1929.

The Great Depression and World War II cooled mergers for two decades, but the third merger wave got under way after the war. More than 200 of the 1,000 largest firms in 1950 disappeared by the early 1960s as a result of the third merger wave, which occurred between 1948 and 1969. In that span, many large firms were absorbed by other, usually larger, firms. The third merger wave peaked during 1964 to 1969, when **conglomerate mergers**, which join firms in different industries, accounted for four-fifths of all mergers. For example, Litton Industries combined firms that made calculators, appliances, electrical equipment, and machine tools. Merging firms were looking to diversify their product mix and perhaps achieve some *economies of scope*—meaning, to reduce average costs by producing a variety of goods.

The fourth merger wave began in 1982 and involved both horizontal and vertical mergers. Some large conglomerate mergers from the third wave were dissolved during the fourth wave, as the core firm sold off unrelated operations. About one-third of mergers in the 1980s resulted from *hostile takeovers,* where one firm would buy control of another against the wishes of the target firm's management. Hostile takeovers dwindled to less than one-tenth of mergers during the 1990s.

Merger activity gained momentum during the latter half of the 1990s, with the dollar value of each new merger topping the previous record. Most mergers during this period were financed by the exchange of corporate stock and were spurred on by a booming stock market (like the mergers of the 1920s). The dissolution of the Soviet Union ended the Cold War and boosted capitalism around the world. Companies merged to achieve a stronger competitive position in global markets. The largest mergers in history were proposed since the late 1990s, with the biggest action in banking, radio and television, insurance, telecommunications, and health services. The fourth merger wave continues. But not all mergers work out. For example, Daimler-Benz bought Chrysler for $36 billion in 1998. After nearly a decade of disappointing results, the merged company had to pay $650 million in 2007 to unload 80 percent of its Chrysler division.[3]

In recent years, there have been fewer objections to mergers on antitrust grounds either from academics or regulatory officials. The government shifted from rules that restrict big mergers to a more flexible approach that allows big companies to merge. For example, after several months of review, the U.S. Justice Department concluded that

3. Stephen Power, "After Pact to Shed Chrysler, Daimler Turns Focus to Other Challenges," *Wall Street Journal,* 15 May 2007.

conglomerate merger a merger of firms in different industries

Exhibit 3

U.S. Merger Waves in the Past Century

Wave	Years	Dominant Type of Merger	Examples	Stimulus
First	1887–1904	Horizontal	U.S. Steel, Standard Oil	Span national markets
Second	1916–1929	Vertical	Copper refiner with fabricator	Stock market boom
Third	1948–1969	Conglomerate	Litton Industries	Diversification
Fourth	1982–present	Horizontal and vertical	Banking, telecommunications, health services, insurance	Span national and global markets, stock market boom

Whirlpool's acquisition of Maytag would not reduce competition substantially and could achieve efficiencies and cost savings. What's more, growing competition from Asia would prevent the merged company from raising prices.[4]

Antitrust officials ask "will the merger hurt competition?"[5] Most, apparently, do not. Regulators ultimately have challenged only about 2 percent of all mergers proposed in recent years, though just the threat of a legal challenge has probably deterred many potentially anticompetitive mergers and acquisitions.

LO6 Competitive Trends in the U.S. Economy

For years, there has been concern about the sheer size of some firms because of the real or potential power they might exercise in the economy. One way to measure the power of the largest corporations is to calculate the share of the nation's corporate assets controlled by the 100 largest manufacturing firms. They now control about half of all manufacturing assets in the United States, up from 40 percent after World War II. We should recognize, however, that size alone is not the same as market power. A very big firm, such as a large automaker, may face stiff competition from other large automakers both foreign and domestic. On the other hand, the only movie theater in an isolated community may be able to raise its price with less concern about competition.

Competition over Time

More important than the size of the largest firms in the nation is the market structure of each industry. Various studies have examined the level of competition by industry and changes in competition over the years. All began with some measure of market share, such as the HHI. Among the most comprehensive is the research of William G. Shepherd, who relied on many sources to determine the competitiveness of each industry in the U.S. economy.[6] He sorted industries into four groups: (1) pure monopoly, in which a single firm controlled the entire market and was able to block entry; (2) dominant firm, in which a single firm had more than half the market share and no close rival; (3) tight oligopoly, in which the top four firms supplied more than 60 percent of market output, with stable market shares and evidence of cooperation; and (4) effective competition, in which firms in the industry exhibited low concentration, low entry barriers, and little or no collusion.

Exhibit 4 presents Shepherd's breakdown of U.S. industries into the four categories for 1939, 1958, and 2000. Between 1939 and 1958, the table shows a modest growth in competition, with the share of those industries rated as "effectively competitive" increasing from 52 percent to 56 percent of all industries. Between 1958 and 2000, however, the share of effectively competitive industries jumped from 56 percent to 77 percent.

According to Shepherd, the growth in competition from 1958 to 2000 can be traced to three sources: (1) *competition from imports,* (2) *deregulation,* and (3) *antitrust policy.* Foreign imports between 1958 and 2000 increased competition in more than a dozen industries, including autos, tires, and steel. The growth in imports accounted for one-sixth of the overall increase in competition. Imports were attractive to consumers because of their higher quality and lower price. Finding themselves at a cost and technological disadvantage, U.S. producers initially sought protection from foreign competitors through trade barriers, such as quotas and tariffs.

Shepherd argues that deregulation accounted for one-fifth of the increase in competition. Trucking, airlines, securities trading, banking, and telecommunications were among the industries deregulated between 1958 and 2000.

Although it is difficult to attribute an increase in competition to specific antitrust cases, Shepherd credits anti-trust policy with two-fifths of the growth in competition between 1958 and 2000.

To summarize: According to Shepherd, the three primary reasons for increased competition were international trade, deregulation, and antitrust policy. One-sixth of the growth in competition between 1958 and 2000 came from imports, one-fifth from deregulation, and two-fifths, the largest

4. Ilan Brat and Richard Gibson, "Whirlpool-Maytag Deal Gets Antitrust Approval," *Wall Street Journal,* 30 March 2006.
5. "Prepared Remarks of Timothy J. Muris, Chairman, Federal Trade Commission," 17 February 2004 at http://www.ftc.gov/speeches/muris/040217hmgwksp.htm#N_4_.
6. William G. Shepherd, "Causes of Increased Competition in the U.S. Economy, 1939–1980," *Review of Economics and Statistics* 64 (November 1982); and William G. Shepherd and Joanna M. Shepherd, *The Economics of Industrial Organization,* 5th ed. (Waveland Press, 2004).

Exhibit 4

Competitive Trends in the U.S. Economy: 1939 to 2000

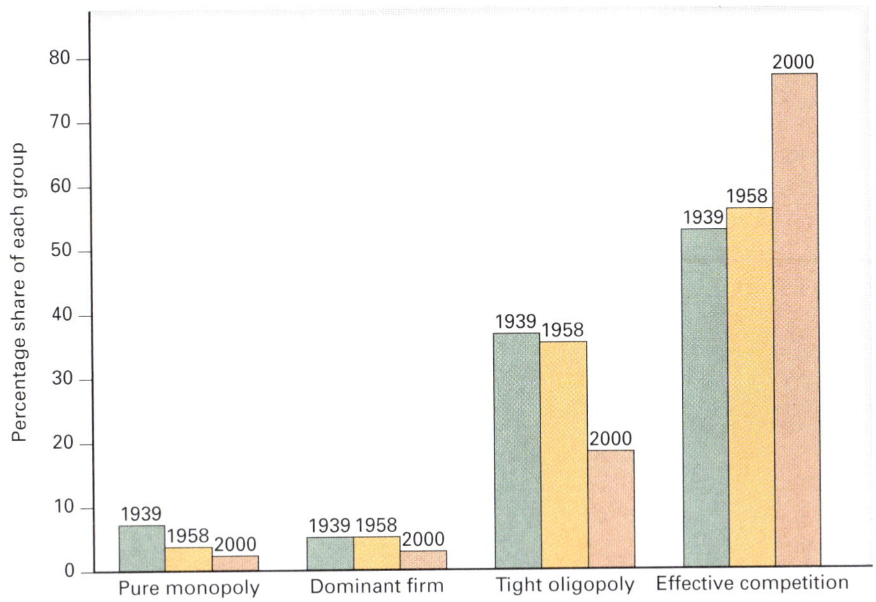

SOURCES: William G. Shepherd, "Causes of Increased Competition in the U.S. Economy, 1939–1980," *Review of Economics and Statistics* 64 (Noovember 1982); and William G. Shepherd and Joanna M. Shepherd, *The Economics of Industrial Organization*, 5th ed. (Long Grove, Ill.: Waveland Press, 2004), 15.

share, from antitrust policy. In light of the important role that Shepherd accords antitrust policy, let's look at the most significant antitrust case of the last decade.

Recent Competitive Trends

Shepherd's analysis of competition extended to 2000. What has been the trend since then? Growing world trade has increased competition in the U.S. economy. For example, the share of the U.S. market controlled by the three major automakers fell from 80 percent in 1970 to 54 percent by 2006. And federal action to deregulate international phone service forced down the average price of international phone calls from $0.88 a minute in 1997 to under $0.10 a minute by 2007. In an effort to reduce international phone rates, federal officials even subpoenaed Filipino phone executives who were attending a conference in Hawaii, alleging they colluded on phone rates to the United States.[7]

Technological change is boosting competition in many markets, especially the market for media. For example, the prime-time audience share of the three major television networks (NBC, CBS, and ABC) dropped from 90 percent in 1980 to under 40 percent today as cable and satellite technology delivered hundreds more networks and channels. About 90 percent of U.S. households have either cable or satellite television. The 14,000 radio stations now available is double the

7. Raissa Robles, "FBI Swoop Sparks Manila-U.S. Row," *South China Morning Post,* 15 January 2004.

Microsoft on Trial

The U.S. Justice Department and 20 state attorneys general filed lawsuits in 1998 alleging that Microsoft tried to protect its operating-system monopoly and to extend that monopoly into Internet software. Microsoft disputed the charges and said the government was interfering with its right to create new products that benefit consumers. Still, after months of proceedings, the judge ruled against Microsoft, maintaining that the company had attempted to monopolize the Web browser market by unlawfully "tying" Internet Explorer with Windows. As a remedy, he proposed restricting Microsoft's business practices and dividing the firm into two companies. Microsoft appealed the decision, arguing that it did not hold a monopoly and had not engaged in anticompetitive practices. Microsoft eventually reached an out-of-court settlement that gave personal-computer makers greater freedom to install non-Microsoft software on new machines. It also banned retaliation against companies that take advantage of these freedoms, prohibited exclusive contracts, and required Microsoft to disclose design information to hardware and software makers so they can build competing products that run smoothly with Windows.

SOURCES: Marc Ferranti, "Iowa Judge Approves Microsoft Class-Action Settlement," *PC World,* 18 April 2007; David Lawsky, "EU Considers New Kind of Microsoft Antitrust Action", *Scientific American,* 23 April 2007.

number in 1970 (satellite radio alone has more than 14 million subscribers). And there are now about 20,000 magazines, an increase of 6,000 since 1993.

Technological change is boosting competition in many markets.

Despite Microsoft's dominance in operating systems, the software market barely existed in 1980 but now flourishes in a technology-rich environment populated by nearly 10,000 producers. And the Internet has opened far-ranging possibilities for greater competition in a number of industries, from online stock trading to all manner of electronic commerce and information distribution.

Problems with Antitrust Policy

Despite the publicity and hoopla surrounding the Microsoft antitrust case (there was even a thinly disguised movie about Microsoft called *Antitrust*), there is growing doubt about the economic value of the lengthy antitrust cases pursued in the past. A case against Exxon, for example, was in the courts for 17 years before the company was cleared of charges in 1992. Another case began in 1969 when IBM, with nearly 70 percent of domestic sales of electronic data-processing equipment, was accused of monopolizing that market. IBM responded that its large market share was based on its innovative products and on its economies of scale. The trial began in 1975, the government took nearly three years to present its case; litigation dragged on for four more years. In the meantime, many other computer makers emerged both in this country and abroad to challenge IBM's dominance. In 1982, the government dropped the case, noting that the threat of monopoly had diminished enough that the case was "without merit." As noted already, the U.S. case against Microsoft took nearly six years to resolve and it dragged on in state courts years longer.

Competition May Not Require That Many Firms

Joseph Schumpeter argued half a century ago that competition should be viewed as a dynamic process, one of "creative destruction." Firms are continually in flux—introducing new products, phasing out old ones, trying to compete for the consumer's dollar in a variety of ways. In light of this, antitrust policy should not necessarily aim at increasing the *number* of firms in each industry. In some cases, firms grow large because they are better than rivals at offering what consumers want. Accordingly, firm size should not be the primary concern. Moreover, as noted in the chapter on perfect competition, economists have shown through market experiments that most of the desirable properties of perfect competition can be achieved with relatively few firms.[8] For example, the two leading chip makers, Intel and Advanced Micro Devices, have been locked in a price war for years, as each fights for market share. Likewise, Boeing, the only U.S. maker of commercial jets, competes fiercely with Europe's Airbus for every new contract.

Abuse of Antitrust

Parties that can show injury from firms that violate antitrust laws can sue the offending company and recover three times the damages sustained. These so-called *treble damage* suits increased after World

8. See, for example, Vernon Smith, "Markets as Economizers of Information: Experimental Examinations of the 'Hayek Hypothesis,'" *Economic Inquiry* 20 (1982); and Douglas Davis and Charles Holt, *Experimental Economics* (Princeton, N.J.: Princeton University Press, 1993).

War II. More than 1,000 are filed each year. Courts have been relatively generous to those claiming to have been wronged. Even foreign firms have started suing in U.S. courts. And, in an unusual twist, foreign firms are now suing other foreign firms using U.S courts, laws, and lawyers. But studies show that such suits can be used to intimidate an aggressive competitor or to convert a contract dispute between, say, a firm and its supplier into treble damage payoffs. The result can have a chilling effect on competition. Many economists now believe that the anticompetitive costs from this abuse of treble damage suits may exceed any competitive benefits of these laws.

Growth of International Markets

Finally, a standard approach to measuring the market power of a firm is its share of the market. With greater international trade, however, the local or even national market share becomes less relevant. General Motors may still dominate U.S. auto manufacturing, accounting for nearly half of national sales by U.S. firms. But when Japanese and European producers are included, GM's share of the U.S. auto market falls to only about one-quarter of all sales. GM's share of world production has declined steadily since the mid-1950s. And in early 2007, for the first time in 76 years, GM failed to lead the world in global sales, ranking just behind Toyota.[9] *Where markets are open to foreign competition, antitrust enforcement that focuses on domestic producers makes less economic sense.* In response to the global nature of markets, antitrust policy is starting to take an international approach. The U.S. government has signed cooperative agreements with some other governments, including Japan and the European Union, to promote antitrust enforcement and reduce conflicting decisions. For example, antitrust investigators from the United States, the European Union, Japan, and Canada simultaneously raided 14 companies in 5 countries in a price fixing probe of the polyvinyl chloride market. Through the International Competition Network, more than 100 nations discuss antitrust procedures and policies. Such discussions have thrown light on anticompetitive regulations in place around the world. Many countries for decades have sheltered firms in some politically powerful industries. For example, until recently, regulations in India restricted entry into the hotel business. As a result, there were fewer hotel rooms in all of India, a country with more than a billion people, than in New York City with less than 1 percent that population.

9. Bob Golfen, "Toyota Top Seller in 1st Quarter," *Arizona Republic*, 25 April 2007.

© BORIS ROESSLER/DPA/LANDOV

Final Word

Competition has been growing in recent decades because of changing technology, greater international trade, industry deregulation, and antitrust policy. Consumers benefit as firms compete by offering lower prices, better products, and new services to keep existing customers and attract new ones. Competition also ensures that the economy's resources find their most efficient uses. Through the process of creative destruction, competition promotes the survival of the fittest. Market forces continuously pressure firms to innovate—that is, to develop new and better products, services, methods of doing business, and technologies.

CHAPTER 16

Public Goods *and* Public Choice

Learning Outcomes

- LO[1] Define public goods
- LO[2] Discuss the role of public choice in representative democracy
- LO[3] Describe the underground economy
- LO[4] Explain bureaucracy and its role in representative democracy

© S. MELTZER/PHOTOLINK/PHOTODISC/GETTY IMAGES

"Why do most people remain largely ignorant about what's happening in the public sector? Why is voter turnout so low?"

How do public goods differ from private goods? Why do most people remain largely ignorant about what's happening in the public sector? Why is it so difficult to interest the public in the public interest? Why is voter turnout so low? Why do some politicians express concern for average Americans, but vote for special interests? Why are incumbents more likely than challengers to support campaign spending limits? Answers to these and related questions are discussed in this chapter, which focuses on the public sector—both the rationale for public goods and public choices about those goods.

What do you think?

There is no completely fair way to pay for public goods.

Strongly Disagree					*Strongly Agree*	
1	2	3	4	5	6	7

The effects of government are all around us. Stitched into the clothes you put on this morning are government-required labels providing washing instructions. Government subsidies affect the price of your Cheerios and the milk and sugar you put on them. Governments regulate the motor vehicle you travel in as well the speed and the sobriety of the driver. Taxpayers subsidize your education in a variety of ways. Yes, government plays a major role in the economy. The federal government alone spends about $3,000,000,000,000—about $3.0 *trillion*—including $1 million for paper clips. State and local governments tax and spend more than $1 trillion on their own.

The role of government has been discussed throughout this book. For the most part, we assumed that government makes optimal adjustments to the shortcomings of the private sector—that is, when confronted with market failure, government adopts and implements the appropriate program to address the problem. But, just as there are limits to the market's effectiveness, there are limits to government's effectiveness. In this chapter, we look at the pros and cons of government activity. We begin with public goods, discuss the decision-making process, and then examine the limitations of that process.

Topics discussed in Chapter 16 include:

- Private versus public goods
- Representative democracy
- Rational ignorance
- Special-interest legislation
- Rent seeking
- The underground economy
- Bureaucratic behavior
- Private versus public production

LO[1] Public Goods

Throughout most of this book, we have been talking about *private goods,* such as pizzas and haircuts. As noted in Chapter 3, private goods have two important features. First, they are *rival* in consumption, meaning that the amount consumed by one person is unavailable for others to consume. For example, when you and friends share a pizza, each slice others eat is one less available for you (which is why you usually eat a little faster when sharing). A second key feature of private goods is that suppliers can easily *exclude* those who don't pay. Only paying customers get pizzas. Thus, private goods are said to be *rival* and *exclusive.*

Private Goods, Public Goods, and In Between

In contrast to private goods, *public goods,* such as national defense, the national weather service, the Centers for Disease Control, or a local mosquito-control program, are *nonrival* in consumption. One person's consumption does not diminish the amount available to others. Once produced, such goods are available to all in equal amount; the good can be supplied to an additional consumer for zero marginal cost. But once a public good is produced, suppliers cannot easily deny it to those who don't pay. There are no vending machines for public goods. For example, if a firm sprays a neighborhood for mosquitoes, all those in the neighborhood benefit. The firm can't easily exclude those who fail to pay. Thus, the mosquito spraying is *nonexclusive*—it benefits all those in the neighborhood. Some people figure, "Since I can enjoy the benefits without paying, why bother paying?" As a consequence, for-profit firms can't profitably sell public goods. In this case of market failure, the government comes to the rescue by providing public goods and paying for them through enforced taxation. Sometimes nonprofit agencies also provide public goods, funding them through contributions and other revenue sources.

But the economy consists of more than just the polar cases of private and public goods. Some goods are *nonrival* but *exclusive.* For example, additional households can watch a TV show without affecting the reception of other viewers. It's not as if there is only so much TV signal to go around. Television signals are nonrival in consumption. Yet the program's producers, should they choose to, could charge each household for reception, as with cable TV, so the TV signal is nonrival but exclusive. A good that is nonrival but exclusive is called a *natural monopoly,* a term already introduced. Along the same lines, short of the point of congestion, additional people can benefit from a golf course, swimming pool, rock concert, or highway without diminishing the benefit to other users. These goods, when not congested, are nonrival. Yet producers can, with relative ease, exclude those who don't pay the greens fee, pool admission, ticket price, or road toll. These uncongested goods are both nonrival and exclusive and are therefore natural monopolies. Once congestion sets in, however, these goods become rival—space is scarce on a backed-up golf course, in a crowded swimming pool, at a jam-packed concert, or on a bumper-to-bumper highway. Once congestion sets in, these natural monopolies morph into private goods—both rival and exclusive.

open-access good
a good such as ocean fish that is rival in consumption but nonpayers cannot be excluded easily

Some other goods are *rival* but *nonexclusive.* The fish in the ocean are rival in the sense that every fish caught is not available for others to catch; the same goes for migratory game, like geese. But ocean fish and migratory game are nonexclusive in that it would be costly if not impossible for a firm to prevent access to these goods. A good that is rival but nonexclusive is called an **open-access good**. We'll examine problems that arise with open-access goods in the next chapter.

Exhibit 1 sorts out the four categories of goods. Across the top, goods are classified as either *rival* or *nonrival,* and along the left margin, goods are either *exclusive* or *nonexclusive.* Private goods are usually provided by the private sector. Natural monopolies are sometimes provided by the private sector, as

Congested public highways may make less-busy (private) toll roads a more attractive option for some commuters.

Exhibit 1

Categories of Goods

	Rival	Nonrival
Exclusive	1. Private Goods —Pizza —Crowded swimming pool 	2. Natural Monopolies —Cable TV —Uncrowded swimming pool 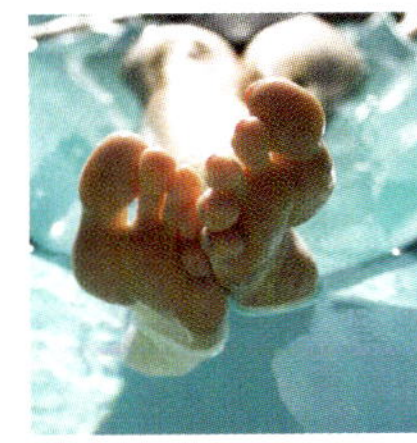
Nonexclusive	3. Open-Access Goods —Ocean fish —Migratory birds 	4. Public Goods —National defense —Mosquito control 

with a private golf course, and sometimes provided by government, as with a municipal golf course. Open-access goods are usually regulated by government, as you will see in the next chapter. And public goods are usually provided by government.

Optimal Provision of Public Goods

Because private goods are rival in consumption, the market demand for a private good at a given price is the sum of the quantities demanded by each consumer. For example, the market quantity of pizza demanded when the price is $10 is the quantity demanded by Alan plus the quantity demanded by Maria plus the quantity demanded by all other consumers in the market. The market demand curve for a private good is the *horizontal* sum of individual demand curves, an idea developed in Exhibit 7 of Chapter 6. The efficient quantity of a private good occurs where the market demand curve intersects the market supply curve.

But a public good is nonrival in consumption, so that good, once produced, is available in that amount to all consumers. For example, the market demand for a given level of mosquito control reflects the marginal benefit that Alan gets from that amount plus the marginal benefit that Maria gets plus the marginal benefit that all others in the community get from that amount of the good. Therefore, the market demand curve for a public good is the *vertical* sum of each consumer's demand for the public good. To arrive at the efficient level of the public good, we find where the market demand curve intersects the marginal cost curve—that is, where the sum of the marginal valuations equals the marginal cost.

Suppose the public good in question is mosquito control in a neighborhood, which, for simplicity, has only two households, one headed by Alan and the other by Maria. Alan spends more time in the yard than does Maria and thus values a mosquito-free environment more than she does. Their individual demand curves are shown in Exhibit 2 as D_a and D_m, reflecting the marginal benefits that Alan and Maria enjoy at each rate of output. Quantity is measured here as hours of mosquito spraying per week. By vertically summing marginal valuations at each rate of output, we derive the neighborhood demand curve, *D*, for mosquito spraying. For example, when the town sprays two hours a week, Maria values the second hour at $5 and Alan values it at $10. To get the market demand for the second hour of spraying, we simply add each resident's marginal benefit to get $15, as identified by point *e*.

How much mosquito spraying should the government provide? Suppose the marginal cost of spraying is a constant $15 an hour, as shown in Exhibit 2 on the next page. The efficient level of output is found where the marginal benefit to the neighborhood equals the marginal cost, which occurs where the neighborhood demand curve intersects the marginal cost curve. In our example, these curves intersect where quantity is two hours per week.

Exhibit 2

Market for Public Goods

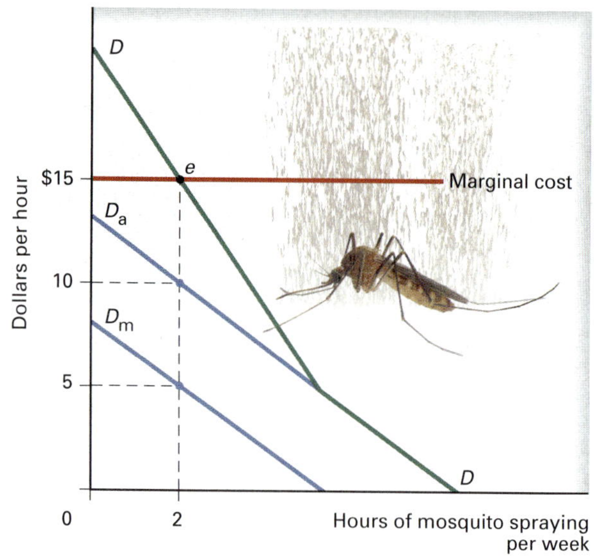

Paying for Public Goods

Suppose the government pays for the mosquito spray through taxes. The efficient approach would be to impose a tax on each resident equal to his or her marginal valuation. Simple enough, but there are at least two problems with this. First, once people realize their taxes are based on government estimates of how much they value the good, people tend to understate their true valuation. Why admit you really value the good if, as a result, you get socked with a higher tax bill? After all, people in the neighborhood can enjoy mosquito abatement whether or not they pay for it. So taxpayers tend to understate their true valuation of public goods. This creates the **free-rider problem**, which occurs because people try to benefit from the public good without paying for it.

But even if the government has accurate information about everyone's marginal valuations, some households have a greater ability to pay taxes than others. In our example, Alan values mosquito control more because he spends more time in the yard than does Maria. What if Alan is around more because he can't find a job? Should his taxes be double those of Maria, who has, say, a high-paying job? *Taxing people according to their marginal valuations of the public good may be efficient, but it may not be fair if the ability to pay differs.*

free-rider problem
because a people cannot be easily excluded from consuming a public good, some people may try to reap the benefits of the good without paying for it

Once the public good is produced, only that quantity is available, such as two hours of mosquito spraying

"Taxing people according to their marginal valuations of the public good may be efficient, but it may not be fair if the ability to pay differs."

per week. With private goods, each consumer can buy any quantity he or she demands and each can purchase a different amount. Thus, *public goods are more complicated than private goods in terms of what goods should be provided, in what quantities, and who should pay.* These decisions are thrashed out through public choices, which we explore in the balance of this chapter.

LO2 Public Choice in Representative Democracy

Government decisions about public goods and taxes are *public choices*. In a democracy, public choices usually require approval by a majority of voters. About 60 percent of the world's 200 independent nations are democracies. Thus, issues raised in this section about majority rule apply to most of the world, including all of Western Europe and nearly all of the Americas.

Median-Voter Model

As it turns out, we can usually explain the outcome of majority rule by focusing on the preferences of the median voter. The *median voter* is the one whose preferences lie in the middle of all voters' preferences. For example, if the issue is the size of the government budget, half the voters prefer a larger budget than the median voter and half prefer a smaller one. The median-voter model predicts that under certain conditions, the preference of the median, or middle, voter will dominate other choices. Here's an example. Suppose you and two roommates have just moved into an apartment, and the three of you must decide on furnishings. You agree to share common expenses equally and to make choices by majority rule. The issue at hand is whether to buy a TV and, if so, of what size. You each have a different preference. Your studious roommate considers a TV an annoying distraction and would rather go without; otherwise, the smaller, the better. Your other roommate, an avid TV watcher, prefers a 48-inch screen but would settle for a smaller one rather than go without. A 27-inch screen is your first choice, but you would accept the 48-inch screen rather than go without. What to do, what to do?

You all agree to make the decision by voting on two alternatives at a time, then pairing the winner against the remaining alternative until one choice dominates the others. When the 27-inch screen is paired with the no-TV option, the 27-inch screen gets both your vote and the TV fan's vote. When the 27-inch screen is then paired with the 48-inch screen, the 27-inch screen wins again, this time because your studious roommate sides with you rather than voting for the super screen.

Majority voting in effect delegates the public choice to the person whose preference is the median for the group. As the median voter in this example, you get your way. You have the votes for any choice between no TV and a 48 incher. Similarly, *the median voter in an electorate often determines public choices. Political candidates try to get elected by appealing to the median voter.* This is why candidates focus their rhetoric on "hard-working Americans," "middle America," or "American families." They are targeting the median voter. This is one reason why candidates often seem so much alike. Note that under majority rule, only the median voter gets his or her way. Other voters must go along with the median choice. Thus, other voters usually end up paying for what they consider to be either too much or too little of the public good. On the contrary, in private markets people get whatever amount they are willing and able to buy.

The median voter in an electorate often determines public choices. Political candidates try to get elected by appealing to the median voter.

People vote directly on issues at New England town meetings and on the occasional referendum, but *direct democracy* is not the most common form of public choice. When you consider the thousands of choices made in the public sector—from the number of teachers to hire to what software to use for municipal records—it becomes clear that direct democracy for all public choices through referenda would be unwieldy and impractical. Rather than make decisions by direct referenda, voters elect *representatives,* who, at least in theory, make public choices that reflect their constituents' views. Under certain conditions, the resulting public choices reflect the preferences of the median voter. Some complications of representative democracy are explored next.

Special Interest and Rational Ignorance

We assume that consumers maximize utility and firms maximize profit, but what about governments? As noted in Chapter 3, there is no common agreement about what, if anything, governments try to maximize or, more precisely, what elected officials try to maximize. One theory that stems from the rational self-interest assumption of economic behavior is that elected officials try to *maximize their political support.*

To maximize political support, elected officials may cater to special interests rather than serve the interest of the public. The possibility arises because of the asymmetry between special interest and public interest, an idea introduced in the previous chapter. Consider only one of the thousands of decisions elected representatives make each year: funding an obscure federal program that subsidizes U.S. wool production. Under the wool-subsidy program, the federal government guarantees that a floor price is paid to sheep farmers for each pound of wool they produce, a

Wool subsidies cost U.S. taxpayers over $75 million per year.

subsidy that costs taxpayers over $75 million per year. During deliberations to renew the program, the only person to testify before Congress was a representative of the National Wool Growers Association, who claimed that the subsidy was vital to the nation's economic welfare. Why didn't a single taxpayer challenge the subsidy? Why were sheep farmers able to pull the wool over taxpayers' eyes?

Households consume so many different public and private goods and services that they have neither the time nor the incentive to understand the effects of public choices on every product. What's more, voters realize that each of them has only a tiny possibility of influencing public choices. And even if an individual voter is somehow able to affect the outcome, the impact on that voter is likely to be small. For example, if a taxpayer could successfully stage a grassroots campaign to eliminate the wool subsidy, the taxpayer would save, on average, less than 50 cents per year in federal income taxes. Therefore, unless voters have a *special* interest in the legislation, they adopt a stance of **rational ignorance**, which means that they remain largely oblivious to most public choices. The cost to the typical voter of acquiring information about each public choice and acting on it usually exceeds any expected benefit. It's not easy to interest the public in the public interest.

In contrast, consumers have much more incentive to gather and act on information about market decisions because they benefit directly and immediately from such information. *Because information and the time required to acquire and digest it are scarce, consumers concentrate on private choices rather than public choices. The payoff in making better private choices is usually more immediate, more direct, and more substantial.* For example, a consumer in the market for a new car has an incentive to examine the performance records of different models, test-drive a few, and check prices at dealerships and online. That same person has less incentive to examine the performance records of candidates for public office because that single voter has virtually no chance of deciding the election. What's more, because candidates aim to please the median voter anyway, they often take positions that are similar.

rational ignorance a stance adopted by voters when they realize that the cost of understanding and voting on a particular issue exceeds the benefit expected from doing so

traditional public-goods legislation legislation that involves widespread costs and widespread benefits—nearly everyone pays and nearly everyone benefits

special-interest legislation legislation with concentrated benefits but widespread costs

pork-barrel spending special-interest legislation with narrow geographical benefits but funded by all taxpayers

populist legislation legislation with widespread benefits but concentrated costs

Distribution of Benefits and Costs

Let's turn now to a different topic—how the benefits and costs of public choices are spread across the population. Depending on the issue, particular legislation may benefit only a small group or much of the population. Likewise, the costs of that legislation may be imposed only on a small group or on much of the population. The combinations of benefits and costs yield four possible categories of distributions: (1) widespread benefits and widespread costs, (2) concentrated benefits and widespread costs, (3) widespread benefits and concentrated costs, and (4) concentrated costs and concentrated benefits.

Traditional public-goods legislation, such as for national defense, a justice system, or cancer research, involves widespread benefits and widespread costs—nearly everyone benefits and nearly everyone pays. Traditional public-goods legislation usually has a positive impact on the economy because total benefits exceed total costs.

With **special-interest legislation**, benefits are concentrated but costs widespread. For example, as you'll see shortly, price supports for dairy products benefit a small group—dairy farmers. To benefit dairy farmers, a special interest, the program spreads costs across nearly all taxpayers and consumers. Legislation that caters to special interests usually harms the economy, on net, because total costs often exceed total benefits. Special-interest legislation benefitting a narrow geographical interest is called **pork-barrel spending**. To boost their reelection prospects, members of Congress "bring home the bacon" by delivering pork-barrel programs for their constituents. For example, a recent federal budget appropriated $50,000 for a tattoo removal program in San Luis Obispo, California; $150,000 to restore the Augusta Historic Theater in Georgia; and $2 million for a statue of a Roman god in Birmingham, Alabama.[1] **Populist legislation** involves widespread benefits but concentrated costs. Populist legislation usually has a tough time getting approved because the widespread group that benefits typically remains rationally ignorant about the proposed legislation, so these voters provide little political support. But the concentrated group who would get whacked

1. Robert Novak, "Senate Sneaks Preserve Pork," *New York Post,* 19 April 2007.

>> $50,000 federal subsidy for a tattoo-removal program in California = pork-barrel spending

by the taxes objects strenuously. Most economists agree that tort-reform legislation, for example, would benefit the economy as a whole by limiting product liability lawsuits, reducing insurance costs, and bringing some goods to the market that, because of liability suits, have all but disappeared, such as personal aircraft. But trial lawyers, the group that would be most harmed by such limits, have successfully blocked reforms for years. Because the small group that bears the cost is savvy about the impact of the proposed legislation but those who would reap the benefits remain rationally ignorant, populist legislation has little chance of approval. The only way such measures get approved is if some political entrepreneur raises enough visibility about the issue to gather public attention and votes. For example, a candidate for governor may run against high electric bills. The key is to somehow get the issue on voters' radar screens.

Finally, **competing-interest legislation** involves both concentrated benefits and concentrated costs, such as labor unions versus employers, or steel makers versus steel-using industries. These are the fierce political battles because both sides have a heavy stake in the outcome.

Exhibit 3 arrays the four categories of distributions. Across the top, benefits of legislation are either *widespread* or *concentrated*, and along the left margin, costs are either *widespread* or

competing-interest legislation legislation that confers concentrated benefits on one group by imposing concentrated costs on another group

Exhibit 3

Categories of Legislation Based on the Distribution of Costs and Benefits

Distribution of Costs \ Distribution of Benefits	Widespread	Concentrated
Widespread	1. Traditional Public Goods —National defense 	2. Special Interest —Farm subsidies 
Concentrated	3. Populist —Tort reform 	4. Competing Interest —Labor union issues 

Farm Subsidies

In much of America, milk prices are the most regulated of farm products. Explaining the intricacies of the price support program for milk takes up three volumes of the *Code of Federal Regulations*. Interpreting and administering regulations employ hundreds of people at the U.S. Department of Agriculture—more than oversee the entire federal budget in the Office of Management and Budget.

Exhibit 4 presents the market for milk. Without government intervention, suppose the market price of milk would average $1.50 per gallon for a market quantity of 100 million gallons per month. In long-run equilibrium, dairy farmers would earn a normal profit in this competitive industry. Consumer surplus is shown by the blue-shaded area. Recall that consumer surplus is the difference between the most that consumers would be willing to pay for that quantity and the amount they actually pay.

Now suppose the dairy lobby persuades Congress that milk should not sell for less than $2.50 per gallon. The higher price encourages farmers to increase their quantity supplied to 150 million gallons per month. Consumers, however, reduce their quantity demanded to 75 million gallons per month. To make the floor price of $2.50 stick, the government must buy the 75 million gallons of surplus milk generated by the floor price or somehow get dairy farmers to cut output to only 75 million gallons per month. For example, to reduce supply, the government could buy dairy cows from farmers (as occurred in the 1980s).

The dairy industry is supported by other legislation. Some states ensure even higher price floors than those imposed by the federal government. Foreign imports of liquid milk are tightly restricted. Other laws promote the consumption of dairy products more generally. For example, some states prohibit restaurants from serving margarine instead of butter unless the customer specifically asks for margarine.

The profound long-run problem for dairy farmers is that technological breakthroughs, such as genetically engineered hormones that stimulate milk production, have increased the milk yield per cow, making each farmer far more productive. Yet, despite the widely advertised "Got milk?" and milk-mustache campaigns, milk consumption remains flat. The combination of increased supply and stagnant demand puts downward pressure on the price.

SOURCES: "Farm Subsidies: Uncle Sam's Teat," *Economist,* 7 September 2006; Juliane Von Reppert-Bismark, "Europe Faults U.S. Farm Proposal," *Wall Street Journal,* 2 February 2007; "Washington Harvest," *Economist,* 27 March 2007; and the U.S. Department of Agriculture's dairy policy site at http://www.ers.usda.gov/Briefing/Dairy/Policy.htm.

Exhibit 4

Effects of Milk Price Supports

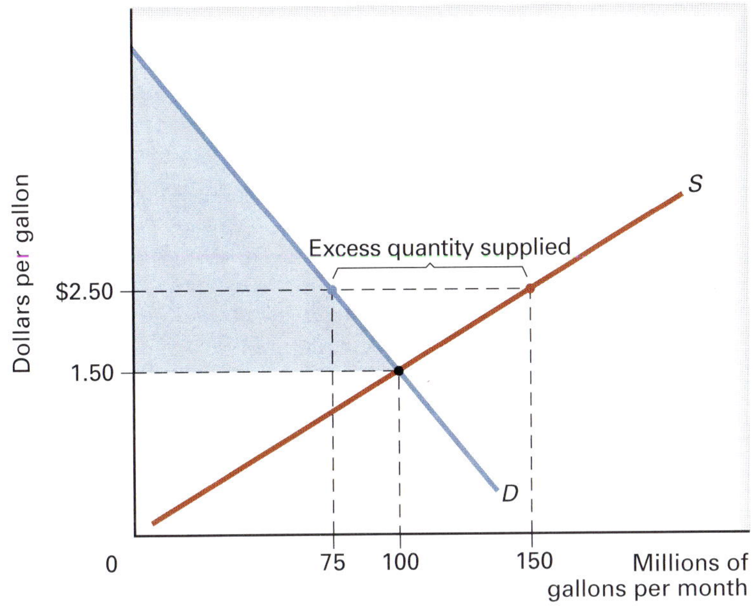

concentrated. Box 1 shows *traditional public-goods legislation,* such as national defense, with both widespread benefits and widespread costs. Box 2 shows *special-interest legislation,* such as farm subsidies, with concentrated benefits but widespread costs. Box 3 shows *populist legislation,* such as tort reform, with widespread benefits but concentrated costs. And box 4 shows *competing-interest legislation,* such as labor union issues, with both concentrated benefits and concentrated costs.

Rent Seeking

An important feature of representative democracy is the incentive and political power it offers interest groups to increase their wealth, either through direct transfers or through favorable public expenditures and regulations. Special-interest groups, such as dairy farmers, trial lawyers, and other producers, seek from government some special advantage or some outright transfer or subsidy. Such benefits are often called *rents* because they exceed what the producer would require to supply the product. Thus, rents represent earnings that exceed opportunity cost. The activity that interest groups undertake to secure these special favors from government is called *rent seeking,* a term already introduced.

The government frequently bestows some special advantage on a producer or group of producers, and abundant resources are expended to acquire these advantages. For example, *political action committees,* known more popularly as PACs, contribute millions to congressional campaigns. About 4,000 PACs try to shape federal legislation. The top contributors recently included the tobacco lobby and the American Trial Lawyers Association. Tobacco interests would like to influence cigarette legislation, and lawyers fear reforms that would limit liability lawsuits.

To the extent that special-interest groups engage in rent seeking, they shift resources from productive endeavors that create output and income to activities that focus more on transferring income to their special interests. *Resources employed to persuade government to redistribute income and wealth to special interests are unproductive because they do nothing to increase total output and usually end up reducing it.* Often many firms compete for the same government advantage, thereby wasting still more resources. If the advantage conferred by government on some special-interest group requires higher income taxes, the earnings people expect from working and investing fall, so they may work less and invest less. If this happens, productive activity declines.

As a firm's profitability relies more and more on decisions made in Washington, resources are diverted from productive activity to rent seeking, or lobbying efforts. One firm may thrive because it secured some special government advantage at a critical time; another firm may fail because its managers were more concerned with productive efficiency than with rent seeking.

"Resources employed to persuade government to redistribute income and wealth to special interests are unproductive because they do nothing to increase total output and usually end up reducing it."

Think of the economy's output in a particular period as depicted by a pie. The pie represents the total value of goods and services produced. In answering the what, how, and for whom questions introduced in Chapter 2, policy makers have three alternatives: (1) they can introduce reforms that increase the size of the pie (that is, positive-sum changes); (2) they can decide simply to carve up the existing pie differently (redistribute income); or (3) they can start fighting over how the pie is carved up, causing some of it to end up on the floor (negative-sum changes).

Special-interest groups have little incentive to make the economy more efficient. In fact, they usually support legislation that transfers wealth to them even if the economy's overall efficiency declines. For example, suppose that the American Trial Lawyers Association is able to change product liability laws in a way that boosts lawyers' annual incomes by a total of $1 billion, or about $1,800 for each of the 550,000 lawyers in private practice. Suppose, too, that this measure drives up insurance premiums, raising the total cost of production by, say, $2 billion per year. Lawyers themselves have to bear part of this higher cost, but because they account for only about 1 percent of the spending in the economy, they bear only about 1 percent of the $2 billion in higher costs, or about $20 million. This amounts to $36 per lawyer per year. Thus, the legislation is a good deal for lawyers because their annual incomes grow about $1,800 each but their annual costs increase only about $36 each, resulting in the net average gain of $1,764 per lawyer in private practice. Much special-interest legislation leads to a net reduction in social welfare. For example, some of the nation's best minds are occupied with devising schemes to avoid taxes or divert income to favored groups at the expense of market efficiency.

There are hundreds of special-interest groups representing farmers, physicians, lawyers, teachers, manufacturers, barbers, and so on.

LO3 The Underground Economy

A government subsidy promotes production, as we saw in the case study on milk price supports. Conversely, a tax discourages production. Perhaps it would be more accurate to say that when government taxes productive activity, less production gets *reported*. If you ever worked as a waitress or waiter, did you faithfully report all your tip income to the Internal Revenue Service? If not, your unreported income became part of the underground economy. The **underground economy** describes all market activity that goes unreported either to avoid taxes or because the activity itself is illegal. Income arising in the underground economy ranges from unreported tips to the earnings of drug dealers.

underground economy
an expression used to describe market activity that goes unreported either because it is illegal or because those involved want to evade taxes

Taxing productive activity has two effects. First, resource owners may supply less of the taxed resource because the after-tax wage declines. Second, to evade taxes, some people shift from the formal, reported economy to an underground, "off the books" economy. Thus, when the government taxes market exchange and the income it generates, less market activity and less income get reported.

We should take care to distinguish between tax *avoidance* and tax *evasion*. Tax avoidance is a *legal* attempt to arrange one's economic affairs to pay the least tax possible, such as buying municipal bonds because they yield interest free of federal income taxes. Tax evasion, on the other hand, is *illegal;* it takes the form of either failing to file a tax return or filing a fraudulent return by understating income or overstating deductions. Research around the world indicates that the underground economy grows more when (1) government regulations increase, (2) tax rates increase, and (3) government corruption is more widespread.[2]

The U.S. Commerce Department estimates that official figures capture only about 90 percent of U.S. income. And an Internal Revenue Service survey estimates that only about 90 percent of taxable income gets reported on tax returns. These studies suggest an underground economy of about $1.4 trillion in 2007.

2. For a summary of these studies, see Simon Johnson et al., "Regulatory Discretion and the Unofficial Economy," *American Economic Review* 88 (May 1998): 387–392.

"Off the books" economic activity generates zero tax dollars.

Those who pursue rent-seeking activity and those involved in the underground economy view government from opposite sides. Rent seekers want government to become actively involved in transferring wealth to them, but those in the underground economy want to avoid government contact. *Subsidies and other advantages bestowed by government draw some groups closer to government; taxes drive some others underground.*

LO4 Bureaucracy and Representative Democracy

Elected representatives approve legislation, but the task of implementing that legislation is typically left to bureaus, which are government departments and agencies whose activities are financed by appropriations from legislative bodies.

Ownership and Funding of Bureaus

We can get a better feel for government bureaus by comparing them to corporations. Stockholders own a corporation and share any profit or loss. Stockholders also get to vote on important corporate matters based on the number of shares owned. Corporate shares can be bought and sold in the stock market: ownership is *transferable* to whomever buys the shares. Taxpayers are in a sense the "owners" of government bureaus. If the bureau earns a "profit," taxes may decline; if the bureau operates at a "loss," as most do, this loss must be made up by taxes. Each taxpayer has just one vote, regardless of the taxes he or she pays. Ownership in the bureau is surrendered only if the taxpayer dies or moves out of the jurisdiction, but ownership is not transferable—it cannot be bought or sold directly.

Because public goods and services are not sold in markets, government bureaus receive less consumer feedback and have less incentive to act on any feedback they do receive.

Whereas corporations cover their costs if enough people purchase their products, bureaus are usually financed by government appropriation. Most funding comes from taxpayers. Bureaus do not have to meet a market test. Some bureaus get revenue through user charges, such as admission fees to state parks or tuition at state colleges, but even these bureaus typically rely on taxes for part of their revenue. Because of these differences in the forms of ownership and in the sources of funding, bureaus have different incentives than do for-profit firms, so they are likely to behave differently, as we'll see next.

Ownership and Organizational Behavior

A central assumption of economics is that people behave rationally and respond to economic incentives. The more tightly compensation is linked to individual incentives, the more people behave in accordance with those incentives. For example, if a letter carrier's pay is based on customer satisfaction, the carrier will make a greater effort to deliver mail promptly and intact.

A private firm receives a steady stream of consumer feedback. If the price is too high or too low to clear the market, surpluses or shortages become obvious. Not only is consumer feedback abundant, but the firm's owners have a profit incentive to act on that information to satisfy consumer wants. The promise of profits also creates incentives to produce output at the least cost. Thus, the firm's owners stand to gain from any improvement in customer satisfaction or any reduction in cost.

Because public goods and services are not sold in markets, government bureaus receive less consumer feedback and have less incentive to act on any feedback they do receive. There are usually no prices and no obvious shortages or surpluses. For example, how would you know whether there was a shortage or a surplus of police protection in your community? Not only do bureaus receive less consumer feedback than firms do, bureaus have less incentive to act on the information available. If a corporation is run poorly, someone could buy most of the shares, improve performance, then reap the benefits of a higher share price. Because the ownership of bureaus is not transferable, there is less incentive to eliminate waste and inefficiency.

Voters could pressure their elected representatives to make bureaus more responsive. But this discipline is rather crude. Most voters remain rationally ignorant about government performance in part because each voter has little impact on the outcome and

bureaus government agencies charged with implementing legislation and financed by appropriations from legislative bodies each stands to gain so little from any increase in efficiency. For example, suppose that you are one of a million taxpayers in a city and you learn that by having FedEx Kinko's do all public copying, the city could save $1 million a year. If, through letters to the editor and calls to local officials, you somehow convince the city to adopt this cost-saving measure, you, as a typical taxpayer, would save yourself about a dollar a year in taxes.

Voters can leave a jurisdiction if they believe government is inefficient. This mechanism, whereby people "vote with their feet," does promote some efficiency and consumer satisfaction at the state and local levels, but it's also crude. What if you like some public programs but not others? Moreover, voters dissatisfied with the biggest spender and taxer, the federal government, cannot easily vote with their feet. Even if you were to move abroad, you, as a U.S. citizen, must still pay U.S. federal taxes on your worldwide income (nearly all other countries tax only domestic income of those living abroad).

Because of differences between public and private organizations—in the owners' ability both to transfer ownership and to appropriate profits—we expect bureaus to be less concerned with satisfying consumer demand or with minimizing costs than private firms are. A variety of empirical studies compares costs for products that are provided by both public bureaus and private firms, such as garbage collection. Of those studies that show a difference, most find private firms are more efficient.

Bureaucratic Objectives

Assuming that bureaus are not simply at the beck and call of the legislature—that is, assuming that bureaucrats have some autonomy—what sort of objectives do *they* pursue? The traditional view is that bureaucrats are "public servants," who try to serve the public as best they can. No doubt many public employees do just that, but is this a realistic assumption for bureaucrats more generally? Why should we assume self-sacrificing behavior by public-sector employees when we make no such assumption about private-sector employees?

One widely discussed theory of bureaucratic behavior claims that bureaus try to *maximize their budget,* for along with a bigger budget come size, prestige, amenities, staff, and pay—all features that are valued by bureaucrats.[3] According to this view, bureaus are monopoly suppliers of their output to elected officials. Rather than charge a price per unit, bureaus offer the entire amount as a package deal in return for the requested appropriation. This theory assumes that the elected officials have only limited ability to dig into the budget and cut particular items. If elected officials do try to cut the bureau's budget, the bureau may threaten to make those cuts as painful to constituents as possible. For example, if city officials attempt to slow the growth of the school budget, school bureaucrats, rather than increase teaching loads or reducing pay raises, may threaten to eliminate kindergarten, abolish the high school football team, disband the school band, or cut textbook orders. If such threats force elected officials to back off, the government budget turns out to be larger than the public would prefer. *Budget maximization results in a larger budget than that desired by the median voter.* The key to this argument is that bureaus are monopoly suppliers of public goods and elected officials have only limited ability to cut that budget. If taxpayers have alternatives in the private sector or if elected officials can dig into the budget, the monopoly power of the bureau is diminished.

> BUREAUS ARE MONOPOLY SUPPLIERS OF PUBLIC GOODS AND ELECTED OFFICIALS HAVE ONLY LIMITED ABILITY TO CUT THAT BUDGET.

Private Versus Public Production

Simply because some goods and services are *financed* by the government, this does not mean that they must be *produced* by the government. Elected officials may contract directly with private firms to produce public output. For example, city officials may contract with a private firm to collect garbage for the city. In some jurisdictions, for-profit firms now provide everything from fire protection to prisons. Elected officials may also use a combination of bureaus and firms to produce the desired output. For example, the Pentagon, a giant bureau, hires and trains military personnel, yet contracts with private firms to develop and produce various weapon systems. State governments typically hire private contractors to build roads but employ state workers to maintain them. The mix of firms and bureaus varies over time and across jurisdictions, but the trend is

3. William A. Niskanen Jr., in *Bureaucracy and Representative Government* (New York: Aldine-Atherton, 1971).

toward increased *privatization,* or production by the private sector, of public goods and services.

When governments produce public goods and services, they are using *the internal organization of the government*—the bureaucracy—to supply the product. When governments contract with private firms to produce public goods and services, they are using *the market* to supply the product. While private firms have more incentives to be efficient than bureaus do, public officials sometimes prefer dealing with bureaus. Public officials may have more control over the bureau than over a private firm. Bureaus may also offer public officials more opportunities to appoint friends and political supporters to government jobs.

In situations where it would be difficult to specify a contract for the public good in question, a bureau may be more responsive to public concerns than a for-profit firm would be. Suppose the service provided by social workers is put out for bid. The firm that wins the bid may be tempted to skimp on quality, particularly if quality can be determined only by direct observation at the time the service is provided. The governments would have difficulty monitoring the quality provided by a private contractor. The services of social workers might be better provided by a government bureau. Because profit is not its goal, a bureau may be less inclined to minimize cost by reducing quality. For example, one study found that privately-operated juvenile correction facilities in Florida had lower costs but experienced higher rates of recidivism than state-operated juvenile correction facilities. The lower costs of privately operated facilities were more than offset by the increased recidivism, making state operation the better choice.[4]

Final Word

Governments attempt to address market failures in the private economy. But simply turning problems of perceived market failure over to government may not always be the best solution, because government has limitations and failings of its own. Participation in markets is based on voluntary exchange. Governments, however, have the legal power to enforce public choices. We should employ at least as high a standard in judging the performance of government, where allocations have the force of law, as we do in judging the private market, where allocations are decided by voluntary exchange between consenting parties. In other words, we should scrutinize a system that is compulsory at least as much as we scrutinize a system that is voluntary. After all, nobody is forcing you to buy tofu, but if you refuse to pay taxes to fund public programs you may not like, you could go to prison.

4. Patrick Bayer and David Pozen, "The Effectiveness of Juvenile Correction Facilities: Public Versus Private Management," *Journal of Law and Economics* 48 (October 2005): 549–89.

$1 million < The amount the federal government spends annually on paper clips

60% < The percentage of the world's 200 independent nations that are democracies

The amount of taxable income that the IRS estimates is actually reported. > **90%**

The estimated value of the underground economy in 2007. > **$1.4 trillion**

The amount the federal government budgeted to restore the Augusta National Theater in Georgia. > **$150,000**

CHAPTER 17

Externalities *and* the Environment

Learning Outcomes

- LO1 Define externalities and explain the common-pool problem
- LO2 Explain the optimal level of pollution
- LO3 Assess the role of environmental problems in the economy
- LO4 Describe positive externalities

"Environmental problems are all negative externalities, which result from the actions of producers or consumers that affect many others."

The rivers in Jakarta, Indonesia, are dead—killed by acid, alcohol, and oil. Coral reefs in the South Pacific are being ripped apart by dynamite fishing. The tropical rainforest is shrinking because of slash-and-burn claims on the land's resources. The build up of greenhouse gases threatens to warm the oceans and near-surface air. Some streams in Colorado are still considered toxic from gold mining that ended more than a century ago. What does all this have to do with economics? These environmental problems are all negative externalities, which result from the actions of producers or consumers that affect many others. Markets can allocate resources efficiently only as long as property rights are well defined and can be easily enforced. But property rights to clean water, air, and soil, to fish in the ocean, to peace and quiet, and to scenic vistas are hard to establish and enforce. This lack of property rights to some resources results in externalities.

Externalities may be either negative, such as air and water pollution, or positive, such as the general improvement in the civic climate that results from better education. This chapter discusses externalities and explores how public policies can reduce negative externalities and increase positive externalities.

What do you think?

Government regulation is the only way to protect citizens' environmental rights.

Strongly Disagree 1 2 3 4 5 6 7 *Strongly Agree*

Topics discussed in Chapter 17 include:

- Exhaustible resources
- Renewable resources
- Common-pool problem
- Private property rights
- Optimal pollution
- Marginal social cost
- Marginal social benefit
- Coase theorem
- Markets for pollution rights
- Environmental protection

LO1 Externalities and the Common-Pool Problem

Let's begin by distinguishing between exhaustible resources and renewable resources. An **exhaustible resource**, such as oil or coal, does not renew itself and so is available in a finite amount. Technology may improve the ability to extract these resources, but each gallon of oil burned is gone forever. Sooner or later, all oil wells will run dry. The world's oil reserves are *exhaustible*.

exhaustible resource
a resource in fixed supply, such as crude oil or coal

Renewable Resources

A resource is renewable if, when used conservatively, it can be drawn on indefinitely. Thus, timber is a renewable resource if trees are cut at sustainable rates and replaced with seedlings. The atmosphere and rivers are renewable resources to the extent that they can absorb and neutralize a certain level of pollutants. More generally, biological resources like fish, game, forests, rivers, grasslands, and agricultural soil are renewable if managed appropriately.

Some renewable resources are also open-access resources, an idea introduced in the previous chapter. An open-access resource is rival in consumption, but exclusion is costly. Fish caught in the ocean, for example, are not available for others to catch, so fish are rival in consumption. Yet it would be difficult, if not impossible, for a person or a firm to "own" fish still swimming in the open ocean and to prevent others from catching them, so ocean fish are nonexclusive. An open-access good is often subject to the common-pool problem, which results because people harvest a resource as long as marginal benefit exceeds marginal cost. For example, people will fish the oceans as long as the marginal benefit of catching more fish exceeds the marginal cost. Practically speaking, people will fish until the oceans become "fished out." Open-access goods are overfished, overhunted, overharvested, and overused. Because the atmosphere is an open-access resource, it's used as a dump for unwanted gases. Air pollution is a negative externality imposed on society by polluters. The problem is that people exploit any resource as long as their personal marginal benefit exceeds their personal marginal cost. As we'll see, personal marginal cost ignores costs imposed on others.

renewable resource
a resource that regenerates itself and so can be used indefinitely if used conservatively, such as a properly managed forest

common-pool problem
unrestricted access to a resource results in overuse; use stops only when the marginal benefit drops to zero

In a market system, specific individuals usually own the rights to resources and therefore have a strong interest in using those resources efficiently. *Private property rights,* a term introduced in Chapter 2, allow individuals to use resources or to charge others for their use. Private property rights are defined and enforced by government, by informal social actions, and by ethical norms. But because defining and enforcing property rights to open-access resources, such as the air, are quite costly or even impossible, these resources usually are not owned as private property.

Pollution and other negative externalities arise because there are no practical, enforceable, private property rights to open-access resources, such as the air. Market prices usually fail to include the costs that negative externalities impose on society. For example, the price you pay for a gallon of gasoline does not reflect the costs imposed by the greenhouse gases, sootier air, and the greater traffic congestion your driving creates. Electric rates do not reflect the negative externalities, or external costs, caused by fossil-fueled power plants. Note that externalities are unintended side effects of actions that are themselves useful and purposeful. Electricity producers, for example, did not go into business to pollute.

Resolving the Common-Pool Problem

Users of the atmosphere, waterways, wildlife, or other open-access resources tend to ignore the impact of their use on the resource's renewal ability. As quality and quantity diminish from overuse, the resource grows scarcer and could disappear. For example, Georges Bank, located off the New England coast, long one of the world's most productive fishing grounds, became so depleted by overfishing that by the 1990s the catch was down 85 percent from peak years. Tuna, once abundant in the Mediterranean, now faces extinction there.[1] The

1. Elisabeth Rosenthal, "Tuna Vanishing from Mediterranean," *International Herald Tribune,* 8 June 2006.

Icelandic Fishing Regulation

The Icelandic government realized that it would have to curb the capacity of its own fleet. But the fishermen compensated by buying more trawlers. Then the government restricted the size of the fleet and the number of days at sea; the fishermen responded by buying larger, more efficient gear. The cod stocks continued to decline. In 1984, the government introduced quotas on species per vessel per season. This was a controversial and often wasteful system. A groundfish hauled up from 50 fathoms [300 feet] is killed by the change in pressure. But if it is a cod and the cod quota has been used up, it is thrown overboard. Or if the price of cod is low that week and cod happens to come in the haddock net, the fishermen will throw them overboard because they do not want to use up their cod quota when they are not getting a good price.[2]

United Nations reports that 11 of the world's 15 primary fishing grounds are seriously depleted.

By imposing restrictions on resource use, government regulations may reduce the common-pool problem. Output restrictions or taxes could force people to use the resource at a rate that is socially optimal. For example, in the face of the tendency to overfish and to catch fish before they are sufficiently mature, the U.S. government has imposed a variety of restrictions on the fishing industry. The laws limit the total catch, the size of fish, the length of the fishing season, the equipment used, and other aspects of the business.

More generally, when imposing and enforcing private property rights would be too costly, government regulations may improve allocative efficiency. For example, stop signs and traffic lights allocate the scarce space at intersections, minimum size restrictions control lobster fishing, hunting seasons control the stock of game, and enforced study hours may calm the din in the college dormitory.

But not all regulations are equally efficient. For example, fishing authorities sometimes limit the total industry catch and allow all firms to fish until that total is reached. Consequently, when the fishing season opens, there is a mad scramble to catch as much as possible before the industry limit is reached. Because time is of the essence, fishing boats make no effort to fish selectively. And the catch reaches processors all at once, creating congestion throughout the supply chain. Also, each firm has an incentive to expand its fishing fleet to catch more in those precious few weeks. Thus, large fleets of technologically efficient fishing vessels operate for a few weeks until the limit is reached and then sit in port for the rest of the year. Each operator is acting rationally, but the collective effect of the regulation is grossly inefficient in terms of social welfare.

Ocean fish remain a common-pool resource because firms have not yet been able to establish and enforce rights to particular schools of fish. But advances in technology may some day allow the creation of private property rights to ocean fish, migrating birds, and other open-access resources. Establishing property rights to cattle on the Great Plains once seemed impossible, but the invention of barbed wire allowed ranchers to fence the range. In a sense, barbed wire tamed the Wild West.

2. Mark Kurlansky, *Cod: A Biography of the Fish That Changed the World* (Walker & Co., 1997), p. 172.

LO[2] Optimal Level of Pollution

Though the science is not fully resolved, fossil fuel used to power the likes of automobiles and electricity generators produces carbon dioxide, which mixes with other greenhouse gases that contribute to global warming. Electricity production from fossil fuels, therefore, involves the external cost of using the atmosphere as a gas dump. This section considers a way to analyze such externalities.

External Costs with Fixed Technology

Suppose *D* in Exhibit 1 depicts the demand for electricity. Recall that a demand curve reflects consumers' marginal benefit of each quantity. The lower horizontal line reflects the marginal private cost of electricity using fossil fuels. If producers base their pricing and output decisions on their private marginal costs, the equilibrium quantity per month is 50 million kilowatt-hours and the equilibrium price is $0.10 per kilowatt-hour. At that price and quantity, identified by point *a*, the marginal private cost of production just equals the marginal benefit enjoyed by consumers of electricity.

Exhibit 1

Negative Externalities: The Market for Electricity in the Midwest

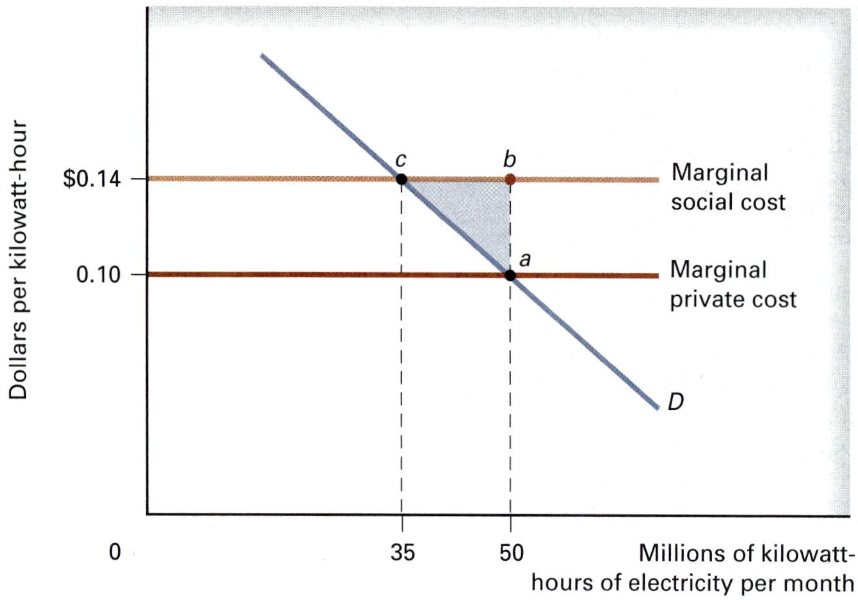

Electricity production involves not only the private cost of the resources employed but also the external cost of using the atmosphere as a dump for greenhouse gases. Suppose that the marginal external cost imposed on the environment by the generation of electricity is $0.04 per kilowatt-hour. If the only way to cut emissions is to reduce electricity production, then the relationship between electricity production and pollution is fixed; the pollution in this case occurs with fixed-production technology.

The vertical distance between the marginal private cost curve and the marginal social cost curve in Exhibit 1 shows the marginal external cost of $0.04 per kilowatt-hour. The marginal social cost includes both the marginal private cost and the marginal external cost that production imposes on society. Because the marginal external cost here is assumed to be a constant $0.04 per kilowatt-hour, the two cost curves are parallel. Notice that at the private-sector equilibrium output level of 50 million kilowatt-hours, the marginal social cost, identified at point *b*, exceeds society's marginal benefit of electricity, identified on the demand curve at point *a*. The 50-millionth kilowatt-hour of electricity costs society $0.14 but yields only $0.10 of marginal benefit. Because the marginal social cost exceeds the marginal benefit, too much electricity is produced.

fixed-production technology occurs when the relationship between the output rate and the generation of an externality is fixed; the only way to reduce the externality is to reduce the output

marginal social cost the sum of the marginal private cost and the marginal external cost of production or consumption

The efficient quantity of 35 million kilowatt-hours is found where the demand, or marginal benefit, curve intersects the marginal social cost curve. This intersection is identified at point *c*. How could output be restricted to the socially efficient amount? If regulators knew the demand and marginal cost curves, they could simply limit production to 35 million kilowatt-hours, the efficient quantity. Or, on each kilowatt hour produced, they could impose a tax equal to the marginal external cost of $0.04. Such a pollution tax would lift the marginal private cost curve up to the marginal social cost curve. Thus, the tax would bring private costs in line with social costs.

With a tax of $0.04 per kilowatt-hour, the equilibrium combination of price and output moves from point *a* to point *c*. The price rises from $0.10 to $0.14 per kilowatt-hour, and output falls to 35 million kilowatt-hours. Setting the tax equal to the marginal external cost results in the efficient level of output. At point *c*, the marginal social cost of production equals the marginal benefit. Notice that greenhouse gas emissions are not eliminated at point *c*, but the utilities no longer generate electricity for which marginal social cost exceeds marginal benefit. The total social gain from reducing production to the socially optimal level is shown by the blue-shaded triangle in Exhibit 1. This triangle also measures the total social cost of allowing firms to ignore the external cost of production. Although Exhibit 1 offers a tidy solution, the external costs of greenhouse gases often cannot be easily calculated or taxed. At times, government intervention may result in more or less production than the optimal solution requires.

External Costs with Variable Technology

The previous example assumes that the only way to reduce greenhouse gases is to reduce output. But power companies, particularly in the long run, can usually change their resource mix to reduce emissions for any given level of electricity. If pollution can be reduced by altering the production process rather than by simply adjusting the quantity, these externalities are said to be produced under conditions of **variable technology**. With variable technology, the idea is to find the optimal level of pollution for a given quantity of electricity.

Let's look at Exhibit 2. The horizontal axis measures greenhouse gas emissions for a given level of electricity production. Emissions can be reduced by adopting cleaner production technology. Yet the production of cleaner air, like the production of other goods, is subject to diminishing returns. Cutting emissions of the most offensive greenhouse gases may involve simply changing the fuel mix, but further reductions call for more sophisticated and more expensive processes. Thus, the marginal social cost of reducing greenhouse gases increases, as shown by the upward-sloping marginal social cost curve in Exhibit 2.

Exhibit 2

The Optimal Reduction in Greenhouse Gas Emissions

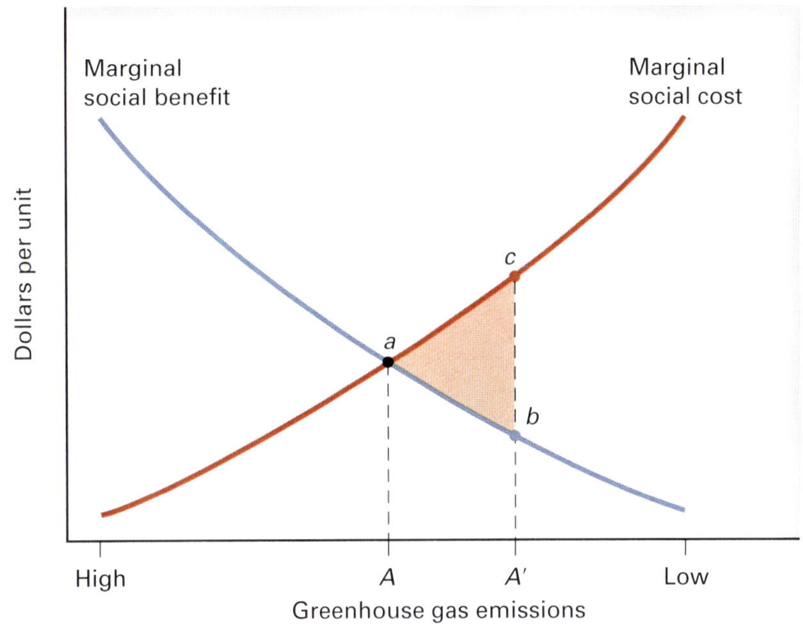

The **marginal social benefit** curve reflects the additional benefit society derives from greenhouse gas reductions. When emissions are high, an improvement can save lives and thus is valued by society more than when emissions are low. Cleaner air, like other goods, has a declining marginal benefit to society (though the total benefit still increases). The marginal social benefit curve from cleaner air therefore slopes downward, as shown in Exhibit 2.

The optimal level of air quality for a given quantity of electricity is found at point *a*, where the marginal social benefit of cleaner air equals the marginal social cost. In this example, the optimal level of greenhouse gas emissions is *A*. If firms made their production decisions based simply on their private cost—that is, if the emission cost is external to the firm—then firms would have no incentive to search for production methods that reduce greenhouse gas emission, so too much production would result.

What if government regulators decree that greenhouse gas emission levels should be no higher than *A*′? For example, suppose a law establishes *A*′ as the maximum acceptable level of emissions. The marginal social cost, identified as *c*, of achieving that level of air quality exceeds the marginal social benefit, identified as *b*. The total social waste associated with imposing a greater-than-optimal level of air quality is shown by the pink-shaded triangle, *abc*. This area is the total amount by which the additional social costs of cleaner air (associated with a move from A to A′) exceed the additional social benefits. Improving air quality benefits society only as long as the marginal social benefit of cleaner air exceeds its marginal social cost.

What would happen to the optimal level of emissions if either the marginal cost curve or the marginal benefit curve shifted? For example, suppose some technological breakthrough reduces the marginal cost of cutting greenhouse gas emissions. As shown in panel (a) of Exhibit 3 on the next page, the marginal social cost curve of reducing emissions would shift downward to *MSC*′, thereby reducing the optimal level of emissions from *A* to *A*′. *The simple logic is that the lower the marginal cost of reducing greenhouse gases, other things constant, the lower the optimal level of such emissions.*

An increase in the marginal benefit of air quality would have a similar effect. For example, suppose research indicates that the

variable technology occurs when the amount of externality generated at a given rate of output can be reduced by altering the production process

marginal social benefit the sum of the marginal private benefit and the marginal external benefit of production or consumption

Exhibit 3

Effect of Changes in Costs or Benefits of Reducing Greenhouse Gas Emissions

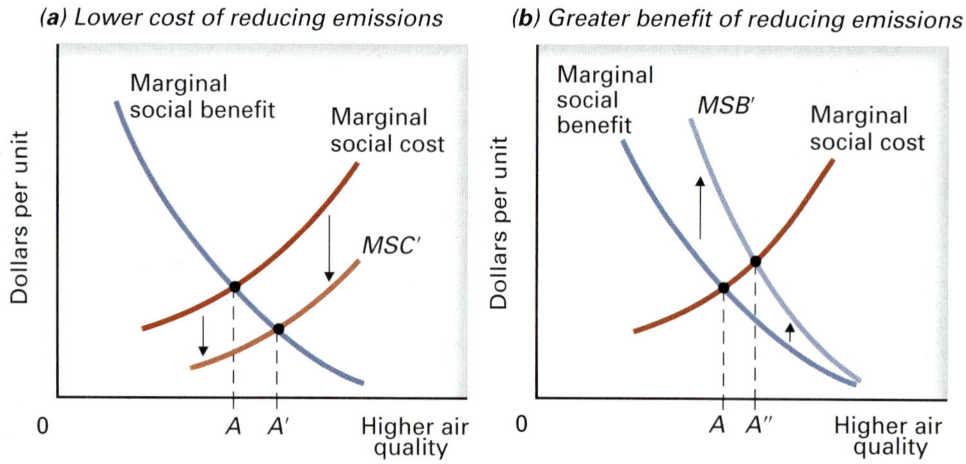

effects of a one degree increase in Earth's average temperature would be much more devastating than previously believed. This finding would increase the perceived benefits of reducing greenhouse gases. Thus, the marginal benefit of cleaner air would increase, as reflected in panel (b) of Exhibit 3 by an upward shift of the marginal social benefit curve to MSB′. As a result, the optimal level of air quality would increase. *The greater the marginal benefit of reducing greenhouse gases, other things constant, the lower the optimal level of emissions.* As another example, recent research indicates that deaths from heart and lung disease would decrease 0.7 percent in large U.S. cities if suspended particulates in the air decrease by just 1/100,000th of a gram per cubic meter of air.[3] This finding increases the perceived benefits of cleaner air, leading to an increase in the optimal quality of clean air.

The Coase Theorem

The traditional analysis of externalities assumes that market failures arise because people ignore the external effects of their actions. For example, suppose a manufacturer of heavy machinery is next door to a research laboratory that tests delicate equipment. The vibrations caused by the manufacturing process throw off the delicate equipment next door. Professor Ronald Coase, who won the Nobel Prize in 1991, would argue that the negative externality in this case is not necessarily imposed by the heavy machinery—rather, it arises from the incompatible activities of the two firms. The externality is the result of both vibrations created by the factory *and* the location of the testing lab next door. Solutions might include modifying the factory, moving the factory, making the test equipment more shock resistant, or moving the testing lab.

Coase theorem
as long as bargaining costs are low, an efficient solution to the problem of externalities is achieved by assigning property rights to one party or the other

3. Jonathan M. Samet et al., "Fine Particulate Air Pollution and Mortality in 20 U.S. Cities, 1987–1994," *New England Journal of Medicine*, 14 December 2000.

According to Coase, the efficient solution depends on which party can avoid the externality at the lower cost. Suppose it would cost $2 million for the factory to reduce vibrations enough for the lab to function normally. On the other hand, if the factory makes no changes, the lab can't insulate equipment enough to operate accurately, so the lab would have to relocate at a cost of $1 million. Based on this information, the least-cost solution would be for the testing lab to relocate at a cost of $1 million. Coase argues that, as long as transaction costs are low, the parties will reach the efficient solution if one party is assigned the property right. And here's Coase's special insight: *This efficient solution will be achieved regardless of which party gets the property right.*

Suppose the testing lab is granted the right to operate free of vibrations from next door, so the testing lab can force the factory to reduce its vibration. Rather than cut vibrations at a cost of $2 million, the factory can pay the lab to relocate. Any payment greater than $1 million but less than $2 million makes both sides better off, because the lab would receive more than its moving cost and the factory would pay less than its cost of reducing vibrations. Thus, the lab will move, which is the efficient outcome.

Alternatively, suppose the factory is granted the right to generate vibrations in its production process, regardless of the impact on the testing lab. For the factory, this means business as usual. Because the minimum payment the factory would accept to reduce vibrations is $2 million, the lab would rather relocate at a cost of $1 million. Thus, whether property rights are granted to the lab or to the factory, the lab will move, which is the efficient, or least-cost, solution. The Coase theorem says that as long as bargaining costs are small, merely assigning the property right will generate an efficient solution to an externality problem regardless of which party is assigned that right. A particular assignment determines which side bears the externality costs but does not affect the efficient outcome.

Inefficient outcomes do occur, however, when the transaction costs of arriving at a solution are high. For example, an airport located in a populated area would have difficulty negotiating noise levels with all the affected residents. Or peasants contemplating clearing a portion of the tropical rainforest would be unable to negotiate with the millions, and perhaps, billions, of people ultimately affected by that decision. *When the number of parties involved in the transaction is large, Coase's solution of assigning property rights may not be enough.*

Markets for Pollution Rights

According to the Coase theorem, the assignment of property rights is often sufficient to resolve the market failure typically associated with externalities. Additional government intervention is not necessary. If pollution can be easily monitored and polluters easily identified, the government may be able to achieve an efficient solution to the problem of pollution simply by assigning the right to pollute. To see how this could work, let's look at an example. Firms that dump into a river evidently value the ability to discharge waste in this way. For them, the river provides a low-cost outlet for by-products that otherwise would have to be disposed of at greater cost. The river provides a disposal service, and the demand curve for that service slopes downward, just like the demand for other resources.

The demand for the river as a discharge system is presented as *D* in Exhibit 4. The horizontal axis measures the tons of discharge dumped into the river per day, and the vertical axis measures firms' marginal benefits of disposing of their waste in this way. The demand curve thus measures the marginal value to firms of using the river as a disposal service. With no restrictions on river pollution—that is, if all firms were free to dump waste into the river—dumping would continue as long it provided firms some marginal benefit. This marginal benefit falls to zero in Exhibit 4 when 250 tons per day are discharged.

The river, like the atmosphere and the soil, can absorb and neutralize a certain amount of discharge per day without deteriorating in quality. What if voters make the public choice that the river should remain clean enough for swimming and fishing? Suppose engineers determine this level of water quality can be maintained as long as no more than 100 tons are discharged per day. Thus, the "supply" of

Exhibit 4

Optimal Allocation of Pollution Rights

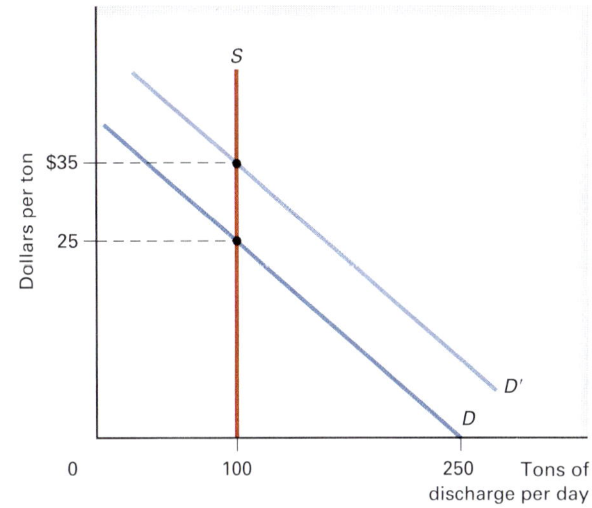

the discharge service provided by the river is fixed at 100 tons per day, shown by the vertical supply curve, *S*, in Exhibit 4.

If government regulators can easily identify polluters and monitor their behavior, authorities can allocate permits to discharge 100 tons per day. If polluters are simply given these permits (that is, if the price of permits is zero), there will be an excess demand for them, because the quantity supplied is 100 tons but the quantity demanded at a price of zero would be 250 tons. An alternative is to sell permits for 100 tons of pollution at the market-clearing price. The intersection of supply curve S and demand curve *D* yields a permit price of $25 per ton, which is the marginal value of discharging the 100th ton into the river each day. To most permit buyers, the marginal value of a permit exceeds $25 per ton.

The beauty of this system is that producers who value the discharge rights the most ultimately end up with them. Producers who attach a lower marginal value apparently have cheaper ways of resolving their waste problems, including changing production techniques. And if conservation groups, such as the Sierra Club, want a higher river quality than the government's standard, such as water clean enough to drink, they can purchase pollution permits but not exercise them.

What if additional firms spring up along the river and are willing to pay more than $25 per ton for pollution rights? This greater demand is reflected in Exhibit 4 by *D*′. This increase of demand would bid up the market price of pollution permits to, say, $35 per ton. Some existing permit holders would sell their rights to those who value them more. Regardless of

© MONTY BRINTON/CBS/LANDOV

the comings and goings of would-be polluters, the total quantity of discharge rights is restricted to 100 tons per day, so the river's quality will be maintained. Thus, *the value of pollution permits, but not the total amount of pollution, may fluctuate over time.*

If the right to pollute could be granted, monitored, and enforced, then what had been a negative externality problem could be solved through market allocation. Historically, the U.S. government had relied on setting discharge standards and fining offenders. But in 1989, a pollution rights market for fluorocarbon emissions was established and was followed in 1990 by a market for sulfur dioxide. During the 1990s, sulfur dioxide emissions in the nation fell by more than half, exceeding the goals of the authorizing legislation. So the market for pollution rights is alive and growing.[4] Even China is now experimenting with this approach. Some companies and even celebrities are using a variant of pollution rights to become "carbon neutral"—that is, by estimating their carbon emissions then offsetting this impact by paying for projects to neutralize, or "sop up," equivalent emissions.[5] For example, Delta Air Lines allows online ticket buyers to pay an extra $5.50 for domestic flights or $11 for international flights for tree plantings to help offset flight emissions. And the band Coldplay funded 10,000 mango trees in India to help sop up emissions related to the release of the band's CD, *A Rush of Blood to the Head*.[6]

command-and-control environmental regulations an approach that required polluters to adopt particular technologies to reduce emissions by specific amounts; inflexible regulations based on engineering standards that ignore each firm's unique ways of reducing pollution

Pollution Rights and Public Choice

Unfortunately, legislation dealing with pollution is affected by the same problems of representative democracy that trouble other public policy questions. Big polluters have a special interest in government proposals relating to pollution, and they fight measures to reduce pollution. But members of the public remain rationally ignorant about pollution legislation. So pollution regulations may be less in accord with the public interest than with the special interests of polluters. This is why a portion of pollution permits are often *given* to existing firms or offered below market prices. For example, under the sulfur dioxide program, the nation's 101 dirtiest power plants receive credits equal to between 30 and 50 percent of the pollution they emitted before the program began. Because they received something of value, polluters were less inclined to oppose the legislation. Once permits were granted, some recipients found it profitable to sell their permits to other firms that valued them more. Thus, a market emerged that led to an efficient allocation of pollution permits. According to some analysts, the sulfur dioxide program saves up to $3 billion annually compared with the old system. More generally, a system of marketable pollution rights can reduce the cost of pollution abatement by as much as 75 percent.

Before 1990, **command-and-control environmental regulations** were the norm—an approach that

4. For a discussion of the market for sulfur dioxide emissions, see Paul Joskow, Richard Schmalensee, and Elizabeth Bailey, "The Market for Sulfur-Dioxide Emissions," *American Economic Review* 88 (September 1998): 669–685.

5. See Andrew Revkin, "Carbon-Neutral Is Hip, But Is It Green?" *New York Times,* 29 April 2007.

6. Michael Hill, "Can Planting a Tree Absolve Your Eco-Sins?" *Arizona Republic,* 28 May 2007.

required polluters, such as electric utilities, to introduce particular technologies to reduce emissions by specific amounts. These regulations were based on engineering standards and did not recognize unique circumstances across generating plants, such as plant design, ability to introduce scrubbers, and the ease of switching to low-sulfur fuels. But the market for pollution rights reflects an economic efficiency approach that offers each electric utility the flexibility to reduce emissions in the most cost-effective manner, given its unique operation. Firms with the lowest costs of emission control have an incentive to implement the largest reduction in emissions and then sell unused pollution permits to those with greater control costs.

Now that you know something about the theory of externalities, let's turn to an important application of the theory—environmental protection.

LO3 Environmental Protection

Federal efforts to address the common-pool problems of air, water, and soil pollution are coordinated by the Environmental Protection Agency (EPA). When the EPA was created in 1970, it began with about 4,000 employees and a budget of $1.1 billion (in 2008 dollars). By 2008, it had about 17,300 employees and a budget exceeding $7.2 billion.

According to EPA estimates, compliance with pollution-control regulations cost U.S. producers and consumers about $270 billion in 2008, an amount equivalent to 2 percent of gross domestic product, the market value of all final goods and services produced in the economy. We can divide pollution control spending into three categories: spending for air pollution abatement, spending for water pollution abatement, and spending for solid waste disposal. About 40 percent of the pollution control expenditures in the United States goes toward cleaner air, another 40 percent goes toward cleaner water, and 20 percent goes toward disposing of solid waste. In this section, we consider, in turn, air pollution, water pollution, Superfund activities, and disposing of solid waste.

Air Pollution

In the Clean Air Act of 1970 and in subsequent amendments, Congress set national standards for the amount of pollution that could be released into the atmosphere. Congress thereby recognized the atmosphere as an economic resource, which, like other resources, has alternative uses. The air can be used as a source of life-giving oxygen, as a prism for viewing breathtaking vistas, or as a dump for carrying away unwanted soot and gases. The 1970 act gave Americans the right to breathe air of a certain quality and at the same time gave producers the right to emit particular amounts of specified pollutants. Research shows that people value clean air and are willing to pay more to live in communities with less pollution.[7]

Smog is the most visible form of air pollution. Automobile emissions account for 40 percent of smog. Another 40 percent comes from consumer products, such as paint thinner, fluorocarbon sprays, dry-cleaning solvents, and baker's yeast by-products. Surprisingly, only 15 percent of smog comes from manufacturing. The 1970 Clean Air Act mandated a reduction of 90 percent in auto emissions, leaving it to the auto industry to achieve this target. At the time, automakers said the target was impossible. Between 1970 and 1990, however, average emissions of lead fell 97 percent, carbon monoxide emissions fell 41 percent, and sulfur dioxide emissions fell 25 percent. In fact, an EPA study concluded that because auto emissions and industrial smoke have been reduced so much, *air pollution on average is now greater indoors than outdoors.* For example, in the Los Angeles area, a smog alert, meaning the air reached dangerous levels, occurred on a weekly basis during the 1980s, but the city has not experienced a smog alert since 2003. U.S. air quality is now considered good compared to the air quality

4 Federal Environmental Laws:

Four federal laws and subsequent amendments underpin U.S. efforts to protect the environment:

- 1970 Clean Air Act
- 1972 Clean Water Act
- 1976 Resource Conservation and Recovery Act (which governs solid waste disposal)
- 1980 Superfund law (legislation focusing on toxic waste dumps)

7. Kenneth Chay and Michael Greenstone, "Does Air Quality Matter? Evidence from the Housing Market," *Journal of Political Economy* 113 (April 2005): 376–424.

economic efficiency approach an approach that offers each polluter the flexibility to reduce emissions as cost-effectively as possible, given its unique cost conditions; the market for pollution rights is an example in much of the world. For example, no U.S. city ranks among the world's worst in sulfur dioxide. Despite recent improvements in air quality, the United States is still a major source of fossil-fuel carbon dioxide emissions, a major greenhouse gas. As you can see from Exhibit 5, which shows the world's 25 worst nations in fossil-fuel carbon dioxide emissions per capita, the United States ranks fourth worst with 5.4 tons per capita.

AIR POLLUTION ON AVERAGE IS NOW GREATER INDOORS THAN OUTDOORS.

The following case study examines air pollution in the capital city of one developing country.

There have been efforts to address greenhouse gases on an international scale. A report by the Intergovernmental Panel on Climate Change, a group sponsored by the United Nations, was approved in May 2007 by more than 120 nations.[8] The study says, to fight global warming, the world must cut emissions of carbon dioxide and other greenhouse gases by (1) sharply improving energy efficiency in buildings, vehicles, and machines; (2) shifting from fossil fuels to nuclear, wind, solar, and other renewable energy sources; (3) preserving forests as absorbers of carbon dioxide, or as "carbon sinks"; and (4) capping agricultural emissions. The United States and China, which account for more

8. For panel reports, go to http://www.ipcc.ch/.

Exhibit 5

Fossil-Fuel Carbon Dioxide Emissions per Capita: The 25 Worst Nations

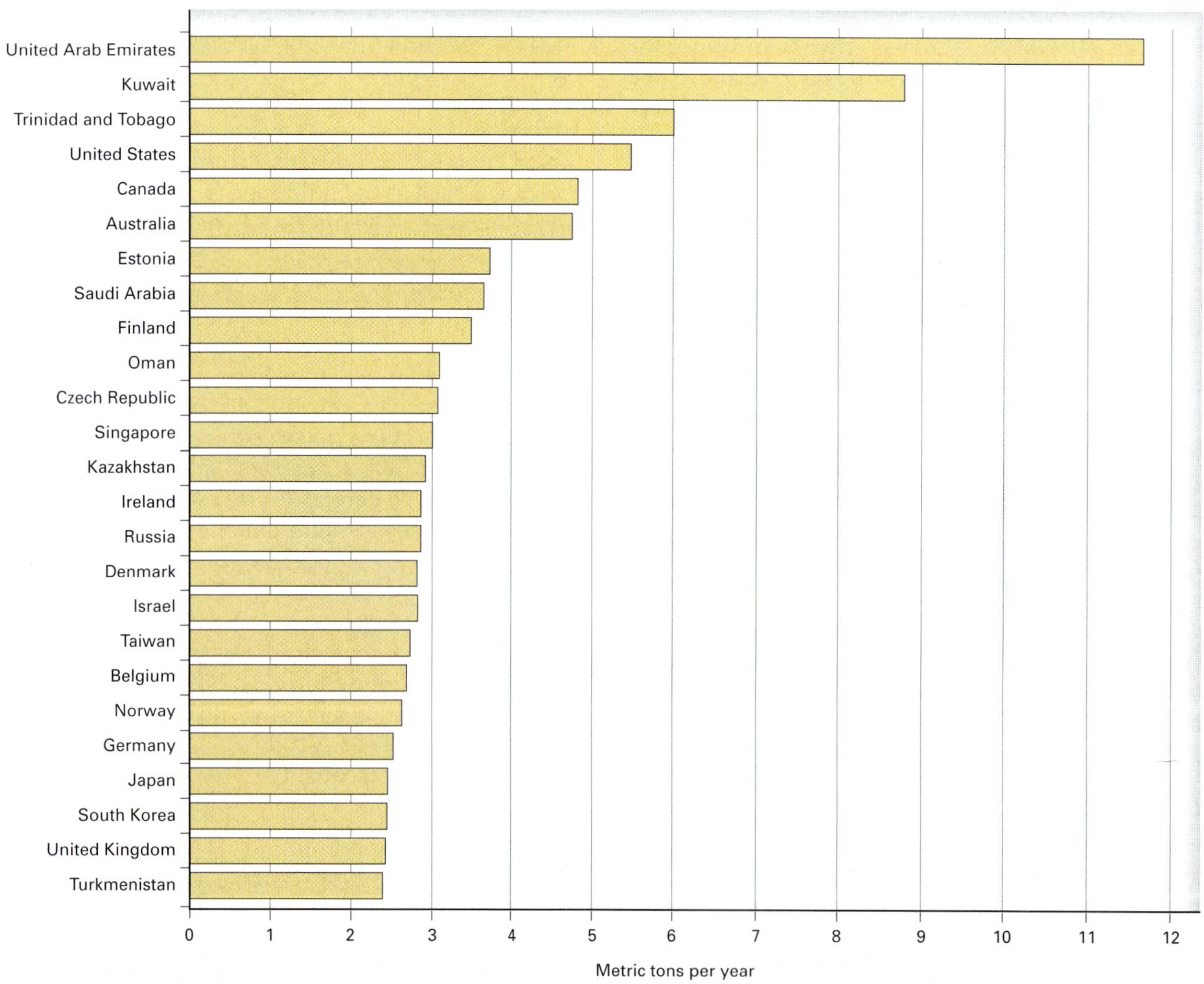

SOURCE: Figures are for 2003 and were estimated by Gregg Marland, Tom Boden, and Bob Andres at the Oak Ridge National Laboratory and can be found at http://cdiac.ornl.gov/trends/emis/top2003.cap. Excluded are nations with fewer than one million people.

than 40 percent of the world's emissions, approved the report but offered no indication that they would reverse their opposition to mandatory emission reductions. The report said that such reforms would require lifestyle changes, increased prices for some basics including gasoline and electricity, and greater investment in research and development.

Water Pollution

Two major sources of water pollution are sewage and chemicals. For decades, U.S. cities had an economic incentive to dump their sewage directly into waterways rather than clean it up first. Water current or tides would carry off the waste to become someone else's problem. Although each community found it rational, based on a narrow view of the situation, to dump into waterways, the combined effect of these local choices was water pollution, a negative externality imposed by one community on other communities. Federal money over the years has funded thousands of sewage treatment plants, which cut water pollution substantially. Nearly all U.S. cities now have modern sewage control systems. Hundreds of once-polluted waterways have been cleaned up enough for swimming and fishing.

Chemicals are another source of water pollution. Chemical pollution may conjure up an image of a pipe spewing chemicals into a river, but only about 10 percent of chemical pollution in the water comes from point pollution—pollution from factories and other industrial sites. About two-thirds come from nonpoint pollution—mostly runoff from agricultural pesticides and fertilizer. Congress has been reluctant to limit the use of pesticides, although pesticides pollute water and contaminate food. Industrial America seems an easier target than Old MacDonald's farm.

In 1970, Congress shifted control of pesticides from the U.S. Department of Agriculture to the newly created Environmental Protection Agency (EPA). But the EPA already had its hands full administering the Clean Water Act, so it turned pesticide regulation over to the states. Most states gave the job to their departments of agriculture, which usually promote the interests of farmers, not restrict what farmers can do. The EPA now reports that in most states pesticides have fouled some groundwater. The EPA also argues that pesticide residue on food poses more health problems than do toxic waste dumps. The EPA's inspector general said that federal and state officials failed to enforce the nation's clean air and water laws. For example, most streams in Missouri are not clean enough for swimming. So that state failed to achieve the Clean Water Act's central goal.[9]

{Makesicko City}

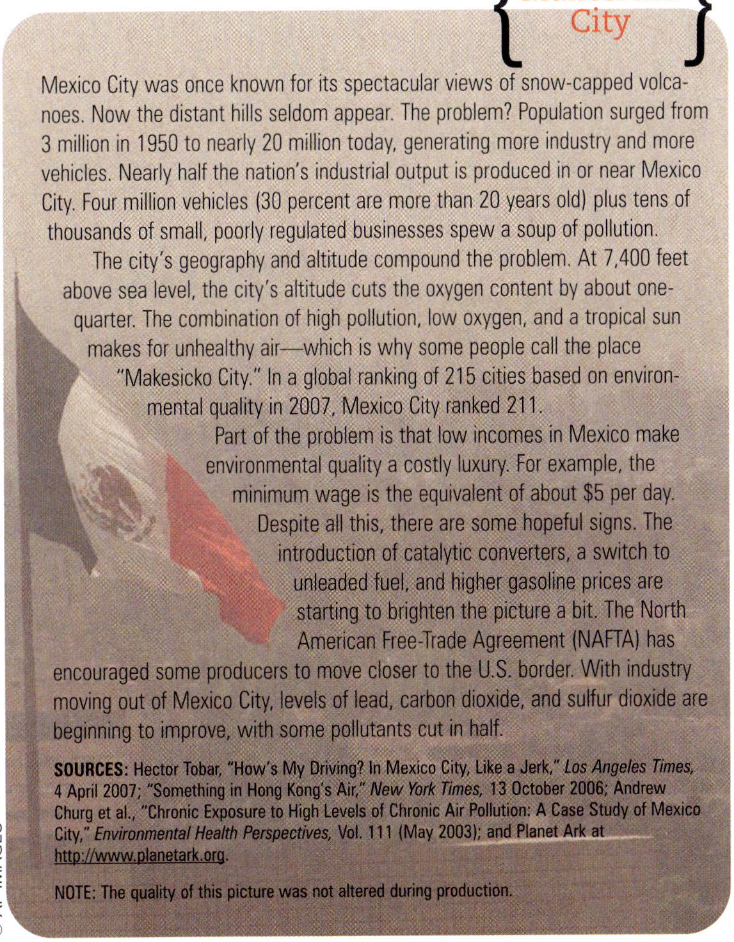

Mexico City was once known for its spectacular views of snow-capped volcanoes. Now the distant hills seldom appear. The problem? Population surged from 3 million in 1950 to nearly 20 million today, generating more industry and more vehicles. Nearly half the nation's industrial output is produced in or near Mexico City. Four million vehicles (30 percent are more than 20 years old) plus tens of thousands of small, poorly regulated businesses spew a soup of pollution.

The city's geography and altitude compound the problem. At 7,400 feet above sea level, the city's altitude cuts the oxygen content by about one-quarter. The combination of high pollution, low oxygen, and a tropical sun makes for unhealthy air—which is why some people call the place "Makesicko City." In a global ranking of 215 cities based on environmental quality in 2007, Mexico City ranked 211.

Part of the problem is that low incomes in Mexico make environmental quality a costly luxury. For example, the minimum wage is the equivalent of about $5 per day.

Despite all this, there are some hopeful signs. The introduction of catalytic converters, a switch to unleaded fuel, and higher gasoline prices are starting to brighten the picture a bit. The North American Free-Trade Agreement (NAFTA) has encouraged some producers to move closer to the U.S. border. With industry moving out of Mexico City, levels of lead, carbon dioxide, and sulfur dioxide are beginning to improve, with some pollutants cut in half.

SOURCES: Hector Tobar, "How's My Driving? In Mexico City, Like a Jerk," *Los Angeles Times,* 4 April 2007; "Something in Hong Kong's Air," *New York Times,* 13 October 2006; Andrew Churg et al., "Chronic Exposure to High Levels of Chronic Air Pollution: A Case Study of Mexico City," *Environmental Health Perspectives,* Vol. 111 (May 2003); and Planet Ark at http://www.planetark.org.

NOTE: The quality of this picture was not altered during production.

Hazardous Waste and the Superfund

The U.S. synthetic chemical industry has flourished in the last 50 years, and over 50,000 chemicals are now in common use. But some have harmful effects on humans and other living creatures. These chemicals can pose risks at every stage of their production, use, and disposal. New Jersey manufactures more toxic chemicals than any other state and, not surprisingly, has the worst toxic waste burden. Prior to 1980, the disposal of toxic waste created get-rich-quick opportunities for anyone who could rent or buy a few acres of land to open a toxic waste dump. As an extreme example, one site in New Jersey took in 71 million gallons of hazardous chemicals during a three-year period.[10]

9. John Cushman, "E.P.A. and States Found to Be Lax on Pollution Law," *New York Times,* 7 June 1998.

10. Jason Zweig, "Real-Life Horror Story," *Forbes,* 12 December 1988.

Before 1980, once a company paid someone to haul away its hazardous waste, the company was no longer responsible. The Comprehensive Environmental Response, Compensation, and Liability Act of 1980, known more popularly as the Superfund law, requires any company that generates, stores, or transports hazardous wastes to pay to clean up any wastes that are improperly disposed. A producer or hauler who is the source of even one barrel of pollution dumped at a site can be held liable for cleaning up the entire site.

The Superfund law gave the federal government authority over sites contaminated with toxins. But to get an offending company to comply, the EPA frequently must sue. The process is slow, and nearly half the budget goes to lawyers, consultants, and administrators rather than to site cleanups. The law did not require that benefits exceed costs or even that such comparisons be attempted. Although billions have been spent so far, a recent EPA study concluded that the health hazards of Superfund sites have been vastly exaggerated. Chemicals in the ground usually move slowly, sometimes taking years to travel a few feet, so any possible health threat is confined to the site itself. People know when they live near toxic waste sites, and they can exert political pressure to get something done, whereas people exposed to polluted air, water, and pesticide residue may develop health problems but never make the connection to their environment. Thus, people see less reason to press public officials for cleaner air and water (though the threat of global warming has focused some attention on greenhouse gas emissions). Toxic waste sites, because of their greater political urgency and media appeal (witness the movies on the subject), tend to receive more attention than air or water pollution. And with the federal government picking up the tab, localities demand all the cleanup they can get.

Solid Waste: "Paper or Plastic?"

Throughout most of history, households tossed their trash outside as fodder for pigs and goats. New York City, like other cities, had no trash collections, so domestic waste was thrown into the street, where it mixed with mud and manure (until recently, many residents of Beijing and other parts of China did the same thing).[11] Decades of such accumulation explain why the oldest Manhattan streets are anywhere from 3 to 15 feet above their original levels. About 200 years ago, people buried their trash near their homes or took it to a local dump. Most cities now forbid burning trash.

U.S. households generate about 4 pounds of garbage per resident per day—more than twice the 1960 level and the most in the world. Much of the solid waste consists of packaging. The question is, how do we dispose of the more than 200 million tons of household garbage generated in this country each year? Advanced economies produce and buy more than less developed economies, so there is more to throw away. And because of higher incomes in advanced economies, the opportunity cost of time is higher, so Americans tend to discard items rather than repair or recycle them. For example, it's cheaper to buy a new toaster for $20 than to pay $40 an hour to fix a broken one, assuming you can even find a repair service. (Look up "Appliance Repair, Small" in the *Yellow Pages* and see if you can find even one such shop in your area.)

About 70 percent of the nation's garbage is bulldozed and covered with soil in landfills. Although a well-managed landfill poses few environmental concerns, at one time, communities dumped all kinds of toxins in them—stuff that could leach into the soil, contaminating wells and aquifers. So landfills got a bad reputation. Now, the prevailing attitude with landfills is Nimby! (Not in my backyard!). We all want our garbage picked up but nobody wants it put down anywhere nearby.

As the cost of solid waste disposal increases, some state and local governments are economizing, charging households by the pound for trash pickups, and requiring more recycling and returnable bottles. **Recycling** is the process of converting waste products into reusable materials. Nearly half of U.S. households participate in curbside recycling programs.

recycling the process of converting waste products into reusable material

11. Laurence Brahm, "Hygiene? It's a Load of Rubbish," *South China Morning Post,* 1 November 2005.

Still, according to the EPA, only about 15 percent of U.S. garbage gets recycled; about 15 percent is incinerated and, as noted already, the remaining 70 percent goes into landfills. Of the recycled material, three-quarters consists of corrugated boxes, newspapers, office paper, newspapers, and other paper products. Some paper is shipped to Korea, Taiwan, and China, where it becomes packaging material for U.S. imports such as DVD players and computer components. Exhibit 6 ranks the world's top 25 recyclers of paper and cardboard among advanced economies. Germany and Finland head the list, recycling 72 percent. Three of the top five are Scandanavian countries. The United States is in a six-way tie for 16th, recycling 45 percent (but more than double that of 1985). Developing countries recycle much less—Mexico, for example, only 7 percent.

Of U.S. Garbage:
15% = recycled
15% = incinerated
70% = trashed

Most of the 15 percent of garbage that is incinerated gets burned in trash-to-energy plants, which generate electricity using the heat from incineration. Until recently, such plants looked like the wave of the future, but less favorable tax treatment and environmental concerns over incinerator locations (Nimby strikes again!) have taken the steam out of the trash-to-energy movement.

To repeat, only 30 percent of U.S. garbage is recycled or incinerated, and about 70 percent goes to landfills. In contrast, the Japanese recycle or incinerate 73 percent, sending only 27 percent to landfills. Japanese households sort their trash into as many as 21 categories. Because land is scarcer in Japan—we know this because it costs relatively more—it is not surprising that the Japanese deposit a smaller share of their garbage in landfills.

Some recycling is clearly economical—such as aluminum cans, which are a relatively cheap source of aluminum compared to producing raw aluminum. About two out of three aluminum cans now get recycled, though only 11 states require returnable deposits. Still, returnable deposit laws increase recycling. Incentives matter. Even if you decide to discard your empties, chances are that someone down the line with a lower opportunity cost than you will find them and return them for the deposits. For example, researchers found an average of 47 bottles or cans along a one-block path of city park each day prior to the enactment of deposit law, but one year after the law was introduced, an average of only two bottles was found each day along the same path.[12]

Recycling paper and cardboard is also economical and occurred long before the environmental

12. J. Trinkaus, "A Bottle Law: An Informal Look," *Perceptual and Motor Skills* 59 (December 1984): 806.

Exhibit 6

Paper and Cardboard Recycling: Top 25 among Advanced Economies

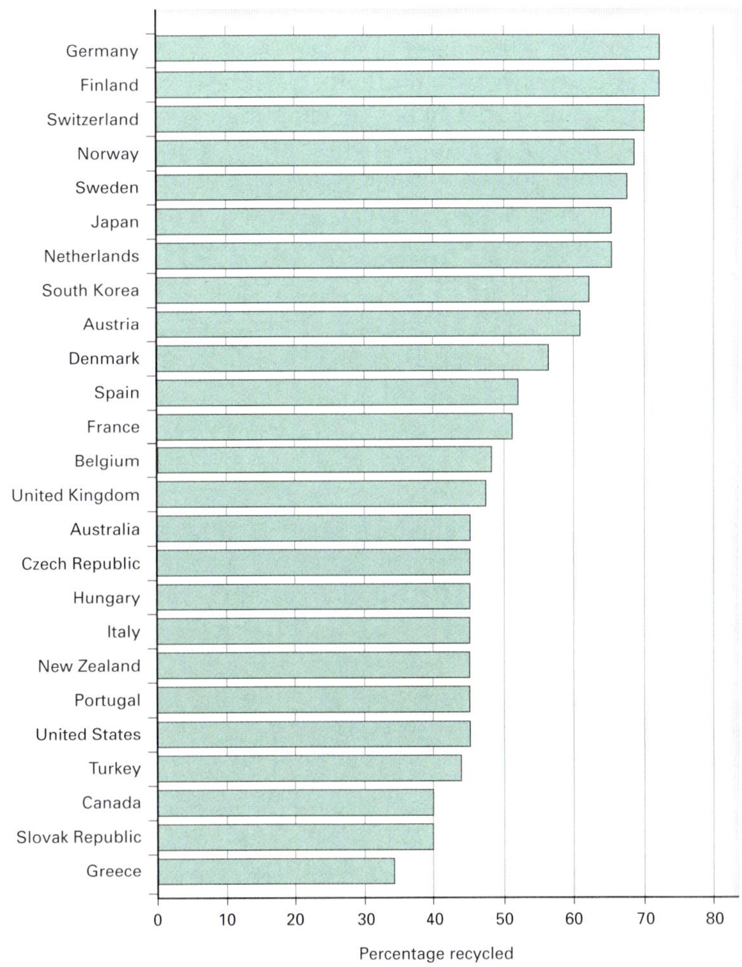

SOURCE: Figures are rankings among members of the Organization of Economic Cooperation and Development as reported in *OECD Environmental Data 2004*. Table 4A, p. 25. This can be found at http://www.oecd.org/dataoecd/60/59/38106368.pdf. Figures are for 2002, except for Canada, Korea, New Zealand, and the U.S., which are for 2001, and Australia, which is for 2000.

© WIDE GROUP/STONE/GETTY IMAGES

movement. Such old standbys as paper drives, drop-off bins, and redemption centers collect more tonnage than curbside programs. Most recycling results from salvaging scrap material from business and industry, a practice that dates back decades.

Governments have tried to stimulate demand for recycled material—for example, by requiring newspapers to use a certain amount of recycled newsprint. Other recycled products are not in such demand. In fact, some recycled products have become worthless and must be hauled to landfills. Recycling imposes its own environmental cost. Curbside recycling requires fleets of trucks that pollute the air. Newsprint must first be de-inked, creating a sludge that must be disposed of. But greater environmental awareness has made consumers more receptive to more efficient packaging. For example, liquid laundry detergent now comes in a concentrated "ultra" form, which cuts volume in half, and Unilever's brand All Small & Mighty cuts volume by two thirds. Labels for all kinds of products proudly identify the recycled content of the packaging.

LO4 Positive Externalities

To this point, we have considered only negative externalities. But externalities are sometimes positive, or beneficial. Positive externalities occur when consumption or production benefits other consumers or other firms. For example, people who get inoculated against a disease reduce their own likelihood of contracting the disease, but they reduce the risk of transmitting the disease to others. Inoculations thus provide external benefits. Likewise, society as a whole receives external benefits from education because those who acquire more education become better citizens, can read road signs, are better able to support themselves and their families, and are less likely to require public assistance or to resort to violent crime for income. Researchers found that more schooling significantly reduces the probability of incarceration.[13] Thus, your education provides personal benefits but it also benefits others.

The effect of external benefits is illustrated in Exhibit 7, which presents the demand and supply of education. The demand curve, *D*, represents the private demand for education, which reflects the marginal private benefit for those who acquire the education. More education is demanded at a lower price than at a higher price.

The benefit of education, however, spills over to others in society. If we add this positive externality, or marginal external benefit, to the marginal private benefit of education, we get the marginal social benefit of education. The marginal social benefit includes all the benefits society derives from education, both private and external. The marginal social benefit curve is above the private demand curve in Exhibit 7. If education were a strictly private decision, the amount purchased would be determined by the intersection of the private demand curve *D* with supply curve *S*. The supply curve reflects the marginal cost of producing each unit of the good. This intersection at point *e* yields education level *E*, where the marginal private benefit of education equals its mar-

13. Lance Lochner and Enrico Moretti, "The Effects of Education on Crime: Evidence from Prison Inmates," *American Economic Review* 94 (March 2004): 155–189.

Exhibit 7

Education and Positive Externalities

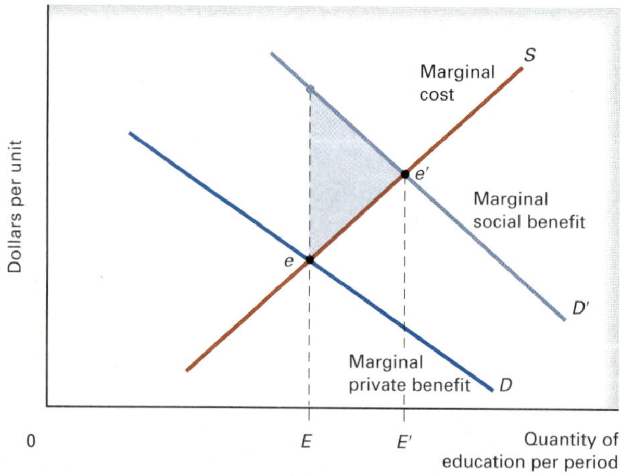

ginal cost, as reflected by the supply curve. But at level E, the marginal social benefit exceeds the marginal cost. Social welfare would increase if education expands beyond E. As long as the marginal social benefit exceeds the marginal cost, social welfare increases as education expands. Social welfare is maximized at point e' in Exhibit 7, where E' units of education are provided—that is, where the marginal social benefit equals the marginal cost. The blue-shaded triangle identifies the increase in social welfare that results from increasing education from E, the private optimum, to E', the social optimum.

Thus, society is better off if the level of education exceeds the private equilibrium. With positive externalities, decisions based on private marginal benefits result in less than the socially optimal quantity of the good. Thus, like negative externalities, positive externalities typically point to market failure, which is why government often gets into the act. When there are external benefits, public policy aims to increase quantity beyond the private optimum. For example, governments try to increase education by providing free primary and secondary education, by requiring students to stay in school until they reach 16 years of age, by subsidizing public higher education, and by offering tax breaks for some education costs.

Final Word

About 6.7 billion people live on the planet, and over 72 million are added each year. World population is projected to reach 9.4 billion by 2050, according to the U.S. Census Bureau, with most of this growth occurring in countries where most people barely eke out a living. Population pressure coupled with a lack of incentives to conserve open-access resources results in deforestation, dwindling fish stocks, and polluted air, land, and water.

Ironically, because of the tighter pollution controls in industrial countries, these countries are less polluted than developing countries, where there is more pollution from what little industry there is. Most developing countries have such profound economic problems that environmental quality is not a priority. For example, when India's Supreme Court tried to close some polluting factories in New Delhi, thousands of workers torched buses, threw stones, and blocked major roads, demanding the factories stay open. Although New Delhi's pollution masks any trace of a blue sky, workers believe their jobs are more important. Here's one account of New Delhi's air quality:

> *In the heat of the afternoons, a yellow-white mixture hung above the city, raining acidic soot into the dust and exhaust fumes. At night the mixture condenses into a dry, choking fog that envelops the headlights of passing cars, and creeps its stink into even the tightest houses. The residents could do little to keep the poison out of their lungs or the lungs of their children, and if they were poor, they could not even try.*[14]

Market prices can direct the allocation of resources only as long as property rights are well defined. Pollution arises not so much from the greed of producers and consumers as from the fact that open-access resources are subject to the common-pool problem.

14. William Langewiesche, "The Shipbreakers," *Atlantic Monthly* (August 2000): 42.

10,000 < Mango trees planted to offset emissions from Coldplay album production

Fee added to Delta domestic flights for tree plantings > $5.50

Smog produced by manufacturing > 15%

120 < Nations approved the UN report on climate change

Mexico City's rank out of 215 cities based on environmental climate > 211

Amount of garbage recycled in Germany & Finland > 72%

CHAPTER 18

Income Distribution *and* Poverty

Learning Outcomes

LO 1 Explain the distribution of household income

LO 2 Describe redistribution programs

LO 3 Explain who the poor are

LO 4 Discuss welfare reform

“Why are some people poor even in the most productive economy on Earth?”

Why are some people poor even in the most productive economy on Earth? Who are the poor, how did they get that way, and how long do they remain poor? What's been the trend in U.S. poverty? What's been the impact of the changing family structure on poverty? What public programs aim to reduce poverty, and how well have they worked? Answers to these and related questions are addressed in this chapter, which discusses income distribution and poverty in America.

To establish a reference point, we first examine the distribution of income in the United States, paying special attention to trends in recent decades. We then examine the "social safety net"—government programs aimed at helping poor people. We also consider the impact of the changing family structure on poverty, focusing in particular on the increase in households headed by women. We close by examining recent welfare reforms.

What do you think?

The government provides more financial help for senior citizens than for teenagers.

Strongly Disagree 1 2 3 4 5 6 7 *Strongly Agree*

LO1 The Distribution of Household Income

In a market economy, income depends primarily on earnings, which depend on the productivity of one's resources. The problem with allocating income according to productivity is that some people have few resources to sell. People with mental or physical disabilities and poor education, those facing discrimination, bad luck, or the demands of caring for small children, and the elderly may be less productive or unable to earn a living.

Topics discussed in Chapter 18 include:

- Distribution of income
- Official poverty level
- Public policy and poverty
- The feminization of poverty
- Poverty and discrimination
- Welfare reforms

Income Distribution by Quintiles

As a starting point, let's consider the distribution of income in the economy and see how it has changed over time, focusing on the household as the economic unit. After dividing the number of U.S. households into five groups of equal size, or *quintiles,* ranked according to income, we can examine the percentage of income received by each quintile. Such a division is presented in Exhibit 1. Take a moment to look over

Exhibit 1

Share of Aggregate Household Income by Quintile: 1970, 1980, 1990, and 2005

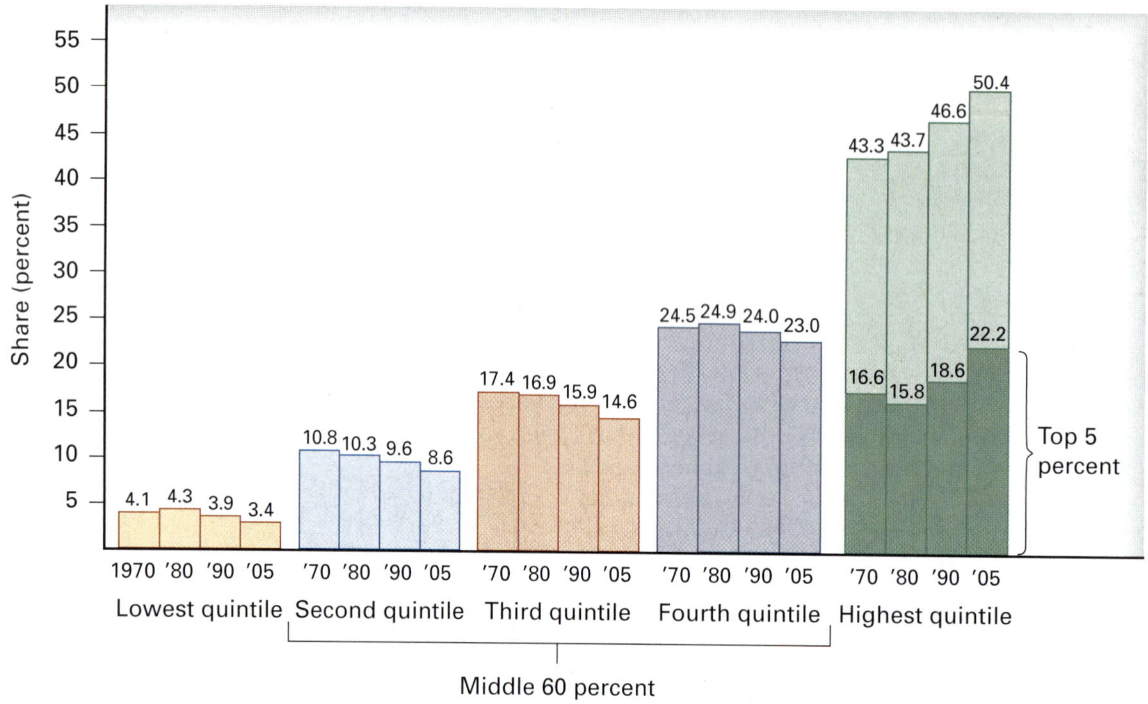

SOURCE: Developed from data found in U.S. Census Bureau, *Income, Poverty, and Health Insurance Coverage in the United States: 2005,* P-60-231, August 2006, Table 1, http://www.census.gov/prod/2006pubs/p60-231.pdf and http://www.census.gov/hhes/www/ income/histinc/h02ar.html.

this exhibit. Notice that households in the lowest, or poorest, fifth of the population received only 4.1 percent of the income in 1970, whereas households in the highest, or richest, fifth received 43.3 percent of the income. The U.S. Census Bureau measures income after cash transfer payments are received but before taxes are paid or in-kind transfers are received (from food stamps, Medicare, Medicaid, public housing, and employer-provided benefits).

In recent decades, the share of income going to the top fifth has increased, and the share going to the bottom fifth has declined. The richest fifth's share of income increased from 43.3 percent in 1970 to 50.4 percent in 2005. A primary contributor to the larger share of income going to the highest group has been the growth of two-earner households in that top group. Three out of four households in the top quintile have two or more people working. A primary contributor to the smaller share going to the lowest group has been the growth of single-parent households in the bottom group. Only one in three households in the bottom quintile has anybody working, and only one in seven has anybody working full time.

Lorenz curve a curve showing the percentage of total income received by a given percentage of recipients whose incomes are arrayed from smallest to largest

Also shown in Exhibit 1 is the share of income going to the top 5 percent of households; that share has grown since 1980, accounting for nearly all the growth of the top 20 percent of households. Because of substantial reductions in the top marginal tax rates in 1981 and 1986, high-income people had less incentive to engage in tax avoidance and tax evasion, so their reported income increased, boosting the share of reported income going to the richest 5 percent of households.

The Lorenz Curve

We have just examined the distribution of income using a bar chart. Another way to picture that distribution is with a Lorenz curve. A **Lorenz curve** shows the percentage of total income received by any given percentage of households when incomes are arrayed from smallest to largest. As shown in Exhibit 2, the cumulative percentage of households is measured along the horizontal axis, and the cumulative percentage of income is measured along the vertical axis. Any given distribution of income can be compared to an equal distribution of income among

Exhibit 2

Lorenz Curves Show That Income Was Less Evenly Distributed Across U.S. Households in 2005 than in 1970

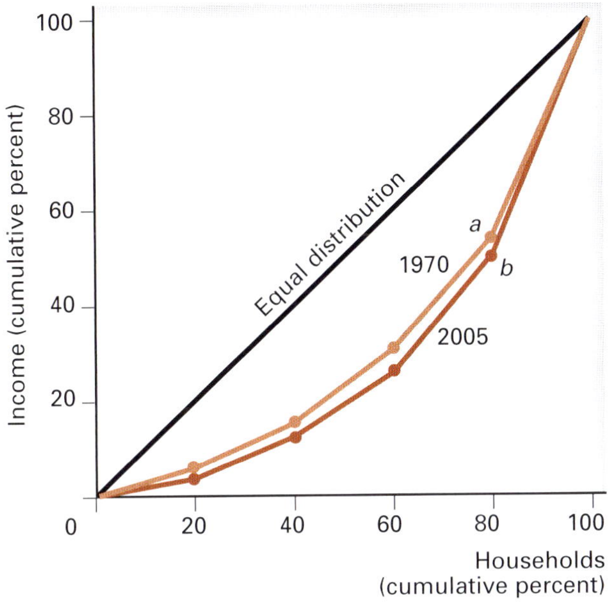

households. If income were evenly distributed, each 20 percent of households would also receive 20 percent of the total income, and the Lorenz curve would be a straight line with a slope equal to 1.0, as shown by the "equal distribution" line in Exhibit 2.

As the distribution becomes more uneven, the Lorenz curve pulls down to the right, away from the line of equal distribution. The Lorenz curves in Exhibit 2 were calculated for 1970 and 2005 based on the data in Exhibit 1. As a reference, point *a* on the 1970 Lorenz curve indicates that in that year, the bottom 80 percent of families received 56.7 percent of the income, and the top 20 percent received 43.3 percent of the income. The Lorenz curve for 2005 is farther from the line of equal distribution than is the Lorenz curve for 1970, showing that income among households has become more unevenly distributed. Point *b* on the 2005 curve shows that the bottom 80 percent received 49.6 percent of the income and the top 20 percent received 50.4 percent of the income.

Why Incomes Differ

Income differences across households stem in part from differences in the *number* of workers in each household. Thus, *one reason household incomes differ is that the number of household members who are working differs*. For example, among households in the bottom 20 percent based on income, only one in seven includes a full-time, year-round worker. Consider the link between median income and the number of workers. The **median income** of all households is the middle income when incomes are ranked from lowest to highest. In any given year, half the households are above the median income and half are below it. The median income for households with two earners is 87 percent higher than for households with only one earner and is about four times higher than for households with no earners.

Incomes also differ for all the reasons labor incomes differ, such as differences in education, ability, job experience, and so on. At every age, those with more education earn more, on average. As noted a few chapters back, those with a professional degree earn nearly six times more than those without a high school diploma. Age itself also has an important effect on income. As workers mature, they acquire valuable job experience, get promoted, and earn more.

Differences in earnings based on age and education reflect a normal *life cycle* pattern of income. In fact, most income differences across households reflect the normal workings of resource markets, whereby workers are rewarded according to their productivity. Because of these lifetime patterns, it is not necessarily the same households that remain rich or poor over time. Indeed, one study of income mobility found that more than three-quarters of people in the bottom 20 percent in one particular year had moved into the top 40 percent for at least one year during the following 16 years.[1]

Despite this mobility over time, we can still characterize rich and poor households at a point in time. A *high-income household usually consists of a well-educated couple with both spouses employed. A low-income household is usually one person living alone or is a family headed by a single parent who is young, female, poorly educated, and not working.* Low incomes are a matter of public concern, especially when children are involved, as we see in the next section.

A College Education Pays More

Also contributing to the dominance of the top group is a growing premium paid those with college educations. In the last two decades, the median wage (adjusted for inflation) for people with only high

1. W. Michael Cox and Richard Arm, "By Our Own Bootstraps," *Federal Reserve Bank of Dallas: 1995 Annual Report*.

median income the middle income when all incomes are ranked from smallest to largest school diplomas declined 6 percent, while the median wage for college graduates rose 12 percent. The **median wage** is the middle wage when wages are ranked from lowest to highest. Why have more-educated workers done better? First, trends such as industry deregulation, declining unionization, and freer international trade and migration have reduced the pay for workers with less education. Labor unions, for example, raised the wages of many workers who would have otherwise ended up in the bottom half of the income distribution. But the share of the workforce that is unionized declined from 26 percent in 1973 to only 12 percent in 2006.

Second, new computer-based information technologies have reduced the demand for low-skilled clerical workers, because their jobs became computerized. Computers also offered more timely and accurate information to management, allowing for organizational innovations that made managers and other professionals more productive.[2] So computers reduced the demand for workers with low skills, such as clerical staff and bank tellers, and increased the demand for those who use computers to boost labor productivity, such as managers and accountants.

Third, the supply of less-educated workers increased more than the supply of more-educated workers, thus increasing the rewards of education. For example, compared to average residents, recent U.S. immigrants tend to be less educated, including an estimated 12 million illegal aliens, more than half from Mexico. The Hispanic population more than doubled between the 1980 census and 2000 census, and the percentage of foreign-born Hispanics increased. Among males age 25 and older, only 57 percent of Hispanics had at least a high school education in 2000, compared with 85 percent of whites and 79 percent of blacks. More generally, the foreign-born share of the U.S. population more than doubled from 5 percent in 1970 to over 12 percent today, the largest share since the 1930s. Thus, immigration has increased the supply of relatively poorly educated workers, which has depressed wages of the less educated generally.

Finally, marriage trends have reinforced the income gap.

So economic forces, immigration, and marriage trends have hurt those at the low end of the income distribution and have benefited those at the high end, and this helps explain the growing disparity in household income.

Income in the United States is less evenly distributed than in other developed countries throughout the world, such as Canada, France, Great Britain, Italy, and Australia, but is more evenly distributed than in most developing countries, such as Brazil, Chile, Mexico, Nigeria, and the Philippines.

Problems with Distribution Benchmarks

One problem with assessing income distributions is that there is no objective standard for evaluating them. The usual assumption is that a more equal distribution of income is more desirable, but is equal distribution most preferred? If not, then how uneven should it be? For example, among major league baseball players, well over half the pay goes to 20 percent of the players. Professional basketball pay skews even more, with top NBA players earning up to 50 times more than the bottom players. Does this mean the economy, as a whole, is in some sense "fairer" than these professional sports?

A second problem is that because Exhibits 1 and 2 measure money income after cash transfers but before taxes they neglect the effects of taxes and in-kind transfers, such as food stamps and free medical care for poor families. The tax system as a whole is progressive, meaning that families with higher incomes pay a larger fraction of their incomes in taxes. In-kind transfers benefit the lowest income

median wage
the middle wage when wages of all workers are ranked from lowest to highest

2. Lex Borghans and Bas ter Weel, "The Diffusion of Computers and the Distribution of Wages," *European Economic Review* (Issue 3, 2007): 715–748.

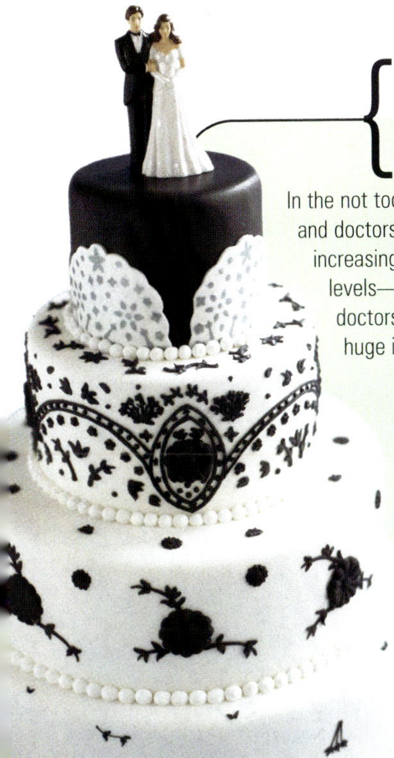

© ALEXANDRA GRABLEWSKI/FOODPIX/JUPITERIMAGES

Marital Sorting and Income Inequality

In the not too distant past, lawyers married secretaries and doctors married nurses. Now, Americans with increasing frequency are pairing off by education levels—lawyers marry lawyers, and doctors marry doctors. Why the change? Women have made huge inroads into the professions.

As a result of their educational strides, particularly in the professions, a growing number of women, for the first time in history, now have high-paying jobs and professional careers. The extent to which couples are educational equals has reached its highest point in decades. Choosing a marriage partner based on income is also on the rise. Studies have found a growing similarity between women's wages before marriage and the future earnings of the men they marry.

The flip side of this is that someone with only a high school education is now less likely to marry a college graduate than was once the case. What's more, among women born after 1960, someone with only a high school education is less likely to ever marry than is someone with a college education.

SOURCES: Raquel Fernández and Richard Rogerson, "Sorting and Long-Term Inequality," *Quarterly Journal of Economics,* Vol. 116 (4, 2001): 1305–1341; Christine Schwartz and Robert Mare, "Trends in Educational Assortative Marriage," *Demography,* Vol. 42, pp. 621–646; Annie Murphy Paul, "The Real Marriage Penalty," *New York Times,* 19 November 2006.

groups the most. Consequently, if Exhibit 1 incorporated the effects of taxes and in-kind transfers, the share of income going to the lower groups would increase, the share going to the higher groups would decrease, and income would become more evenly distributed.

Third, focusing on the share of income going to each income quintile overlooks the fact that household size differs across quintiles. Most households in the bottom quintile consist of one person living alone. Only one in 16 households in the top quintile consists of one person living alone. Fourth, Exhibits 1 and 2 include only *reported* income. If people receive payment "under the table" to evade taxes, or if they earn money through illegal activities, their actual income will exceed their *reported* income. The omission of unreported income distorts the data if unreported income as a percentage of total family income differs across income levels.

Finally, Exhibits 1 and 2 focus on the distribution of *income,* but a better measure of household welfare would be the distribution of *spending.* Available evidence indicates that *spending by quintiles is much more evenly distributed than income by quintiles.*

LO[2] Redistribution Programs

Because poverty is such a relative concept, how do we measure it objectively, and how do we ensure that the measure can be applied with equal relevance over time? The federal government has developed a method for calculating an official poverty level, which serves as a benchmark for poverty analysis in the United States.

Official Poverty Level

To derive the **U.S. official poverty level,** the U.S. Department of Agriculture in 1959 first estimated the cost of a nutritionally adequate diet. Then, based on the assumption that the poor spend about one-third of their income on food, the official poverty level was calculated by multiplying this food cost by three. The U.S. Census Bureau tracks the official poverty level, making adjustments for family size and for inflation. For example, the official poverty level of money income for a family of four was $19,971 in 2005; a family of four at or below that income threshold was regarded as living in poverty. Poverty levels in 2005 ranged from $9,973 for a person living alone to $40,288 for a family of nine. The poverty definition is based on pretax money income, including cash transfers, but it excludes the value of noncash transfers such as food stamps, Medicaid, subsidized housing, or employer-provided health insurance.

Each year since 1959, the Census Bureau has conducted a survey comparing each family's cash income to the annual poverty level applicable to that family. Results of this survey are presented in Exhibit 3, which indicates both the millions of people living below the official poverty level and the percentage of the U.S. population below that level. Periods of U.S. recession are also shown (a recession is defined as two or more successive quarters of declining output in the economy). Note that poverty increased during recessions.

The biggest decline in poverty occurred before 1970; *the poverty rate dropped from 22.4 percent in 1959 to 12.1 percent in 1969.* During that period, the number of poor people decreased from about 40 million to 24 million. The poverty rate has not shown huge fluctuations since that initial drop. After declining from 1994 to 2000, the poverty rate and the number of poor people drifted higher over the next five years because of the national recession in 2001.

U.S. official poverty level benchmark level of income computed by the federal government to track poverty over time; initially based on three times the cost of a nutritionally adequate diet

Exhibit 3

Number and Percentage of U.S. Population in Poverty: 1959–2005

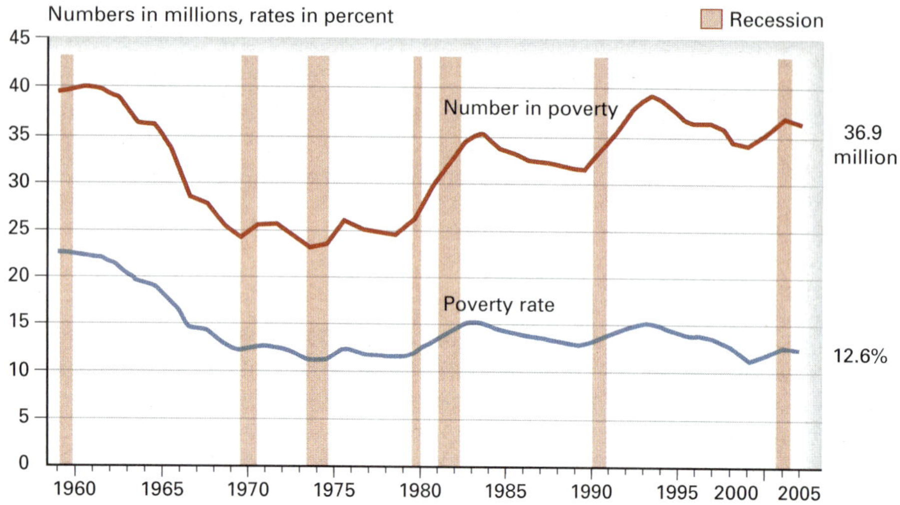

SOURCE: U.S. Census Bureau, *Poverty in the United States, 2005.* Current Population Reports, September 2006. Figure 1, p. 3, http://www.census.gov/ hhes/www/poverty/histpov/hstpov2.html.

Poverty is a relative term. If we examined the distribution of income across countries, we would find huge gaps between rich and poor nations. The U.S. official poverty level of income is many times greater than the average income for three-fourths of the world's population. The U.S. poverty level for a family of four in 2005 works out to be $13.70 per person per day. Most nations employ a much lower poverty threshhold. For example, the World Bank uses an *international poverty line* of $1 per person per day. Based on that benchmark, 24 percent of people in Nepal, 56 percent of those in Tanzania, 71 percent of those in Nigeria, and 76 percent of those in Zambia live in poverty.[3]

social insurance government programs designed to help make up for lost income of people who worked but are now retired, unemployed, or unable to work because of disability or work-related injury

Social Security supplements retirement income to those with a record of contributing to the program during their working years; by far the largest government redistribution program

Programs to Help the Poor

What should society's response to poverty be? The best predictor of family poverty is whether someone in that family has a job. Those families with a full-time worker in 2005 had a poverty rate of 2.8 percent; those families without someone working had a rate of 21.8 percent. One way government can try to to reduce poverty, therefore, is to promote a healthy economy. The stronger the economy, the greater the job opportunities, and the more likely people will find work. Perhaps the best indicator of whether or not jobs are readily available is the *unemployment rate,* which shows the percentage or the labor force out of work. The *lower* the unemployment rate, the *higher* the likelihood that someone who wants a job can find one. Thus, the lower the unemployment rate, the lower the poverty rate. Exhibit 4 shows poverty rates and unemployment rates in the United States each year since 1969. As you can see, the poverty rate, shown by the top line, tends to rise when the unemployment rate increases and fall when the unemployment rate declines.

Thus, the government's first line of defense in fighting poverty is promoting a healthy economy. Yet even when the unemployment rate is low, some people are still poor. Although some antipoverty programs involve direct market intervention, such as minimum-wage laws, the most visible antipoverty programs redistribute income after the market has made an initial distribution. Since the mid-1960s, social welfare expenditures at all levels of government have increased significantly. We can divide these programs into two broad categories: social insurance and income assistance.

Social Insurance

Social insurance programs are designed to help make up for the lost income of people who worked but are now retired, temporarily unemployed, or unable to work because of disability or work-related injury. The major social insurance program is **Social Security**, established during the Great Depression to sup-

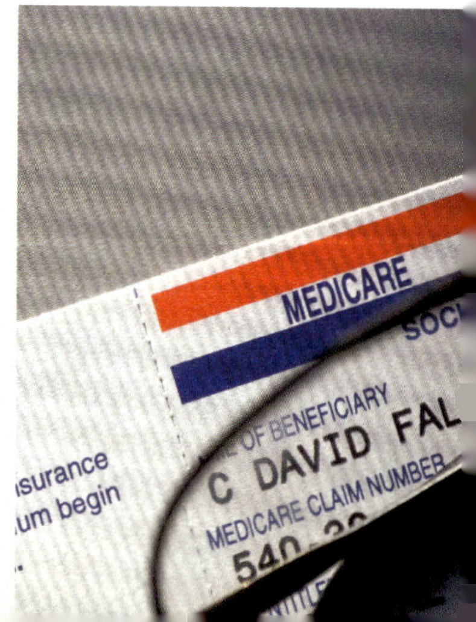

3. Poverty rates can be found at the World Bank Group's site at http://iresearch.worldbank.org/PovcalNet/jsp/index.jsp.

Exhibit 4

U.S. Poverty Rates and Unemployment Rates

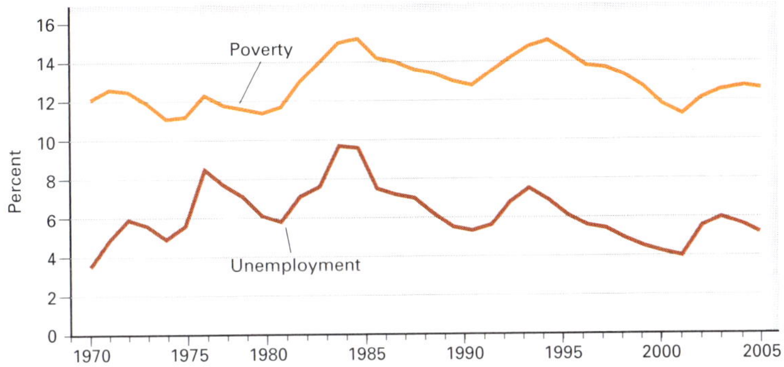

SOURCE: U.S. Census Bureau and U.S. Bureau of Labor Statistics.

plement retirement income of those with a work history and a record of contributing to the program. **Medicare**, another social insurance program, provides health insurance for short-term medical care, mostly to those ages 65 and older, regardless of income. There are over 44 million Social Security and Medicare beneficiaries. Other social insurance programs include *unemployment insurance,* which supports those who have lost jobs, and *workers' compensation*, which supports workers injured on the job; both programs require that beneficiaries have a prior record of employment.

The social insurance system deducts "insurance premiums" from workers' pay to provide benefits to other retired, disabled, and unemployed individuals. These programs protect some families from poverty, particularly the elderly, but they are aimed more at those with a work history. Still, the social insurance system tends to redistribute income from rich to poor and from young to old. Most current Social Security beneficiaries receive far more in benefits than they paid into the program, especially those with a brief work history or a record of low wages.

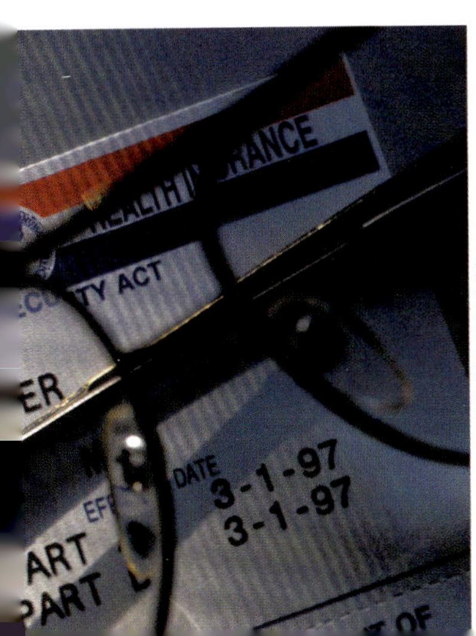

Income Assistance

Income assistance programs—what we usually call welfare programs—provide cash and in-kind assistance to the poor. Unlike social insurance programs, income assistance programs do not require recipients to have a work history or to have paid into the program. Income assistance programs are means tested. Those with sufficient means are not eligible. In a **means-tested program**, a household's income and assets must be below a certain level to qualify for benefits. The federal government funds about two-thirds of welfare spending, and state and local governments fund about one-third.

The two primary *cash transfer* programs are **Temporary Assistance for Needy Families (TANF)**, which provides cash to poor families with dependent children, and **Supplemental Security Income (SSI)**, which provides cash to the elderly poor and the disabled. Cash transfers vary inversely with family income from other sources. In 1997, TANF replaced Aid for Families with Dependent Children (AFDC), which began during the Great Depression and originally supported widows with young children. Whereas AFDC was a federal *entitlement* program, meaning that anyone who met the criteria was *entitled* to benefits, TANF is under the control of each state and carries no federal entitlement. The federal government gives each state a fixed grant to help fund TANF programs.

The SSI program provides support for the elderly and disabled poor. It is the fastest-growing cash transfer program. SSI coverage has been broadened to include people addicted to drugs and alcohol, children with learning disabilities, and, in some cases, the homeless. The federal portion of this program is uniform across states, but states can supplement federal aid. For example, benefit levels in California average twice those in Alabama. Most states also offer modest *General Assistance* aid to those who are poor but do not qualify for TANF or SSI. The federal government also provides

Medicare
social insurance program providing health insurance for short-term medical care to older Americans, regardless of income

income assistance programs
welfare programs that provide money and in-kind assistance to the poor; benefits do not depend on prior contributions

means-tested program
a program in which, to be eligible, an individual's income and assets must not exceed specified levels

Temporary Assistance for Needy Families (TANF)
an income assistance program funded largely by the federal government but run by the states to provide cash transfer payments to poor families with dependent children

Supplemental Security Income (SSI)
an income assistance program that provides cash transfers to the elderly poor and the disabled; a uniform federal payment is supplemented by transfers that vary across states

an **earned-income tax credit**, which supplements wages of the working poor. For example, a low-income family with two children would not only pay no federal income tax but would receive a cash transfer of up to $4,700 in 2007. More than 20 million tax filers received such transfers in 2006, when outlays of $35 billion for the program were double federal spending of $17 billion on TANF. The earned-income tax credit lifts millions of families out of poverty. Twenty states also offer earned-income tax credits on top of the federal plan.

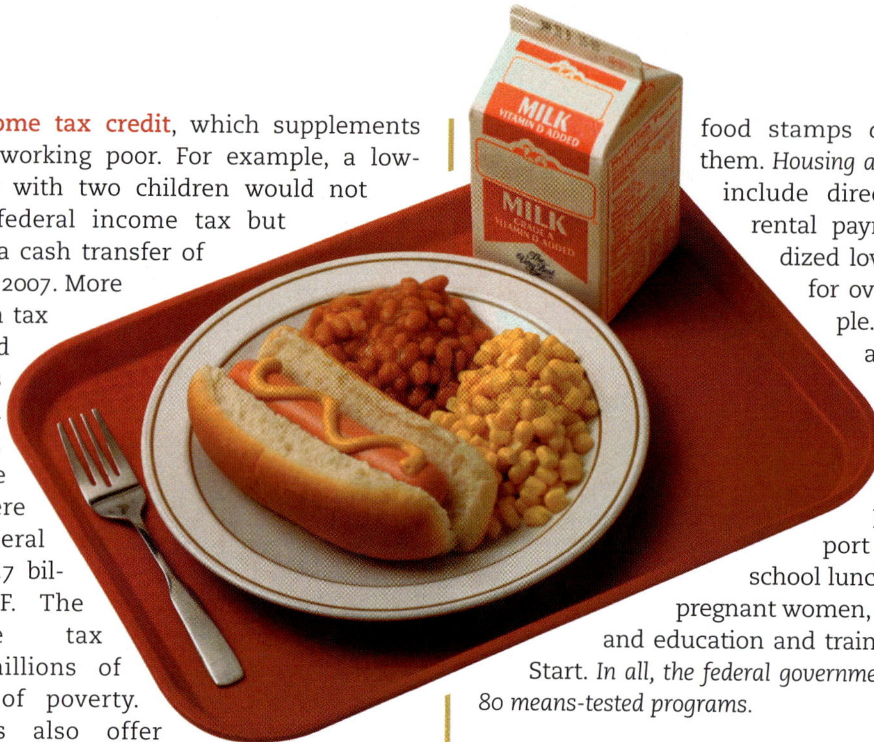

In addition to cash transfers, a variety of *in-kind transfer* programs provide health care, food stamps, and housing assistance to the poor. **Medicaid** pays for medical care for those with low incomes who are aged, blind, disabled, or are in families with dependent children. *Medicaid is by far the largest welfare program, costing more than all cash and other in-kind transfer programs combined.* It has grown more than any other poverty program, quadrupling in the last decade and accounting for nearly a quarter of the typical state's budget (though states receive federal grants covering half or more of their Medicaid budget). The qualifying level of income is set by each state, and some states are stricter than others. Therefore, the proportion of poor people covered by Medicaid varies across states. More than 56 million, or more than one in six U.S. residents, received Medicaid benefits at a total cost of over $350 billion in 2007. For many elderly, Medicaid covers long-term nursing care, which can cost the taxpayers up to $100,000 a year per recipient.

earned-income tax credit
a federal program that supplements the wages of the working poor

Medicaid
an in-kind transfer program that provides medical care for poor people; by far the most costly welfare program

food stamps
an in-kind transfer program that offers low-income households vouchers redeemable for food; benefit levels vary inversely with household income

Food stamps are vouchers that the poor can redeem for food. Twenty-six million people received food stamps in an average month of 2007, and the monthly benefit averaged $212 per household. But nearly half those eligible for food stamps do not apply for them. *Housing assistance* programs include direct assistance for rental payments and subsidized low-income housing for over 10 million people. Federal spending alone came to about $40 billion in 2007. Other in-kind transfer programs for the poor include support for day care, school lunches, extra food for pregnant women, energy assistance, and education and training, such as Head Start. *In all, the federal government funds more than 80 means-tested programs.*

To review: Federal programs were budgeted to exceed $1.4 trillion, more than twice the amount spent on national defense. Adding in state and local outlays pushes the total over $2.0 trillion. Exhibit 5 shows the growth in federal redistribution programs since 1962. To eliminate the effects of inflation, figures are expressed in dollars of 2008 purchasing power. Overall, redistribution outlays grew at an annual average of 6 percent since 1962, even after netting out the effects of inflation. Social Security and Medicare, programs that benefit the elderly primarily, make up the greatest share throughout the period. Next is Medicaid, which, as noted earlier, exceeds outlays for cash transfers and other in-kind transfers combined. Although more than half the federal welfare budget goes for health care, about 47 million U.S. residents still lacked health insurance in 2006.

Some countries also have far more extensive redistribution programs than does the United States, basing a variety of public policies on income. For example, Finland's traffic fines increase with the driver's income. One young tycoon speeding 43 miles per hour in a 25-mile-an-hour zone paid a $71,400 fine.[4]

LO3 Who Are the Poor?

Who are the poor, and how has the composition of this group changed over time? We will slice poverty statistics in several ways to examine

4. Seven Stecklow, "Finnish Drivers Don't Mind Sliding Scale, But Instant Calculation Gets Low Marks," *Wall Street Journal,* 2 January 2001.

Exhibit 5

Federal Redistribution Outlays Each Year by Category: 1962 to 2008

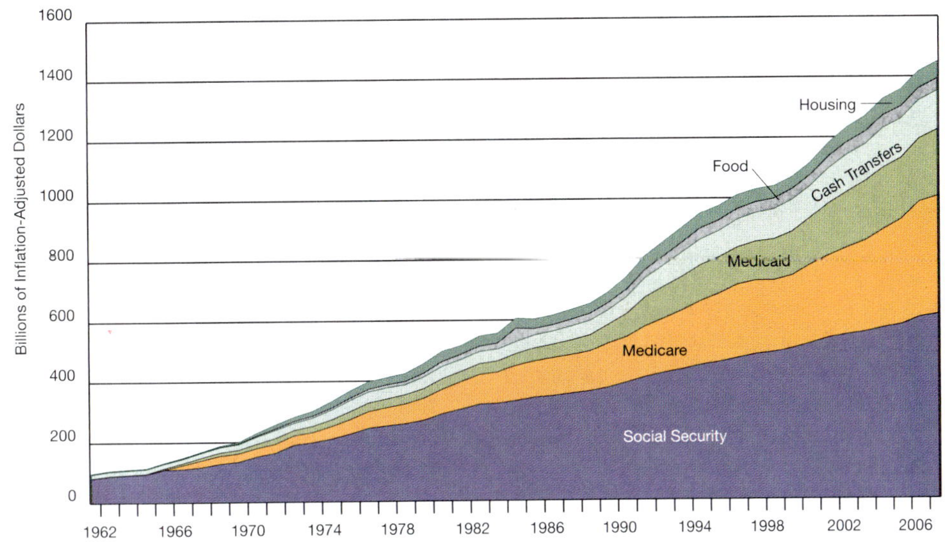

SOURCE: Developed from figures in *Historical Tables, Budget of the United States,* Fiscal Year 2008. Figures are in 2008 purchasing power using the GDP Price Index. Data for 2008 are projections.

the makeup of the group. Keep in mind that we are relying on official poverty estimates, which ignore the value of in-kind transfers, so, to that extent, official estimates overstate poverty.

Poverty and Age

Earlier we looked at poverty among the U.S. population. Here we focus on poverty and age. Exhibit 6 presents the poverty rates for three age groups since 1959: people less than 18 years old, those between 18 and 64, and those 65 and older. As you can see, poverty rates for each group declined between 1959 and 1968. Between the mid-1970s and the early 1980s, the rate among those under 18 trended upward, but then declined from 22.7 percent in 1993 to 17.6 percent in 2005.

In 1959, the elderly were the poorest group, with a poverty rate of 35 percent. Poverty among the elderly declined to 10.1 percent by 2005, slightly below the rate of 11.1 percent for people 18 to 64 years of age. The decline in poverty among the elderly stems from the tremendous growth in spending for Social Security and Medicare. In real terms—that is, after adjusting for the effects of inflation—those two programs have grown more than twelvefold since 1959 (Medicare didn't even exist until 1965). *Although not welfare programs in a strict sense, Social Security and Medicare have been hugely successful in reducing poverty among the elderly.*

Poverty and Public Choice

In a democracy, public policies depend very much on the political influence of the interest groups involved. In recent years, the elderly have become a powerful political force. The voter participation rate of those 65 and over is higher than that of any other age group. For example, people 65 years of age and older vote at triple the rate of those between 18 and 24 and four times that of welfare recipients. The political muscle of the elderly has been flexed whenever a question of Social Security or Medicare benefits is considered.

Unlike most interest groups, the elderly make up a group we all expect to join one day. The elderly are actually supported by five constituencies: (1) the elderly themselves; (2) people under 65 who are concerned about the current benefits to their parents or other elderly relatives; (3) people under 65 who are concerned about their own benefits in the future; (4) people who earn their living by caring for the elderly, such as doctors, nurses, and nursing-home operators; and (5) candidates for office who want to harvest the votes that seniors deliver. So the elderly have a broad constituency, and this pays off in terms of redistribution of wealth to the elderly and in the reduction of poverty among this group.

The Feminization of Poverty

Another way to look at poverty is based on the status of the household head. Exhibit 7 on page 267 compares poverty rates among families headed by females with no husband present with poverty rates for other families. Two trends are unmistakable. First, poverty rates among families headed by females are much higher than rates among other families—about five times higher on average. Second, poverty rates among female-headed families have trended down since the early 1990s, falling from 39.7 percent in 1991 to 31.1 percent in 2005.

The exhibit compares poverty among female householders to other families. What it doesn't show is the growth in female-headed households. The number of families headed by women increased 158 percent between 1965 and 2005, while all other families grew just 23 percent. The percentage of births to unmarried mothers is five times greater today than in the 1960s. In 1960, only 1 in 200 children lived with a single parent who had never married. Today, 1 in 10 children lives with a single parent who has never married.

The United States has the highest teenage pregnancy rate in the developed world—twice the rate of Great Britain and 15 times that of Japan. More than 80 percent of teen mothers are unmarried. Because fathers in such cases typically provide little support, children born outside marriage are likely to be poorer than other children. *The growth in the number of poor families since 1965 resulted overwhelmingly from a growth in the number of female householders.* The number of jobs in the U.S. economy more than doubled in the last four decades. Families with a female householder were in the worst position to take advantage of this job growth. *Children of female householders are five times more likely to live in poverty than are other children. Young, single motherhood is a recipe for poverty.* Often the young mother drops out of school, which reduces her future earning possibilities when and if she seeks work outside the home. Even a strong economy is little help to households with nobody in the labor force. Worse yet, young, single mothers-to-be are less likely to seek adequate medical care; the result is a higher proportion of premature, underweight babies. This is one reason why the U.S. infant mortality rate exceeds that of some other industrialized countries. Compared to two-parent families, children in one-parent families are twice as likely to drop out of school, and girls from one-parent families are twice as likely to become single mothers themselves.

Because of a lack of education and limited job skills, most single mothers go on welfare. Before recently imposed lifetime limits on welfare, the average never-married mother had been on welfare for a decade, twice as long as divorced mothers on welfare. Of all teenagers who gave birth, the proportion

Exhibit 6

U.S. Poverty Rates by Age: 1959–2005

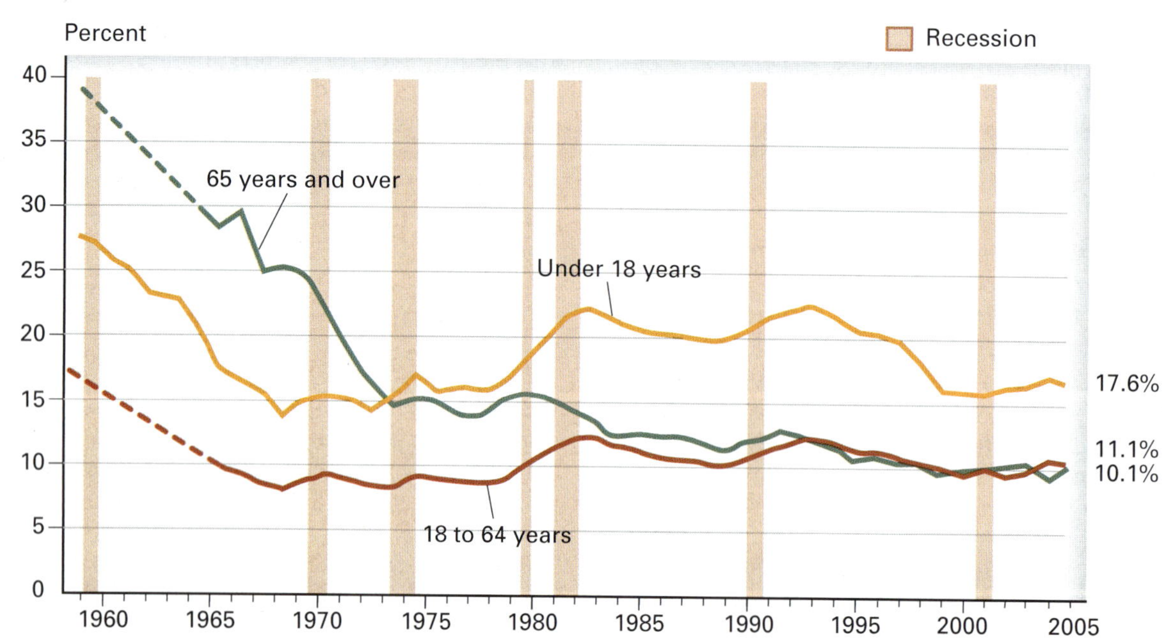

SOURCE: U.S. Census Bureau, *Poverty in the United States 2005,* Current Population Reports, September, 2006. Figure 2, http://www.census.gov/hhes/www/poverty/histpov/hstpov3.html.

unmarried was 13 percent in 1950, 30 percent in 1970, 67 percent in 1990, and 83 percent in 2005.[5]

Poverty has therefore become increasingly feminized, mostly because female householders have become more common. Children from mothers who finished high school, married before having a child, and gave birth after age 20 are 10 times less likely to be poor than children from mothers who fail to do these things.[6] Because the number of female householders has grown more rapidly among African Americans, the feminization of poverty has been more dramatic in those households. Seventy percent of all births to non-Hispanic black mothers in 2005 were to unmarried women, compared with 48 percent of all births among women of Hispanic origin, and 25 percent of births among non-Hispanic whites.[7] But we should be careful in drawing conclusions about the role of race or ethnicity per se, because black and Hispanic households are poorer on average than white households. Low income alone could account for much of the difference in birth rates. In other words, a better comparison would adjust for income differences across groups, but such data are not available.

Exhibit 8 shows the poverty rates for each of the 50 states. States with a deeper shade of red have higher poverty rates. States with no shading have lower rates. As you can see, poverty rates are higher across the bottom half of the United States. Poverty rates tend to be higher in states where births to single mothers make up a larger percentage of all births. For example, New Mexico, Louisiana, and Mississippi had the highest poverty rates. They also had the highest rates of births to unmarried mothers. Nearly half of all births in these three states were to unmarried mothers.

5. "Births: Preliminary Data for 2005," *National Vital Statistics Report* 55, No. 11 (28 December 2006), Table C; also at http://www.cdc.gov/nchs/data/nvsr/nvsr55/nvsr55_11.pdf.
6. James Q. Wilson, "Human Remedies for Social Disorder," *Public Interest* (Spring 1998): 27.

7. "Births: Preliminary Data for 2005," *National Vital Statistics Report* 55, No. 11 (28 December 2006), Table A; also found at http://www.cdc.gov/nchs/data/nvsr/nvsr55/nvsr55_11.pdf.

Exhibit 7

Poverty Rates Are Much Higher for Families Headed by Females But Have Declined in the Last Decade

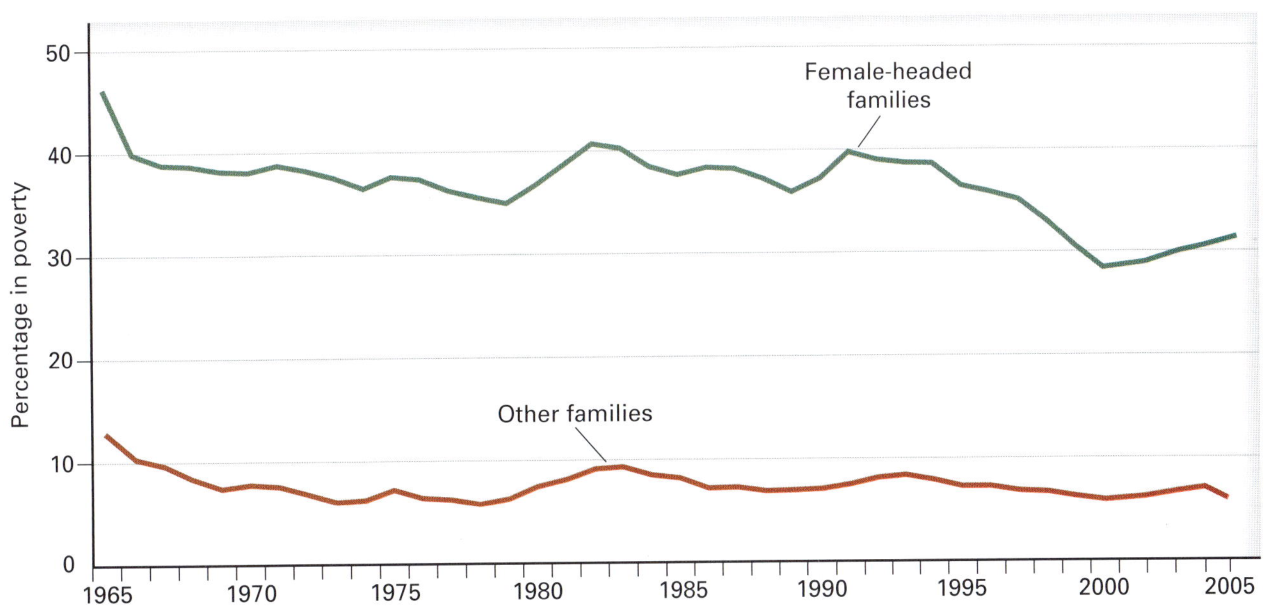

SOURCE: Developed from data in U.S. Census Bureau, *Income, Poverty, and Health Insurance Coverage in the United States: 2005,* Current Population Reports, August 2006, Table B-1, http://www.census.gov/prod/2006pubs/p60-231.pdf.

Exhibit 8

Percent of Population Living in Poverty by State

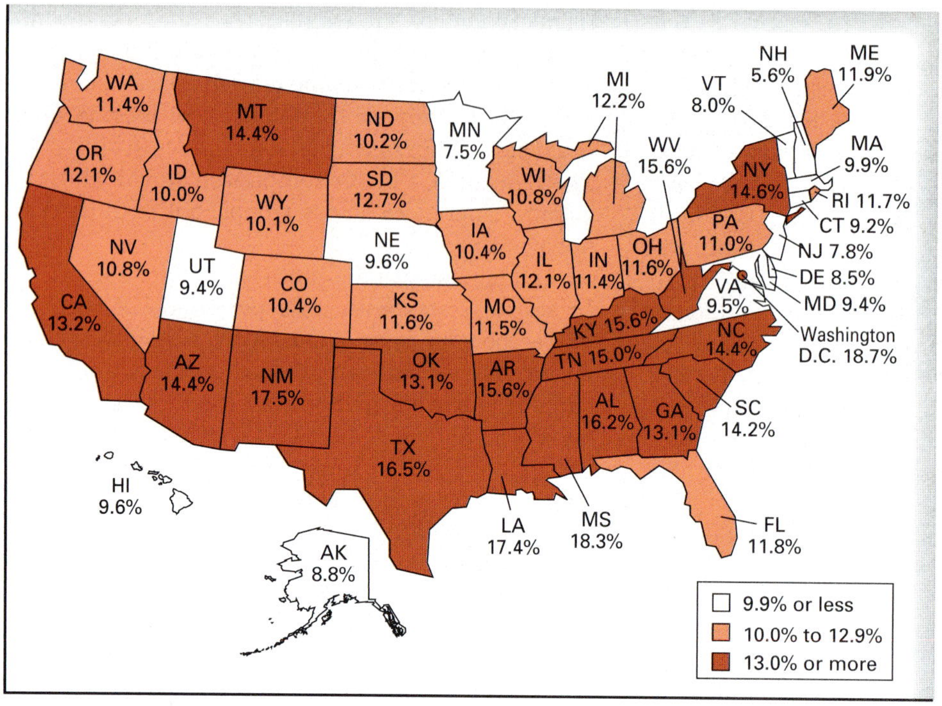

SOURCE: Poverty in the United States: 2005, U.S. Census Bureau, September 2006, Table 19, http://www.census.gov/hhes/www/poverty/histpov/hstpov19.html. Rates are averaged for 2003, 2004, and 2005 to provide more reliable figures.

Poverty and Discrimination

To what extent has racial discrimination limited job opportunities and increased poverty among minorities? Discrimination can occur in many ways: in school funding, in housing, in employment, in career advancement. Also, discrimination in one area can affect opportunities in another. For example, housing discrimination can reduce job opportunities if a black family cannot move within commuting distance of the best jobs. Job-market discrimination can take many forms. An employer may fail to hire a black job applicant because the applicant lacks training. But this lack of training can arise from discrimination in the schools, in union apprenticeship programs, or in training programs run by other employers. For example, evidence suggests that black workers receive less on-the-job training than otherwise similar white workers.

After adjusting for a variety of factors that could affect the wage, such as education and work experience, research shows that white workers earn more than black workers. The gap between the two narrowed between 1940 and 1976 to the point where black workers earned only 7 percent less than white workers; then it widened somewhat.[8] Since 1993, the gap has again narrowed. Could explanations besides job discrimination account for the wage gap? Though the data adjust for *years* of schooling, some research suggests that black workers received a lower *quality* of schooling than white workers. For example, black students are less likely to use computers in school. Inner-city schools often have more problems with classroom discipline, which takes time and attention away from instruction. Such quality differences could account for at least a portion of the remaining gap in standardized wages.

Evidence of discrimination comes from studies where otherwise similar white and black candidates are sent to the same source to seek jobs, rent apartments, or apply for mortgages. For example, white and black job applicants with similar qualifications and résumés applied for the same job. These studies find that employers are less likely to interview or offer a job to minority applicants. Minority applicants also tend to be treated less favorably by real estate agents and lenders. The President's Council of Economic Advisers concluded that discrimination against members of racial and ethnic minorities, while "far less pervasive and overt" than in the past, still persists.[9]

Affirmative Action

The Equal Employment Opportunity Commission, established by the Civil Rights Act of 1964, monitors cases involving unequal pay for equal work and

8. M. Boozer, A. Krueger, and S. Wolken, "Race and School Quality Since Brown v. Board of Education," *Brookings Papers on Economic Activity: Microeconomics* (1992): 269–326.
9. *Economic Report of the President,* February 1998, 152.

unequal access to promotion. All companies doing business with the federal government had to set numerical hiring, promotion, and training goals to ensure that these firms did not discriminate in hiring on the basis of race, sex, religion, or national origin. Black employment increased in those firms required to file affirmative action plans.[10] The fraction of the black labor force employed in white-collar jobs increased from 16.5 percent in 1960 to 40.5 percent in 1981—an increase that greatly exceeded the growth of white-collar jobs in the labor force as a whole. Research also suggests that civil rights legislation played a role in narrowing the black–white earnings gap between 1960 and the mid-1970s.[11]

Attention focused on hiring practices and equality of opportunity at the state and local levels as well, as governments introduced so-called *set-aside* programs to guarantee minorities a share of contracts. But a 1995 U.S. Supreme Court decision challenged affirmative action programs, ruling that Congress must meet a rigorous legal standard to justify any contracting or hiring practice based on race, especially programs that reserve jobs for minorities and women. Programs must be shown to be in response to injustices created by past discrimination, said the Court.

In summary, evidence suggests that black workers earn less than white workers after adjustment for other factors that could affect wages, such as education and job experience. Part of this wage gap may reflect differences in the quality of education, differences that could themselves be the result of discrimination.[12] Keep in mind that unemployment rates are higher among blacks than among whites and are higher still among black teenagers, the group most in need of job skills and job experience. *But we should also note that black families are not a homogeneous group. In fact, the distribution of income is more uneven among black families than it is among the population as a whole.*

On the upside, in the last decade the median income of black families has risen faster than that of white families. The proportion of black families living below the poverty line fell to a record low. And there is a growing middle class among black households. According to the most recent five-year survey of U.S. business ownership, the number of black-owned businesses rose 45 percent to 1.2 million. This growth rate was more that four times that of the 10 percent growth in the number of all businesses. Since 1970, the number of black doctors, nurses, college professors, and newspaper reporters has tripled; the number of black engineers, computer programmers, accountants, managers, and administrators has quadrupled; the number of black elected officials has increased fivefold; and the number of black lawyers has increased more than sixfold. In Georgia, for example, the number of black lawyers increased from just 54 in 1970 to about 2,000 today. Two of the most admired Americans are black—talk show host Oprah Winfrey and presidential candidate Senator Barack Obama.

Unintended Consequences of Income Assistance

On the plus side, antipoverty programs increase the consumption possibilities of poor families, and this is a good thing, especially because children are the largest poverty group. But programs to assist the poor have secondary effects that limit their ability to reduce poverty over time. Here we consider some unintended consequences.

Society, through government, tries to provide families with an adequate standard of living, but

© AP IMAGES

10. James Smith and Finis Welch, "Black Economic Progress After Myrdal," *Journal of Economic Literature* 27 (June 1989): 519–563.
11. David Card and Alan Krueger, "Trends in Relative Black-White Earnings Revisited," *American Economic Review* 83 (May 1993): 85–91.
12. Huoying Wu, "Can the Human Capital Approach Explain Life-Cycle Wage Differentials Between Races and Sexes?" *Economic Inquiry* 45 (January 2007): 24–39.

society also wants to ensure that only the needy receive benefits. As we have seen, income assistance consists of a combination of cash and in-kind transfer programs. Because these programs are designed to help the poor and only the poor, benefits decrease as income from other sources increases. With transfers declining sharply as earned income increases, welfare recipients face a high marginal tax rate on earned income. An increase in earnings may reduce benefits from TANF, Medicaid, food stamps, housing assistance, energy assistance, and other programs. With a loss in support from each program as earned income increases, working may lead to little or no increase in total income. Over certain income ranges, a welfare recipient may lose more than $1 in welfare benefits for each additional $1 in earnings. Thus, the *marginal tax rate* on earned income could exceed 100 percent!

Holding even a part-time job involves some costs—for clothing, transportation, and child care, for instance—not to mention the loss of free time. Such a system of perverse incentives can frustrate people trying to work their way off welfare. *The high marginal tax rate discourages employment and self-sufficiency.* In many cases, welfare benefits exceed the income resulting from full-time employment.

The longer people stay out of the labor force, the more their job skills deteriorate, so when they do look for work, their productivity is lower than when they were last employed. This reduces their expected wage, making work even less attractive. Some economists argue that in this way, welfare benefits can lead to long-term dependency. While welfare seems to be a rational choice in the short run, it has unfavorable long-term consequences for the family, for society, and for the economy.

The longer people stay out of the labor force, the more their job skills deteriorate, so when they do look for work, their productivity is lower than when they were last employed.

Welfare programs can cause other disincentives. For example, children may be eligible for Supplemental Security Income if they have a learning disability. According to one firsthand account, some low-income parents encouraged poor performance in school so their children could qualify for this program.[13]

A serious concern is whether children on welfare are more likely to end up on welfare as adults. Is there a cycle of dependency? Why might we expect one? Children in welfare households may learn the ropes about the welfare system and may come to view welfare as a normal way of life rather than as a temporary bridge over a rough patch. Research indicates that daughters from welfare families are more likely than daughters in other families to participate in the welfare system themselves and are more likely to have premarital births.[14] It is difficult to say whether welfare "causes" the link between mother and daughter, because the same factors that contribute to a mother's welfare status can also contribute to her daughter's welfare status. Evidence of a link is weaker when it comes to sons from welfare families.

LO4 Welfare Reform

There has been much dissatisfaction with the welfare system, among both those who pay for the programs and direct beneficiaries. Welfare reforms introduced more than a decade ago have been aimed at reducing long-term dependency.

Recent Reforms

Some analysts believe that one way to reduce poverty is to provide welfare recipients with job skills and make them find jobs. Even before the 1996 federal reform of welfare, to be discussed shortly, some sort of "workfare" component for welfare recipients operated in most states. In these states, as a condition of receiving welfare, the head of the household had to participate in education and training programs, search for work, or take some paid or unpaid position. The idea was to expose people on welfare to the job market. Evidence from various states indicates that programs involving mandatory job searches, short-term unpaid work, and training could operate at low cost and could increase employment. The government saved money because those in welfare-to-work programs left welfare rolls sooner. Exhibit 9 shows how welfare recipients as a percentage of the population declined after reforms.

Reforms at the state level set the stage for federal reforms. By far the biggest reform in the welfare

13. Jacqueline Goldwyn Kingon, "Education Life: A View from the Trenches," *New York Times,* 8 April 2001.

14. Robert Moffit, "Welfare Reform: The U.S. Experience," Paper Presented at the Economic Council of Sweden Conference, 7 May 2007.

system in the last 70 years came with the 1996 legislation that replaced Aid to Families with Dependent Children (AFDC) with Temporary Assistance for Needy Families (TANF). Whereas the AFDC program set eligibility rules and left federal costs open-ended through matching grants to the states, TANF offers a fixed grant to the states to run their welfare programs. States ended AFDC and began TANF by July 1, 1997. Under the new system, states have much more control over their own welfare programs. But concerns about welfare dependency fostered some special provisions. The act imposes a five-year lifetime limit on cash transfers and requires states to move a certain percentage of people from welfare to work.

Aside from the time limits and work participation rates imposed by the federal government, states are free to set benefit levels and experiment however they choose. For example, about half the states impose time limits shorter than five years. Some observers fear that states now have an incentive to keep welfare costs down by cutting benefits. To avoid becoming destinations for poor people—that is, to avoid becoming "welfare magnets"—states may be tempted to offer relatively low benefits. The fear is that states will undercut benefits in what has been called a "race to the bottom."

Final Word

Government redistribution programs have been most successful at reducing poverty among the elderly. But until recently, poverty rates among children increased because of the growth in the number of female householders. We might ask why transfer programs have reduced poverty rates more among the elderly than among female householders. Transfer programs do not encourage people to get old; that process occurs naturally and is independent of the level of transfers. But the level and availability of transfer programs at the margin could influence some young unmarried women as they are deciding whether or not to have a child and may, at the margin, influence a married mother's decision to get divorced.

Most transfers in the economy are not from the government but are in-kind transfers within the family, from parents to children. Thus, any change in a family's capacity to earn income has serious consequences for dependent children. *Family structure is a primary determinant of family income.* About one in six children in the United States lives in poverty. Children are the innocent victims of the changing family structure. Recent welfare reforms have succeeded in reducing welfare roles and increasing employment among single mothers.

Exhibit 9

Welfare Recipients as a Percentage of the U.S. Population Declined Sharply After 1994

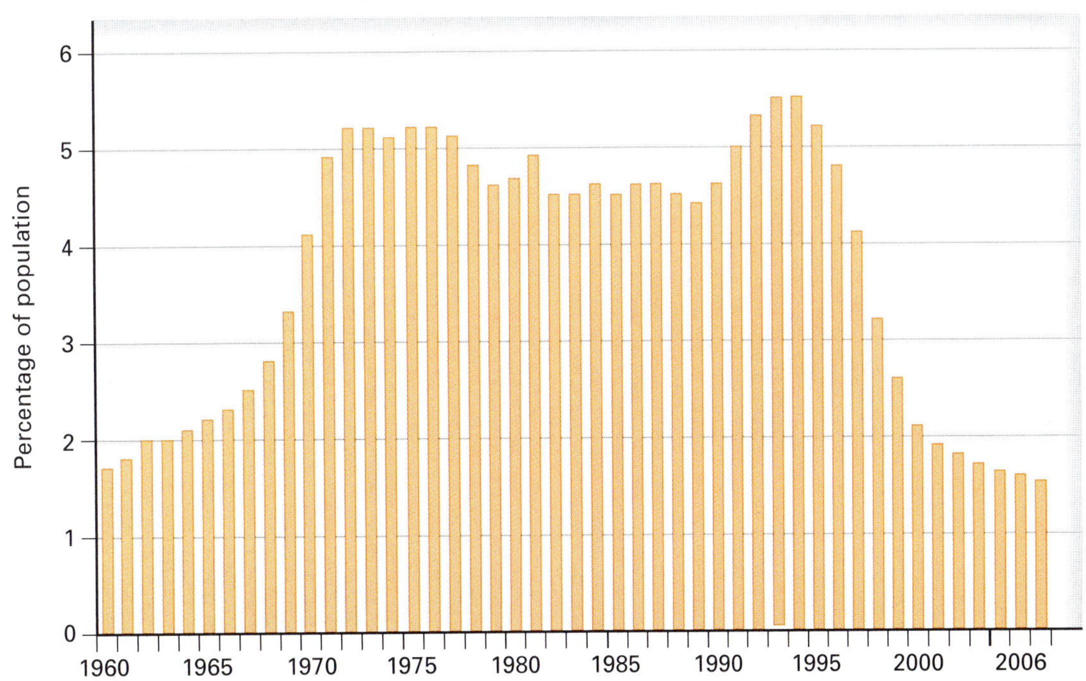

SOURCE: Developed from data from the U.S. Department of Health and Human Services. Figures are for AFDC recipients before 1997 and TANF recipients for 1997 and later. Figures are found at http://www.acf.hhs.gov/programs/ofa/caseload/2006/tanf_recipients.htm.

CHAPTER 19

International Trade

Learning Outcomes

LO 1 Describe the gains that trade brings

LO 2 Discuss the reasons for international specialization

LO 3 Explain trade restrictions and welfare loss

LO 4 Describe ways countries have reduced or eliminated trade barriers

LO 5 List and describe the arguments in favor of trade restrictions

"The world is a giant shopping mall, and Americans are big spenders."

This morning you pulled on your Levi's jeans from Mexico, pulled your Benetton sweater from Italy over your head, and laced up your Timberland boots from Thailand. After a breakfast that included bananas from Honduras and coffee from Brazil, you climbed into your Volvo from Sweden fueled by Venezuelan oil and headed for a lecture by a visiting professor from Hungary. If the United States is such a rich and productive country, why do we import so many goods and services? Why don't we produce everything ourselves? And why do some producers try to restrict foreign trade? Answers to these and other questions are addressed in this chapter.

What do you think?

The U.S. government should eliminate all trade restrictions.

Strongly Disagree						Strongly Agree
1	2	3	4	5	6	7

The world is a giant shopping mall, and Americans are big spenders. For example, the U.S. population is less than 5 percent of the world's population, but Americans buy more than half the Rolls Royces and diamonds sold around the world. Americans also buy Japanese cars, French wine, European vacations, Chinese products galore, and thousands of other goods and services from around the globe. Foreigners buy U.S. products too—grain, aircraft, movies, software, trips to New York City, and thousands of other goods and services. In this chapter, we examine the gains from international trade and the effects of trade restrictions on the allocation of resources. The analysis is based on the familiar tools of demand and supply.

Topics discussed in Chapter 19 include:

- Gains from trade
- Absolute and comparative advantage revisited
- Tariffs
- Quotas
- Welfare loss from trade restrictions
- Arguments for trade restrictions

LO1 The Gains from Trade

A family from Virginia that sits down for a meal of Kansas prime rib, Idaho potatoes, and California string beans, with Georgia peach cobbler for dessert, is benefiting from interstate trade. You already understand why the residents of one state trade with those of another. Back in Chapter 2, you learned about the gains arising from specialization and exchange. You may recall how you and your roommate could maximize output when you each specialized. The law of comparative advantage says that the individual with the lowest opportunity cost of producing a particular good should specialize in that good. Just as individuals benefit from specialization and exchange, so do states and, indeed, nations. To reap the gains that arise from specialization, countries engage in international trade. *Each country specializes in making goods with the lowest opportunity cost.*

Exhibit 1

Composition of U.S. Merchandise Exports and Imports in 2006

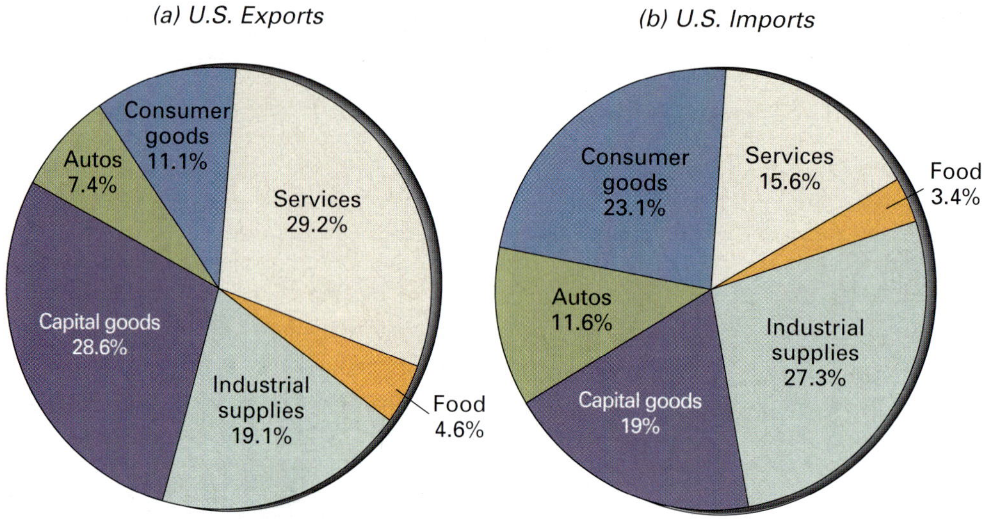

A Profile of Exports and Imports

Just as some states are more involved in interstate trade than others, some nations are more involved in international trade than others. For example, exports account for about one-quarter of the gross domestic product (GDP) in Canada and the United Kingdom; about one-third of GDP in Germany, Sweden, and Switzerland; and about half of GDP in the Netherlands. Despite the perception that Japan has a huge export sector, exports make up only about one-sixth of its GDP.

U.S. Exports

U.S. exports of goods and services amounted to $1.4 trillion, or about 11 percent of GDP in 2006. The left panel of Exhibit 1 shows the composition by major category. The largest category is services, which accounted for the 29.2 percent of U.S. exports. U.S. service exports include transportation, insurance, banking, education, consulting, and tourism. Capital goods ranked second at 28.6 percent of exports in 2006. Capital goods include high-tech products, such as computers and jet aircraft. Third most important are industrial supplies, at 19.1 percent of the total. Capital goods and industrial supplies help foreign producers make stuff and accounted for nearly half of U.S. exports. Consumer goods (except food, which appears separately) accounted for only 11.1 percent of exports. Consumer goods include entertainment products, such as movies and recorded music.

U.S. Imports

U.S. imports of goods and services in 2006 totaled $2.2 trillion, or about 16 percent relative to GDP. The right panel of Exhibit 1 shows the composition of U.S. imports. The most important category, at 27.3 percent, is industrial supplies, such as crude oil from Venezuela and raw metals, including lead, zinc, and copper, from around the world. Whereas consumer goods accounted for only 11.1 percent of U.S. exports, they were 23.1 percent of imports. Imported consumer goods include electronics from Taiwan, shoes from Brazil, and all kinds of products from China. Ranked third in importance is capital goods, at 19.0 percent, such as printing presses from Germany. Note that services, which accounted for 29.2 percent of U.S. exports, were only 15.6 percent of imports.

Trading Partners

To give you some feel for America's trading partners, here are the top 10 destinations for merchandise exports in 2006: Canada, Mexico, Japan, China, United Kingdom, Germany, South Korea, Netherlands, France, and Singapore. The top 10 sources of merchandise imports are Canada, China, Mexico, Japan, Germany, United Kingdom, South Korea, Taiwan, Venezuala, and France.

Production Possibilities Without Trade

The rationale behind most international trade is obvious. The United States grows little coffee because the climate is not suited to coffee. More revealing, however, are the gains from trade where the comparative advantage is not so obvious. Suppose that just two goods—food and clothing—are produced and consumed and that there are only two countries in the world—the United States, with

Exhibit 2

Production Possibilities Schedules for the United States and Izodia

(a) United States

	Production Possibilities with 100 Million Workers (millions of units per day)					
	U_1	U_2	U_3	U_4	U_5	U_6
Food	600	480	360	240	120	0
Clothing	0	60	120	180	240	300

(b) Izodia

	Production Possibilities with 200 Million Workers (millions of units per day)					
	I_1	I_2	I_3	I_4	I_5	I_6
Food	200	160	120	80	40	0
Clothing	0	80	160	240	320	400

a labor force of 100 million workers, and the mythical country of Izodia, with 200 million workers. The conclusions derived from this simple model have general relevance for international trade.

Exhibit 2 presents production possibilities tables for each country, based on the size of the labor force and the productivity of workers in each country. The exhibit assumes that each country has a given technology and that labor is efficiently employed. If no trade occurs between countries, Exhibit 2 also represents each country's *consumption possibilities* table. The production numbers imply that each worker in the United States can produce either 6 units of food or 3 units of clothing per day. If all 100 million U.S. workers produce food, they make 600 million units per day, as shown in column U_1 in panel (a). If all U.S. workers make clothing, they turn out 300 million units per day, as shown in column U_6. The columns in between show some workers making food and some making clothing. Because a U.S. worker can produce either 6 units of food or 3 units of clothing, *the opportunity cost of 1 more unit of food is 0.5 units of clothing.*

Suppose Izodian workers are less educated, work with less capital, and farm less fertile soil than U.S. workers, so each Izodian worker can produce only 1 unit of food or 2 units of clothing per day. If all 200 million Izodian workers specialize in food, they can make 200 million units per day, as shown in column I_1 in panel (b) of Exhibit 2. If they all make clothing, total output is 400 million units per day, as shown in column I_6. Some intermediate production possibilities are also listed in the exhibit. Because an Izodian worker can produce either 1 unit of food or 2 units of clothing, *their opportunity cost of 1 more unit of food is 2 units of clothing.*

We can convert the data in Exhibit 2 to a production possibilities frontier for each country, as shown in Exhibit 3. In each diagram, the amount of food produced is measured on the vertical axis and the amount of clothing on the horizontal axis. U.S. combinations are shown in the left panel by U_1, U_2, and so on. Izodian combinations are shown in the right panel by I_1, I_2, and so on. Because we assume for simplicity that resources are perfectly adaptable to the production of each commodity, each production possibilities curve is a straight line. The slope of this line differs between countries because the opportunity cost of production differs between countries.

Exhibit 3 illustrates possible combinations of food and clothing that residents of each country can produce and consume if all resources are efficiently employed and there is no trade between the two countries. **Autarky** is the situation of national self-sufficiency, in which there is no economic interaction with foreign producers or consumers. Suppose that U.S. producers

Exhibit 3

Production Possibilities Frontiers for the United States and Izodia Without Trade (millions of units per day)

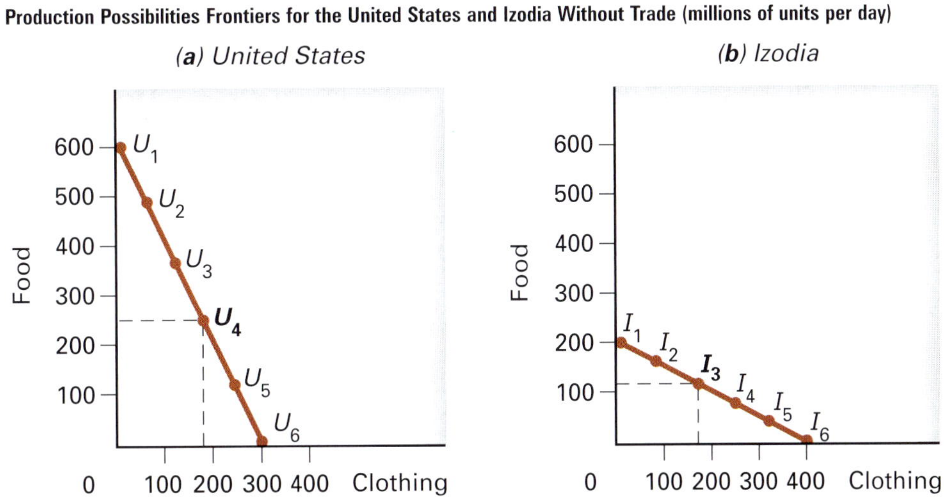

autarky
national self-sufficiency; no economic interaction with foreigners

maximize profit and U.S. consumers maximize utility with the combination of 240 million units of food and 180 million units of clothing—combination U_4. This is called the *autarky equilibrium*. Suppose also that Izodians are in autarky equilibrium, identified as combination I_3, of 120 million units of food and 160 million units of clothing.

Consumption Possibilities Based on Comparative Advantage

In our example, each U.S. worker can produce more clothing and more food per day than can each Izodian worker, so Americans have an *absolute advantage* in the production of both goods. Recall from Chapter 2 that having an absolute advantage means being able to produce something using fewer resources than other producers require. Should the U.S. economy remain in autarky—that is, self-sufficient in both food and clothing productions—or could there be gains from specialization and trade?

As long as the opportunity cost of production differs between the two countries, there are gains from specialization and trade. *According to the law of comparative advantage, each country should specialize in producing the good with the lower opportunity cost.* The opportunity cost of producing 1 more unit of food is 0.5 units of clothing in the United States compared with 2 units of clothing in Izodia. Because the opportunity cost of producing food is lower in the United States than in Izodia, both countries gain if the United States specializes in food and exports some to Izodia, and Izodia specializes in clothing and exports some to the United States.

Before countries can trade, however, they must agree on how much of one good exchanges for another—that is, they must agree on the **terms of trade**. As long as Americans can get more than 0.5 units of clothing for each unit of food produced, and as long as Izodians can get more than 0.5 units of food for each unit of clothing produced, both countries will be better off specializing. Suppose that market forces shape the terms of trade so that 1 unit of clothing exchanges for 1 unit of food. Americans thus trade 1 unit of food to Izodians for 1 unit of clothing. To produce 1 unit of clothing themselves, Americans would have to sacrifice 2 units of food. Likewise, Izodians trade 1 unit of clothing to Americans for 1 unit of food, which is only half what Izodians would sacrifice to produce 1 unit of food themselves.

terms of trade
how much of one good exchanges for a unit of another good

Exhibit 4 shows that with 1 unit of food trading for 1 unit of clothing, Americans and Izodians can consume anywhere along their blue consumption possibilities frontiers. *The consumption possibilities frontier* shows a nation's possible combinations of goods available as a result of specialization and exchange. (Note that the U.S. consumption possibilities curve does not extend to the right of 400 million units of clothing, because Izodia could produce no more than that.) The amount each country actually consumes depends on the relative preferences for food and clothing. Suppose Americans select combination *U* in panel (a) and Izodians select point *I* in panel (b).

Without trade, the United States produces and consumes 240 million units of food and 180 million units of clothing. With trade, the Americans specialize to produce 600 million units of food; they eat 400 million units and exchange the rest for 200 million units of Izodian clothing. This consumption combination is reflected by point *U*. Through exchange, Americans increase their consumption of both food and clothing.

Without trade, Izodians produce and consume 120 million units of food and 160 million units of

Exhibit 4

Production (and Consumption) Possibility Frontiers with Trade (millions of units per day)

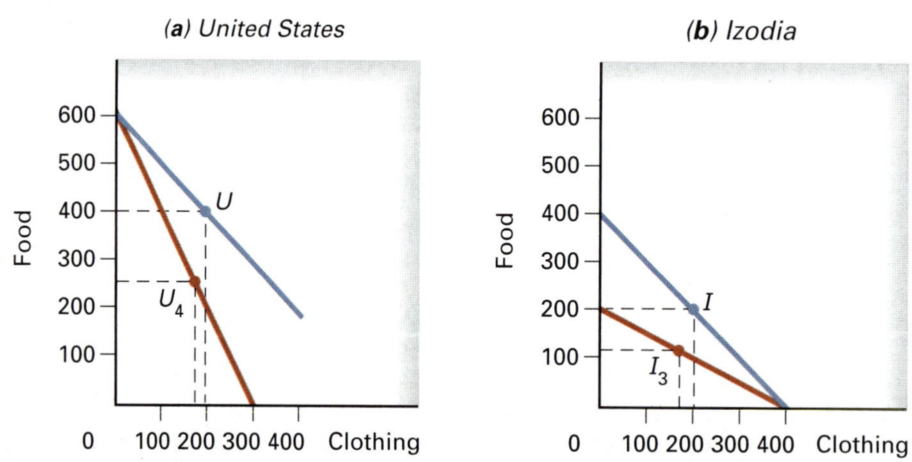

clothing. With trade, Izodians specialize to produce 400 million units of clothing; they wear 200 million and exchange the rest for 200 million units of U.S. food. This consumption combination is shown by point *I*. Through trade, Izodians, like Americans, are able to increase their consumption of both goods. How is this possible?

Because Americans are more efficient in the production of food and Izodians are more efficient in the production of clothing, total output increases when each specializes. Without specialization, total world production was 360 million units of food and 340 million units of clothing. With specialization, food increases to 600 million units and clothing to 400 million units. Thus, both countries increase consumption with trade. *Although the United States has an absolute advantage in both goods, differences in the opportunity cost of production between the two nations ensure that specialization and exchange result in mutual gains.* Remember that comparative advantage, not absolute advantage, creates gains from specialization and trade. The only constraint on trade is that, for each good, *total world production must equal total world consumption*.

> "Total world production must equal total world consumption."

We simplified trade relations in our example to highlight the gains from specialization and exchange. We assumed that each country would completely specialize in producing a particular good, that resources were equally adaptable to the production of either good, that the costs of transporting goods from one country to another were inconsequential, and that there were no problems in arriving at the terms of trade. The world is not that simple. For example, we don't expect a country to produce just one good. Regardless, specialization based on the law of comparative advantage still leads to gains from trade.

LO2 Reasons for International Specialization

Countries trade with one another—or, more precisely, people and firms in one country trade with those in another—because each side expects to gain from exchange. How do we know what each country should produce and what each should trade?

Differences in Resource Endowments

Differences in resource endowments often create differences in the opportunity cost of production across countries. Some countries are blessed with an abundance of fertile land and favorable growing seasons. The United States, for example, has been called the "breadbasket of the world" because of its rich farmland ideal for growing corn. Coffee grows best in the climate and elevation of Colombia, Brazil, and Jamaica. Honduras has the ideal climate for bananas. Thus, the United States exports corn and imports coffee and bananas. Seasonal differences across countries also encourage trade. For example, in the winter, Americans import fruit from Chile, and Canadians travel to Florida for sun and fun. In the summer, Americans export fruit to Chile, and Americans travel to Canada for camping and hiking.

Resources are often concentrated in particular countries: crude oil in Saudi Arabia, fertile soil in the United States, copper ore in Chile, rough diamonds in South Africa. The United States grows abundant supplies of oil seeds such as soybeans and sunflowers, but does not have enough crude oil to satisfy domestic demand. Thus, the United States exports oil seeds and imports crude oil. More generally, *countries export products they can produce more cheaply in return for products that are unavailable domestically or are cheaper elsewhere.* Remember, trade is based on comparative advantage, which is the ability to produce something at a lower opportunity cost than other producers face.

Exhibit 5 on the next page shows, for 12 key commodities, U.S. production as a percentage of U.S. consumption. If production falls short of consumption, this means the United States imports the difference. For example, because America grows coffee only in Hawaii, U.S. production is only 1 percent of U.S. consumption, so nearly all coffee is imported. The exhibit also shows that U.S. production falls short of consumption for oil and for metals such as lead, zinc, copper, and aluminum. If production exceeds consumption, the United States exports the difference. For example, U.S.-grown cotton amounts to 281 percent of U.S. cotton consumption, so most U.S. grown cotton is exported. U.S. production also exceeds consumption for other crops, including wheat, oil seeds, and coarse grains (corn, barley,

Exhibit 5

U.S. Production as a Percentage of U.S. Consumption for Various Commodities

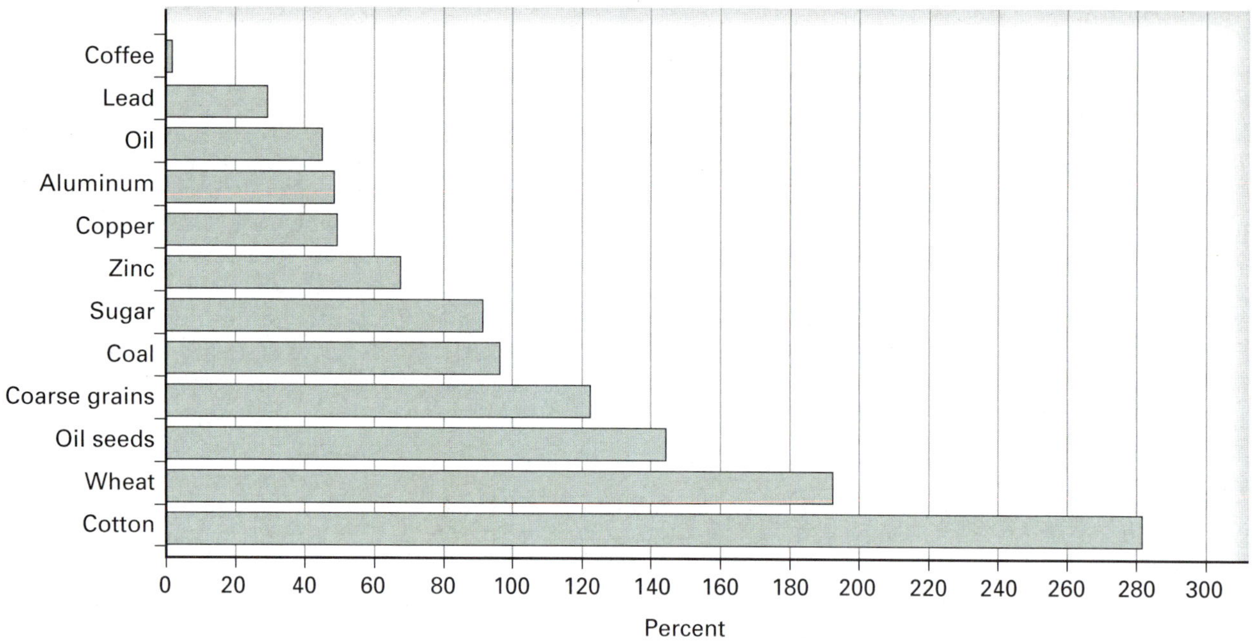

SOURCE: Based on annual figures from *The Economist World in Figures: 2007 Edition* (London: Profile Books, 2007).

oats). In short, when it comes to basic commodities, the United States is a net importer of oil and metals and a net exporter of farm crops.

Economies of Scale

If production is subject to *economies of scale*—that is, if the long-run average cost of production falls as a firm expands its scale of operation—countries can gain from trade if each nation specializes. Such specialization allows firms in each nation to produce more, which reduces average costs. The primary reason for establishing the single integrated market of the European Union was to offer producers there a large, open market of now more than 500 million consumers. Producers could thereby achieve economies of scale. Firms and countries producing at the lowest opportunity costs are most competitive in international markets. For example, 60 percent of the world's buttons come from a single Chinese city.

Differences in Tastes

Even if all countries had identical resource endowments and combined those resources with equal efficiency, each country would still gain from trade as

>> Different tastes result in different consumption patterns, which affect trade.

© DIGITAL ANIMAL FARM/ WORKBOOK STOCK/JUPITERIMAGES

© MIKE KEMP/RUBBERBALL/ JUPITERIMAGES

long as tastes differed among countries. Consumption patterns differ across countries and some of this results from differences in tastes. For example, the Czechs and Irish drink three times as much beer per capita as do the Swiss and Swedes. The French drink three times as much wine as do Australians. The Danes eat twice as much pork as do Americans. Americans eat twice as much chicken as do Hungarians. Soft drinks are four times more popular in the United States than in Europe. The English like tea; Americans, coffee. Algeria has an ideal climate for growing grapes (vineyards there date back to Roman times). But Algeria's population is 99 percent Muslim, a religion that forbids alcohol consumption. Thus, Algeria exports wine.

LO[3] Trade Restrictions and Welfare Loss

Despite the benefits of exchange, nearly all countries at one time or another erect trade barriers, which benefit some domestic producers but harm other domestic producers and all domestic consumers. In this section, we consider the effects of trade barriers and the reasons they are imposed.

Consumer Surplus and Producer Surplus from Market Exchange

Before we explore the net effects of world trade on social welfare, let's review a framework showing the benefits that consumers and producers get from market exchange. Consider a hypothetical market for chicken, shown in Exhibit 6. As discussed way back in Chapter 4, the height of the demand curve shows what consumers are willing and able to pay for each additional pound of chicken. In effect, the height of the demand curve shows the *marginal benefit* consumers expect from that pound of chicken. For example, the demand curve indicates that some consumers in this market are willing to pay $1.50 or more per pound for the first few pounds of chicken. But every consumer gets to buy chicken at the market-clearing price, which here is $0.50 per pound. Most consumers thus get a bonus, or a surplus, from market exchange.

Exhibit 6

Consumer Surplus and Producer Surplus

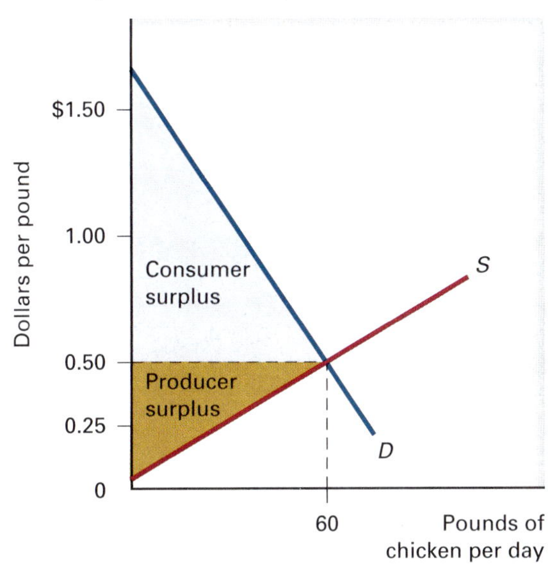

The blue-shaded triangle below the demand curve and above the market price reflects the *consumer surplus* in this market, which is the difference between the most that consumers would pay for 60 pounds of chicken per day and the actual amount they do pay. We all enjoy a consumer surplus from most products we buy.

Producers usually derive a similar surplus. The height of the supply curve shows what producers are willing and able to accept for each additional pound of chicken. That is, the height of the supply curve shows the expected *marginal cost* from producing each additional pound of chicken. For example, the supply curve indicates that some producers face a marginal cost of $0.25 or less per pound for supplying the first few pounds of chicken. But every producer gets to sell chicken for the market-clearing price of $0.50 per pound. The gold-shaded triangle above the supply curve and below the market price reflects the *producer surplus,* which is the difference between the actual amount that producers receive for 60 pounds of chicken and what they would accept to supply that amount.

The point is that market exchange usually generates a surplus, or a bonus, for both consumers and producers. In the balance of this chapter, we will continue to look at the gains from international trade and how trade restrictions affect consumer and producer surplus.

Tariffs

A *tariff,* a term first introduced in Chapter 3, is a tax on imports. (Tariffs can apply to exports, too, but we will focus on import tariffs.) A tariff can be either *specific,* such as a tariff of $5 per barrel of oil, or *ad valorem,* such as 10 percent on the import price of jeans. Consider the effects of a specific tariff on a particular good. In Exhibit 7 on the next page, *D* is the U.S. demand for sugar and S is the supply of sugar from U.S. growers (there were about 10,000 U.S. sugarcane growers in 2007). Suppose that the world price of sugar is $0.10 per pound, as it was in June 2007. The world price is determined by the world supply and demand for a product. It is the price at which any supplier can sell output on the world market and at which any demander can purchase output on the world market.

With free trade, any U.S. consumers could buy any amount desired at the world price of $0.10 per pound, so the quantity demanded is 70 million pounds per month, of which U.S. producers supply 20 million pounds and importers supply 50 million pounds. Because U.S. buyers can purchase sugar at the world price, U.S. producers can't charge more than that. Now suppose that a specific tariff of $0.05 is imposed on each pound of imported sugar, raising its price from $0.10 to $0.15 per pound. U.S. producers can therefore raise their own price to $0.15 per pound as well without losing business to imports. At the higher price, the quantity supplied by U.S. producers increases to 30 million pounds, but the quantity demanded by U.S. consumers declines to 60 million pounds. Because quantity demanded has declined and quantity supplied by U.S. producers has increased, U.S. imports fall from 50 million to 30 million pounds per month.

Because the U.S. price is higher after the tariff, U.S. consumers are worse off. Their loss in consumer surplus is identified in Exhibit 7 by the combination of the blue- and pink-shaded areas. Because both the U.S. price and the quantity supplied by U.S. producers have increased, their total revenue increases by the areas *a* plus *b* plus *f*. But only area *a* represents an increase in producer surplus. Revenue represented by the areas *b* plus *f* merely offsets the higher marginal cost U.S. producers face in expanding sugar output from 20 million to 30 million pounds per month. Area *b* represents part of the net welfare loss to the domestic economy because those 10 million pounds could have been imported for $0.10 per pound rather than produced domestically at a higher marginal cost.

Government revenue from the tariff is identified by area *c*, which equals the tariff of $0.05 per pound multiplied by the 30 million pounds imported, for tariff revenue of $1.5 million per month. Tariff revenue is a loss to consumers, but because the tariff goes to the government, it can be used to lower taxes or to increase public services, so it's not a loss to the U.S. economy. Area *d* shows a loss in consumer sur-

Exhibit 7

Effect of a Tariff

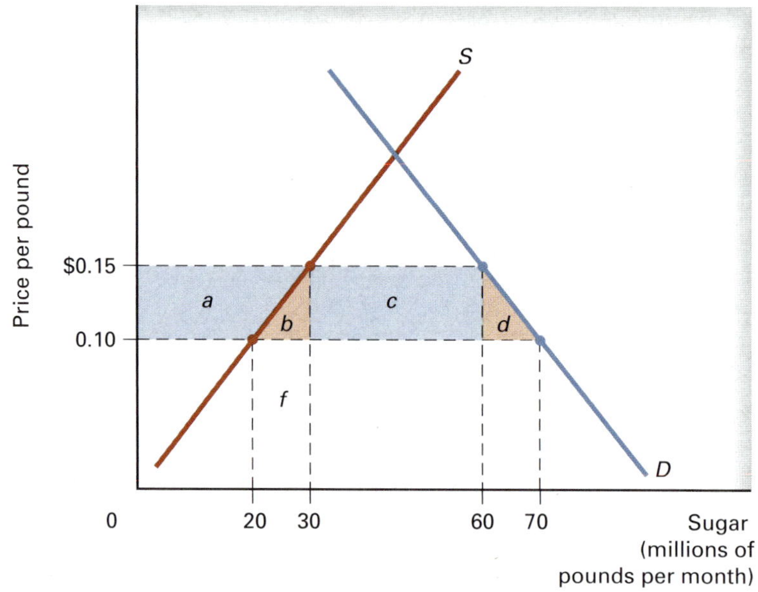

© PETER SZEKELY/ALAMY

world price the price at which a good is traded on the world market; determined by the world demand and world supply for the good plus because less sugar is consumed at the higher price. This loss is not redistributed to anyone else, so area *d* reflects part of the net welfare loss of the tariff. Therefore, areas *b* and *d* show the domestic economy's net welfare loss of the tariff; *the two triangles measure a loss in consumer surplus that is not offset by a gain to anyone in the domestic economy*.

In summary: Of the total loss in U.S. consumer surplus (areas *a*, *b*, *c*, and *d*) resulting from the tariff, area *a* goes to U.S producers, area *c* becomes government revenue, but areas *b* and *d* are net losses in domestic social welfare.

Import Quotas

An *import quota* is a legal limit on the amount of a commodity that can be imported. Quotas usually target imports from certain countries. For example, a quota may limit furniture from China or shoes from Brazil. To have an impact on the domestic market, a quota must be set below what would be imported with free trade. Consider a quota on the U.S. market for sugar. In panel (a) of Exhibit 8, *D* is the U.S. demand curve and S is the supply curve of U.S. sugar producers. Suppose again that the world price of sugar is \$0.10 per pound. With free trade, that price would prevail in the U.S. market as well, and a total of 70 million pounds would be demanded per month. U.S. producers would supply 20 million pounds and importers, 50 million pounds. With a quota of 50 million pounds or more per month, the U.S. price would remain the same as the world price of \$0.10 per pound, and quantity would be 70 million pounds per month. In short, a quota of at least 50 million pounds would not raise the U.S. price above the world price because 50 million pounds were imported without a quota. A more stringent quota, however, would cut imports, which, as we'll see, would raise the U.S. price.

Suppose U.S. trade officials impose an import quota of 30 million pounds per month. As long as the U.S. price is at or above the world price of \$0.10 per pound, foreign producers will supply 30 million pounds. So at prices at or above \$0.10 per pound, the total supply of sugar to the U.S. market is found by adding 30 million pounds of imported sugar to the amount supplied by U.S. producers. U.S. and foreign producers would never sell in the U.S. market for less than \$0.10 per pound because they can always get that price on the world market. Thus, the supply curve that sums domestic production and imports is horizontal at the world price of \$0.10 per pound and remains so until the quantity supplied reaches 50 million pounds.

Again, for prices above \$0.10 per pound, the new supply curve, S', adds horizontally the 30-million-pound quota to S, the supply curve of U.S. producers. The U.S. price is found where this new supply curve, S', intersects the domestic demand curve, which in the left panel of Exhibit 8 occurs at point *e*. *By limiting imports, the quota raises the domestic price of sugar above the world price and reduces quantity below the free trade level.* (Note that to compare more easily the effects of tariffs and quotas, this quota is designed to yield the same equilibrium price and quantity as the tariff examined earlier.)

Exhibit 8

Effect of a Quota

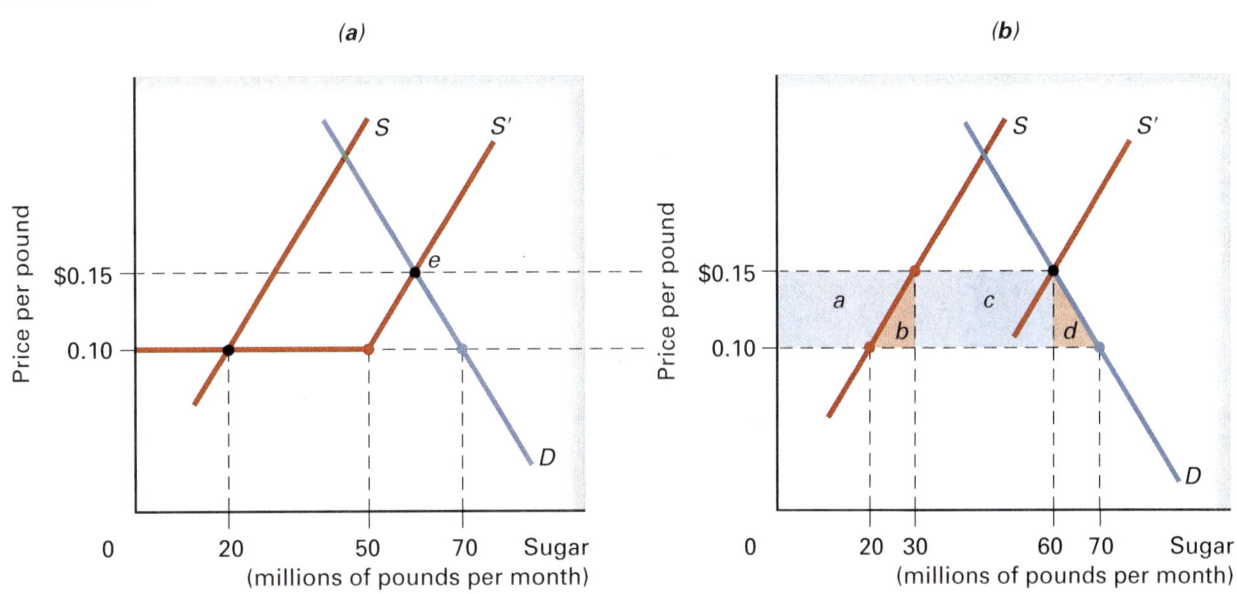

Panel (b) of Exhibit 8 shows the distribution and efficiency effects of the quota. As a result of the quota, U.S. consumer surplus declines by the combined blue and pink areas. Area *a* becomes producer surplus and thus involves no loss of U.S. welfare. Area *c* shows the increased economic profit to those permitted by the quota to sell Americans 30 million pounds for $0.15 per pound, or $0.05 above the world price. If foreign exporters rather than U.S. importers reap this profit, area *c* reflects a net loss in U.S. welfare.

Area *b* shows a welfare loss to the U.S. economy, because sugar could have been purchased abroad for $0.10 per pound, and the U.S. resources employed to increase sugar production could have been used more efficiently producing other goods. Area *d* is also a welfare loss because it reflects a reduction in consumer surplus with no offsetting gain to anyone. Thus, areas *b* and *d* in panel (b) of Exhibit 8 measure the minimum U.S. welfare loss from the quota. If the profit from quota rights (area *c*) accrues to foreign producers, this increases the U.S. welfare loss.

Quotas in Practice

The United States has granted quotas to specific countries. These countries, in turn, distribute these quota rights to their exporters through a variety of means. *By rewarding domestic and foreign producers with higher prices, the quota system creates two groups intent on securing and perpetuating these quotas.* Lobbyists for foreign producers work the halls of Congress, seeking the right to export to the United States. This strong support from producers, coupled with a lack of opposition from consumers (who remain rationally ignorant for the most part), has resulted in quotas that have lasted decades. For example, sugar quotas have been around more than 50 years. In June 2007, the world price of sugar was about $0.10 a pound, but U.S. businesses that need sugar to make products, such as candy, paid more than $0.20 a pound, costing consumers an extra $2 billion annually. Sugar sales, which account for only 1 percent of U.S. farm sales, have accounted for 17 percent of political contributions from agriculture since 1990.[1]

Some economists have argued that if quotas are to be used, the United States should auction them off to foreign producers, thereby capturing at least some of the difference between the world price and the U.S. price. Auctioning off quotas would not only increase federal revenue but would reduce the profitability of quotas, which would reduce pressure on Washington to perpetuate them. American consumers are not the only victims of sugar quotas. Thousands of poor farmers around the world miss out on an opportunity to earn a living growing sugarcane for export to America.

1. Michael Schroeder, "Sugar Growers Hold Up Push for Free Trade," *Wall Street Journal,* 3 February 2004.

Tariffs and Quotas Compared

Consider the similarities and differences between a tariff and a quota. Because both have identical effects on the price in our example, they both lead to the same change in quantity demanded. In both cases, U.S. consumers suffer the same loss of consumer surplus, and U.S. producers reap the same gain of producer surplus. The primary difference is that the revenue from the tariff goes to the U.S. government, whereas the revenue from the quota goes to whoever secures the right to sell foreign goods in the U.S. market. *If quota rights accrue to foreigners, then the domestic economy is worse off with a quota than with a tariff.* But even if quota rights go to domestic importers, quotas, like tariffs, still increase the domestic price, restrict quantity, and thereby reduce consumer surplus and economic welfare. Quotas and tariffs can also raise production costs. For example, U.S. candy manufacturers face higher production costs because of sugar quotas, making them less competitive on world markets. Finally, and most importantly, *quotas and tariffs encourage foreign governments to retaliate with quotas and tariffs of their own, thus shrinking U.S. export markets, so the loss is greater than shown in Exhibits 7 and 8.*

Other Trade Restrictions

Besides tariffs and quotas, a variety of other measures limit free trade. A country may provide *export subsidies* to encourage exports and *low-interest loans* to foreign buyers. Some countries impose *domestic content requirements* specifying that a certain portion of a final good must be produced domestically. Other requirements concerning health, safety, or technical standards often discriminate against foreign goods. For example, European countries prohibit beef from hormone-fed cattle, a measure aimed at U.S. beef. Purity laws in Germany bar many non-German beers. Until the European Community adopted uniform standards, differing technical requirements forced manufacturers to offer as many as seven different versions of the same TV for that market. Sometimes exporters will voluntarily limit exports, as when Japanese automakers agreed to cut exports to the United States. The point is that *tariffs and quotas are only two of many devices used to restrict foreign trade.*

Recent research on the cost of protectionism indicates that international trade barriers slow the introduction of new goods and better technologies. So, rather than simply raising domestic prices, trade restrictions slow economic progress.

LO4 Reduction of Trade Barriers

In recent decades, countries have worked to reduce trade barriers and increase the flow of international trade. Let's examine multilateral agreements, the World Trade Organization, and common markets more closely.

Freer Trade by Multilateral Agreement

Mindful of how high tariffs cut world trade during the Great Depression, the United States, after World War II, invited its trading partners to negotiate lower tariffs and other trade barriers. The result was the General Agreement on Tariffs and Trade (GATT), an international trade treaty adopted in 1947 by 23 countries, including the United States. Each GATT member agreed to (1) reduce tariffs through multinational negotiations, (2) reduce import quotas, and (3) treat all members equally with respect to trade.

Trade barriers have been reduced through trade negotiations among many countries, or "trade rounds," under the auspices of GATT. Trade rounds offer a package approach rather than an issue-by-issue approach to trade negotiations. Concessions that are necessary but otherwise difficult to defend in domestic political terms can be made more acceptable in the context of a package that also contains politically and economically attractive benefits. Most early GATT trade rounds were aimed at reducing tariffs. The Kennedy Round in the mid-1960s included new provisions against dumping, which is selling a commodity abroad for less than is charged in the home market or less than the cost of production. The Tokyo Round of the 1970s was a more sweeping attempt to extend and improve the system.

The most recently completed round was launched in Uruguay in September 1986 and ratified by 123 participating countries in 1994. The number of signing countries now exceeds 140. This so-called Uruguay Round, the most comprehensive of the eight postwar multilateral trade negotiations, included 550 pages of tariff reductions on 85 percent of world trade. The Uruguay Round also created the World Trade Organization (WTO) to succeed GATT.

The World Trade Organization

The World Trade Organization (WTO) now provides the legal and institutional foundation for world trade. Whereas GATT was a multilateral agreement with no institutional foundation, the WTO is a permanent institution in Geneva, Switzerland. A staff of about 500 economists and lawyers helps shape policy and resolves trade disputes between member countries. Whereas GATT involved only merchandise trade, the WTO also covers services and trade-related aspects of intellectual property, such as books, movies, and computer programs. The WTO will eventually phase out quotas, but tariffs will remain legal. As a result of the Uruguay Round, average tariffs fell from 6 percent to 4 percent of the value of imports (when GATT began in 1947, tariffs averaged 40 percent).

Whereas GATT relied on voluntary cooperation, the WTO settles disputes in a way that is faster, more automatic, and less susceptible to blockage than the GATT system was. The WTO resolved more trade disputes in its first decade than GATT did in nearly 50 years. Since 2000, developing countries have filed 60 percent of the disputes. But the WTO has also become a lightning rod for globalization issues, as discussed in the following case study.

Common Markets

Some countries looked to the success of the U.S. economy, which is essentially a free trade zone across 50 states, and have tried to develop free trade zones of their own. The largest and best known is the European Union, which began in 1958 with a half dozen countries and expanded by 2007 to 27 countries and about 500 million people. The idea was to create a barrier-free

General Agreement on Tariffs and Trade (GATT) an international tariff-reduction treaty adopted in 1947 that resulted in a series of negotiated "rounds" aimed at freer trade; the Uruguay Round created GATT's successor, the World Trade Organization (WTO)

dumping selling a product abroad for less than charged in the home market or for less than the cost of production

Uruguay Round the final multilateral trade negotiation under GATT; this 1994 agreement cut tariffs, formed the World Trade Organization (WTO), and will eventually eliminate quotas

World Trade Organization (WTO) the legal and institutional foundation of the multilateral trading system that succeeded GATT in 1995

© LEE JAE-WON/REUTERS/LANDOV

European market like that of the United States in which goods, services, people, and capital are free to flow to their highest-valued use. Thirteen members of the European Union have also adopted a common currency, the *euro,* which replaced national currencies in 2002.

The United States, Canada, and Mexico have developed a free trade pact called the North American Free Trade Agreement (NAFTA). Through NAFTA, Mexico hopes to attract more U.S. investment by guaranteeing companies that locate there duty-free access to U.S. markets, which is where over two-thirds of Mexico's exports go. Mexico's 110 million people represent an attractive export market for U.S. producers, and Mexico's oil reserves could ease U.S. energy problems. The United States would also like to support Mexico's efforts to become more market oriented, as is reflected, for example, by Mexico's privatization of its phone system and banks. Creating job opportunities in Mexico also reduces pressure for Mexicans to cross the U.S. border illegally. After more than a decade of NAFTA, agricultural exports to Mexico have doubled, as has overall trade among the three nations, but Americans still buy much more from Mexicans and Canadians than the other way around.

Free trade areas are springing up around the world. The United States and other countries are negotiating a free trade agreement with the Dominican Republic and five Central American countries, called DR-CAFTA. A half dozen Latin American countries form Mercosur. In southeast Asia, ten nations have come together to form ASEAN, the Association of Southeast Asian Nations. And South Africa and its four neighboring countries form the Southern African Customs Union. Regional trade agreements require an exception to WTO rules because bloc members can make special deals among themselves and thus discriminate against outsiders. Under WTO's requirements, any trade concession granted one country must usually be granted to *all other* WTO members.

LO5 Arguments for Trade Restrictions

Trade restrictions are often little more than handouts for the domestic industries they protect. Given the loss in social welfare that results from these restrictions, it would be more efficient simply to transfer money from domestic consumers to domestic producers. But such a bald transfer would be politically unpopular. Arguments for trade restrictions avoid mention of transfers to domestic producers and instead cite loftier goals. As we shall now see, none of these goals makes a strong case for restrictions, but some make more sense than others.

National Defense Argument

Some industries claim they need protection from import competition because their output is vital for national defense. Products such as strategic metals and military hardware are often insulated from foreign competition by trade restrictions. Thus, national defense considerations outweigh concerns about efficiency and equity. How valid is this argument? Trade restrictions may shelter the defense industry, but other means, such as government subsidies, might be more efficient. Or the government could stockpile basic military hardware so that maintaining an ongoing productive capacity would become less essential. Still, technological change could make certain weapons obsolete. Because most industries can play some role in national defense, instituting trade restrictions on this basis can get out of hand. For example, many decades ago U.S. wool producers secured trade protection at a time when some military uniforms were made of wool.

Infant Industry Argument

The infant industry argument was formulated as a rationale for protecting emerging domestic industries from foreign competition. In industries where a firm's average cost of production falls as output expands, new firms may need protection from imports until these firms grow enough to become competitive. Trade restrictions let new firms achieve the economies of scale necessary to compete with mature foreign producers.

But how do we identify industries that merit protection, and when do they become old enough to look after themselves? Protection often fosters inefficiencies. The immediate cost of such restrictions is the net welfare loss from higher domestic prices.

These costs may become permanent if the industry never realizes the expected economies of scale and thus never becomes competitive. As with the national defense argument, policy makers should be careful in adopting trade restrictions based on the infant industry argument. Here again, temporary production subsidies may be more efficient than import restrictions.

Antidumping Argument

As we have noted already, *dumping* is selling a product abroad for less than in the home market or less than the cost of production. Exporters may be able to sell the good for less overseas because of export subsidies, or firms may simply find it profitable to sell for less in foreign markets where consumers are more sensitive to prices. But why shouldn't U.S. consumers pay as little as possible? If dumping is *persistent,* the increase in consumer surplus would more than offset losses to domestic producers. *There is no good reason why consumers should not be allowed to buy imports for a persistently lower price.*

An alternative form of dumping, termed *predatory dumping,* is the *temporary* sale abroad at prices below cost to eliminate competitors in that foreign market. Once the competition is gone, so the story goes, the exporting firm can raise the price in the foreign market. The trouble with this argument is that if dumpers try to take advantage of their monopoly position by sharply increasing the price, then other firms, either domestic or foreign, could enter the market and sell for less. There are few documented cases of predatory dumping.

There is no good reason why consumers should not be allowed to buy imports for a persistently lower price.

Sometimes dumping may be *sporadic,* as firms occasionally try to unload excess inventories. Retailers hold periodic "sales" for the same reason. Sporadic dumping can be unsettling for domestic producers, but the economic impact is not a matter of great public concern. Regardless, all dumping is prohibited in the United States by the Trade Agreements Act of 1979, which calls for the imposition of tariffs when a good is sold for less in the United States than in its home market or less than the cost of production. In addition, WTO rules allow for offsetting tariffs when products are sold for "less than fair value" and when there is "material injury" to domestic producers. For example, U.S. producers of lumber and beer often accuse their Canadian counterparts of dumping.

Jobs and Income Argument

One rationale for trade restrictions that is commonly heard in the United States, and is voiced by WTO protestors, is that they protect U.S. jobs and wage levels. Using trade restrictions to protect domestic jobs is a strategy that dates back centuries. One problem with such a policy is that other countries usually retaliate by restricting *their* imports to save *their* jobs, so international trade is reduced, jobs are lost in export industries, and potential gains from trade fail to materialize. That happened big time during the Great Depression, as high tariffs choked trade and jobs.

Wages in other countries, especially developing countries, are often a small fraction of wages in the United States. Looking simply at differences in wages, however, narrows the focus too much. Wages represent just one component of the total production cost and may not necessarily be the most important. Employers are interested in the labor cost per unit of output, which depends on both the wage and labor productivity. Wages are high in the United States partly because U.S. labor productivity remains the highest in the world. High productivity can be traced to better education and training and to the abundant computers, machines, and other physical capital that make workers more productive. U.S. workers also benefit greatly from a stable business climate.

But what about the lower wages in many developing countries? Low wages are often linked to workers' lack of education and training, to the meager physical capital available to each worker, and to a business climate that is less stable and hence less attractive for producers. But once multinational firms build plants and provide technological know-how in developing countries, U.S. workers lose some of their competitive edge, and their relatively high wages could price some U.S. products out of the world market. This has already happened in the consumer electronics and toy industries. China makes 80 percent of the toys sold in the United States. Some U.S. toy sellers, such as the makers of Etch A Sketch, would no longer survive if they had not outsourced manufacturing to China.

Domestic producers do not like to compete with foreign producers whose costs are lower, so they often push for trade restrictions. But if restrictions negate any cost advantage a foreign producer might have, the law of comparative advantage becomes

prices resulting from trade restrictions meant that U.S. consumers paid two to three times more than apparel workers earned. Trade restrictions in the U.S. clothing and textile industry started phasing out in 2005 under the Uruguay Round of trade agreements.

Free trade may displace some U.S. jobs through imports, but it also creates U.S. jobs through exports. When people celebrate a ribbon-cutting ceremony for a new software company, nobody credits free trade for those jobs, but when a steel plant closes, everyone talks about how those jobs went overseas. What's more, many foreign companies have built plants in the United States and employ U.S. workers. For example, a dozen foreign television manufacturers and all major Japanese automakers now operate plants in the United States.

The number of jobs in the United States has more than doubled in the last four decades. To recognize this job growth is not to deny the problems facing workers displaced by imports. Some displaced workers, particularly those in blue-collar jobs in steel and other unionized industries, are not likely to find jobs that will pay nearly as well as the ones they lost. As with infant industries, however, the problems posed by declining industries need not require trade restrictions. To support the affected industry, the government could offer wage subsidies or special tax breaks that decline over time. The government has also funded programs to retrain affected workers for jobs that are in greater demand.

inoperative and domestic consumers are denied access to the lower-priced goods.

Over time, as labor productivity in developing countries increases, wage differentials among countries will narrow, much as wage differentials narrowed between the northern and southern United States. As technology and capital spread, U.S. workers, particularly unskilled workers, cannot expect to maintain wage levels that are far above those in other countries. So far, research and development has kept U.S. producers on the cutting edge of technological developments, but staying ahead in the technological race is a constant battle.

Declining Industries Argument

Where an established domestic industry is in jeopardy of closing because of lower-priced imports, could there be a rationale for *temporary* import restrictions? After all, domestic producers employ many industry-specific resources—both specialized labor and specialized machines. This human and physical capital is worth less in its best alternative use. If the extinction of the domestic industry is forestalled through trade restrictions, specialized workers can retire voluntarily or can gradually pursue more promising careers. Specialized machines can be allowed to wear out naturally.

Thus, in the case of declining domestic industries, trade protection can help lessen shocks to the economy and can allow for an orderly transition to a new industrial mix. But the protection offered should not be so generous as to encourage continued investment in the industry. Protection should be of specific duration and should be phased out over that period.

The clothing industry is an example of a declining U.S. industry. The 22,000 U.S. jobs saved as a result of one trade restriction paid an average of less than $30,000 per year. But a Congressional Budget Office study estimated that the higher domestic clothing

Problems with Trade Protection

Trade restrictions raise a number of problems in addition to those already mentioned. First, protecting one stage of production usually requires protecting downstream stages of production as well. Protecting the U.S. textile industry from foreign competition, for example, raised the cost of cloth to U.S. apparel makers, reducing their competitiveness. Thus, when the government protected domestic textile manufacturers, the domestic garment industry also needed protection. Second, the cost of protection includes not only the welfare loss from the higher domestic price but also the cost of the resources used by domestic producer groups to secure the favored protection. The cost of *rent seeking*—lobbying fees, propaganda, and legal actions—can sometimes equal or exceed the direct welfare loss from restrictions. A third problem with trade restrictions is the transaction costs of enforcing the myriad quotas, tariffs, and other trade restrictions. These often lead to smuggling and black markets. A fourth problem is that economies insulated from foreign competition become less innovative and less efficient. The final and biggest problem with imposing trade restrictions is that other countries usually retaliate, thus shrinking the gains from trade. Retaliation can set off still greater trade restrictions, leading to an outright trade war.

Final Word

International trade arises from voluntary exchange among buyers and sellers pursuing their self-interest. Since 1950 world output has risen eightfold, while world trade has increased nearly twentyfold. World trade offers many advantages to the trading countries: access to markets around the world, lower costs through economies of scale, the opportunity to utilize abundant resources, better access to information about markets and technology, improved quality honed by competitive pressure, and, most importantly, lower prices for consumers. Comparative advantage, specialization, and trade allow people to use their scarce resources most efficiently to satisfy their unlimited wants.

Despite the clear gains from free trade, restrictions on international trade date back centuries, and pressure on public officials to impose trade restrictions continues today. Domestic producers (and their resource suppliers) benefit from trade restrictions in their markets because they can charge domestic consumers more. Trade restrictions insulate domestic producers from the rigors of global competition, in the process stifling innovation and leaving the industry vulnerable to technological change from abroad. With trade quotas, the winners also include those who have secured the right to import goods at the world prices and sell them at the domestic prices. Consumers, who must pay higher prices for protected goods, suffer from trade restrictions, as do the domestic producers who import resources. Other losers include U.S. exporters, who face higher trade barriers as foreigners retaliate with their own trade restrictions.

Producers have a laser-like focus on trade legislation, but consumers remain largely oblivious. Consumers purchase thousands of different goods and thus have no special interest in the effects of trade policy on any particular good. Congress tends to support the group that makes the most noise, so trade restrictions often persist, despite the clear and widespread gains from freer trade.

© AP IMAGES

<< This kiosk is the gateway to New York City's garment district, an area that continues to be severely affected by low-price competition from overseas markets.

CHAPTER 20

International Finance

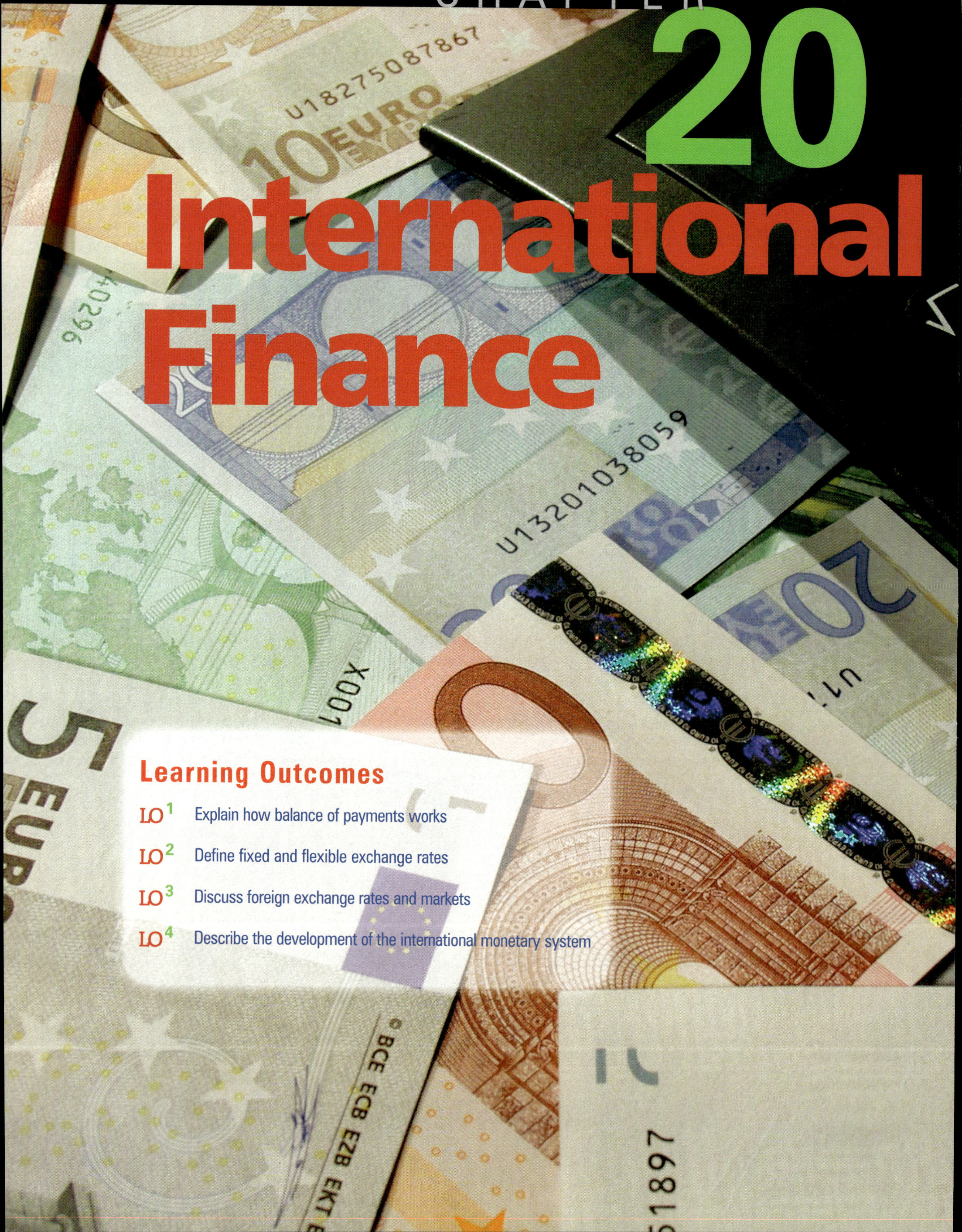

Learning Outcomes

LO[1] Explain how balance of payments works

LO[2] Define fixed and flexible exchange rates

LO[3] Discuss foreign exchange rates and markets

LO[4] Describe the development of the international monetary system

“Why do nations try to influence the value of their currency?”

How can the United States export more than any other country yet still have the world’s highest trade deficit? Are high trade deficits a worry? What’s the official “fudge factor” used in computing the balance of payments? What’s a “strong dollar”? Why do nations try to influence the value of their currency? And what’s up with China? Answers to these and other questions are explored in this chapter, which focuses on international finance.

If Starbucks wants to buy 1,000 espresso machines from the German manufacturer, Krups, it will be quoted a price in euros. Suppose the machines cost a total of 1 million euros. How much is that in dollars? The dollar cost will depend on the exchange rate. When trade takes place across international borders, two currencies are usually involved. Supporting the flows of goods and services are flows of currencies that fund international transactions. The *exchange rate* between currencies—the price of one in terms of the other—is how the price of a product in one country translates into the price quoted a buyer in another country. Cross-border trade therefore depends on the exchange rate. In this chapter we examine the market forces that affect the relative value of one currency in terms of another.

What do you think?

The current euro exchange rate makes this a good time for a European vacation.

Strongly Disagree 1 2 3 4 5 6 7 *Strongly Agree*

Topics discussed in Chapter 20 include:

- Balance of payments
- Trade deficits and surpluses
- Foreign exchange markets
- Purchasing power parity
- Flexible exchange rates
- Fixed exchange rates
- International monetary system
- Bretton Woods agreement
- Managed float

LO[1] Balance of Payments

A country’s gross domestic product, or GDP, measures the economy’s income and output during a given period. To account for dealings abroad, countries must also keep track of international transactions. A country’s *balance of payments,* as introduced in Chapter 3, summarizes all economic transactions during a given period between residents of that country and residents of other countries. *Residents* include people, firms, organizations, and governments.

International Economic Transactions

The balance of payments measures economic transactions between a country and the rest of the world, whether these transactions involve goods and services, real and financial assets, or transfer payments. The balance of payments measures a *flow* of transactions during a particular period, usually a year. Some transactions do not involve actual payments. For example, if *Time* magazine ships a new printing press to its Australian subsidiary, no payment is made, yet an economic transaction involving another country has occurred. Similarly, if CARE sends food to Africa or the Pentagon provides military assistance to the Middle East, these transactions must be captured in the balance of payments. So remember, although we speak of the *balance of payments,* a more descriptive phrase would be the *balance of economic transactions.*

Balance-of-payments accounts are maintained according to the principles of *double-entry bookkeeping.* Some entries are called *credits,* and others are called *debits.* As you will see, the balance of payments consists of several individual accounts. An individual account may not balance, but a deficit in one or more accounts must be offset by a surplus in the other accounts. Because total credits must equal total debits, there is a *balance* of payments—hence, the name. During a given period, such as a year, the inflow of receipts from the rest of the world, which are entered as credits, must equal the outflow of payments to the rest of the world, which are entered as debits.

The first of two major categories in the balance of payments is the current account. The current account records *current* flows of funds into and out of the country, including imports and exports of goods and services, net income earned by U.S. residents from foreign assets, and net transfer payments from abroad. These are discussed in turn.

The Merchandise Trade Balance

The *merchandise trade balance,* a term introduced in Chapter 3, equals the value of merchandise exports minus the value of merchandise imports. The merchandise account reflects trade in goods, or tangible products (stuff you can put in a box), like French wine or U.S. computers, and is often referred to simply as the *trade balance.* The value of U.S. merchandise exports is a credit in the U.S. balance-of-payments account because U.S. residents get *paid* for the exported goods. The value of U.S. merchandise imports is a debit in the balance-of-payments account because U.S. residents *pay* foreigners for imported goods.

If merchandise exports exceed merchandise imports, the trade balance is in *surplus.* If merchandise imports exceed merchandise exports, the trade balance is in *deficit.* The merchandise trade balance, which is reported monthly, influences foreign exchange markets, the stock market, and other financial markets. The trade balance depends on a variety of factors, including the relative strength and competitiveness of the domestic economy compared with other economies and the relative value of the domestic currency compared with other currencies. Strong economies with growing incomes tend to buy more of everything, including imports.

U.S. merchandise trade since 1960 is depicted in Exhibit 1, where exports, the blue line, and imports, the red line, are expressed as a percentage of GDP. During the 1960s, exports exceeded imports, and the resulting trade surpluses are shaded blue. Since 1976, imports have exceeded exports, and the resulting trade deficits are shaded pink. Trade deficits as a percentage of GDP increased from 1.3 percent in 1991 to 6.3 percent in 2006, when the deficit reached a record $838.3 billion. Notice in Exhibit 1 that exports as a percentage of GDP dipped during the 1980s, when the value of the dollar rose sharply relative to other currencies (more on this later). Despite that dip, merchandise exports since 1980 have remained in the

Exhibit 1

U.S. Imports Have Exceeded Exports Since 1976, and the Trade Deficit Has Widened

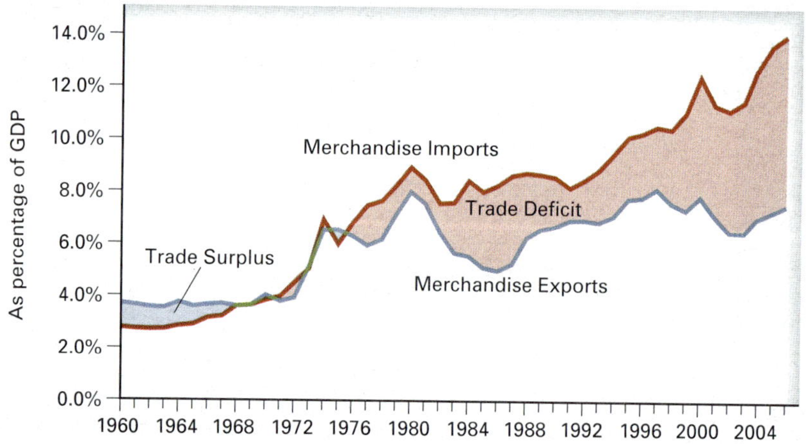

SOURCE: Developed from merchandise trade data from the *Economic Report of the President,* February 2007, and *Survey of Current Business,* June 2007. U.S. Department of Commerce. For the latest data, go to http://www.bea.gov.

range of about 5 percent to 8 percent of GDP. But merchandise imports have trended up from about 9 percent in 1980 to about 14 percent in 2006.

Because per capita income in the United States is the highest in the world, the United States imports more goods from each of the world's major economies than it exports to them. Exhibit 2 shows the U.S. merchandise trade deficit with major economies or regions of the world in 2006. The $233 billion trade deficit with China was by far the largest, double that with Latin America, the European Union, or the OPEC nations. The Chinese bought $55 billion in U.S. goods in 2006, but Americans bought $288 billion in Chinese goods, or about $2,400 per U.S. household. So China sells America five times more than it buys from America. Chances are, most of the utensils in your kitchen were made in China; most toys are also Chinese made. The United States does not have a trade surplus with any major economy in the world and is the world's biggest importer.

Balance on Goods and Services

The merchandise trade balance focuses on the flow of goods, but services are also traded internationally. *Services* are intangibles, such as transportation, insurance, banking, education, consulting, and tourism. Services are often called "invisibles" because they are not tangible. The value of U.S. service exports, as when an Irish tourist visits New York City, is listed as a credit in the U.S. balance-of-payments account because U.S. residents get paid for these services. The value of U.S. service imports, like computer programming outsourced to India, is listed as a debit in the balance-of-payments account because U.S. residents must pay for the imported services.

Because the United States exports more services than it imports, services have been in surplus for the last three decades. The **balance on goods and services** is the export value of goods and services minus the import value of goods and services, or *net exports,* a component of GDP.

Exhibit 2

U.S. Trade Deficits in 2006 by Country or Grouping

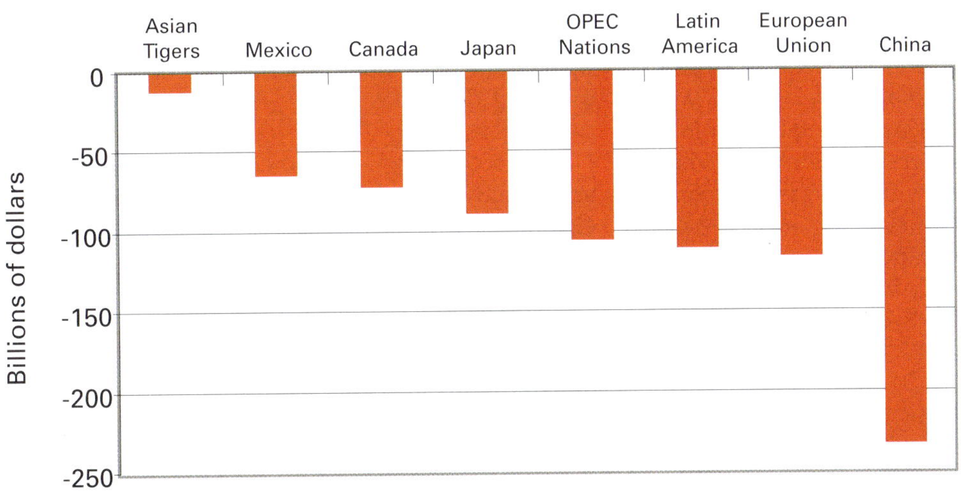

SOURCE: Developed from data in "Exports, Imports, and Trade Balance by County and Area: 2006 Annual Totals," Table 13, U.S. Bureau of Economic Analysis, 8 June 2007. Asian Tigers are Hong Kong, Singapore, South Korea, and Taiwan.

balance on goods and services
the portion of a country's balance-of-payments account that measures the value of a country's exports of goods and services minus the value of its imports of goods and services

Net Investment Income

U.S. residents earn investment income, such as interest and dividends, from assets owned abroad. This investment income flows to the United States and is a credit in the balance-of-payments account. On the other side, foreigners earn investment income on assets owned in the United States, and this payment flows out of the country. This outflow is a debit in the balance-of-payments account. **Net investment income from abroad** is U.S. investment earnings from foreign assets minus foreigners' earnings from their U.S. assets. From year to year, this figure bounces around between a positive and a negative number. In 2006, net investment income from foreign holdings was $36.6 billion.

Unilateral Transfers

Unilateral transfers consist of government transfers to foreign residents, foreign aid, money workers send to families abroad, personal gifts to friends and relatives abroad, charitable donations, and the like. Money sent out of the country is a debit in the balance-of-payments account. For example, immigrants to the United States often send money to families back home. **Net unilateral transfers abroad** equal the unilateral transfers received from abroad by U.S. residents minus unilateral transfers sent to foreign residents by U.S. residents. U.S. net unilateral transfers have been negative since World War II, except for 1991, when the U.S. government received sizable transfers from foreign governments to help pay their share of the Persian Gulf War. In 2006, net unilateral transfers were a negative $89.6 billion, with private transfers accounting for nearly two-thirds of that. Net unilateral transfers abroad averaged about $300 per U.S. resident in 2006.

net investment income from abroad
investment earnings by U.S. residents from their foreign assets minus investment earnings by foreigners from their assets in the United States

net unilateral transfers abroad
the unilateral transfers (gifts and grants) received from abroad by U.S. residents minus the unilateral transfers U.S. residents send abroad

balance on current account
the portion of the balance-of-payments account that measures that country's balance on goods and services, net investment income from abroad, plus net unilateral transfers abroad

financial account
the record of a country's international transactions involving purchases or sales of financial and real assets

The United States places few restrictions on money sent out of the country. Other countries, particularly developing countries, strictly limit the amount that may be sent abroad. More generally, many developing countries, such as China, restrict the convertibility of their currency into other currencies.

When we add net unilateral transfers to net exports of goods and services and net income from assets owned abroad, we get the **balance on current account**, which is reported quarterly. Thus, *the current account includes all international transactions in currently produced goods and services, net income from foreign assets, and net unilateral transfers.* It can be negative, reflecting a current account deficit; positive, reflecting a current account surplus; or zero.

The Financial Account

The current account records international transactions in goods, services, asset income, and unilateral transfers. The **financial account** records international purchases of assets, including financial assets such as stocks, bonds, and bank balances, and real assets such as land, housing, factories, and other physical assets. For example, U.S. residents purchase foreign securities to earn a higher return and to diversify their portfolios. Money flows out when Americans buy foreign assets or build factories overseas. Money flows in when foreigners buy U.S. assets or build factories here. The international purchase or sale of assets is recorded in the financial account.

Between 1917 and 1982, the United States ran a financial account deficit, meaning that U.S. residents purchased more foreign assets than foreigners purchased assets from the United States. The net income from these foreign assets improved our current account balance. But in 1983, for the first time in 65 years, foreigners bought more assets in the United States than U.S. residents purchased abroad. Since 1983, foreigners have continued to buy more U.S. assets most years than the other way around, meaning there has usually been a surplus in the financial account.

By 2006, foreigners owned $16.3 trillion in U.S. assets and U.S. residents owned $13.8 trillion in foreign assets. Thus, foreigners owned $2.5 trillion more assets in the United States than U.S. residents owned abroad. This is not as bad as it sounds, because foreign purchases of assets in the United States add to America's productive capacity and promote employment and labor productivity here. But the income from these assets flows to their foreign owners, not to Americans. Remember, the investment income from these assets shows up in the current account.

Deficits and Surpluses

Nations, like households, operate under a budget constraint. Spending cannot exceed income plus cash on hand and borrowed funds. We have distinguished between *current* transactions, which include exports, imports, asset income, and unilateral transfers, and *financial* transactions, which reflect purchases of foreign real and financial assets. Any surplus or deficit in one account must be offset by deficits or surpluses in other balance-of-payments accounts.

Exhibit 3 presents the U.S. balance-of-payments statement for 2006. All transactions requiring payments from foreigners to U.S. residents are entered as credits, indicated by a plus sign (+), because they result in an inflow of funds from foreign residents to U.S. residents. All transactions requiring payments to foreigners from U.S. residents are entered as debits, indicated by a minus sign (−), because they result in an outflow of funds from U.S. residents to foreign residents. As you can see, a surplus in the financial account of $829.3 billion more than offsets a current account deficit of $811.5 billion. A *statistical discrepancy* is required to balance the payments, and that amounts to a negative $17.8 billion. Think of the statistical discrepancy as the official "fudge factor" that (1) measures the error in the balance of payments and (2) satisfies the double-entry bookkeeping requirement that total debits must equal total credits.

Exhibit 3

U.S. Balance of Payments for 2006 (billions of dollars)

Current Accounts	
1. Merchandise exports	+1,023.1
2. Merchandise imports	−1,861.4
3. Merchandise trade balance (1 + 2)	−838.3
4. Service exports	+422.6
5. Service imports	−342.8
6. Goods and services balance (3 + 4 + 5)	−785.5
7. Net investment income from abroad	+36.6
8. Net unilateral transfers	−89.6
9. Current account balance (6 + 7 + 8)	−811.5
Financial Accounts	
10. Change in U.S.-owned assets abroad	−1,059.1
11. Change in foreign-owned assets in U.S.	+1,888.4
12. Financial account balance (10 + 11)	+829.3
13. Statistical discrepancy	−17.8
TOTAL (9 + 12 + 13)	**0.0**

SOURCE: Computed from estimates in "News Release: U.S. International Transactions," Bureau of Economic Analysis, U.S. Department of Commerce, Table 1, 15 June 2007.

Foreign exchange is the currency of another country needed to carry out international transactions. A country runs a deficit in its current account when the amount of foreign exchange received from exports, from holding foreign assets, and from unilateral transfers falls short of the amount needed to pay for imports, pay foreigners for their U.S. assets, and make unilateral transfers. If the current account is in deficit, the necessary foreign exchange must come from a net inflow in the financial account. Such an inflow in the financial account could stem from borrowing from foreigners, selling domestic stocks and bonds to foreigners, selling a steel plant in Pittsburgh or a ski lodge in Aspen to foreigners, and so forth.

If a country runs a current account surplus, the foreign exchange received from exports, from holding assets abroad, and from unilateral transfers exceeds the amount needed to pay for imports, to pay foreign holders for U.S. assets, and to make unilateral transfers. If the current account is in surplus, this excess foreign exchange results in a net outflow in the financial account through lending abroad, buying foreign stocks and bonds, buying a shoe plant in Italy or a villa on the French Riviera, and so forth.

When all transactions are considered, accounts must always balance, though specific accounts usually don't. A deficit in a particular account should not necessarily be viewed as a source of concern, nor should a surplus be a source of satisfaction. The deficit in the U.S. current account in recent years has been offset by a financial account surplus. As a result, foreigners are acquiring more claims on U.S. assets.

LO2 Foreign Exchange Rates and Markets

Now that you have some idea about international flows, we can take a closer look at the forces that determine the underlying value of the currencies involved. Let's begin by looking at exchange rates and the market for foreign exchange.

Foreign Exchange

Foreign exchange, recall, is foreign money needed to carry out international transactions. The **exchange rate** is the price measured in one country's currency of

exchange rate the price measured in one country's currency of purchasing 1 unit of another country's currency

© PETER GRIFFIN/ALAMY

buying one unit of another country's currency. Exchange rates are determined by the interaction of the households, firms, private financial institutions, governments, and central banks that buy and sell foreign exchange. The exchange rate fluctuates to equate the quantity of foreign exchange demanded with the quantity supplied. Typically, foreign exchange is made up of bank deposits denominated in the foreign currency. When foreign travel is involved, foreign exchange often consists of foreign paper money.

The foreign exchange market incorporates all the arrangements used to buy and sell foreign exchange. This market is not so much a physical place as a network of telephones and computers connecting financial centers all over the world. Perhaps you have seen pictures of foreign exchange traders in New York, Frankfurt, London, or Tokyo in front of computer screens amid a tangle of phone lines. The foreign exchange market is like an all-night diner—it never closes. A trading center is always open somewhere in the world.

currency depreciation
with respect to the dollar, an increase in the number of dollars needed to purchase 1 unit of foreign exchange in a flexible rate system

currency appreciation
with respect to the dollar, a decrease in the number of dollars needed to purchase 1 unit of foreign exchange in a flexible rate system

We will consider the market for the euro in terms of the dollar. But first, a little more about the euro. For decades the nations of Western Europe have tried to increase their economic cooperation and trade. These countries believed they would be more productive and more competitive with the United States if they acted less like many separate economies and more like the 50 United States, with a single set of trade regulations and one currency. Imagine the hassle involved if each of the 50 states had its own currency.

In 2002, euro notes and coins entered circulation in the 12 European countries adopting the common currency. The big advantage of a common currency is that Europeans no longer have to change money every time they cross a border or trade with another country in the group. Again, the inspiration for this is the United States, arguably the most successful economy in world history.

So the euro is the common currency of the *euro area*,or *euro zone*, as the now 13-country region is usually called. The price, or exchange rate, of the euro in terms of the dollar is the number of dollars required to purchase one euro. An increase in the number of dollars needed to purchase a euro indicates weakening, or **depreciation**, of the dollar. A decrease in the number of dollars needed to purchase a euro indicates strengthening, or **appreciation**, of the dollar. Put another way, a decrease in the number of euros needed to purchase a dollar is a depreciation of the dollar, and an increase in the number of euros needed to purchase a dollar is an appreciation of the dollar.

Because the exchange rate is usually a market price, it is determined by demand and supply: The equilibrium price is the one that equates quantity demanded with quantity supplied. To simplify the analysis, suppose that the United States and the euro area make up the entire world, so the demand and supply for euros in international finance is the demand and supply for foreign exchange from the U.S. perspective.

The Demand for Foreign Exchange

Whenever U.S. residents need euros, they must buy them in the foreign exchange market, which could include their local banks, paying for them with dollars. Exhibit 4 depicts a market for foreign exchange—in this case, euros. The horizontal axis shows the quantity of foreign exchange, measured here in millions of euros. The vertical axis shows the price per unit of foreign exchange, measured here in dollars per euro. The demand curve *D* for foreign exchange shows the inverse relationship between the dollar price of the euro and the quantity of euros demanded, other things assumed constant. Assumed constant along the demand curve are the incomes and preferences of U.S. consumers, expected inflation in the United States and in the euro area, the euro price of goods in the euro area, and interest rates in the United States and in the euro area. People have many reasons for demanding foreign exchange, but in the aggregate, the lower the dollar price of foreign exchange, other things constant, the greater the quantity of foreign exchange demanded.

A drop in the dollar price of foreign exchange, in this case the euro, means that fewer dollars are needed to purchase each euro, so the dollar prices of euro area products (like German cars, Italian shoes, tickets to Euro Disney, and euro area securities), which list prices in euros, become cheaper. The cheaper it is to buy euros, the lower the dollar price of euro area products to U.S. residents, so the greater the quantity of euros demanded by U.S. residents, other things constant. For example, a cheap enough euro might persuade you to tour Rome, climb the Austrian Alps, wander the museums of Paris, or crawl the pubs of Dublin.

The Supply of Foreign Exchange

The supply of foreign exchange is generated by the desire of foreign residents to acquire dollars—that is, to exchange euros for dollars. Euro area residents want dollars to buy U.S. goods and services, acquire U.S. assets, make loans in dollars, or send dollars to their U.S. friends and relatives. Euros are supplied in the foreign exchange market to acquire the dollars people want. An increase in the dollar-per-euro exchange rate, other things constant, makes U.S. products cheaper for foreigners because foreign residents need fewer euros to get the same number of dollars. For example, suppose a Dell computer sells for $600. If the exchange rate is $1.20 per euro, that computer costs 500 euros; if the exchange rate is $1.25 per euro, it costs only 480 euros. The number of Dell computers demanded in the euro area increases as the dollar-per-euro exchange rate increases, other things constant, so more euros will be supplied on the foreign exchange market to buy dollars.

The positive relationship between the dollar-per-euro exchange rate and the quantity of euros supplied on the foreign exchange market is expressed in Exhibit 4 by the upward-sloping supply curve for foreign exchange (again, euros in our example). The supply curve assumes that other things remain constant, including euro area incomes and tastes, expectations about inflation in the euro area and in the United States, and interest rates in the euro area and in the United States.

Exhibit 4

The Foreign Exchange Market

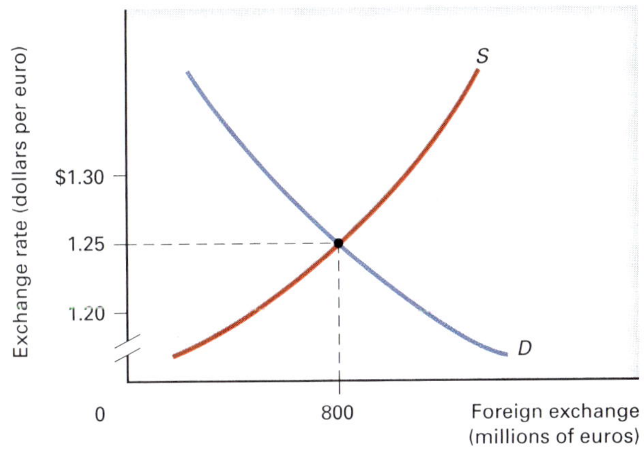

Determining the Exchange Rate

Exhibit 4 brings together the demand and supply for foreign exchange to determine the exchange rate. At a rate of $1.25 per euro, the quantity of euros demanded equals the quantity supplied—in our example, 800 million euros. Once achieved, this equilibrium rate will remain constant until a change occurs in one of the factors that affect supply or demand. If the exchange rate is allowed to adjust freely, or to *float*, in response to market forces, the market will clear continually, as the quantities of foreign exchange demanded and supplied are equated.

What if the initial equilibrium is upset by a change in one of the underlying forces that affect demand or supply? For example, suppose higher U.S. incomes increase American demand for all normal goods, including those from the euro area. This shifts the U.S. demand curve for foreign exchange to the right, as Americans buy more Italian marble, Dutch chocolate, German machines, Parisian vacations, and euro area securities.

This increased demand for euros is shown in Exhibit 5 by a rightward shift of the demand curve for foreign exchange. The demand increase from *D* to *D*' leads to an increase in the exchange rate per euro from $1.25 to $1.27. Thus, the euro increases in value, or appreciates, while the dollar falls in value, or depreciates. An increase in U.S. income should not affect the euro supply curve, though it does increase the *quantity of euros supplied*. The higher exchange value of the euro prompts those in the euro area to buy more American products and assets, which are now cheaper in terms of the euro.

If the exchange rate is allowed to adjust freely, or to float, in response to market forces, the market will clear continually, as the quantities of foreign exchange demanded and supplied are equated.

© DON FARRALL/GETTY IMAGES

To review: Any increase in the demand for foreign exchange or any decrease in its supply, other things constant, increases the number of dollars required to purchase one unit of foreign exchange, which is a depreciation of the dollar. On the other hand, any decrease in the demand for foreign exchange or any increase in its supply, other things constant, reduces the number of dollars required to purchase one unit of foreign exchange, which is an appreciation of the dollar.

Arbitrageurs and Speculators

Exchange rates between two currencies are nearly identical at any given time in markets around the world. For example, the dollar price of a euro is the same in New York, Frankfurt, Tokyo, London, Zurich, Hong Kong, Istanbul, and other financial centers. **Arbitrageurs**—dealers who take advantage of any difference in exchange rates between markets by buying low and selling high—ensure this equality. Their actions help to equalize exchange rates across markets. For example, if one euro costs \$1.24 in New York but \$1.25 in Frankfurt, an arbitrageur could buy, say, \$1,000,000 worth of euros in New York and at the same time sell them in Frankfurt for \$1,008,060, thereby earning \$8,060 minus the transaction costs of the trades.

arbitrageur
someone who takes advantage of temporary geographic differences in the exchange rate by simultaneously purchasing a currency in one market and selling it in another market

speculator
someone who buys or sells foreign exchange in hopes of profiting from fluctuations in the exchange rate over time

Because an arbitrageur buys and sells simultaneously, little risk is involved. In our example, the arbitrageur increased the demand for euros in New York and increased the supply of euros in Frankfurt. These actions increased the dollar price of euros in New York and decreased it in Frankfurt, thereby squeezing down the difference in exchange rates. Exchange rates may still change because of market forces, but they tend to change in all markets simultaneously.

The demand and supply of foreign exchange arises from many sources—from importers and exporters, investors in foreign assets, central banks, tourists, arbitrageurs, and speculators. **Speculators** buy or sell foreign exchange in hopes of profiting by trading the currency at a more favorable exchange rate later. By taking risks, speculators aim to profit from market fluctuations—they try to buy low and sell high. In contrast, arbitrageurs take less risk, because they *simultaneously* buy currency in one market and sell it in another.

Finally, people in countries suffering from economic and political turmoil, such as occurred in Russia, Indonesia, and the Philippines, may buy *hard* currency as a hedge against the depreciation and instability of their own currencies. The dollar has long been accepted as an international medium of exchange. It is also the currency of choice in the world markets for oil and illegal drugs. But the euro eventu-

Exhibit 5

Effect on the Foreign Exchange Market of an Increased Demand for Euros

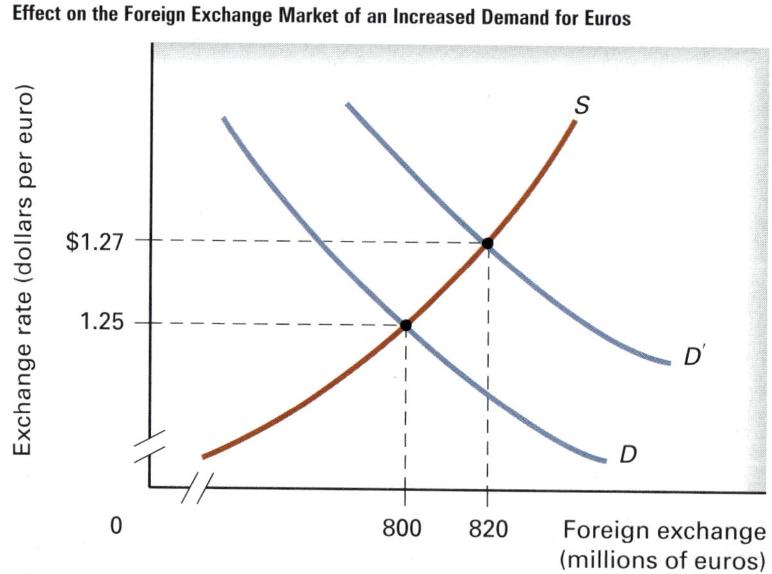

ally may challenge that dominance, in part because the largest euro denomination, the 500 euro note, is worth about six times the largest U.S. denomination, the $100 note. So it would be six times easier to smuggle euro notes than U.S. notes of equal value.

Purchasing Power Parity

As long as trade across borders is unrestricted and as long as exchange rates are allowed to adjust freely, the purchasing power parity (PPP) theory predicts that the exchange rate between two currencies will adjust in the long run to reflect price differences between the two currency regions. *A given basket of internationally traded goods should therefore sell for about the same around the world (except for differences reflecting transportation costs and the like).* Suppose a basket of internationally traded goods that sells for $10,000 in the United States sells for 8,000 euros in the euro area. According to the purchasing power parity theory, the equilibrium exchange rate should be $1.25 per euro. If this were not the case—if the exchange rate were, say, $1.20 per euro—then you could exchange $9,600 for 8,000 euros, with which you buy the basket of commodities in the euro area. You could then sell that basket of goods in the States for $10,000, yielding you a profit of $400 minus any transaction costs. Selling dollars and buying euros will also drive up the dollar price of euros.

The purchasing power parity theory is more of a long-run predictor than a day-to-day indicator of the relationship between changes in the price level and the exchange rate. For example, a country's currency generally appreciates when inflation is low compared with other countries and depreciates when inflation is high. Likewise, a country's currency generally appreciates when its real interest rates are higher than those in the rest of the world, because foreigners are more willing to buy and hold investments denominated in that high-interest currency. As a case in point, the dollar appreciated during the first half of the 1980s, when real U.S. interest rates were relatively high, and depreciated during 2002 to 2004, when real U.S. interest rates were relatively low.

Because of trade barriers, central bank intervention in exchange markets, and the fact that many products are not traded or are not comparable across countries, the purchasing power parity theory usually does not explain exchange rates at a particular point in time that well. For example, if you went shopping in London tomorrow, you would soon notice a dollar does not buy as much there as it does in the United States.

LO3 Fixed and Flexible Exchange Rates

Flexible Exchange Rates

For the most part, we have been discussing a system of flexible exchange rates, with rates determined by demand and supply. Flexible, or *floating*, exchange rates adjust continually to the myriad forces that buffet foreign exchange markets. Consider how the exchange rate is linked to the balance-of-payments accounts. Debit entries in the current or financial accounts increase the demand for foreign exchange, resulting in a depreciation of the dollar. Credit entries in these accounts increase the supply of foreign exchange, resulting in an appreciation of the dollar.

Fixed Exchange Rates

When exchange rates are flexible, governments usually have little direct role in foreign exchange markets. But if governments try to set exchange rates, active and ongoing central bank intervention is often necessary to establish and maintain these fixed exchange rates. Suppose the European Central Bank selects what it thinks is an appropriate rate of exchange between the dollar and the euro. It attempts to *fix*, or to *peg*, the exchange rate within a narrow band around the particular value selected. If the euro threatens to climb above the maximum acceptable exchange rate, monetary authorities must sell euros and buy dollars, thereby keeping the dollar price of the euro down. Conversely, if the euro threatens to drop below the minimum acceptable exchange rate, monetary authorities must sell dollars and buy euros. This increased demand for the euro will keep its value up relative to the dollar. Through such intervention in the foreign exchange market, monetary authorities try to stabilize the exchange rate, keeping it within the specified band.

If monetary officials must keep selling foreign exchange to keep the value

purchasing power parity (PPP) theory the idea that the exchange rate between two countries will adjust in the long run to equalize the cost between the countries of a basket of internationally traded goods

flexible exchange rate rate determined in foreign exchange markets by the forces of demand and supply without government intervention

fixed exchange rate rate of exchange between currencies pegged within a narrow range and maintained by the central bank's ongoing purchases and sales of currencies of their domestic currency from falling, they risk running out of foreign exchange reserves. Faced with this threat, the government has several options for eliminating the exchange rate disequilibrium. First, the pegged exchange rate can be increased, which is a **devaluation** of the domestic currency. (A decrease in the pegged exchange rate is called a **revaluation**.) Second, the government can reduce the domestic demand for foreign exchange directly by imposing restrictions on imports or on financial outflows. Many developing countries do this. Third, the government can adopt policies to slow the domestic economy, increase interest rates, or reduce inflation relative to that of the country's trading partners, thereby indirectly decreasing the demand for foreign exchange and increasing the supply of foreign exchange. Several Asian economies, such as South Korea and Indonesia, pursued such policies to stabilize their currencies. Finally, the government can allow the disequilibrium to persist and ration the available foreign reserves through some form of foreign exchange control.

This concludes our introduction to the theories of international finance. Let's examine international finance in practice.

LO4 Development of the International Monetary System

currency devaluation an increase in the official pegged price of foreign exchange in terms of the domestic currency

currency revaluation a reduction in the official pegged price of foreign exchange in terms of the domestic currency

gold standard an arrangement whereby the currencies of most countries are convertible into gold at a fixed rate

International Monetary Fund (IMF) an international organization that establishes rules for maintaining the international monetary system and makes loans to countries with temporary balance-of-payments problems

From 1879 to 1914, the international financial system operated under a **gold standard**, whereby the major currencies were convertible into gold at a fixed rate. For example, the U.S. dollar could be redeemed at the U.S. Treasury for one-twentieth of an ounce of gold. The British pound could be redeemed at the British Exchequer, or treasury, for one-fourth of an ounce of gold. Because each British pound could buy five times as much gold as each dollar, one British pound exchanged for $5.

The gold standard provided a predictable exchange rate, one that did not vary as long as currencies could be redeemed for gold at the announced rate. But the money supply in each country was determined in part by the flow of gold between countries, so each country's monetary policy was influenced by the supply of gold. A balance-of-payments deficit resulted in a loss of gold, which theoretically caused a country's money supply to shrink. A balance-of-payments surplus resulted in an influx of gold, which theoretically caused a country's money supply to expand. The supply of money throughout the world also depended on the vagaries of gold discoveries. When gold production did not keep pace with the growth in economic activity, the price level dropped. When gold production exceeded the growth in economic activity, the price level rose. For example, gold discoveries in Alaska and South Africa in the late 1890s expanded the U.S. money supply, leading to inflation.

The Bretton Woods Agreement

During World War I, many countries could no longer convert their currencies into gold, and the gold standard eventually collapsed, disrupting international trade during the 1920s and 1930s. Once an Allied victory in World War II appeared certain, the Allies met in Bretton Woods, New Hampshire, in July 1944 to formulate a new international monetary system. Because the United States had a strong economy and was not ravaged by the war, the dollar was selected as the key reserve currency in the new international monetary system. All exchange rates were fixed in terms of the dollar, and the United States, which held most of the world's gold reserves, stood ready to convert foreign holdings of dollars into gold at a rate of $35 per ounce. Even though the rate that dollars could be exchanged for gold was fixed by the Bretton Woods agreement, *other* countries could adjust *their* exchange rates relative to the U.S. dollar if they found a chronic disequilibrium in their balance of payments—that is, if a country faced a large and persistent deficit or surplus.

The Bretton Woods agreement also created the **International Monetary Fund (IMF)** to set rules for maintaining the international monetary system, to standardize financial reporting for international trade, and to make loans to countries with temporary balance-of-payments problems. The IMF lends a revolving fund of about $350 billion to economies in need of reserves. Headquartered in Washington, D.C., the IMF has more than 180 member countries and a staff of 2,500 drawn from around the world.

The Demise of the Bretton Woods System

During the latter part of the 1960s, inflation began heating up in the United States. Because of U.S. inflation, the dollar had become *overvalued* at the official exchange rate, meaning that the gold value of the dollar exceeded the exchange value of the dollar. In 1971, U.S. merchandise imports exceeded merchandise exports for the first time since World War II. Foreigners exchanged dollars for gold. To stem this gold outflow, the United States stopped exchanging gold for dollars, but this just made the dollar less attractive. In December 1971, the world's 10 richest countries met in Washington and devalued the dollar by 8 percent. They hoped this devaluation would put the dollar on firmer footing and would save the "dollar standard." With prices rising at different rates around the world, however, an international monetary system based on fixed exchange rates was doomed.

When the U.S. trade deficit tripled in 1972, it became clear that the dollar was still overvalued. In early 1973, the dollar was devalued another 10 percent, but this did not quiet foreign exchange markets. The dollar, for three decades the anchor of the international monetary system, suddenly looked vulnerable, and speculators began betting that the dollar would fall even more. Dollars were exchanged for German marks because the mark appeared to be the most stable currency. Bundesbank, Germany's central bank, tried to defend the dollar's official exchange rate by selling marks and buying dollars. Why didn't Germany want the mark to appreciate? Appreciation would make German goods more expensive abroad and foreign goods cheaper in Germany, thereby reducing German exports and increasing German imports. So the mark's appreciation would reduce German output and employment. But after selling $10 billion worth of marks, the Bundesbank gave up defending the dollar. As soon as the value of the dollar was allowed to float against the mark, the Bretton Woods system, already on shaky ground, collapsed.

The Current System: Managed Float

The Bretton Woods system has been replaced by a **managed float system**, which combines features of a freely floating exchange rate with sporadic intervention by central banks as a way of moderating exchange rate fluctuations among the world's major currencies. Most small countries, particularly developing countries, still peg their currencies to one of the major currencies (such as the U.S. dollar) or to a "basket" of major currencies. What's more, in developing countries, private international borrowing and lending are severely restricted; some governments allow residents to purchase foreign exchange only for certain purposes. In some countries, different exchange rates apply to different categories of transactions.

Critics of flexible exchange rates argue that they are inflationary, because they free monetary authorities to pursue expansionary policies, and they have often been volatile. This volatility creates uncertainty and risk for importers and exporters, increasing the transaction costs of international trade. Furthermore, exchange rate volatility can lead to wrenching changes in the competitiveness of a country's export sector. These changes cause swings in employment, resulting in louder calls for import restrictions. For example, the exchange rate between the Japanese yen and the U.S. dollar has been relatively unstable, particularly because of international speculation.

Policy makers are always on the lookout for a system that will perform better than the current managed float system, with its fluctuating currency values. *Their ideal is a system that will foster international trade, lower inflation, and promote a more stable world economy.* International finance ministers have acknowledged that the world must find an international standard and establish greater exchange rate stability.

Final Word

The United States is very much a part of the world economy, not only as the largest exporter nation but also as the largest importer nation. Although the dollar remains the unit of transaction in many international settlements—OPEC, for example, still states oil prices in dollars—gyrations of exchange rates have made those involved in international finance wary of putting all their eggs in one basket. The international monetary system is now going through a difficult period as it gropes for a new source of stability nearly four decades after the collapse of the Bretton Woods agreement.

managed float system
an exchange rate system that combines features of freely floating rates with sporadic intervention by central banks

CHAPTER 21

Developing and Transitional Economies

Learning Outcomes

- LO 1 Describe the worldwide variation in economic vitality
- LO 2 Explain why productivity is the key to development
- LO 3 Discuss international trade and development
- LO 4 Describe the role of foreign aid in economic development
- LO 5 Define transitional economies
- LO 6 Discuss markets and institutions

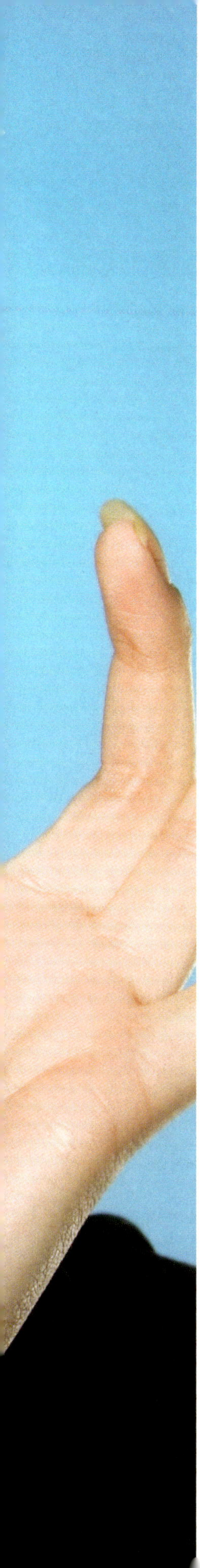

© ISTOCKPHOTO.COM/ALEKSEY POPRUGIN

“A billion people need eyeglasses but can't afford them. Why are some countries so poor while others are so rich?”

People around the world face the day under quite different circumstances. Most Americans rise from a comfortable bed in a nice home, select the day's clothing from a wardrobe, choose from a variety of breakfast foods, and drive to school or to work in one of the family's personal automobiles. But many of the world's 6.6 billion people have little housing, clothing, or food. They have no automobile, and no formal job. Their health is poor, as is their education. Many cannot read or write. A billion people need eyeglasses but can't afford them. Why are some countries so poor while others are so rich? What determines the wealth of nations?

What do you think?

Poverty is a self-perpetuating cycle.

Strongly Disagree 1 2 3 4 5 6 7 *Strongly Agree*

In this chapter, we sort out rich nations from poor ones and try to explain the difference. Although there is no widely accepted theory of how best to achieve economic development, one approach that seems to be gaining favor is the introduction of market forces, especially in formerly socialist countries. Around the world, the demise of central planning has been stunning and pervasive. We close the chapter with a discussion of these rich experiments—these works in progress.

Topics discussed in Chapter 21 include:

- Developing countries
- Obstacles to development
- Import substitution
- Export promotion
- Foreign aid
- Transitional economies
- Big bang versus gradualism
- Privatization

LO1 Worlds Apart

Differences in economic vitality among countries are huge. Countries are classified in a variety of ways based on their economic development. The yardstick most often used to compare living standards across nations is the amount an economy produces per capita, or *output per capita*. The World Bank, an economic development institution affiliated with the United Nations (UN), estimates output per capita figures and then uses these figures to classify economies. The measure used by the World Bank to classify countries begins with *gross national product (GNP)*. GNP measures the market value of all goods and services produced by resources supplied by the countries' residents and firms, regardless of the location of the resource. For example, U.S. GNP includes profit earned by a Ford factory in Great Britain but excludes profits earned by a Toyota factory in Kentucky.

GNP measures both the value of output produced and the income that output generates. The World Bank computes the GNP per capita, which also measures income per capita, then adjusts figures across countries based on the purchasing power of that income in each country. Using this measure, the World Bank sorts countries around the world into three major groups: *high-income economies, middle-income economies,* and *low-income economies.*

Data on world population and world output are summarized in Exhibit 1. High-income economies in 2006 made up only 16 percent of the 6.6 billion people on Earth, but accounted for 54 percent of world output. So high-income economies, *with only about one-eighth of the world's population, produced more than half the world's output.* Middle-income economies made up 47 percent of the world's population, but accounted for 36 percent of the world output. And low-income countries made up 37 percent of the world's population, but accounted for only 10 percent of the world output.

Developing and Industrial Economies

The low- and middle-income economies are usually referred to as **developing countries**. Most high-income economies are also referred to as **industrial market countries**. So low- and middle-income economies, what are called developing countries, made up 84 percent of the world's population in 2006 but produced only 46 percent of the output. Compared to industrial market countries, developing countries usually have higher rates of illiteracy, higher unemployment, faster population growth, and exports consisting mostly of agricultural products and raw materials.

On average, more than 50 percent the labor force in developing countries works in agriculture, versus only about 3 percent in industrial market countries. Because farming methods are relatively primitive in developing countries, farm productivity is low and many barely subsist. Industrial market countries, or *developed countries,* are primarily the economically advanced capitalist countries of Western Europe, North America, Australia, New Zealand, and Japan. They were the first to experience long-term economic growth during the 19th century.

developing countries
nations typified by high rates of illiteracy, high unemployment, high fertility rates, and exports of primary products; also known as low-income and middle-income economies

industrial market countries
economically advanced capitalist countries of Western Europe, North America, Australia, New Zealand, and Japan; also known as developed countries and high-income economies

Exhibit 1

Share of World Population and Output

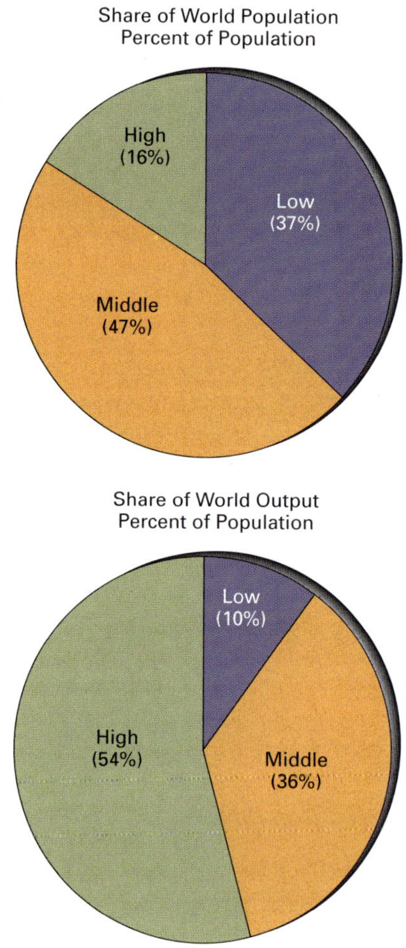

SOURCE: Based on population and output estimated from the *World Bank's World Development Report: 2007,* Table 1. Find the World Bank at http://web.worldbank.org.

Exhibit 2 presents income per capita in 2006 for a sample of high-, middle-, and low-income economies. Because most countries in the sample have a large population, together they account for 56 percent of world population. Countries are listed from top to bottom in descending order based on income per capita. Again, figures have been adjusted to reflect the actual purchasing power of the native currency in its respective economy. The bars in the chart are color-coded, with high-income economies in blue, middle-income economies in orange, and low-income economies in red. Per capita income in the United States, the top-ranked country, was more than five times that of China, a middle-income economy. But per capita in China, in turn, was about five times that of Nigeria and 11 time that of Burundi, poor African nations. Residents of China likely feel poor relative to America,

Exhibit 2

Per Capita Income for Selected Countries in 2006

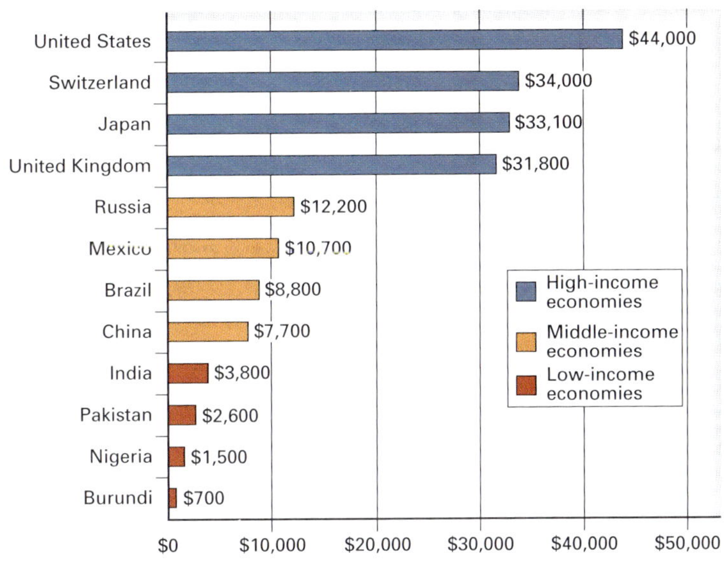

SOURCE: Developed from estimates from the Central Intelligence Agency *World Factbook: 2007* at www.cia.gov/library/publications/the-world-factbook/index.html. Figures are based on the purchasing power of each country's currency.

but they appear well off compared to the poorest developing nations. U.S per capita income was 29 times that of Nigeria, and 63 times that of Burundi, the poorest nation on Earth. Thus, there is a tremendous range in productive performance around the world.

Health and Nutrition

Differences in stages of development among countries are reflected in a number of ways besides per capita income. For example, many people in developing countries suffer from poor health as a result of malnutrition and disease. AIDS is devastating some developing countries, particularly those in sub-Saharan Africa. In 2005, one in five adults in Zimbabwe and South Africa had HIV, compared to only one in 200 among those living in high-income economies. In sub-Saharan Africa, life expectancy at birth averaged 46 years, versus 79 years in high-income economies, 70 years in middle-income economies, and 59 years in all low-income economies.

Malnutrition

Those in the poorest countries consume only half the calories of those in high-income countries. Even if an infant survives the first year, malnutrition can turn normal childhood diseases, such as measles, into life-threatening events. Malnutrition is a primary or contributing factor in more than half of the deaths of children under the age of 5 in low-income countries. Diseases that are well controlled in the industrial countries—malaria, whooping cough, polio, dysentery, typhoid, and cholera—can become epidemics in poor countries. Many of these diseases are waterborne, as safe drinking water is often hard to find. In low-income countries, about 40 percent of children under the age of 5 suffered from malnutrition in 2004. Among middle-income countries the figure was about 10 percent. Among high-income countries, it was 3 percent.

Exhibit 3

Child Mortality Rates Per 1,000 Live Births for the Sample of High-, Middle-, and Low-Income Economies

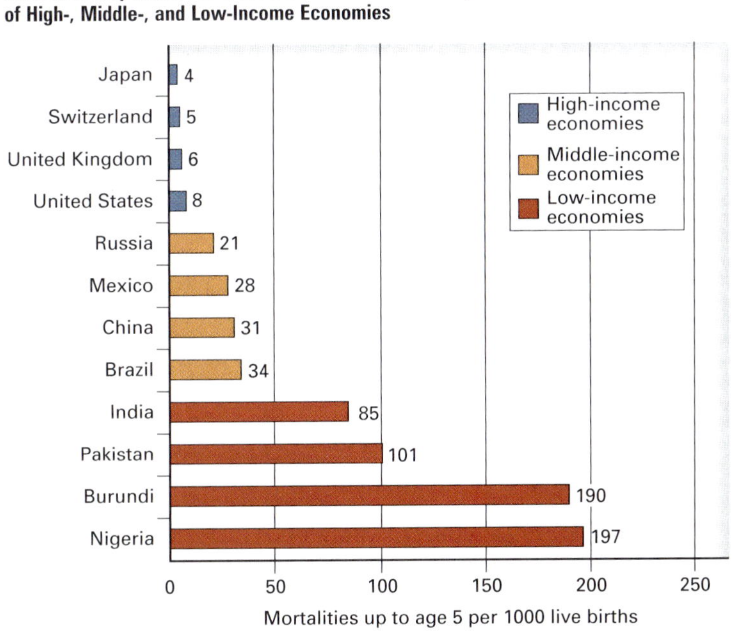

SOURCE: Based on figures from the World Bank's *World Development Report: 2007,* Table 1. Find the World Bank at http://web.worldbank.org.

Infant Mortality

Health differences among countries are reflected in child mortality. Child mortality rates are much greater in low-income countries than in high-income countries. As of 2006, the mortality rate for children up to 5 years of age was 7 per 1,000 live births in high-income economies, 39 in middle-income economies, and 122 in low-income economies. Rates for our representative sample of high-, middle-, and low-income economies appear in Exhibit 3. Again, high-income economies appear as blue bars, middle-income as orange bars, and low-income as red bars. Among the dozen

© JANINE WEIDEL PHOTOLIBRARY/ALAMY

countries shown, child mortality was highest in the sub-Saharan African nations of Nigeria and Burundi. Child mortality among all 48 sub-Saharan African countries averaged 24 times that in high-income countries.

High Birth Rates

Developing countries are identified not only by their low incomes and high mortality rates but also by their high birth rates. This year, more than 80 million of the 90 million people added to the world's population will be born in developing countries. In fact, the birth rate is one of the clearest ways of distinguishing between industrial and developing countries. Very few low-income economies have a fertility rate below 2.2 births per woman, but only one of 57 high-come countries, Israel, has a fertility rate above that level.

Exhibit 4 presents total fertility rates per woman for selected countries as of 2007. Burundi, the world's poorest country, had one the world's highest fertility rates at 6.5. This means each woman in Burundi on average gives birth to 6.5 children during her lifetime. Note that the four low-income economies, shown as red bars, have the highest fertility rates. Historically, families tend to be larger in poor countries because children are viewed as a source of farm labor and as economic and social security as the parents age. Most developing countries have no pension or social security system for the aged. The higher child mortality rates in poorer countries also engender higher birth rates, as parents strive to ensure a sufficiently large family.

Sub-Saharan African nations are the poorest in the world and have the fastest-growing populations. Because of high fertility rates in the poorest countries, children under 15 make up nearly half the population there. In industrial countries, children make up less than a quarter of the population. Italy, an industrial economy, became the first country in history with more people over the age of 65 than under the age of 15. Germany, Greece, Spain, Portugal, and Japan have since followed.

In some developing countries, the population growth rate has exceeded the growth rate in total production, so the standard of living as measured by per capita output has declined. Still, even in the poorest of countries, attitudes about family size are changing. According to the United Nations, the birth rate during a typical woman's lifetime in a developing country has fallen from six children in 1965 to under three children today. Evidence from developing countries more generally indicates that when women have employment opportunities outside the home, fertility rates decline. And as women become better educated, they earn more and tend to have fewer children.

Exhibit 4

Average Number of Births During a Woman's Lifetime as of 2007

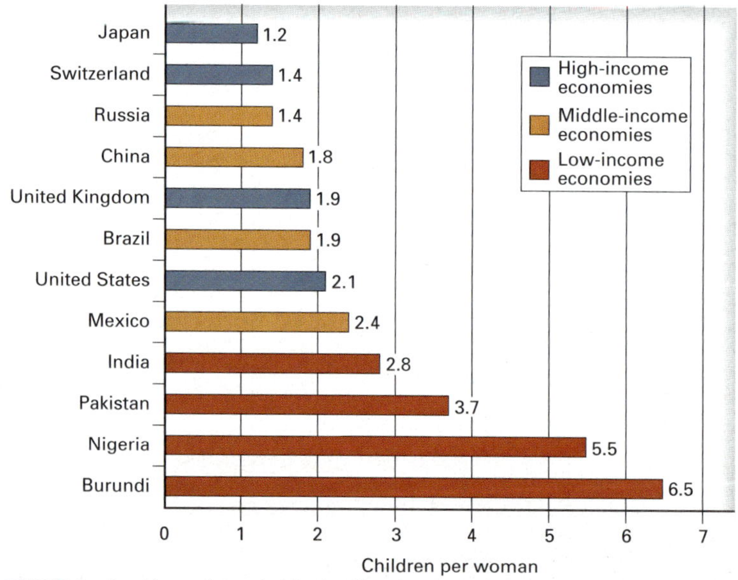

SOURCE: Developed from estimates found at http://en.wikipedia.org/wiki/List_of_countries_and_territories_by_fertility_rates.

Women in Developing Countries

Throughout the world, poverty is greater among women than men, particularly women who head households. The percentage of households headed by women varies from country to country, but nears 50 percent in some areas of Africa and the Caribbean. Because women often must work in the home as well as in the labor market, poverty can impose a special hardship on them. In many cultures, women's responsibilities include gathering firewood and carrying water, tasks that are especially burdensome if firewood is scarce and water is far from home.

Women in developing countries tend to be less educated than men. In the countries of sub-Saharan Africa and South Asia, for example, only half as many women as men complete high school. And in Indonesia, girls are six times more likely than boys to drop out of school before the fourth grade. Women have fewer employment opportunities and earn lower wages than men do. For example, Sudan's Muslim fundamentalist government bans women from working in public places after 5:00 P.M. In Algeria, Egypt, Jordan, Libya, and Saudi Arabia, women account for only about one-quarter of the work force. Women are often on the fringes of the labor market, working long hours in agriculture. They also have less access to other resources, such as land, capital, and technology.

LO2 Productivity: Key to Development

We have examined some symptoms of poverty in developing countries, but not why poor countries are poor. At the risk of appearing simplistic, we might say that poor countries are poor because they do not produce many goods and services. In this section, we examine why some developing countries experience such low productivity.

© IMAGEBROKER/ALAMY

Low Labor Productivity

Labor productivity, measured in terms of output per worker, is by definition low in low-income countries. Why? Labor productivity depends on the quality of the labor and on the amount of capital, natural resources, and other inputs that combine with labor. For example, as mentioned earlier, one certified public accountant with a computer and specialized software can sort out a company's finances more quickly and more accurately than can a thousand high-school–educated file clerks with pencils and paper.

One way a country raises its productivity is by investing more in human and physical capital. This investment must be financed by either domestic savings or foreign funds. Income per capita in the poorest countries is often too low to support much investments. In poor countries with unstable governments, the wealthy minority frequently invests in more stable foreign economies. This leaves less to invest domestically in either human or physical capital; without sufficient capital, workers remain less productive.

Technology and Education

What exactly is the contribution of education to the process of economic development? Education helps people make better use of the resources available. If knowledge is lacking, other resources may not be used efficiently. For example, a country may be endowed with fertile land, but farmers may lack knowledge of irrigation and fertilization techniques. Or farmers may not know how to rotate crops to avoid soil depletion. In low-income countries, 38 percent of those 15 and older were illiterate during the period 2000 to 2004, compared to 10 percent in middle-income countries, and less than 5 percent in high-income countries. In the low-income economies of Burundi and Pakistan only about one quarter complete ninth grade. In the middle-income economies of Brazil and Mexico about half do. Children drop out of school because the family can't afford it or would rather put the child to work. Child labor in developing countries obviously limits educational opportunities.

Education also makes people more receptive to new ideas and methods. Countries with the most advanced educational systems were also the first to develop. In the 20th century, the leader in schooling and economic development was the United States. In Latin America, Argentina was the most educationally advanced nation 100 years ago, and it is one of the most developed Latin American nations today. The growth of education in Japan during the 19th

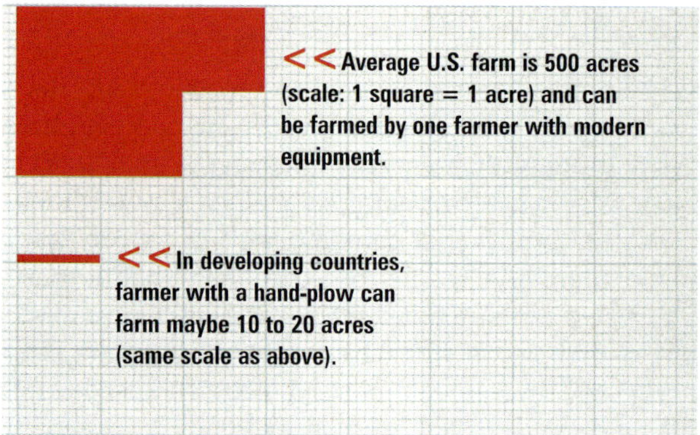

century contributed to a ready acceptance of technology and thus to Japan's remarkable economic growth in the 20th century.

Inefficient Use of Labor

Another feature of developing countries is that they use labor less efficiently than do industrial nations. Unemployment and underemployment reflect inefficient uses of labor. *Underemployment* occurs when skilled workers are employed in low-skill jobs or when people are working less than they would like—a worker seeking full-time employment may find only a part-time job. *Unemployment* occurs when those willing and able to work can't find jobs.

Unemployment is measured primarily in urban areas, because in rural areas farm work is usually an outlet for labor even if many workers are underemployed there. The unemployment rate in developing nations on average is about 10 to 15 percent of the urban labor force. Unemployment among young workers—those aged 15 to 24—is typically twice that of older workers. In developing nations, about 30 percent of the combined urban and rural work forces is either unemployed or underemployed. In Zimbabwe the unemployment rate was 80 percent in 2007.

LOW INCOME AND LOW PRODUCTIVITY MAY REINFORCE EACH OTHER IN A CYCLE OF POVERTY.

In some developing countries, the average farm is as small as two acres. Productivity is also low because few other inputs, such as capital and fertilizer, are used. *Although more than half the labor force in developing countries works in agriculture, only about one-third of output in these countries stems from agriculture.* In the United States, where farmers account for only 2 percent of the labor force, a farmer with modern equipment can farm hundreds or even thousands of acres (the average farm is about 500 acres). In developing countries, a farmer with a hand plow or an ox-drawn plow can farm maybe 10 to 20 acres. U.S. farmers, though only one-fiftieth of the labor force, grow enough to feed a nation and to lead the world in farm exports. The average value added per U.S. farm worker is about 50 times that of farm workers in low and middle-income countries.

Low productivity obviously results in low income, but low income can, in turn, affect worker productivity. Low income means less saving and less saving means less investment in human and physical capital. Low income can also mean poor nutrition during the formative years, which can retard mental and physical development. These difficult beginnings may be aggravated by poor diet and insufficient health care in later life, making workers poorly suited for regular employment. Poverty can result in less saving, less education, less capital formation, a poor diet, and little health care—all of which can reduce a worker's productivity. Thus, *low income and low productivity may reinforce each other in a cycle of poverty.*

Natural Resources

Some countries are rich in natural resources. The difference is most striking when we compare countries with oil reserves and those without. The Middle East countries of Bahrain, Kuwait, Qatar, Saudi Arabia, and the United Arab Emirates are developing countries classified as high-income economies because they were lucky enough to be sitting atop huge oil reserves. But oil-rich countries are the exception. Many developing countries, such as Chad and Ethiopia, have little in the way of natural resources. Most developing countries without oil reserves were in trouble when oil prices rose in 2006. Since oil must be imported, high oil prices drained oil-poor countries of precious foreign exchange.

Oil-rich countries also show us that an abundant supply of a natural resource is not in itself enough to create a modern industrial economy. On the other hand, Japan has one of the most developed economies in the world, yet has few natural resources. Connecticut is consistently the most productive of the United States measured in per capita income, but the state has little in the way of natural resources (its main natural resource is gravel). In fact, many researchers believe that reliance on resource wealth can be something of a curse for a nation, as you will see in an upcoming case study.

Financial Institutions

Another requirement for development is an adequate and trusted system of financial institutions. An important source of funds for investment is the savings of households and firms. People in some developing countries have little confidence in their currency because some governments finance a large fraction of public outlays by printing money. This practice results in high inflation and sometimes very high inflation, or hyperinflation, as has occurred recently in Zimbabwe, where annual inflation topped 1,000 percent. High and unpredictable inflation discourages saving and hurts development.

Developing countries have special problems because banks are often viewed with suspicion. At the first sign of economic problems, many depositors withdraw their funds. Because banks cannot rely on a continuous supply of deposits, they cannot make loans for extended periods. If financial institutions fail to serve as intermediaries between savers and borrowers, the lack of funds for investment becomes an obstacle to growth. One measure of banking presence is the credit provided by banks as a percent of a nation's total output. This percentage is more than five times greater in high-income countries than in low-income countries.

Capital Infrastructure

Production and exchange depend on a reliable infrastructure of transportation, communication, sanitation, and electricity. Roads, bridges, airports, harbors, and other transportation facilities are vital to commercial activity. Reliable mail service, telephone communication, clean water, and electricity are also essential for advanced production techniques. Imagine how difficult it would be to run even a personal computer if the supply of electricity and access to the Internet were unavailable or continually interrupted, as is often the case in many developing countries.

Some developing countries have serious deficiencies in their physical infrastructures. As just one measure, Exhibit 5 shows the number of fixed and mobile telephone lines per 1,000 people in 2006 for the 12 countries examined earlier. The top four countries, which are high-income economies, have about 10 times more phones per 1,000 people than the bottom four countries, which are low-income economies. The United States, the top-rated in this category, had 1,607 phone lines per 1,000 people. Bottom-ranked Burundi had just 22 phones lines per 1,000 people.

Phone lines help knit together an economy's communications network. Countries without reliable phone service have difficulty not only communicating but reaping the benefits of other technology advances, such as the Internet. Exhibit 6 shows Internet users as a percent of the population in 2006 for our sample countries. There is an unmistakable digital divide between high-income and low-income economies. In the four high-income economies, an average 66.3 percent of the population used the Internet. The United States, which developed the Internet, topped the group at 68.2 percent. In low-income economies, just 3.9 percent used the Internet on average. At the bottom is Burundi, where only 0.3 percent, or three out of every 1,000 people, used the Internet. Even in India, which has a reputation as computer savvy, what with all the online support centers and software companies we read about, only 5.3 percent of the population were Internet users. Indian colleges average only one computer for every 229 students.[1]

1. Shailaja Neelakantan, "India's Prime Minister Assails Universities as Below Average and 'Dysfunctional,'" *Chronicle of Higher Education,* 25 June 2007.

Exhibit 5

Phone Lines Per 1,000 People for the Sample of High-, Middle-, and Low-Income Economies

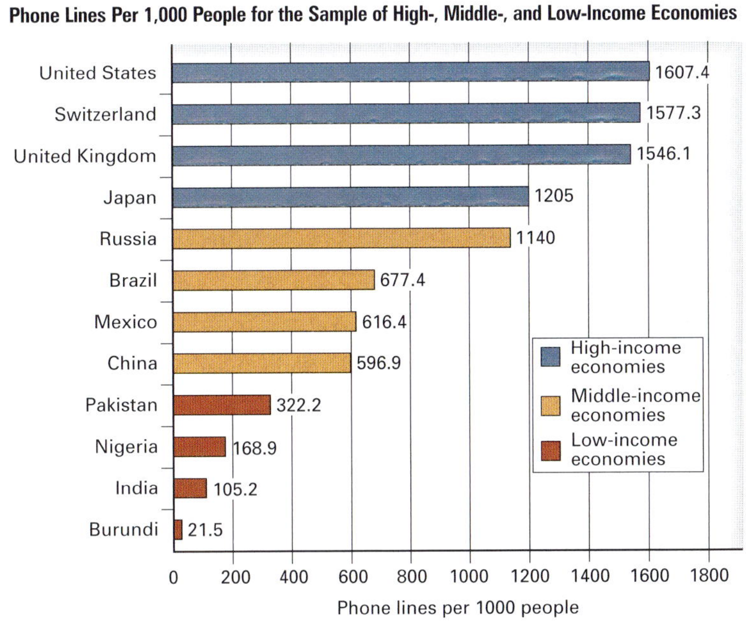

SOURCE: Computed based on fixed and mobile line estimates from the Central Intelligence Agency's *World Factbook: 2007* at www.cia.gov/library/publications/the-world-factbook/index.html.

Exhibit 6

Internet Users as Percent of Population for the Sample of High-, Middle-, and Low-Income Economies

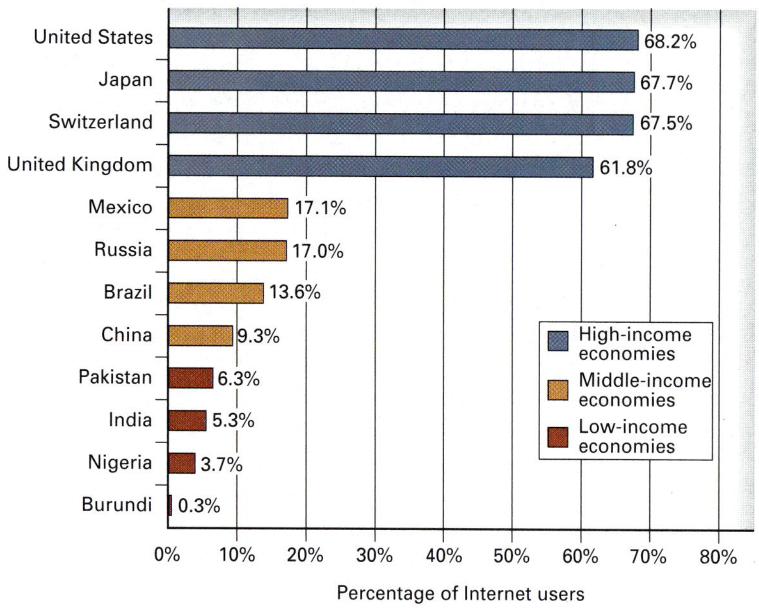

SOURCE: Computed from used estimates in the Central Intelligence Agency's *World Factbook: 2007* at www.cla.gov/library/publications/the-world-factbook/index.html.

Entrepreneurial Ability

An economy can have abundant supplies of labor, capital, and natural resources, but without entrepreneurial ability, the other resources will not be combined efficiently to produce goods and services. Unless a country has entrepreneurs who are able to bring together resources and take the risk of profit or loss, development may never get off the ground. Many developing countries were once under colonial rule, a system of government that offered the local population fewer opportunities to develop entrepreneurial skills.

Government officials sometimes decide that entrepreneurs are unable to generate the kind of economic growth the country needs. State enterprises are therefore created to do what government believes the free market cannot do. But state-owned enterprises may have objectives other than producing goods efficiently—objectives that could include providing jobs for friends and relatives of government officials.

Rules of the Game

social capital the shared values and trust that promote cooperation in the economy

Finally, in addition to human capital, natural resources, financial institutions, capital infrastructure, and entrepreneurial ability, a successful economy needs reliable *rules of the game*. Perhaps the most elusive ingredients for development are the formal and informal institutions that promote production and exchange: the laws, customs, conventions, and other institutional elements that sustain an economy. A stable political environment with well-defined property rights is important. Little private-sector investment will occur if potential investors believe their capital might be appropriated by government, destroyed by civil unrest, or stolen by thieves.

High-income economies have developed a reliable and respected system of property rights and customs and conventions that nurture productive activity. These successful economies have cultivated the social capital that helps the economy run more smoothly. **Social capital** consists of the shared values and trust that promote cooperation in the economy. Low-income economies typically have poorly defined property rights, less social capital, and, in the extreme, customs and conventions where bribery is commonplace and government corruption is an everyday practice. Worse still, civil wars have ravaged some of the poorest countries on Earth. Such violence and uncertainty make people less willing to invest in their own future or in the future of their country.

Although it is common to sort countries into advanced industrial economies and developing economies, there are broad differences among developing economies.

Income Distribution Within Countries

Thus far the focus has been on income differences across countries, and these differences can be vast. But what about income differences within a country. Are poor countries uniformly poor or are there sizable income differences within a given nation's population. One way to measure inequality across households is to look at the share of national income going to the poorest fifth of the population. As a point of reference, in the unlikely event that income in an economy were evenly distributed across all households, then the poorest fifth would also receive exactly one fifth, or 20 percent, of national income. More realistically, the poorest fifth receives less than 20 percent of the income, but how much less? Is the percentage of income going to the poorest fifth higher for low-income countries than for high-income countries? In other words, is income more evenly distributed among people in poor countries than among people in rich countries? Not necessarily. Among our 12 nations, the poorest fifth of the population got an average of 7.4 percent of the income in the high-income countries, 4.4 percent in middle-income countries, and 7.1 percent in low-income countries. So, at least in this sample, income was less evenly distributed in middle-income countries than in high- or low-income countries.

LO3 International Trade and Development

Developing countries need to trade with developed countries to acquire the capital and technology that will increase labor productivity on the farm, in the factory, in the office, and in the home. To import capital and technology, developing countries must first acquire the funds, or foreign exchange, needed to pay for imports. Exports usually generate more than half of the annual flow of foreign exchange in developing countries. Foreign aid and private investment make up the rest.

Trade Problems for Developing Countries

Primary products, such as agricultural goods and other raw materials, make up the bulk of exports from developing countries, just as manufactured goods make up the bulk of exports from industrial countries. About half the merchandise exports from low-income countries consist of raw materials, compared to only 20 percent from high-income countries. A problem for developing countries is that the prices of primary products, such as coffee, cocoa, sugar, and rubber, fluctuate more widely than do the prices of finished goods, because crop supply fluctuates with the weather.

When developing countries experience trade deficits, they often try to restrict imports. Because imported food is sometimes critical to survival, developing countries are more likely to cut imports of capital goods—the very items needed to promote long-term growth and productivity. Thus many developing countries cannot afford the modern machinery that will help them become more productive. Developing countries must also confront industrial countries' trade restrictions, such as tariffs and quotas, which often discriminate against primary products. For example, the United States strictly limits sugar imports.

Migration and the Brain Drain

Migration plays an important role in the economies of developing countries. A major source of foreign exchange in some countries is the money sent home by migrants who find jobs in industrial countries. According to the World Bank, migrants sent home about $240 billion in 2007. Thus migration provides a valuable safety valve for poor countries. But there is a downside. Often the best and the brightest professionals, such as doctors, nurses, and engineers, migrate to developed countries. For example, every year thousands of nurses migrate from countries such as Kenya and the Philippines to the United States, where half the world's nurses are employed. The financial attraction is powerful: a nurse in the Philippines would start there at less than $2,000 a year, compared with at least $36,000 in the United States.[2]

The Philippines economy benefits from the billions sent home by overseas workers. So the upside of the brain drain for the poor country is the remittance sent home by overseas worker. Still, a nation is hurt when its best and brightest leave for opportunities elsewhere. Some African countries are demanding compensation for educating the doctors and nurses who move to high-income economies.

Import Substitution Versus Export Promotion

An economy's progress usually involves moving up the production chain from agriculture and raw material to manufacturing and then to services. If a country is fortunate, this transformation occurs gradually through

2. Celia Dugger, "U.S. Plan to Lure Nurses May Hurt Poor Countries," *New York Times,* 24 May 2006.

natural market forces. For example, in 1850 most U.S. jobs were in agriculture. Now most jobs are in the service sector. Sometimes governments try to speed up the evolution. Many developing countries, including Argentina and India, pursued a strategy called **import substitution**, whereby domestic manufacturers would make products that until then had been imported. To insulate domestic manufacturers from foreign competition, the government imposed stiff tariffs and quotas. This development strategy became popular for several reasons. First, demand already existed for these products, so the "what to produce" question was easily answered. Second, import substitution provided infant industries a protected market. Finally, import substitution was popular with those who supplied resources to the favored domestic industries.

Like all trade protection, however, import substitution erased the gains from specialization and comparative advantage among countries. Often the developing country replaced low-cost foreign goods with high-cost domestic goods. And domestic producers, shielded from foreign competition, usually failed to become efficient. Worse still, other countries often retaliated with their own trade restrictions.

Critics of import substitution claim that export promotion is a surer path to economic development. **Export promotion** concentrates on producing for the export market. This development strategy begins with relatively simple products, such as textiles. As a developing country builds its technological and educational base—that is, as the developing economy learns by doing—producers can then make more complex products for export. Economists favor export promotion over import substitution because the emphasis is on comparative advantage and trade expansion rather than on trade restriction. Export promotion also forces producers to become more efficient in order to compete on world markets. Research shows that facing global competition boosts domestic efficiency.[3] What's more, export promotion requires less government intervention in the market than does import substitution.

Of the two approaches, export promotion has been more successful around the world. For example, the newly industrialized countries of East Asia have successfully pursued export promotion, while Argentina, India, and Peru have failed with their import substitution approach. In 1965, the newly industrialized economies of Hong Kong, Korea, Singapore, and Taiwan had an average income only 20 percent that of high-income countries. Now these four are themselves high-income countries. Most Latin American nations, which for decades had favored import substitution, are now pursuing free trade agreements with each other and with the United States. Even India is dismantling trade barriers, with an emphasis on importing high-technology capital goods. One slogan of Indian trade officials is "Microchips, yes! Potato chips, no!"

import substitution
a development strategy that emphasizes domestic manufacturing of products that are currently imported

export promotion
a development strategy that concentrates on producing for the export market

3. See Martin Baily and Hans Gersbach, "Efficiency in Manufacturing and the Need for Global Competition," in *Brookings Papers on Economic Activity: Microeconomics*, M. Baily, P. Reiss, and C. Winston, eds. (Brookings Institution, 1995): 307-347.

"One slogan of Indian trade officials is "Microchips, yes! Potato chips, no!""

Trade Liberalization and Special Interests

Although most people would benefit from freer international trade, some would be worse off. Consequently, governments in some developing countries have difficulty pursuing policies conducive to development. Often the gains from economic development are widespread, but the beneficiaries, such as consumers, do not recognize their potential gains. On the other hand, the losers tend to be concentrated, such as producers in an industry that had been sheltered from foreign competition, and they know quite well the source of their losses. So the government often lacks the political will and support to remove impediments to development, because the potential losers fight reforms that might harm their livelihood while the potential winners remain largely unaware of what's at stake. What's more, consumers have difficulty organizing even if they become aware of what's going on. A recent study by the World Bank suggests a strong link in Africa between governments that cater to special-interest groups and low rates of economic growth.

Nonetheless, many developing countries have been opening their borders to freer trade. People around the world have been exposed to information about the opportunities and goods available on world markets. So consumers want the goods and firms want the technology and capital that are available abroad. Both groups want government to ease trade restrictions. Studies by the World Bank and others have underscored the successes of countries that have adopted trade liberalization policies.

LO4 Foreign Aid and Economic Development

We have already seen that because poor countries do not generate enough savings to fund an adequate level of investment, these countries often rely on foreign financing. Private international borrowing and lending are heavily restricted by the governments of developing countries. Governments may allow residents to purchase foreign exchange only for certain purposes. In some developing countries, different exchange rates apply to different categories of transactions. Thus the local currency is not easily convertible into other currencies. Some developing countries also require foreign investors to find a local partner who must be granted controlling interest. All these restrictions discourage foreign investment. In this section, we will look primarily at foreign aid and its link to economic development.

Foreign Aid

Foreign aid is any international transfer made on *concessional* (i.e., especially favorable) terms for the purposes of promoting economic development. Foreign aid includes grants, which need not be repaid, and loans extended on more favorable repayment terms than the recipient could normally secure. Concessional loans have lower interest rates, longer repayment periods, or grace periods during which repayments are reduced or even waived (similar to some student loans). Foreign aid can take the form of money, capital goods, technical assistance, food, and so forth.

Some foreign aid is granted by a specific country, such as the United States, to another specific country, such as the Philippines. Country-to-country aid is called *bilateral* assistance. Other foreign aid goes through international bodies such as the World Bank. Assistance provided by organizations that use funds from a number of countries is called *multilateral*. For example, the World Bank provides loans and grants to support activities that are viewed as prerequisites for development, such as health and education programs or basic development projects like dams, roads, and communications networks. And the International Monetary Fund extends loans to countries that have trouble with their balance of payments.

During the last four decades, the United States has provided the developing world with over $400 billion in aid. Since 1961, most U.S. aid has been coordinated by the U.S. Agency for International Development (USAID), which is part of the U.S. Department of State. This agency concentrates primarily on health, education, and agriculture, providing both technical assistance and loans. USAID emphasizes long-range plans to meet the basic needs of the poor and to promote self-sufficiency. Foreign aid is a controversial, though relatively small, part of the federal budget. Since 1993, official U.S. aid has been less than 0.2 percent of U.S. GDP, compared to an average of 0.3 percent from 21 other industrialized nations.

Does Foreign Aid Promote Economic Development?

In general, foreign aid provides additional purchasing power and thus the possibility of increased investment, capital imports, and consumption. But it remains unclear whether foreign aid *supplements* domestic saving, thus increasing investment, or simply *substitutes* for domestic saving, thereby increasing consumption rather than investment. What is clear is that foreign aid often becomes a source of discretionary funds that benefit not the poor but their leaders. Historically, more than 90 percent of the funds distributed by USAID have gone to governments, whose leaders assume responsibility for distributing these funds.

Much bilateral funding is tied to purchases of goods and services from the donor nation, and such programs can sometimes be counterproductive. For example, in the 1950s, the United States began the Food for Peace program, which helped sell U.S. farm products abroad, but some

foreign aid
an international transfer made on especially favorable terms for the purpose of promoting economic development

recipient governments sold that food to finance poorly conceived projects. Worse yet, the availability of low-priced food from abroad drove down farm prices in the developing countries, hurting poor farmers there.

Foreign aid may have raised the standard of living in some developing countries, but it has not necessarily increased their ability to become self-supporting at that higher standard of living. Many countries that receive aid are doing less of what they had done well. Their agricultural sectors have suffered. For example, though we should be careful when drawing conclusions about causality, per capita food production in Africa has fallen since 1960. Outside aid has often insulated government officials from their own incompetence and fundamental troubles of their own economies. No country receiving U.S. aid in the past 25 years has moved up in status from developing to industrial. And most countries today that have achieved industrial status did so without foreign aid.

Because of disappointment with the results of government aid, the trend is toward channeling funds through private nonprofit agencies such as CARE. More than half of foreign aid now flows through private channels. The privatization of foreign aid follows a larger trend toward privatization around the world. We discuss that important development in the balance of this chapter.

LO5 Transitional Economies

As we have seen, there is no widely accepted theory of economic development, but around the world, markets have replaced central plans in once-socialist countries. Economic developments in these emerging market economies have tremendous significance for those who study economics. Like geologists, economists must rely primarily on natural experiments to figure out how things work. *The attempt to replace central planning with markets has been one of the greatest economic experiments in history.* In the study of geology, this would be comparable to a huge earthquake. In this section, we take a look at these so-called transitional economies.

Types of Economic Systems

First, let's briefly review economic systems. Chapter 2 considered the three questions that every economic system must answer: what to produce, how to produce it, and for whom to produce it. Laws regarding resource ownership and the role of government in resource allocation determine the "rules of the game"—the incentives and constraints that guide the behavior of individual decision makers. Economic systems can be classified based on the ownership of resources, the way resources are allocated to produce goods and services, and the incentives used to motivate people.

soft budget constraint
the budget condition faced by socialist enterprises that are subsidized if they lose money

As we discussed in Chapter 2, resources in *capitalist* systems are owned mostly by individuals and are allocated through market coordination. In socialist economies, resources other than labor are owned by the state. For example, a country such as Cuba or North Korea carefully limits the private ownership of resources such as land and capital. Each country employs a slightly different system of resource ownership, resource allocation, and individual incentives to answer the three economic questions.

So under capitalism, the rules of the game include private ownership of most resources and the coordination of economic activity by price signals generated by market forces; market coordination answers the three questions. Under socialism, the rules of the game include government ownership of most resources and the allocation of resources through central plans.

Enterprises and Soft Budget Constraints

In the socialist system, enterprises that earn a "profit" see that profit appropriated by the state. Firms that end up with a loss find that loss covered by a state subsidy. Thus socialist enterprises face what has been called a soft budget constraint. This can lead to inefficiency, a lack of response to changes in supply or demand, and poor investment decisions. Quality has also been a problem under central planning, because plant managers would rather meet production quotas than satisfy consumer demand. For example, plant managers do not score extra bureaucratic points by producing garments

© IGOR GAVRILOV/TIME-LIFE PICTURES/GETTY IMAGES

that are in style and in popular sizes. Tales of shoddy products in socialist systems abound.

Most prices in centrally planned economies are established not by market forces but by central planners. As a result, consumers have less say in what to produce. Once set, prices tend to be inflexible. For example, in the former Soviet Union, the price of a cabbage slicer was stamped on the metal at the factory. In the spirit of equity, Soviet planners priced most consumer goods below the market-clearing level, so shortages (or "interruptions in supply," as they were called) were common. For example, as of 1990, the price of bread in the former Soviet Union had not changed since 1954, and that price in 1990 amounted to just 7 percent of bread's production cost. Meat prices had not changed since 1962. Some rents had not changed in 60 years.

Capitalist economies equate quantity demanded with quantity supplied through the *invisible hand* of market coordination; centrally planned economies try to equate the two using the *visible hand* of bureaucratic coordination assisted by taxes and subsidies. If quantity supplied and quantity demanded are not in balance, something has to give. In a capitalist system, what gives is the price. In a centrally planned economy, what usually gives is the central plan itself. A common problem in the Soviet system was that the amount produced often fell short of planned production. When the quantity supplied fell below the planned amount, central planners reduced the amount supplied to each sector, cutting critical sectors such as heavy industry and the military the least and cutting lower-priority sectors such as consumer products the most. Evidence of shortages of consumer goods included long waiting lines at retail stores; empty store shelves; the "tips," or bribes, shop operators expected for supplying scarce consumer goods; and higher prices for the same goods on the black market. Shoppers would sometimes wait in line all night and into the next day. Consumers often relied on "connections" through acquaintances to obtain most goods and services. Scarce goods were frequently diverted to the black market.

LO6 Markets and Institutions

A study of economic systems underscores the importance of institutions in the course of development. *Institutions,* or "rules of the game," are the incentives and constraints that structure political, economic, and social interaction. They consist of (1) formal rules of behavior, such as a constitution, laws, and property rights, and (2) informal constraints on behavior, such as sanctions, manners, customs, traditions, and codes of conduct. Throughout history, institutions have been devised by people to create order and reduce uncertainty in exchange. Thus underlying the surface of economic behavior is a grid of informal, often unconscious, habits, customs, manners, and norms that make markets possible. *A reliable system of property rights and enforceable contracts is a prerequisite for creating incentives that support a healthy market economy.*

A reliable system of property rights and enforceable contracts is a prerequisite for creating incentives that support a healthy market economy.

Together with the standard constraints of economics, such as income, resource availability, and prices, institutions shape the incentive structure of an economy. As the incentive structure evolves, it can direct economic change toward growth, stagnation, or decline. Economic history is largely a story of economies that have failed to produce a set of economic rules of the game that lead to sustained economic growth. After all, most of the world's economies are still developing—still trying to get their act together.

Customs and conventions can sometimes be obstacles to development. In developed market economies, resource owners tend to supply their resources where they are most valued; but in developing countries, links to the family or clan may be the most important consideration. For example, in some cultures, children, particularly male children, are expected to remain in their father's occupation even though some are better suited for other lines of work. Family businesses may resist growth because such growth would involve hiring people from outside the family.

Institutions and Economic Development

Institutions shape the incentive structure of an economy, but, as already noted, most countries in the world have failed to come up with the rules of the game that lead to sustained economic growth. Although political and judicial decisions may change formal rules overnight, informal constraints embodied in manners, customs, traditions, and codes of conduct are more immune to deliberate policies. For example, respect for the law cannot be legislated.

Prior to the market reforms in the former Soviet Union, widespread corruption and a lack of faith in formal institutions were woven into the social fabric. Workers bribed officials to get good jobs and consumers bribed clerks to get desired products. Bribery became a way of life, a way of dealing with the distortions that arise when prices are not allowed to allocate resources efficiently.

In centrally planned economies, the exchange relationship was typically personal, based as it was on bureaucratic ties on the production side and inside connections on the consumption side. But in the United States and other market economies, successful institutional evolution permits the impersonal exchange necessary to capture the potential economic benefits of specialization and modern technology. Impersonal exchange allows for a far greater division of labor, but it requires a richer and more stable institutional setting.

The Big Bang Versus Gradualism

The Hungarian economist Janos Kornai believes that a market order should be grown from the bottom up. First, small-scale capitalism in farming, trade, light manufacturing, and services thrives. These grass-roots markets can serve as a foundation for the privatization of larger industrial sectors. Large industrial enterprises should quickly find the market-clearing price so that input and output decisions are consistent with market preferences. In the meantime, state-owned enterprises should be run more like businesses in which state directors attempt to maximize profit. Money-losing enterprises should be phased out. This "bottom-up" approach proposed by Kornai could be termed **gradualism**, which can be contrasted with a **big-bang theory**, whereby the transition from central planning to a market economy would occur in a matter of months.

gradualism a "bottom-up" approach to moving gradually from a centrally planned to a market economy by establishing markets at the most decentralized level first, such as on small farms or in light industry

big-bang theory the argument that the transition from a centrally planned to a market economy should be broad and swift, taking place in a matter of months

privatization the process of turning public enterprises into private enterprises

transparent finances a firm's financial records that clearly indicate the economic health of the company

One example of gradualism is taking place in China. In 1978, the government began dismantling agricultural communes in favor of a "household-responsibility" system of small-farm agriculture. Land was assigned to individual families, who could keep any excess production after meeting specific state-imposed goals. Initially the system was to be applied only to the poorest 20 percent of rural areas. Once the positive effects became apparent, however, the system spread on its own. Eventually farmers established their own wholesale and retail marketing systems and were allowed to sell directly to urban areas at market-clearing prices. This gave rise to a market for truckers to buy, transport, and resell farm products. Over the next seven years, agricultural output increased by an impressive 8 to 10 percent per year.

Privatization

Privatization is the process of turning public enterprises into private enterprises. It is the opposite of *nationalization* (what Cesar Chavez has been doing in Venezuela). For example, Russian privatization began in April 1992 with the sale of municipally owned shops. Although most property in countries of the former Soviet Union was nominally owned by the state, it often remained unclear who had the authority to sell the property and who should receive the proceeds. This ambiguity resulted in cases in which the same property was purchased from different officials by different buyers. Yet *there was no clear legal process for resolving title disputes*. Worse still, some enterprises have been stripped of their assets by self-serving managers, a process that derisively came to be called "spontaneous" privatization. The necessarily complex process of privatization was undermined because the general population perceived it as unfair.

Privatization also requires modern accounting and other information systems, the training of competent managers, and the installation of adequate facilities for telecommunication, computing, travel, and transportation. This transformation cannot be accomplished overnight. Consider just the accounting problem. A market economy depends on financial accounting rules as well as on an independent system for auditing financial reports. The needed information must show up in a company's balance sheet and income statement. Prospective buyers of enterprises need such information, as do banks and other lenders. Thus, a firm's finances should be **transparent**, meaning someone should be able to look at the books and the balance sheet and tell exactly what's going on.

By all reports, the accounting systems of most formerly socialist firms are almost worthless. For decades, data had been aimed more at central planners, who wanted to know about *physical* flows, than at someone who wanted to know about the efficiency and financial promise of the firm. So there is much information, but little that is relevant. Incidentally, the major advantage of the market economy is that it minimizes the need for the kind of resource-flow data that had been reported under central planning. *Prices convey most of the information necessary to coordinate economic activity among firms.*

Institutional Requirements of Efficient Markets

Some may look at the initial instability that resulted from the dismantling of socialist states and argue that the move toward markets has been a failure. But in the former Soviet Union the state dismantled central controls before institutions such as property rights, customs, codes of conduct, and a legal system were in place.

Tax laws are applied unevenly and the rates change frequently. For example, the personal income tax in Russia jumped from a graduated rate topping at 13 percent to a flat rate of 60 percent, to a graduated rate topping at 40 percent, then 30 percent, then to a flat rate of 13 percent. The low flat rate seems to be popular and has increased revenue more than 10 percent a year since its adoption in 2001. Russian expert Marshall Goldman has argued that "tax evasion by both enterprises and individuals is a source of pride dating back to czarist times."[4] Millions of Russians carry out their business in the underground economy.

The shift from central planning to a market economy has been rough going in Russia. Simply loosening constraints to create private property may not be enough for successful reform. The development of supporting institutions is essential, but *there is no unified economic theory of how to construct the institutions that are central to the success of capitalism.* Most so-called economists employed in Soviet-type systems did not understand even the basics of how markets work. They had been trained to regard the alleged "anarchy" of the market as a primary defect of capitalism.

Prices convey most of the information necessary to coordinate economic activity among firms.

A more fundamental problem is that, although Western economic theory focuses on the operation of efficient markets, *even market economists usually do not understand the institutional requirements of efficient markets.* Market economists often take the necessary institutions for granted. Those involved in the transition must develop a deeper appreciation for the institutions that nurture and support impersonal market activity.

So the jury is still out on the transition to markets. Exhibit 7 presents, for 10 key transitional economies, the gross domestic product (GDP) per capita in 2006 based on the purchasing power of the domestic currency. Notice the dramatic differences across these economies, with GDP per capita in the Czech Republic about seven times greater than that of Vietnam.

4. Marshall Goldman, "Russian Tax Evasion Is Source of Pride," letter to the editor, *New York Times*, 9 August 1998.

Exhibit 7

GDP Per Capita for Transitional Economies in 2006

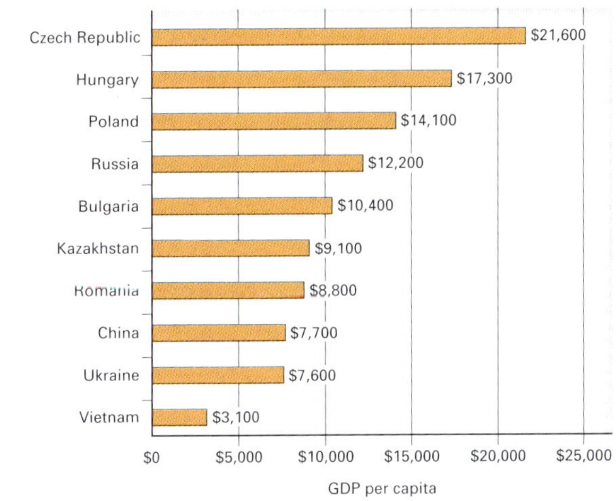

SOURCE: Computed from estimates in the Central Intelligence Agency's *World Factbook: 2007* at www.cia.gov/library/publications/the-world-factbook/index.html. Figures are based on the purchasing power of the local currency.

Russia ranked about halfway between those two. Nine of the 10 countries are middle-income economies. Vietnam, the exception, is a low-income economy but on the way up. Thus, no transitional economy has yet become a high-income nation.

Lessons about the nature of economic processes will likely emerge from the analysis of these transitional economies. The course of economic reform will provide insights into both the potential and the limits of economics itself.

Final Word

Because no single theory of economic development has become widely accepted, this chapter has been more descriptive than theoretical. We can readily identify the features that distinguish developing from industrial economies. Education is key to development, both because of its direct effect on productivity and because those who are more educated tend to be more receptive to new ideas. A physical infrastructure of transportation and communication systems and utilities is needed to link economic participants. And trusted financial institutions help link savers and borrowers. A country needs entrepreneurs with the vision to move the economy forward. Finally, the most elusive ingredients are the laws, manners, customs, and ways of doing business that nurture economic development. Economic history is largely a story of economies that have failed to produce a set of economic rules of the game that lead to sustained economic growth. Some newly emerging industrial countries in Asia show that economic development is still achievable.

egokast
1 Ton
GRAND
OPENING

Problems Appendix

CHAPTER 1

LO1 Explain the economic problem of scarce resources and unlimited wants

1.1. *(Definition of Economics)* What determines whether or not a resource is scarce? Why is the concept of scarcity important to the definition of economics?

LO2 Describe the forces that shape economic choices

2.1. *(Rational Self-Interest)* Discuss the impact of rational self-interest on each of the following decisions:
   a. Whether to attend college full time or enter the workforce full time
   b. Whether to buy a new textbook or a used one
   c. Whether to attend a local college or an out-of-town college

2.2. *(Rational Self-Interest)* If behavior is governed by rational self-interest, why do people make charitable contributions of time and money?

2.3. *(Marginal Analysis)* The owner of a small pizzeria is deciding whether to increase the radius of delivery area by one mile. What considerations must be taken into account if such a decision is to increase profitability?

2.4. *(Time and Information)* It is often costly to obtain the information necessary to make good decisions. Yet your own interests can be best served by rationally weighing all options available to you. This requires informed decision making. Does this mean that making uninformed decisions is irrational? How do you determine how much information is the right amount?

LO3 Explain the relationship between economic theory and economic reality

3.1. *(Role of Theory)* What good is economic theory if it can't predict the behavior of a specific individual?

LO4 Identify some pitfalls of economic analysis

4.1. *(Pitfalls of Economic Analysis)* Review the discussion of pitfalls in economic thinking in this chapter. Then identify the fallacy, or mistake in thinking, in each of the following statements:
   a. Raising taxes always increases government revenues.
   b. Whenever there is a recession, imports decrease. Therefore, to stop a recession, we should increase imports.
   c. Raising the tariff on imported steel helps the U.S. steel industry. Therefore, the entire economy is helped.
   d. Gold sells for about $625 per ounce. Therefore, the U.S. government could sell all the gold in Fort Knox at $625 per ounce and reduce the national debt.

4.2. *(Association Versus Causation)* Suppose I observe that communities with lots of doctors tend to have relatively high rates of illness. I conclude that doctors cause illness. What's wrong with this reasoning?

LO5 Describe several reasons to study economics

5.1. According to the text, economics majors on average make more money than most other majors and have more job opportunities. Are these the primary motivations one might have for studying economics? What are your motivations for studying economics?

CHAPTER 2

LO1 Describe the impact of choice on opportunity

1.1. *(Sunk Cost and Choice)* Suppose you go to a restaurant and buy an expensive meal. Halfway through, despite feeling quite full, you decide to clean your plate. After all, you think, you paid for the meal, so you are going to eat all of it. What's wrong with this thinking?

1.2. *(Opportunity Cost)* You can either spend spring break working at home for $80 per day for five days or go to Florida for the week. If you stay home, your expenses will total about $100. If you go to Florida, the airfare, hotel, food, and miscellaneous expenses will total about $700. What's your opportunity cost of going to Florida?

LO2 Explain how comparative advantage, specialization, and exchange affect economic outcomes (output)

2.1. *(Absolute and Comparative Advantage)* You have the following information concerning the production of wheat and cloth in the United States and the United Kingdom:

	Labor Hours Required to Produce One Unit	
	United Kingdom	**United States**
Wheat	2	1
Cloth	6	5

   a. What is the opportunity cost of producing a unit of wheat in the United Kingdom? In the United States?
   b. Which country has an absolute advantage in producing wheat? In producing cloth?
   c. Which country has a comparative advantage in producing wheat? In producing cloth?

d. Which country should specialize in producing wheat? In producing cloth?

2.2. *(Specialization)* Provide some examples of specialized markets or retail outlets. What makes the Web so conducive to specialization?

LO3 Outline how economies function as production systems

3.1. *(Shape of the PPF)* Suppose a production possibilities frontier includes the following combinations:

Cars	Washing Machines
0	1,000
100	600
200	0

a. Graph the PPF, assuming that it has no curved segments.
b. What is the cost of producing an additional car when 50 cars are being produced?
c. What is the cost of producing an additional car when 150 cars are being produced?
d. What is the cost of producing an additional washing machine when 50 cars are being produced? When 150 cars are being produced?
e. What do your answers tell you about opportunity costs?

3.2. *(Production Possibilities)* Suppose an economy uses two resources (labor and capital) to produce two goods (wheat and cloth). Capital is relatively more useful in producing cloth, and labor is relatively more useful in producing wheat. If the supply of capital falls by 10 percent and the supply of labor increases by 10 percent, how will the PPF for wheat and cloth change?

3.3. *(Production Possibilities)* There's no reason why a production possibilities frontier could not be used to represent the situation facing an individual. Imagine your own PPF. Right now—today—you have certain resources—your time, your skills, perhaps some capital. And you can produce various outputs. Suppose you can produce combinations of two outputs, call them studying and partying.

a. Draw your PPF for studying and partying. Be sure to label the axes of the diagram appropriately. Label the points where the PPF intersects the axes, as well as several other points along the frontier.
b. Explain what it would mean for you to move upward and to the left along your personal PPF. What kinds of adjustments would you have to make in your life to make such a movement along the frontier?
c. Under what circumstances would your personal PPF shift outward? Do you think the shift would be a "parallel" one? Why, or why not?

3.4. *(Shifting Production Possibilities)* Determine whether each of the following would cause the economy's PPF to shift inward, outward, or not at all:

a. An increase in average length of annual vacations
b. An increase in immigration
c. A decrease in the average retirement age
d. The migration of skilled workers to other countries

LO4 Describe different economic systems and the decision-making rules that define them

4.1 *(Economic Systems)* The United States is best described as having a mixed economy. What are some elements of command in the U.S. economy? What are some elements of tradition?

CHAPTER 3

LO1 Explain the role of the household in an economic system

1.1. *(Evolution of the Household)* Determine whether each of the following would increase or decrease the opportunity costs for mothers who choose not to work outside the home. Explain your answers.

a. Higher levels of education for women
b. Higher unemployment rates for women
c. Higher average pay levels for women
d. Lower demand for labor in industries that traditionally employ large numbers of women

1.2. *(Household Production)* Many households supplement their food budget by cultivating small vegetable gardens. Explain how each of the following might influence this kind of household production:

a. Both husband and wife are professionals who earn high salaries.
b. The household is located in a city rather than in a rural area.
c. The household is located in a region where there is a high sales tax on food.
d. The household is located in a region that has a high property tax rate.

1.3. *(Household Production)* What factors does a householder consider when deciding whether to produce a good or service at home or buy it in the marketplace?

1.4. *(Objectives of the Economic Decision Makers)* In economic analysis, what are the assumed objectives of households, firms, and the government?

LO2 Identify the different types of firms and describe their role in the economy

2.1. *(Corporations)* How did the institution of the firm get a boost from the advent of the Industrial Revolution? What type of business organization existed before this?

2.2. *(Sole Proprietorships)* What are the disadvantages of the sole proprietorship form of business?

2.3. *(Cooperatives)* How do cooperatives differ from typical businesses?

2.4. *(Evolution of the Firm)* Explain how production after the Industrial Revolution differed from production under the cottage industry system.

LO3 Outline the ways governments affect their economies

3.1. *(Government)* Complete each of the following sentences:

a. When the private operation of a market leads to overproduction or underproduction of some good, this is known as a(n) ________.

b. Goods that are nonrival and nonexcludable are known as ___________.

c. _________ are cash or in-kind benefits given to individuals as outright grants from the government.

d. A(n) _________ confers an external benefit on third parties that are not directly involved in a market transaction.

e. _________ refers to the government's pursuit of full employment and price stability through variations in taxes and government spending.

3.2. *(Tax Rates)* Suppose taxes are related to income level as follows:

Income	Taxes
$1,000	$200
$2,000	$350
$3,000	$450

a. What percentage of income is paid in taxes at each level?

b. Is the tax rate progressive, proportional, or regressive?

c. What is the marginal tax rate on the first $1,000 of income? The second $1,000? The third $1,000?

3.3. *(Government Revenue)* What are the sources of government revenue in the United States? Which types of taxes are most important at each level of government? Which two taxes provide the most revenue to the federal government?

3.4. *(Externalities)* Suppose there is an external cost, or negative externality, associated with production of a certain good. What's wrong with letting the market determine how much of this good will be produced?

LO4 Outline the international influences on an economy

4.1. *(International Trade)* Why does international trade occur? What does it mean to run a deficit in the merchandise trade balance?

4.2. *(International Trade)* Distinguish between a tariff and a quota. Who benefits from and who is harmed by such restrictions on imports?

CHAPTER 4

LO1 Explain how the law of demand affects market activity

1.1. *(Shifting Demand)* Using demand and supply curves, show the effect of each of the following on the market for cigarettes:

a. A cure for lung cancer is found.

b. The price of cigars increases.

c. Wages increase substantially in states that grow tobacco.

d. A fertilizer that increases the yield per acre of tobacco is discovered.

e. There is a sharp increase in the price of matches, lighters, and lighter fluid.

f. More states pass laws restricting smoking in restaurants and public places.

1.2. *(Substitutes and Complements)* For each of the following pair of goods, determine whether the goods are substitutes, complements, or unrelated:

a. Peanut butter and jelly

b. Private and public transportation

c. Coke and Pepsi

d. Alarm clocks and automobiles

e. Golf clubs and golf balls

LO2 Explain how the law of supply affects market activity

2.1. *(Supply)* What is the law of supply? Give an example of how you have observed the law of supply at work. What is the relationship between the law of supply and the supply curve?

LO3 Describe how the interaction between supply and demand create markets

3.1. *(Demand and Supply)* How do you think each of the following affected the world price of oil? (Use demand and supply analysis.)

a. Tax credits were offered for expenditures on home insulation.

b. The Alaskan oil pipeline was completed.

c. The ceiling on the price of oil was removed.

d. Oil was discovered in the North Sea.

e. Sport utility vehicles and minivans became popular.

f. The use of nuclear power declined.

3.2. *(Demand and Supply)* What happens to the equilibrium price and quantity of ice cream in response to each of the following? Explain your answers.

a. The price of dairy cow fodder increases.

b. The price of beef decreases.

c. Concerns arise about the fat content of ice cream. Simultaneously, the price of sugar (used to produce ice cream) increases.

LO4 Describe how markets reach equilibrium

4.1. *(Equilibrium)* "If a price is not an equilibrium price, there is a tendency for it to move to its equilibrium level. Regardless of whether the price is too high or too low to begin with, the adjustment process will increase the quantity of the good purchased." Explain, using a demand and supply diagram.

4.2. *(Equilibrium)* Assume the market for corn is depicted as in the table that appears below.

a. Complete the table below.

b. What market pressure occurs when quantity demanded exceeds quantity supplied? Explain.

c. What market pressure occurs when quantity supplied exceeds quantity demanded? Explain.

d. What is the equilibrium price?

e. What could change the equilibrium price?

f. At each price in the first column of the table below, how much is sold?

Price per Bushel	Quantity Demanded (millions of bushels)	Quantity Supplied (millions of bushels)	Surplus/ Shortage	Will Price Rise or Fall?
$1.80	320	200	______	______
2.00	300	230	______	______
2.20	270	270	______	______
2.40	230	300	______	______
2.60	200	330	______	______
2.80	180	350		

4.3. *(Market Equilibrium)* Determine whether each of the following statements is true, false, or uncertain. Then briefly explain each answer.
a. In equilibrium, all sellers can find buyers.
b. In equilibrium, there is no pressure on the market to produce or consume more than is being sold.
c. At prices above equilibrium, the quantity exchanged exceeds the quantity demanded.
d. At prices below equilibrium, the quantity exchanged is equal to the quantity supplied

4.4. *(Changes in Equilibrium)* What are the effects on the equilibrium price and quantity of steel if the wages of steelworkers rise and, simultaneously, the price of aluminum rises?

LO5 Explain how markets react during periods of disequilibrium.

5.1. *(Price Floor)* There is considerable interest in whether the minimum wage rate contributes to teenage unemployment. Draw a demand and supply diagram for the unskilled labor market, and discuss the effects of a minimum wage. Who is helped and who is hurt by the minimum wage?

CHAPTER 5

LO1 Define and graph the price elasticity of demand

1.1. *(Calculating Price Elasticity of Demand)* Suppose that 50 units of a good are demanded at a price of $1 per unit. A reduction in price to $0.20 results in an increase in quantity demanded to 70 units. Show that these data yield a price elasticity of 0.25. By what percentage would a 10 percent rise in the price reduce the quantity demanded, assuming price elasticity remains constant along the demand curve?

1.2. *(Price Elasticity and Total Revenue)* Fill in the blanks for each price-quantity combination listed in the following table. What relationship have you depicted?

P	Q	Price Elasticity	Total Revenue
$9	1	______	______
$8	2	______	______
$7	3	______	______
$6	4	______	______
$5	5	______	______
$4	6	______	______
$3	7	______	______
$2	8	______	______

1.3. *(Categories of Price Elasticity of Demand)* For each of the following absolute values of price elasticity of demand, indicate whether demand is elastic, inelastic, perfectly elastic, perfectly inelastic, or unit elastic. In addition, determine what would happen to total revenue if a firm raised its price in each elasticity range identified.

	Absolute Value	Elasticity	Affect of Price Increase
a	$E_D = 2.5$		
b	$E_D = 1.0$		
c	$E_D = \infty$		
d	$E_D = 0.8$		

LO2 Identify the determinants of the price elasticity of demand

2.1. *(Determinants of Price Elasticity)* Why is the price elasticity of demand for Coca-Cola greater than the price elasticity of demand for soft drinks generally?

2.2. *(Determinants of Price Elasticity)* Would the price elasticity of demand for electricity be more elastic over a shorter or a longer period of time?

LO3 Define and graph the price elasticity of supply

3.1. *(Price Elasticity of Supply)* Calculate the price elasticity of supply for each of the following combinations of price and quantity supplied. In each case, determine whether supply is elastic, inelastic, perfectly elastic, perfectly inelastic, or unit elastic.
a. Price falls from $2.25 to $1.75; quantity supplied falls from 600 units to 400 units.
b. Price falls from $2.25 to $1.75; quantity supplied falls from 600 units to 500 units.
c. Price falls from $2.25 to $1.75; quantity supplied remains at 600 units.
d. Price increases from $1.75 to $2.25; quantity supplied increases from 466.67 units to 600 units.

LO4 Describe other measures of elasticity

4.1. *(Cross-Price Elasticity)* Rank the following in order of increasing (from negative to positive) cross-price elasticity of demand with coffee. Explain your reasoning.

Bleach ______ Tea ______ Cream ______ Cola ______

4.2. *(Income Elasticity of Demand)* Calculate the income elasticity of demand for each of the following goods:

	Quantity Demanded When Income Is $10,000	Quantity Demanded When Income Is $20,000
Good 1	10	25
Good 2	4	5
Good 3	3	2

4.3. *(Other Elasticity Measures)* Complete each of the following sentences:
a. The income elasticity of demand measures, for a given price, the ________ in quantity demanded divided by the ________ income from which it resulted.
b. If a decrease in the price of one good causes a decrease in demand for another good, the two goods are ________.
c. If the value of the cross-price elasticity of demand between two goods is approximately zero, they are considered ________.

CHAPTER 6

LO1 Explain the basics of utility analysis

1.1. *(Law of Diminishing Marginal Utility)* Some restaurants offer "all you can eat" meals. How is this practice related to diminishing marginal utility? What restrictions must the restaurant impose on the customer to make a profit?

1.2. *(Law of Diminishing Marginal Utility)* Complete each of the following sentences:

a. Your tastes determine the ________ you derive from consuming a particular good.

b. ________ utility is the change in ________ utility resulting from a ________ change in the consumption of a good.

c. As long as marginal utility is positive, total utility is ________.

d. The law of diminishing marginal utility states that as an individual consumes more of a good during a given time period, other things constant, total utility ________.

1.3. *(Marginal Utility)* Is it possible for marginal utility to be negative while total utility is positive? If yes, under what circumstances is it possible?

LO2 Describe how to measure and maximize utility

2.1. *(Utility Maximization)* The following tables illustrate Eileen's utilities from watching first-run movies in a theater and from renting movies from a video store. Suppose that she has a monthly movie budget of $36, each movie ticket costs $6, and each video rental costs $3.

Movies in a Theater

Q	*TU*	*MU*	*MU/P*
0	0	____	____
1	200	____	____
2	290	____	____
3	370	____	____
4	440	____	____
5	500	____	____
6	550	____	____
7	590	____	____

Movies from a Video Store

Q	*TU*	*MU*	*MU/P*
0	0	____	____
1	250	____	____
2	295	____	____
3	335	____	____
4	370	____	____
5	400	____	____
6	425	____	____

a. Complete the tables.

b. Do these tables show that Eileen's preferences obey the law of diminishing marginal utility? Explain your answer.

c. How much of each good does Eileen consume in equilibrium?

d. Suppose the prices of both types of movies drop to $1 while Eileen's movie budget shrinks to $10. How much of each good does she consume in equilibrium?

2.2. *(Utility Maximization)* Suppose that a consumer has a choice between two goods, *X* and *Y*. If the price of *X* is $2 and the price of *Y* is $3, how much of *X* and *Y* does the consumer purchase, given an income of $17? Use the following information about marginal utility:

Units	MU_X	MU_Y
1	10	5
2	8	4
3	2	3
4	2	2
5	1	2

LO3 Explain how marginal utility and the law of demand can create consumer surplus

3.1. *(The Law of Demand and Marginal Utility)* Daniel allocates his budget of $24 per week among three goods. Use the following table of marginal utilities for good *A*, good *B*, and good *C* to answer the questions below:

Q_A	MU_A	Q_B	MU_B	Q_C	MU_C
1	50	1	75	1	25
2	40	2	60	2	20
3	30	3	40	3	15
4	20	4	30	4	10
5	15	5	20	5	7.5

a. If the price of *A* is $2, the price of *B* is $3, and the price of *C* is $1, how much of each does Daniel purchase in equilibrium?

b. If the price of *A* rises to $4 while other prices and Daniel's budget remain unchanged, how much of each does he purchase in equilibrium?

c. Using the information from parts (a) and (b), draw the demand curve for good *A*. Be sure to indicate the price and quantity demanded for each point on the curve.

3.2. *(Consumer Surplus)* Suppose the linear demand curve for shirts slopes downward and that consumers buy 500 shirts per year when the price is $30 and 1,000 shirts per year when the price is $25.

a. Compared to the prices of $30 and $25, what can you say about the marginal valuation that consumers place on the 300th shirt, the 700th shirt, and the 1,200th shirt they might buy each year?

b. With diminishing marginal utility, are consumers deriving any consumer surplus if the price is $25 per shirt? Explain.

c. Use a market demand curve to illustrate the change in consumer surplus if the price drops from $30 to $25.

3.3. *(Consumer Surplus)* Suppose supply of a good is perfectly elastic at a price of $5. The market demand curve for this good is linear, with zero quantity demanded at a price of $25. Given that the slope of this linear demand curve is –0.25, draw a supply and demand graph to illustrate the consumer surplus that occurs when the market is in equilibrium.

LO4 Describe the role of time in demand

4.1. *(Role of Time in Demand)* In many amusement parks, you pay an admission fee to the park but you do not need to pay for individual rides. How do people choose which rides to go on?

CHAPTER 7

LO1 Explain the relationship between cost and profit

1.1. *(Explicit and Implicit Costs)* Amos McCoy is currently raising corn on his 100-acre farm and earning an accounting profit of $100 per acre. However, if he raised soybeans, he could earn $200 per acre. Is he currently earning an economic profit? Why or why not?

1.2. *(Explicit and Implicit Costs)* Determine whether each of the following is an explicit cost or an implicit cost:

a. Payments for labor purchased in the labor market

b. A firm's use of a warehouse that it owns and could rent to another firm

c. Rent paid for the use of a warehouse not owned by the firm

d. The wages that owners could earn if they did not work for themselves

1.3. *(Alternative Measures of Profit)* Calculate the accounting profit or loss as well as the economic profit or loss in each of the following situations:

a. A firm with total revenues of $150 million, explicit costs of $90 million, and implicit costs of $40 million

b. A firm with total revenues of $125 million, explicit costs of $100 million, and implicit costs of $30 million

c. A firm with total revenues of $100 million, explicit costs of $90 million, and implicit costs of $20 million

d. A firm with total revenues of $250,000, explicit costs of $275,000, and implicit costs of $50,000

1.4. *(Alternative Measures of Profit)* Why is it reasonable to think of normal profit as a type of cost to the firm?

LO2 Identify the elements that affect production in the short term

2.1. *(Production in the Short Run)* Complete the following table. At what point does diminishing marginal returns set in?

Units of the Variable Resource	Total Product	Marginal Product
0	0	—
1	10	______
2	22	______
3	______	9
4	______	4
5	34	______

2.2. *(Costs in the Short Run)* Identify each of the curves in the following graph:

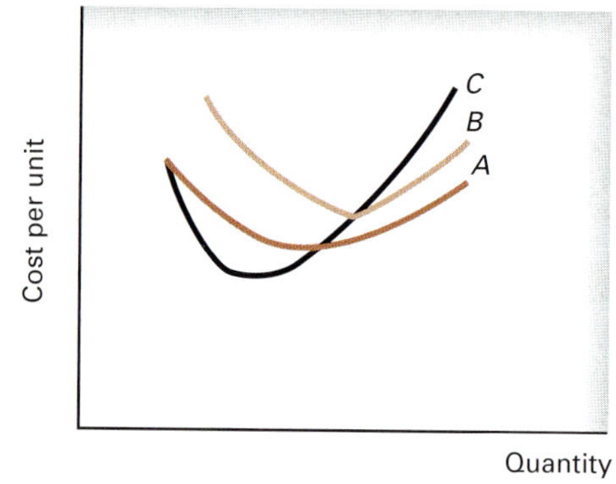

LO3 Explain how the costs of production vary with output in the short run

3.1. *(Total Cost and Marginal Cost)* Complete the following table, assuming that each unit of labor costs $75 per day.

Quantity of Labor per Day	Output per Day	Fixed Cost	Variable Cost	Total Cost	Marginal Cost
0	______	$300	$______	$______	$______
1	5	______	75	______	15
2	11	______	150	450	12.5
3	15	______	______	525	______
4	18	______	300	600	25
5	20	______	______	______	37.5

a. Graph the fixed cost, variable cost, and total cost curves for these data.

b. What is the marginal product of the third unit of labor?

c. What is average total cost when output is 18 units per day?

3.2. *(Total Cost and Marginal Cost)* Complete the following table, where *L* is units of labor, *Q* is units of output, and *MP* is the marginal product of labor.

L	*Q*	*MP*	*VC*	*TC*	*MC*	*ATC*
0	0	______	$ 0	$12	______	______
1	6	______	$ 3	15	______	______
2	15	______	$ 6	______	______	______
3	21	______	$ 9	______	______	______
4	24	______	$12	______	______	______
5	26	______	$15	______	______	______

a. At what level of labor input do the marginal returns to labor begin to diminish?

b. What is the average variable cost when $Q = 24$?

c. What is this firm's fixed cost?

d. What is the wage rate per day?

3.3. *(Relationship Between Marginal Cost and Average Cost)* Assume that labor and capital are the only inputs used by a firm. Capital is fixed at 5 units, which cost $100 each. Workers can be hired for $200 each. Complete the following table to show average variable cost *(AVC)*, average total cost *(ATC)*, and marginal cost *(MC)*.

Quantity of Labor	Total Output	*AVC*	*ATC*	*MC*
0	0	____	____	____
1	100	____	____	____
2	250	____	____	____
3	350	____	____	____
4	400	____	____	____
5	425	____	____	____

LO4 Describe how firms use the long-run average cost curve to make choices about production

4.1. *(Long-Run Costs)* Suppose the firm has only three possible scales of production as shown below:

a. Which scale of production is most efficient when $Q = 65$?

b. Which scale of production is most efficient when $Q = 75$?

c. Trace out the long-run average cost curve on the diagram.

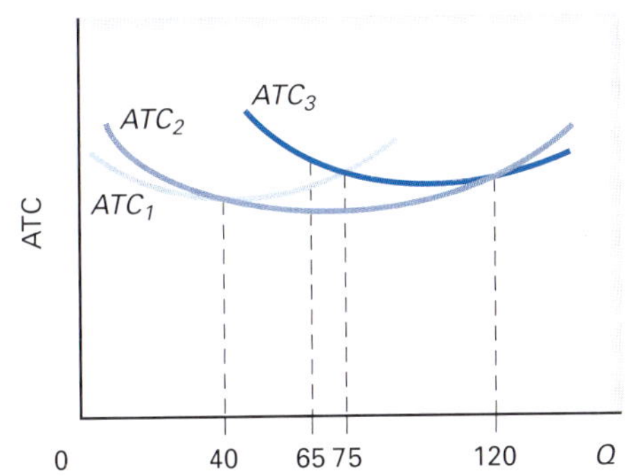

CHAPTER 8

LO1 Define a perfectly competitive market and explain its effect on demand

1.1. *(Market Structure)* Define *market structure.* What factors are considered in determining the market structure of a particular industry?

1.2. *(Demand Under Perfect Competition)* What type of demand curve does a perfectly competitive firm face? Why?

LO2 Explain how firms maximize profit in the short run

2.1. *(Short-Run Profit Maximization)* A perfectly competitive firm has the following fixed and variable costs in the short run. The market price for the firm's product is $150.

Output	*FC*	*VC*	*TC*	*TR*	Profit/ Loss
0	$100	$ 0	____	____	____
1	$100	$100	____	____	____
2	$100	$180	____	____	____
3	$100	$300	____	____	____
4	$100	$440	____	____	____
5	$100	$600	____	____	____
6	$100	$780	____	____	____

a. Complete the table.

b. At what output rate does the firm maximize profit or minimize loss?

c. What is the firm's marginal revenue at each positive level of output? Its average revenue?

d. What can you say about the relationship between marginal revenue and marginal cost for output rates below the profit-maximizing (or loss-minimizing) rate? For output rates above the profit-maximizing (or loss-minimizing) rate?

LO3 Identify ways firms minimize short-run losses

3.1. Explain the different options a firm has for minimizing losses in the short run.

LO4 Explain how firms manage short-run supply

4.1. *(The Short-Run Firm Supply Curve)* Use the following data to answer the questions below:

Q	*VC*	*MC*	*AVC*
1	$10	____	____
2	$16	____	____
3	$20	____	____
4	$25	____	____
5	$31	____	____
6	$38	____	____
7	$46	____	____
8	$55	____	____
9	$65	____	____

a. Calculate the marginal cost and average variable cost for each level of production.

b. How much would the firm produce if it could sell its product for $5? For $7? For $10?

c. Explain your answers.

d. Assuming that its fixed cost is $3, calculate the firm's profit at each of the production levels determined in part (b).

4.2. *(The Short-Run Firm Supply Curve)* Each of the following situations could exist for a firm in the short run. In each case, indicate whether the firm should produce in the short run or shut down in the short run, or whether additional information is needed to determine what it should do in the short run.

a. Total cost exceeds total revenue at all output levels.

b. Total variable cost exceeds total revenue at all output levels.

c. Total revenue exceeds total fixed cost at all output levels.

d. Marginal revenue exceeds marginal cost at the current output level.

e. Price exceeds average total cost at all output levels.

f. Average variable cost exceeds price at all output levels.

g. Average total cost exceeds price at all output levels.

LO5 Describe how taking the long-run view affects economic factors

5.1. *(The Long-Run Industry Supply Curve)* A normal good is being produced in a constant-cost, perfectly competitive industry. Initially, each firm is in long-run equilibrium.

a. Graphically illustrate and explain the short-run adjustments for the market and the firm to a decrease in consumer incomes. Be sure to discuss any changes in output levels, prices, profits, and the number of firms.

b. Next, show on your graph and explain the long-run adjustment to the income change. Be sure to discuss any changes in output levels, prices, profits, and the number of firms.

5.2. *(Long-Run Industry Supply)* Why does the long-run industry supply curve for an increasing-cost industry slope upward? What causes the increasing costs in an increasing-cost industry?

LO6 Describe how different cost structures influence an industry's long-run supply curve

6.1. *(Perfect Competition in the Long Run)* Draw the short- and long-run cost curves for a competitive firm in long-run equilibrium. Indicate the long-run equilibrium price and quantity.

a. Discuss the firm's short-run response to a reduction in the price of a variable resource.

b. Assuming that this is a constant-cost industry, describe the process by which the industry returns to long-run equilibrium following a change in market demand.

6.2. *(The Long-Run Industry Supply Curve)* The following graph shows possible long-run market supply curves for a perfectly competitive industry. Determine which supply curve indicates a constant-cost industry and which an increasing-cost industry.

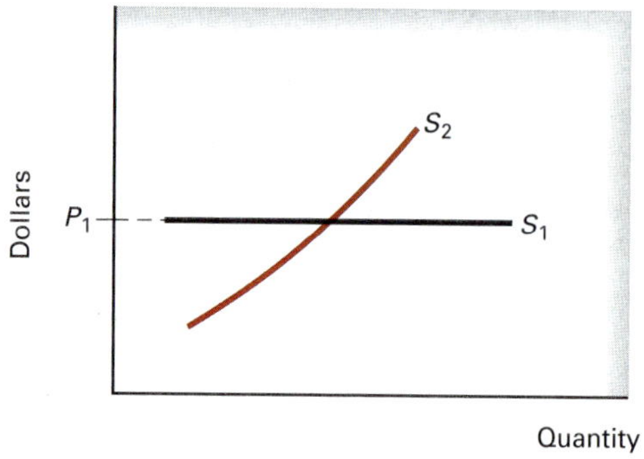

a. Explain the difference between a constant-cost industry and an increasing-cost industry.

b. Distinguish between the long-run impact of an increase in market demand in a constant-cost industry and the impact in an increasing-cost industry.

LO7 Identify how concepts of efficiency are used to judge market performance

7.1. *(What's So Perfect About Perfect Competition)* Use the following data to answer the questions.

Quantity	Marginal Cost	Marginal Benefit
0	—	—
1	\$ 2	\$10
2	\$ 3	\$ 9
3	\$ 4	\$ 8
4	\$ 5	\$ 7
5	\$ 6	\$ 6
6	\$ 8	\$ 5
7	\$10	\$ 4
8	\$12	\$ 3

a. For the product shown, assume that the minimum point of each firm's average variable cost curve is at \$2. Construct a demand and supply diagram for the product and indicate the equilibrium price and quantity.

b. On the graph, label the area of consumer surplus as *f*. Label the area of producer surplus as *g*.

c. If the equilibrium price were \$2, what would be the amount of producer surplus?

CHAPTER 9

LO1 List and describe barriers to market entry

1.1. *(Barriers to Entry)* Explain how economies of scale can be a barrier to entry.

LO2 Explain sources of revenue for the monopolist

2.1. *(Monopoly)* Suppose that a certain manufacturer has a monopoly on the sorority and fraternity ring business (a constant-cost industry) because it has persuaded the "Greeks" to give it exclusive rights to their insignia.

a. Using demand and cost curves, draw a diagram depicting the firm's profit-maximizing price and output level.

b. Why is marginal revenue less than price for this firm?

c. On your diagram, show the deadweight loss that occurs because the output level is determined by a monopoly rather than by a competitive market.

d. What would happen if the Greeks decided to charge the manufacturer a royalty fee of \$3 per ring?

LO3 Describe a firm's costs and its opportunities for profit maximization

3.1. *(Short-Run Profit Maximization)* Answer the following questions on the basis of the monopolist's situation illustrated in the following graph.

a. At what output rate and price does the monopolist operate?

b. In equilibrium, approximately what is the firm's total cost and total revenue?

c. What is the firm's economic profit or loss in equilibrium?

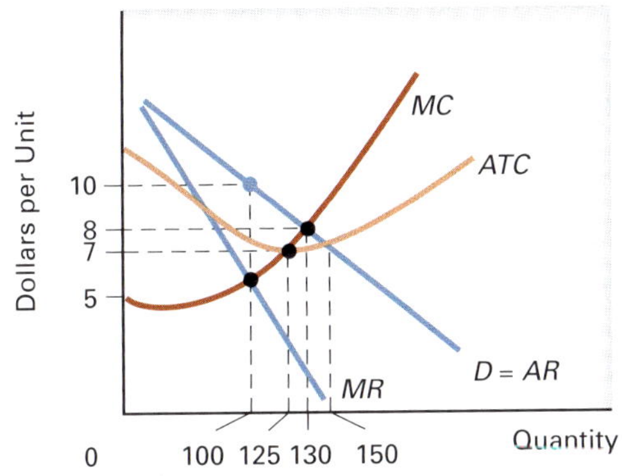

LO4 Explain monopoly and the allocation of resources

4.1. *(Monopoly and the Allocation of Resources)* What is the problem with monopoly? Compare monopoly to the benchmark of perfect competition established in the previous chapter. Use the exhibit below for reference.

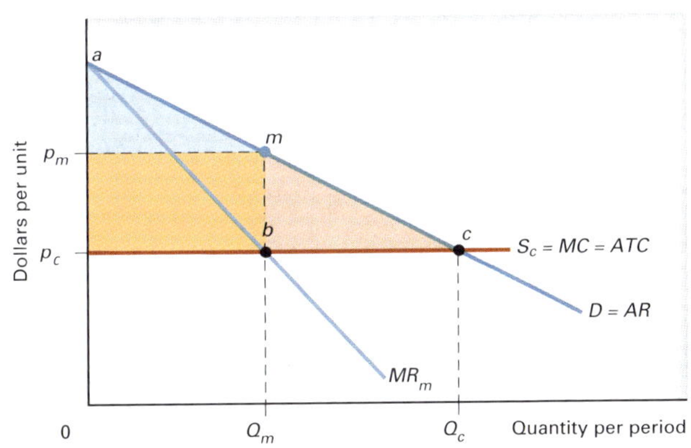

LO5 Describe the problems that interfere with estimating the deadweight loss of a monopoly

5.1. *(Allocative and Distributive Effects)* Why is society worse off under monopoly than under perfect competition, even if both market structures face the same constant long-run average cost curve?

5.2. *(Welfare Cost of Monopoly)* Explain why the welfare loss of a monopoly may be smaller or larger than the loss shown in the exhibit above.

LO6 Describe conditions that create price discrimination

6.1. *(Conditions for Price Discrimination)* List three conditions that must be met for a monopolist to price discriminate successfully?

6.2. *(Price Discrimination)* Explain how it may be profitable for South Korean manufacturers to sell new autos at a lower price in the United States than in South Korea, even with transportation costs included.

6.3. *(Perfect Price Discrimination)* Why is the perfectly discriminating monopolist's marginal revenue curve identical to the demand curve it faces?

CHAPTER 10

LO1 Discuss factors that lead to monopolistic competition

1.1. *(Short-Run Profit Maximization)* A monopolistically competitive firm faces the following demand and cost structure in the short run:

Output	Price	FC	VC	TC	TR	Profit/ Loss
0	$100	$100	$0	___	___	___
1	90	___	50	___	___	___
2	80	___	90	___	___	___
3	70	___	150	___	___	___
4	60	___	230	___	___	___
5	50	___	330	___	___	___
6	40	___	450	___	___	___
7	30	___	590	___	___	___

a. Complete the table.

b. What is the highest profit or lowest loss available to this firm?

c. Should this firm operate or shut down in the short run? Why?

d. What is the relationship between marginal revenue and marginal cost as the firm increases output?

1.2. *(Monopolistic Competition and Perfect Competition Compared)* Illustrated below are the marginal cost and average total cost curves for a small firm that is in long-run equilibrium.

a. Locate the long-run equilibrium price and quantity if the firm is perfectly competitive.

b. Label the price and quantity p_1 and q_1.

c. Draw in a demand and marginal revenue curve to illustrate long-run equilibrium if the firm is monopolistically competitive. Label the price and quantity p_2 and q_2.

d. How do the monopolistically competitive firm's price and output compare to those of the perfectly competitive firm?

e. How do long-run profits compare for the two types of firms?

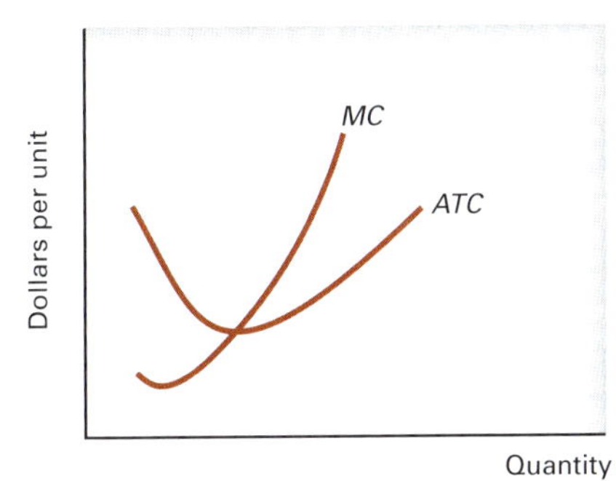

LO2 Explain the concept of oligopoly

2.1. *(Varieties of Oligopolies)* Do the firms in an oligopoly act independently or interdependently? Explain your answer.

LO3 Identify models of oligopoly

3.1. *(Price Leadership)* Why might a price-leadership model of oligopoly not be an effective means of collusion in an oligopoly?

3.2. *(Collusion and Cartels)* Why would each of the following induce some members of OPEC to cheat on their cartel agreement?

a. Newly joined cartel members are less-developed countries.
b. The number of cartel members doubles from 11 to 22.
c. International debts of some members grow.
d. Expectations grow that some members will cheat.

LO4 Explain how game theory helps predict cartel behavior

4.1. *(Collusion and Cartels)* Use revenue and cost curves to illustrate and explain the sense in which a cartel behaves like a monopolist.

4.2. *(Game Theory)* Suppose there are only two automobile companies, Ford and Chevrolet. Ford believes that Chevrolet will match any price it sets, but Chevrolet too is interested in maximizing profit. Use the following price and profit data to answer the following questions.

Ford's Selling Price	Chevrolet's Selling Price	Ford's Profits (millions)	Chevrolet's Profits (millions)
$ 4,000	$ 4,000	$ 8	$ 8
4,000	8,000	12	6
4,000	12,000	14	2
8,000	4,000	6	12
8,000	8,000	10	10
8,000	12,000	12	6
12,000	4,000	2	14
12,000	8,000	6	12
12,000	12,000	7	7

a. What price will Ford charge?
b. What price will Chevrolet charge once Ford has set its price?
c. What is Ford's profit after Chevrolet's response?
d. If the two firms collaborated to maximize joint profits, what prices would they set?
e. Given your answer to part (d), how could undetected cheating on price cause the cheating firm's profit to rise?

4.3. *(Game Theory)* While grading a final exam, an economics professor discovers that two students have virtually identical answers. She is convinced the two cheated but cannot prove it. The professor speaks with each student separately and offers the following deal: Sign a statement admitting to cheating. If both students sign the statement, each will receive an "F" for the course. If only one signs, he is allowed to withdraw from the course while the other student is expelled. If neither signs, both receive a "C" because the professor does not have sufficient evidence to prove cheating.

a. Draw the payoff matrix.
b. Which outcome do you expect? Why?

LO5 Compare oligopoly and perfect competition

5.1. *(Market Structures)* Determine whether each of the following is a characteristic of perfect competition, monopolistic competition, oligopoly, and/or monopoly:

a. A large number of sellers
b. Product is a commodity
c. Advertising by firms
d. Barriers to entry
e. Firms are price makers

CHAPTER 11

LO1 Identify examples of resource demand and supply in daily life

1.1. *(Resource Demand)* How do firms and individuals determine if it's worth it to (a) invest in capital improvements, (b) hire additional workers, or (c) decide where to work?

LO2 Explain resource supply and demand

2.1. *(Resource Demand and Supply)* Answer each of the following questions about the labor market:

a. Which economic decision makers determine the demand for labor? What is their goal, and what decision criteria do they use in trying to reach that goal?
b. Which economic decision makers determine the supply of labor? What is their goal and what decision criteria do they use in trying to reach that goal?
c. In what sense is the demand for labor a derived demand?

LO3 Define opportunity cost and economic rent

3.1. *(Opportunity Cost and Economic Rent)* Define economic rent. In the graph below, assume that the market demand curve for labor is initially D_1.

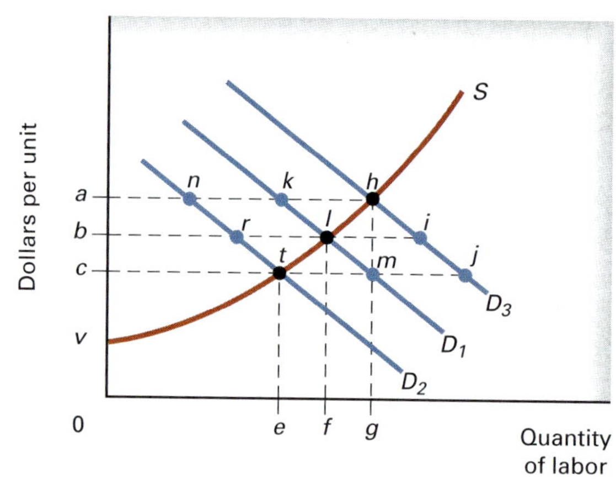

a. What are the equilibrium wage rate and employment level? What is the economic rent?
b. Next assume that the price of a substitute resource increases, other things constant. What happens to demand for labor? What are the new equilibrium wage rate and employment level? What happens to economic rent?
c. Suppose instead that demand for the final product drops, other things constant. Using labor demand curve D_1 as your starting point, what happens to the demand for labor? What are the new equilibrium wage rate and employment level? Does the amount of economic rent change?

LO4 Analyze the factors influencing resource demand

4.1. *(Firm's Demand for a Resource)* Use the following data to answer the questions that follow. Assume a perfectly competitive product market.

Units of Labor	Units of Output
0	0
1	7
2	13
3	18
4	22
5	25

a. Calculate the marginal revenue product for each additional unit of labor if output sells for $3 per unit.
b. Draw the demand curve for labor based on the above data and the $3-per-unit product price.
c. If the wage rate is $15 per hour, how much labor will be hired?
d. Using your answer to part (c), compare the firm's total revenue to the total amount paid for labor. Who gets the difference?
e. What would happen to your answers to parts (b) and (c) if the price of output increased to $5 per unit, other things constant?

4.2. *(Shifts of Resource Demand)* A local pizzeria hires college students to make pizza, wait on tables, take phone orders, and deliver pizzas. For each situation described, determine whether the demand for student employees by the restaurant would increase, decrease, or remain unchanged. Explain each answer.
a. The demand for pizza increases.
b. Another pizzeria opens up next door.
c. An increase in the minimum wage raises the cost of hiring student employees.
d. The restaurant buys a computer system for taking phone orders.

4.3. *(Selling Output as a Price Taker)* If a competitive firm hires another full-time worker, total output increases from 100 units to 110 units per week. Suppose the market price of output is $25 per unit. What is the maximum weekly wage at which the firm would hire that additional worker?

CHAPTER 12

LO1 Discuss issues affecting labor supply and utility maximization

1.1. *(Market Supply of Labor)* The following table shows the hours per week supplied to a particular market by three individuals at various wage rates. Calculate the total hours per week (Q_T) supplied to the market.

Hourly Wage	Hours per Week			
	Q_1	Q_2	Q_3	Q_T
$ 5	20	0	0	____
6	25	0	0	____
7	35	10	0	____
8	45	25	10	____
9	42	40	30	____
10	38	37	45	____

Which individuals, if any, have backward-bending supply curves in the wage range shown? Does the market supply curve bend backward in the wage range shown in the table?

1.2. *(Substitution and Income Effects)* Suppose that the cost of living increases, thereby reducing the purchasing power of your income. If your money wage doesn't increase, you may work *more* hours because of this cost-of-living increase. Is this response predominantly an income effect or a substitution effect? Explain.

1.3. *(Nonwage Determinants of Labor Supply)* Suppose that two jobs are exactly the same except that one is performed in an air-conditioned workplace. How could you measure the value workers attach to such a job amenity?

LO2 Explain the market supply factors that lead to differing wages

2.1. *(Why Wages Differ)* Why might permanent wage differences occur between different markets for labor or within the same labor market?

LO3 List types of unions and describe their collective bargaining strategies

3.1. *(Craft Unions)* Both industrial unions and craft unions attempt to raise their members' wages, but each goes about it differently. Explain the difference in approaches and describe the impact these differences have on excess quantity of labor supplied.

LO4 Describe the relationship between union wages and employment

4.1. *(Industrial Unions)* Review the logic underlying the exhibit below. Then determine the effect, on the industry and a typical firm, of an increase in the demand for industry output. Show your conclusions on a graph. Does the magnitude of the increase in demand make a difference?

Effects of Labor Union's Wage Floor

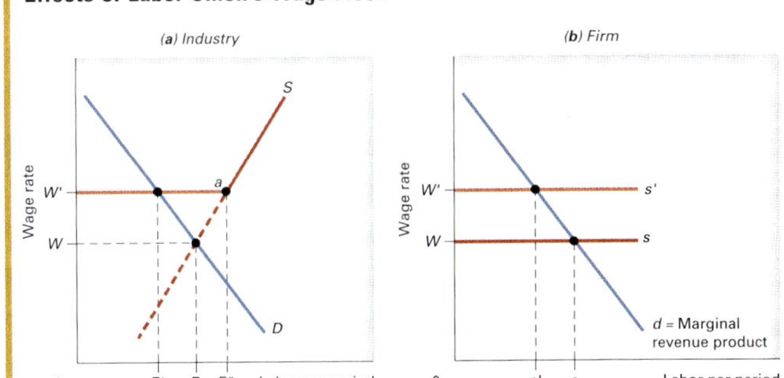

4.2. *(The Strike)* Why might firms in industries with high fixed costs be inclined to prevent strikes or end strikes quickly?

4.3. *(Industrial Unions)* Why are unions more effective at raising wages in oligopolistic industries than in competitive industries?

CHAPTER 13

LO1 Discuss the role of time in production and consumption

1.1. *(Role of Time)* Complete the following sentences with a word or a phrase:

a. If Bryan values current consumption more than future consumption, he has a ___________.

b. The reward to households for forgoing current consumption is _______.

c. Producing capital goods rather than producing final goods is known as ____________.

1.2. *(Consumption, Saving, and Time)* Explain why the supply of loanable funds curve slopes upward to the right.

LO2 Describe the factors that determine optimal investment

Marginal Rate of Return per Year on Investment in Farm Equipment

(1) Farm Equipment	(2) Total Product (bushels)	(3) Marginal Product (bushels)	(4) Marginal revenue Product (4) = (3) × \$4	(5) Marginal Resource Cost	(6) Marginal Rate of Return (6) = (4) / (5)
No equipment	200	—	—	—	—
Tractor-tiller	1,200	1,000	\$4,000	\$10,000	40%
Combine	2,000	800	3,200	10,000	32
Irrigator	2,600	600	2,400	10,000	24
Harrow	3,000	400	1,600	10,000	16
Crop sprayer	3,200	200	800	10,000	8
Post-hole digger	3,200	0	0	10,000	0

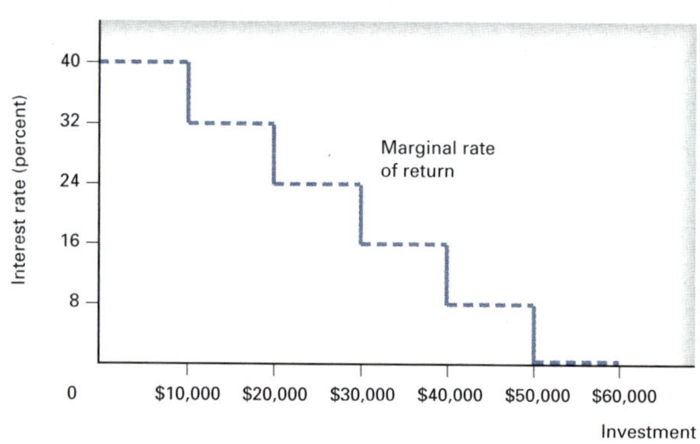

2.1. *(Optimal Investment)* Look back at the exhibit above in this chapter. If the marginal resource cost rose to \$24,000 what would be the optimal investment at a market interest rate of 10 percent? If the interest rate then rose to 16.6 percent, what would be the optimal level of investment?

2.2. *(Market for Loanable Funds)* Using the demand-supply for loanable funds diagram, show the effect on the market interest rate of each of the following:

a. An increase in the marginal resource cost of capital

b. An increase in the marginal productivity of capital

c. A shift in preferences toward present consumption and away from future consumption

LO3 Explain present value and discounting

3.1. *(Present Value)* Calculate the present value of each of the following future payments. (For some of these problems you may wish to use the online calculator available at **http://www.moneychimp.com/articles/finworks/fmpresval.htm**.)

a. A \$10,000 lump sum received 1 year from now if the market interest rate is 8 percent

b. A \$10,000 lump sum received 2 years from now if the market interest rate is 10 percent

c. A \$1,000 lump sum received 3 years from now if the market interest rate is 5 percent

d. A \$25,000 lump sum received 1 year from now if the market interest rate is 12 percent

e. A \$25,000 lump sum received 1 year from now if the market interest rate is 10 percent

f. A perpetuity of \$500 per year if the market interest rate is 6 percent

3.2. *(Present Value of an Income Stream)* Suppose the market interest rate is 10 percent. Would you be willing to lend \$10,000 if you were guaranteed to receive \$1,000 at the end of each of the next 12 years plus a \$5,000 payment 15 years from now? Why or why not?

LO4 Analyze different corporate finance strategies

4.1. *(Securities Exchanges)* What role do securities exchanges play in financing corporations?

CHAPTER 14

LO1 Explain the rationale for the firm and describe its scope of operation

1.1. *(Bounds of the Firm)* Ashland Oil buys its crude oil in the market. Larger oil refiners, such as Texaco, drill for their own crude oil. Why do some oil companies drill for their own crude oil and others buy crude oil in the market?

1.2. *(Economies of Scope)* Distinguish between economies of scale and economies of scope. Why do some firms produce multiple product lines, while others produce only one?

LO2 Discuss the ways in which imperfect information influences market behavior

2.1. *(Search with Imperfect Information)* The following questions concern the accompanying graph.

a. Identify the two curves shown on the graph, and explain their upward or downward slopes.

b. Why does curve *A* intersect the horizontal axis?

c. What is the significance of quantity *d*?

d. What does *e* represent?

e. How would the optimal quantity of information change if the marginal benefit of information increased—that is, if the marginal benefit curve shifted upward?

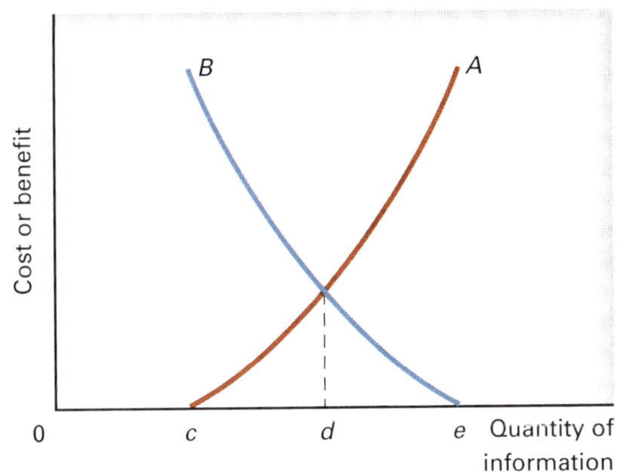

2.2. *(Search with Imperfect Information)* Determine the effect of each of the following on the optimal level of search.

a. The consumer's wage increases.
b. One seller guarantees to offer the lowest price on the market.
c. The technology of gathering and transmitting market information improves.

LO3 Explain how asymmetric information affects product markets

3.1. *(Asymmetric Information)* Define asymmetric information. Distinguish between hidden characteristics and hidden actions. Which type of asymmetric information contributes to the principal-agent problem?

3.2. *(The Principal-Agent Problem)* Discuss the nature of the principal-agent problem. Determine which is the principal and which is the agent in each of the following relationships:

a. A firm that produces export goods and the export management company that helps market its goods overseas
b. The management of a firm and its stockholders
c. A homeowner and the plumber hired to make repairs
d. A dentist and a patient
e. An employee-pension management firm and the company using its services

3.3. *(Adverse Selection and Moral Hazard)* Describe the problems faced by health insurance companies as a result of adverse selection and moral hazard. How do insurance companies try to reduce these problems?

LO4 Describe the way asymmetric information influences labor markets

4.1. *(Signaling)* Give an example of signaling in each of the following situations:

a. Choosing a doctor
b. Applying to graduate school
c. Filling out a form for a dating service

CHAPTER 15

LO1 Describe the different types of government regulation

1.1. *(Business Behavior and Public Policy)* Define market power, and then discuss the rationale for government regulation of firms with market power.

LO2 Explain how natural monopolies are regulated

2.1. *(Regulating Natural Monopolies)* The following graph represents a natural monopoly.

a. Why is this firm considered a natural monopoly?
b. If the firm is unregulated, what price and output would maximize its profit? What would be its profit or loss?
c. If a regulatory commission establishes a price with the goal of achieving allocative efficiency, what would be the price and output? What would be the firm's profit or loss?
d. If a regulatory commission establishes a price with the goal of allowing the firm a "fair return," what would be the price and output? What would be the firm's profit or loss?
e. Which one of the prices in parts b, c, and d maximizes consumer surplus? What problem, if any, occurs at this price?

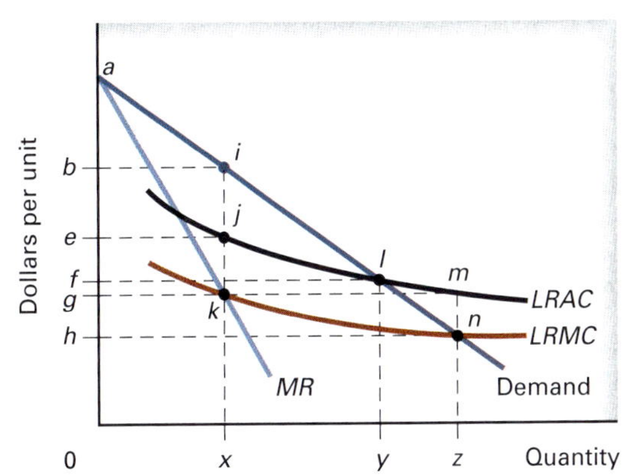

LO3 Explain why producers are interested in economic regulation

3.1. *(Theories of Regulation)* Why do producers have more interest in government regulations than consumers do?

a. Compare and contrast the public-interest and special-interest theories of economic regulation. What is the capture theory of regulation?
b. Which of these theories best describes the case of airline deregulation? Which best explains the government's case against Microsoft?

LO4 Discuss anti-trust laws and their enforcement

4.1. *(Origins of Antitrust Policy)* Identify the type of anticompetitive behavior illustrated by each of the following:

a. A university requires buyers of season tickets for its basketball games to buy season tickets for its football games as well.

b. Dairies that bid on contracts to supply milk to school districts collude to increase what they charge.
c. The same individual serves on the boards of directors of General Motors and Ford.
d. A large retailer sells merchandise below cost in certain regions to drive competitors out of business.
e. A producer of carbonated soft drinks sells to a retailer only if the retailer agrees not to buy from the producer's major competitor.

LO5 Describe the relationship between public policy and merger activity

5.1. *(Mergers and Public Policy)* Calculate the Herfindahl-Hirschman Index (HHI) for each of the following industries. Which industry is the most concentrated?
   a. An industry with five firms that have the following market shares: 50 percent, 30 percent, 10 percent, 5 percent, and 5 percent
   b. An industry with five firms that have the following market shares: 60 percent, 20 percent, 10 percent, 5 percent, and 5 percent
   c. An industry with five firms, each of which has a 20 percent market share

LO6 List competitive trends in the U.S. economy

6.1. *(Competitive Trends in the U.S. Economy)* William Shepherd's study of U.S. industries showed a clear increase in competition in the U.S. economy between 1958 and 2000. How did Shepherd explain this trend?

CHAPTER 16

LO1 Define public goods

1.1. *(Optimal Provision of Public Goods)* Using at least two individual consumers, show how the market demand curve is derived from individual demand curves (a) for a private good and (b) for a public good. Once you have derived the market demand curve in each case, introduce a market supply curve and then show the optimal level of production.

1.2. *(Private and Public Goods)* Distinguish among private goods, natural monopolies, open-access goods, and public goods. Provide examples of each.

LO2 Discuss the role of public choice in representative democracy

2.1. *(Distribution of Costs and Benefits)* Suppose that the government decides to guarantee an above-market price for a good by buying up any surplus at that above-market price. Using a conventional supply-demand diagram, illustrate the following gains and losses from such a price support:
   a. The loss of consumer surplus
   b. The gain of producer surplus in the short run
   c. The cost of running the government program (assuming no storage costs)
   d. What is the total cost of the program to consumers?
   e. Are the costs and benefits of the support program widespread or concentrated?

2.2. *(Median Voter Model)* In a single-issue majority vote, such as the TV example in this chapter, does the median voter always get his or her most preferred outcome?

2.3. *(Representative Democracy)* Major political parties typically offer "middle of the road" platforms rather than take extreme positions. Is this consistent with the concepts of the median voter and rational ignorance discussed in this chapter?

LO3 Describe the underground economy

3.1. *(Rent Seeking)* Explain how rent seeking can lead to a drop in production of goods and services. What role might the underground economy play in lessening the drop in productive activities?

LO4 Explain bureaucracy and its role in representative democracy

4.1. *(Bureaucracy and Representative Democracy)* How do the incentives and feedback for government bureaus differ from those for profit-making firms?

4.2. *(Bureaucracy and Representative Democracy)* A firm is described as combining managerial coordination with market exchange in order to produce its good or service. Does similar behavior occur in government bureaus? Explain.

CHAPTER 17

LO1 Define externalities and explain the common-pool problem

1.1. *(Negative Externalities)* Suppose you wish to reduce a negative externality by imposing a tax on the activity that creates that externality. When the amount of the externality produced per unit of output increases as output increases, the correct tax can be determined by using a demand-supply diagram; show this. Assume that the marginal private cost curve slopes upward.

1.2. *(Externalities)* Complete each of the following sentences:
   a. Resources that are available only in a fixed amount are ________ resources.
   b. The possibility that a open-access resource is used until the net marginal value of additional use equals zero is known as the ________.
   c. Resources for which periodic use can be continued indefinitely are known as ________ resources.

1.3. *(Resolving the Common-Pool Problem)* Why have authorities found it so difficult to regulate the fishing catch in the open ocean to allow for a sustainable yield?

LO2 Explain the optimal level of pollution

Negative Externalities: The Market for Electricity in the Midwest

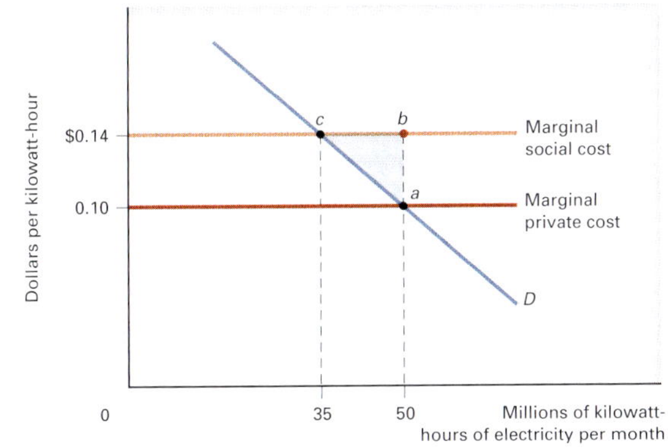

2.1. *(External Costs with Fixed-Production Technology)* Review the situation illustrated in the graph above. If the government sets the price of electricity at the socially optimal level, why is the net gain equal to triangle *abc,* even though consumers now pay a higher price for electricity? What would the net gain be if the government set the price above the optimal level?

2.2. *(External Costs)* Use the data in the table below to answer the following questions.
   a. What is the external cost per unit of production?
   b. What level is produced if there is no regulation of the externality?
   c. What level should be produced to achieve economic efficiency?
   d. Calculate the dollar value of the net gain to society from correcting the externality.

Quantity	Marginal Private Benefit (demand)	Marginal Private Cost (supply)	Marginal Social Cost
0	—	$0	$0
1	$10	2	4
2	9	3	5
3	8	4	6
4	7	5	7
5	6	6	8
6	5	7	9
7	4	8	10
8	3	9	11
9	2	10	12
10	1	11	13

2.3. *(External Costs with Variable Technology)* Think of an industry that pollutes the water and has access to variable technology for reducing that pollution. Graphically illustrate and explain the impact of each of the following, other things constant, on the optimal level of water quality:
   a. New evidence is discovered about a greater risk of cancer from water pollution.
   b. The cost of pollution-control equipment increases.
   c. A technological improvement reduces the cost of pollution control.

2.4. *(Market for Pollution Rights)* The following graph shows the market for pollution rights.
   a. If there are no restrictions on pollution, what amount is discharged?
   b. What is the quantity supplied and the quantity demanded if the government restricts the amount of discharge to Q* but gives the permits away?
   c. Where is market equilibrium if the government sells the permits? Illustrate this on the graph.
   d. What happens to market equilibrium if the government reduces the amount of discharge permitted to Q**? Illustrate this on the graph.

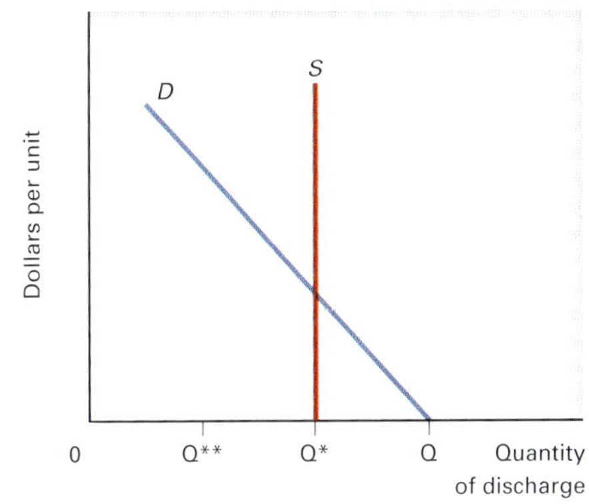

LO3 Assess the role of environmental problems in the economy

3.1. Four federal laws and subsequent amendments underpin U.S. environmental protection. Identify these laws.

LO4 Describe positive externalities

4.1. *(Positive Externalities)* The value of a home depends in part on how attractive other homes and yards in the neighborhood are. How do local zoning ordinances try to promote land uses that generate external benefits for neighbors?

CHAPTER 18

LO1 Explain the distribution of household income

1.1. *(Distribution of Household Income)* Look at the graph below. How would you explain the shift of the U.S. income distribution in the last two decades?

Share of Aggregate Household Income by Quintile: 1970, 1980, 1990, and 2005

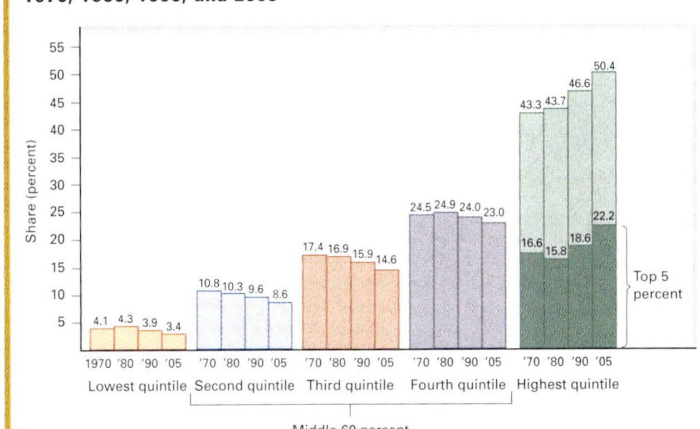

1.2. *(Lorenz Curve)* What is a Lorenz curve? What does the Lorenz curve below illustrate?

Lorenz Curves Show That Income Was Less Evenly Distributed Across U.S. Households in 2005 than in 1970

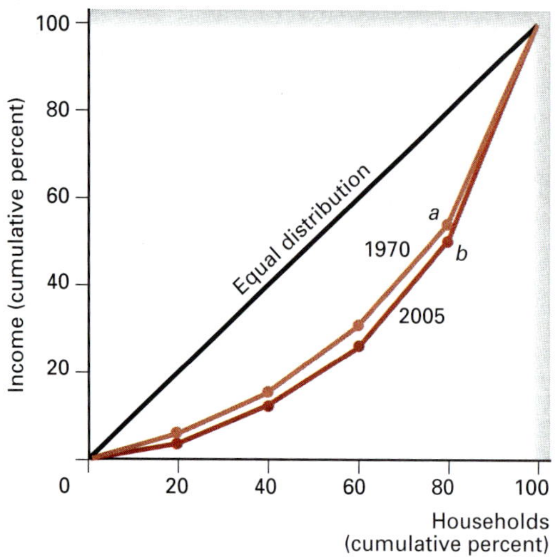

LO2 Describe redistribution programs

2.1. *(Official Poverty Level)* Although the poverty rate among single mothers has decreased since 1960, the number of poor children from such families has more than doubled. Explain.

2.2. *(Income Differences)* List some reasons why household incomes differ. Which factors are the most important?

2.3. *(Official Poverty Level)* How does the U.S. Department of Agriculture calculate the official poverty level? What government assistance programs does the Census Bureau consider when calculating household income? What programs are ignored?

LO3 Explain who the poor are

3.1. *(Poverty and Age)* Poverty among the elderly fell dramatically between 1959 and 1974 and has continued to decline. However, poverty among that portion of the U.S. population that is less than 18 years old is no lower today than in the 1970s. Why have the experiences of these two age groups differed?

3.2. *(Disincentives)* How does the implicit tax on earned income (in the form of lost benefits from government assistance programs as earned income increases) affect work incentives? How do some people avoid the implicit tax?

LO4 Discuss welfare reform

4.1. *(Welfare Reform)* What has happened to the number of people on welfare since 1994? What explains the change over time?

CHAPTER 19

LO1 Describe the gains that trade brings

1.1. *(Comparative Advantage)* Suppose that each U.S. worker can produce 8 units of food or 2 units of clothing daily. In Fredonia, which has the same number of workers, each worker can produce 7 units of food or 1 unit of clothing daily. Why does the United States have an absolute advantage in both goods? Which country enjoys a comparative advantage in food? Why?

1.2. *(Comparative Advantage)* The consumption possibilities frontiers shown in the following exhibit assume terms of trade of 1 unit of clothing for 1 unit of food. What would the consumption possibilities frontiers look like if the terms of trade were 1 unit of clothing for 2 units of food?

Production (and Consumption) Possibility Frontiers with Trade (millions of units per day)

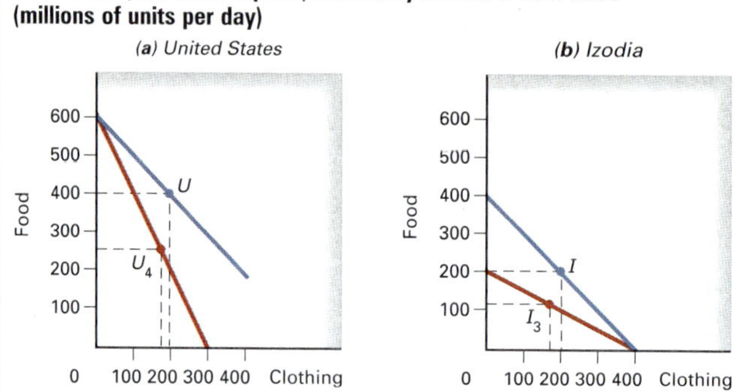

LO2 Discuss the reasons for international specialization

2.1. *(Reasons for International Specialization)* What determines which goods a country should produce and export?

LO3 Explain trade restrictions and welfare loss

3.1. *(Import Quotas)* How low must a quota be in effect to have an impact? Using a demand-and-supply diagram, illustrate and explain the net welfare loss from imposing such a quota. Under what circumstances would the net welfare loss from an import quota exceed the net welfare loss from an equivalent tariff (one that results in the same price and import level as the quota)?

3.2. *(Trade Restrictions)* Suppose that the world price for steel is below the U.S. domestic price, but the government requires that all steel used in the United States be domestically produced.

   a. Use a diagram like the one below to show the gains and losses from such a policy.
   b. How could you estimate the net welfare loss (deadweight loss) from such a diagram?
   c. What response to such a policy would you expect from industries (like automobile producers) that use U.S. steel?
   d. What government revenues are generated by this policy?

Effect of a Tariff

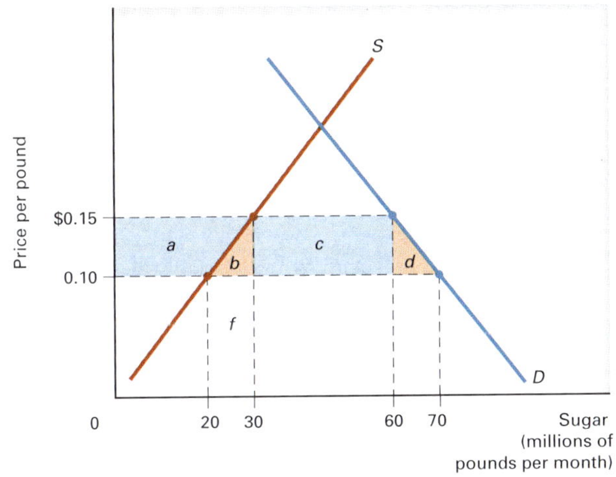

Effect of a Quota

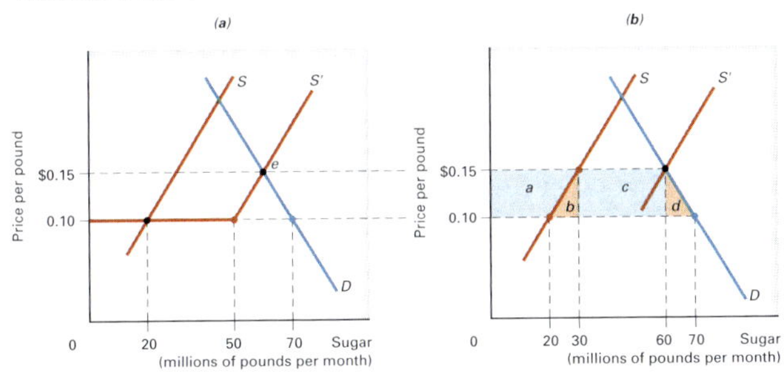

3.3. *(Trade Restrictions)* The previous three graphs show net losses to the economy of a country that imposes tariffs or quotas on imported sugar. What kinds of gains and losses would occur in the economies of countries that export sugar?

LO4 Describe ways countries have reduced or eliminated trade barriers

4.1. *(The World Trade Organization)* What is the World Trade Organization (WTO) and how does it help foster multilateral trade? (Check the WTO Web site at **http://www.wto.org/**.)

LO5 List and describe the arguments in favor of trade restrictions

5.1. *(Arguments for Trade Restrictions)* Explain the national defense, declining industries, and infant industry arguments for protecting a domestic industry from international competition.

5.2. *(Arguments for Trade Restrictions)* Firms hurt by cheap imports typically argue that restricting trade will save U.S. jobs. What's wrong with this argument? Are there ever any reasons to support such trade restrictions?

CHAPTER 20

LO1 Explain how balance of payments works

1.1. *(Balance of Payments)* The following are hypothetical data for the U.S. balance of payments. Use the data to calculate each of the following:

a. Merchandise trade balance
b. Balance on goods and services
c. Balance on current account
d. Capital account balance
e. Statistical discrepancy

	Billions of Dollars
Merchandise exports	350.0
Merchandise imports	2,425.0
Service exports	170.0
Service imports	2,145.0
Net income and net transfers	221.5
Outflow of U.S. capital	245.0
Inflow of foreign capital	70.0

1.2. *(Balance of Payments)* Explain where in the U.S. balance of payments an entry would be recorded for each of the following:

a. A Hong Kong financier buys some U.S. corporate stock.
b. A U.S. tourist in Paris buys some perfume to take home.
c. A Japanese company sells machinery to a pineapple company in Hawaii.
d. U.S. farmers make a gift of food to starving children in Ethiopia.
e. The U.S. Treasury sells a bond to a Saudi Arabian prince.
f. A U.S. tourist flies to France on Air France.
g. A U.S. company sells insurance to a foreign firm.

LO2 Discuss foreign exchange rates and markets

2.1. *(Determining the Exchange Rate)* Use these data to answer the following questions about the market for British pounds:

Pound Price (in $)	**Quantity Demanded (of pounds)**	**Quantity Supplied (of pounds)**
$4.00	50	100
3.00	75	75
2.00	100	50

a. Draw the demand and supply curves for pounds, and determine the equilibrium exchange rate (dollars per pound).
b. Suppose that the supply of pounds doubles. Draw the new supply curve.
c. What is the new equilibrium exchange rate?
d. Has the dollar appreciated or depreciated?
e. What happens to U.S. imports of British goods?

LO3 Define fixed and flexible exchange rates

3.1. Discuss the differences between a flexible exchange rate and a fixed exchange rate. What measures can the government take to maintain fixed exchange rates?

LO4 Describe the development of the international monetary system

4.1. *(The Current System: Managed Float)* What is a managed float? What are the disadvantages of freely floating exchange rates that led countries to the managed float system?

CHAPTER 21

LO1 Describe the worldwide variation in economic vitality

1.1. *(Worlds Apart)* GDP Per capita income most recently was about 63 times greater in the richest country on Earth than in the poorest country. Suppose GDP per capita grows an average of 3 percent per year in the richest country and 6 percent per year in the poorest country. Assuming such growth rates continue indefinitely into the future, how many years would it take before per capita in the poorest country exceed that of the richest country? (To simplify the math, suppose at the outset per capita income is $63,000 in the richest country and $1,000 in the poorest country.)

LO2 Explain why productivity is the key to development

2.1. *(Import Substitution versus Export Promotion)* Explain why domestic producers who supply a good that competes with imports would prefer an import-substitution approach to trade policy rather than an export-promotion approach. Which policy would domestic consumers prefer and why?

LO3 Discuss international trade and development

3.1. *(International Trade and Development)* From the perspective of citizens in a developing country, what are some of the benefits and drawbacks of international trade?

LO4 Describe the role of foreign aid in economic development

4.1. *(Foreign Aid and Economic Development)* Foreign aid, if it is to be successful in enhancing economic development, must lead to a more productive economy. Describe some of the problems in achieving such an objective through foreign aid.

LO5 Define transitional economies

5.1. *(Transitional Economies)* What special problems are faced by Eastern European economies as they make the transition from central planning to competitive markets?

LO6 Discuss markets and institutions

6.1. *(Markets and Institutions)* Why is a system of well-defined and enforceable property rights crucial when a country is converting to a market-based system of resource allocation?

VS.

Index

D

E

J

K

L

M

Q

R

S

T

U

V

W

Z

THE ART AND SCIENCE OF ECONOMIC ANALYSIS

Prep Card

What's a Prep Card?

To help you prepare, we've developed a Prep Card for each chapter. Each card starts with a short list of key concepts covered in the chapter.

In this chapter:

The economic problem; scien... tive versus positive analysis... nomic thinking.

Learning Outcomes

LO 1 Explain the economic problem of scarce resources and unlimited wants

LO 2 Describe the forces that shape economic choices

LO 3 Explain the relationship between economic theory and economic reality

LO 4 Identify some pitfalls of economic analysis

LO 5 Describe several reasons to study economics

Chapter Exhibits

Chapter Elements

This column contains a list of learning outcomes, chapter exhibits, key terms with page references, and chapter equations.

Key Terms

economics 4

resources 4

labor 4

capital 4

natural resources 4

entrepreneurial ability 5

entrepreneur 5

wages 5

Outline

Chapter at a Glance

The outline with page references gives you a quick snapshot of the content covered in the chapter.

Assignments

Case assignments are available on the web for students to download.

Case Assignments

Assign students to read the case studies on why Japan has so many vending machines (or combining resources to conserve those resources that are most costly) and on how choice of college major relates to earnings potential. Both cases have related questions and problems and are posted for download at www.econ4me.com.

Teaching Points

- This course will provide the first exposure to the economic way of thinking for many of your students. Although it seems natural to you, economic analysis presents a formidable challenge to many students. You may wish to consider presenting economics as one of many approaches to describing human behavior rather than as a body of established doctrines. Introducing a topic with relevant questions to which economics provides an answer generally enhances student interest in economics. Such questions appear at the beginning of each chapter.
- Students are generally eage... the semester. Chapters 1 an... week, and you can move alm... production possibilities, the... marginal analysis, and comp... should also be easy to meld... in the Chapter 1 Appendix w...

Quick Tips

Teaching points from the Instructor Manual help you engage your students. The teaching points also give suggestions on ways to deliver the material to ensure maximum student understanding.

interest 5
rent 5
profit 5
good 5
service 5
scarcity 5
market 6
product market 6
resource market 6
circular-flow model 6
rational self-interest 7
marginal 8
microeconomics 8
macroeconomics 9
economic theory (economic model) 9
variable 10
other-things-constant assumption 10
behavioral assumption 10
hypothesis 10
positive economic statement 11
normative economic statement 11
association-is-causation fallacy 12
fallacy of composition 12
secondary effects 12

Appendix Key Terms

origin 15
horizontal axis 15
vertical axis 15
graph 15
dependent variable 15
independent variable 15
positive, or direct, relation 16
negative, or inverse, relation 16
slope of a line 16
tangent 18

Chapter Equations

$$\text{Slope} = \frac{\Delta x}{\Delta y}$$

Discussion questions, PowerPoint indications, and video topics are all elements on chapter cards.

- One point to stress in discussing the role and importance of economic analysis is that while individual responses to changes in an economic environment are not always predictable, the aggregate response often is. The use of such knowledge is valuable in virtually any context in which individuals, households, firms, resource owners, and so on, are faced with changing opportunities and costs. You might use some examples to illustrate this, such as what is the predicted response to a tax on gasoline and who ends up paying for the tax or the impact of a tax refund on consumer behavior.
- From a purely analytical perspective, the most important concept introduced in this chapter is the idea that decisions are made on the basis of marginal analysis. You might stress that marginal analysis is a cornerstone of economics.
- Some terminology in the text may deviate from your own lecture notes. If you intend to use any of the Test Banks, try to mention deviations between the text's usage and the terms you use in your lectures. For example, the text uses the word *resources* whereas you might use *factors of production* in your lecture notes.
- Some students think that economics is synonymous with business. You may wish to explain the difference, since many of your students will be studying business administration.
- Many students will be apprehensive about the mathematics used in the course. A good way for students to master the few mathematical tools needed in class is by through application and by using the Interactive Study Center and the Study Guides. It is essential for students to become comfortable with reading and shifting graphs as well as dividing fractions. The appendix to Chapter 1 provides a good foundation for the tools needed.
- Many beginning students do not understand what economists mean by the statement "consumers are rational." It is helpful to emphasize that rationality does not imply that all consumers must be identical or that all consumers make "good" decisions all the time. Individuals can have dramatically different tastes for goods and service and yet all can be considered rational.

Discussion Questions

What factors do *you* take into account when you're choosing which of your wants you will try to satisfy and how you will go about satisfying them?

Consider Albert Einstein's quote, "Sometimes one pays the most for things one gets for nothing," and the Russian proverb, "The only place you find free cheese is in a mousetrap." Do you agree with these statements? Why or Why not?

PowerPoint

A full PowerPoint list and script for Chapter 1 are in the Instructor Manual on the Instructor Resource CD-ROM and online at www.econ4me.com.

Video

In the Ask the Author videos for Chapter 1, the author asks these questions:

- Why are economists always talking about money and wealth?
- Why is economics difficult for so many students?
- Why do economists emphasize marginal analysis?

Download the clips from the web at www.econ4me.com.

1

THE ART AND SCIENCE OF ECONOMIC ANALYSIS

Prep Card

In this chapter:

The economic problem; scientific method; marginal analysis; normative versus positive analysis; rational self-interest; pitfalls of economic thinking.

Learning Outcomes

LO 1 Explain the economic problem of scarce resources and unlimited wants

LO 2 Describe the forces that shape economic choices

LO 3 Explain the relationship between economic theory and economic reality

LO 4 Identify some pitfalls of economic analysis

LO 5 Describe several reasons to study economics

Chapter Exhibits

Key Terms

economics 4

resources 4

labor 4

capital 4

natural resources 4

entrepreneurial ability 5

entrepreneur 5

wages 5

Outline

Case Assignments

Assign students to read the case studies on why Japan has so many vending machines (or combining resources to conserve those resources that are most costly) and on how choice of college major relates to earnings potential. Both cases have related questions and problems and are posted for download at www.econ4me.com.

Teaching Points

- This course will provide the first exposure to the economic way of thinking for many of your students. Although it seems natural to you, economic analysis presents a formidable challenge to many students. You may wish to consider presenting economics as one of many approaches to describing human behavior rather than as a body of established doctrines. Introducing a topic with relevant questions to which economics provides an answer generally enhances student interest in economics. Such questions appear at the beginning of each chapter.
- Students are generally eager and very fresh at the beginning of the semester. Chapters 1 and 2 can be assigned during the first week, and you can move almost immediately into discussions of production possibilities, the idea of opportunity cost, the use of marginal analysis, and comparative advantage (see Chapter 2). It should also be easy to meld a discussion of the points contained in the Chapter 1 Appendix with the analytics of Chapter 2.

interest 5
rent 5
profit 5
good 5
service 5
scarcity 5
market 6
product market 6
resource market 6
circular-flow model 6
rational self-interest 7
marginal 8
microeconomics 8
macroeconomics 9
economic theory (economic model) 9
variable 10
other-things-constant assumption 10
behavioral assumption 10
hypothesis 10
positive economic statement 11
normative economic statement 11
association-is-causation fallacy 12
fallacy of composition 12
secondary effects 12

Appendix Key Terms

origin 15
horizontal axis 15
vertical axis 15
graph 15
dependent variable 15
independent variable 15
positive, or direct, relation 16
negative, or inverse, relation 16
slope of a line 16
tangent 18

Chapter Equations

$$\text{Slope} = \frac{\Delta x}{\Delta y}$$

- One point to stress in discussing the role and importance of economic analysis is that while individual responses to changes in an economic environment are not always predictable, the aggregate response often is. The use of such knowledge is valuable in virtually any context in which individuals, households, firms, resource owners, and so on, are faced with changing opportunities and costs. You might use some examples to illustrate this, such as what is the predicted response to a tax on gasoline and who ends up paying for the tax or the impact of a tax refund on consumer behavior.
- From a purely analytical perspective, the most important concept introduced in this chapter is the idea that decisions are made on the basis of marginal analysis. You might stress that marginal analysis is a cornerstone of economics.
- Some terminology in the text may deviate from your own lecture notes. If you intend to use any of the Test Banks, try to mention deviations between the text's usage and the terms you use in your lectures. For example, the text uses the word *resources* whereas you might use *factors of production* in your lecture notes.
- Some students think that economics is synonymous with business. You may wish to explain the difference, since many of your students will be studying business administration.
- Many students will be apprehensive about the mathematics used in the course. A good way for students to master the few mathematical tools needed in class is by through application and by using the Interactive Study Center and the Study Guides. It is essential for students to become comfortable with reading and shifting graphs as well as dividing fractions. The appendix to Chapter 1 provides a good foundation for the tools needed.
- Many beginning students do not understand what economists mean by the statement "consumers are rational." It is helpful to emphasize that rationality does not imply that all consumers must be identical or that all consumers make "good" decisions all the time. Individuals can have dramatically different tastes for goods and service and yet all can be considered rational.

Discussion Questions

What factors do *you* take into account when you're choosing which of your wants you will try to satisfy and how you will go about satisfying them?

Consider Albert Einstein's quote, "Sometimes one pays the most for things one gets for nothing," and the Russian proverb, "The only place you find free cheese is in a mousetrap." Do you agree with these statements? Why or Why not?

PowerPoint

A full PowerPoint list and script for Chapter 1 are in the Instructor Manual on the Instructor Resource CD-ROM and online at www.econ4me.com.

Video

In the Ask the Author videos for Chapter 1, the author asks these questions:

- Why are economists always talking about money and wealth?
- Why is economics difficult for so many students?
- Why do economists emphasize marginal analysis?

Download the clips from the web at www.econ4me.com.

2

ECONOMIC TOOLS AND ECONOMIC SYSTEMS

Prep Card

In this chapter:

Opportunity cost; production possibilities frontier; division of labor; three economic questions; comparative advantage; economic systems; specialization.

Learning Outcomes

LO 1 Describe the impact of choice on opportunity

LO 2 Explain how comparative advantage, specialization, and exchange affect economic outcomes (output)

LO 3 Outline how economies function as production systems

LO 4 Describe different economic systems and the decision-making rules that define them

Chapter Exhibits

Exhibit 1 The Economy's Production Possibilities Frontier

Exhibit 2 Shifts of the Economy's Production Possibilities Frontier

Exhibit 3 Best 10 and Worst 10 Among 175 Countries Based on Ease of Doing Business

Key Terms

opportunity cost 22
sunk cost 23
law of comparative advantage 24
absolute advantage 24
comparative advantage 24
barter 25
division of labor 26
specialization of labor 26
production possibilities frontier (PPF) 27
efficiency 27
law of increasing opportunity cost 27
economic growth 28
rules of the game 29
economic system 30
pure capitalism 31
private property rights 31
pure command system 32
mixed system 32

Outline

Experiential Assignment

Following are some data on the U.S. economy taken from the *Economic Report of the President* at http://www.access.gpo.gov/eop/. (Reports from before 2004 can be found at http://fraser.stlouisfed.org/publications/ERP/.)

Year	Unemployment Rate	Real Government Spending (billions)	Real Civilian Spending (billions)
1982	9.7%	$ 947.7	$3,672.6
1983	9.6	960.1	3,943.6
1996	5.4	1,257.9	5,670.5
1997	4.9	1,270.6	5,920.8

a. Have students sketch a production possibilities frontier for the years 1982 and 1983, showing the trade-off between public sector (government) and private-sector (civilian) spending. Assume that resource availability and technology were the same in both years, but notice that the unemployment rate was relatively high.

b. Have students sketch a PPF for the years 1996 and 1997. Assume that resource availability and technology were the same in both years but higher than in 1982 and 1983. Note that the unemployment rate in the late 1990s was much lower than in the early 1980s.

c. Ask them what lessons they learned about the U.S. economy of the past 20 years?

Case Assignments

Assign students to read the case studies on the opportunity cost of college and on the rules of the game. Both cases have related questions and problems and are posted for download at www.econ4me.com.

Teaching Points

- This chapter contains several fundamental concepts that should be fully discussed because they are used throughout the text to discuss economic choice in a variety of settings. When discussing opportunity cost and choice, be sure to distinguish between those costs that are associated with marginal decision making and those that are not (i.e., sunk costs). Also, many students will not immediately recognize that non-monetary costs are components of opportunity costs so it helps to emphasize this point.
- Comparative advantage is a second important concept emphasized in this chapter. For additional examples of comparative advantage, consider the classic example in which an attorney can type and file faster and more accurately than a secretary. Because of comparative advantage, it will usually pay the lawyer to hire a secretary rather than to do the typing and filing since the opportunity cost is lower. Another example would be for Hawaii to specialize in pineapple growing and then trade with Idaho for potatoes. This chapter makes the point that opportunity cost is a relative concept, based on relative rather than absolute resource requirements in the production of goods. Because comparative advantage implies the specialization of resource use, trade becomes important in allocating goods to consumers. Students often note that self-reliance is an admirable concept. The discussion of comparative advantage shows that specialization and exchange lead to a more efficient allocation of resources.
- When drawing the production possibilities frontier, partition the horizontal axis into equal segments, and then show the ever-increasing amounts of the alternative good that must be sacrificed to obtain more of the good in question. You thereby illustrate the law of increasing opportunity costs. Students often confuse increasing total and increasing marginal opportunity costs. You should emphasize, through your construction, that it is incremental costs that are increasing. Draw your curve large with plenty of bow in it. Numerical examples are helpful to some students.
- Sometimes people claim that the PPF is bowed out because of the law of diminishing returns. Diminishing returns, of course, assumes an increase in one type of resource, holding other resources constant. This is not the case along the PPF, since all resources tend to be reallocated between goods with movement along the PPF. You could incorporate the law of diminishing returns into your discussion by fixing capital between the sectors and then shifting only labor resources. The text's approach, however, is to assume that resources are not homogeneous; some are specific to the production of a particular good. The result is increasing opportunity costs and a bowed-out PPF.
- Once the PPF is understood in terms of its construction and shape, it is important to emphasize the concepts that it illustrates. Scarcity is reflected by the fact that some output combinations are not feasible. The infinite number of output combinations that are feasible illustrates choice. Efficiency is illustrated when production occurs along the PPF, and the shape of the PPF illustrates the law of increasing opportunity costs. Furthermore, if resources are different, then the required specialization of resource usage implies that some form of trading occurs in order for each resource owner to consume all (both) goods.
- A discussion of shifts in the production possibilities frontier leads naturally to a consideration of the sources of economic growth. Technological advance shifts the PPF. Such advances take time and require society to save, just as with the accumulation of physical capital. Emphasize that the PPF need not always shift out in a balanced way. Technological advance is often specific to an industry. Improvements the rules of the game and in the education and health of the population may also lead to an outward shift in the PPF.
- This chapter closes by considering how different economic systems answer the three economic questions. You may wish to discuss how numerous political systems have shifted toward more market-based economies over the past century to emphasize the capitalist approach. The chapter contains a fairly short reference to Adam Smith and his notion of the "invisible hand". You may want to discuss this important concept in more detail.

PowerPoint

A full PowerPoint list and script for Chapter 2 are in the Instructor Manual on the Instructor Resource CD-ROM and online at www.econ4me.com.

Video

In the Ask the Author video for Chapter 2, the author asks this question:

- How is our economy related to the rest of the world?

Download the clip from the web at www.econ4me.com.

3

ECONOMIC DECISION MAKERS

Prep Card

In this chapter:

Evolution of the household; evolution of the firm; types of firms; market failures and government remedies; taxing and public spending; international trade and finance.

Learning Outcomes

LO 1 Explain the role of the household in an economic system

LO 2 Identify the different types of firms and describe their role in the economy

LO 3 Outline the ways governments affect their economies

LO 4 Outline the international influences on an economy

Chapter Exhibits

Exhibit 1 Where U.S. Personal Income Comes From and Where It Goes

Exhibit 2 Number and Sales of Each Type of Firm

Exhibit 3 Redistribution Has Grown and Defense Has Declined as Share of Federal Outlays Since 1960

Exhibit 4 Payroll Taxes Have Grown as a Share of Federal Revenue Since 1960

Exhibit 5 Top Marginal Rate on Federal Personal Income Tax Since 1913

Key Terms

utility 36
transfer payments 37
Industrial Revolution 38
firms 38
sole proprietorship 38
partnership 39
corporation 39
cooperative 39
not-for-profit organizations 41
market failure 42
monopoly 42
natural monopoly 42
private good 43
public good 43
externality 43
fiscal policy 43
monetary policy 43
ability-to-pay tax principle 46
benefits-received tax principle 46
tax incidence 46

Outline

Experiential Assignments

1. Have students get a library copy of *The Wealth and Poverty of Nations*, by David Landes, and read pages 207–210. Ask them how they would interpret Landes's story about mechanization using the ideas developed in this chapter.
2. The household is the most important decision-making unit in our economy. Have students look through the rotating columns (e.g.,"Work and Family" and "Personal Technology") in the *Wall Street Journal* this week, and find a description of some technological change that might affect household production. Ask them to explain how production would be affected.

Case Assignments

Assign students to read the cases on user-generated content and on how technology is creating a return to a cottage industry structure with people working from home. Both cases have related questions and are posted for download at www.econ4me.com.

proportional taxation 46
progressive taxation 46
marginal tax rate 46
regressive taxation 47
merchandise trade balance 48
balance of payments 48
foreign exchange 48
tariff 49
quota 49

Teaching Points

- This chapter discusses the principal players in the economy and also reviews the historical development of the institutions of the economy. For example, the evolution of the firm and the household are discussed, and both are integrated with the concepts of specialization and comparative advantage from Chapter 2.
- Students should be familiar with the idea of household production. A common example would be fixing the evening meal rather than dining out. Fixing the auto, painting the house, and cultivating a garden are all examples of household production.
- It might be instructive to point out how certain inventions, such as the vacuum cleaner, have expanded the degree of household production. An interesting question to raise is whether such changes were supply induced or demand induced. That is, did the need for vacuum cleaners appear in the market and give rise to the invention, or did the invention give rise to the market and thus the increased household production of cleaning?
- Many students will not know the basic structure of corporate finance. It is therefore advisable to discuss the difference between corporate stocks and corporate bonds, one implying ownership and the other implying debt. The stock financing of corporations is an interesting application of specialization. The owners of the corporation may know little about the actual production of the firm's product but are able to supply capital and earn a return.
- In discussing the section on the rationale for government, you may wish to emphasize the basic ideas of public goods and externalities. It is interesting to note that while pollution abatement equipment may be produced and sold by private business, it is government that creates demand for the goods. Private sellers of such equipment would have a hard time finding customers in the absence of government mandates.
- It is important to stress externalities as examples of situations where the market outcome may not be optimal. Externalities can be negative or positive. Cigarette smoking, for example, is an activity that generates a negative externality with possibly harmful medical side effects. As a result, all domestic air travel is now smoke free and many states have passed legislation outlawing smoking in public places. This subject will be of interest to almost everyone whether or not they smoke. Positive externalities may flow from public education, immunizations, and government funded research.
- Although students are probably aware of the recent large U.S. trade deficits, they probably do not know what these deficits mean or why the foreign sector is of increasing importance to the U.S. economy. While detailed discussion of these topics is deferred to later chapters, it is useful to link briefly the notions of trade and comparative advantage (a world PPF) and to tie into this discussion the relevance of exchange rates and trade restrictions to the operation of international markets. You might even wish to bring in the recent volatility in world capital markets as a possible by product of the increasing importance of international trade.

Discussion Question

Often it is said that government is necessary when private markets fail to work effectively and fairly. How might private markets break down?

PowerPoint

A full PowerPoint list and script for Chapter 3 are in the Instructor Manual on the Instructor Resource CD-ROM and online at www.econ4me.com.

Video

In the Ask the Author video for Chapter 3, the author asks this question:

- How big is government and what are its major functions?

Download the clip from the web at www.econ4me.com.

4 DEMAND, SUPPLY, AND MARKETS Prep Card

In this chapter:

Topics discussed in chapter 4 include: Demand and quantity demanded; movement along a supply curve; movement along a demand curve; shift of a supply curve; shift of a demand curve; markets and equilibrium; supply and quantity supplied; disequilibrium.

Learning Outcomes

LO 1 Explain how the law of demand affects market activity

LO 2 Explain how the law of supply affects market activity

LO 3 Describe how the interaction between supply and demand create markets

LO 4 Describe how markets reach equilibrium

LO 5 Explain how markets react during periods of disequilibrium

Chapter Exhibits

Key Terms

Outline

Case Assignments

Assign students to read the chapter cases on the market for professional basketball players and on rent ceilings in New York City. Both cases have related questions and are posted for download at www.econ4me.com.

PowerPoint

A full PowerPoint list and script for Chapter 4 are in the Instructor Manual on the Instructor Resource CD-ROM and online at www.econ4me.com.

Video

In the Ask the Author video for Chapter 4, the author asks this question:

- Why do some prices adjust more slowly?

Download the clip from the web at www.econ4me.com.

inferior good 55
substitutes 55
complements 55
tastes 56
movement along a demand curve 56
shift of a demand curve 56
supply 56
law of supply 56
supply curve 56
quantity supplied 57
individual supply 57
market supply 57
relevant resources 58
alternative goods 58
movement along a supply curve 59
shift of a supply curve 59
transaction costs 59
surplus 60
shortage 60
equilibrium 61
disequilibrium 63
price floor 64
price ceiling 64

Teaching Points

- Students are usually confused by the distinction between demand and quantity demanded. Such confusion can be reduced by continually reminding students that *demand is a curve* that depicts the relationship between price and quantity demanded assuming that all other factors (which may affect demand) are held constant. *Quantity demanded is a point on the curve* that shows the quantity demanded at a given price. Quantity demanded will increase as the price falls. An increase in demand, by definition, is a shift of the demand curve. Another way to emphasize the distinction is to emphasize that because we graph the current quantity demanded (holding all other factors constant) against price:
  - A change in price leads to a movement along the demand curve.
  - ONLY changes in factors other than price can lead to a change or shift in demand (curve) since once we allow these factors to change, the original curve is no longer valid (because it assumed all other factors were held constant).
- You may wish to begin the discussion of demand and supply by creating both curves through an example in class (i.e., ask students how many cookies they would like to buy next class at different prices. Then ask what they would be willing to supply at various prices). Briefly discuss the equilibrium process, making sure that students understand the importance of market forces. This will provide a context for the textbook's development of demand, then supply, and then market equilibrium.
- The income and substitution effects can be presented as the direct consequence of the *ceteris paribus* assumption. Holding other prices constant while changing the price of the good whose demand curve is being constructed results in a change in its opportunity cost because its relative price has changed. Holding money income constant while changing the price of the good results in a change in the purchasing power or real income of the person whose demand curve is being constructed.
- You should use examples to discuss how the demand for a particular good changes when the price of a substitute or a complement changes. Students may have trouble with this concept, but if concrete examples are used it becomes clear (i.e. if Pepsi is on sale, those who normally purchase Coca Cola may switch).
- Students frequently become mixed up in distinguishing between movements along and shifts in the demand and supply curves. It is best to use MANY examples to illustrate the difference. Numerical examples are helpful to some students since they see clearly price changes as well as changes in the equilibrium price and quantity. Work through the comparative statics adjustment of quantity and price very carefully. You may wish to emphasize the fact that shifts in supply move you "along the demand curve," and vice versa, leading to predictable changes in equilibrium price and quantity in both instances. You may also wish to talk specifically about the quantities of goods purchased at nonequilibrium prices. This will be useful in discussing efficiency later in the course.
- You may want to get into the normative aspects of equilibrium price changes to answer the question "Is the equilibrium price a desirable price?" This will lead to a discussion of who gains and who loses from such price changes as well as keying in on the importance of the ability (as well as the willingness) to pay underlying the demand curve.
- By the end of the chapter, students may still have difficulty understanding how markets are able to identify the equilibrium price. Charles Holt, in a 1996 article published in the Journal of Economic Perspectives, shows how instructors can use playing cards to illustrate the interaction of demand and supply in competitive markets. This method can also be used to illustrate how price ceilings, price floors, and shifts in demand and supply influence equilibrium price and quantity. The method is very easy to use in the classroom and should generate much interest among students.

Discussion Questions

Discuss how particular markets, such as professional sports or fast food, might bring suppliers and demanders together. Which methods might be unique to these industries and which might be similar?

How would the various factors that cause shifts in the supply curve, such as technology and prices of resources, influence each other?

5

ELASTICITY OF DEMAND AND SUPPLY

Prep Card

In this chapter:

Price elasticity of demand; price elasticity of supply; determinants of price elasticity; income elasticity of demand; price elasticity and total revenue; cross-price elasticity of demand.

Learning Outcomes

LO 1 Define and graph the price elasticity of demand

LO 2 Identify the determinants of the price elasticity of demand

LO 3 Define and graph the price elasticity of supply

LO 4 Describe other measures of elasticity

Chapter Exhibits

Outline

Experiential Assignments

1. The Campaign for Tobacco Free Kids maintains a Web site with articles on the economics of tobacco policy at http://tobaccofreekids.org/campaign/global/worldconference.shtml. For additional background information in the form of the transcript of a five-part television series, have students check *The Tobacco Wars*, by Walter Adams and James Brock (Cincinnati, OH: South-Western College Publishing Co., 1999).
2. Farm problems are not unique to the United States. Send students to the Web page for "Policy Coherence in Trade and Agriculture" at http://www.tcd.ie/iiis/policycoherence/index.php/iiis/home. Have them review the material presented there and determine to what extent agricultural issues in the European Union (EU) are similar to those experienced in the United States. Ask them what role economics plays in the analysis of EU farm policy.
3. In the computer industry, cross-elasticities of demand are quite important. For example, we know that computers and computer software are complements, and the cross-elasticity of demand would tell us how strong that relationship is. Ask students to read the "Personal Technology" column in a Thursday *Wall Street Journal* and find a story that describes pricing of computer hardware or software. Based on what is known about the relationships among different types of computers and different types of software, and between computers and software, have students try to predict the effects of the price change. Ask them how the change will affect the quantity demanded of the item described, and how it will affect the demand for substitutes and complements to that item.

Key Terms

price elasticity of demand 68
price elasticity formula 68
inelastic demand 69
unit-elastic demand 69
elastic demand 69
total revenue 69
linear demand curve 70
perfectly elastic demand curve 71
perfectly inelastic demand curve 72
unit-elastic demand curve 72
constant-elasticity demand curve 72
price elasticity of supply 75
inelastic supply 76
unit-elastic supply 76
elastic supply 76
perfectly elastic supply curve 76
perfectly inelastic supply curve 76
unit-elastic supply curve 77
income elasticity of demand 78
cross-price elasticity of demand 79

Chapter Equations

$$\text{Price elasticity of demand} = \frac{\text{Percentage change in quantity demanded}}{\text{Percentage change in price}}$$

Elasticity of Demand

$$E_D = \frac{\Delta q}{(q + q')/2} \div \frac{\Delta p}{(p + p')/2}$$

Total Revenue

$$TR = p \times q$$

Elasticity of Supply

$$E_S = \frac{\Delta q}{(q + q')/2} \div \frac{\Delta p}{(p + p')/2}$$

Teaching Points

- After establishing how to calculate price elasticity, it is easy to illustrate the relationship between elasticity and total revenue. Try the following steps using a numerical example:
  - Assume a small rise in the price of the good.
  - Note that this causes the quantity demanded to fall.
  - Because the change in total revenue depends on the changes in both quantity demanded and price, the direction of change in total revenue depends on which of the two changes (quantity demanded or price) is larger.
  - If demand is elastic, the quantity effect is larger and therefore total revenue changes in the same direction as quantity (i.e., falls in this example). If demand is inelastic, the price effect is larger and, therefore, total revenue changes in the same direction as price (i.e., increases in this example).

  This exercise completes a circle of ideas. First was the relationship among the points on the demand curve, price change, and total revenue. Next was the relationship between price-induced changes in total revenue and elasticity. Therefore, a natural connection exists between the points on the demand curve and the elasticity measure. Elasticity decreases as we move down along the demand curve.
- The elasticity formula is very useful. Consider a grocery store that sells, among other things, peanut butter. One month it sets its price and observes its sales. The next month it raises the price by 10 percent and observes the effect on total revenue. This is an experiment, and a very inexpensive one. Cross-price elasticities with goods such as grape jelly are also easy to calculate.
- Remind students that this chapter focuses on revenues only—costs are not yet considered. Thus, maximizing total revenue by selling at the unitary elastic price will almost never be an optimum. The unitary elasticity problem forms a good basis for a question for students to ponder.
- Aside from the obvious need for business owners to understand elasticity in their revenue calculations, knowledge of elasticities is important for policymakers as well. It is important to carefully go through the examples of tax incidence and agricultural public policy. .

Discussion Questions

Consider the analysis for price elasticity of demand for cigarettes in the "Smoke Out" box. What are some other products that are similarly price elastic in their demand, and what factors influence their elasticity?

Aside from the examples given of Coke and Pepsi or gasoline and tires, what are some other pairs of goods that are substitutes or complements?

PowerPoint

A full PowerPoint list and script for Chapter 5 are in the Instructor Manual both at www.econ4me.com and on the Instructor Resource CD-ROM.

Video

In the Ask the Author video for Chapter 5, the author answers the question:

- Is price elasticity of demand the same thing as slope?

Download the clip from www.econ4me.com.

6

CONSUMER CHOICE AND DEMAND

Prep Card

In this chapter:

Total and marginal utility; utility-maximizing conditions; law of diminishing; consumer surplus; marginal utility; role of time in demand; measuring utility; time price of goods.

Learning Outcomes

LO 1 Explain the basics of utility analysis

LO 2 Describe how to measure and maximize utility

LO 3 Explain how marginal utility and the law of demand can create consumer surplus.

LO 4 Describe the role of time in demand

Chapter Exhibits

Key Terms

Chapter Equations

Consumer Equilibrium

$$\frac{MU_P}{p_p} = \frac{MU_V}{p_v}$$

Outline

Experiential Assignments

1. For more about the economics of consumption, have students read Jane Katz's "The Joy of Consumption: We Are What We Buy," in the Federal Reserve Bank of Boston's *Regional Review* at http://www.bos.frb.org/economic/econbios/katz.htm#publications. Ask students to discuss the evidence that Katz cites about how the rising value of time has affected consumer spending patterns.
2. In this chapter, students learned that the cost of consumption involves both a money price and a time price. In a Wednesday *Wall Street Journal* issue, have your students find the "Work and Family" column. See if they can find some examples of changes in new goods, services, government policies, or institutional arrangements that work by reducing the time price of a product. Ask them how they think that change will affect the demand for the product. Will demand for any related products be affected?

Case Assignments

Assign students to read the more detailed explanation of the water-diamond paradox and the case study on the marginal value of free medical care. Both cases have related questions and problems and are posted for download at www.econ4me.com.

Teaching Points

- This chapter and the next provide the foundation for microeconomics. This chapter will be the first look most students will have at the concept of utility, and therefore many will be skeptical in regard to its existence or relevance. In response to this skepticism you need to emphasize the fact that we all subconsciously act as if we are utility maximizers in our daily decision making even though utility itself is completely subjective. As such, utility maximization becomes the underlying framework for the analysis of many forms of outcome assessment. Furthermore, the fact that utility itself cannot be measured objectively does not mean that it can't be meaningfully quantified.

- Diminishing marginal utility is easy to explain, but you should point out that some goods may have ranges over which marginal utility increases. For example, the first gallon of gasoline you put in your car may not yield as much marginal utility as the tenth. You can point out to skeptics that it is not necessary to measure utility objectively (e.g., in utils) in order to have diminishing marginal utility. This will probably be the first time students have had to think in marginal terms. It will be useful to distinguish between marginal and average. Students often find it confusing that total utility is at a maximum when marginal utility is zero. This point should be emphasized and demonstrated through problems.
- An important point to make is that movements in relative prices, rather than movements in the overall price level, cause alterations in consumer allocations. You can illustrate this by setting the ratio of marginal utilities equal to the ratio of prices. If a doubling or tripling of prices occurs, there will be no change in consumer allocation. This also illustrates the utility-maximization rule for allocating spending. It is the relative price rather than the absolute price level that is critical in the allocation process. If one good costs twice as much as another, the rational consumer must get at least twice the benefit from the higher-priced good if he or she is going to consume it.
- Consumer surplus is discussed at some length in this chapter. It is a subject that will be of considerable importance in measuring efficiency gains and losses at later stages of the course. It is essential that students recognize that the height of the demand curve represents the marginal benefit (in dollar terms) for each unit of the good consumed. In developing consumer surplus, this idea should be emphasized.

Discussion Questions

How does an increase in total number of available goods affect the marginal utility of each good, and what factors ultimately determine what and how much you consume?

Why is marginal utility subjective? How do objective factors, such as needs, influence utility?

PowerPoint

A full PowerPoint list and script for Chapter 6 are in the Instructor Manual both at www.econ4me.com and on the Instructor Resource CD-ROM.

Video

In the Ask the Author videos for Chapter 6, the author answers the following questions:

- How is weight gain related to the Law of Diminishing Marginal Utility?
- Why can't we feed the world from a flower pot?
- Are the demand curves and indifference curves the same?

Download the clips from www.econ4me.com.

7

PRODUCTION AND COST IN THE FIRM

Prep Card

In this chapter:

Explicit and implicit costs; short-run costs; economic and normal profit; long-run costs; increasing and diminishing returns; economies and diseconomies of scale.

Learning Outcomes

LO 1 Explain the relationship between cost and profit

LO 2 Identify the elements that affect production in the short term

LO 3 Explain how the costs of production vary with output in the short run

LO 4 Describe how firms use the long-run average cost curve to make choices about production

Chapter Exhibits

Key Terms

Outline

Experiential Assignments

1. The terms "diminishing returns" and "economies of scale" are often referred to in everyday discussions and in the popular press. Have students use an Internet search engine to search for diminishing returns or economies of scale. They should check the first five sites they find and, in each case, decide whether the term is being used correctly or incorrectly. If the latter, they should try to determine the nature of the writer's confusion. For example, they can check "The Concepts of Increasing and Diminishing Returns" (http://www. useit.com/alertbox/increasingreturns.html), in which the author manages to compare a short-run concept (diminishing marginal returns) with a long-run concept (increasing returns to scale).
2. Have students read Erik Brynjolfsson and Shinkyu Yang's "Information Technology and Productivity: A Review of the Literature," online at http://ccs.mit.edu/papers/ccswp202/. Using the concepts learned in this chapter, they should try to explain the expected long-run impact of information technology on productivity and costs.

Case Assignments

Assign students to read the case studies on the economies and diseconomies of scale at the movies and at McDonald's. Both cases have related questions and problems and are posted for download at www.econ4me.com.

long run 97
total product 98
production function 98
marginal product 98
increasing marginal returns 98
law of diminishing marginal returns 98
fixed cost 99
variable cost 99
total cost 100
marginal cost 100
average variable cost 101
average total cost 101
economies of scale 103
diseconomies of scale 104
long-run average cost curve (planning curve) 105
constant long-run average cost 105
minimum efficient scale 105

Chapter Equations

Total Cost

$$TC = FC + VC$$

Marginal Cost

$$MC = \Delta TC/\Delta q$$

Average Variable Cost

$$AVC = VC/q$$

Average Total Cost

$$ATC = TC/q$$

PowerPoint

A full PowerPoint list and script for Chapter 7 are in the Instructor Manual both at www.econ4me.com and on the Instructor Resource CD-ROM.

Video

In the Ask the Author videos for Chapter 7, the author answers the following questions:

- What do we mean by fixed versus variable costs?
- Why do economists and accountants disagree?

Download the clips from www.econ4me.com.

Teaching Points

- This chapter presents the construction of cost curves for the individual firm. Students who master this material should have no problem understanding the sections of the text dealing with market structure. The cost curves discussed in this chapter are inherently quantitative, and those students with weaker math backgrounds need exercises that force them to derive average cost and marginal cost from the basics. The Interactive Learning Center and Study Guide provide additional exercises and also help students learn how to utilize graphic techniques—something that will be essential in the discussion of competitive equilibrium.
- The chapter begins with a discussion of the meaning of the total and marginal products of labor, which is the only variable resource considered in the short run. Exhibit 2 shows the relationship between labor employed and output generated. Note that both increasing and diminishing returns are discussed. Point out that marginal product can be negative while total product is still positive. Ask the students to explain how this can happen.
- It should not be hard to explain the concept of diminishing marginal returns. It is important to emphasize that the additional units of the variable resource are not less capable than earlier units. As an example, you might have students think about how total output at a fast food restaurant will change as additional workers are added.
- Exhibit 4 is particularly useful for class discussion. Some students find the numerical examples particularly illuminating. An interesting way to approach this material is to leave certain parts of the table blank and ask students to use the filled-in parts to guide them in completing the table. You need delete only one table entry per line to make this an interesting exercise.
- Exhibit 5 shows the relationship between the total cost curve and the marginal cost curve. Since marginal cost is the slope of the total cost curve, it is natural to use the word *slope* in the classroom. Another word that might prove illuminating for students is *steepness*. As the total cost curve becomes steeper, marginal cost increases.
- Exhibits 6 and 7 are crucial to understanding cost in the short run and must be covered with great care. Because the marginal cost curve ultimately drives the variable and total cost curves, understanding why diminishing marginal productivity leads to increasing marginal costs is absolutely essential. Once this is understood, relating marginal to average results in the characteristic U-shaped average variable and average total cost curves. A clear way to depict the relationship between marginal and average is to use the impact on the average class height when a tall or short student joins the class.
- The long-run average cost curve should be presented as an envelope curve based on selection of the best scale of production from the many possible scales for each output level on the basis of cost. The shape of the long-run curve then does not depend on diminishing marginal product but on the existence of economies and diseconomies of scale.

Discussion Questions

In spite of the fact that firms do not make payments on resources they own, these resources still have an opportunity cost. How is this possible, and how does this affect a firm's efforts to maximize profits?

Choose an example like the movie theater discussed in the chapter (perhaps baseball stadiums or farmland). What factors contribute to economies of scale? Diseconomies of scale?

PERFECT COMPETITION

Prep Card

In this chapter:

Market structure; short-run supply curve; price takers; long-run supply curve; marginal revenue; competition and efficiency; golden rule of profit maximization; producer surplus; gains from exchange; loss minimization.

Learning Outcomes

LO 1 Define a perfectly competitive market and explain its effect on demand

LO 2 Explain how firms maximize profit in the short run

LO 3 Identify ways firms minimize short-run losses

LO 4 Explain how firms manage short-run supply

LO 5 Describe how taking the long-run view affects economic factors

LO 6 Describe how different cost structures influence an industry's long-run supply curve

LO 7 Identify how concepts of efficiency are used to judge market performance

Chapter Exhibits

Outline

Experiential Assignment

Financial markets are quintessential examples of perfectly competitive markets. And, of course, the *Wall Street Journal* features in-depth coverage of these markets. Have students go to the Money and Investing section of today's *Wall Street Journal,* and choose one or two articles that seem interesting to them. Then ask them to determine how financial markets contribute to productive and allocative efficiency in the U.S. economy.

Case Assignments

Assign students to read the case studies on the auction markets and on experimental economics. Both cases have related questions and problems and are posted for download at www.econ4me.com.

Discussion Question

What factors might detract from a firm's ability to achieve perfect competition?

Key Terms

market structure 109
perfect competition 110
commodity 110
price 111
marginal revenue *(MR)* 112
golden rule of profit maximization 112
average revenue 113
short-run firm supply curve 116
short-run industry supply curve 117
long-run industry supply curve 122
constant-cost industry 122
increasing-cost industries 122
productive efficiency 123
allocative efficiency 124
producer surplus 125
social welfare 125

Chapter Equation

Market price = Marginal revenue = Average revenue

Teaching Points

- A thorough understanding of the perfectly competitive market is essential to understanding the other market structures. Reiterate that in the perfectly competitive model no firm has control over the market price. Students often find this assumption unrealistic since firms should have control over the price they charge. The point to stress is that firms can certainly choose any price for their product, but setting a price above market equilibrium results in no sales at all, and setting a price below equilibrium is not rational for the firm since it can sell the same quantity at the higher market equilibrium price. The key to this result is that firms must face competitors offering exactly the same product at the market price. Unless a firm can somehow differentiate its product from the competition, it cannot raise its price above the competitive market price. This ability to differentiate, of course, distinguishes the monopolistically competitive model from the perfectly competitive model.
- The perfectly competitive model is often attacked because of its many supposedly unrealistic assumptions. The purpose of the model is to illustrate competitive forces that are present in many sectors of the economy and to differentiate the purely competitive situation with other market structures. Point out that commodities trade in such markets. Students find discussions of the commodities markets interesting. You may ask students to track a market for a few days as an assignment.
- Students sometimes object to the idea that firms make output decisions based on marginal analysis. The important point to stress is that although firms may not make marginal decisions explicitly, they nevertheless cannot ignore the force of the marginal logic. When deciding to alter production, firms must consider the change in costs and revenues that will result. To do this, they need not have exact knowledge of the shapes of the marginal curves. They need understand only the marginal magnitudes centered about the current level of production.
- It is important to work through the firms' decision process using numerical examples. For instance, students often become confused as to why firms do not operate at the lowest point of average cost in the short run, since this is the point of lowest cost per unit produced and the highest per-unit profit. This psychological trap is caused by the appearance of the curves. Ask students whether they would rather sell 8 units with a profit per unit of $10 or 12 units with an average profit of $7.
- Students sometimes wonder why zero profits in the long run represent a stable, normal situation. The key is to have them recall that this is economic profit. Zero profit means that all resources are being paid exactly enough to keep them in the industry (i.e., their opportunity cost).
- Aside from applying marginal analysis and understanding how firms make profit-maximizing decisions in the perfectly competitive model, the importance of this chapter is in its implications for economic efficiency. In the previous chapter, students were introduced to the notion of consumer surplus, considering the demand curve to be a marginal benefit curve. Similarly, in this chapter, students will discover that for the competitive firm, the supply curve is the marginal cost curve. Just as consumer surplus exists whenever the price is lower than the marginal benefit associated with units of the good consumed, so producer surplus exists whenever the price received by the firm exceeds the marginal cost associated with the units of the good produced. Thus, a competitive industry, by producing where quantity supplied equals quantity demanded, is actually causing the production of all units of output that have a marginal benefit at least as great as the marginal cost. Furthermore, this result means that the sum of consumer and producer surpluses is maximized at the competitive equilibrium solution. This concept will be important later when considering the social welfare implications of the various market structures.

PowerPoint

A full PowerPoint list and script for Chapter 8 are in the Instructor Manual both at www.econ4me.com and on the Instructor Resource CD-ROM.

Video

In the Ask the Author videos for Chapter 8, the author answers these questions:

- Is the used car market perfectly competitive?
- What factors affect the auction price of your house?
- Do competitive firms earn economic profit in the long run?

Download the clips from www.econ4me.com.

9 MONOPOLY

Prep Card

In this chapter:

Barriers to entry; monopoly and resource allocation; price elasticity and marginal revenue; welfare cost of monopoly; price discrimination; profit maximization and monopolist's dream; the loss minimization.

Learning Outcomes

- LO 1 List and describe barriers to market entry
- LO 2 Explain sources of revenue for the monopolist
- LO 3 Describe a firm's costs and its opportunities for profit maximization
- LO 4 Explain monopoly and the allocation of resources
- LO 5 Describe the problems that interfere with estimating the deadweight loss of a monopoly
- LO 6 Describe conditions that create price discrimination

Chapter Exhibits

- Exhibit 1 Economies of Scale as a Barrier to Entry
- Exhibit 2 A Monopolist's Gain and Loss in Total Revenue from Selling One More Unit
- Exhibit 3 Revenue for De Beer's, a Monopolist
- Exhibit 4 Monopoly Demand and Marginal Total Revenue
- Exhibit 5 Short-Run Costs and Revenue for a Monopolist
- Exhibit 6 Monopoly Cost and Revenue
- Exhibit 7 The Monopolist Minimizes Losses in the Short Run
- Exhibit 8 Perfect Competition and Monopoly
- Exhibit 9 Price Discrimination with Two Groups of Consumers
- Exhibit 10 Perfect Price Discrimination

Key Terms

Outline

Experiential Assignment

In many large U.S. cities, monopoly owners of sports franchises have been lobbying local governments for new publicly-financed sports stadiums. Is this a form of rent seeking? Have students go to Heartland Institute's Web site at http://www.heartland.org/Index.cfm, conduct a search for sports stadiums, and look at one of the documents collected there. Ask them if there is convincing evidence of rent seeking? If so, how does that relate to the welfare cost of monopoly?

Case Assignments

Assign students to read the case studies on the monopolies held by De Beers and the U.S. Postal Service. Both cases have related questions and problems and are posted for download at www.econ4me.com.

Chapter Equations

Total Revenue

$$TR = p \times Q$$

Marginal Revenue

$$MR = \Delta TR/\Delta Q$$

Teaching Points

- Monopoly is always an interesting topic to discuss in class. The text takes the view that monopoly refers to a single seller of a good. Some economists prefer to use the term more loosely, since a single seller of a product is quite difficult to find. The first issue to deal with in this chapter is that of barriers to entry. The text identifies three main barriers that are the sources of monopoly—legal restrictions, economies of scale, and control of an essential resource.
- To fully appreciate the difference between monopoly and competitive profit maximization solutions, it is important to recognize an important similarity—that both maximize profits where marginal revenue equals marginal cost. Assuming identical market demand and cost curves, the difference between profit-maximizing quantity and price occurs because for the monopolist the relevant demand curve is the market demand curve, and hence marginal revenue is less than price. It is vital for the student to appreciate the relationship between demand and marginal revenue before adding cost data to the picture. Many students will find numerical examples the most compelling evidence.
- Sometimes students have the idea that monopolies are immune to losses. Remind them that even monopolies may need to shut down in the short run.
- Students often have the idea that monopoly is bad because of the excessive profits that a monopoly makes. Actually, what is bad is not making profits but the deadweight loss created as the monopolist reduces output below the competitive level. A related point to make is that monopoly does not lead to efficient pricing. There is always a divergence between marginal cost and price. Marginal cost is the additional cost to society of using certain resources in a particular way. Presumably these resources should be used to produce the goods that consumers value most highly. A monopoly produces less than the amount of a good for which society is willing and able to pay. Resources are therefore redirected toward the production of other, less desirable goods. Monopoly underproduces goods that society wants.
- The latter part of the chapter is concerned with price discrimination. For example, senior citizens are often given discounts on meals at restaurants, students are given discounts on movie tickets, and so on. You might encourage students to find their own examples of price discrimination. It is tempting to argue that price discrimination is bad because it flies in the face of our view of fairness. However, it is easy to show that overall resource allocation is actually improved when a monopolist is allowed to price discriminate because such behavior leads to an increase in output. Thus, the argument against this behavior is purely a distributional one. When a monopolist price discriminates, monopoly profits are increased and the price to some consumers is also increased relative to the pure monopoly result. However, other consumers enjoy lower prices, and total output is increased (toward the competitive industry level). Because additional units of the good are produced, this generates a net gain to consumers because the value (marginal benefit) exceeds the alternative resource use value (marginal cost) of those units.

PowerPoint

A full PowerPoint list and script for Chapter 9 are in the Instructor Manual both at www.econ4me.com and on the Instructor Resource CD-ROM.

Video

In the Ask the Author videos for Chapter 9, the author answers these questions:

- Why are cable rates so high?
- Why do professions try to limit entry?

Download the clips from www.econ4me.com.

10

MONOPOLISTIC COMPETITION AND OLIGOPOLY

Prep Card

In this chapter:

Monopolistic competition; oligopoly; product differentiation; collusion; excess capacity; prisoner's dilemma.

Learning Outcomes

LO 1 Discuss factors that lead to monopolistic competition

LO 2 Explain the concept of oligopoly

LO 3 Describe models of oligopoly

LO 4 Explain how game theory heps predict cartel behavior

LO 5 Compare oligopoly and perfect competition

Chapter Exhibits

Key Terms

monopolistic competition 144
excess capacity 148
oligopoly 148
undifferentiated oligopoly 148
differentiated oligopoly 148
collusion 151
cartel 151
price leader 152
game theory 153
prisoner's dilemma 153
strategy 153
payoff matrix 153
dominant-strategy equilibrium 154
duopoly 154

Outline

Case Assignments

Assign students to read the case studies on creative destruction and on Zara's speed to market. Both cases have related questions and problems and are posted for download at www.econ4me.com.

Teaching Points

- A point that may be useful to stress in your lecture is that monopolistic competition is an intermediate market structure that displays characteristics of both perfect competition and monopoly. Like perfect competition, there are many buyers and sellers and there is free entry and exit of firms. Like monopoly (because products are not perfectly substitutable), each firm faces a downward-sloping demand curve for its product and thus has some influence over price. Therefore, like a monopoly, the monopolistically competitive firm always prices its product above its marginal cost of production. In the long run, the monopolistically competitive firm earns only a normal profit, as is the case for the perfect competitor.
- Monopolistic competition is sometimes called the "brand name" model of market structure because firms may choose to differentiate their products by means of brand names and then compete on the basis of advertising as well as price. However, as the text points out, monopolistic competition need not require brand names. Firms may produce a relatively homogeneous product, as in the case of non-specialty steel or oil. Typically, when advertising

Nash equilibrium 154
tit-for-tat 156
coordination game 156

is used to differentiate the products of different firms, costs are higher than they would otherwise be. An interesting question for discussion is whether or not these extra costs are incurred to offer consumers a choice of varieties. Students are also likely to be interested in discussing whether it matters if the choice of products involves real differences in product characteristics or merely the perception that such differences exist.

- One interesting feature of monopolistic competition is that a firm is in long-run equilibrium when the demand curve it faces is tangent to its average cost curve. The key concept is that entry of competing firms shifts the demand curve to the left, reducing profits of each firm as a consequence. The extent to which the tangency point deviates from minimum average cost is determined by the degree to which the entering firms can closely duplicate the product of already successful firms. The closer competitors are to each other, the flatter each firm's demand curve is, and the closer the tangency is to minimum average cost. The efficiency implication of this is that the same total output could be produced at a lower resource cost if there were fewer firms, yet a less differentiated product would be the result.
- You may wish to examine a number of industries with many products (e.g., cereals, soaps) to determine whether they are monopolistically competitive or oligopolistic. The idea that individual firms deliberately market sets of products that compete with each other may seem irrational to some students. A discussion of why firms might do this gives a real-world flavor to the analysis of industry behavior and leads directly into the theory of oligopoly.
- The latter part of the chapter is devoted to a discussion of oligopoly—the kinked demand model is dropped in this edition but the discussion of game theory is enhanced. The text considers cartels, price leadership, and game theory models.
- While a variety of models has been developed to explain firm behavior in oligopolistic industries, no one model characterizes the structure. This makes oligopoly analysis difficult yet fascinating for economic researchers. This variation in firm behavior often occurs because of different operating assumptions by the firms, a situation highlighted in the game theory approach.
- A good example of an oligopoly is the toothpaste industry. The firms involved parry back and forth with "new, improved formulas." They segment the market by appealing to the young, the old, and smokers. If any particular brand "catches fire" and sales are hot, very similar products are almost immediately introduced. The same may be said for soaps and laundry detergents.

PowerPoint

A full PowerPoint list and script for Chapter 10 are in the Instructor Manual both at www.econ4me.com and on the Instructor Resource CD-ROM.

Video

In the Ask the Author videos for Chapter 10, the author answers these questions:

- What are the differences among the four market structures?
- How do educational vouchers relate to market structure?

Download the clips from www.econ4me.com.

11

RESOURCE MARKETS

Prep Card

In this chapter:

Demand and supply of resources; marginal revenue product; marginal resource cost; opportunity cost and economic rent; changes in resource demand.

Learning Outcomes

LO 1 Identify examples of resource demand and supply in daily life

LO 2 Explain resource supply and demand

LO 3 Define opportunity cost and economic rent

LO 4 Analyze the factors influencing resource demand

Chapter Exhibits

Exhibit 1 Resource Market for Carpenters

Exhibit 2 Market for Carpenter in Alternative Uses

Exhibit 3 Opportunity Cost and Economic Rent

Exhibit 4 Marginal Revenue Product When a Firm Sells in a Competitive Market

Exhibit 5 The Marginal Revenue Product When a Firm Sells with Market Power

Exhibit 6 Market Equilibrium for a Resource and the Firm's Employment Decision

Key Terms

derived demand 161

economic rent 164

marginal revenue product 166

marginal resource cost 167

resource substitutes 169

resource complements 169

Chapter Equations

Marginal revenue product = Marginal resource cost

Outline

Experiential Assignment

The *Occupational Outlook Handbook* (OOH) is a U.S. Department of Labor publication that projects employment trends. Using the search feature available at the OOH Web site at http://www. bls.gov/oco/, have students research several occupations. Ask them: What factors seem to affect employment prospects in those fields? What role does derived demand play? How about technological change?

Case Assignments

Assign students to read the case studies on the lumber prices and housing markets and on the minimum wage. Both cases have related questions and problems and are posted for download at www.econ4me.com.

Teaching Points

- This chapter is important because it provides the foundation for understanding different resource markets. Later chapters deal with markets for particular resources, such as labor or capital. The principles developed in this chapter are used repeatedly. Perhaps the most important of these ideas is the concept of derived demand. A resource is demanded to the extent that the goods that it helps produce are demanded. Any increase in the demand for a good produces a corresponding increase in the demand for the resources used to produce that good.

- There are two parts to the initial discussion of resource markets. The first is the distinction between temporary and permanent resource price differences, and the second is the distinction between opportunity cost and economic rent. A good example of the first is the case of an unemployed plumber who is offered a job in another state. Whether he or she takes the job depends on whether the differential in wages between the two states is sufficiently high. If the wage differential is too low, the plumber will stay put. This means that the differential is permanent because it does not result in a reallocation of resources. If the plumber decides to move to take the job, the differential can be considered temporary.
- This distinction may spark interest in discussing circumstances in which differentials seem to be permanent but not explainable by differences in nonmonetary job attributes or employee training or skills. You may wish to defer such discussion until the next chapter.
- The total remuneration of a resource is divided into two categories—economic rent and opportunity cost. Economic rent is a type of supplier's surplus since it equals the amount of income received by households over and above that necessary to attract the resource to the market. Opportunity cost is the amount of income that households must receive if they are to be willing and able to sell their resources in their best alternative use.
- The second part of the chapter is devoted to explaining the derivation of resource demand by use of marginal productivity and marginal revenue. After students feel comfortable with the marginal product curve, it is not hard to move on to the marginal revenue product curve. For competitive product markets, marginal product multiplied by the price of output yields marginal revenue product.
- Students should realize that the demand for a resource can change in two basic ways. The first occurs when the price (or marginal revenue) of output changes. The second occurs when the marginal productivity curve of the resource shifts.
- It is easy to become lost in the details of resource market analysis and fail to make the essential point to the students: Firms are willing to hire an additional unit of a resource only if that unit can generate revenue for the firm in excess of its cost. The amount brought in is the marginal revenue product, and the amount it costs the firm is the marginal resource cost. The resource demand curve is derived from the revenue associated with hiring the resource.
- You may wish to extend the discussion of optimal resource use with more than one resource. With a little algebra, you can show that the rule that each resource is used to the point where the marginal revenue product equals the marginal resource cost is equivalent to the rule that resources are used in combination so that the marginal product per dollar spent on each resource is equalized. This in turn means that the marginal rate of technical substitution between resources equals the ratio of resource prices.

PowerPoint

A full PowerPoint list and script for Chapter 11 are in the Instructor Manual both at www.econ4me.com and on the Instructor Resource CD-ROM.

Video

In the Ask the Author videos for Chapter 11, the author answers these questions:

- How would a zero-radius lawn mower affect your productivity?
- Should you have gone to college?

Download the clips from www.econ4me.com.

12

LABOR MARKETS AND LABOR UNIONS

Prep Card

In this chapter:

Theory of time allocation; why wages differ; backward-bending labor supply curve; unions and collective bargaining; union wages and employment; nonwage factors in labor supply; trends in union membership.

Learning Outcomes

- **LO 1** Discuss issues affecting labor supply and utility maximization
- **LO 2** Explain the market supply factors that lead to differing wages
- **LO 3** List types of unions and describe their collective bargaining strategies
- **LO 4** Describe the relationship between union wages and employment

Chapter Exhibits

- Exhibit 1 Individual Labor Supply Curve for Unskilled Work
- Exhibit 2 Deriving the Market Labor Supply Curve from Individual Labor Supply Curves
- Exhibit 3 Average Hourly Wage by Occupation in the United States as of May 2006
- Exhibit 4 Age, Education, and Pay
- Exhibit 5 Effects of Labor Union's Wage Floor
- Exhibit 6 Median Weekly Earnings Are Higher for Union Than Nonunion Workers
- Exhibit 7 Effect of Reducing Labor Supply or Increasing Labor Demand
- Exhibit 8 Unionization Rates by Age and Gender

Key Terms

- **market work** 174
- **nonmarket work** 174
- **leisure** 174
- **substitution effect of a wage increase** 176
- **income effect of a wage increase** 176
- **backward-bending supply curve of labor** 176
- **winner-take-all labor markets** 180
- **labor union** 182
- **craft union** 182
- **industrial union** 182
- **collective bargaining** 182
- **mediator** 182
- **binding arbitration** 182
- **strike** 182

Outline

Experiential Assignments

1. Ask students to interview five classmates to determine the nature of their labor supply curves for a summer job. Students should ask each of them how many hours of work he or she would be willing to supply at wage rates of $10, $15, $20, $25, and $30 per hour. They should then plot the results on a labor supply diagram. Do any of these individuals exhibit a backward-bending labor supply curve? Is the market supply curve for these five individuals backward bending?
2. Robert Frank's "Talent and the Winner-Take-All-Society" appeared in *The American Prospect* (21 March, 1994) at http://www.prospect.org/cs/articles?article=talent_and_the_winnertakeall_society. Have students read this non-technical article and discuss some of the problems that Frank identifies.

Case Assignments

Assign students to read the case studies on the winner-take-all labor markets and on dock-worker unions. Both cases have related questions and problems and are posted for download at www.econ4me.com.

featherbedding **186**
right-to-work states **186**

Teaching Points

- The first part of this chapter deals with the important problem of time allocation. Time can be allocated to three distinct uses: market work, nonmarket work, and leisure. These are some examples of each. Market work includes working on the assembly line, driving a taxi, providing secretarial work, managing a bank, and shining other people's shoes. Nonmarket work includes working in the yard, spraying for bugs in your own house, taking a self-study course, cutting and styling your own hair, shining your own shoes, and going to college. Leisure includes sleeping, reading a book for pleasure, watching television, and playing tennis or swimming (nonprofessionally).
- The interplay of the substitution and income effects of a wage change may be difficult for some students to grasp at first. Most will have a reasonably intuitive feel for the substitution effect, but the income effect will remain a stumbling block. One way to make the point is to exaggerate the increase in the wage, say from $10 per hour to $1,000 per hour. Most will begin to see that an income effect is lurking in the background. This will also point out the fact that the backward-bending portion of the labor supply curve should appear at high wage rates, although the exact rate will differ across people.
- There may be a tendency for students to believe that fair and nondiscriminatory wages should depend strictly on an individual's training, ability, and experience. It is therefore important to emphasize that the nonwage attributes of a job also typically play a role in establishing the relative attractiveness of different jobs. Consequently, the existence of wage differentials is not, by itself, evidence of discrimination in employment. On the other hand, long-standing wage differences among jobs requiring equal training and skills as well as possessing equal nonwage characteristics can occur only if some form of barrier to job mobility exists.
- An important section of this chapter deals with the ways in which a union can increase employment for its members. Many of them are subtle and will be of interest to your students. For example, when unions pay for television time to urge consumers to buy particular products, they are helping not only themselves but also the companies for which they work. This type of shared interest will no doubt be surprising to students who all too often see unions as an eternal adversary of management.

PowerPoint

A full PowerPoint list and script for Chapter 12 are in the Instructor Manual both at www.econ4me.com and on the Instructor Resource CD-ROM.

Video

In the Ask the Author videos for Chapter 12, the author answers these questions:

- Why do language teachers earn less?
- What would happen if everyone were paid the same?

Download the clips from www.econ4me.com.

13 CAPITAL, INTEREST, AND CORPORATE FINANCE Prep Card

In this chapter:

Production, saving, and time; loanable funds market; consumption, saving, and time; present value and discounting; corporate finance; optimal investment; stocks, bonds, and retained earnings.

Learning Outcomes

LO 1 Discuss the role of time in production and consumption

LO 2 Describe the factors that determine optimal investment

LO 3 Explain present value and discounting

LO 4 Analyze different corporate finance strategies

Chapter Exhibits

Key Terms

Outline

Experiential Assignments

1. Although the article is dated, have students read Jane Katz, "Who Should Be in Charge," in the Federal Reserve Bank of Boston's *Regional Review* at http://www.bos.frb.org/economic/nerr/rr1997/fall/katz97_4.htm. What are some of the issues in corporate finance as outlined by Katz? Do they hold true today?
2. Each day, the *Wall Street Journal* highlights a key interest rate in a graph on the first page of the Money and Investing section. Have students compare the graphs over several days to see the movements in rates for different securities. How have interest rates changed over the past year? Ask students to compare the graphs for several different securities. Have the rates on the various securities moved identically?

Case Assignments

Assign students to read the case studies on the intellectual property and million-dollar-lottery winners. Both cases have related questions and problems and are posted for download at www.econ4me.com.

Teaching Points

- The decision of whether to borrow to invest in capital formation is complicated by the element of time. When the benefits and costs of such a decision are spread over time, the manner in which time is discounted and the opportunity cost of time become important.

Chapter Equations

$$\text{Present value} = \frac{\text{Amount received one year from now}}{1 + \text{interest rate}}$$

$$\text{Present value} = \frac{M}{(1 + i)^t}$$

$$\text{Present value of receiving } M \text{ dollars each year forever} = \frac{M}{i}$$

- The idea that present consumption is more highly valued than future consumption is one with which most students will readily agree. However, connecting future income to present value by means of the interest, or discount, rate is frequently hard for students to understand. One way to foster such understanding is to have students calculate the amount of money that must be invested, given an interest rate, to obtain each bit of future income when such income is received over several years. If they can do this, they have grasped the idea of present value calculation.
- An important distinction (not yet brought up in the text) should be made between the rate of interest that is figured in nominal terms and the real rate of interest—the rate calculated from real sums paid and received. In a world without inflation, this distinction disappears and real and nominal rates are equal. If inflation is present, however, the nominal rate must be adjusted to obtain the real rate. A commonly used approximation of the expected real rate is obtained by subtracting an inflation premium (or expected inflation rate) from the nominal rate.
- You may wish to introduce the concept of risk into the present value calculations. This is one of the most poorly understood ideas in security valuation, and grasping this concept will help students in other business courses they might take. Try emphasizing that future cash flows should be discounted for both the time value of money and the riskiness or likelihood of actually receiving the anticipated cash flow or income stream.

Discussion Questions

Would you rather receive $10 today or $100 in ten years? Explain.

Ethically speaking, should interest rates fluctuate according to the borrower's ability to repay, as they do, or should interest rates be the same for all borrowers?

PowerPoint

A full PowerPoint list and script for Chapter 13 are in the Instructor Manual both at www.econ4me.com and on the Instructor Resource CD-ROM.

Video

In the Ask the Author videos for Chapter 13, the author answers these questions:

- Why do interest rates vary?
- What is the actual value of lottery winnings?

Download the clips from www.econ4me.com.

14 TRANSACTION COSTS, IMPERFECT INFORMATION, AND MARKET BEHAVIOR

Prep Card

In this chapter:

Transaction costs; asymmetric information; vertical integration; adverse selection; economies of scope; principal-agent problem; optimal search; moral hazard; winner's curse; signaling and screening.

Learning Outcomes

LO 1 Explain the rationale for the firm and describe its scope of operation

LO 2 Discuss the ways in which imperfect information influences market behavior

LO 3 Explain how asymmetric information affects product markets

LO 4 Describe the way asymmetric information influences labor markets

Chapter Exhibits

Exhibit 1 Minimum Efficient Scale and Vertical Integration

Exhibit 2 Optimal Search with Imperfect Information

Key Terms

vertical integration 203
bounded rationality 203
outsourcing 205
core competency 205
economies of scope 205
winner's curse 207
asymmetric information 207
hidden characteristics 207
adverse selection 208
hidden actions 208
principal-agent problem 208
principal 208
agent 208
moral hazard 209
efficiency wage theory 210
signaling 211
screening 211

Outline

Experiential Assignments

1. Nobel laureate Kenneth Arrow has contributed many important ideas to the economics of information. Ask students to read the interview with Arrow in *The Region* at http://woodrow.mpls.frb.fed.us/pubs/region/95-12/int9512.cfm. What does Arrow think are the policy implications that arise because of imperfect information?
2. Once students learn about the economics of asymmetric information, they can begin to see examples all around them. To demonstrate this point, have them check today's *Wall Street Journal* for a story that describes some new development that is a response to an asymmetric information problem. Look on the Economy page in the First Section or in the Marketplace section. When they've found an article, have them analyze it using the ideas developed in this chapter.
3. Many firms utilize both the concepts of outsourcing and economies of scope. Ask students to find an example of a firm using one of these concepts in the *Wall Street Journal* (the lead stories, or Industry/Corporate Focus, which appear daily, or the Monday Outlook sections). Then have them analyze the firm's decision in the context of the theories developed in this chapter.

Case Assignments

Assign students to read the case studies on outsourcing and on the reputation of the Big Mac. Both cases have related questions and problems and are posted for download at www.econ4me.com.

Teaching Points

- Those who are interested in industrial organization will find the first part of this chapter especially engaging. It concerns the reasons why firms exist. What do they do? What governs their size? What limits their scope of operation?
- The firm arises as a response to transaction costs. In a perfectly frictionless world of perfect information, households would simply contract with other households to supply goods. It might be interesting to consider the relation this would have to the concept of economies of scale. If there were no economies of scale, could a single household still produce its own products?
- The latter part of this chapter makes microeconomics more real by looking at the causes and consequences of imperfect information problems. Students should be able to relate to many examples including buying a used car, buying car insurance, and interviewing for a job. None of the material is technical, and the students can get deeply involved in these issues if you let them.

Discussion Questions

McDonald's has 30,000 restaurants in more than 100 countries and employs about a million people. The secret to its success and reputation is that customers around the world can count on product consistency because it has attracted competent and reliable franchise owners and has provided them with appropriate incentives and constraints to offer a product of consistent quality. How do you think McDonald's avoids adverse selection?

When you plan your next vacation, will you do it yourself or use a travel agent? What kind of hidden characteristics and hidden actions might be present or occur if you use an agent? How could you reduce the consequences of any asymmetric information?

PowerPoint

A full PowerPoint list and script for Chapter 14 are in the Instructor Manual both at www.econ4me.com and on the Instructor Resource CD-ROM.

Video

In the Ask the Author videos for Chapter 14, the author answers these questions:

- Why does asymmetric information create problems?
- How does "adverse selection" affect markets?

Download the clips from www.econ4me.com.

15 ECONOMIC REGULATION AND ANTITRUST POLICY
Prep Card

In this chapter:

Regulating natural monopolies; per se illegality; theories of economic regulation; rule of reason; deregulation; merger waves; antitrust policy; competitive trends.

Learning Outcomes

LO 1 Describe the different types of government regulation

LO 2 Explain how natural monopolies are regulated

LO 3 Explain why producers are interested in economic regulation

LO 4 Discuss antitrust laws and their enforcement

LO 5 Describe the relationship between public policy and merger activity

LO 6 List competitve trends in the U.S. economy

Chapter Exhibits

Exhibit 1 Regulating a Natural Monopoly

Exhibit 2 Herfindahl-Hirschman Index (HHI) Based on Market Share in Three Industries

Exhibit 3 U.S. Merger Waves in the Past Century

Exhibit 4 Competitive Trends in the U.S. Economy: 1939 to 2000

Key Terms

market power 214
social regulation 214
economic regulation 214
antitrust policy 214
public utilities 215
capture theory of regulation 217
trust 218
Sherman Antitrust Act of 1890 218
Clayton Act of 1914 218
tying contract 218
exclusive dealing 218
interlocking directorates 218
Federal Trade Commission (FTC) Act of 1914 218
horizontal merger 219
vertical merger 219
consent decree 219
per se illegal 219
rule of reason 219
predatory pricing 219

Outline

Experiential Assignments

1. Find the Department of Justice and Federal Trade Commission merger guidelines at http://www.usdoj.gov/atr/public/guidelines/horiz_book/toc.html. How does the government use the Herfindahl-Hirschman Index to determine which proposed mergers to allow and which to challenge? Do these guidelines indicate that the Justice Department is using the per se illegality or rule-of-reason approach to antitrust enforcement?
2. Microsoft's legal issues have been ongoing since 2000. The latest information on the Justice Department's case against Microsoft is available at http://www.usdoj.gov/atr/cases/ms_index.htm.To get the other side of the story, check Microsoft's PressPass page at http://www.microsoft.com/presspass/legalnews.mspx. What has happened with the case in Europe since this textbook went to press?

Case Assignments

Assign students to read the case studies on airline regulation and deregulation and the antitrust litigation against Microsoft. Both cases have related questions and problems and are posted for download at www.econ4me.com.

Herfindahl-Hirschman Index, or HHI **220**

conglomerate merger **221**

Teaching Points

- This chapter is divided into three parts: a review of economic regulation and deregulation (LOs 1–3), an analysis of antitrust laws (LO4), and a survey of recent trends in U.S. competitiveness (LOs 5–6).
- Regulation of natural monopoly is reviewed early in the chapter. This introduces the central problem with marginal cost pricing regulation of a natural monopoly—that is, how to control market power but still keep the firm afloat. The dilemma facing regulators is whether to require the monopolist to charge the socially optimal price and then subsidize the firm or to permit the monopolist to set a price that is higher than the socially optimal price but that allows for a normal profit. None of the solutions—monopoly pricing, marginal cost pricing, or average cost pricing—is without problems.
- One important point to stress in discussing regulation and deregulation is that there are always winners and losers from such actions. Often the consumer is supposed to be the beneficiary of regulation. The regulations, however, often have negative side effects. Regulated industries can often use regulations to stabilize their control of the market. This is a good point at which to review "Case Study: Airline Regulation and Deregulation."
- The text considers three pieces of antitrust legislation: the Sherman Act of 1890, the Clayton Act of 1914, and the Federal Trade Commission Act of 1914.
- Finally, William G. Shepherd's analysis of U.S. competitiveness is discussed, as are some of the consequences of deregulation in the 1980s on the telephone industry.

Discussion Question

A topic that might generate good discussion is whether the government should continue to subsidize Amtrak. Depending on where your college or university is located, students may have very strong feelings one way or the other. If that is the case, be prepared to play an equally strong devil's advocate to push your students beyond their personal feelings to economic analysis. Alternatively, require your students to argue against their own personal opinions and use economic concepts to support the opposing arguments.

PowerPoint

A full PowerPoint list and script for Chapter 15 are in the Instructor Manual both at www.econ4me.com and on the Instructor Resource CD-ROM.

Video

In the Ask the Author videos for Chapter 15, the author answers these questions:

- Is the auto industry more competitive now than in the past?
- Which antitrust cases have received a lot of attention?

Download the clips from www.econ4me.com.

16 PUBLIC GOODS AND PUBLIC CHOICE

Prep Card

In this chapter:

Private versus public goods; rent seeking; representative democracy; the underground economy; rational ignorance; bureaucratic behavior; special-interest legislation; private versus public production.

Learning Outcomes

LO 1 Define public goods

LO 2 Discuss the role of public choice in representative democracy

LO 3 Describe the underground economy

LO 4 Explain bureaucracy and its role in representative democracy

Chapter Exhibits

Key Terms

Outline

Experiential Assignments

1. Loren Lomasky, in "The Booth and Consequences" at http://perspicuity.net/sd/tbac.html, wrestles with the question of why people bother to vote. Have students read the article and decide for themselves if voting is rational.
2. "The Politics & Policy" column in the *Wall Street Journal* is a good source for articles on politics at every level. Ask students to choose one such article and decide which it describes: special-interest or traditional public-goods legislation. Have them classify the benefits and the costs as either concentrated or widespread.
3. The federal budget revenues and expenditures are detailed at http://www.whitehouse.gov/omb/budget. Have students browse the site and locate the section detailing spending to find several expenditures that seem interesting. They should then identify the groups bearing the costs and those reaping the benefits of the expenditures.

Case Assignments

Assign students to read the case studies on the farm subsidies and campaign finance reform. Both cases have related questions and problems and are posted for download at www.econ4me.com.

Teaching Points

- Much of this material will be new to principles students. The first new concepts discussed in this chapter are the problems associated with defining majority rule and the median voter model. A majority vote leading to the median voter position could seem desirable. After all, this is a centrist position—but in fact it has many drawbacks, including inefficiency, unresponsiveness to changes in voter preferences, and—of course—the fact that everyone but the median voter is unhappy with the result! It also tends to lead to indistinguishable differences in political candidates' positions and voter apathy.

- Students may be surprised to learn that the median voter position is not likely to be the economically efficient outcome. The reason is that intensities of preferences are not reflected when everyone has an "equal voice" in the voting outcome.
- Rational ignorance is often the reason given for poor turnouts on Election Day. The benefits to each individual voter from voting do not appear to outweigh the cost of voting. One should definitely use the word *appear* since this is a matter of perception as the presidential election of 2000 made clear.
- The farm subsidies case study merits additional consideration. If government policies are made in response to special-interest groups rather than to consumer interests, a useful exercise is analyzing the efficiency losses associated with these policies. This case study describes the steps needed to identify the relative sizes of the gains and losses associated with policy that supports agricultural production.

Discussion Questions

Should the concept of utility inform how we fund public goods? What are the advantages of taking a solely utilitarian approach to paying for public goods? Are there any dangers to focusing on utilitarian benefit when making funding decisions?

Will we ever see the death of pork-barrel spending? Why or why not?

PowerPoint

A full PowerPoint list and script for Chapter 16 are in the Instructor Manual both at www.econ4me.com and on the Instructor Resource CD-ROM.

Video

In the Ask the Author videos for Chapter 16, the author answers these questions:

- Why do we keep the income tax if it is so unpopular?
- What is the meaning of public goods?

Download the clips from www.econ4me.com.

17 EXTERNALITIES AND THE ENVIRONMENT Prep Card

In this chapter:

Exhaustible resources; marginal social cost; renewable resources; marginal social benefit; common-pool problem; Coase theorem; private property rights; markets for pollution rights; optimal pollution; environmental protection.

Learning Outcomes

LO 1 Define externalities and explain the common-pool problem

LO 2 Explain the optimal level of pollution

LO 3 Assess the role of environmental problems in the economy

LO 4 Describe positive externalities

Chapter Exhibits

Exhibit 1 Negative Externalities: The Market for Electricity in the Midwest

Exhibit 2 The Optimal Reduction in Greenhouse Gas Emissions

Exhibit 3 Effect of Changes in Costs or Benefits of Reducing Greenhouse Gas Emissions

Exhibit 4 Optimal Allocation of Pollution Rights

Exhibit 5 Fossil-Fuel Carbon Dioxide Emissions per Capita: The 25 Worst Nations

Exhibit 6 Paper and Cardboard Recycling: Top 25 among Advanced Economies

Exhibit 7 Education and Positive Externalities

Key Terms

exhaustible resource 241
renewable resource 242
common-pool problem 242
fixed-production technology 244
marginal social cost 244
variable technology 245
marginal social benefit 245
Coase theorem 246
command-and-control environmental regulations 248
economic efficiency approach 249
recycling 252

Outline

Experiential Assignments

1. Suggest the following scenario to your students: Suppose you are the mayor of Mexico City. How can you use some of the techniques outlined in this chapter to control pollution there? (For background information, have students check http://www.ess.co.at/GAIA/CASES/MEX/index.html.)
2. Garrett Hardin's 1968 article, "The Tragedy of the Commons," is available online at http://www.garretthardinsociety.org/articles/art_tragedy_of_the_commons.html. Ask students to read it and describe some examples of the common-pool problem or, as he calls it, the tragedy of the commons.
3. Students should read Betty Joyce Nash's "Pollution Allowances Help Clear the Air" at http://www.richmondfed.org/publications/economic_research/cross_sections/winter_1996/feature2.cfm. Based on what they've learned in this chapter, have them evaluate Nash's case for pollution allowances as a way of controlling negative externalities.
4. The Marketplace section of the *Wall Street Journal* is a good place to look for information related to externalities. On a given day, see how many stories your students can find that deal with externalities—positive or negative. Are businesses taking steps to "internalize" externalities? What role does technology play in controlling negative externalities?

Case Assignments

Assign students to read the case studies on the rainforests and on Mexico City. Both cases have related questions and problems and are posted for download at www.econ4me.com.

Teaching Points

- A review of exhaustible and renewable resources is recommended to establish a foundation for identification of what an externality is and is not. The key factor is that some benefit or cost associated with consumption or production activity is not reflected in the price. Air pollution—the act of "using up" clean air—is a negative externality if the monetary cost of clean air to the producer is zero when in fact it is a scarce resource. Housing rents to locals driven up by college students living off campus are not an externality, however. The external cost borne by the locals is picked up in the price of housing to students. You may wish to give the class a set of externalities and have members determine which are true externalities and which are not.
- Externalities are typically the consequences of nonexistent or unenforceable property rights. One of the easiest to understand is the common-pool resource, which is a resource that belongs to everybody and therefore is free to all. Such common-pool resources—such as fish, ocean minerals, and ocean water—are overused. In other cases, the result can be more difficult to analyze because the property rights issue may be problematic. Do smokers generate a negative externality, or do they have the right to blow smoke without "compensating" anyone? Does a state have the right to seed clouds to get rain when states to the east of it have less rainfall as a result? In these cases, the externality may exist, but the solution is difficult.
- To determine the "cost" of an uncorrected externality, the class needs to be able to determine the economically efficient level of the externality-producing activity. This is done by vertically adding private and external costs (or benefits) to find the point at which marginal social benefits equal marginal social costs. This will be easily understood only if the class recognizes that the demand curve measures marginal (private) benefits for different amounts of activity. One implication of the analysis of correction for externalities is that the optimal amount of an externality is generally nonzero. Students often find this surprising when the externality is a negative one, such as pollution, and may suggest that the optimal amount of pollution is zero. Remind them that this is a direct consequence of comparing marginal benefits and costs and that given scarce resources, there is a limit to what people are willing to spend on eliminating pollution.
- Another interesting idea developed in this chapter is the Coase theorem. It states that if property rights can be assigned (and enforced), who actually obtains the property rights is of no importance in determining the economically efficient level of the externality-producing activity. In other words, because a lack of property rights created the externality, it is corrected by establishing property rights. The property rights assignment decision will have distributional consequences but the same correct result will be achieved in all cases.

PowerPoint

A full PowerPoint list and script for Chapter 17 are in the Instructor Manual both at www.econ4me.com and on the Instructor Resource CD-ROM.

Video

In the Ask the Author videos for Chapter 17, the author answers these questions:

- How does government affect the economy?
- What does barbed wire have to do with externalities?

Download the clips from www.econ4me.com.

18 INCOME DISTRIBUTION AND POVERTY
Prep Card

In this chapter:

Distribution of income; the feminization of poverty; official poverty level; poverty and discrimination; public policy and poverty; welfare reforms.

Learning Outcomes

LO 1 Explain the distribution of household income

LO 2 Describe redistribution programs

LO 3 Explain who the poor are

LO 4 Discuss welfare reform

Chapter Exhibits

Exhibit 1 Share of Aggregate Household Income by Quintile: 1970, 1980, 1990, and 2005

Exhibit 2 Lorenz Curves Show That Income Was Less Evenly Distributed Across U.S. Households in 2005 than in 1970

Exhibit 3 Number and Percentage of U.S. Population in Poverty: 1959–2005

Exhibit 4 U.S. Poverty Rates and Unemployment Rates

Exhibit 5 Federal Redistribution Outlays Each Year by Category: 1962 to 2008

Exhibit 6 U.S. Poverty Rates by Age: 1959–2005

Exhibit 7 Poverty Rates Are Much Higher for Families Headed by Females But Have Declined in the Last Decade

Exhibit 8 Percent of Population Living in Poverty by State

Key Terms

Lorenz curve 258
median income 259
median wage 260
U.S. official poverty level 261
social insurance 262
Social Security 262
Medicare 263
income assistance programs 263
means-tested program 263
Temporary Assistance for Needy Families (TANF) 263
Supplemental Security Income (SSI) 263
earned-income tax credit 264
Medicaid 264
food stamps 264

Outline

Experiential Assignments

1. Have students visit the Census Bureau's page on poverty statistics at http://www.census.gov/hhes/www/poverty.html to check the Small Area Income and Poverty Estimates, and find the latest poverty estimate for their county. How does the poverty rate there compare with the overall rate in their state and in the United States as a whole?
2. The front page of the Marketplace section of the *Wall Street Journal* often carries articles on income distribution and the personal impact of poverty. Ask students to pay particular attention to the "Work & Family" and "Business and Race" columns that appear in the Wednesday edition of paper. How are the actions of U.S. businesses affecting income distribution and poverty?

Case Assignments

Assign students to read the case studies on marital sorting and income inequality and on welfare-to-work programs. Both cases have related questions and problems and are posted for download at www.econ4me.com.

Teaching Points

- Considerable disagreement regarding the facts of poverty and income distribution is common, even among economists. Exhibits 1, 2, 4, and 5 should stimulate classroom discussion.
- An issue related to the measurement of poverty is why family incomes differ. If, for example, family incomes differ largely on the basis of the number of earners or the position of the family income level on the life-cycle pattern of income, the response probably should be different than if income differences were generated by educational or job discrimination reasons. The question of whether aid should or should not be given strictly on the basis of poverty may be interesting to pose to the class.

- The text asks, "Who are the poor?" Here are some things to consider:
  - Poverty is highest for households headed by people under the age of 25.
  - The elderly have become increasingly better off, owing in no small measure to Social Security.
  - Much of the increase in poverty has fallen on families headed by females.
- This chapter contains a section on discrimination. Evidence suggests that blacks earn less than whites even after adjusting for factors that could affect wages such as education and job experience. Black teenagers have especially high unemployment rates. However, it is difficult to address this issue with one type of policy because black families are not a homogeneous group and in fact the distribution of income is more uneven among black families than it is among the population as a whole.
- The section on disincentives should highlight how difficult it can be to create effective policy.

Discussion Questions

What trade-offs are made when income is distributed more equally across a society (i.e. redistributed from high-income citizens to low- or no-income citizens)?

How beneficial do you think income redistribution is for the overall economy? Why do you think as you do? (Give an economic rationale for your position, not just an emotional one.)

PowerPoint

A full PowerPoint list and script for Chapter 18 are in the Instructor Manual both at www.econ4me.com and on the Instructor Resource CD-ROM.

Video

In the Ask the Author videos for Chapter 18, the author answers these questions:

- Will there always be poverty?
- How does income distribution in the U.S. compare?

Download the clips from www.econ4me.com.

19

INTERNATIONAL TRADE

Prep Card

In this chapter:

Gains from trade; quotas; absolute and comparative advantage revisited; welfare loss from trade restrictions; tariffs; arguments for trade restrictions.

Learning Outcomes

LO 1 Describe the gains that trade brings

LO 2 Discuss the reasons for international specialization

LO 3 Explain trade restrictions and welfare loss

LO 4 Describe ways countries have reduced or eliminated trade barriers

LO 5 List and describe the arguments in favor of trade restrictions

Chapter Exhibits

Key Terms

Outline

Experiential Assignments

1. Send your students to the Office of the U.S. Trade Representative at http://www.ustr.gov/. The U.S. Trade Representative is a cabinet member who acts as the principal trade advisor, negotiator, and spokesperson for the president on trade and related investment matters. Have them read some of the most recent press releases. What are some of the trade-related issues the United States is currently facing?
2. The *Wall Street Journal* is one of the world's best sources of information regarding international trade—the International page inside the first section of each day's edition. Ask students to find an article in today's issue (or some recent issue) dealing with trade barriers—tariffs, quotas, and so on. If the article provides sufficient information to estimate costs and benefits in dollar terms, have them model the trade barrier using a graph, and determine who benefits and who bears the costs.

Case Assignments

Assign students to read the case studies on the Doha Round and on steel tariffs. Both cases have related questions and problems and are posted for download at www.econ4me.com.

Teaching Points

- While this chapter contains potentially difficult material, most students are interested in international trade and the topic can lead to fruitful classroom discussion.
- Although the principle of comparative advantage may have made sense to students when you discussed the importance of specialization and trade in the context of the production possibilities frontier, the emotional elements surrounding the discussion of trade and trade barriers may cause students to miss its relevance in the context of international trade. You should stress that the same principle applies and that students should think of a world production possibilities frontier. You will probably get into a discussion of the costs of free trade (or benefits of limiting trade), and therefore you must stress that the fact that each country realizes net gains from trade does not mean that everyone gains. After all, if the world price of a product (such as steel) is above the U.S. price, U.S. consumers lose when we export steel; therefore, the price for it rises in the United States. Students must become aware that goods consumption (not production) is the key to the standard of living. Review *CaseStudy: Bush's Steel Tariffs*.
- The text discusses tariffs and quotas as well as their impacts. Exhibits 7 and 8 are very useful in illustrating these concepts. The principal difference between tariffs and quotas is that tariffs generate government revenue for the country imposing them, whereas quotas generate revenue for firms that are able to secure the licenses to import at the world price and sell at the higher domestic price.

Discussion Questions

Is there a downside to the global economy evolving to be based completely and wholly on the law of comparative advantage?

What risks if any does a country assume by making production decisions only according to the law of comparative advantage?

PowerPoint

A full PowerPoint list and script for Chapter 19 are in the Instructor Manual both at www.econ4me.com and on the Instructor Resource CD-ROM.

Video

In the Ask the Author videos for Chapter 19, the author answers these questions:

- What are the arguments for trade restrictions?
- Why don't we restrict trade among states?

Download the clips from www.econ4me.com.

INTERNATIONAL FINANCE

Prep Card

In this chapter:

Balance of payments; fixed exchange rates; trade deficits and surpluses; international monetary system; foreign exchange markets; Bretton Woods agreement; purchasing power parity; managed float; flexible exchange rates.

Learning Outcomes

LO 1 Explain how balance of payments works

LO 2 Define fixed and flexible exchange rates

LO 3 Discuss foreign exchange rates and markets

LO 4 Describe the development of the international monetary system

Chapter Exhibits

Exhibit 1 U.S. Imports Have Topped Exports Since 1976, and the Trade Deficit Has Widened

Exhibit 2 U.S. Trade Deficits in 2006 by Country or Region

Exhibit 3 U.S. Balance of Payments for 2006 (billions of dollars)

Exhibit 4 The Foreign Exchange Market

Exhibit 5 Effect on the Foreign Exchange Market of an Increase Demand for Euros

Exhibit 6 In June 2007, A Big Mac Cost More in the U.S. Than in Most Other Countries

Key Terms

Outline

Experiential Assignments

1. Trade among European nations has been bolstered by the introduction of the euro a few years ago. Have students visit http://www.euro.gov.uk/home.asp?f=1 to review the latest developments in the use and value of the euro. How is it performing in comparison to the dollar?
2. Send students to *Time* magazine's Global Business Web site at http://www.time.com/time/global_business to determine if the Asian economic situation seems to be better or worse than that of the U.S. or some other Western country. The site's *Global Competitive Report* might help—they can easily compare countries. They can also try http://www.nni.nikkei.co.jp and http://www.thehindu.com/2007/12/07/01hdline.htm, for additional perspectives.
3. The latest data on exchange rates appear in the "Currency Trading" column in the Money and Investing section of the daily *Wall Street Journal*. Have students try tracking a particular foreign currency over the course of several weeks. Has the dollar been appreciating or depreciating relative to that currency? Try to explain why it has been appreciating or depreciating.

Case Assignments

Assign students to read the case studies on the Big Mac index and on China and the trade deficit. Both cases have related questions and problems and are posted for download at www.econ4me.com.

Teaching Points

- Students typically have preconceptions about international finance. Some believe that the laws of supply and demand are somehow mysteriously suspended and that a handful of people control the fates of millions by moving exchange rates and interest rates at their discretion. It is therefore important to explain very carefully the forces influencing the supply and demand for dollars in foreign exchange markets. If students can understand what forces influence these curves, they will be better prepared for determining exchange rate pressures generated by a variety of circumstances including inflation rate differences. Explaining the purchasing power parity concept as a long-run exchange rate determinant is also useful.
- By distinguishing between current and financial account balances within the overall balance-of-payments mechanism, you can easily discuss the reasoning underlying the so-called twin deficits problem. You might also want to discuss what running a surplus in the financial account at the expense of the balance in the current account means in the long run. Are we mortgaging our future? How do we pay off the foreign-held debt?

Discussion Questions

Although many countries in the European Union use the euro as their currency, not all do. Denmark, Lichtenstein, Sweden, Switzerland, and the United Kingdom do not use the euro at all; Andorra, Montenegro, and Kosovo use the euro, but not exclusively. What do you think are the advantages of retaining a national currency? Are there disadvantages?

There are countries that use more than one currency (the EU countries mentioned above are not the only examples of this). How do you think they manage two currencies? What benefits do you think they derive from having more than one currency in circulation?

PowerPoint

A full PowerPoint list and script for Chapter 20 are in the Instructor Manual both at www.econ4me.com and on the Instructor Resource CD-ROM.

Video

In the Ask the Author videos for Chapter 20, the author answers these questions:

- How do we pay for imports?
- What causes the demand for foreign exchange to change?

Download the clips from www.econ4me.com.